# THE BIBLE WORD OF GOD

With consummate pedagogical skill, Pierre Grelot of the Institut Catholique of Paris has gathered and skillfully arranged all materials indispensable to a serious, well-grounded study of Scripture.

His theological introduction to Scripture, which is divided in two main parts— Sacred Scripture and the Interpretation of Scripture—is a goldmine of information on the problems raised by the Bible.

" *A major work of Roman Catholic scholarship.* "—H. H. Rowley commenting on the French edition in *The Expository Times*.

Pierre GRELOT

*Professor at the Catholic Institute of Paris*

# THE BIBLE
# WORD OF GOD

A THEOLOGICAL INTRODUCTION TO THE STUDY OF SCRIPTURE

*Translated from the second French edition by*

Peter NICKELS, O.F.M. Conv.

DESCLEE COMPANY

NEW YORK

First published in French under the title *La Bible, parole de Dieu* (Desclée & Co., Tournai, Belgium).

Nihil Obstat:
R.A.F. MacKenzie, S.J., Censor Deputatus.
Rome, November 10, 1968.

Imprimatur:
Hector Cunial, Vicar General.
Rome, November 18, 1968.

Library of Congress Catalog Card Number: 68-31196.

Printed and bound in Belgium by Desclée & Co., S. A., Tournai.

# TABLE OF CONTENTS

## PART II. THE INTERPRETATION OF SCRIPTURE

CHAPTER V.   HISTORY OF THE PROBLEM OF BIBLICAL
INTERPRETATION . . . . . . . . . . . . . . . . . . . . . 185

# AUTHOR'S PREFACE

The tract *On Sacred Scripture* has an importance all its own.  In a certain sense it dominates all of theology, because it concerns the texts which are the basis of theological reflection, and which indicate as well the manner in which that reflection should proceed.  But it occupies a dominant position in biblical exegesis too, since it points out to the exegete the particular character of the texts he interprets, and shows him the requirements he must face in order not to distort their mysterious content.  For this reason, the tract has a place both in manuals of theology and in general introductions to Sacred Scripture.  In the first case it usually takes on a more theoretical character, leaving aside the historical and critical questions which the theologian considers outside his field, or in any case, secondary to his purpose.  In the second case, without neglecting fundamental problems, the tract tends more to develop whatever has practical value for exegesis : methods of textual or literary criticism, history of the canon, etc. . . .

In this work I have taken the point of view of a theologian.  As a consequence, I have left aside the technical aspects of biblical criticism.  To that extent, this work is purposely incomplete.  But I have not lost sight of the particular interests of exegesis.  As a matter of fact, on the one hand every theologian has to be aware of not only the results, but even the method of exegesis, if he expects to make intelligent use of Scripture in his work.  The meaning of biblical texts cannot be determined *a priori;* the positions of theologians of the past need continually to be reexamined—in a word, the Word of God concealed in the Scriptures can be understood in all its depth only through methodical effort.  On the other hand, exegesis, even in its most technical aspects, belongs rightfully to theology from the moment that it is exercised under the light of faith.  For the effort of the human intelligence which applies itself to the Word of God, even if it is intent on clarifying its slightest detail, is not dependent on profane sciences alone, even when it employs their services.  It is therefore important to make clear from the outset the rule of exegesis as a task of the Church, so that it can come to full bloom and bear fruit.  When an apparent cleft is drawn between theology and exegesis, as sometimes happened in the field of biblical criticism during the past hundred years, the reason is not that there is any opposition between them.   The responsibility must rather be laid, according to the case, to exegetes who fail to understand the place that their work occupies among the functions of the Church, or who fail to situate the diverse elements properly, or to theologians whose unilateral formation renders them insensitive to a method of which they are in practice ignorant.   The former should be asked whether it is possible to interpret critically the texts of either Testament without concerning oneself with the doctrinal questions that exegesis raises; the latter, whether one can usefully discuss the meaning of biblical texts or the problem of their literary genres without becoming aware of the manner in which concrete problems arise, and whether one can correctly make use of scriptural texts without having first placed them in their proper context.   While the complexity of the problems makes speciali-zation in ecclesial functions necessary today, still this very specialization becomes harmful when it ends in a compartmentalization in which each specialist remains ignorant of the work of his colleagues.

The tract *On Sacred Scripture* therefore demands a continual give-and-take between the interests of the exegete and those of the theologian, a conscious exchange of positions and points of view.   But something else is needed: the exegete and the theologian, even if they work in harmony, risk cutting themselves off from the pastoral activity of the Church, in whose service they are theoretically working.   Before Sacred Scripture becomes the property of exegetical technicians and professional theologians, it already belongs to this pastoral activity, because it contains, or better, it attests the Word of God, the multiformed expression of the one Gospel which the Church has the mission to announce to men through the centuries. It is therefore important that a theological introduction to the study of Sacred Scripture, while endeavoring to bridge the gap between exegesis and theology, should not lose sight of its vital relationship to all the pastoral activities in which Scripture is involved: the liturgy, catechetics, apologetics, etc.   It was with all this in mind that I selected as title for my work *The Bible, Word of God*.   The Word of God is actually the only thing which we ought to search for in the Bible, the unique mystery the Bible conceals beneath its outer vest of human book, and which the science of interpretation ought to bring to light for men to live.

The first part, *Sacred Scripture*, attempts to analyze this mystery by examining in order its essential aspects: I. How was the Word of God finally crystallized in these books without prejudicing its living transmission in the Church?   II. What charism of the Holy Spirit made the sacred authors the transmitters and determiners of this Word?   III. What consequences for the books they have written flow from inspiration of the sacred authors, especially as concerns their value in the realm of truth?   IV. How can we in practice recognize the authentic list of books which are the word of God, and distinguish them from others, themselves excellent, which are not? The questions treated in chapters II, III, and IV are the classic ones. But it seemed useful to treat them, with chapter I as introduction, in a larger framework, so that their true dimensions would become more apparent.

After having examined Scripture in itself, in the Second Part, *The Interpretation of Scripture*, I have attempted to show how men can comprehend its mysterious meaning and acquire a correct understanding of it. This is a complex problem, and one as old as Scripture itself. Its solution involves, and has always involved, unchangeable principles, but in practice it can differ in subtle and various ways. My investigation unfolds in three stages: V. The history of the problem, which provides the best introduction to its present state. VI. Its classic formulation as the doctrine of the senses of Scripture, reexamined in the light of new discoveries, leads first of all to an examination of the meaning of biblical realities in the whole of revelation. VII. From that standpoint, I have attempted to solve the problem of the meaning of the inspired texts, and have outlined a methodology which seeks to satisfy the demands of critical science, theology, and pastoral need at the same time. The questions treated in this Second Part were in part the object of one of my earlier works, *Sens chrétien de l'Ancien Testament*. They have been reexamined here from a wider point of view; useless repetitions have been avoided as much as possible.

Naturally I do not flatter myself to have solved definitively all the problems encountered along the way. Quite a number of them are still the object of discussion among specialists. For some of them, even the recent bibliography would quickly have become cumbersome if I had made an attempt to present it in exhaustive fashion: the problem of interpretation in contemporary Protestantism, and the endless discussions surrounding the work of R. Bultmann come immediately to mind. In such cases I have attempted no more than to mark out a helpful path through difficult terrain without trying to treat everything in depth. Two chapters of this book appeared previously in print as articles: chapter II on scriptural inspiration in *Recherches de science religieuse*, 1963, and chapter III on the sacred books in *Nouvelle revue théologique*, 1963. But the studies which have appeared since then on the questions they treat have obliged me to revise them in order to bring them up to date.

To anyone who reflects upon the problems which the evangelization of the modern world poses for the Church, Scripture presents itself as the point where faith and reason, apologetics and liturgy, theological investigation and mystical contemplation necessarily meet. It is not surprising then that over the centuries the unity of religious thought in the Church was produced through the medium of exegesis, in the practical framework of the four senses of Scripture, as H. de Lubac has so well shown. After a period of division, in which the diverse disciplines failed to achieve unity, is it too much to hope to see that unity rebuilt around a revitalized biblical exegesis? That would be my earnest wish as I undertake a work which aims less to propose new or original solutions than to take its place in the broad current of traditional theology, even if on occasion I feel constrained to appeal from a recent and debatable tradition to a deeper and truer one.

# ABBREVIATIONS

I. Books of the Bible (cf. *The Jerusalem Bible*)
II. Encyclopedia and Periodical Literature

| | |
|---|---|
| AER | *American Ecclesisastical Review*, Washington |
| ANET | J. B. Pritchard, *Ancient Near Eastern Texts Relating to the O. T.* |
| AOT | H. Gressmann, *Altorientalische Texte zum A.T.* |
| ATD | *Das Alte Testament Deutsch*, Göttingen |
| BASOR | *Bulletin of the American School of Oriental Research*, Baltimore |
| BCE | *Bulletin du Comité des Études* (Compagnie de S. Sulpice), Paris |
| BPC | *La sainte Bible*, ed. L. Pirot and A. Clamer, Paris |
| BT | *Babylonian Talmud* |
| BVC | *Bible et vie chrétienne*, Maredsous-Paris |
| BZ | *Biblische Zeitschrift*, Paderborn |
| CBQ | *Catholic Biblical Quarterly*, Washington |
| CCL | *Corpus Christianorum Latinorum*, Turnhout |
| CS | *Cahiers sioniens*, Paris |
| DAFC | *Dictionnaire apologétique de la foi catholique*, ed. A. d'Alès |
| DBS | *Dictionnaire de la Bible, Supplément*, ed. A. Pirot, A. Robert, H. Cazelles and A. Feuillet |
| DTC | *Dictionnaire de théologie catholique*, ed. A. Vacant, A. Mangenot and E. Amann |
| EB | *Études bibliques*, Paris |
| Ench.B. | *Enchiridion Biblicum*, 4 ed., Rome, 1961 |
| Ench.P. | M. J. Rouet de Journel, *Enchiridion Patristicum* |
| Ench.S. | H. Denzinger, *Enchiridion Symbolorum*, 34 ed. (1967), A. Schonmetzer |
| EstB | *Estudios Biblicos*, Madrid |
| ETL | *Ephemerides Theologicae Lovanienses*, Louvain |
| HUCA | *Hebrew Union College Annual*, New York |
| ICC | *International Critical Commentary*, Edinburgh |
| JB | *The Jerusalem Bible*, London-New York |
| JBL | *Journal of Biblical Literature*, Philadelphia |
| JQR | *Jewish Quarterly Review*, Philadelphia |
| JTS | *Journal of Theological Studies*, London |
| LMD | *La Maison-Dieu*, Paris |
| NRT | *Nouvelle revue théologique*, Louvain |
| NTS | *New Testament Studies*, Cambridge |
| OS | *Orient syrien*, Paris |
| PG | J. P. Migne, *Patrologia graeca* |
| PL | J. P. Migne, *Patrologia latina* |
| RB | *Revue biblique*, Paris |
| RGG | *Die Religion in Geschichte und Gegenwart*, 3 ed., Tübingen |
| RHPR | *Revue d'histoire et de philosophie religieuse*, Strasbourg |
| RQ | *Revue de Qumran*, Paris |
| RSPT | *Revue des sciences philosophiques et religieuses*, Le Saulchoir |

RSR      *Revue de science religieuse,* Paris
RTh      *Revue thomiste,* Paris-Toulouse
RTP      *Revue de théologie et de philosophie,* Lausanne
TLZ      *Theologische Literaturzeitung,* Berlin
TWNT     *Theologisches Wörterbuch zum Neuen Testament,* ed. R. KITTEL
TZ       *Theologische Zeitschrift,* Basel
VC       *Verbum Caro,* Lausanne
VT       *Vetus Testamentum,* Leiden
VTB      *Vocabulaire de théologie biblique,* ed. X. LÉON-DUFOUR
ZAW      *Zeitschrift für die alttestamentliche Wissenschaft,* Giessen-Berlin
ZTK      *Zeitschrift für Theologie und Kirche,* Tübingen

# PART I

# SACRED SCRIPTURE

# CHAPTER I

# THE WORD OF GOD AND SACRED SCRIPTURE

The Old Alliance, which was in its entirety salvation history, law and promise,[1] exists for us, since Christ has fulfilled it, only under the concrete form of the sacred books which were born of it. It is the same with the New Alliance, inasmuch as it was the fulfilment of the mystery of salvation by Christ and the inauguration of the time of the Church through the ministry of the apostles. Still, the collection in which the books of the two Testaments have found their place is for us not just a witness of a past that is completed, like the collections of documents historians gather as the basis for their work. The titles which this collection, the Bible, that is to say the Book *par excellence*, receives in Christian theology, make this evident. They are "the holy scriptures" (2 Tm 3:15), "the scriptures" (Rm 1:2), "the holy scriptures given through the Holy Spirit" (1 Clem 45:2), or simply "Scripture" (Rm 4:3; Jm 2:8.23 etc.). As to their content, they are "God's message" (Rm 3:2), or simply "God's word" (Mk 7:13; Jn 10:35, etc.). It is not at all necessary to name the human authors to whom its several parts are due to measure its authority. The value of "that which is written" comes from the fact that in every instance it is God himself who speaks, and through the first recipients of each book men of all times are directly affected by the message which comes from him.

It would be nevertheless dangerous to retain this fundamental identification of word of God and Sacred Scripture without defining its exact meaning, because it is not valid in the same degree and the same respect in both directions. Sacred Scripture is always the word of God. But must we hold that we attain the word of God only through Sacred Scripture? And can the content of the word of God be reduced to the explicit affirmations of Scripture? The problem is important, because it brings into play the manner in which we can in fact attain the word of God. In order to clarify it, we shall examine in succession three questions: 1) the notion of the word of God in its relations with the people of God. 2) The channels of transmission of the word of God in the two Testaments. 3) The reception and conservation of the word of God in the Church.

---

[1] On these general aspects of the Old Testament, see *Sens chrétien de l'ancien Testament* (Paris : Desclée, 1962), Ch. IV-VI.

## § 1. THE WORD OF GOD AND THE PEOPLE OF GOD

We are here faced with a general truth, one which is treated in detail in every work on the knowledge of faith. [2] We will content ourselves with repeating only what is necessary for the subject we are going to study, namely: 1. The word of God as means of revelation, and 2. The intrinsic relationship between the word of God and the people of God.

## I. REVELATION AND WORD OF GOD

### I. KNOWLEDGE OF DIVINE MYSTERIES AND REVELATION

Left only to our natural powers, we can know of God only that which is perceptible through creatures in which his being is reflected. [3] In this respect, two points of departure are open to us. On the one hand, our experience of the world and of other men: "Ever since God created the world his everlasting power and deity—however invisible—have been there for the mind to see in the things he has made" (Rm 1:20). On the other, our interior experience in which our moral conscience [4] reveals to us the divine law written in our being (Rm 2:15), while the dynamism of our Ego [5] in search of the absolute appears as the hidden sign of our having been destined for God ("You made us for yourself, and our heart is restless, until it rests in you," as St. Augustine put it). This general view, however, is only a theoretic statement of the problem. For so great is the spiritual misery which is our condition at birth that the natural language of God risks being understood only faintly by many men, and even literaly perverted. [6] While knowable, God will be poorly understood, misunderstood, misrepresented (Rm 1:21-23). The intelligence of man needs redeeming as much as his

---

[2] Y. Congar, *La foi et la théologie* (Tournai-Paris : Desclée, 1962), pp. 3-40.

[3] *Ibid.*, pp. 9-12 (with a bibliography on the question). See the more detailed development of F. M. Genuyt, *Le mystère de Dieu* (Tournai-Paris : Desclée, 1963).

[4] The importance given the moral conscience in the knowledge of God by Newman is well known : J. H. Newman, *Grammar of Assent*, Ch. 5, I and Ch. 10, I, 1.

[5] The best analysis of this dynamism is probably the one that underlies the thesis of M. Blondel, *L'action* (1893). Among the works that have been devoted to it we note B. Romeyer, *La philosophie religieuse de Maurice Blondel* (Paris : Aubier, 1943), pp. 43-110; Y. de Montcheuil, *Pages religieuses de Maurice Blondel* (Paris, 1941).

[6] Blondel is here speaking of superstition as the necessary substitute for religion for the man who has not found the true God. The perversions of ancient cults and their mythologies are well known. Modern perversions rather take the form of atheistic humanism, or the varnish of atheism covers a superstitious cult of man under one form or another (cf. H. de Lubac, *Recherche de l'Homme nouveau* [Paris, 1949], pp. 15-92).

free will. Even more, setting aside this difficulty of understanding God, knowledge of his intimate mystery would remain for us forever impossible, since neither his natural language nor the natural exercise of our faculties reaches his level.

It is at this point that revelation enters. [7] Through revelation God accomplishes in one act two complementary things. In the first place he reveals to men the profound mystery of his being, while at the same time introducing them into it by allowing them to participate in it through grace in Christ Jesus. In the same act he heals the weakness of their wounded nature, giving them through grace a right understanding of what in principle should have been accessible to their natural faculties, but in fact was not. Through this healing action of grace, [8] the functioning of human intelligence in the order of religious understanding becomes, one might say, normalized; by its elevating action it is rendered capable of a new mode of understanding which implies a participation in God's own understanding. As far as the revelation of man's being and the meaning of his existence is concerned, it arises jointly from the two orders. Moreover, the two actions of grace which we here distinguish are really overlapping: it is in and through the elevation of man to the knowledge of faith that his natural understanding of God is normalized; it is in and through his admission to intimacy with the living God that he is able to find His likeness in himself and in every creature. Revelation, as the supernatural language of God, thus assumes in its own way all the import of his natural language—not only to enlighten what the shadow of sin had darkened, but to make the whole a part of the new order of things into which man has been gratuitously introduced. [9] Revelation thus appears as an essential aspect of the mystery of salvation which unfolds in sacred history, and which has as its center the cross and resurrection of Christ. And just as sacred history is not simply an external framework within which the mystery of salvation unrolls, but is an integral part of it, so is it likewise bound to revelation in the strictest manner, since

---

[7] Y. Congar, *op. cit.*, pp. 3-4 (with bibliography). R. Latourelle, *The Théology of Revelation* (Staten Island : Alba) "Révélation," *VTB*, cols. 925-935. G. Moran, "What is Revelation?," *Theological Studies* 25 (1964), 217-231.

[8] In scholastic terminology, *gratia sanans*. It is somewhat surprising to note that this aspect of healing grace is totally absent from the work of C. Baumgartner, *La grâce du Christ* (Tournai-Paris : Desclée, 1963). The separation of the problem of faith from that of morality in theological discussions of the past few centuries is most likely responsible for this.

[9] In speaking here of the natural and the supernatural, we are omitting a discussion of the problem of pure nature. Concretely, the nature of man was always ordered to the supernatural. Still it remains useful and legitimate to distinguish in our being different orders which must not be confused : our participation in divine life remains in every way a gratuitous gift.

it is its medium. [10]   In effect, it is in being realized in time that salvation is revealed to men.   The events in which it is accomplished have two aspects: while they are historical facts for the outside observer, they are also acts of the living God.   With them as a starting point, then, an unlimited perspective opens upon the intimate being of him who produces them.   God becomes perceptible through his interventions in time.   In a word, sacred history as such performs an irreplaceable revealing function.

## II. THE WORD OF GOD [11]

Our analysis, however, remains incomplete unless we bring into play the word of God, the true medium of revelation.   It is important, though, to have a proper notion of this word.   A philosophical tradition which issues from far off Greece would lead us to see in it only a reality of the intelligible order: a message, a teaching, through which God enters into contact with men. [12]   That is not the biblical notion of the word.   It is first of all a dynamic reality through which God acts in the world, creates, brings events into being: having gone out from the mouth of God, it "does not return to him empty, without carrying out his will and succeeding in what it was sent to do" (Is 55:11).   To recognize in certain facts of human history the acts of God here below is to discern there the effect of this active word, which carries out the design of creation and the plan of salvation.   It is at the same time to discover there the visible expression of a sovereign thought—the Old Testament would put it better: of divine counsel—which by directing the course of things concretely manifests itself in significative acts.   The events in question, considered under their external appearances, obviously remain accessible to every man's natural perception.   But the same cannot be said of their internal nature.   Inasmuch as they are the words of God in act, they are full of religious meaning, which is in this case accessible to faith alone.   There is, to be sure, an intrinsic relation between their external aspects and this deeper meaning which gives them their worth, and it will be necessary to determine the nature of that relationship.   But already an important consequence can be drawn: since God reveals his plan of salvation, and even his intimate being, through the medium of the

---

[10] R. Latourelle, "Revelation, histoire et incarnation," *Gregorianum* 44 (1963), 225-262.

[11] "Λέγω/Λόγος," *TWNT* 4, pp. 69-140; *La Parole de Dieu en Jésus-Christ* (Cahiers de l'actualité religieuse 15), (Tournai-Paris : Desclée, 1961) (with ample bibliography).   "Parole de Dieu," *VTB*, cols. 750-758.

[12] On this too narrow view, see J. Dupont, "Écriture et Tradition," *NRT* 85 (1963), 459 ff., who cites many examples taken from modern theologians.

events of sacred history, the intelligible content of these events includes virtually the whole of revelation.

Nevertheless, in order to become accessible to us, that intelligible content must become explicit and be translated into human words. The realization of the plan of salvation includes the sending of messengers of God, whose message unveils the meaning of events and makes the acts of God recognizable in them. In their mouths the word of God takes on the form of understandable language. Not that their message, which is necessarily an analytic translation of divine mysteries, captures all their richness in a conceptual formulation that would serve as an adequate definition of them. Those mysteries, offered by the Word for human contemplation, retain in every respect an unfathomable richness. But nonetheless, some of their aspects are positively unveiled with more or less exactness, and are expressed in words which we can understand. By that token they enter the field of our comprehension. The acts of God in time and the message of those he sends thus appear as correlative realities; it is through their joint intervention that the revealing word reaches us. As for the dispensation of this word, the earthly echo of the Word of God who is his uncreated word,[13] it has gone through several successive stages: the Old Testament, in which the word spoke through the prophets (in the wide sense of the word); the New Testament, in which he assumed flesh within the human race in order to make himself known personally here below while accomplishing our salvation, and then sent his apostles to make his gospel known to all men.

## II. WORD OF GOD AND PEOPLE OF GOD

Our discussion of the word of God would remain incomplete if it did not include, finally, the concrete conditions in which it is communicated to the human race. Despite the fact that the word was pronounced for the benefit of all men, it could not reach them all at once in the course of its dispensation in history, which, for that matter, remains incomplete, since it continues in the evangelization of the world. God, by an act of his providence, set apart from the rest of the human race a particular community which he constituted his people[14]: in the Old Testament, Israel; in the New Testament, the Church, the new Israel open to all the nations. In the Old, just as in

---

[13] On this presence of the Word *(Verbum)* in every divine word addressed to men, see *Sens chrétien de l'A.T.*, pp. 132 ff. (with select bibliography). L. Charlier, "Le Christ, Parole de Dieu," *La Parole de Dieu en Jésus-Christ* (Tournai-Paris : Desclée, 1961), pp. 121-139. L. M. Dewailly, *Jésus-Christ, Parole de Dieu* (Paris : Cerf, 1945).

the New Testament, this community is the exclusive depository of the divine word, to which it must respond with its faith. The result is that it is impossible for any man to have access to the word without participating in that community's life. [15] It is in effect in the history of this community that the word, as an active principle, manifests its efficacious presence through meaningful events. As a prophetic message, it is principally to this community that it is addressed through the intervention first of the prophets, then of the word made flesh, and finally of the apostles, his messengers. Or better, through the message that it brings and through the effects that it produces, this word creates the salvation community, which has no existence outside it. The word is the hidden principle of its life; and it is the reason that the community itself is the living sign of its presence and action in the midst of a sinful world.

This close relationship between the word of God and the people of God naturally has its consequences for the manner in which the word is dispensed to men. In order to be accessible to them, it is allotted first of all to the limited community which receives it in trust. It assumes forms and adopts a language that root it deeply in the culture of that community. It inserts itself in precise stages into the community's historical experience: as an act of God, to give meaning to the various aspects of that experience; as a message, to make clear that hidden meaning. At whatever level, then, one might wish to consider divine revelation, it is essential, if its mode of expression and its content are to be understood, not to lose sight of the relation of the word to the people to whom it is addressed.

## § II. THE WORD OF GOD
## AND ITS CHANNELS OF TRANSMISSION

The problem now is to determine the way in which God's message, made known to men through his word, has been preserved and transmitted to us. Analogies taken from the history of religions and cultures suggest two possible ways: that of Tradition, and that of Scripture. [16] In civilizations

---

[14] Art. "Λαός," *TWNT* 4, pp. 29-57. Cf. *Sens chrétien de l'A.T.*, pp. 134 ff.

[15] This general formula does not take into consideration the particular case of those men who, in good faith, have no knowledge of the word of God addressed to his people in the two Testaments. These men do have some link with the people of God, to whom they are ordered (cf. Vatican II, Constitution *Lumen gentium*, n⁰ 16).

[16] J. Leipoldt—S. Morenz, *Heilige Schriften* (Leipzig : Harrassowitz, 1953).

without writing, religious ideas and cultic practices are passed on exclusively by way of tradition. By that must be understood not only the handing down of teachings by word of mouth openly (preaching, etc.) or secretly (secret initiation), but likewise the religious customs (rites, actions, taboos, etc.) which imply a certain ideological content and often express it in appropriate formulas. In civilizations with writing, on the other hand, there are cases in which the activity and the teaching of a founder, very soon collected in a sacred book, dominate all the further development of the religious tradition. The best example is Islam, in which tradition plays a quite restricted role alongside the Koran. Between these two extremes can be found many intermediate cases. Most often, Tradition, while still being transmitted in many ways, tends to become crystallized in writings destined to serve as a norm. The role of these writings is greater in proportion as the religion in question attaches itself to the revelation or illumination received by a real or legendary founder, who in relation to other men occupies the position of mediator or initiator. We might mention here the case of Buddhism, [17] in which the fundamental teaching is sought in the original tradition (sanscrit *Agama*), identical with the written canon *(pali Nikaya)* of the school of the ancients (Theravada, or Hinayana).

It should not be surprising, then, to find this problem of Scripture-Tradition in Judeo-Christian revelation. At no time did the latter present itself as a " religion of the book" in the strict sense of the term. Scripture [18] always appeared in this religion joined to a certain Tradition, by the very reason of the framework in which revelation is received and transmitted: the people of God. It will be helpful, therefore, to determine more precisely their respective position in their common relation to the word of God. In order to do this, we shall distinguish two stages: the first, which includes all the Old Testament, culminates in Christ; the second, which begins with Christ, reaches the Church through the apostles.

---

[17] W. Rahula, *L'enseignement du Bouddha d'après les textes les plus anciens* (Paris : Seuil, 1961). See the presentation of the book by P. Demiéville on p. 10.

[18] "Γράφω, etc.," *TWNT* I, pp. 742-773; " βίβλος, " *ibid.*, pp. 613-620. "Écriture," *VTB*, cols. 241-244; "Livre," *VTB*, cols. 538-540.

## I. FROM THE PROPHETS TO CHRIST [19]

### I. TRADITION AND SCRIPTURE IN THE OLD TESTAMENT

#### 1. From Tradition to Scripture

At the origin of the religion of Israel, and at every stage of its development, there was always a message transmitted by one sent by God, joined to something experienced by the people of God itself. Thus at the time of the constitution of Israel on the slopes of Sinai, there was the message of Moses joined to the experience of the exodus. Now the first mode of conservation of these two united elements was not Scripture; it was rather the continuity of a *praxis* of the community in which the traditional actions and rites were accompanied by formulas which explained them. The typical example is the Passover, [20] whose ritual recalls the divine actions which it commemorates (Ex 12:25-27).

It would be useful here to analyze in detail all the aspects of this living tradition, [21] which concerned beliefs and practical wisdom as well as customs and rites, and to discover all the techniques of transmission it made use of. It would become clear how it involved the whole life of the Israelite community. Nevertheless, to fill the practical needs of the community, certain of the traditional elements always ended up being fixed in written form. The resulting text fixed the word of God less in its original sense, than in the form given it by the tradition which received it, was nourished by it, faithfully preserved it, and finally developed some of its implications. As a typical example, we might take the decalogue, [22] the written norm of morality which

[19] P. Auvray, "Écriture et tradition dans la communauté d'Israël," *BVC* 12 (1955), 19-34.
[20] For further detail, see H. Haag, "Pâque," *DBS* 6, cols. 1120-1149; R. Le Déaut, *La nuit pascale* (Rome : Pontifical Biblical Institute, 1963).
[21] In J. J. von Allmen, *Vocabulaire biblique*, P. H. Menoud, art. "Tradition," p. 293 writes : "Word and idea are unknown in the Old Testament." This statement probably depends on "Παραδίδωμι/Παράδοσις," *TWNT* 2, pp. 172-175. Compare "Tradition," *VTB*, cols. 1064-1067. The positive study of tradition in the Old Testament owes much to Scandinavian exegetes beginning with J. Pedersen, *Israel, Its Life and Culture* (London-Copenhagen : Poul-Branner, 1926-1940). But this study too often restricts itself to the sole problem of the transmission of the texts; cf. J. van der Ploeg, "Le rôle de la Tradition orale du texte de l'Ancien Testament," *RB* 54 (1947), 5-41. For briefer studies : E. Nielsen, *Oral Tradition* (London : SCM Press, 1954); B. S. Childs, *Memory and Tradition in Israel* (London : SCM Press, 1962).
[22] Bibliography in J. J. Stamm, *Le Décalogue à la lumière des recherches contemporaines* (Cahiers théologiques 43), (Neuchâtel-Paris : Delachaux, 1959); cf. *Theologische Rundschau* 26 (1961), 189-239; 281-305.

Israel's tradition attributed to Moses and to the alliance forged on Sinai, but in which literary criticism detects later developments.[23] It is true that in other cases the written text closely resembles the announcement made by God's messenger, to the point of seizing it at its source. Such is the case of a prophet who personally put his oracles down in writing, or dictated them to a secretary. But even then this announcement, first proclaimed *viva voce*, and then set down in a book, never constituted a reality unrelated to the tradition which surrounded it. While an heir to that which preceded it, it in turn became one of its composite parts. Whatever followed it assimilated its contribution and in its turn influenced its interpretation.

## 2. Interdependence of Tradition and Scripture

It is obvious how false it would be to study Scripture independently of the tradition to which it belongs. Both of them retain the memory of the acts of God in history and of the message of those he sent. It is apparent that a constant interplay goes on between them. On the one hand, living tradition retains the message only by adapting it to changing circumstances and by developing what is implicit in it. Only thus can it continue to play its normative role in the faith and life of the people of God. On the other hand, the message itself, or the tradition born of it, tends to become fixed in written form, in order the better to avoid the hazards of oral or customary transmission. Scripture born in these circumstances serves afterwards as a touchstone for the living tradition; it permits the latter to test its fidelity to the word of God. But in return, Scripture itself is not preserved without the support of a traditional interpretation which makes it understandable to its readers, which makes explicit the content of the ancient texts in a way that makes them actual.

Throughout the course of the Old Testament, the unfolding of revelation was thus the fruit of a complex process, in which, on the one hand, intervened the prophets, the personal bearers of an original message, and on the other, the institutional organs of living tradition: priests in charge of the law and cult, singers dedicated to sacred song, scribes trained to teach wisdom. The corpus of the scriptures grew from century to century, but it never dispensed with the need for a multiform tradition, for which it provided a set norm, but which had the task of interpreting it and making it actual. As a result, the word of God was preserved conjointly in the

[23] H. Graf Reventlow, *Gebot und Predigt im Dekalog* (Gütersloh : Gütersloher Verlag, 1952), criticized by N. Lohfink, "Zur Dekalogfassung von Dt 5," *BZ* N.F. 9 (1965), 17-32.

sacred books and in the tradition which it nourished. The books, for their part, played an irreplaceable role; nevertheless, they did not necessarily set everything down explicitly. A simple example: the meaning of Pentecost [24] as memorial of the Sinaitic alliance is nowhere attested in the canonical writings of the Old Testament. But this important element of later Jewish tradition was none the less called upon to play a part in revelation, for it reappears as the background and outline of the Christian Pentecost (Ac 2).

In order, then, to discover the word of God in its entirety in the Old Testament, it is essential not to separate Scripture from the living tradition in which it took root, in which it was preserved, and which continued without interruption to the New Testament. But at the same time it must be noted that in Christ's time this tradition was not as yet fixed in every point. It still retained disputed questions, and was divided into different currents, [25] its understanding of scriptural texts was not unified. Things proceeded as if an absolute principle of unity, an unquestionable criterion of interpretation, were still lacking for the manifold words of God spoken by the prophets "in various times and in various different ways" (Heb 1:1).

## II. CHRIST THE WORD OF GOD [26]

This principle of unity and criterion of interpretation was provided by Christ. He was not only a depository of the word among many others. He did not announce only a partial message in which the mysteries of God and of salvation were only imperfectly unveiled. He was the word in person, presented in its totality in a man who expressed it in its fulness. To be sure, the humanity of Christ constituted in some manner a veil, beneath which the divine glory was hidden from human eyes. But at the same time that it was a veil, it was also a sign through which that glory could be genuinely perceived. [27]

---

[24] "Πεντηκοστή," *TWNT*, 6, pp. 45-49; G. F. Moore, *Judaism in the First Centuries of the Christian Era* 2 (Cambridge, Mass. : Harvard U. Press, 1927-1930), p. 48; K. Hruby, "Shabu'ôt ou la Pentecôte," *OS* 8 (1963), 395-412; R. Le Déaut, "Pentecôte et tradition juive," *Fête de la Pentecôte* (Assemblées du Seigneur 51), pp. 22-38, reprinted in *Spiritus* 7 (1961), 127-144.

[25] It is an anachronism to transfer to the time of Christ the idea of a Jewish orthodoxy which did not develop until after the year 70 when the Pharisaic party took control of the threatened community (cf. D. S. Russell, *The Method and Message of Jewish Apocalyptic* [London : SCM Press, 1964], pp. 20-23). The attempts made in our days to connect Jesus and primitive Christianity either to Pharisaism, or to Essenism, ignore what is in fact its genuine originality.

[26] See the bibliography above, p. 7, note 13.

[27] R. Thibault, *Le sens de l'Homme-Dieu* (Bruxelles-Paris : Desclée de Brouwer, 1942).

## 1. The Two Aspects of the Word of God

Here, as in the Old Testament, the word of God made itself known in two related ways: in meaningful acts that were a part of the unfolding of history, and in human words which made the meaning of those acts explicit. But there is a considerable difference between the meaningful acts in which the faith of Israel recognized the acts of God, and the acts performed by the Word Incarnate. God no longer intervened only with that sovereign power which directs the course of secondary causes by subordinating them to the realization of a transcendent plan, in such a way that the latter is both brought about and signified by the former. Now the word of God entered the course of secondary causes in person; he made himself directly accessible to men. Thus the deeds and acts of Jesus Christ, his social attitudes, his human experiences which culminated in the final drama of his death and return from this world to the Father, all signify the mystery of the living God in an absolute manner, in its relations with the human race that he came to save, as well as in its ineffable innermost being.

Naturally, the meaning of these deeds and events, inasmuch as they are acts of God, is not of itself apparent to everyone. It is necessary for that reason that God himself unveil it. That is precisely the role of the words of Jesus, which do not express a timeless teaching, but rather manifest the rich content of a revelation accomplished in deeds. Now these deeds and words of the word made flesh respond to the demands of our temporal character.[28] They take their place, each at its proper time, in a progressive pedagogy. The concrete relation of Christ to the community in which he was born thus went through successive stages. While those who believed in him grew in nearness to him and in understanding of his mystery, the authorities of his people sank into a rejection which unknown to them prepared the final sacrifice. Jesus adapted his dispensation of the divine word to this situation. It was not finally handed over in its fulness until the mystery of salvation was accomplished through the cross and resurrection.[29] Then all the previous deeds, all the words pronounced in the course of his ministry, took on their full meaning. It was due to their contact with the glorified Christ that the apostles apprehended their definitive meaning, which was partially hidden from their eyes until that supreme moment.

---

[28] J. Mouroux, *Le mystère du temps* (Paris : Aubier, 1962), pp. 79-167. Eng. trans. : *The Mystery of Time* (New York : Desclée, 1964), pp. 85-176.

[29] X. Léon-Dufour, *Les évangiles et l'histoire de Jésus* (Paris : Seuil, 1963), pp. 451 ff. Eng. trans. : *The Gospels and the Jesus of History* (New York : Desclée, 1968), pp. 259 ff.

## 2. Normative Character of Christ, the Word of God

By[thus expressing the word of God in total fashion, Christ accomplished [30] the preparatory revelation which preceded him. Whether it is a question of the acts of God upon his people, or of messages given out by the prophets in the course of time, or of the living tradition born of the divine word and developed with it as basis, or of writings which fixed certain elements of it—everything now received its full meaning in virtue of the mystery of salvation which Christ accomplished and of the revelation which he brought in its fulness. The previous acts of God did no more than prepare for and prefigure him. Prophetic words speak only of him, sketching his traits in various ways. Even the law was training in preparation for understanding his gospel. In him, then, they converged and found their true meaning. He provided the sole norm which makes possible a proper understanding of past sacred history, the law of Israel, and the prophetic promises. This absolute norm replaced that of living tradition whose representatives [31] until then were the Jewish doctors. Not that Jesus was opposed at every point to the tenets of tradition, but he alone provided the decisive criterion for discerning what was to be retained and what was to be abandoned (or better, perfected). In the midst of a community bound in many ways by tradition, he acted and taught with authority (Mk 1:22). From then on, he was the only foundation of faith. The Scripture and tradition of former times, each in its own way, were to be taken into account only insofar as they witnessed him or led to him. In him took place what Origen called the mutation of the scriptures. [32]

---

[30] "Πληρόω," *TWNT* 6, pp. 285-296; for a complete view of "accomplishment" it is necessary to take into account the articles Τελέω and Τελειόω.  On Τελειόω, see C. Spicq, *Épître aux Hébreux* [2] (Paris : Cerf, 1957), pp. 214-225.

[31] P. Lengsfeld, *Überlieferung, Tradition und Schrift in der evangelischen und katholischen Theologie der Gegenwart* (Paderborn : Bonifacius, 1960); French trans. *Tradition, Écriture et Église dans le dialogue œcuménique* (Paris : L'Orante, 1964), cited here.

[32] *In Joannen,* I, 8; cf. *Sens chrétien de l'A.T.,* p. 403.

## II. FROM CHRIST TO THE APOSTLES

### I. APOSTOLIC TRADITION [33]

#### *1. Apostolic Tradition and the Gospel*

Christ wrote nothing. During his earthly life he acted, spoke, shared the condition of men even unto suffering and death. A relatively large number of Jews entered into direct contact with him; as a result, in the following decades a human tradition could arise and preserve the memory of his words, his deeds, his death, etc. But this human tradition would not suffice to found the gospel tradition. This was bound to the ministry of the men called by Jesus to the apostolate [34] and appointed by him witnesses of his resurrection (Ac 1:8.21-22). An immediate contact with the risen Christ was therefore essential to the gospel tradition. But even among those who had that honor (quite numerous according to 1 Co 15:6), and who as a consequence could have recounted the deeds and words of Jesus "from the time when John was baptizing until the day when he was taken up" (Ac 1:22), those whom Luke questioned about "the whole story from the beginning" (Lk 1:3), not all received an apostolic mission properly so called. That was essentially the office of the twelve, thanks to whom the primitive Church had the appearance of a solidly structured organism (Ac 1:13.21-26; 2:14; 5:9). On the other hand, Paul, who was called directly by the risen Christ without having known him during his terrestrial life, is for that reason an apostle (Ga 1:2.12; Rm 1:4ff.) and minister of the gospel on a par with the twelve.

[33] The problem of tradition has been the object of numerous studies in the past ten years. A general orientation will be found in H. Holstein, *La tradition dans l'Église* (Paris : Grasset, 1960); Y. M.-J. Congar, *La Tradition et les traditions : I. Essai Historique, II. Essai Théologique* (Paris : Fayard, 1960-1963); Eng. trans. *Tradition and Traditions* (London : Burns & Oates, 1966). *Idem, La Tradition et la vie de l'Église* (Paris : Fayard, 1963); Eng. trans. *Tradition and the Life of the Church* (London : Burns & Oates, 1965). J. R. Geiselmann, "La tradition," *Questions théologiques aujourd'hui* 1 (Bruges-Paris : Desclée de Brouwer, 1964), pp. 95-148. For the Protestant viewpoint, see "Tradition," *RGG* 3rd. ed., Vol. 6, cols 966-984. We will have occasion frequently to cite the studies collected in the volume *De Scriptura et Traditione* (Roma : Pontificia Academia Mariana Internationalis, 1963); ample bibliography on the question on pp. 85-112.

[34] On the apostolate and the title of apostle, see J. Dupont, "Le nom d'apôtres a-t-il été donné aux Douze par Jésus?" *OS* 1 (1956), 267-290; 425-444. L. Cerfaux, "Pour l'histoire du titre *Apostolos* dans le Nouveau Testament," *RSR* 48 (1960), 76-92 (reprinted in *Recueil L. Cerfaux* 3 [Gembloux : Duculot, 1954], pp. 185-200). P. Lengsfeld, *op. cit.*, p. 38, accepts the criteria of apostolate put forward by K. H. Rengstorf in *TWNT* 1, pp. 431 ff.

For this apostolic group, whose individual members were responsible for witnessing the gospel, Jesus was not an object of free speculation, but the starting point of a sacred tradition [35] which he had charged them to make known to the world. While he wrote nothing, yet he left two things: his words, which were retained in a more or less literal form, understood in depth in the light of his resurrection, assimilated and accepted as the principle and rule of faith; and the memory of his deeds, which were preserved with more or less detail, and understood from the point of view of his total mystery as visible revelations of him who presently acts in his Church in his capacity as Lord. All of this made up the gospel, [36] and this latter contains all the real content of apostolic tradition, [37] the permanent norm of the Church's faith and life.

Naturally, this tradition is of its nature manifold. [38] It covers all the aspects of ecclesial life: the proclamation of the gospel to lead men to the faith, the spiritual instruction of the baptized, the liturgy in all its forms (from prayer meetings copied from the synagogue to wholly Christian services such as the breaking of bread), defense of the faith, a rudimentary juridical organization of the communities, the hierarchical structure of the ministry, etc. Alongside the detailed formulations of the faith, there existed a complex of usages implying doctrinal content. It is understood that the deeds and words of Jesus played a decisive role in this tradition, because they lie at its very source. But they are found there with explanation and commentary which reveal their practical value for the day to day life of the Church. As far as the ancient scriptures and the Jewish tradition which until then proclaimed its meaning are concerned, they were now looked upon in a different light, from the exclusive point of view of the gospel,

---

[35] X. Léon-Dufour, *The Gospels and the Jesus of History*, pp. 193 ff.

[36] Y. Congar, *Tradition and Traditions*, pp. 274-283 makes use of the word "gospel" (following the Council of Trent) to define the deposit of faith. Similarly, J. Dupont, "Écriture et Tradition," *NRT* 85 (1963), 344 ff.

[37] It is on this apostolic tradition that the accent is put in H. Holstein, *op. cit.*, 169 ff. See similarly J. R. Geiselmann in *Questions théologiques aujourd'hui*, pp. 113-136; R. Bandas, "Biblia et Traditio juxta Scripturam," *De Scriptura et Traditione*, pp. 171-180; P. Lengsfeld, *Tradition, Écriture et Église*, pp. 37-72.

[38] P. Lengsfeld, *op. cit.*, pp. 41-44, 54-72 analyzes these various forms of the apostolic *paradosis*. But he does it to underline in his conclusion (pp. 65-72) that it does not consist only in a transmission of words (verbal transmission); it comprises the transmission of a *res* (real transmission) which is no other than the gift of the Holy Spirit and grace itself. Verbal transmission does no more than announce (always in a more or less inadequate way) the content of real transmission signified by the activity of the Church. It is in this same sense that we here speak of the practice of the Church, which, in perpetuating itself, forever contains a body of thought—verbal transmission is implied in real transmission. This fact begins at the level of apostolic tradition.

and as witnesses to Christ. As a result, while the Scriptures were preserved in whole by reason of their sacred character, tradition became the object of meticulous selection [39]; in any case, the interpretation given to the legacy received from Judaism underwent a profound change under the influence of the originality of the gospel.

## 2. Diversity and Development of Apostolic Tradition

Apostolic tradition differed according to the personality of those who transmitted it. For example, Peter does not bring Jesus alive in the same way as John, as a comparison of the gospel of Mark ("the memoirs of Peter" according to St. Justin [40]) with the fourth gospel shows. As for Paul, for the whole time of the terrestrial life of Jesus and even for his apparitions after the resurrection, he could appeal only to the tradition [41] which he had received, as he explicitly states (1 Co 11:23; 15:3). But that did not prevent him from developing a particularly original gospel. Now Paul was deeply aware of the absolute unity of the gospel (2 Co 11:4; Ga 1:6-9). This unity, however, must be rightly understood: the single-mindedness of the witnesses, their sharing in the same faith, their agreement in understanding the mystery of Christ—these do not demand uniformity. Divine revelation, given in its totality in Christ, now found its adequate formulation in this manifold teaching which brought its content to light under the direction of the Holy Spirit. [42] In order, therefore, to gather the full testimony, it is necessary to gather what all the witnesses said. They complement one another, and the variety of their points of view contributes to the richness of the gospel which they all served.

[39] The distinction made by the Jewish doctors between *halakah* and *haggadah* is here of significance. The opposition of Jesus to the tradition of the ancients (Mk 7 : 5) refers essentially to rabbinic *halakah*. Primitive Christian theology was much more receptive to the *haggadah*, which enriched it both in matter and in form.

[40] St. Justin, *Dialogue with Trypho* 106, 3 (the allusion to Mk 3:16 ff. is attributed to the Memoirs of Peter).

[41] L. Cerfaux, "La Tradition selon saint Paul," *Recueil L. Cerfaux* 2, pp. 253-264; "Les deux points de départ de la tradition chrétienne," *ibid.*, pp. 265-282. B. Rigaux, "De traditione apud S. Paulum," *De Scriptura et traditione*, pp. 137-169 (with bibliography). Reservations must be made about the work of K. Wegenast, *Das Verständnis der Tradition bei Paulus und Deuteropaulinen* (Neukirchen: Neukirchener Verlag, 1962). In the passages cited here, Paul uses the vocabulary of rabbinic tradition. It is necessary, therefore, to take account of the techniques of the latter in order to understand the formation of apostolic tradition when it has to do with the words of Jesus or with accounts about him. Cf. B. Gerhardsson, *Memory and Manuscript: Oral Tradition and Written Transmission in Rabbinic Judaism and Early Christianity* (Uppsala: C. W. K. Gleerup, 1961); M. Smith, "A Comparison of Early Christian and Early Rabbinic Tradition," *JBL* 92 (1963), 169-176.

[42] A. Feuillet, "De munere doctrinali a Paraclito in Ecclesia expleto juxta evangelium sancti Joannis," *De Scriptura et Traditione*, pp. 115-136.

In the same way, the tradition they represent should not be looked upon as something static, something set down from the first day in a complete and definitive form. It rather grew with the times, in proportion as the apostolic Church faced new problems or enriched its language in order to announce the gospel in new circumstances. The passage from a Jewish to a pagan world, the crisis raised by Judaizers, contact with Alexandrian culture (Ac 18:24 and the letter to the Hebrews), the growing opposition of Judaism which ended in expulsion of Christians from the synagogue, the necessity of defending the genuine gospel against arising heresies—all of these were decisive experiences which contributed to the enrichment of the apostolic tradition. It is certain that the apostles properly so called (the twelve and Paul) were not the only ones who had a hand in facing and solving these problems; all those who in practice had some responsibility took part, each according to the position he held. Still the testimony and the authority of the apostles remained the supreme norm, and even the exclusive one. As far as possible, they were consulted directly, since they controlled the life of the churches. Once their approval was obtained, the undertakings of local ministers were incorporated into the apostolic tradition. The case of the evangelization of the pagans at Antioch furnishes a good example (Ac 11:20-24), and better still the settling of the problem of the circumcised and uncircumcised at the same table (Ga 2:1-10; Ac 15:1-29). Still, in many cases the way in which this collegial authority, [43] whether in matters of doctrine or discipline, was exercised remains unknown to us. Perhaps it was a case of tacit agreement (the same which even now permits a custom to prevail by prescription over a written law), or of general conformity without formal approbation. It is only in such vague ways that the apostolicity of certain New Testament writings can be understood.

## II. THE APOSTOLIC WRITINGS

Apostolic tradition did indeed tend spontaneously to become fixed in written texts, either in general outlines which were amplified to fit the needs of preaching or the liturgy, or in precise formulas, traces of which can already be found in the letters of St. Paul (1 Co 11:23-26; 15:2 ff.). This is not the place to examine the question in detail. [44] Suffice it to say that a functional literature [45] was already well on the way to formation in the apostolic age.

---

[43] On this solidarity of apostolic responsibility, see J. Colson, *L'épiscopat catholique, Collégialité et primauté dans les trois premiers siècles de l'Église* (Paris: Cerf, 1963), pp. 15-29; Vatican II, Dogmatic Constitution *Lumen gentium*, N° 19.

[44] P. Lengsfeld, *Tradition, Écriture et Église*, pp. 55-62.

[45] We will develop this point later (below, pp. 82 ff.).

Its core was obviously first of all the gospel material, or in other words, the formulation of the words of Jesus, which were used according to the needs of the communities, and of the recollections of Jesus, which served to nourish Christian faith by providing material for it to contemplate its Lord. [46] Around the gospel thus narrowly defined other texts arose, which more directly filled the daily needs of ecclesiastical life. It was in this framework that the books of the New Testament came into being. Some of them, as the letters of St. Paul, have an immediate connection with an apostle. For others, it was a disciple who collected the apostolic testimony, as Mark did for the gospel of Peter. [47] The collaboration of secretaries from among the followers of the apostles is sometimes clearly evident, as that of Silas in the first letter of Peter (1 P 5:12). Finally, there are cases in which an author acted on his own authority, leaving the mark of his own personality or of his theology on his presentation of the gospel or on his reflections on Christian life. Such is the case of the writings of Luke and the letter to the Hebrews, without mentioning the pseudonymous second letter of Peter. [48] It makes little difference, since all these works have something in common: they are rooted in the world in which the apostles exercised their normative authority, or at least in the life of the churches which were directly influenced by apostolic tradition, and they have no other goal but to fix that same tradition, [49] moved by the necessity of defending it against heretical teachers who distorted its sense (the case of 2 P 3:16).

It must however be noted that these are no more than occasional crystallizations of apostolic tradition, and they are therefore necessarily partial. There exists no complete collection of the deeds and sayings of Jesus, and no gospel that presents the whole of the testimony (cf. Jn 20:30; 21:25). There is no systematic exposition of the faith, even from the particular point of view of only one apostle or one doctor; no liturgical and sacramentary collection that reproduces fully the texts used in even one church, and that would give a full picture of its cultic life; no collection of laws, no speculative synthesis of the structure of the Church and its ministry.

[46] X. Léon-Dufour, *op. cit.*, pp. 256-280. Eng. tran., pp. 175-187.

[47] On the relation of Mark to the Gospel of Peter, see M. J. Lagrange, *Évangile selon saint Marc* (Paris : Lecoffre, 5th ed., 1929) pp. xvi-xxxii; L. Vaganay, *Le problème synoptique* (Tournai-Paris : Desclée, 1954), pp. 152 ff. Of the two traditions, that of Clement of Alexandria and that of Irenaeus, the second must certainly be preferred; it places the final edition of the gospel after the death of Peter.

[48] On the problem of authenticity which this book poses, see below, p. 36, note 4.

[49] P. Lengsfeld, *op. cit.*, pp. 74-75. Likewise, R. Geiselmann in *Questions théologiques aujourd'hui* I, pp. 133-136, who, following Moehler, shows the importance of this written fixation of apostolic tradition for the Church in every age. Cf. J. A. Moehler, *Die Einheit in der Kirche* (Köln: Hegner, 1957).

All of these things certainly existed in the life of the communities, and it would be extremely useful for us to be acquainted with them directly. But we must resign ourselves to our ignorance; form criticism of the apostolic writings enlightens us only on insignificant points. [50] It is obvious that this fragmentary character of the New Testament books must be taken into consideration if one is to use them correctly. [51] They are authentic representatives of apostolic tradition from which they proceed and to which they belong with full right. It is quite unlikely that any essential doctrinal element is completely lacking in them. But they certainly do not explicitly express all the richness of that tradition, no more than they put all of its elements in order and indicate their relative importance. Therefore, to undertake to reconstruct that tradition on the basis of the New Testament alone would produce only a mutilated image of it, one with many obscure points, both in doctrine and even more in practice. Christian theology must keep this difficulty ever present to mind; it is the stumbling block for the principle of *Scripture alone* taken in its strictest sense.

## § III. THE CHURCH BEFORE THE WORD OF GOD

The question here is not the attitude the Church ought to take in regard to the word of God, but the practical way in which it can actually know it fully in order to make it operative in its faith and life. We touch here a sore point, on which it is not just Catholic and Protestant theology that find themselves in opposition. [52] Within Protestantism a fundamentalist current

---

[50] Concerning the form criticism of the Pauline letters, consult B. Rigaux, *Saint Paul et ses lettres* (Bruges-Paris: Desclée de Brouwer, 1962), pp. 163-199. To be noted is the extent to which the Pauline texts allow us to uncover the tradition which precedes them. A further example in M. E. Boismard, *Quatre hymnes baptismales dans la première épître de Pierre* (Paris: Cerf, 1961).

[51] Concerning this "contingent and occasional character of Scripture," Cardinal Journet remarks that "the oral preaching of the apostles was likewise in part occasioned by contingent events. The important thing is to know that God is the Lord of contingency, and he uses it to realize his plan" (*Le message révélé: Sa transmission, son développement, ses dépendances* [Bruges-Paris: Desclée de Brouwer, 1964] p. 38). Assuredly; but the problem here is to recover apostolic tradition *in its entirety* with admittedly partial documentation as a starting point. What practical means has God provided for this?

[52] Concerning the history of this theological problem, consult the work of Y. Congar, *Tradition and Traditions*, Part I, Historical Essay. The exposition of A. Michel, "Tradition," *DTC* 15, cols. 1252-1350, is dominated by the anti-Protestant controversy (on the 16th century, see cols. 1306-1317) but the patristic evidence is quite ample (cols. 1256-1300). Concerning the crisis of the 16th century, consult G. H. Tavard, *Écriture ou Église? La crise de la Réforme* (Paris: Cerf, 1963). Concerning modern times, P. Lengsfeld, *Tradition, Écriture et Église dans le dialogue œcuménique* (Paris: L'Orante, 1964).

continues to hold for *Scripture alone* in an intransigent manner, while other theologians are searching in various ways to make a positive reevaluation of ecclesiastical tradition.[53] This has become more apparent since the Fourth World Faith and Order Conference[54] (Montreal, 1963). On the other hand, Catholic theologians themselves are divided over what is called "the problem of the two sources," as the first session of Vatican II made strikingly apparent. The Council of Trent admittedly chose a prudent wording on this point, one that did not prejudice any of the real relations between Scripture and Tradition.[55] But theologians soon thereafter returned to the wording contained in the text of the decree proposed to the council fathers for discussion. That text stated revealed truth *"partim contineri in libris scriptis, partim in traditionibus non scriptis,"* not without emphasis on the meaning of *"partim...partim."*[56] This view is today rejected by a

[53] See the exposition of the dogmatic problem and the recent bibliography in the article by G. Ebeling, *RGG*, 3rd. ed., Vol. 6, cols. 976-984. Among the works devoted to the question, we note: O. Cullmann, *Die Tradition* (Zürich: Zwingli-Verlag, 1954); A. C. Outler, *The Christian Tradition and the Unity We Seek* (New York: Oxford Univ. Press, 1957); E. Schlink, *Der kommende Christus und die kirchliche Tradition* (Göttingen: Vandenhoeck, 1961); A. Benoit, *L'actualité des Pères de l'Église* (Neuchâtel-Paris: Delachaux, 1961); F. Leenhardt, "'Sola scriptura' ou 'Écriture et Tradition'?"; *Études théologiques et religieuses* 36 (1961), 5-46; M. Thurian, *L'unité visible des chrétiens et la Tradition* (Paris: Epi, 1961). General discussions may be found in Y. Congar, *op. cit.*, pp. 459-493; R. Beaupère, *De Scriptura et traditione*, pp. 527-541.

[54] Cf. particularly the position of J. L. Leuba in *Tradition et traditions* (Publication of the work of the Congress's preparatory commission) pp. 67 ff. For the continuation of the discussion after the Conference: J. P. Gabus, "Comment repenser dans une perspective protestante le rapport Écriture-Tradition," *Istina* 8 (1963), 305-318; J. Leuba, "La Tradition et les traditions: Essai de systématique chrétienne," *VC* 18 (1964), 75-92.

[55] The history of the redaction of the Tridentine decree is complex. Cf. G. H. Tavard, *op. cit.*, pp. 294-303. Y. Congar, *op. cit.*, pp. 164-169. A discussion on this point was set in motion by J. R. Geiselmann, "Das Konzil von Trient über das Verhältnis der Heiligen Schrift und der nicht geschriebenen Traditionen," *Die mündliche Überlieferung*, ed. M. Schmaus (Munich: Max Hueber, 1957), pp. 123-206. Remarks by J. Beumer, "Die Frage nach Schrift und Tradition bei Robert Bellarmin," *Scholastik* 34 (1959), 1-22. More radical criticism by H. Lennerz in *Gregorianum* 40 (1959), 38-53, 624-635; 42 (1961), 517-521; H. Schauf, "Schrift und Tradition," *Antonianum* 39 (1964), 200-209.

[56] J. Dupont, "Écriture et Tradition," *NRT* 85 (1963), 337-346, 449-468. J. Beumer, *Die mündliche Überlieferung als Glaubensquelle* (Freiburg i. Br.: Herder, 1962). A. Trapè, "De Traditionis relatione ad S. Scripturam juxta concilium Tridentinum," *Augustinianum* 3 (1963), 253-289; P. de Vooght, "Remarques sur l'évolution du problème Écriture-Tradition chez les théologiens de Salamanque," *Istina* 8 (1963), 279-304. It should be noted that Latin style gives the expression *"partim...partim"* a less exact meaning than that which the theologians of the schools arrived at in the post-Tridentine period, as has been demonstrated by A. M. Dubarle, "Quelques notes sur Écriture et Tradition," *RSPT* 48 (1964), 274-280—from Cicero through St. Thomas to the 16th century, *"partim...partim"* is found in the very vague sense of "on the one hand...on the other."

number of theologians, who hold it contrary to patristic thought and even that of the Middle Ages. [57] Following the latter, they willingly accept the idea of the "sufficiency of Scripture," [58] in a sense, evidently, which does not coincide with the *Scripture alone* of the Protestant reformers.

We will not be able here to treat this complex question in detail. But we must at least clarify certain points that are involved in the particular problem we are dealing with: that of Scripture, its place in the Church and its interpretation. What we have just said about apostolic tradition furnishes us the best starting point. For that tradition is, in fact, the unique source [59] of the faith and of theology, both as expression of the word of God addressed to men in Christ, and as criterion of interpretation for all his previous words. It remains for us then to examine two points: 1) the relation of ecclesiastical tradition to apostolic tradition, and consequently, 2) the relation of ecclesiastical tradition to Scripture.

## I. APOSTOLIC TRADITION AND ECCLESIASTICAL TRADITION

### I. THE PROBLEM OF TRANSFERAL

In relation to the word of God, the supreme rule of faith, apostolic tradition and ecclesiastical tradition are in quite different situations. The first is the medium through which that word reached men and took the form of human language. The second is the living environment which received it, conserved it, and made it flourish. The passage from one to the other did not take place at a determined moment in time, for example, at the passage from the first to the second century, or at the death of the last apostle. It was taking

---

[57] J. R. Geiselmann, *Die Heilige Schrift und die Tradition. Zu neueren kontroversen über das Verhältnis der Heiligen Schrift zu der nichtgeschriebenen Traditionen* (Freiburg i. Br.: Herder, 1962); Eng. trans. *The Meaning of Tradition* (London: Burns & Oates, 1966).

[58] Y. Congar, *op. cit.*, pp. 107-118; A. Lang, "Sacrae Scripturae sufficientia?" *De Scriptura et Traditione*, pp. 62-65; G. Barauna, "Quaenam Sacrae Scripturae sufficientia in Ecclesia catholica teneatur," *ibid.*, pp. 73-84.

[59] It should be noted that the language of theology is equivocal in its use of the word "source." From the standpoint of its particular understanding of its task, which was to establish dogmas by founding them on scriptural texts, 19th-century theology distinguished Scripture and Tradition as *two sources*; "*Scripturam et traditiones fontes esse divinae revelationis*," wrote Pius IX in the letter *Inter gravissimas* (1870). The schema presented in the first session of Vatican II employed the same language. But if one places himself in the perspective of the history of salvation, in which revelation reaches man through the word of God, there can be question of only *one source*: the preaching of the gospel by the apostles, or, if one prefers, apostolic tradition (cf. the text of the Council of Trent cited below, p. 32, note 97). This manner of approaching the question does not touch the problem of the relation between Scripture and ecclesiastical tradition.

place while the apostles were still alive, since they confided the care of the gospel and custody of some churches to others who were not, as they were, direct witnesses of Christ. Thus the churches of Thessalonia and Corinth have the obligation of preserving faithfully the tradition [60] (or traditions) of the founding apostle (2 Th 2.15; 3:6; 1 Co 11:2), and the responsibility fell primarily on the "overseers" (1 Th 5:12) whom Paul placed at their head (cf. 1 Co 16:16). This is even clearer in the pastoral letters [61]: those sent by the apostle must "take great care of all that has been entrusted to them" (1 Tm 6:20; 2 Tm 1:12-14; 3:14; Tt 2:1) and then entrust it to some tried persons who will instruct the others (2 Tm 2:2).

That is exactly the definition of ecclesiastical tradition. Its content includes both teaching and practice, which are to be preserved as equally important. This does not prejudice the existence of apostolic writings, nor the role which they play in this tradition. It means simply that ecclesiastical tradition is a unique means of transmitting the legacy of the apostles. [62] The attitude demanded of Titus and Timothy defines that which the whole Church ought consequently to adopt in its hierarchical structure established by the apostles: the exercise of the ministry, in teaching as well as in practice, remains forever linked to the original deposit which is its only norm. It is obvious how narrow and finally false it would be to reduce this tradition to the mere oral transmission of certain sayings handed down from Christ, or to certain recollections of him, around the edges of the New Testament. [63] This manner of conceiving it can only cloud the problem, and lead its discussion into ways that leave no hope for a positive solution.

## II. THE PROBLEM OF CONTINUITY AND FIDELITY

The radical difference of situation between apostolic tradition and ecclesiastical tradition in relation to the word of God has no effect on their perfect

---

[60] For a more detailed study, see that of B. Rigaux in *De Scriptura et traditione*, pp. 137 ff.

[61] This point is touched upon by H. Schlier, "La hiérarchie de l'Église d'après les épîtres pastorales," *Le temps de l'Église* (French trans. Tournai-Paris: Desclée, 1961), pp. 140-156. Concerning the notion of deposit in the pastoral epistles, see the study of C. Spicq, *Les épîtres pastorales* (Paris: Lecoffre-Gabalda, 1947), pp. 327-335; S. Cipriani, "La dottrina del Depositum nelle lettere pastorali," *Studiorum paulinorum congressus internationalis catholicus* 2 (Roma: Pont. Biblical Institute, 1963), pp. 129-142.

[62] Y. Congar, *op. cit.*, pp. 348-375, underlines the fecundity of Blondel's thought on this point, as does likewise H. Holstein, *op. cit.*, pp. 134-140.

[63] The confusion is classic. An example is the work of R.P.C. Hanson, *Tradition in the Early Church* (London: SCM Press, 1962); see the pertinent criticism of J. Daniélou, "Écriture et tradition," *RSR* 51 (1963), 550-557.

continuity and substantial identity, allowing for the qualifications we are about to make. This is the result, first of all, of a historically established fact. There is not the slightest doubt that the churches of the second century took great care to preserve intact the legacy received from the apostles, no matter what might have been its form: the gospel message proper and the interpretation of the ancient scriptures made in light of it; ecclesiastical organization, beliefs, customs and rites; oral teachings and written texts. The permanence of religious thought and practice, assured by the permanence of community structures and ministers, forbade in the churches that spiritual foment exemplified in the various sects of every age. Ideas and practices, as well as writings, certainly passed from one church to another. But such conservatism existed as could provoke conflicts when local traditions differed, as happened in the Easter question. [64] Even more, the struggle against false teachers, begun at the end of the apostolic age (pastoral letters, Jude, first letter of John, second of Peter), increased with the passage of time until it reached its height in the age of St. Irenaeus. In this struggle the defenders of orthodoxy had as their principal weapon the apostolicity both of doctrine and practices held in the churches. [65] These fundamental preoccupations remained the same in all the following centuries. And whenever there was a question of having recourse to ancient ecclesiastical tradition to ascertain the content of the gospel or the way to live according to it, it was not a matter of recognizing in that tradition a self-sufficient authority, but solely one of finding in it a testimony for some element which it considered apostolic.

It might be asked whether such a fidelity to the original deposit is possible, given the many historical factors that have influenced ecclesiastical tradition over twenty centuries. Since the sixteenth century Protestant theology has systematically depreciated that tradition, considering it a mere human tradition, subject to all the hazards which such traditions undergo. [66] But this stand neglects an essential element of the life of the Church as Body of Christ, which Moehler so well made clear in his presentation of living tradition [67]: the presence and activity of the Holy Spirit. The promise of perpetual assistance made by the risen Christ to his apostles (Mt 28:20) is fulfilled in the mission of the Paraclete (cf. Jn 15:26 ff.; 16:7-11). If the

---

[64] J. Lebreton in Fliche et Martin, *Histoire de l'Église* 2, pp. 87-93. The two practices, Roman and Asiatic, both claimed apostolic origin.

[65] *Ibid.*, pp. 54-56. I. Ortiz de Urbina, "Traditio et Scriptura apud primaevos Patres orientales," *De Scriptura et traditione*, pp. 185-203; Y. Congar, *op. cit.*, pp. 26 ff.

[66] See the texts cited by E. Stakemeier in *De Scriptura et traditione*, pp. 505-526.

[67] J. A. Moehler, *Die Einheit in der Kirche*; French trans. *L'unité dans l'Église* (Paris: Cerf, 1938), pp. 10-12. Cf. Y. Congar, *op. cit.*, pp. 193 ff.

word spoken by God to men in Christ is, in the Church, something more than a document of the past, if every man can receive it as a living and actual reality, it is all due to that activity of the Spirit. It was thus already for the apostolic announcement of the gospel: the testimony of the Spirit went hand in hand with the testimony of the twelve (Jn 15:26 ff.; Ac 1:8) at the same time that it manifested itself in the hearts of believers (Rm 8:16). The Church's proclamation of the gospel received from the apostles is in the same condition. [68] That is precisely the fundamental element of tradition in every age of history. When it is asked in what this activity of the Spirit consists, it is necessary to avoid reducing it to the interior illumination of the hearts of believers. [69] In reality, it accompanies, animates, and assists with graces the same ministers who give tradition a definite form. [70] All of these are concrete means through which the Spirit assures the Church's indefectibility in faith. [71]

That being the case, it is clear that the tradition of the Church cannot be likened to any human tradition. Apostolic tradition is preserved in the Church in its integrity, authentically and faithfully. It must be noted, however, that it is not preserved after the fashion of unused capital. Both as to doctrine and to practice it undergoes a legitimate development. If the successive experiences of the apostolic Church contributed positively to the formulation of revelation itself, [72] the experiences of the following centuries had as their natural fruit the manifestation of the hidden riches

[68] This point is admitted to a certain extent by some Protestant theologians: "There is no break between apostolic times and the time of the Church in the sense that the real presence of Christ continues from the first to the second. The time of the Church must not be emptied of its Christological content. Jesus Christ willed to be present among his own until the end of the world..., and this presence is the apostolate, which Christ instituted as the instrument of his presence" (F. J. Leenhardt, "'Sola Scriptura' ou 'Écriture et tradition'?" *Études théologiques et religieuses* 36 [1961] 31.) "The apostolate as such did not disappear with the disappearance of the persons of the first apostles; the apostolate perpetuates itself as a constitutive function of the Church, because Jesus Christ continues to will to actualize his word and make his person present to all nations until the end of the world" (*ibid.*, 34). By putting the accent on the action of Jesus Christ, the author leaves open the question of the mode of action of the Holy Spirit in the Church.

[69] It is at this level only that Calvin establishes a relationship between the word of God and the activity of the Holy Spirit. Cf. G. H. Tavard, *Écriture ou Église?*, pp. 145 ff.

[70] It is at this point that the proper role of the ecclesiastical magisterium in tradition must be placed. Cf. H. Holstein, *La Tradition dans l'Église*, pp. 207-229; Y. Congar, *op. cit.*, pp. 328 ff.

[71] We do not propose to treat here in detail the problem of the infallibility of the Church. As a property of living tradition directed by the Holy Spirit, it operates at every level of the hierarchical body of the Church, according to the proper role of each.

[72] Above, pp. 17 ff.

of that primitive deposit. That is the meaning of the development of dogma: it adds nothing to the apostolic heritage; it only brings to light certain of its implications, which were perhaps attested in the beginning only under the form of a practice. [73] It is important nonetheless not to confuse the tradition of the Church with the manifold forms which the development of the apostolic deposit might have taken on in one or the other age, or in one or the other particular church. Ecclesiastical traditions do not all represent Tradition with the same right or in the same degree, [74] any more than the theologians' presentation of dogma represents doctrine as such. [75]

These remarks show that the faithful preservation of tradition is not a simple matter. It constantly demands of those in positions of responsibility a twofold effort: on the one hand, they must seek to grasp apostolic tradition in its entirety in order to make it bear fruit in response to the needs of the times; on the other, they must test the quality of the traditions (doctrinal and practical) handed down from the previous age, in order to avoid being pulled by the weight of history toward a deviation from the apostolic deposit. What means do they have to accomplish this? It is here that the problem of the relation between ecclesiastical tradition and Scripture enters.

## II. ECCLESIASTICAL TRADITION AND SCRIPTURE

### I. PARTIAL SOLUTIONS

The problem becomes clear when one contemplates the activity of the Holy Spirit since Pentecost in its totality and in its diverse forms. In order effectively to bring about the salvation of men, the Spirit forms the Church and animates it from within. [76] But here too his activity takes on quite particular forms: he inspired the apostles to be witnesses of Jesus Christ

---

[73] Concerning this "progress of the Church in understanding the faith," see Y. Congar, La foi et la théologie, pp. 93-120.

[74] The confusion between Tradition and traditions has undoubtedly introduced a pernicious equivocation into the controversy between Catholics and Protestants. The historical determination given by the Church (or a part of the Church) to the various elements which constitute Tradition cannot to that extent claim apostolic origin; as a result, they are subject to revision and reform.

[75] Not even conciliar definitions escape the relativity of history: they refer to a particular problem; the terminology used in their formulation is that of a given language and a given time. It is necessary to keep these determinant elements in mind to understand their intent, and thus their real content.

[76] The idea is well known in theology. It is beautifully developed by Dom A. Vonier, The Spirit and the Bride (London: Burns, Oates & Washburn, 1935), pp. 13-33, 73-84.

and formulators of revelation; he inspired the sacred writers who set the apostolic tradition down in writing, no matter how occasional and incomplete their works; he then produced in the Church a *sensus fidei* which provides it with a proper understanding of the original deposit; he assists the magisterium in its proper tasks; he gives to pastors, prophets and doctors (to use the Pauline vocabulary of ministries) an understanding of the faith in order to promote dogmatic progress. [77] In this general outline, Scripture and ecclesiastical tradition occupy definite places, which determine their relationship.

God willed the existence of Scripture in order to permit his Church to touch the apostolic tradition directly, the supreme norm of its faith and life. [78] This fact alone confers on the New Testament an incomparable dignity. But to use it correctly, it is well not to forget its limits. The books of which it is made up, as we saw above, [79] have by no means captured explicitly all the richness of apostolic tradition, nor announced clearly the totality of doctrine which then sustained the life of faith, nor described in detail the full content of the practice of the Christian churches. They have even less explained under all its aspects the authentic interpretation of the ancient Scriptures considered as the word of God accomplished in Christ. It would likewise be an error to suppose *a priori* that they necessarily determined every essential, giving each a place proportionate to its importance. In the life of a society, is it not rather the controversial points that have a better chance of being noted, rather than those that are taken for granted and are commonly admitted? So the silence of the New Testament on such or such a point of doctrine or practice must not be taken, by itself alone, as an indication of non-existence. Consequently, if it were applied as a mechanical rule, rejecting from the faith and from Church life everything that is not expressly mentioned there, the end would surely be a mutilation of the word of God, an amputation or minimization of a part of its authentic content. This would be to reconstruct the faith and Christian life artificially on the basis of fragmentary documentation. It would be uncertain even how much such an operation would retain of the primitive deposit, and how much it would allow to fall by the way. The principle of *Scripture alone*, if strictly applied,—supposing that that is

---

[77] This manifold activity of the Holy Spirit in the economy of salvation is used by K. Rahner, *Inspiration in the Bible* (New York: Herder & Herder, 1961) to illuminate the problem of scriptural inspiration: only the Church assisted by the Spirit possesses the understanding of Scripture inspired by the Spirit.

[78] "Sacred Scripture is the normative externalization of the normative faith of the apostolic Church," wrote K. Rahner in "Écriture et tradition," *L'homme devant Dieu. Mélanges H. de Lubac* 3 (Paris: Montaigne, 1964), p. 219.

[79] Above, p. 19.

possible—grinds to a halt in this disastrous quandary.[80] And who can admit that Christ destined his Church to so unfortunate a plight?

At the opposite pole from this position, an unrestrained glorification of tradition would result in no less serious pitfalls. Let us take our bearing within this opposite approach.[81] Since the Holy Spirit's assistance of the Church is assured, the conformity of ecclesiastical tradition with apostolic tradition is also assured. So too with the development of dogma and the infallibility of the magisterium. Scripture generally provides a partial proof of this. But precisely where it does not, one can pass on in peace. The presence of a common belief in ecclesiastical tradition in a given age supplies in some manner for its silence, and that suffices to prove a theological thesis or lay down a dogma. Revelation is preserved *partim in Scriptura, partim in Traditione.* The accent should perhaps be put on the *partim... partim,* because the absence of certain facts in Scripture rightly demonstrates the independence of the traditional source from the scriptural source.[82] In this view, the word of God as conserved in the Church in its living form takes precedence in practice over the word of God in its written form, even if in principle the preeminence of the latter is recognized in any matter it treats.

In reality, these two opposite positions seem to share a similar juridical conception of a theological proof, a heritage perhaps of medieval scholasticism. According to this conception, a proof arises out of a sort of syllogistic reasoning founded upon a normative text. That is why, on the one hand, in laying down the principle "Word of God=Scripture," everything that is not found there is eliminated as something foreign to the apostolic deposit; on the other hand, given the principle that ecclesiastical tradition is undoubtedly faithful to apostolic tradition, it is permissible to leap over the divinely established medium (Scripture) to allow the Church to lay hold of the latter. The one position risks mutilating the apostolic tradition; the other, canonizing as word of God mere ecclesiastical traditions.[83]

[80] This position, which was that of orthodox Lutheranism, is not in perfect agreement with the thought of Luther himself. The latter sought the norm of faith, beyond the Bible itself, in what constitutes its heart: its witness to salvation accorded by grace. Cf. F. Refoulé, "L'Église et le Saint-Esprit chez Luther," *RSPT* 48 (1964), 451-453.

[81] We are not here presenting a precise thesis which can be attributed to any particular theologian. Our aim is just to push to their extreme the tendencies of a current of academic theology, whose outlines unfortunately dominate more than a few works on the subjects.

[82] Concerning this limiting of the sense given to "*partim...partim,*" see the remarks of A. M. Dubarle in the article cited above, p. 56, note 21.

[83] The risk is not just imaginary, for the expressions used by certain fathers at the Council of Trent, and by some theologians since, give substance to the tendency. Cf. the declaration of Tomaso Casella cited by G. H. Tavard, *Écriture ou Église ?,* pp. 290 f.

## II. THE POSITION OF THE PATRISTIC AND MIDDLE AGES [84]

### 1. Second Century Theology

Instead of discussing the problem theoretically, there are advantages in having recourse to the ancient tradition of the Church to discover its attitude in the matter. That of the second century has a particular interest because of its proximity to the apostolic age. As we saw above, [85] in order to combat rising heresies and to present a firm foundation for every doctrine, the authors of the time appealed to the criterion of apostolic origin. But they applied that criterion without distinguishing between Scripture and the traditions that are not to be found in it. [86] It is true that during the same age, in the face of a proliferation of apocryphal and especially heretical literature which circulated under well-known names, an effort was made to determine concretely the list of the books in which authentic apostolic tradition was preserved with the guarantee of the Holy Spirit. There were indeed hesitations concerning one or the other book in particular, but the principle of a canon was not for that any less clearly set down. [87] Only this did not make those books an automatic rule, whose application, for the rest, would have mutilated the current tradition by eliminating elements which were not explicitly attested in Scripture, but which were in peaceful and uncontested possession.

Oral traditions relative to the words of Christ or to recollections of his life are here much less in question than church practices and the interpretation of the Scriptures. If it were a question only of the first, we would be forced to admit the legacy of the presbyters preserved by Papias or by Irenaeus was often of quite mediocre quality, for example, in the question of millenarianism [88] (which is, as a matter of fact, a problem of interpretation of the New Testament on which ecclesiastical tradition appears divided [89]).

[84] Besides the general works already cited, see D. van der Eynde, *Les normes de l'enseignement chrétien dans la littérature patristique des trois premiers siècles* (Gembloux-Paris: Duculot, 1933); J. Daniélou, *Message évangélique et culture hellénistique aux IIe et IIIe siècles* (Tournai-Paris: Desclée, 1961), pp. 131-145.

[85] Above, p. 24.

[86] For St. Ignatius of Antioch this fact is underlined by R. M. Grant, "Scripture and Tradition in St. Ignatius of Antioch," *CBQ* 25 (1963), 322-335.

[87] There is basic agreement on this point between O. Cullmann, *La Tradition*, pp. 41 ff., and Y. Congar, *op. cit.*, pp. 417-420. Their disagreement concerns the interpretation of this fact (Y. Congar, *ibid.*, pp. 38-42). See also P. Lengsfeld, *Tradition, Écriture et Église*, pp. 78-83.

[88] Cf. J. Lebreton in Fliche et Martin, *Histoire de l'Église* 2, pp. 61 ff.

[89] St. Justin, *Dialogue with Trypho* 80-81, makes this clear, since he explicitly cites the sources for his belief in the millennium, and says that "some Christians of sound and pious doctrine know nothing of it."

But the same Irenaeus, who was so firmly attached to the apostolicity of
doctrine, points to Mary as the new Eve, [90] a point which Scripture nowhere
explicitly attests, though the theme is not without discreet points of contact
with it. [91] For the writers of the second century, then, Scripture is not
a source which limits meaning, as Protestant theology understands it. It is
at one and the same time a mysterious word whose depths must be
investigated, and a touchstone which provides a means of testing the value
of doctrines and practices. Recourse is had to it to keep ecclesiastical
tradition faithful to its apostolic norm, but at the same time all of its hidden
riches are given their due. It is scarcely disputable, therefore, that some
non-written traditions, linked to Christian practices of every sort, were
preserved as an authentic legacy of the apostles. [92] But effort was always
made to compare them with Scripture in order to trace their roots—somewhat
in the manner in which the Jewish doctors labored to found the *halakah*
and *haggadah* on the sacred texts.

## 2. The Following Centuries

This procedure prevailed throughout the patristic age, modified only by
the fact that the apostolic age was ever more distant. In this age Scripture
was for tradition *the* essential reference and the norm constantly invoked,
by reason of its character as word of God. But in return, Scripture itself
was read within this tradition, systematically compared with it, and
understood in its light. In this situation ecclesiastical and sacramentary
practice, full of ideas more or less clearly perceived, played an essential role,
inasmuch as it was the faithful prolongation of the practice bequeathed from
apostolic times. Doctrinal disputes and pastoral problems provided little
by little the occasion for bringing to light the hidden content of that practice,
and by the same token the sacred texts themselves became clearer. In them
were found the faint outlines of some given point which tradition had always
held without being able to indicate by what way or under what form it had
received it from the apostles. After the example of the New Testament,
the whole Old Testament bit by bit acquired its Christian meaning, which
was then widely employed in the liturgy and preaching.

[90] The theme is found already in St. Justin, *Dialogue with Trypho*, 100. On the
Mariological doctrine of St. Irenaeus, see the bibliography provided by J. Quasten,
*Patrology I. The Beginnings of Patristic Literature* (Utrecht: Spectrum, 1950),
p. 299.

[91] Contemporary exegesis has undertaken to set forth these first outlines of the
theme, especially in the Johannine writings. Consult the bibliography given below,
p. 293f and p. 381.

[92] A number of examples will be found in the work of Y. Congar, *op. cit.*, pp. 50 ff.

In a word, the truths of the faith were not deduced from scriptural texts by syllogistic reasoning. Rather, the mystery of Christ in its totality was contemplated in it by applying to it a very flexible method of interpretation, one always attentive to the internal coherence of the faith and concerned with drawing out the latent power of the word of God. Scripture thus remained the starting point of all theological reflection, and the need was never felt to search for a second source of the faith alongside it. [93] But its understanding was received from living tradition, within which every pastor, every one of the faithful, took care to place himself. Anything that contradicted its explicit indications was immediately cast aside. But it was held as certain that its least words concealed in their depths all the divine secrets; by referring to the faith held in peaceful possession or to the constant practice of the Church, Christians uncovered that virtual content which belonged part and parcel to the word of God. Thus the absolute respect given the sacred texts did not enclose the interpreter within the limits of what we today call the literal sense.

It was no different in the Middle Ages. To be sure, theological method underwent a profound change in the twelfth and thirteenth centuries. Deductive reasoning and Aristotelian logic were introduced into it as instruments of reflection and expression. But Scripture retained its place as source of sacred doctrine, and its reading remained fundamentally the same as it had been in the patristic age. [94] If the accent was put on the literal sense, the only one capable of providing theology irrefutable arguments, this literal sense was not reduced to the resources of human reason alone, to grammar and rhetoric; it was contained in the tradition of the Church. [95] St. Thomas' biblical commentaries, which are the foundation of his theological syntheses, are an abundant proof of this.

[93] J. Plagneux, *Saint Grégoire de Nazianze théologien* (Paris: Éd. Franciscaines, 1951), pp. 37-59, is visibly impeded by the principle of "two sources," which he struggles to find in the great Greek theologian. In spite of this handicap, he shows clearly that, for Gregory, "if Scripture does not stand without Tradition, the reason is that the latter has as its primary task the authentic interpretation of the former....Most often, it is as an exegetical method, and not as a distinct source, that (Tradition) is cited by our Doctor" (p. 49).

[94] P. de Vooght, "Le rapport Écriture-Tradition d'après saint Thomas d'Aquin et les théologiens du XIIIᵉ siècle," *Istina* 7 (1962), 71-85; Y. Congar, "Tradition et 'Sacra doctrina' chez saint Thomas d'Aquin" in J. Betz—H. Fries, *Église et Tradition* (Le Puy-Lyon: Mappus, 1963), pp. 157-194; *idem, Tradition and Traditions*, pp. 111 ff.; E. Ménard, *La Tradition: Révélation, Écriture et Église selon saint Thomas d'Aquin* (Bruges-Paris: Desclée de Brouwer, 1964) studies this aspect of the doctrine of St. Thomas in detail.

[95] We will return later to this Thomistic conception of the *sensus litteralis* (below, pp. 201 ff.); cf. C. Spicq, *Esquisse d'une histoire de l'exégèse latine au moyen âge* (Paris: Vrin, 1944), pp. 273-281.

## III. CONCLUSION [96]

This, then, is the relationship of Scripture to tradition. It follows that the theological argument from Scripture and that from tradition cannot be placed side by side in equal rank, because they are not of the same order and do not answer the same needs. True, in a way common to both of them, it is always apostolic tradition that is sought. But ecclesiastical tradition, as the medium in which this latter is preserved and operates, presents it only indirectly, and even then without guaranteeing the various elements which compose it. Scripture, on the other hand, allows direct contact with it; it presents it in its primitive freshness, at the moment in which the word of God took on written form. We do not say that the argument from Scripture possesses an eminent dignity alongside an argument from tradition which is sometimes sufficient in itself. This position, which comes from counter-reformation theology, leans too heavily on reform theology, to which it acts as counter balance. The declarations of Trent were more attentive to shades of meaning in giving preeminence to the gospel and apostolic tradition, both in regard to Scripture and in regard to unwritten traditions. [97]

Having found the fathers and medieval theologians in agreement on the matter, we conclude that Scripture and Tradition must both enter into every theological investigation, but with different roles. To search in Scripture for the root of every truth of the faith, in order to use it as the starting point for its explanation, is to place oneself immediately within the apostolic tradition itself, with the vivid knowlegde that everything is contained there, that the texts which are an integral part of it and the realities of which these texts speak conceal profound mysteries. Now to reach these depths, it is necessary to put oneself into the living stream of tradition and from that standpoint gauge the currents of Scripture. The patristic and medieval

[96] We agree substantially with the position of J. R. Geiselmann, "Écriture, Tradition, Église: Un problème œcuménique," *Catholiques et protestants, Confrontations théologiques* (Paris: Seuil, 1961), pp. 48-79; Y. Congar, *op. cit.*, pp. 376-408; *idem*, "Bible et Parole de Dieu," *Les voies du Dieu vivant* (Paris: Cerf, 1962), pp. 25-43; *idem*, "Le débat sur la question du rapport entre Écriture et Tradition au point de vue de leur contenu matériel," *RSPT* 48 (1964), 645-657; K. Rahner, "Écriture et tradition," in *L'homme devant Dieu* 3, pp. 209-221; C. Journet, *Le message révélé*, pp. 32-39, 43-45; P. Lengsfeld, *Tradition, Écriture et Église*, pp. 200-228.

[97] See the text of the 4th session, *Ench. S.* 1501: "In order that the purity of the gospel might be preserved in the Church, our Lord Jesus Christ, the Son of God, first promulgated by his own word what had been previously promised through the prophets in Sacred Scripture, and then ordered it to be preached through his apostles to every creature as the source of every saving truth and rule of conduct." It should be noted that this text uses the word "source" *(fontem)* in the singular. The only theological problem it poses is that of the transmission of the apostolic source in its purity and integrity by means of the gospel.

thesis of the sufficiency of Scripture was never separated from a kind of interpretation which went beyond the limits of the letter to reach the spirit hidden beneath it. All sorts of reservations might be made concerning the exegetical methods used to attain this end. Its principle and its spirit constitute an essential aspect of the apostolic legacy; it is expressly attested in the New Testament. [98] If one is so inclined, he can continue to profess the sufficiency of Scripture, since Scripture yields its riches only on condition that it is read within tradition. [99] The more difficult problem to be resolved, then, is that of interpretation, for a method of interpretation must provide access to the totality of apostolic revelation with occasional and fragmentary texts as a starting point—unless those texts belong to an already completed dispensation. If the exegetical methods of Alexandrian allegory or the Antiochean theory are today hopelessly out of date, is there still some way to go beyond the letter of Scripture without betraying its deep purpose? We are made aware at the beginning of our exposition that everything in it is interrelated. The problem of Scripture and Tradition already appears as one with that of the method of interpretation which we will take up in the final chapter.

[98] We will return to these problems in chapter V.

[99] It might be noted in passing that this view is not so very far from that found among certain theologians of the separated oriental churches. See the texts analyzed by B. Schultze, "Traditio et Scriptura juxta theologos orientales disjunctos," *De Scriptura et traditione*, pp. 543-572. They have been somewhat influenced by the reform and counter-reform statement of the problem, but they are closer to the positions of the patristic age, not without a certain lack of precision in their exposition of doctrine.

# CHAPTER II

# SCRIPTURAL INSPIRATION [1]

Two New Testament texts have provided theology with the term it uses to define the fundamental property of Scripture: inspiration (2 Tm 3:16 and 2 P 1:20-21). In 2 Tm 3:16, after mentioning the instruction Timothy received (3:14) and the sacred writings he has known from his youth, the text continues: "All scripture is inspired by God and can profitably be used for teaching, for refuting error, for guiding people's lives and teaching them to be holy." [2] By scripture here must be understood the books of the Old Testament. But the context shows that in their use they are to be given a Christian interpretation, in line with the teachings received from the apostles. The value of the texts "inspired by God" is, then, inseparable from apostolic tradition, through which their real import has been made apparent.

In 2 P 1:20-21, the context is likewise that of the defense of the faith against false doctors (1:9.16), by fidelity to the apostolic witness (1:12-18) and the prophetic word (1:19) whose true sense is made known by that

---

[1] General treatments of the question: C. Pesch, *De inspiratione S. Scripturae* (Freiburg i. Br.: Herder, 1906); *idem, Supplementum continens disputationes recentiores et decreta de inspiratione S. Scripturae* (Freiburg i. Br.: Herder, 1926). E. Mangenot, "Inspiration," *DTC* 7, cols. 2068-2266. H. Lusseau, *Essai sur la nature de l'inspiration scripturaire* (Paris: Geuthner, 1930). J. M. Vosté, *De divina inspiratione et veritate S. Scripturae*, 2nd ed. (Roma: Angelicum, 1932). A. Bea, *De Scripturae sacrae inspiratione quaestiones historicae et dogmaticae* (Roma: Pont. Bibl. Inst., 1947). P. Benoit, "L'inspiration scripturaire," *La Prophétie* (Paris: Desclée,1947), pp. 293-376; *idem,* "Inspiration" in A. Robert and A. Tricot, *Guide to the Bible*, 2nd ed. (New York: Desclée, 1960), I, pp. 9-52; *idem,* "Note complémentaire sur l'inspiration," *RB* 65 (1956), 416-422. G. Courtade, "Inspiration et inerrance," *DBS* 4, cols. 482-520. J. Schildenberger, *Vom Geheimnis des Gotteswortes* (Heidelberg: F. H. Kerle, 1950), pp. 17-37. A. Merk and A. Bea, "De inspiratione Sacrae Scripturae," *Institutiones Biblicae*, 6th ed. (Roma: Pont. Bibl. Inst., 1951), pp. 12-108. S. Tromp, *De Scripturae Sacrae inspiratione*, 5th ed. (Roma: Univ. Gregoriana, 1953). H. Höpfl—L. Leloir, *Introductio generalis in Sacram Scripturam*, 3rd ed. (Naples-Rome: D'Auria, 1958), pp. 19-78. R.A.F. MacKenzie, "Some Problems in the Field of Inspiration," *CBQ* 20 (1958), 1-8. A. Barucq—H. Cazelles, "The Inspired Books" in A. Robert—A. Feuillet, *Introduction à la Bible I*, 2nd ed. (Tournai-Paris: Desclée, 1959), pp. 3-30. M. Adinolfi, *Ispirazione e inerranza* (Roma: Paoline, 1962). More detailed bibliography can be found in *DTC, DBS* and *Institutiones Biblicae*.

[2] See the commentary of C. Spicq, *Les épîtres pastorales* (Paris: Lecoffre-Gabalda, 1947), pp. 375-379. Cf. E. Schweizer, "Θεόπνευστος," *TWNT* 6, pp. 452 ff.

testimony: "... the interpretation of scriptural prophecy is never a matter
for the individual. Why? Because no prophecy ever came from man's
initiative. When men spoke for God it was the Holy Spirit that moved them
(ὑπὸ πνεύματος ἁγίου φερόμενοι)." [3]   Scripture is here considered under
its prophetic aspect, as an anticipated testimony to Jesus Christ. But if
these texts can be called divinely inspired, the reason is that the men who
wrote them were moved by the Holy Spirit. The fact of inspiration, therefore, must first be studied in these men before being studied in the texts.
Further, to give this prophetic Scripture its correct explanation, it is necessary to leave behind its proper sense and adopt the tradition which issues
from apostolic testimony, because the same Spirit who moved the prophets
has also moved the apostles and continues his activity in the Church which
has received their testimony. This implicit fact suggests that the principle
of inspiration should not be restricted to the books of the Old Testament;
elsewhere the second letter of Peter explicitly likens the letters of St. Paul
to the "rest of scripture" (2 P 3:15-16). [4]

The problem of inspiration is thus placed in a broad context: the
scriptural charism is not separate from other charisms having to do with
revelation and the word of God, especially those of prophecy and the
apostolate. This is the point of view we have adopted in our study of
inspiration. After tracing rapidly the history of the question, we will discuss
the related charisms and the place scriptural inspiration occupies among
them; we will then be in a good position to examine the nature of inspiration.

[3] See the commentary of J. Chaine, *Les épîtres catholiques* (Paris: Lecoffre-
Gabalda, 1939), pp. 54-57.

[4] This awareness of a collection of Pauline letters supposes that the author
was some distance from apostolic times—hence the hypothesis of a pseudonym,
which is held by J. Chaine *(op. cit.,* pp. 28-31); J. Cantinat (in Robert—Feuillet,
*Introduction to the New Testament* [New York: Desclée, 1965], pp. 588-590);
K. H. Schelkle *(Die Petrusbriefe. Der Judasbrief* [Freiburg i. Br.: Herder, 1961],
pp. 178-181) and many others. This is a fortunate situation for us, since it enables
us to view the birth of the New Testament as a collection of canonical scriptures.
On the first letter of Peter considered as a legitimate development of apostolic doctrine,
see K. H. Schelkle, "Spätapostolische Briefe als frühkatholischen Zeugnis," *Neutestamentliche Aufsätze. Festschrift J. Schmid* (Regensburg: Pustet, 1963), pp. 225-232.

## § I. HISTORY OF THE PROBLEM [5]

### I. THE PATRISTIC AGE [6]

It would hardly be convenient to list the patristic texts in which the doctrine of inspiration is attested. Many of them do no more than repeat the expressions of 2 Tm and 2 P which we have examined above. [7] But traces of two doctrinal points are to be found there, and it is on them that later theological reflection built: the sacred authors are instruments of God, and God is the author of Scripture.

#### I. THE SACRED AUTHORS, INSTRUMENTS OF GOD

In ancient times the sacred authors were always included in the category of prophets through whom God has spoken to us. The author of the *Cohortatio ad Graecos* presents them as offering themselves to the divine Spirit, so that he, the divine plectrum, playing upon them as he would a cithara or a lyre, might communicate to us knowledge of things divine. [8] It is in the same sense that the Nicaean Creed says of the Holy Spirit: "he spoke through the prophets." [9] Still, the fact that these prophets actually speak to men is a reason for relating them to the Word from whom every word of God goes forth to men. It was the word, says Theophilus of Antioch, [10] who spoke through Moses in Genesis "as if through an instrument " (ὡς δι ὀργάνου). The joint action of the Word and the Spirit, then, is to be acknowledged as the source of prophetic writings. That is why the sacred authors, "prepared by the prophetic Spirit and properly honored by the

---

[5] A historical summary and a more detailed bibliography can be found in the articles by E. Mangenot *(DTC)*, A. Merk and A. Bea *(Institutiones Biblicae)*, and G. Coutarde *(DBS)* which we will have occasion to cite frequently.

[6] For Christian antiquity, many of the texts cited here can be found in M. J. Rouët de Journel, *Enchiridion Patristicum (Ench. P.)*. For a systematic exposition, G. M. Perrella, "La nozione dell'ispirazione scritturale secondo primitivi documenti cristiani," *Angelicum* 19 (1943), 32-52.

[7] Some characteristic examples: Athenagoras, *Legatio pro christianis*, 7 *(PG 6, 904; Ench. P.* 162)*; Theophilus of Antioch, *Ad Autolycum*, 1, 14 *(PG 6, 1045; Ench. P.* 175)*; Gregory of Nyssa, *Contra Eunomium*, 7 *(PG 45, 741; Ench. P.* 1045)*; Ambrose, *De Spiritu Sancto*, 3, 16, 112 *(PL 16, 803; Ench. P.* 1286)*; Theodoretus, *In Psalmos*, Praef. *(PG 80, 861; Ench. P.* 2158)*.

[8] *Cohortatio ad Graecos*, 8 *(PG 6, 256; Ench. P.* 149)*. The same figure of speech was used by Athenagoras, *Legatio*, 7 *(PG 6, 904; Ench. P.* 162)*.

[9] Cf. the expressions of Origen, *In psalmos*, 1, 4 *(PG 12, 1081; Ench. P.* 483)* and *In Jeremiam*, 21, 2 *(PG 13, 536; Ench. P.* 488)*.

[10] *Ad Autolycum*, 2, 10 *(PG 6, 1064; Ench. P.* 179)*.

Word himself, united to the Word as instruments, had him always within them as a sort of plectrum, in such a manner that under his action they announced precisely what God wanted them to; for the prophets did not speak of their own power, and it was not what they themselves chose that they preached." These words of Hippolytus [11] are an excellent summary of the doctrine which became classic in the 4th and 5th centuries. [12]

## II. GOD THE AUTHOR OF THE SCRIPTURES

Thus far the accent has been on the cooperation of God and men in the expression, oral or written, of revelation. In other places, it is the primary responsibility of God that is underlined, and sometimes that alone. The formula "God the author of the Scriptures" is not the most ancient one in this regard. Originally, in fact, this formula meant (against the Gnostics, Marcionites or Manichaeans) that it was one and the same God who authored the two Testaments which together compose the Scriptures. This is the sense given the phrase, for example, by St. Irenaeus, [13] St. Augustine, [14] St. Leo, [15] and on into the late Middle Ages, by the Council of Florence. [16] But the doctrine underlies other expressions, of which that of St. Jerome may serve as an example: "*Scripturae sacrae a Spiritu Sancto conscriptae sunt et editae*," [17] as well as that of St. Augustine, speaking of Christ and his evangelists: "*Nequaquam dicendum est quod ipse non scripserit, quandoquidem membra ejus id operata sunt, quod dictante capite cognoverunt.*" [18] This concept of dictation gained strength from that time on. In St. Gregory, for example, it takes over from the formula "God author" in a text in which the sacred writer is relegated to a secondary place so that the action of Him who inspired him will be more apparent: "*Quis haec scripserit, valde supervacue quaeritur, cum tamen auctor libri Spiritus Sanctus fideliter credatur. Ipse igitur haec*

[11] *De antichristo*, 2 (*PG* 10, 728; *Ench. P.* 388).

[12] See the similar expressions of Jerome and Theodoretus cited in *Institutiones Biblicae*, Nos. 17-18.

[13] "...The founder of the law and the gospel is one and the same" (*Adversus Haereses*, 4, 12, 3; *PG* 7, 1005; *Ench. P.* 230).

[14] *Contra adversarium legis et prophetarum*, 1, 17, 35 (*PL* 42, 623; *Ench. B.* 1895).

[15] *Sermon* 63, 5 (*PL* 54, 356; *Ench. P.* 2205).

[16] *Ench. S.* 1334.

[17] "Sacred Scripture was written and edited by the Holy Spirit." *In Micheam* 7, 5-7 (*PL* 25, 1224). Other texts are cited in the encyclical *Spiritus Paraclitus* (*Ench. P.* 469).

[18] "It must never be said that he did not write, since his members set down what they knew from the dictation of the head." *De consensu evangelistarum*, 1, 35 (*PL* 34, 1070; *Ench. P.* 1609).

*scripsit, qui scribenda dictavit.*[19] It was this statement of the traditional doctrine that St. Gregory bequeathed to medieval theology. Taken as it stands, it is not without danger, in the measure, that is, that it pushes into the shadows the properly human activity of the sacred writers.

## II. FROM THE MIDDLE AGES TO THE 18th CENTURY

### I. THE PROBLEM OF PROPHECY

As a prolongation of patristic theology, medieval scholasticism continued to consider the question of scriptural inspiration within the category of prophecy. Whatever traditional expressions they repeated can be left aside. Our interest centers rather on those theologians who attempted to analyze, with the aid of philosophical concepts, the classic themes of God as author and the sacred writers as instruments. In his commentary on St. John, Albert the Great[20] finds in divine wisdom, manifested in the Word Incarnate, the primary efficient cause that directed John and enabled him to write; John was the proximate efficient cause who translated the divine secrets he received from the Word. Henry of Ghent's explanation is more systematic[21]: he distinguishes the principal author from the ministerial authors, and brings all three divine persons into the act of inspiration by recurring to the theory of appropriation. In the Thomistic synthesis, finally, the Holy Spirit is called the principal author of Scripture, while man is the instrumental author.[22] But this comment made in passing is not developed, because nowhere does St. Thomas elaborate the particular doctrine of scriptural inspiration. It is only in speaking of prophecy that he treats the problem of the relation between the two authors, divine and human: the case of the sacred writers who were that alone is, in his eyes, an imperfect realization of prophecy.[23] Several consequences flow from this. First of all, the accent is put upon the problem of charismatic knowledge, which is common to the prophets and sacred writers albeit in different

---

[19] "It is a waste of time to inquire who wrote these things, since we firmly believe that the Holy Spirit is the author of the book. He, therefore, who dictated these things is their author." *Moralia in Job*, 1, 2 (*PL* 75, 517; *Ench. P.* 2302).

[20] *Institutione Biblicae*, No. 20.

[21] *Ibid.*, No. 21.

[22] "The principal author of Scripture is the Holy Spirit; man was the instrumental author" (*Quolibet* 7, art. 14, ad 5). This remark was made only in passing, for questions 14-16 of *Quodlibet* 7 deal with the senses of Scripture.

[23] See IIª, IIᵃᵉ, qq. 171-174.

forms, rather than on the proclamation of the word of God, either orally or in writing. From this it follows that the question of revelation and that of inspiration become confused, while the problems raised by the human activity of man under inspiration are never examined in detail. [24]

## II. THE PROBLEM OF SCRIPTURAL INSPIRATION

From the 16th century, on the contrary, scriptural inspiration became an object of study in itself. This was an indirect consequence of the rise of Protestantism, which forced the attention of theologians to Scripture. At the Council of Trent, the question was treated only indirectly, as a part of the decree on the canon of Scriptures. [25] In refusing to separate the Scriptures from the apostolic traditions preserved by the Church, the Council took up again the formula *"Deus (est) auctor utriusque Testamenti,"* [26] which came to dominate the view of post-Tridentine theology. This latter, in fact, considered the activity of the sacred writer only under the divine movement which directed it, inasmuch as the writer's activity is no more than the expression in human language of a revelation which comes from God. Thus the Thomistic doctrine on prophecy, only now applied to the particular case of the sacred books, reappeared. Revelation and inspiration continued to be more or less confused. But now the problems posed by the activity of the inspired writer could not be avoided. There was likewise an apologetic reason for this, for from this time on theology had to defend not only the inspiration of Scripture, but its inerrancy as well. That is why authors began to inquire to what extent the divine action determines the activity of the inspired writers, and what form that action takes.

Some traditional texts speak, in this regard, of divine dictation. [27] The theologians of the 16th century were one in taking up the expression.

---

[24] Concerning this limitation of Thomistic doctrine, see especially the excellent article of P. Benoit, "Révélation et inspiration," *RB* 72 (1963), 331-334.

[25] *Ench. B.* 57.

[26] It will be noted that the Council did not apply the formula "at the dictation of the Holy Spirit" to the inspired texts of the New Testament, but to the apostolic traditions the Church received through other channels. Once again, it is the problem of revelation that is in the forefront of attention.

[27] To cite a few of the quotations gathered in *Institutiones Biblicae*, Nos. 24-26: it would be heretical to pretend that in Scripture "not everything was written at the dictation of the Holy Spirit" (S. Robert Bellarmine); "God wrote the whole Bible through the men to whom he dictated it" (N. Sérier); "Scripture was written at the movement of the Holy Spirit who dictated not only its meaning, but also its words" (Suarez).

From there it was only a short step to arrive at speaking of verbal inspiration [28]; the difficulty then became one of sufficiently softening the supernatural action so that the human instrument fully retains his own activity. [29]  At this point Suarez supplied the most useful comments. Conscious that each sacred author *"modo sibi accommodato et secundum suum ingenium, eruditionem et linguam singula scribat,"* he distinguishes two types of inspiration: *"aut per specialem motionem antecedentem, aut tantum per assistentiam et quasi custodiam" ;* this second type applies *"quando Spiritus Sanctus auctori specialiter assistat et custodiat illum ab omni errore et falsitate et ab omnibus verbis quae non expediunt vel decent talem Scripturam."* [30]  This is a wholly negative concept of verbal inspiration; it was drawn up with inerrancy in mind. Lessius later dangerously exaggerated its consequences. [31]  Jahn, going further in the same direction, arrived at identifying inspiration with the simple privilege of inerrancy, [32] and Haneberg, with the subsequent approbation of the sacred books by the Church (in the case of certain historical books). [33]

[28] This notion has a whole tradition behind it. The notion of mechanical verbal dictation is found in Philo (cf. J.-B. Frey, "La révélation d'après les conceptions juives au temps de Jésus-Christ," *RB* 26 [1916], 495-501) and some ancient ecclesiastical writers (*Institutiones Biblicae*, Nos 55-56; *DBS, art. cit.*, cols. 503-504). It was taken up again in a much more flexible sense in post-Tridentine theology by Bañez, Gregory of Valencia, Billuart, etc. (*Inst. Bibl.*, No 58). Bañez, for example, wrote, "The Holy Spirit...prompted and, as it were, dictated...the individual words" (*Scholastica commentaria in Iᵃᵐ Partem*, q. 1, art. 8).

[29] In the same age, verbal dictation was understood in a much more strict sense by some Protestants (*Inst. Bibl.*, No. 57). We might cite the Swiss confession of faith of 1675, which in this point depends on the ideas of J. Buxtorf: "The Hebrew text of the Old Testament...both as regards consonants and vowel points, or at least the significance of those points, (is) Θεόπνευστος." This position has lived on with certain fundamentalists, and especially in the sects which have broken off the Protestant trunk, who take from the Bible the texts which serve to confirm their particular beliefs.

[30] In *Inst. Bibl.*, No. 26. These two modes of dictation were admitted by N. Sérier ("by dictation in a strict or a broad sense," *ibid.*, No. 25) and by Cornelius a Lapide (*ibid.*, No. 27).

[31] Concerning the theses of Lessius which were censured by the faculty of Louvain, see *Inst. Bibl.*, Nos. 41 and 60. In fact, the explanations Lessius gave show that his doctrine was not really so heterodox (cf. H. Holstein, "Lessius a-t-il été condamné par le Concile du Vatican?" *RSR* 42 [1951], 219-226). The same viewpoint was held by Bonfrère (*Inst. Bibl.*, No. 42) and a few others (*DBS, art. cit.*, col. 509).

[32] *Inst. Bibl.*, No. 43; *DBS, art. cit.*, col. 509.

[33] *Inst. Bibl.*, No. 42; *DBS, art. cit.*, col. 508: "A Council can make an ordinary but pious book Sacred Scripture by declaring it free of error and placing it in the canon."

## III. FROM THE 19th CENTURY TO THE PRESENT

### I. INSPIRATION AND INERRANCY

It was with these two insufficient notions in mind that Vatican Council I declared in regard to the sacred books: their canonical character is not the result of the fact that the Church has approved them, nor of the fact that they contain revelation without error, but *"quod Spiritu sancto inspirante conscripti Deum habent auctorem."* [34]   This doctrine is forcefully repeated in the decree *Lamentabili* (prop. 9-12). [35]   But it is obvious that the then current discussions of the problem considered inspiration in relation to inerrancy, which was then under strong rationalist attack.   It was from this point of view that Leo XIII gave Catholic doctrine a formulation that was to become classic: "Hence, the fact that it was man whom the Holy Spirit took up as his instrument for writing does not mean that it was these inspired instruments —but not the primary author—who might have made an error.   For, by supernatural power, he so moved and impelled them to write—he so assisted them when writing—that the things which he ordered, and those only, they, first, rightly understood, then willed faithfully to write down, and finally expressed in apt words and with infallible truth.   Otherwise, it could not be said that he was the author of the entire Scripture." [36]

These words were repeated by Benedict XV [37] for a precise purpose: to reject those theories which restricted the inspiration of the biblical books to matters of dogma and morality alone, to the exclusion of science and history. [38]   Pius XII himself speaks in the same vein in the opening paragraphs of *Divino Afflante Spiritu.* [39]   It must be admitted that the problems posed by the apparent errors in the Bible, in scientific matters, and even in history, had led some theologians to seek a means of escape,

---

[34] "Because they were written at the inspiration of the Holy Spirit, they have God as their author." (*Ench. B.* 77; cf. N. Weyns, "De notione inspirationis biblicae juxta concilium vaticanum," *Angelicum* 29 [1953] 315-336.)

[35] *Ench. B.* 200-203, with the explanations of the encyclical *Pascendi, ibid.,* 258-259.   These texts were aimed at the modernist ideas which radically distorted the notion of inspiration.

[36] *Ench. B.* 125.   (Translation from *Rome and the Study of Scripture,* 7th ed. [St. Meinrad, Ind.: Grail, 1962], p. 24).   This text comes immediately after the quotation from the Vatican Council I (above, note 34).

[37] Encyclical *Spiritus Paraclitus,* in *Ench. B.* 452.

[38] *Ibid.,* 454.

[39] *Ibid.,* 538 (which repeats the doctrine of the Council of Trent) and 539 (which quotes Leo XIII).

either by restricting inspiration to certain realms of knowledge,[40] or by removing from its influence certain parts of Scripture (the *obiter dicta*[41] or implicit citations[42]). This persistent confusion of the two questions of inspiration and inerrancy obviously did not facilitate their harmonious solution.

## II. THE PSYCHOLOGY OF INSPIRATION

Happily, since the end of the 19th century, the statement of the problem has become much clearer. After Vatican I, theologians thought at first that they had found a balanced solution in the theory of Franzelin.[43] Taking as his starting point the notion of "God the author of Scripture," he distinguished in the sacred books a formal element, the thought to be expressed, and a material element, the words and phrases used to express it. The first constituted the essential object of the divine action, by reason of its intrinsic connection with revelation; the second was left to the liberty of each author. This opened a dangerous dichotomy: it scarcely saves the concrete unity of thought and language which is essential to every human work.

That is why Fr. Lagrange and certain others, in 1895 and the years following, seized upon the Thomistic notion of principal and instrumental causality, and proposed to apply it to the problem of inspiration.[44] The two

[40] See the article by Mgsr. d'Hulst in *Le Correspondant* in 1893, cited by G. Courtade, *DBS*, art. cit., col. 522.

[41] This is the expression used by Newman in his tract in 1884 (*ibid.*, col. 498). Newman's mind on this subject cannot be reduced to this groping phrase; on this point see the discussion of J. Seynaeve, "Newman," *DBS* 4, cols. 430-447.

[42] G. Courtade, art. cit., *DBS* 4, cols. 548 ff. Ecclesiastical documents on the question can be found in *Ench. B.* 160, 273, 461. Cf. A. Lemonnyer, "Citations implicites," *DBS* 2, cols. 51-55.

[43] J. B. Franzelin, *Tractatus de divina Traditione et Scriptura*, 4th ed. (Rome: S.C. de Prop. Fide, 1896). The same viewpoint was retained by C. Pesch, *Zur neusten Geschichte der katholischen Inspirationslehre* (Freiburg i. Br.: Herder, 1902); *idem*, *De inspiratione Sacrae Scripturae* (Freiburg i. Br.: Herder, 1906). It was criticized by D. Zanecchia, *Scriptor sacer sub divina inspiratione juxta sententiam Cardinalis Franzelin* (Rome: Pustet, 1903). See the brief summaries in *Inst. Bibl.*, Nos 62-63; *DBS*, art. cit., cols. 518 ff.; L. Arnaldich, "La naturaleza de la inspiración según el Card. Franzelin," *XIV Semana Bíblica Española* (Madrid: Consejo, 1954), pp. 131-163.

[44] E. Lévesque, "Questions actuelles d'Écriture Sainte," *RB* 4 (1895), 421-423; T. M. Pègues, "Une pensée de saint Thomas sur l'inspiration scripturaire," *RTh* 3 (1895), 95-112. D. Zanecchia, *Divina inspiratio Sacrarum Scripturarum ad mentem S. Thomae Aquinatis* (Rome: Pustet, 1898). M.-J. Lagrange, "Une pensée de saint Thomas sur l'inspiration scripturaire," *RB* 4 (1895), 563-571; *idem*, "L'inspiration des livres saints," *RB* 5 (1896), 199-220; *idem*, "L'inspiration et les exigences de la critique," *RB* 5 (1896), 496-518; *idem*, *La méthode historique* (Paris: Lecoffre, 1903), pp. 71-109.

authors of Scripture, divine and human, concur equally in its production, each at his own level; they are therefore equally the cause of everything it contains, its language as well as its thought. In this view it is permissible to adopt the thesis of verbal inspiration, so long as the human authors are allowed to retain fully their human activity under the divine action. These views were proposed on the vigil of the modernist crisis. That fact did not favor their immediate adoption, but they made inroads nonetheless. Already in the encyclical *Spiritus Paraclitus*, while explaining St. Jerome's doctrine on the sacred books, Benedict XV declared: "The individual authors of these books worked in full freedom under the divine *afflatus*, each of them in accordance with his individual nature and character." [45] The accent is clearly on the human aspect of Scripture. In the encyclical *Divino afflante Spiritu*, Pius XII was even clearer in presenting the sacred author as a living and free instrument of the Holy Spirit; in order to explain his work properly, it is necessary to study his character, conditions of life and manner of writing. [46] So a correct solution of the problem was finally reached. That does not mean, however, that no questions remain to be considered.

### III. THE SOCIAL DIMENSION OF SCRIPTURAL INSPIRATION

This conception of inspiration lacks first of all an essential aspect which contemporary exegesis has brought to the fore, and has obliged theologians to consider seriously. Though personally inspired by God, the sacred writer is not by that fact isolated. The economy of salvation, in which he plays an essential role, has a social structure, and he receives his charism from God only in view of the salvation community. If the social aspect of inspiration is not given its just due, how will it be possible to appreciate sufficiently the organic bonds which bind the sacred books to the people of God? Dom C. Charlier wrote in this vein in 1950: "Biblical inspiration (in Israel) could only be one form of the wider inspiration that affected the whole life of the people.... A book was said to be inspired because the author was acknowledged to be an inspired man. The author was seen to be inspired because he served the community in a social capacity that had been given

---

[45] *Ench. B.* 448 (translation from *Rome and the Study of Scripture*, p. 47). The encyclical goes on to insist upon the peculiarities of each author as regards his style of composition, his language, his manner of expression. When the encyclical reacts against the abuse of the principle of literary genres (*ibid.*, 461), it is in order to counter any attack on the inerrancy of the sacred books.

[46] *Ibid.*, 556-557.

him by God." [47]  The thought was correct, but a lack of precision in ist theological formulation left it open to criticism. [48]

### *1. Scripture, an Essential Element of the Church*

K. Rahner approached the problem by another route in a brief work published in 1958. [49]  After having shown to what insoluble difficulties the "classic" thesis leads, he goes on to say that the same divine will to which is owed the eschatological realization of salvation in the foundation of the Church is responsible too for Scripture as a constituent element of the Church. [50] Such is the meaning of scriptural inspiration, which is thus organically related to every salvific action of the Spirit.  This explains why New Testament Scripture expressed the faith of the apostolic Church; why its authors were conscious of working in the service of that Church; why the post-apostolic Church saw in Scripture its rule of faith, since it recognized in itself a certain natural identity with it; why the magisterium, which continues to guide living tradition, can neither oppose Scripture, nor range itself alongside it.

This view of the matter considerably widens the horizon of classic theology, but it does not really come to grips with the specific problem of scriptural inspiration as such.  Since it is strictly speaking applicable only to the books of the New Testament, it cannot serve as the basis for a general theory which must take all the facts into consideration. [51]  The notion of Scripture as a constituent element of the Church is surely to be retained, but it must be noted that this function is fulfilled in a much more fundamental way by the apostolic word, the one and only rule of faith to which the Church must in every age have recourse.  It is as the authentic fixation of this word—occasional and partial, but immediate—that Scripture

[47] Dom C. Charlier, *The Christian Approach to the Bible*, 5th ed. (Westminster: Newman, 1965), pp. 111-112.

[48] A more qualified and more exact presentation can be found in A. Barucq and H. Cazelles in Robert—Feuillet, *Introduction à la Bible* 1, 2nd ed., pp. 27-29.

[49] K. Rahner, *Inspiration in the Bible* (New York: Herder and Herder, 1961).

[50] This position is adopted by P. Lengsfeld: "God in some manner willed to fortify his Church with these writings, which are the normative deposit of the history of its preaching, which is itself a bearer of revelation.  By revealing himself as the God who founded a Church, and by simultaneously establishing in that Church Scripture as the canon of its preaching, he also revealed himself as the author of Scripture, in the very same way that he is the author of the Church" (*Tradition, Écriture et Église*, p. 213).  See likewise the substantial agreement of B. Brinkmann in *Scholastik* 33 (1958), 208-233 (except for some reservations with regard to the problem of the canon) and of J. Schildenberger in *Questions théologiques aujourd'hui* 1 (Paris: Desclée de Brouwer, 1964), pp. 160-167.

[51] See the remarks of P. Benoit in *RB* 69 (1960), 278; and of A.-M. Dubarle in *RSPT* 43 (1959), pp. 106 ff.

possesses unequaled authority and plays an essential role in the Church. [52] It is not a question of the apostolic word remaining unattainable except through Scripture, nor of the living tradition of the Church having no function in this regard. It is simply that Scripture and ecclesiastical tradition are not in the same situation in relation to the apostolic word. [53] Moreover, it is through them jointly that the word is actually accessible to us. Once these points have been admitted, the limits of the problem of the nature of inspiration will have been set.

## 2. Types of Inspiration

P. Benoit has recently put forward a more exact formulation of the problem, at the heart of which are the analogies of inspiration. [54] In realizing the history of salvation at all its levels, the Holy Spirit is active among the people of God through all sorts of charisms, which one can rightfully group together under the generic term of inspiration. These charisms correspond to the various functions confided to men in salvation history: some must act in such a manner that an event might take its place in God's design; others must speak to announce the word of God as prophets or apostles; still others must write in order that the word of God might not exist only for the tradition that experienced it, but for all future generations. These three types of inspiration are evidently correlative. The last two, moreover, imply a prior action of the Holy Spirit, which has to do with knowledge of the word to be transmitted; it is no longer a question only of the knowledge of faith, but of real prophetic knowledge, which, following the statements of St. Thomas, is susceptive of varying degrees. [55] Finally, this manifold inspiration, which accompanied the people of God for the whole time when revelation was still growing, has its real prolongation today in the Holy Spirit's assistance of the Church—that assistance which the theology of the ancients did not hesitate to call inspiration. [56]

This explanation is helpful and well put; a few observations, however, ought to be made. Inspiration to act is only of indirect interest here, even though it does bridge the gap between the word of God and salvation history.

[52] Cf. Y. Congar, "Inspiration et apostolicité de l'Église," *RSPT* 45 (1961), 32-42 (reprinted in *Sainte Église, Études et approches ecclésiologiques* [Paris: Cerf, 1963], pp. 187-200).

[53] Cf. above, p. 32 ff.

[54] P. Benoit, "Les analogies de l'inspiration," *Sacra Pagina* 1 (Paris-Gembloux: Duculot, 1959), pp. 86-99.

[55] See the explanation of P. Benoit, *La prophétie*, pp. 269 ff.

[56] G. Bardy, "L'inspiration des Pères de l'Église," *Mélanges J. Lebreton* 2 (*RSR*, 1951-1952), pp. 7-26; Y. Congar, *Tradition and Traditions*, pp. 125-129.

Inspiration to write is correctly defined in relation to its purpose and within its limits. There remains inspiration to speak. It seems to us that P. Benoit's description remains incomplete, since the only cases he explicitly considers are those of the prophets in the Old Testament and of the apostles in the New. But the two Testaments present examples of other charismatic functions related to the word of God. The prophets and apostles proclaim this word as essential mediators of revelation. But after them that word is gathered, preserved, utilized within a tradition that brings it to fruition under the guidance of the Holy Spirit. Inspiration to speak, distinct from the prophetic and apostolic charisms, ought additionally to be attributed to the organs of that tradition. [57]

### 3. *The Sacred Authors and the People of God*

In this state of affairs, J. L. McKenzie, with the remarks of Rahner and Benoit in mind, has attempted to define more precisely this social character of inspiration. [58] But instead of taking as his starting point the theology of charisms as it has been developed over the ages, he has sought a new approach in facts provided by biblical criticism itself. In the New Testament, he notes, the authors of the sacred books are generally known. But in the Old, they are very often anonymous, just as in most ancient oriental literatures. This fact is not without importance: it shows that those authors considered themselves as fulfilling a social function. Through them the society of which they were members put its thought into writing; they were its spokesmen, and for that reason the society was the real author of what they wrote, [59] since they desired nothing more than "to be the voice of Israel and of the Church." [60]

This position, while fundamentally correct in insisting on the insertion of the biblical authors into the tradition of the people of God, actually conceals several questionable points. While it is true that the composers of the psalms, for example, desired to be "the praying voice of Israel," the more usual case must, in fact, be understood the other way around: what the biblical authors intended to set down in writing was "the voice of God

---

[57] P. Benoit *(loc. cit.)* classes this inspiration *to speak* under the various degrees of prophecy. It is in part a question of terminology. That of St. Thomas is poorly suited for the problem we are here discussing, as can be gathered from the following paragraph.

[58] J. L. McKenzie, "The Social Character of Inspiration," *CBQ* 24 (1962), 115-124. See also D. J. McCarthy, "Personality, Society and Inspiration," *Theological Studies* 24 (1963), 553-576.

[59] *Art. cit.*, p. 119.

[60] *Ibid.*, p. 120.

for Israel," received either directly through prophetic revelation or from the channel of a tradition which preserved it. That tradition itself should not be deified, as if the word of God could be preserved in the community as such. As a matter of fact, the community's operation is due to charismatic functions, which in this respect play a decisive role. If, therefore, it is necessary to relate scriptural inspiration to these charismatic functions in order to understand correctly its social character, it is no less necessary to insist on its personal character, even if that means recognizing its intervention at several redactional stages, since the composition of the sacred books took place in successive stages or involved "reinterpretations." The activity of the Holy Spirit in the community of salvation has always manifested itself in individual charisms, at the level of revelation as well as at that of the proclamation or writing of the word.

### 4. The Responsibility of the Apostolic Church

Nevertheless, the whole of the Old Testament poses a peculiar problem in this respect, to which N. Lohfink has called attention. [61] If it is true that the definitive meaning of a book within revelation is that which its final author or editor gave it, how are we to describe the responsibility of the apostolic Church in regard to the books of the Old Testament? Did that Church not, on the one hand, determine its canonical list, and on the other, determine its exact meaning from the standpoint of the gospel of Jesus Christ? Did it not by that fact produce a Christian edition of the Old Testament, in which the individual books were brought together into a unique collection, Scripture, in such a way that the Church in fact accepted the responsibility of author of that collection?

Such a view does not contradict what we have said above. In fact, this final application of scriptural inspiration to the books of the Old Testament would be organically connected to the functional charism of the apostolate, considered as the indivisible possession of the twelve and Paul, and it is not difficult to understand how the integration of the ancient Scriptures to the apostolic tradition—which remains the rule of faith for the Church of all times [62]—could take place. Nevertheless, it is best not to confuse under the same heading the composition or edition of the inspired books on the one hand, and the fixing of their list and determination of their meaning through charismatic interpretation on the other. These last two

[61] N. Lohfink, "Über die Irrtumlosigkeit und die Einheit der Schrift," *Stimmen der Zeit* 174 (1964), 161-181.

[62] Above, pp. 15 ff.

operations, the only ones which must be attributed to the apostolic Church, do not pertain to the properly literary functions to which scriptural inspiration is ordered. It suffices to admit that the meaning of the biblical books which antedate Christ remained always open to further deepening, inasmuch as revelation had not yet reached its completion. That meaning became known through the preaching of the gospel; that is one of the purposes of the charism of the apostolate. But even for the apostles, the text of the sacred books constituted an inspired Scripture (2 Tm 3:16) which they presented without claiming for themselves any right to modify its purport.

## IV. INSPIRATION AND REVELATION

Finally, there is in the doctrine proposed by P. Lagrange and since become common, another weak point, as P. Benoit made clear in an article which appeared in 1963. [63] We noted in passing that the problem of charismatic knowledge dominated the whole Thomistic development of the doctrine of prophecy. As a result the latter was studied essentially as the medium of divine revelation, in the sense that it brought to the prophet an intellectual illumination in which he understood the message he was to transmit to men. But the communication of that message was not considered in itself. St. Thomas did not himself confuse inspiration and revelation, but the way of treating the problem common to his time hardly permitted him to explain their relationship with sufficient exactness, because the communication of the prophetic message through human words posed no problem to the theologians of that day. [64] And, it should be noted, the modern concept of scriptural inspiration has developed as a prolongation of the Thomistic tract on prophecy. Even more, in order to distinguish the case of the sacred authors from that of the prophets properly so called, ever since Fr. Lagrange, authors have had recourse to the degrees which St. Thomas distinguished in prophecy: at its height, a charismatic knowledge in the full sense, including the infusion into the prophet's mind of *lumen* and *species;* beneath that, an imperfect realization of the same charism, which implied only the charismatic *lumen.* This second is the case of scriptural inspiration as such. [65]

Fr. Benoit rightly observes that it is precisely here that the Thomistic doctrine has been misused, by applying it to a matter with which it had nothing to do when it was drawn up. The problem of scriptural inspiration

[63] P. Benoit, "Révélation et inspiration," *RB* 72 (1963), 321-370.
[64] *Art. cit.*, pp. 325-336.
[65] *Ibid.*, pp. 322-324.

as such has to do less with the knowledge of supernatural truths to be transmitted either orally or in writing as with the transmission of those truths
and all that this implies.  A certain charismatic knowledge must certainly
be attributed to the sacred authors; it is only by reason of such knowledge
that their works can represent the word of God in the full sense of the term.
But, on the one hand, the biblical notion of revelation and of knowledge
carries with it a concrete richness which medieval theology, under the
influence of Greek philosophy, could not completely fathom [66]; secondly,
inspiration ought to be analyzed in the whole practical activity of the sacred
authors.  The close association of inspiration and revelation should not,
then, blur their formal distinction.  Moreover, it is not proper, on the basis
of the presence or absence of infused *species* in the mind of the one inspired,
to distinguish the prophets as bearers of revelation from the sacred writers
who reveal nothing new, for the formal element of charismatic knowledge
consists less in these *species* than in the judgment made under the influence
of the supernatural *lumen*.  Otherwise, the result is to put in opposition,
in an arbitrary manner, the passivity of the prophet who receives everything
from God, and the activity of the inspired writer who is no more than aroused
and guided by the divine *lumen*. [67]  It is necessary, therefore, to break out
of the narrowness of the medieval treatment of the problem in order to give
all the elements concerned their just due.  Through the studies of P. Benoit,
K. Rahner and J. L. McKenzie, we have arrived at the most recent state of
the question [68]: our historical summary has led us to the heart of the matter.


## § II. CHARISMS RELATED TO THE WORD OF GOD

To begin with, an investigation of positive theology will bring to light the
ways in which God provided in the two Testaments for the announcement
and preservation of his word.  On this point the New Testament theology
of charisms furnishes an adequate doctrinal formulation; the Old, without
the same precision, presents already the essential outlines of it, on condition
that one know how to find them.  As in every investigation of this type,
care must be taken to analyze the texts objectively, without imposing on

---

[66] *Ibid.*, pp. 336-343.

[67] See the typical quotation of E. Lévesque, *RB* 4 (1895), 421 reproduced by
P. Benoit, *art. cit.*, p. 365, note 105.

[68] Add W. Harrington, "The Inspiration of Scripture," *Irish Theological Quar-
terly* 29 (1962), 3-24.  Protestant theology has not neglected this problem.  An
explanation of the school of Barth's point of view can be found in D. Beegle, *The
Inspiration of Scripture* (Philadelphia: Westminster, 1963).

them *a priori* the categories of later theology. Nevertheless, later theological developments are not without usefulness, for they will aid us to classify the results of our investigations by distinguishing the various ways in which the Holy Spirit intervened in the salvation community.

## I. IN THE OLD TESTAMENT

The Old Testament contains no *ex professo* statement on the present question, but it does speak clearly of the divine action by which the word of God was proclaimed, preserved and explained in his people. This doctrine is not expressed in a set vocabulary. On the one hand, in the prophetic tradition, it is the Holy Spirit who intervenes, [69] or in some places God himself who confides his word to men. [70] On the other hand, in the wisdom tradition, the assistance of divine wisdom produces the same effects. [71] We shall in our discussion unite these two types of expression; certain later writings noted their tendency to converge (Si 24:30-34; Ws 9:17). Two different cases are to be distinguished. At the birth of Israel's faith, and at every stage of its progress, the word of God in a revealing function was always present; the person who transmitted it possessed the prophetic charism in the full sense of the term. Then this word was preserved and its dynamism harnessed by all the means and under all the forms at the disposal of living tradition; all those involved in this operation received functional charisms corresponding to their various responsibilities. The composition of the sacred books was always in relation with both the prophetic charism and one or the other of the functional charisms.

[69] Concerning the theology of the Spirit of God, see J. Lebreton, *Histoire du dogme de la Trinité* I (Paris: Beauchesne, 1927), pp. 111-122; F. Baumgärtel, W. Bieder and E. Sjöberg, "Πνεῦμα," *TWNT* 6, pp. 357-387; P. van Imschoot, *Theology of the Old Testament* I (New York: Desclée, 1965), pp. 172-188; J. Guillet, *Thèmes bibliques* (Paris: Aubier, 1951), pp. 208-253; "Esprit de Dieu," *VTB*, cols. 313-317; W. Eichrodt, *Theology of the Old Testament* 2 (London: SCM Press, 1967), pp. 46-68.

[70] On the theology of the Word of God, see J. Lebreton, *op. cit.*, pp. 131-133, 209-251; O. Procksch, "Λέγω," etc., *TWNT* 4, pp. 89-100; A. Robert, "Logos," *DBS* 5, cols. 442-483; P. van Imschoot, *op. cit.*, pp. 188-195; W. Eichrodt, *op. cit.*, Vol. 2, pp. 69-79; the collective volume *La Parole de Dieu en Jésus-Christ* (Tournai-Paris: Desclée de Brouwer, 1962); "Parole de Dieu," *VTB*, cols. 750-758.

[71] On the theology of the Wisdom of God, see J. Lebreton, *op. cit.*, pp. 122-131; P. van Imschoot, "Sagesse et Esprit dans l'Ancien Testament," *RB* 47 (1938), 23-49; *idem*, "Sagesse," *Dictionnaire encyclopédique de la Bible*, cols. 1651-1656; W. Eichrodt, *op. cit.*, Vol. 2, pp. 80-92; *idem*, "Sagesse," *VTB*, cols. 974-981. It will be noted that there is no entry under "Sagesse" in the *DTC*; the article on "Trinité" gives some indications, but they are quite insufficient.

## I. THE PROPHETIC CHARISM

Leaving aside patriarchal revelation, which is more difficult to grasp historically, we find this charism at work in the case of Moses and that of the prophets, [72] in whom the Deuteronomist sees the authentic successors of Moses (Dt 18:15-19). It always presents a twofold aspect: first a divine revelation received in any one of many ways (Nb 12:6-8); and secondly a personal mission to transmit the revelation received to the people of God. In more concrete terms, God "puts his words into the mouth" of the man he calls (Jr 1:9; cf. Is 6:6-7; Ezk 2:8—3:3; Dt 18:18), with the result that one must listen to the words of that man as the words of God himself (Dt 18:19). Elsewhere the proclamation of the word of God is related to his Spirit, the principle of supernatural operation that transforms the acts of man: God sends the Spirit upon his servant to "bring true justice to the nations" (Is 42:1); he makes the Spirit rest upon the anonymous messenger on whom he confers the prophetic anointing to bring to his people the good news of salvation (Is 61:1).

The word of God thus confided to the prophet may take on various aspects. [73] In the case of Moses, along with the strictly religious message concerning the name of God, his plan of salvation (Ex 3:14-20), and his alliance (Ex 19:3-8), it included the commandments, principles of justice and of cult, etc. In the case of the other prophets, it was sometimes a message of conversion accompanied by threats, sometimes a promise of salvation which sketched the future action of God. It is true to a certain extent that these prophets, as true servants of an already formed tradition, repeated some of the older words. [74] But each of them was also the bearer of a particular message whose revealed origin they attested. No matter in what form this message reached men, and no matter what traditional elements the prophet incorporated in it, it was wholly under the influence of the prophetic charism and had the value of a word of God.

[72] On the notion of prophecy in the Old Testament, see P. van Imschoot, *op. cit.*, Vol. 1, pp. 148-171; J. Lindblom, *Prophecy in Ancient Israel* (Oxford: Blackwell, 1962). The concept of prophetism in Christian theology does not exactly correspond to that of the Old Testament; it concerns more exclusively the problem of revelation itself (see, for example, II[a]-II[æ], qq. 171-174, and the remarks of P. Benoit, *La Prophétie*, pp. 270-272). A. Michel, art. "Prophétie," *DTC*, treats the question exclusively from an apologetic point of view, which is of no interest here.

[73] See *Sens chrétien de l'A.T.*, pp. 128-131 (a rational synthesis rather than a descriptive analysis).

[74] Cf. "Tradition," *VTB*, cols. 873-875. Compare the negative position of of P. H. Menoud, "Tradition" in J. J. von Almen, *Vocabulaire biblique*, p. 293: "The word and the idea of tradition are unknown in the Old Testament" (cf. above, p. 10, note 21).

## II. THE OTHER FUNCTIONAL CHARISMS

The prophet had a wholly distinct function in the people of God. But his message, once proclaimed, was not abandoned to the hazards of a human tradition which could evolve in its own fashion. The *milieu* in which it was transmitted is in fact an organic community, held together by activities which played a determining role in the transmission of the word of God. The exact nature of these functions is not so easily determined as in the New Testament, but those that have to do with the law and cult, and those which the lay scribes fulfil, are sufficiently clear. For these the texts foresee a divine assistance, which, according to the function of each, depended upon the prophetic charism.

### *1. Elders, Priests, Chanters*

The oldest collections of traditions mention elders who fulfilled the office of commissioners (šōṭᵉrim: Nb 11:16) and applied the Mosaic law in ordinary cases [75] (Ex 18:19-26). For that reason they partook of the spirit of Moses (Nb 11:16-17) and were likened to the prophets (Nb 11:24-25). Joshua's role was not only a military one; it included the duty to recall the divine commands, and to preserve the cultic tradition and the law as well (Jos 24). Joshua too received the spirit of Moses (Nb 27:15-23), which is a spirit of wisdom (Dt 24:8), and later tradition considered him the successor of Moses in the prophetic office (Si 46:1, Greek text). The levitic priests watched over the word of God [76] when they taught the law (Dt 33:10) and judged in Israel (Dt 17:8-13). Nothing is said of the divine assistance they then received, but since their office continued that of the elders mentioned above, it can be assumed that their charism was passed on to them. Nothing further is said about the cultic function of the priests, but the rite of anointing by which they were consecrated from the time of the exile [77] (Lv 8:12.30) was usually connected with the Spirit of God who envelops a man in order to destine him for a particular mission. Finally, to the chanters, whose songs were a vehicle of the community's tradition, later texts attribute sometimes the prophetic charism (1 Ch 25:1-3), sometimes the gift of wisdom (Si 15:9-10).

[75] On this office of commissioner and of judge entrusted to the elders, see R. de Vaux, *Ancient Israel, Its Life and Institutions*, 2nd ed. (New York: McGraw-Hill, 1965), pp. 152-155.

[76] *Ibid.*, pp. 353-355. G. Schrenk, " Ἱερεύς, " *TWNT* 3, pp. 256-263. A. Gelin, "Le sacerdoce de l'ancienne alliance," *La tradition sacerdotale* (LePuy: Mappus, 1959), pp. 27-60; A. George, art. "Sacerdoce," *VTB*, cols. 962 ff.

[77] R. de Vaux, *op. cit.*, pp. 105, 400.

## 2. The Scribes and Wisdom

The scribes we are going to discuss here were not just educated men, those who possessed a certain human culture. This point is clear enough from the reaction of the prophets against the profane wisdom of the royal advisors. [78] But there was another sort of wisemen in Israel, who found the source of their wisdom in the law of God. (cf. Dt 4:4.6). Especially after the exile, certain lay scribes put their knowledge in the service of the word of God and the tradition founded upon it, either by laboring to collect and transmit already existent scriptures, or by setting down the content of their own personal teaching. [79] These masters of wisdom, along with a specialized priesthood and prophetism which tended to disappear, became pillars of the Jewish community. It is exclusively in their regard that there can be a question of a charism.

Ben Sira [80] presents the scribe receiving an intimate infusion of wisdom (Si 15:1-6). Wisdom actually resided in Israel under the form of the law (24:23 ff.), and assisted the man who meditated on the scriptures in which it is expressed (24:20-27). It is for this reason that the teacher could transmit to his disciples the wisdom he possessed (51:22-30). Having nourished his thought on the scriptures (39:1-3; prol. 7-11), he in his turn dispensed an authentic teaching (39:6-8), assisted by the Spirit of understanding (39:6). His teaching, moreover, though it aimed at no more than to explain the content of the law (24:23-29), took on the character of true prophecy (24:33), since it supposed a charismatic understanding of the scriptures (39:1-3). Besides, in that age the charismatic interpretation of scriptures became one of the forms of prophetic revelation (Dn 9:22). Thus the wiseman, though he was not properly speaking the recipient of the prophetic charism, nevertheless partook of it in some measure.

The book of Wisdom says the same thing no less clearly. [81] The wiseman's knowledge is a pure gift of God (Ws 7:15-21; 8:21). It can be compared to prophetic knowledge, because for God it is one and the

---

[78] See the examination of the question in H. Duesberg, Les Scribes inspirés I (Bruges-Paris: Desclée de Brouwer, 1939), pp. 191-232.

[79] Ibid., Vol. I, pp. 501-573. It should be noted that even at a very ancient age this religious evolution of Israelite wisdom had already commenced, as Dom Duesberg shows in the preceding chapters of the same work (pp. 232 ff.).

[80] For a more detailed study of the texts cited here, see H. Duesberg, op. cit., Vol. 2, pp. 235-440, as well as commentaries on the book.

[81] Ibid., Vol. 2, pp. 485 ff. A good exposition is that of L. Bigot, "Sagesse (Livre de la)," DTC 14, cols. 703-744. There are some useful remarks, insufficiently developed, in G. Ziener, Die theologische Begriffssprache im Buche der Weisheit (Bonn: P. Hanstein, 1956), pp. 91 and 113.

same thing to confer wisdom and to send forth his Spirit (9:17); by coming among men, divine wisdom makes prophets of them (7:27). This view agrees with the new concept of prophecy which arose in the apocalyptic current: the revelation of divine secrets is there likewise attributed to transcendent wisdom whose source is the spirit of God (Dn 5:11-14).

The existence, in the Old Testament, therefore, of particular charisms related to the functions through which living tradition operates must be admitted. Not that there existed then an infallible magisterium analogous to that found in the Church, but the faithful preservation of the word of God, its proclamation, its application for the good of the community, could not have taken place without some sort of intervention of the Spirit and wisdom of God. One could even say that there is no authentic tradition except where the Spirit and wisdom are at work. These functional charisms even contribute in some measure to the development of revelation, first as complements of prophecy, then as its perpetuators. The boundaries of the two are imprecise: there are borderline cases in which the wiseman speaks as a prophet, and others in which the prophet takes on the qualities of the wiseman. The problem now is to discover in what relation scriptural inspiration stands to this whole group of charisms.

### III. THE SCRIPTURAL CHARISM

The message of the prophets and the tradition developed upon it were collected in writing through complex processes and under very different forms. Were the men who had a part in this work aided by a special charism? In order to reply, we will distinguish two cases: that of the prophets, and that of the custodians of tradition.

#### 1. *The Case of the Prophets*

The word of a prophet, in whatever form expressed and however it reaches men, has the normative value of a word of God, since it is guaranteed by the prophetic charism. Whether the prophet himself put his message in writing (Jr 29), whether he dictated it to a secretary (Jr 36:4), or whether he entrusted it to the memory of his disciples (Is 8:16), it comes practically to the same thing: the scriptural charism connected with the literary fixation of the message does no more in these cases than prolong the action of the divine Spirit which had enveloped the prophet in the first place. Such a prolongation is not obligatory: the discourses of some prophets have not been preserved in their literal form. But when it does exist, it always implies the divine assistance to write. The situation, however, is rarely so simple.

The notes and recollections of disciples can include a certain literary activity for which they alone were responsible. They are usually the composers of the biographical accounts (thus Baruch wrote the life of Jeremias). In the case of Moses, an initiator of revelation, the message went through a long development in living tradition before receiving, in stages, its definitive literary form. [82]   In such circumstances, the prophet's personal charism does not sufficiently account for the text that preserves the memory of his deed or in which his message is expressed. That text can be an authentic, but only mediate, witness of the message.

## 2. The Other Cases

There is no reason to attribute to the redactors of the Mosaic or prophetic books a direct participation in the charism proper to Moses or to the prophets, except in the sense in which Nb 11:16-17 says of the elders that they received " some of the spirit which is on Moses." The required charism had less connection with the person of these men than with their function. For that reason, it can already be said that their work was accomplished under the movement of the Spirit and wisdom of God. Still, scriptural inspiration does not necessarily accompany all the literary activity that they might perform in such cases. A particular grace is needed, one conferred in an unforeseeable fashion and with a limited scope: the production of a book which will be the word of God. Where this grace exists, the functional charism is likewise at its maximum of effectiveness, so that the message received from a prophet or gathered in tradition might be expressed in authentic form. That is why the book to which these men contributed in a positive way retained, in their eyes, the authority of Moses (the only authority cited in the Pentateuch!), or of Jeremias, or of some other prophet. The sacred writers were in such cases, therefore, linked to these prophetic (in the strict sense of the term) authorities by tradition, where their charismatic function placed them. But they enjoyed, in addition, a properly scriptural charism, which rendered them also transmitters of the word of God.

All other things being equal, the same can be said of those authors who were in no way dependent on Mosaic tradition or that of the prophets,

---

[82] Even if the literary solution of the problem of the Pentateuch remains disputable in detail, the development of the Mosaic tradition in the course of ages remains an established fact (cf. *Sens chrétien de l'A.T.*, pp. 192-195 for a theological estimation of this fact). Concerning the critical discussion, see H. Cazelles in Robert—Feuillet, *Introduction to the Old Testament*, pp. 164 ff.; "Pentateuque," *DBS* 7, cols. 687-858.

and who produced original works on their own authority: historians, psalmists, masters of wisdom, etc. Whether priests or laymen, it was always in the exercise of a charismatic function that they served the word of God in the community of salvation. It is unthinkable that any book of the Old Testament should have been published, at least in the definitive form in which the Church has received it, outside such conditions, even if it is difficult to determine in detail what functions existed in the community of salvation at that time, and if some of them had little apparent importance, that of the grandson of Ben Sira, for example (Si prol.), or the author who condensed the work of Jason of Cyrene (2 M 2:19-30). From this it follows that just by reason of their function, the sacred authors were already seized in some measure by the Spirit and wisdom of God. When scriptural inspiration was added, it prolonged and specified for a determined scope that potentially broader charism, assuring it at the same time a quasi-prophetic effectiveness (cf. Si prol. 4-14). Recognition of this fact is at the basis of the canon of Scriptures. In fact, from their oldest traces on, it is apparent that all the works that make up Scripture were equally considered the word of God, but at the same time several categories, which correspond to different charismatic functions, were admitted (Si 39:1-3; prol. 1. 7-10). The New Testament will likewise recognize in them "scriptures inspired by God" (2 Tm 3:16), but it retained the principle of their different classes (cf. Lk 24:44, etc.).

## II. IN THE NEW TESTAMENT

The question is more easily circumscribed in the New Testament, because the relations between tradition and Scripture take on a more exact form in it, ecclesiastical offices are more clearly outlined, and its theology of charisms [83] is much more developed. But here too, in order to study the framework in which the scriptures were born, it is necessary to distinguish two kinds of charism: the apostolic charism, which is at the source of all the others, and the various functional charisms which served to give ecclesiastical tradition its form.

---

[83] On charisms, see the commentaries on the Pauline letters under that reference, especially E. B. Allo, *Première épître aux Corinthiens* (Paris: Lecoffre, 1935), pp. 317-339; F. Prat, *The Theology of St. Paul* (London: Burns, 1964), pp. 423-428; L. Cerfaux, *The Christian in the Theology of St. Paul* (New York: Herder & Herder, 1967), pp. 242-261. It is not our purpose here to examine all the charisms, but only those which are bound to some ecclesiastical function.

## I. THE APOSTOLIC CHARISM [84]

The apostolate is at the head of every Pauline list of charisms (1 Co 12:28; Ep 4:11). Through it the word of God takes form in the New Testament. From this point of view, it implies a gift of knowledge that is to the fulness of revelation what prophetic illumination was to preparatory revelation. Certainly, the words and acts of Jesus, crowned by his appearance after the resurrection, were at the source of this knowledge [85] (Ep 3:3-5) and constituted its fundamental object. But that knowledge was finally communicated in full only "through the Spirit" (Ep 3:5). In the Acts, the Spirit is given to the twelve in consideration of the testimony they are to render to Christ (Ac 1:8; 5:32). The fourth gospel [86] is still more precise: the Spirit given to the apostles will render testimony to Christ, so that they in their turn might also testify to him (Jn 15:26-27; cf. 1 Jn 5:6); he will teach them every truth and call to their minds the teaching of Jesus (14:26); he will guide them to the fulness of truth and instruct them about things to come (16:13); it is therefore due to the Spirit that the apostles will be able to understand the meaning of the words of Jesus (2:19-22), of his significant acts (13:7), and of the scriptures which speak of him (12:16; 20:9).

These facts show that the substantial progress of revelation that took place while the apostles were alive must be attributed to the aspotolic charism. Everything was given in Christ, in his words, his deeds, the historical accomplishment of his mystery. But following that, everything had to be expressed and handed over to the Church. [87] This development took place

---

[84] J. Colson, *Les fonctions ecclésiales aux deux premiers siècles* (Bruges-Paris: Desclée de Bouwer, 1956), pp. 11-71 (with a good bibliography on the question); L. Cerfaux, *op. cit.*, pp. 116-128, 486 ff. We are here examining the apostolate only under the aspect of its relation to the word of God, leaving aside its other aspects.

[85] Y. Congar, *La foi et la théologie*, pp. 13-15.

[86] See the commentaries on the 4th gospel, on the verses cited above, especially M. J. Lagrange, pp. 391-392 and 421-423. St. Augustine, in the corresponding passages of the *Tractatus in Joannem* (77, 2; 92; 96), hardly insists on this aspect of the question, except to say that the Spirit of Pentecost gave the apostles the strength to give witness (cf. *Tract.* 92). For a systematic treatment of the question, see A. Feuillet, "De munere doctrinali a Paraclito in Ecclesia expleto juxta Evangelium sancti Joannis," *De Scriptura et traditione* (Rome: Pont. Academia Mariana Internat., 1963), pp. 115-136. In a broader perspective, J. Giblet, "Les promesses de l'Esprit et la mission des apôtres dans les évangiles," *Irenikon* 30 (1957), 5-43.

[87] Many Catholic commentators apply these promises directly to the Church, which the Holy Spirit forever assists. That is to mix unjustly two questions: that of the assistance of the Spirit given the apostles to bear witness, which is the foundation of faith, and that of the assistance given the Church to preserve and make fruitful that apostolic testimony. The texts cited here concern principally the first, as J. B. Franzelin well noted in *De divina traditione et scriptura* (Rome: S.C. de Prop. Fide, 1896), pp. 268 ff.

under the movement of the Spirit, just as the doctrinal development in the Old Testament, whose essential medium was the prophetic word. The proclamation of the gospel by the apostles could also be presented as the eschatological manifestation of the prophetic Spirit (Ac 2:16-18). In the respective plans of the two Testaments, the two charisms are, from this point of view, of the same nature. They have to do not only with the manifestation of the divine word to the conscience of the prophet or apostle, but include also its formulation and proclamation to men.

## II. THE FUNCTIONAL CHARISMS

It is nevertheless necessary to go beyond this view of the matter, for the Spirit's assistance to the apostles required a prolongation in the structure of the Church. [88] Jesus promised the twelve that he would be with them "to the end of time" (Mt 28:20). This active presence of the Lord cannot be dissociated from the mission of the Spirit (cf. Jn 14:16-19); but the mention of a duration covering all the time of the Church necessarily demands an assistance that will continue after the age of the apostles. To determine its forms, attention might first of all turn to the grace of interior illumination which the Spirit gives to every Christian to enable him to understand the mystery of Christ revealed in the word of the gospel [89] (Ep 1:17-18; 1 Jn 2:20.27; cf. Jn 6:44-45). Nevertheless, this general grace should not mask a more particular action which invests the ecclesiastical hierarchy. Already in Ac 15:28 the decision made "by the Holy Spirit and by ourselves" obliges not only the apostles present in Jerusalem, but the heads of local churches as well [90] (Ac 15:22-23); while the apostolic authority dominates and still embraces ecclesiastical authority, the two act in harmony with the assistance and under the guaranty of the same Spirit.

In the letters, especially those of St. Paul, the theology of charisms shows how, in fact, this assistance passed from one stage to the other. Leaving aside the particular gifts which are signs of the word, such as miracles,

[88] Concerning the custodians of these ecclesiastical offices, see J. Colson, *Les fonctions ecclésiales*, pp. 72-174 (a study of ecclesiastical offices in New Testament times). For an Anglican point of view, see G. Dix, "The Ministry in the Early Church" in K. Kirk, ed., *The Apostolic Ministry* (London: Hodder & Stoughton, 1946).

[89] See the commentary of J. Chaine, *Les épîtres catholiques* (Paris: Lecoffre, 1939), pp. 173-175. J. Bonsirven, *Épîtres de saint Jean*, 2nd ed. (Paris: Beauchesne, 1954), pp. 143-152 (excellent quotes from St. Augustine and St. Thomas). See the texts of St. Augustine, *In epistulam Joannis*, 3, 13.

[90] This point is independent of the critical discussion on the origin of the apostolic decree (cf. J. Dupont, *Les problèmes du livre des Actes* (Louvain: Univ. of Louvain, 1950), pp. 67-70. L. Cerfaux in Robert—Feuillet, *Introduction to the New Testament*, pp. 344-346.

the gift of tongues, etc. (1 Co 12:8-10; cf. Mk 16:17-18), there are some
that are connected to the functions which the apostles confided to responsible
persons in every community they founded. [91] We have selected here those
that have to do with the word of God. Prophecy [92] is not easily defined,
and its relation to other functions is no longer very clear (1 Co 12:10.28;
Rm 12:6; Ep 4:11). It always includes a message to be delivered to the
community on the part of God (cf. Rv 1:1-3; 22:10-18), but it must submit
to critical examination (1 Co 14:32; 1 Th 5:19) and to community discipline
(1 Co 14:29-30.37). It is not, therefore, in exactly the same situation as
prophecy in the Old Testament. [93] Two other functions directly concern
instruction: that of teacher (1 Co 12:28; Rm 12:7; Ep 4:11), which is exercised
by Timothy (1 Tm 4:13.16), Titus (Tt 2:1.7), the elders of the churches
(1 Tm 5:17); and that of evangelist (Ep 4:11) exercised by Philip (Ac 21:8)
and Timothy (2 Tm 4:5). Finally, the office of officials or overseers (Rm 12:8;
1 Th 5:12), which most probably is to be identified with that of pastor
(Ep 4:11), is confided to some elders (Ac 20:28; cf. 1 P 5:1-2), and without
doubt it includes a certain responsibility in regard to the apostolic message
(Ac 20:29-31). The special position of Titus and Timothy bears no special
title, [94] but it is stated that their mission is charismatic (1 Tm 4:14; 2 Tm 1:6).

Those who fill these positions are the organs of ecclesiastical tradition [95]
even during the life of the apostles. The apostolic word has been confided
as the deposit [96] which they must guard (1 Tm 4:6.11; 5:17.22; 6:20; 2 Tm
3:14; 4:2.5; Tt 1:7-9; 2:15). Their charge includes teaching doctrine,
explaining the sacred scriptures (2 Tm 3:14-15), and defending tradition

[91] On the importance of these charisms for the theology of the sacrament of
orders, see P. Grelot, "Le sacerdoce chrétien dans l'Écriture," *BCE* (1962), 279-337.

[92] G. Friedrich, "Προφήτης," *TWNT* 6, pp. 829-863. J. Colson, *op. cit.*, pp. 354-
366 (*excursus* devoted to the question). L. Cerfaux, *The Christian in the Theology
of St. Paul*, pp. 94-96 (reduces to prophecy certain secondary charisms: gnosis,
wisdom, revelation), 247-249, 251-255.

[93] In the Church, just as in Israel, the message of the prophet actualizes the
word of God as it applies to the concrete problems of a particular age. But while
in the Old Testament that message was delivered within revelation in growth, and
contributed to its development, in the New it adds substantially nothing to a revelation which depends upon the apostolic charism alone, even when it contributes
toward bringing to light the potentialities of the tradition in which it takes its place.

[94] These co-workers of Paul are "apostles through the mediation of men"
(J. Colson, *op. cit.*, pp. 72-91 and 146-150).

[95] On this notion of tradition, see L. Cerfaux, "La tradition selon saint Paul"
and "Les deux points de départ de la tradition chrétienne" in *Recueil L. Cerfaux* 2
(Gembloux: Duculot, 1954), pp. 253-282.

[96] C. Spicq, *Les épîtres pastorales*, pp. 214-217 and 327-335. This deposit
is certainly broader than the "truths of the faith," for it includes the whole practice
of the churches, which had a rich content of thought that was to unfold with the
passage of time (above, p. 22f).

against the false doctors, who, in distorting the sense of Scripture to their own purposes (1 Tm 4:1-3; 2 Tm 4:3-4), the letters of the apostles included (2 P 3:16), are successors to the false prophets of the Old Testament (2 P 2:1). The comparison is illuminating: when the ecclesiastical defenders of authority and doctrine defend the apostolic tradition against those who pervert it, they are in the same situation as the prophets of another age, in that they defend the authentic word of God against those who falsify it.

The idea of a magisterium assisted by the Holy Spirit can be read between the lines of the texts cited. The ways it functions need not concern us here. It suffices to note that ecclesiastical tradition is built up by ministerial charisms to enable it to preserve intact the apostolic tradition and to bring its potential riches to light. Such is the framework in which the inspired literature of the New Testament was born.

### III. THE SCRIPTURAL CHARISM

Even when compared with the Old Testament, the New makes only scanty explicit mention of this particular point. There are, however, a number of positive indications of it. The author of Revelation himself attaches divine authority to his prophetic writing (Rv 22:18-19). In 1 Tm 5:18 two texts are cited on the same footing as Scripture: Dt 25:4 and a saying of Christ preserved in Lk 10:7. More precisely, 2 P 3:15-16 likens the Pauline letters to the other scriptures, that is, to the books of the Old Testament. This is somewhat meager data, but it is possible to draw conclusions from it by inference, as long as the case of the apostles is distinguished from that of the other sacred writers.

### 1. The Case of the Apostles

The apostolic charism affected every act performed by its recipients in the exercise of their office. It conferred the worth of the word of God to their proclamation of the gospel, to their charismatic interpretation of Scripture, and to the practical directives they laid down for the Christian communities. There is no reason here to distinguish between the word of God preached orally and the same word written. The scriptural charism then necessarily prolonged the apostolic charism, whenever an apostle had recourse to the written word to accomplish his mission. This principle applies to written or dictated letters, as well as to the gospel texts which preserve the apostolic preaching in its raw form. The secretaries employed in similar cases (Tertius, in Rm 16:22) had no need to partake of a special charism. [97] But

---

[97] See however J. M. Vosté, "Utrum amanuenses, quibus hagiographi usi sunt, fuerint inspirati?" *Angelicum* 6 (1930), 61-64.

the situation is different when the apostolic message was formulated by a redactor who left the mark of his own personality, such as Silvanus on the first letter of St. Peter [98] (I P 5:12); his activity then required an appropriate charism to insure that the apostolic message was authentically interpreted and could thus exercise its full authority. The case is similar to that of the editors who collaborated to produce the prophetic books.

## 2. The Other Cases

There remain those books which were not directly authored by an apostle. In the case of these authors, the scriptural charism is grafted to an already existent functional charism. Only one case involved the charism of prophecy, that of Revelation, if its author is not to be identified with John the apostle. [99] Its prophetic author is conscious of being inspired by God, both as far as the revelation of the message he is to transmit (Rv 1:2) is concerned, and as to putting it in writing (10:4; 22:7.10). Psychologically, this situation is similar to that of ancient prophetism. But it cannot be concluded that Christian prophetism necessarily required scriptural inspiration as a consequence when its recipient made his message known in writing. In this regard, the situation is completely different, for now revelation (in its strict sense) is made through the apostolic charism, and no longer through the prophetic charism. His charism classes the prophet—if he is not himself an apostle, as is perhaps the case of John—among the recipients and guardians of tradition. It is just such a case that we are going to examine now.

The responsible authors of all the other books of the New Testament, whether of the gospels in which apostolic testimony is transformed into ecclesiastical catechesis, or of the letters in which analysis reveals the hand of various editors, undoubtedly belonged to the category of ministers, men who performed some charismastic function in the communities. [100] They

---

[98] J. Cantinat in Robert—Feuillet, Introduction to the New Testament, pp. 578 f.

[99] See M. E. Boismard, L'Apocalypse, BJ, pp. 16-20; Robert—Feuillet, Introduction to the New Testament, pp. 710-722.

[100] The clearest cases are those of Luke and Mark. Mark was "a useful helper in my work" (2 Tm 4:11), and Papias later called him Peter's interpreter. Luke must have been more than "my dear friend, the doctor" of Col 4:14. Why should their literary work not be referred to the office of evangelist (Ep 4:11)? For the fourth gospel, the epilogue (Jn 21:24) gives to understand that John's disciples took part in the editing of the work. As for the text of Matthew, between the gospel "in the Hebrew language" of which Papias speaks and the present text a literary elaboration certainly took place, one that present day exegesis would like to attribute to a "school of Matthew" (K. Stendahl, The School of St. Matthew [Uppsala: Almquist, 1954]). All these indications direct our attention to the teachers of the primitive Church. Similar remarks could be made for a good number of the letters. Concerning Silas and the First Letter of Peter, cf. above, note 98; the letter to the Hebrews

did not write on their own authority, but in the exercise of the duties of their office. There is, then, a close connection between their scriptural inspiration and their functional charism. Not that this latter *ipso facto* entails inspiration, but by a particular disposition of providence, having been destined in a precise case to put the word of God in writing, they received whatever was necessary to accomplish that end. It should be noted that these complementary graces have a great importance, for the books which result will not be considered only as excellent witnesses of ecclesiastical tradition, but will finally enjoy an authority equal to that of the apostolic writings. In other words, such writings represent an integral part of Christian revelation. That supposes that their authors were the recipients of an interior illumination analogous to that of the prophet in the Old Testament and that of the apostle.

The analysis we have made, therefore, shows that there is always an organic relation between scriptural inspiration and the other charisms which have to do with the word of God. Nevertheless, the first does not flow from the second, except in two instances: prophecy in the Old Testament and the apostolate in the New. This is due to the particular nature of these two charisms, which make of their recipients the direct organs of revelation in every act of their ministry.

The relation of Scripture to the economy of salvation is now quite clear. In the Old Testament, prophecy (in the strict sense) in some manner founded the community of salvation by bringing to it the word of God. Then other charisms appeared to give the community its structure, so that it could preserve the word and develop its potentialities. During all of this development, scriptural inspiration occasionnally gave that word a written form, so that the community could refer to this scripture as a rule of faith. In the fulness of time, Christ, the word of God made flesh, brought to men the fulness of revelation by his words and deeds. At the same time, he unveiled the definitive sense of the ancient scriptures. But only the gospel message proclaimed after Pentecost made that revelation explicit; thus the role of the apostolic charism as foundation of the Church (Ep 2:20; Rv 21:14) to which it brought the word. After that, other charisms gave form to ecclesiastical tradition to enable it to preserve the word and make it produc-

---

is the work of a Christian teacher who might be Apollos (C. Spicq, *Épître aux Hébreux* I, p. 218). James of Jerusalem does not seem to have been one of the twelve, but he presided over the assembly of elders; there are other reasons for posing the problem of a secondary redactor for his letter. Concerning the Second Letter of Peter, cf. above, p. 36, notes 3 and 4. In the Pauline collection, the question of a redactor has been raised for the letter to the Ephesians (state of the question by L. Cerfaux in Robert—Feuillet, *Introduction to the New Testament*, pp. 502-504) and even more for the pastoral letters (*ibid.*, pp. 518-525).

tive through the course of time. Such is the meaning of the hierarchical magisterium which, with the assistance of the Holy Spirit, still continues to guard the apostolic deposit. Still, that deposit has been fixed in writing, thanks to scriptural inspiration, which was accorded to certain men who exercised charismatic functions and were still near enough to the apostles to be direct witnesses to the deposit bequeathed by them.

This connection between scriptural inspiration and the various charisms which could be grouped under the generic name inspiration throws light as well upon the relation of the sacred writers to revelation. Revelation comes to us primarily through the agency of the prophets, then of the apostles. Those who exercised charismatic functions could positively collaborate with them on occasion, if God so willed, by developing the material they gathered from tradition. The sacred writers cooperated with them in every case, if not by making known new truths, at least by setting down what was revealed, with the guarantee of God himself, in the books which are the word of God.

## § III. THE NATURE OF SCRIPTURAL INSPIRATION

Having determined the place of scriptural inspiration among the manifold gifts of the Holy Spirit, we can now turn to an examination of its nature. In our brief historical summary of the problem, we have already seen its outline gradually become clearer. Following some introductory remarks, we will now analyze the elements of scriptural inspiration. In conclusion, we will consider some questions brought up by our analysis.

### I. PRELIMINARY REMARKS

#### I. ON THE NOTION OF INSTRUMENT OF GOD

##### *1. Metaphor or Philosophical Concept?*

No philosophical consideration influenced the fathers when they called God the author of the sacred books, and the inspired authors the instruments of the word or of the Holy Spirit. On the first point, the expression represented the reaction of the Church against the dualist heresies. In their regard, the Church insisted on the responsibility of God for the two Testaments, that is, for the two dispensations of which the scriptures are a part. [101]

---

[101] Above, p. 38, notes 13 to 16.

But afterwards the expression gradually passed over to the literary field, as the text of St. Gregory cited above [102] shows. Concerning the second point, the metaphoric nature of the expression was still more evident, as is apparent from its earliest use (in the *Cohortatio ad Graecos* or by Hippolytus). [103] This figurative language was not, however, without its perils, for metaphors can always be abused. For example, one theologian might not lose sight of the properly human activity of the sacred authors, free and intelligent instruments; another might tend to understand the expression mechanically and practically overlook that human activity, as if the word of God could be understood without any attention given to the diversity of human expressions it took on. [104]

Scholastic theology of the 13th century attempted to eliminate these equivocations by examining the question more rigorously. It was with that in mind that it introduced the Aristotelian concept of efficient cause, principal and instrumental, and applied it to the collaboration of God and man, both in the case of prophecy and in that of the sacred books. [105] It should not be concluded that from that time onward this philosophical concept was intrinsically linked to the dogma it helped to explain. It just seemed to be an excellent tool of expression, because it respected, on the one hand, the transcendence and sovereign power of God, who controls all secondary causes as their Creator, and, on the other, the full originality of the inspired writers, whom the divine action caused to act always in conformity with their human nature. [106]

## 2. The Sacred Authors and the Humanity of Jesus Christ

The utility of the concept of instrument applies also to another case, which we will now examine. It can be applied in every instance where God operates here below through the intermediation of men (for example, in the administration of the sacraments), and particularly through the humanity

---

[102] Above, p. 39, note 18.

[103] Above, p. 37, note 8.

[104] See the text of St. Gregory, above, p. 39, note 19, and especially those on p. 40, note 27 and on p. 41, note 28.

[105] Above, p. 39, notes 20 to 22. Concerning the use of this philosophical notion, see E. Hugon, *La causalité instrumentale en théologie*, 2nd ed. (Paris: Tequi, 1924).

[106] This notion of instrumental causality is explained in regard to the sacraments in III[a], q. 61, art. 1, *in corp.* and ad 2. The proper action of the created cause is then ordered to its instrumental effect, which in itself would surpass its nature, but that proper action retains its integrity. Cf. also III[a], q. 18, art. 1, ad 2. See the explanation of G. Courtade, "Inspiration," *DBS* 4, cols. 511-514.

of Christ, the instrument of divinity par excellence. [107] Now the comparison between the humanity of Christ and the sacred authors is not a fortuitous one. It recalls an idea which was current in the patristic age, [108] and which had its source in the letter to the Hebrews and the fourth gospel: in the Old Testament the Word spoke to men through the prophets in a still imperfect manner; in the New, he assumed a human nature in order to speak to them in person, and then made the apostles ministers of his word by entrusting the gospel to them. Nevertheless, the very comparison of these diverse cases underlines their profound difference: the instrumental character of the Word is neither realized in the same degree, nor in the same manner. To use the language of St. Thomas, in the case of the humanity of Christ the instrument is personally united to the word of God [109]; in all the others —whether it be the prophets, apostles, ministers of the word, or the sacraments of the Church—there can be no question of more than separated instruments. [110]

The comparison is, therefore, helpful, since it helps to understand how the Word assumes the activity of the prophets and sacred writers through the charism of inspiration. But it should not be pushed too far, because that assumption does not have the fulness it possesses in the unique case of the hypostatic union. In Jesus Christ the human instrument never acted except in the very person of the Word, whose perfect medium of expression it was. In all other instruments, the Word leaves to the autonomous human persons the complete control of their spontaneous activity, even at the moment he uses them for his own purposes. For that reason, the human instrument who proclaims or writes the word of God does it within certain limits: those of his time and his personality, of his mission and the grace he has received; he might even prove to be a deficient instrument. [111] That makes it necessary to examine closely the conditions in

---

[107] IIIᵃ, q. 13, art. 3, *in corp.*; q. 19, art. 1, *in corp.*; q. 43, art. 2, *in corp.*; q. 48, art. 6, *in corp.*; q. 49, art. 1, ad 1; q. 56, art. 1, art. 3, etc.

[108] J. W. Crehans, "The Analogy between *Verbum Dei incarnatum* and *Verbum Dei scriptum* in the Fathers," *JTS* n.s. 6 (1955), 87-90. P. Bellet, "Il sentido de la analogia *Verbum Dei incarnatum—Verbum Dei scriptum*," *EstB* 14 (1955), 415-428.

[109] "An instrument united to the word of God in person" (IIIᵃ, q. 13, art. 3, *in corp.*).

[110] The explicit distinction is utilized in IIIᵃ, q. 62, art. 5, *in corp.*, where it is applied to the ministers of the sacraments. These ministers are the instruments of the sanctifying word of Christ, just as the sacred writers were of his revealing word.

[111] We repeat that in treating prophecy St. Thomas directed his attention to the prophet's knowledge, rather than to his office of herald of the word of God. But the notion of human instrument cannot be applied in the same way in the two cases. Concerning the first, see the qualifications of P. Benoit, *La Prophétie*, pp. 286-292. Concerning the second, which is closely related to the activity of the sacred writers, *ibid.*, pp. 303-310. The prophet's "deficiency" is mentioned by St. Thomas in regard

which this human word is formulated, to scrutinize mental processes and motivation, since the revelatory action of the Word makes use of all these factors without suppressing their peculiarities and limitations. In brief, the philosophical concept of instrumentality must be flexible enough to encompass the structure of a complex reality such as nature assumed by the supernatural.

## II. CONDITIONS FOR THE REALIZATION OF SCRIPTURAL INSPIRATION

Many doctrinal expositions of scriptural inspiration, in order the better to analyze it in itself, end up treating it as if it were an isolated phenomenon. But it is essential never to lose sight of its organic relation to a life of faith and a charismatic function which are its necessary support.

### *1. Inspiration and Life of Faith*

All the charisms which have to do with the word of God have similarly a link with the life of faith. In order to bring the word to men or to set it down in writing, one must first have received it himself. The cases of Balaam, a prophet in spite of himself, and of Caiaphas, an unwilling prophet, are not valid objections. [112] They do not fit into the ordinary notion of prophet, which supposes that the inspired person personally shares the faith he intends to arouse or nourish in the people of God by proclaiming the word to them. This applies to very diverse situations: that of the prophet or apostle, who are bearers of revelation, is not the same as that of mere sacred writers; that of Moses, founder of the faith of Israel, is not realized in the other prophets who had behind them a tradition already formed.

Thus, in most cases, even before receiving the prophetic or scriptural charism, a man's spirit is already formed by his faith. This not only gives a certain direction to his thought, and gives him a certain understanding of divine realities (more or less complete according to the stage revelation has reached), but consequently influences all his physical life, his emotions, his imagination, his language, thus providing a positive preparation for the task he will be called upon to undertake. When through inspiration the

to the prophet who unwittingly prophesies (II^a-II^æ, q. 173, art. 4, *in corp.*). But the principle can be applied to other cases. Especially does it explain the divergence between the literal and fuller senses in texts of the Old Testament (cf. *Sens chrétien de l'A.T.*, pp. 448-455).

[112] II^a-II^æ, q. 173, art. 4. In fact, St. Thomas says of Caiaphas himself, in his commentary on St. John, "He can no more be called a prophet than Balaam's donkey" (*In Joh.*, 11, 51).

Word takes possession of that man and makes him his instrument, he takes him just as his life of faith has formed him. It would be useless to attribute to a charism as such what is quite simply the result of this life of faith. It is necessary, though, to recognize that that man is assumed by the charism, completed by it, directed to a precise task: the proclamation of the word of God, its preservation, or its expression in writing.

## 2. Inspiration and Functional Charism

We have seen too that the mission of a sacred writer is always superadded to a charismatic function, one fulfilled in the people of God for the common good. This connection between the two charisms can take on two different forms. In the prophets and apostles the functional charism necessarily entails the scriptural charism whenever the prophet or apostle makes use of writing to fulfill his ministry. In all others, the relation is only accidental, and it depends upon a free decision of God in each particular case. That the scriptural charism is never superimposed upon the functional charism as an independent reality which could be studied in its own right is only a theoretical difficulty. In the prophets and apostles, the one is the organic prolongation of the other; in the others, the scriptural charism assumes the functional to direct it to put the word of God in writing. In the act of writing, the sacred author is moved by both at the same time, even if in some way they then constitute only one charism. It remains necessary to distinguish them since they are different in nature. But at the same time that a distinction is made, an awareness of their concrete unity in the activity of the author who possesses them must not be lost. If, in effect, the act of writing is in itself identical in every case, it is colored according to the situations which those who exercise it occupy. Now this diversity in the sacred writers corresponds to that of the functional charisms. This distinction allows us to reconcile the individual character of the scriptural charism, which must be retained at every stage of the discussion, with the facts upon which Fr. McKenzie[113] based his insistence upon its social character.

## II. ANALYSIS OF SCRIPTURAL INSPIRATION

The diverse charisms relative to the word of God take their specific distinction from their purpose. Scriptural inspiration has as its purpose the expression of the word in writing, a book in which that word will be authentically expressed under the guarantee of the Holy Spirit. Its precise goal, then, is to

[113] Above, p. 47.

direct all the activity of a man, including his life of faith and his functional charism, to the production of such a book, no matter in what manner the inspired person collaborates in it. Consequently, whatever does not directly tend toward that end does not depend on the charism. Such a charism is unique in its class, but it is identical in all the men it seizes. There is no room for distinctions of degree or mode.

It will not be useless here to recall that Suarez in the 16th century proposed two distinct modes of inspiration: antecedent movement, always accompanied by a revelation strictly so called, comprising *lumen et species;* simple assistance in all other cases. [114] Isaias and the author of the second book of Maccabees seemed to him to provide the best illustration of this fundamental distinction. In fact, his conclusion was the result of an unfortunate statement of the problem. As Fr. Benoit [115] has stressed, revelation and inspiration are two distinct problems; the mode of prophetic knowledge proper to each sacred writer ought not then to enter into consideration when it is a question of studying scriptural inspiration as such. It is true that, as far as revelation is concerned, the prophets and apostles were in a much different situation from that of all the other sacred writers. But, we want to repeat, that difference is to be situated at the level of the functional charisms, not at that of scriptural inspiration, whose nature never changes of itself.

Now that that point is clear, we can proceed to an examination of the various aspects of the sacred writer's activity that are affected by the charism. Since the 16th century, a method of analysis has become classic; it makes use of the data of Aristotelico-Thomistic psychology. [116] Thus, in succession, the sacred authors' intellect, their will, and their executive faculties are passed in review. The principle is right, so long as it does not result in automatically attributing to scriptural inspiration what perhaps in reality depends upon something else.

### I. ACTION OF THE CHARISM ON THE INTELLECTUAL FACULTIES [117]

The intellectual activity of a writer forms a whole whose elements are difficult to separate: concepts and judgments, both speculative and practical, enter

---

[114] Above, p. 41, note 30.

[115] Above, p. 49 ff.

[116] See, for example, the analysis of Nicholas Sérier (Serarius), summarized in *Institutiones Biblicae*, pp. 35 f. The same distinctions are employed by G. Courtade, *art. cit.*, DBS 4, cols. 514-517; A. Barucq and H. Cazelles in Robert—Feuillet, *Introduction à la Bible* 1, pp. 18-24.

[117] See the excellent thesis of A. Desroches, *Jugement spéculatif et jugement pratique chez l'écrivain inspiré* (Ottawa, 1958).

continually at every stage of the literary composition. The problem is to determine exactly at what point in this process properly scriptural inspiration enters. In this matter a controversy divides modern Thomists. [118] Some, in order the better to distinguish revelation and inspiration, attribute to the former the sacred author's speculative judgments, and their practical judgments to the latter, inasmuch as they are immediately concerned with the written expression of divine truths. Others find traces of inspiration already at the level of the speculative judgment. Before examining the two sides of the question, it is well to remark, with Fr. Benoit, [119] that in the course of the composition of a book, the speculative ideas that are going to figure in it are already sorted out and set aside for a well determined purpose, and therefore under the influence of a quite general practical judgment that gives the whole work its direction. The author does not devote himself to speculation for its own sake, but to express one or the other aspect of the divine message. Put in these terms, the problem is not exactly the same as that treated by St. Thomas in those questions he devoted to prophetic knowledge. The conclusions he reached, therefore, will have at least to be adapted to the point of view we are taking.

## 1. *Speculative Knowledge*

In whatever concerns knowledge of the divine mysteries of which he speaks, no sacred author was left to the sole exercise of his natural faculties, nor even to the sole exercise of his faith. His understanding of the word of God is always charismatic. But let there be no misunderstanding. The sacred books are not tracts of abstract theology. The word of God takes no form in them except by inserting itself in a concrete context in which many other elements come into play, notably human facts which of themselves have no need to be revealed in order to be known (anthropology, history, etc.). The only point, therefore, that depends upon revelation is the relation of all these things to the mystery of salvation. That remains true even if an intellectual charism seizes the writer in such a fashion that all the judgments made by him in regard to his book depend upon what is called, in Thomistic language, prophetic knowledge. [120] We purposely said *judgments*. It is, as a matter of fact, at this level that the formal element of knowledge is to be found, whatever might be the origin of the concepts *(species)* which are included

---

[118] The controversy is clearly explained by P. Benoit, "Révélation et inspiration," *RB* 70 (1963), 349-356.

[119] *Ibid.*, pp. 356-363.

[120] For more detail, see P. Benoit, *La Prophétie*, pp. 242-247 (degrees and modes of prophetic knowledge).

in it. From this point of view the reception of infused *species* by a prophet has no effect on the question: it is always in the activity of knowing (the act of judgment) that the prophet or the sacred writer is enveloped by the divine light. [121] But is that the effect of scriptural inspiration as such? The question comes up if one supposes that scriptural inspiration is always organically related to a functional charism in which prophetic knowledge might have a part.

Two cases are to be distinguished in theory: 1) Either the man has a revelatory function, as a mediator of the word in the people of God (prophets in the Old Testament, apostles in the New). Then his functional charism already includes a prophetic knowledge of the divine message organically connected to his literary activity. 2) Or his essential function is to preserve authentically the word of God within the framework of living tradition. Then the question is more complicated, because the functional charism does not of itself entail that prophetic illumination, even if in fact it could be given him in a muted form [122] which St. Thomas, following St. Augustine, called a "prophetic instinct." [123] Now it is clear that this "sapiential" illumination (if one may use the expression) is indispensable to all the sacred authors who were neither apostles nor prophets, in order that their books should be the word of God. Neither in the case of the sages of the Old Testament nor in that of the Christian doctors did the functional charism *ipso facto* assure such a degree of supernatural knowledge that the judgments they made in the exercise of their duties were equivalent to prophecy or to apostolic testimony. It might be supposed that this was often the case with those who guarded over revealed truth, but it must be proven in each particular case. Such was certainly the case for those who positively contributed to the progress of revelation, even if they left no written work, but how can the fact be proven? By the same token, it must have been so for the sacred writers, thanks to a particular disposition of providence which made them mediators of the divine word. It is not necessary that they should bring new revelations to men; they at least put into writing traditional data under the guarantee of God. It would have been impossible for them to do that without a charismatic illumination which enveloped their speculative judgments, already conditioned by the practical goal to which they were directed. [124]

---

[121] P. Benoit, "Révélation et inspiration," *RB* 70 (1963), rightly reacts against a notion of revelation that would make of the prophet a passive instrument of God.

[122] Above, p. 54 f.

[123] P. Benoit, *La Prophétie*, pp. 232-234.

[124] The identical conclusion is reached by P. Benoit, "Révélation et inspiration," *RB* 70 (1963), 356-363.

## 2. The Practical Judgment

Naturally, the practical judgments necessary to the composition of the sacred books fall with full right under the domain of scriptural inspiration. Through them the author consciously orients his intellectual activity toward a work which, in whatever manner it might, will give testimony to the word of God. This is a complex operation, which involves not only the choice of ideas to be employed, the materials to use, etc., but the choice of a literary form, the selection of words and expressions which aptly express the thought, etc. It is in all of this that the specific nature of the scriptural charism is to be found, whatever might have been the origin of the data which goes into the work: some acquired perhaps by prophetic knowledge, others received from tradition or acquired through natural means, but aided by sapiential illumination.

This illumination of the pratical judgment by inspiration can be applied without difficulty to all situations in which the sacred authors composed their books: a prophet dictating his prophecies, an apostle dictating his letters, a psalmist composing or retouching a poem, an evangelist presenting in his own particular way traditional material, an Israelite jurist adapting the Mosaic law to changing circumstances, a Christian teacher composing an exhortation (cf. Heb 13:22), a glossator adding to a prophetic work, an editor giving a literary form to apostolic instruction (2 P), an historian recounting a factual summary for the edification of the faithful (for example, 2 M or Ac), a master of wisdom passing on the results of his personal reflections. [125] The list could be lengthened, but to no purpose. [126] Naturally, the diversity of functional charisms is relative to this diversity of concrete situations: the two are correlative.

## II. CHARISM AND THE ACHIEVEMENT OF THE LITERARY WORK

It is only a short step from the pratical judgment to the will and the execution of the work. Concerning these two, it would be naive to ask just how far the influence of inspiration extends: it obviously extends the whole way, since the author is an instrument of God in all the acts that go into the production of his book. There is no need to fear that having thus postu-

---

[125] These are only a few examples; cf. P. Benoit in *Guide to the Bible* I, p. 24.

[126] Thus allotment is made for the legitimate requirements of J. L. McKenzie, "The social Character of Inspiration," *CBQ* 24 (1962), 117 ff. The distinction of the speculative and practical judgment, which is useful for a theoretic analysis, must allow for the diversity of concrete situations, such as biblical criticism reveals them to be.

lated a divine impulse at the origin of every act, [127] we have subtracted anything from man's free spontaneity: he is all the more free wherever he is roused, enveloped and sustained by the Holy Spirit in his activity. [128] It is possible, then, to analyze carefully every phase of his labor, to examine his intentions as a writer, and the practical manner in which he realized them, scrutinize the working of his imagination and the peculiarities of his language, study the environment in which his age, his culture, the society in which he lived influenced him—in all these respects it must be admitted that he acted only under the hand of God. This will even show that there exists the strictest of relations between his functional charism and the literary forms which he used, since these latter were dictated by the function he exercised in the people of God and the role his writings were to play in it. In brief, the problem of verbal inspiration, raised by the theologians of the 16th century and since then become classic, finds in this view its positive solution [129] far from mechanical dictation, since it supposes the full use of all the human faculties of the inspired writer.

## III. PROBLEMS RAISED BY SCRIPTURAL INSPIRATION

By placing the problem of inspiration in the broader framework of the charisms related to the word of God, we have been able to bring to light its social dimension, which has been stressed by contemporary exegesis and theology. [130] Not only does the inspired man belong to a community for which he labors, in a tradition on which he depends and which enriches him, but this very charism, while conferring on him a particular mission whose aim is the sacred book, is always connected to a community function which is not his alone, and which is ordered to the common good. That is far from the idea of a collective inspiration whose recipient would be the community as such. Applied to revelation, this concept would not be far from certain modernist views, in which the community was presented as the creator of its own faith under the impulse of the Spirit who fashioned it. [131] Applied to the

[127] "He so moved and impelled them to write—He so assisted them when writing" (Leo XIII, Encyclical *Providentissimus*, cited above, p. 42).

[128] See the remarks of G. Courtade on the instrumental activity of the sacred writers, *DBS* 4, cols. 511 f.

[129] *Institutiones Biblicae*, Nos. 64-71.

[130] Above, pp. 44-49.

[131] This is the collective aspect of a theory of revelation which was adopted by a good number of liberal Protestants in the 19th century (cf. G. Courtade, *art. cit.*, *DBS* 4, cols. 506-507), and which appears also in Catholic modernism. This reduction of the charism to an individual or collective natural religious experience included a certain assimilation of scriptural inspiration to poetic inspiration (cf. the encyclical *Pascendi*, Ench. B. 258, confirmed by the reflections of Loisy on the encyclical).

sacred books, that concept would manifest a total lack of understanding of the literary problem those views pose, since of itself a community writes nothing. In fact, when one examines the matter closely, he is aware that the assistance of the Holy Spirit to the community always passes through the intermediary of individual charisms. Having made this point clear, we still have two classic questions to examine: the extension of inspiration, and the consciousness the sacred writer has of it.

## I. EXTENSION OF INSPIRATION

What we have said about the role of inspiration in the execution of the sacred books supplies an answer to this first question, in the form in which theologians generally ask it: inspiration extends to all the acts which have a part in the production of these books, to every part of them, to everything taught in them. [132] This manner of speaking does not transform all the phrases of the Bible into divine oracles, to be used independently of their context, like so many statements of truths to be believed. It rather requires that the reader respect the character proper to each writing and to each of its parts, that he search for the meaning and value that its author purposely put into it. This point will have its importance in our discussion of the truth of Scripture. [133] Two questions might nonetheless be asked: 1) When the author makes use of sources, at what level can the passages that depend on them be said to be inspired? 2) Must inspiration be restricted only to those works preserved in our canon?

### 1. Sources of the Sacred Books

Concerning the sources of the sacred books, a distinction must be made immediately. The sacred authors could have drawn from sources of quite different character: collections of laws, books of history, psalms, wisdom writings. Some of their sources were mere profane documents, [134] from which they drew with full knowledge whatever they judged useful to their purpose, whether that might be material of foreign origin (Edomite documents reproduced in Gn 36; a Cananean myth in Is 14:12-14; the Assyrian story of Ahikar used in Tb 14:10) or Israelite material which was not considered

---

[132] P. Benoit, *La Prophétie*, pp. 328-340; in *Guide to the Bible* I, p. 30, the same author states quite clearly, "Inspiration extends to everything, but in an analogous way..."

[133] Below, pp. 110 ff.

[134] Lest there be some misunderstanding, we have in mind documents which did not have the sacred character of the canonical books; it could very well have been religious documents which were involved.

a normative expression of the word of God (the annals of the kings of Israel and Judah cited in the books of Kings; data from archives cited by the Chronicler in Ezr 4—7). In such cases the material was covered by inspiration from the moment that it became an integral part of the author's own work. To have recourse to the theory of implicit citations in order to restrict the authority of the sacred text in this regard would be only a false escape, the result of a misunderstanding of the problem. [135] Every citation, even if implicit, comes under the movement of inspiration, but obviously its meaning depends on what the author purposely intended it to express.

The situation is quite different when the author uses or reproduces a text that he himself considers as normative for the faith of the people of God, as the word of God. His attitude then shows that he considered that text inspired, and that is sufficient proof that it was. [136] For example, it was in this spirit that the last compiler of the Pentateuch reproduced his sources, as sacred documents which were authoritative because they contained the word of God expressed by Moses. It can be concluded that at every stage of its redaction the Mosaic tradition was put into writing by inspired authors. This principle applies even to the sources of the first written collections of traditions, in the measure that they already constituted texts or schemas fixed in oral recitation; for scriptural inspiration is bound less to the fact of setting down a text in writing than to its literary fixation. To be sure, in this question of the Pentateuch, spreading out inspiration over the various stages of redaction still implies at every level the exercise of a functional charism common to all those who perpetuated the Mosaic tradition.

The same reasoning can be applied to the redactional stages which preceded the fixation of our canonical gospels. When they drew already formed material from the ecclesiastical *milieu*, the evangelists did not treat it as profane material, but as an authentic witness of the apostolic tradition. How can inspiration be denied to these normative texts whose authority the evangelists themselves recognized? It suffices to recall that the use of a canonical text by an inspired author never excludes a certain amount of freedom to adapt it, as religious teaching might require. The classic case of the Chronicler reshaping the book of Kings is sufficient proof of that. [137]

But between these two extremes, there can exist intermediate cases which at first glance are not so clear. It happened, in fact, that the inspired writers borrowed material from the religious literature of the people of God,

---

[135] Above, p. 43, note 42.

[136] The same position is held by P. Benoit in *Sacra Pagina* I (Gembloux: Duculot, 1959), p. 92.

[137] A. M. Brunet, "Le Chroniste et ses sources," *RB* 60 (1953), 481-508; 61 (1954), 349-386.

recognizing in it witnesses of authentic tradition. In the New Testament, citations of, or allusions to, the apocrypha of the Old Testament [138] and the Targums [139] have been detected. The Pauline and Catholic letters contain fragments of hymns which were borrowed from the liturgical literature of primitive Christianity. [140] Are such borrowings an indirect proof of the inspiration of the texts in question? We must reply in the negative, and that for two reasons. 1) St. Paul is aware that a traditional literature had begun to develop in the churches (Col 3:16; Ep 5:19). It was the result of Christian prophecy whose value he recognized; but nothing permits us to suppose that he attributed to it authority of the same sort the apostolic tradition possesses: it belongs to the province of ecclesiastical tradition. 2) For the baptismal hymn cited in Ep 5:14, Clement of Alexandria has preserved a further strophe whose authenticity is probable.[141] But except for the fragment cited by Paul, no part of this text was ever considered canonical. In brief, the same principle applied to profane texts must be applied here: even if they were from their origin covered by functional charisms, even if they are a faithful echo of the word of God, they are not *ipso facto* the word of God.

## 2. *Inspired Books That Have Been Lost*

Now let us turn to the other question. It is certain that all of the books preserved in the canon are inspired. But were there any inspired books that have been lost in the course of time? Our reply must certainly be in the affirmative. In 1 Co 5:9 St. Paul alludes to a letter which is now lost (2 Co 6:14—7:1 could perhaps constitute a part of it). It appears beyond doubt that this letter, like all the acts performed by Paul in the exercise of his ministry, fell under the apostolic authority, and that scriptural inspiration prolonged the apostolic charism from the moment Paul dictated it, just as in all similar cases. Similarly, in the Pentateuch, it is well known that the Yahwist and Elohist sacred histories (especially the second) have come down

---

[138] See Jude 9. 13-16 (allusions to the *Assumption of Moses* and to the *Book of Enoch*); Heb 11:37 alludes to the *Ascension of Isaiah* (or to a Palestinian Targum of the prophets).

[139] The rabbinic tradition mentioned in 1 Co 10:4 seems to come from the Palestinian Targum to the Pentateuch (cf. *RB* 66 [1959] 369-374). On the importance of this Targum for the study of the New Testament, see R. Le Déaut, *La nuit pascale* (Rome: Pont. Bibl. Inst., 1963).

[140] Concerning this question, see M. E. Boismard, *Quatre hymnes baptismales dans la première épître de Pierre* (Paris: Cerf, 1961), pp. 7-14. A number of these texts have been collected, and a commentary written by A. Hamman, *La Prière. I. Le Nouveau Testament* (Tournai-Paris: Desclée, 1959).

[141] See Clement of Alexandria, *Protrepticus* 9, 84 (*PG* 8, 495 f.).

in incomplete form. [142] There is no reason why the lost fragments should have escaped the scriptural charism, if the parts preserved were covered by it. The principle is more difficult to apply, though, when the works considered were not covered, right from the beginning, by the prophetic or apostolic charism. In such cases, some positive indications are required to prove that the author's functional charism was really prolonged by scriptural inspiration, and that his writing was not simply a witness of Jewish or Christian tradition, the same as the writings of the fathers of the Church.

In fact, the only concrete cases which deserve more profound investigation are those books of the Old Testament whose original Semitic text has been lost [143] (which text is inspired: the original Semitic or the Greek translation?), those of which we possess several differing versions (for example, the Greek versions of Tobit [144]), and more generally, the case of the Greek version of the Septuagint, which was the Bible of the primitive Church. Standing merely on the theology of inspiration, nothing forbids us to suppose that it could not have extended to translators or adaptors. [145] This is a question of fact which depends on the problem of the canon of Scripture. It is merely a question of knowing whether the translations and adaptations in question were, as they stand, considered the word of God by the apostolic Church, which passed on their text to the Church of the following centuries. This point does not further concern us here.

## II. CONSCIOUSNESS OF INSPIRATION

Was inspiration always consciously apprehended? In its Thomistic treatment, this question was considered only for the case of prophecy. [146] It is admitted that in certain circumstances a prophet might have received only

[142] On this problem, see H. Cazelles in Robert—Feuillet, *Introduction to the Old Testament*, pp. 130-151.

[143] The question becomes more complicated when some part of it is found that does not exactly agree with the Greek version, as is the case with Ecclesiasticus (see H. Duesberg and P. Auvray, *L'Ecclésiastique*, *BJ*, pp. 18-22). It is still too early to draw conclusions from the Hebrew or Aramaic fragments of Tobit found at Qumran.

[144] See A. Lefèvre in A. Robert and A. Feuillet, *Introduction to the Old Testament*, pp. 514 ff.

[145] P. Auvray, "Comment se pose le problème de l'inspiration des Septante," *RB* 59 (1952), 321-336. P. Benoit, "La Septante est-elle inspirée?" *Vom Wort des Lebens. Festschrift M. Meinerz* (Münster: Aschendorff, 1951); P. Grelot, "Sur l'inspiration et la canonicité de la Septante," *Sciences Ecclésiastiques* 16 (1964), 387-418. We will return to this question further on (below, pp. 170-178.)

[146] III^a, q. 171, art. 5; cf. q. 173, art. 4. S. M. Zarb, "Num hagiographi sibi conscii fuerint charismatis divinae inspirationis?" *Angelicum* 10 (1934), 228-244.

a prophetic instinct of which he was not aware, in such a way that he "was not able to discern whether his words and his thoughts were the result of a divine inspiration or of his own spirit." [147]   Commenting on this text, Fr. Benoit remarks that it applies to the usual case of the sacred writers. [148]   But in reality, it seems that the problem has not been correctly considered.   For the consciousness of inspiration that St. Thomas has in mind is exclusively that which is related to the revelation a prophet is to transmit.   To use Thomistic language, when God infuses in a man *lumen et species*, the inspiration is consciously apprehended; when he infuses only the *lumen propheticum*, it is not. [149]   Now we have seen that the charism of revelation must be carefully distinguished from the scriptural charism.   It would then in itself be unconscious, and would not become conscious except *per accidens*, if the author, that is, were to write directly under the impulse of a prophetic revelation, understood in its strict sense [150] (Jr 29; Rv 1:19).

But the problem has another aspect.   For scriptural inspiration is always linked to a functional charism which controls, in each particular case, the composition of the sacred book.   Now the sacred writer was always fully conscious of the function he exercised in the people of God; he was also conscious, more or less clearly, that some divine assistance was connected with that function.   This is evident for the prophets in the Old Testament and the apostles in the New, whose functions were always exercised under the impulse of the Spirit.   As for the other functions, it is a fact that in the Old Testament the theology of the Spirit and of Wisdom provided for a special assistance for them, while in the New the theology of charisms was applied to them in full.   From this angle, scriptural inspiration enters in some way into the field of consciousness, since the sacred writer, following the impulse of the Wisdom or the Spirit of God, always proposed to exercise his charismatic function for the benefit of the community of salvation.   We share here a conclusion already reached by Fr. Rahner in his study of the inspiration of the sacred books. [151]

---

[147] IIIª, q. 171, art. 5, *in corp.*

[148] P. Benoit, *La Prophétie*, pp. 282-284.

[149] *Ibid.*, pp. 272-277.

[150] It should be noted that this applies to the prophetic charism in both Testaments, and for that reason prophecy is in a quite different situation than divine revelation (above, p. 60, note 93).   Even the apostles, who were conscious of speaking "with the Holy Spirit" (Ac 5:32) of the mystery of Christ which they had "seen with their own eyes" (1 Jn 1:1) did not for that receive that *lumen* and *species*, allowance made for the possibility of visions properly so called.

[151] K. Rahner, *Inspiration in the Bible*, p. 66 f.   The author, however, emphasizes consciousness of the message transmitted to the salvation community more than the charismatic office in whose name this message is transmitted.

It is now apparent how important it is to distinguish the scriptural charism from the functional charisms, while still insisting on their close relationship. And how important too to distinguish inspiration from revelation, so as not to attribute to the first what really has to do with the diverse forms of the second. We will come back later to the practical consequences of these preliminary considerations, notably when we search for the angle from which divine inspiration could determine the practical choice of literary forms employed in the sacred books. The author's charismatic function and the circumatances surrounding its exercise will furnish us the key to the problem.

# CHAPTER III

# THE SACRED BOOKS

After having studied the fact of inspiration in the sacred authors, we must now examine its consequences for the books which constitute its result. Authors who treat this question usually employ one of two methods according to their intellectual formation and the disciplines to which they are accustomed. Some, like deductive theologians, draw from the doctrine of inspiration the consequences which seem to them to follow necessarily, endeavoring to make them flexible enough to adapt to the various cases which must be considered. [1] Others begin with the biblical books just as they appear after their critical study, and strive to discover beneath these human words the divine message which is expressed therein. Correctly applied, the two methods ought to complement one another, but one runs great risks to practice them in isolation. The first has the grave inconvenience of failing sufficiently to integrate the results of critical study into theological reflection, as if critical study were a worldly task with which theology, if it wished, could dispense. By the same token, the theologian risks being in a state of perpetual tension with the exegete, without mentioning the deadlocks at which he can arrive, as the multitude of discussions about biblical inerrancy during the past century has shown. [2] In the second method, the danger is on the contrary to be so concerned about the human aspect of Scripture that its transcendence is more or less hidden from view: instead of finding there divine revelation as an absolute fact, will one not first see in Scripture the record of human thought through which that fact is somehow refracted? Thus result the mutual accusations which critics and theologians cast at each other. Some very recent controversies show that the possibility is not just imaginary. [3]

Basically, these two contrary dangers are identical with those which torment the theology of the incarnation: pure critics easily fall back into a sort of biblical Nestorianism, and pure theologians, into unconscious monophy-

---

[1] Paging through the standard treatments of the subject, one will note that these consequences are usually reduced to inerrancy. This somewhat shortsighted view of the problem was overcome by J. Schildenberger, *Vom Geheimnis des Gotteswortes* (Heidelberg: Kehrle, 1950), pp. 38-69: "Intent and content of Scripture."

[2] Below, pp. 102-104.

[3] Below, p. 123, note 134.

sism. It is necessary to avoid both these dangers at once, and it is not sufficient for one side to denounce the other from across the chasm. The only valid middle position is to be acquainted with both approaches, to have recourse both to the results of exegesis and to the fruit of theological reflection in order to combine their contributions. The solid results of a sane critical study offer the means to draw up such a synthesis without further difficulty. [4] Two questions will occupy us in succession. First we shall examine in a general way the consequences of inspiration for the sacred books. This introductory exposition will permit us then to treat the most delicate point, that of inerrancy, or better, of the truth of Scripture.

## § I. THE WORD OF GOD IN HUMAN LANGUAGE

The first consequence of inspiration is the human-divine nature of Scripture: it contains the word of God in human language. Here one must be aware of an over-simplification, as if Scripture pertained to theology as the word of God, and to critical science as human language. Such a dichotomy overlooks the reality of the matter: in Scripture the whole is of God, and the whole is of man; it all comes from God, but everything passes through man. Whether the thought or the language is under study, therefore, it is important to take a point of view that makes this common action of God and man apparent. A particular aspect of the sacred books furnishes us the desired element that permits us to join theology and critical science: their place in the life of the people of God and the specific functions they fulfil. In fact, our lengthy study of the scriptural charism made evident that in the sacred authors it always grafts itself onto a functional charism corresponding to their respective missions [5]: prophet, apostle, priest, scribe, teacher, etc. Likewise, the books written by them have a very close relationship to the life of the community in which they are born, whether in Israel or in the primitive Church. They constitute a functional literature for it, and their content and forms correspond to its structure, its practical needs, its specific activities. In noting this paramount fact, criticism and theology are one. Its consequences have the highest importance.

In every age, two factors control the life of the people of God. 1) The first is the word of God, to which man must respond with his faith. In this

---

[4] Outstanding success in joining criticism and theology was achieved by G. Auzou, *La Parole de Dieu. Approches du mystère des saintes Écritures*, 2nd ed. (Paris: L'Orante, 1960); but the aim and type of this work excluded a technical discussion of the problems we are treating here.

[5] Above, pp. 55-57, 61-64.

regard the life of the people of God is essentially a dialogue between God and man. As the functional literature of this people, the sacred books had as their purpose to fix in writing, under the guarantee of God himself, the two sides of this dialogue, capturing them live during the centuries that revelation was in its course of development. It is in this concrete form that the word of God is presented to us when it eventually reaches us to demand our faith. 2) But on the other hand, the life of the people of God is also subject constantly to all sorts of human conditions: a history, the institutional structures of a society which undergoes many successive changes, a civilization and a culture in continual evolution.... As the functional literature of this human community, the sacred books made use of a language suitable in each particular case to the men for whom they were written. The word of God thus assumed all the variations of which the human word is susceptible, in the living circumstances in which it took on literary form.

## I. SCRIPTURE AS WORD OF GOD

Scripture contains the word of God addressed to men for their salvation. As a result, beyond its surface differences, it possesses a profound unity: a unity of object, or more exactly, of point of view.

### I. THE SOLE OBJECT OF SCRIPTURE

The sacred books are just as much an essential element of the economy of salvation as the incarnation and the Church. They translate its mystery into human language; this is in fact their sole object, as it is also the sole object of revelation. It must not be supposed, however, that this mystery appears there under the form of an ideological system, carefully constructed and thought out in every point, whose conclusions can be deduced with the aid of some principles, and whose individual tenets form a logical chain like a philosophical tract. Its unity is of another order, that of a supernatural organism based entirely, at the level of history and institutions as at that of doctrine, on the person of the Word made flesh. It is true that Jesus Christ, the cornerstone of the whole edifice, did not appear here below until very late, "when the appointed time came" (Ga 4:4). But once this historic manifestation had taken place, he rightly appeared as the focal point at which the lines of preparatory revelation had already converged. [6] Thus the mystery of our salvation in Christ constitutes the unique object of which every page of the

[6] *Sens chrétien de l'A.T.*, pp. 424-427.

two Testaments speaks to us, even if in the Old Testament its literary formulation remains veiled, imperfect, and partially implicit.

The presentation of this mystery does not have the attraction of the systematic expositions to which our theological minds are accustomed. It is entwined, we have just said, in the dialogue between God and man which goes on from century to century: the word of God speaks to men (through the prophets, then in person, and finally through his ministers), and his word arouses in them a response of faith. This communication and reponse can be heard alternately in the sacred books, and it is in this manner that revelation of the mystery took on literary form. From this it follows that the word which it reveals is always profoundly rooted in time. At whatever level one might consider it, it is a particular message destined for particular men of a particular time, whom God thus called to form his community of salvation. The very authors who transmit it did not address this community from without; quite the contrary, they participated in its faith, its life, its drama. They were familiar with the dialogue between God and man from within, through their personal experience; they themselves lived the mystery of which they were witnesses. That does not suffice, though, to make their books a word of God in the full sense of the term; but it does establish a strong link between their message and the circumstances in which they lived. The scriptural charism is grafted on from above, always connected with a functional charism which exactly corresponds to the situation. Then, under the divine impulse, the sacred authors transmit in authentic form the two sides of the dialogue between God and man. It is in this manner that the mystery of Christ was progressively unveiled, to the extent that it unfolded in human history. Evidently, before the coming of Christ, the authors' understanding of faith and charismatic knowledge never reached this mystery except as hidden by a veil which each in his turn partially removed. [7] But however imperfect their manner of expressing it might have been, it is still no less than the unique object of their testimony.

## II. THE SCRIPTURAL POINT OF VIEW

Let us attempt to be more precise about what we mean by unique object. It is well known that Scripture involves a multitude of domains: as the functional literature of the people of God it usually reflects all the aspects of

---

[7] It is proper to insist on the reality of this faith in the mystery of Christ in the Old Testament, on the condition that it be added that its content remains in large part implicit. Christ was known only "under the veil of figures" until the day when his appearance in human history signaled their withdrawal in the presence of the reality they signified. Cf. *Sens chrétien de l'A.T.*, pp. 149f., 427.

its life, its experience, its thought, during the two thousand years that the history of revelation lasted. But there is a factor that profoundly unifies this apparent diversity. None of the particular elements which figure in the sacred books has taken its place there in an unconditional fashion. Even one that occupies an important place in them, or is right in the forefront, was of interest to the sacred authors always from just one point of view, related to the life of faith: its relation to the mystery of salvation. In scholastic language, which is useful here because it is precise, one would say that this is the *objectum formale quo* of their testimony, no matter what might be the *objectum materiale*. This fact is a direct consequence of scriptural inspiration, which had as its effect the elevation of the sacred author to an outlook which was subordinated to that of the Word himself, whose instrument that man had become. Consequently, the judgments concerning truth and value that he made when he proceeded to write his book, his choice of materials, and finally his actual assertions were all accomplished in this unique perspective which gave them their distinctive character. Here once again theological reasoning has no difficulty in assimilating the findings of critical science. For the life of the salvation community, of which the biblical books are the functional literature, has itself only one center of interest: the relation of men to the living God in the religious dispensation defined by the two alliances, their participation in the mystery of salvation, in the measure and manner which befits each age.

By thus considering Scripture as the word of God, we discern a fundamental principle which will have important applications later. When we consider the discussions stirred up by critical science in regard to the truth of Scripture, it will enable us to reject erroneous statements of the problem and fallacious solutions.

## II. THE WORD OF GOD IN ITS HUMAN EXPRESSION

We come now to the other side of the matter. In order to reach men's spirits, the word of God assumed the peculiarities of human language, such as they were in the environment in which its recipients lived. [8] This common sense statement raises two sorts of questions. 1) Granted the originality of revelation in relation to every other current of thought, even and especially religious, ought it not to be expected that it would create a language and specific literary forms? 2) But on the other hand, given the insertion of

---

[8] A sketchy treatment may be found in J. Levie, *The Bible, Word of God in Words of Men* (New York: Kenedy, 1961), pp. 214-246. A fuller treatment of the problem in G. Auzou, *op. cit.*, pp. 88-163.

revelation in a determined historical community, would not that language and those literary forms be subject to all sorts of cultural modifications which would put them in strict relation to neighboring civilizations?

## II. THE SPECIFIC CHARACTER OF BIBLICAL LITERATURE

### 1. *The Problem of Language* [9]

a) *From common language to religious language.*—Human language, which is the expression of thought and the medium of social communication, [10] is conditioned by the sense experience in relation to which it was developed. No matter what degree of abstraction it reaches, one can still apply to it a principle parallel to the well known one: *nihil in intellectu, quod non prius fuerit in sensu.* If then it is to be employed to express the original experience which the relation of men to God is, a real transmutation must be made: after the words, associations, and images have been selected, they must be transported, overloaded, and finally given a meaning they did not have in the beginning. In this way a technical language is created, one adapted to the needs of a specific domain, that of religious experience. Such creation is not left to chance or whim. It is based on a more or less clear and conscious perception of the connections and analogies that exist between the two orders of experience life implies: external experience of our relations with the world and other men, and inner experience of our relations with God. That is the basis of the symbols which make possible, on the one hand, a representation of the divine world, and on the other, an expression of our relations with God.[11] To think of the creator or to speak of him, man takes as his starting point the reflections which he left in his creatures (Rm 1:20). To speak to him, he uses the expressive or measured language that commonly serves as the vehicle of human relations.

In practice, however, the matter is not simple. For natural revelation of God remains ambiguous for sinful humanity. For more than one reason,

---

[9] *Sens chrétien de l'A.T.*, pp. 427-430. X. Léon-Dufour, *Dictionary of Biblical Theology* (New York: Desclée, 1967), pp. XVIII-XXI. J. A. Hutchinson, *Language and Faith: Studies in Sign, Symbol and Meaning* (Philadelphia, 1963).

[10] On the general problems of language, see below, p. 94, note 31.

[11] We do not intend here to examine all the various functions of words in religion; cf. G. van der Leeuw, *La religion dans son essence et ses manifestations* (Paris: Payot, 1955), pp. 394-438. Concerning the role of symbols in the expression of religious thought and in the field of rites, see M. Eliade, *Traité d'histoire des religions* (Paris: Payot, 1949) (a systematic gathering of the general symbols employed in various religious currents); P. Ricœur, *Finitude et culpabilité. II. La symbolique du mal* (Paris: Aubier, 1960), pp. 11-25, 154-165; "Symbolique et temporalité," *Herméneutique et tradition* (Congress of International Center of Humanistic Studies) (Paris: Vrin; Padua: CEDAM, 1963), pp. 5-31.

its understanding can go awry. Then the objective symbols to which religious language spontaneously has recourse become degraded and take on erroneous meanings. That is the usual outcome of pagan religious myths and rites. One of the principal aspects of biblical revelation consists in its restitution of those symbols in the creation of a correct religious language. It is apparent on every page of Scripture that many symbols common to all religious languages and consecrated by long use in the Orient are borrowed and developed. Rightly understood, they express authentically the knowledge of the living God and the relations his people have with him. For example, God is given the titles of king, father, bridegroom, etc. These expressions can be understood by everyone, because they refer to common human experience. But they have been purified of the particular significance they have taken on in polytheistic myths. [12] The use of cultic symbols in the Old Testament likewise involves a resumption of sacrificial offerings, of sacred times and places, etc.; but these rites, which are common to all religious traditions, were purified of the ambiguities and deviations which marked them in the nature worship cults of the ancient Orient.

b) *The specific language of revelation.* [13]—The purification of the common religious language, however, is not the essential point of biblical revelation. Its principal aim is to inform men of the mystery of salvation whose center is Christ. It could not do that without inventing an adequate language, it too symbolic, but different from that based on universal human experience. Its symbols would have to be rooted in a particular experience, intrinsically connected to the mystery of salvation itself. That experience is above all that which was the privilege of the apostles: immediate contact with the Word made flesh (cf. 1 Jn 1:1-3). The humanity of Christ was indeed not just another symbol of divine realities; it was their perfect sign, their sacrament. Still it was necessary that Christ too should have a means to communicate with his contemporaries, in order to make them understand what he did and what he was; it was necessary thereafter that his witnesses should have at their disposition a language capable of correctly expressing their experience. The Old Testament provided for the formulation of this specific language; it prepared to translate the mystery of Christ. From that time on, it served furthermore to express an anticipated revelation of that mystery considered in some of its essential aspects. And it had a very precise basis: the original experience of the people to whom revelation was accorded.

---

[12] For the image of God as Father, see W. Marchel, *Abba, Père! La prière du Christ et des chrétiens* (Rome: Pont. Biblical Institute, 1963), pp. 9-97.

[13] Cf. Y. Congar, *La foi et la théologie* (Tournai-Paris: Desclée, 1962), pp. 26-32.

Actually, revelation did not have as its sole vehicle the word of the divine messengers. The events of Israel's history, its civil and religious institutions, the personalities who gave its destiny a decisive orientation, were also ordained by God with the mystery of salvation in view, not only because they prepared its future coming, but also because in various ways they prefigured its characteristics. [14] By the same token, the most concrete human experience, and the most involved in the visible world, but the most private as well, took on the worth of an experience of faith, whose meaning the divine messengers progressively clarified. Thus was born a new symbolism, unlike those of other religions because it was bound to something which had never before entered into religious thought: human history with its irreversible progress and unique events. [15] In this context the most common symbols of religious language took on a new meaning. For example, the ideas of God as Father and as bridegroom took on an entirely new meaning by being linked to the experience of the exodus and the Sinaitic pact. [16] In a word, the very experience of Israel as the people of God forged the categories of thought in which the mystery of salvation came to be expressed. In effect, the New Testament always used these categories to announce its message: Christ himself began the process by being born in Israel and by receiving a Jewish education. [17] Following him, witnesses, basing themselves on Scripture, employed them to announce his gospel.

c) *The normative character of biblical language.*—The sacred books, then, speak a specific language, which is not reducible to any other, and which remains the norm for all times. The history of the two Testaments is actually the only point in space and time in which a human experience performed that revelatory function, and the basic symbols of biblical language have consecrated it forever. Biblical history is the only place where the categories of man's thought have thus been recast under the direct force of revelation, with a view to the mystery of Christ, which they were to serve as the medium of its authentic expression. The fact that the two Testaments used in succession Hebrew (or Aramaic) and Greek does not mean that the categories of thought natural to these languages were themselves raised to the

---

[14] *Sens chrétien de l'A.T.*, pp. 290-296.  G. Auzou, *La Parole de Dieu*, pp. 167 ff.: History which is Revelation.  See below, pp. 269 ff.

[15] See especially M. Eliade, *Le mythe de l'éternel retour*, 2nd ed. (Paris: Gallimard, 1949), pp. 139-240, and especially pp. 152-156: History Considered as a Theophany; Eng. trans. *The Myth of the Eternal Return* (New York: Pantheon, 1954). H. Duméry, *Phénoménologie et religion* (Paris, 1958), pp. 6-26.

[16] P. Grelot, *Man and Wife in Scripture* (New York: Herder, 1964), pp. 57 ff. For the title of father, see W. Marchel, *op. cit.*, pp. 39-41, 45-52.

[17] Below, Ch. VI, pp. 260 ff.

level of norms. [18] Rather they were the first to undergo that recasting which adapted them to the demands of a unique experience: that of life in Christ, incompletely anticipated in the Old Testament, fully realized in the New. As a result, their words, phraseology, figures of speech, etc., acquired a particular density which is substantially identical under their twofold exterior, Semitic and Greek.

In this specific language, abstraction plays almost no part at all. This fact has the inestimable advantage of not identifying it with any particular philosophic system. But when Christian theology has recourse to the language of one philosophy or another in order to make revelation accessible to minds accustomed to that form of thought, it is to the specific language of Scripture that they ought to resort, in order in their turn to recast that philosophical language and impose on it a density of thought which pagan philosophers could not have foreseen. [19] Human words have acquired a real normative value since the word of God has used them to speak to men, whether in person, or through the medium of his prophets and apostles.

## 2. *The Problem of Literary Forms* [20]

a) *General Principle.*—In every literary work, whatever its nature, human language is poured into general molds which determine the scope of its words, phrases, and all its component elements. Here it is not just a question of stylistic forms, but of literary genres which include those forms. Such genres are never left to the whim of the individual author. They are imposed on him by his social environment, even when he uses them in an original way that will influence their further evolution. They define, one might say, the conventions of language within which communication between the writer and his public becomes possible. They correspond to the mentality, the culture, the customs of a particular social group whose needs or desires the writer wishes to satisfy. The sacred books cannot escape this law, and it is

[18] C. Tresmontant, *A Study of Hebrew Thought* (New York: Desclée, 1960) excessively identifies Hebrew thought and biblical thought, using Greek thought as his term of contrast. This viewpoint should not be pushed too far, as we will have occasion to point out further on.

[19] See the examples, taken from medieval theology, provided by M. D. Chenu, "Vocabulaire biblique et vocabulaire théologique," *NRT* 74 (1952), 1029-1041 (reprinted in *La foi dans l'intelligence* [Paris, 1964], pp. 171-186).

[20] A. Robert, "Littéraires (Genres)," *DBS* 5, cols. 405-421. While still making use of the conclusions of critical study here, we restrict ourselves to general views. The important thing is to determine what place literary genres occupy in the theology of the inspired book.

therefore understandable that the encyclical *Divino Afflante Spiritu*, developing a suggestion of *Spiritus Paraclitus*, [21] strongly insisted on it. [22]

Nevertheless, the very statement of the problem often remains equivocal, for two questions, which are in fact connected, but which must be carefully distinguished, are confused. The first, which is evident to everyone, is the difference between modern literary genres and those used in the ancient Orient, in recounting history, for example. There it is a question of culture, and it was on this that the encyclical insisted. [23] That is not, however, the most important question; another arises, one that touches more intimately the nature of the sacred books. These books constitute, we have said, the functional literature of the people of God. It ought to be asked, then, whether as such they do not make use of specific literary genres, or do not confer upon genres in general use a particular character.

b) *The Bible as functional literature.*—We here return to an aspect of Scripture which has already provided us valuable information. The sacred books, written by men who filled certain offices in the people of God, were written to meet the demands of its life by playing a specific role in it. This purpose enlightens the design, the general direction, and the manner of expression of each one of them, since their respective place in the community's life determined in practice their literary structure. [24] To be content, therefore, to classify the sacred books artificially according to the broad divisions to which our modern literatures have accustomed us would be to touch only the surface, and to compromise their proper understanding. From such a point of view, the Old Testament would consist of historical books, prophetical books, and poetic or sapiential books; the New Testament, historical books (the gospels and Acts), letters, and a prophetic book (Revelation). The result of such a pragmatic classification would be to assimilate completely the historical genre found in the two Testaments to that practiced by modern historians, allowing for some unimportant conventions in writing. This is an

---

[21] *Ench. B.* 448.

[22] *Ench. B.* 556-561. Cf. P. Eufrasio di Cristo Re, "I generi letterari e l'enciclica 'Divino afflante Spiritu'," *Questioni bibliche alla luce dell'enciclica* I (Biblical Weeks, 1947-1948) (Rome: Pont. Biblical Institute, 1949), pp. 1-30 (includes a history of the question since the encyclical *Providentissimus*). *Los generos literarios de la S. Escritura* (Congress, 7th centenary Univ. of Salamanca), (Barcelona: J. Flors, 1957).

[23] *Ench. B.* 558-559.

[24] This will have been recognized as one of the fundamental principles of the *formgeschichtliche Methode*, which is directed toward research into the *Sitz im Leben* of the texts and into the literary form determined by it. If those who use this method have committed errors in its application, that does not cancel the fact that it fills an essential requirement of the theology of inspiration, as we are pointing out. Everything rests in making proper use of it (cf. below, pp. 351 ff.). Those who attack it in principle simply show that they have not understood either its nature or its real value.

erroneous view of the matter, because it neglects to inquire first of all of the community of each Testament what it thought of its own literature, what functions it attributed to each of the books in question, to what purpose and in what spirit they were composed.

The problem ought to be approached the other way around, without any prejudice whatsoever. Then it becomes apparent that neither our modern literatures, nor those of classical or oriental antiquity, provide us all the necessary elements to appreciate the literary genres of the Bible in all their originality and irreducibility. The reason for that is simple: neither the Israelite community at the various stages of its development, nor the primitive Church, were religious groups identical in every point with those which surrounded them. Their faith had its own characteristics, from which certain particular needs result: its relation to the word of God determined the structure of the tradition which preserved it, and it explains the place alotted to prophetic literature; its relation to historical experience, understood as an experience of the plan of salvation, determined the attention paid to events, and it explains the place alotted to historical recollection in very different types of literary works. The Israelite and Christian communities had their own forms of worship and instruction, depended upon certain officials, and so on. All these factors determined even more directly the forms of expression found in their literature. We will present two examples of what we mean, one from each Testament.

Grand literary collections like Deuteronomy and the books permeated with its spirit, from Joshua to the second book of Kings, can be properly understood only by discovering their exact relation to the Israelite community of that age,[25] with its problems (religious, moral and social), its worship, its environmental influences, its outstanding personalities, etc. The literary genres that are found there (legal, ritual, exhortatory, historical, etc.) not only have a general existence in the Old Testament which shapes them everywhere to a uniform pattern; each of their particular realizations bears the mark of the time in which they came into existence. In other words, the forms the word of God took on in Deuteronomic literature were conditioned by a particular religious sociology which explains its fine points and justifies its content.

That is still only the first step in the work to be done. For after having established the place which Deuteronomy and the works connected with it occupy in the life and history of Israel at the level of their final redaction, the same investigation must be repeated concerning all the materials which

[25] Concerning these problems, see H. Cazelles in Robert—Feuillet, *Introduction to the Old Testament*, pp. 152-155; J. Delorme, *ibid.*, pp. 173-176, 191-194, 208-212.

make them up. For example, if there are literary affinities between the profession of faith in Dt 26:5-10, the instruction to be imparted within the family in Dt 6:20-25, and the priestly discourse of Jos 24:1-15 followed by a ritual profession of faith (Jos 24:16-24), this is not the result of chance, but the sign of a common relation of all these passages with a certain form of worship. [26] And if these various passages do not at length fit into any of the classic patterns found in the literatures of the ancient Orient, this literary originality indicates a deeper originality, which reaches a level of thought, and which puts the religion of the Old Testament in a situation all its own. Whatever might be the genre of the texts, they attest the close bonds which worship retained with a certain historical experience, which in Israel was a medium of revelation. The analysis of literary form, then, permits a proper appreciation of the import of the texts in question, whether it be historical, dogmatic, or cultic. It is in this way that their significance as word of God can be understood. The same process must be repeated for all the writings of the Old Testament, both at the stage of their final redaction, and at that of their most ancient redaction or of their sources.

In the New Testament, the life of the primitive Church affected the redaction of the sacred books in the same manner. Take the example of the gospels. These brief books are not "Lives of Christ," written with the interests and the methods employed by modern historians, or even of Greek historians. [27] Each one of them, taken as a whole, presents concretely the good news of the kingdom of God and of salvation, realized in Jesus Christ according to the promises of the scriptures. As such, the gospel genre has no equivalent in any other religion, not even in Judaism, with whose literature it nonetheless supposes an acquaintance. It is a specifically Christian literary form, which cannot be understood except in relation to Christian preaching, such as can be found in the discourses of Acts or in the Pauline letters. The works which employ that form thus have a very definite place in the life of Christian communities: they fill their most basic catechetic needs. Still, one can, and ought to go beyond this final stage of their literary composition and make the same inquiries concerning each of the elements that make them up. In each particular case, in the background of the texts will be found the centers of interest of the apostolic Church, the various aspects of its community life, the hierarchical functions which gave it a certain structure,

---

[26] This point was stressed by G. von Rad, *Das formgeschichtliche Problem des Hexateuch* (Stuttgart: Kohlhammer, 1938), pp. 23-30 (reprinted in *Gesammelte Studien zum Pentateuch* [Munich: C. Kaiser, 1958], pp. 33-41).

[27] J. Huby—X. Léon-Dufour, *L'Évangile et les évangiles* (Paris: Beauchesne, 1954), (especially chapter I). X. Léon-Dufour, *The Gospels and the Jesus of History* (New York: Desclée, 1968), pp. 152-155. D. M. Stanley, *The Apostolic Church in the New Testament* (Westminster, Md.: Newman, 1965).

etc. [28] In other words, within the gospel genre, the materials brought together in our books can be distinguished and divided among a certain number of more specialized genres, all of which correspond to practical aims which are easy enough to discern. The study of these genres cannot be done without a parallel study of the milieu in which the gospel traditions were formed, since their form, in practice, was dictated by the exigencies of that milieu. Thus the proper value of all the elements included in the texts, and their exact signification as word of God, will become apparent.

This gives some idea of how the study of literary genres in the biblical books ought to proceed, and how the relation of this functional literature to the religious milieu in which it was born provides the key to the problem.

## II. THE HUMAN LIMITATIONS OF THE WORD OF GOD

After having insisted upon the specific character of the language and the literary forms employed in the Bible, it is necessary now to consider the other aspect of the question. When it took form in a definite society, the word of God subjected itself to all sorts of unavoidable human limitations, those of the make-up of spirit and mentality, of the degree and forms of culture.

This fact could be examined in the case of Jesus Christ himself. He spoke Hebrew or Aramaic; he adjusted the expression of his message and the presentation of his mystery to the mentality of his listeners and to their degree of culture; he used literary forms which were familiar to them, even if he was original in his use of them; he employed the principal terms of Jewish theology, though he gave them new meaning; he adapted himself to a view of the world, of man, of society, and history which was current in his time, correcting it only when it would have betrayed the mysterious reality he was to reveal. When he became flesh, when he assumed an individual humanity, the Word therefore not only limited his contact with the societies and cultures which succeed one another in the course of time; he also bound himself to accept the language and customs of the rather limited milieu in which he chose to be born, to a degree that might seem to us self-defeating. This condescension, [29] tied to the incarnation, is an essential aspect of the divine pedagogy.

All this is true *a fortiori* in the case of the sacred authors, whose activity was assumed by the Word in a degree obviously less than in the case of the

---

[28] X. Léon-Dufour in Robert—Feuillet, *Introduction to the New Testament*, pp. 305-310; in *L'Évangile et les évangiles*, pp. 58-75; in *The Gospels and the Jesus of History*, pp. 181-187.

[29] Encyclical *Divino afflante Spiritu*, *Ench. B.* 559 (including the reference to St. John Chrysostom).

hypostatic union [30]: inspiration fully respected the individual traits of those human instruments, necessarily limited, imperfect, and even deficient in some respects. Two consequences of this will be noted here. They concern the problem of the language of Scripture and that of literary genres.

## I. The Problem of Language

a) *Languages and mentalities in the actual condition of man.*—Verbal expression takes the form of a determined language. [31] But a language is not just a system of audible sounds, interchangeable with any parallel system. It eflects a certain mental framework, which supposes an original perception of the world and of existence, closely related to the deeper layers of psychic life. Such a view of things seems completely natural to those who speak that same language, since they are not far enough away from it to pass judgment on it. No language can lay claim to be universal, nor identify itself with the absolute of the human spirit; of that any one of them is never more than a particular actualization, more or less rich, more or less extensive, more or less suitable for assessing and expressing its values, which it estimates spontaneously in a way that is all its own. No man is capable of separating his way of thinking from the system of mental reference which he acquired in the environment in which he was brought up. Even if he is led to break through those limitations to express new ideas or experiences, he can succeed only by respecting the genius proper to the language which he speaks.

Communication between languages remains possible because the human spirit is basically the same everywhere. But its languages are no less irreducible one to another, for the diverse aspects of the human experience are apprehended and expressed differently in each of them, so much so that to make oneself understood from one to another always requires a great

---

[30] Above, pp. 65 f.

[31] Apart from technical analyses (cf. below, p. 348), contemporary thought has frequently turned its attention to the philosophical problem of language. See for example: B. Parain, *Recherches sur la nature et les fonctions du langage* (Paris, 1942); L. Lavelle, *La parole et l'écriture* (Paris: L'artisan du livre, 1947); M. Merleau-Ponty, *Phénoménologie de la perception*, 3rd ed. (Paris: Gallimard, 1945), pp. 203-232; G. Gusdorf, *La Parole* (Paris: Presses Univ. de France, 1953). However, in abstract analysis of the phenomenon of language, the questions raised by the diversity of languages is not treated (this is the case too with F. Gaboriau, *Phénoménologie de l'existence, Gravitations* 2 [Paris: Casterman, 1963], pp. 67-109, especially pp. 70 ff.). But this problem is of the utmost importance for an appreciation of biblical language. This point was raised by F. de Saussure, *Cours de linguistique général* (Paris: Payot, 1964), and serves as the basis of C. Lévi-Strauss, *Anthropologie structurale* (Paris: Plon, 1962) which was criticized by P. Ricoeur, "Symbolique et temporalité," *Herméneutique et tradition*, pp. 1-31. It is not for us to enter into a detailed study of this problem, but we cannot afford to omit some points of it.

effort of detachment from self and understanding of the other. This spiritual fragmentation of the human spirit, a sure indication of its sinful condition (Gn 11:1-9), will be overcome only at the eschatological accomplishment of salvation (Is 66:18; Rv 7:9). Until then, the riches of the human spirit can be expressed only by means of a dialogue between languages and cultures in an effort toward integration always under way but never achieved. [32]

This diversity of languages is closely mingled with that of mentalities which lie at a somewhat shallow level of mental life, and are not exactly coextensive with languages. The fact has been analyzed a number of times by J. Guitton, and justifiably as it concerns the sacred books. [33] The expression of human thought can never abstract from a certain outer wrapping which, like language, is a social phenomenon and corresponds to a particular experience of life. It varies according to times and environments; it gives a special color to that grasp of existence which, each according to its genre, every literary work aims to translate. It also becomes one with a man's mind, so that every person perceives the mentality of others without being able to determine exactly the characteristics of his own. It would be no less a serious mistake to hypostatize mentality by attributing to it universal and absolute value.

b) *Languages and mentalities in Scripture.*—Scripture is not exempt from these fundamental laws of human psychology. It is true that in order to transmit divine revelation, human language had to undergo a recasting. But it does not follow that the supernatural mystery revealed by the word of God and the necessarily particular and limited means of expression it makes use of can be put on the same level. The real understanding of the mystery of faith took the form of ideas in the mind of the sacred authors, and was poured out in words in order to reach the minds of other men and arouse in them the experience of faith. But to retain their full signifying value, those ideas and words have to be understood according to their intent. [34] Thus everything in them that displays a relative character will be at once understood and transcended.

[32] J. Daniélou, "La division des langues," *Essai sur le mystère de l'histoire* (Paris: Seuil, 1953), pp. 46-60.

[33] J. Guitton, "Esprit et mentalité," (IXe congrès de philosophie, 1937), reprinted in "Jean Guitton," *Revue Montalembert*, special issue (1963), 339-344; *Portrait de Monsieur Pouget* (Paris: Gallimard, 1941), pp. 107-137; *Le développement des idées dans l'Ancien Testament* (Paris: Aubier, 1947), pp. 33-36, 85-88; *Difficultés de croire* (Paris: Plon, 1948), pp. 76-82.

[34] This point will be contested by those theologians who seem to admit a total equivalence between the knowledge of faith and its conceptual expression, and who thus confuse the concrete knowledge of revealed realities with the attempt to capture it in verbal expressions. But the richer the knowledge of faith, the more the man who possesses it is conscious of the incapacity of his concepts and language to express all

As far as languages are concerned, revelation assumed primarily the mental categories of Semitic languages (Hebrew and Aramaic), not without reshaping them according to its own ends. It is therefore impossible to know exactly what God says to us in Scripture without knowing them well. [35] This does not mean that those mental categories have been canonized as such, but that they served as the providential instrument in the first announcement of revealed truths. The later passage from Hebrew to Greek showed that the mystery of salvation could be translated into any language, provided it undergoes the recasting operation which revelation always demands. [36] In thus becoming the vehicle of the word of God, the Greek of the Septuagint [37] and of the New Testament conferred on them its own coloring. In return, divine truth planted itself firmly in Greek culture. That was the first step toward the final state of the people of God, in which the good news will be announced and the praise of God proclaimed in every language (cf. Ac 2:6-11). In effect, the unity of minds in the same faith in the Church has not been realized by the canonization of a particular language (Syriac, Greek, or Latin, for example), but through a harmonious dialogue between languages and cultures recast through contact with the normative language of Scripture.

As for mentalities, which limit the literary expression of revelation at every stage of its unfolding, it is even more important not to confuse them with the absolute of the word of God. They are only its outer wrapping. But if one wants to estimate properly their relativity and limits, he cannot take as his norm the western mentality of the 20th century. [38] On the

its content. He can only attempt to do so in various ways, and it is the mode of that intentional attempt that determines the meaning of his concepts and his words. These latter, therefore, cannot be exactly understood unless the subjective intention is taken into account. Scriptural affirmations must be treated the same way: since they are in human language, they must not be dissociated from the intention which determined their expression, for our purpose is to reach objectively the profound thought of the sacred authors in all its richness through the medium of language.

[35] G. Auzou, La Parole de Dieu, pp. 151-163.

[36] Along with well made points, there are obvious exaggerations in the work of T. Boman, Hebrew Thought Compared with Greek (Philadelphia: Westminster, 1961). An incisive critique of this work can be found in J. Barr, The Semantics of Biblical Language (Oxford: Oxford U., 1962), pp. 8-20 and passim.

[37] C. H. Dodd, The Bible and the Greeks (London: Hodder & Stoughton, 1934), pp. 1-95. J. Coste, "La première expérience de traduction biblique: la Septante," LMD 53 (1958), 56-88. The linguistic influence of Hebrew on the Greek of the Septuagint is underscored by H. S. Gehman, "The Hebraic Character of Septuagint Greek," VT 1 (1951), 81-90.

[38] Does it never happen that Christian theologians judge the language of the sacred books too rudimentary or too imprecise, or the concepts it supposes too comprehensive? For example, the sacred authors' anthropology might be considered very primitive when it is compared to that of the Greek philosophers or of modern man. What ought to be thought of this superiority complex?

contrary, he must approach them with understanding and sympathy, so as to view the problem, in some manner, with the eyes of the sacred writers. Then the peculiarities of their mind will no longer be a barrier between the word of God and modern man.

## 2. The Problem of Literary Genres

a) *The Bible and ancient literature.*—We have already called attention to the specific characteristics of the literary genres employed in the Bible. We did not mean to indicate that they were created all at once.

Literary genres in the Old Testament developed from current formulas which were recast to adapt them to the needs and demands of the religion of Israel. There were laws and rites before the writing of the Mosaic code, divinatory writings before the oracles of the prophets, liturgical hymns before the composition of the psalms, collections of wisdom writings before the writing of Proverbs, etc. It is always possible then to search in the oriental milieu for texts which served as points of departure for biblical literary genres, or for others which might have influenced their development. [39] Only it is necessary to avoid exaggerating the similarities to the point of overlooking the specific traits which distinguish the biblical texts from their oriental parallels.

For example, there are in fact parallels in formula and phraseology between the oracular responses given by Mesopotamian and Syrian diviners and the oracles of the Israelite prophets. But the latter no longer belong to the literature of divination: while they bring to men a message from God, it is no longer in order to put the divine knowledge at the service of their daily interests through some sort of secret consultation, but to reveal to them the plan of God in human history with all that implies. In these conditions, the genre is completely changed. [40]

In the New Testament, the state of the problem is different. For although the primitive Church developed chiefly in a Greek milieu, its literary texts have their roots in Judaism (of Greek or Hebrew-Aramaic language), even if some side influence of Hellenism is perceptible here or there. [41] It is

[39] H. Cazelles and P. Grelot in Robert—Feuillet, *Introduction à la Bible* I, 2nd ed., pp. 126-131.

[40] See the investigations of A. Néher, *L'essence du prophétisme* (Paris: Presses Univ. de France, 1955) and J. Lindblom, *Prophecy in Ancient Israel* (Oxford: Blackwell, 1962).

[41] A. Feuillet and P. Grelot in Robert—Feuillet, *Introduction à la Bible* I, 2nd ed., pp. 142-151. Cf. L. Cerfaux in Robert—Feuillet, *Introduction to the New Testament*, pp. 338-341 (Acts); J. Cambier, *ibid.*, pp. 383-385 (epistles); M. E. Boismard, *ibid.*, pp. 693 ff. (Revelation). St. Paul's debt to Hellenism is strongly upheld by L. Cerfaux, *Le chrétien dans la théologie paulinienne* (Paris: Cerf, 1962), p. 22.

therefore in Jewish literature that texts which might enlighten the origin of New Testament genres must be sought: biographical anecdotes about famous rabbis, apocalypses, rabbinic opinions and parables, letters exchanged between communities (cf. 2 M 1), exegesis of the type practiced by the rabbis, by the Qumran community, or by Philo, etc. On the basis of parallels uncovered, however, one cannot conclude to an identity of spirit and thought: New Testament genres have their own specific traits, which are the result of the originality of the doctrine and of the spiritual experience they transmit. It is obvious what service comparative literature can render: by illuminating the biblical texts from without, it allows a better understanding of what is proper to them, and what their true meaning is. [42]

b) *Literary genres and the evolution of culture.*—From the age of the patriarchs to the end of the apostolic age, the people of God were in a constant state of cultural evolution, just as every human community in history.[43] They were successively in contact with very different civilizations (Egyptian, Mycenaean, Canaanean, Mesopotamian, Persian, Greek, Roman) and assimilated many elements from them. They passed from an oral culture (in all of Genesis, writing is not mentioned once![44]) to a culture in which writing

For a graphic idea of how the approach to the problem has changed in the past fifty years, one might compare P. Wendland, *Die urchristliche Literaturformen* (Tübingen: Mohr, 1912) with A. N. Wilder, *The Language of the Gospel: Early Christian Rhetoric* (New York: Harper, 1964).

[42] The more attention is given to the roots of texts in the religious life of the people of God, the less the temptation to search for purely profane genres in the Bible, such as erotic poetry with no specifically moral reference (the problem of the Song of Songs), wisdom reflection unrelated to religion (the problem of certain proverbs), scientific history preoccupied solely with the external appearance of events, etc. It is not excluded that indirect traces of these genres can be found, either as quotations or as imitations of a model (cf. A. Bentzen, *Introduction to the Old Testament* 1 [Copenhagen: G.E.C. Gads, 1948], pp. 124 ff.; O. Eissfeldt, *The Old Testament: An Introduction* [Oxford: Blackwell, 1965], pp. 129 ff.). But at that rate, the poetry of Prudentius could also be compared with that of Ausonius or Horace!

[43] Cf. P. Grelot, "The Formation of the Old Testament," Robert—Feuillet, *Introduction to the Old Testament*, pp. 556-605, where this cultural evolution is sketched in broad terms as the framework for the literary history of the Old Testament.

[44] From this point of view the heroes of the *Iliad* are in the same situation as that of the biblical patriarchs. The only mention of writing in the epic poem is found in the marginal episode of Bellerophon: falsely accused by Stheneboea, the wife of Proetus, Bellerophon was sent by Proetus to Lycia with tablets on which he had written "fatal signs," that is, an order to put him to death (Song 6, 168-179). The conduct of Stheneboea is curiously parallel to that of Potiphar's wife toward Joseph; but the resemblance ends there, for Bellerophon's exploits seem to be distantly inspired by those of Gilgamesh. As far as writing is concerned, it cannot be concluded that Agamennon's Achaeans were ignorant of it, since the Mycenaean tablets in linear B contain some archaic Greek. But its use remained restricted, as must have been the case in Canaan in the age of the patriarchs as well (in Gn 38:18 Judah has a seal which must have served to seal contracts). Besides, it was oral tradition which served as the vehicle of culture. Parallels between the Old Testament and the

became more and more important. All of these factors had obvious effects on literature. The means of expression which suited the needs and the mentality of ancient Israel had become practically outdated in the age of the kings, and those which the Jewish scribes had employed at the time of the exile and the postexilic restauration were no longer apt in the Hellenistic and Roman ages. The continuity of literary forms from one age to another was never realized except at the price of an often profound alteration, like that which transformed the prophetic oracle into apocalypse. [45] Understanding these texts, therefore, demands constant attention to the evolution of the forms in which the word of God was cast.

It is perhaps in the matter of history that this evolution and diversity are most apparent; they are more noticeable to us, since our culture has completely different ideas on that point from those of antiquity. [46] In general, the word history is applied to any text which preserves a recollection of the past, whether as a document, or as a systematic reconstruction. Now there are a thousand ways to write history, each depending upon the mentality and the degree of culture which marks a given social group. When the didactic intent of the biblical authors refers in some manner to history, it can never be stated *a priori* what literary conventions the texts they composed or the sources they used or reproduced follow. There are as many problems as there are particular cases. The historical genre is in reality manifold, in the Bible as everywhere else. To overlook this under the pretext that Scripture is the word of God would be to fall into biblical monophysism, whose danger we have pointed out, and to leave one open to the charge of talking nonsense. It is not with our European (Western) yardstick of the 20th century that we ought to measure the human instruments whom the word made use of to speak to men of other times, with those of all times after them in view. In assuming the normal psychology of each sacred author, inspiration respected the manner of expression of each of them. However great might be the difficulty of the problems this diversity of literary forms poses, they must be faced squarely in order to obtain an exact understanding of God's message. To decide *a priori* that all of the accounts of sacred history belong to the same category would mean arbitrarily to project into the biblical past a uniformity that contradicts the history of all human cultures.

poems of Homer have been particularly underscored by C. H. Gordon, "Homer and the Bible," *HUCA* 26 (1955), 43-108; *Before the Bible* (London: Collins, 1962); H. Haag, "Homer und das Alte Testament," *Tübinger Theologische Quartalschrift* 141 (1961), 1-24.

[45] E. B. Allo, *Saint Jean: L'Apocalypse*, 3rd ed. (Paris: Lecoffre-Gabalda, 1933), pp. xxix-xxxiv. B. Vawter, "Apocalyptic: Its Relation to Prophecy," *CBQ* 22 (1960), 33-46.

[46] We will return to this point more in detail as regards the truth of Scripture (below, pp. 129 ff.). For now it is sufficient to note it in passing.

## § II. THE TRUTH OF SCRIPTURE

### I. BRIEF HISTORY OF THE PROBLEM

The problem we are about to treat is usually treated under the title of biblical inerrancy. [47] But such a formulation is doubly defective. 1) It presents in negative form (absence of error) what is a positive privilege of Scripture: as the word of God and the written record of revelation, Scripture participates in the very truth of God. 2) Anxiety to defend the Bible against the rationalists who pretend to find errors in it is not without its dangers, for it risks restricting the apologist to a narrow statement of the problem which he should be the first to criticize. Besides, the theological study of a supernatural mystery like Scripture should not allow itself to be limited to questions of passing interest which apologetics is obliged to examine in detail. This position will receive confirmation from a brief history of the problem, which serves as the best introduction to its proper formulation.

#### I. FROM CHRISTIAN ORIGINS TO THE 16TH CENTURY

Belief in the truth of Scripture underlies the whole theological literature of the Church; it is included in the very definition of Scripture as the word of God. On this point it would be useless to multiply citations. But it was in defending this belief against the attacks which came from several sides that little by little the problems it gives rise to were recognized. The earliest reference is to be found in St. Justin's *Dialogue with Trypho.* [48] The Christian apologist accuses his Jewish adversary of intending to embarrass him by making him admit that the scriptures contradict one another. He replies vigorously, and shows in the Christian interpretation of the prophetic promises the way to reconcile them with one another. The controversy became more heated when pagan criticism entered the field with Celsus,

---

[47] E. Mangenot, "Inspiration," *DTC* 7-2, cols. 2207-2266 (appeared in 1926, but the bibliography and discussion of questions reflect the outlook of 1910-1912). G. Courtade, "Inspiration-Inerrance," *DBS* 4, cols. 520-550. P. Benoit, *La Prophétie,* pp. 340-353; *idem* in Robert—Tricot, *Guide to the Bible* 1, 2nd ed., pp. 40-52 (cf. *RB* 65 [1956], 418-421). A. Bea in *Institutiones biblicae,* 3rd ed., pp. 85-98. J. Schildenberger, *Das Geheimnis des Gotteswortes,* pp. 70-86; *idem,* "Inspiration et inerrance de la sainte Écriture," *Questions théologiques aujourd'hui* (Bruges-Paris: Desclée de Brouwer, 1964), pp. 149-169. G. Castellino, *L'inerranza della S. Scrittura* (Turin: Sales, 1949). H. Höpfl—L. Leloir, *Introductio generalis in Sacram Scripturam,* 3rd ed., pp. 79-118. M. Adinolfi, *Ispirazione e inerranza* (Rome: Paoline, 1962). J. Schildenberger is the only one who entitles his treatment "The Truth of Scripture," but he immediately returns to the classical approach to inerrancy.

[48] *Dialogue with Trypho* 65, 2.

Porphyrus, and Julian the Apostate. [49] They pointed especially to contradictions between the two Testaments and between the four gospels. It was when faced with these assertions that St. Jerome and St. Augustine made an effort to formulate some principles. St. Jerome [50] distinguished error properly so called from a lack of exactness in form, which he admits finding in some gospel passages. St. Augustine held that in case of apparent contradiction, *"vel mendosum esse codicem, vel interpretem non assecutum esse quod dictum est, vel me minime intellexisse non ambiguam."* [51] For a long time, Catholic exegesis was content with these generalities.

In St. Thomas, however, we find a noticeably more precise statement of the problem. Considering the difficulties of chapter I of Genesis, [52] following St. Augustine, he observes: 1) it is essential to hold fast to the truth of Scripture; 2) in the case of several interpretations of Scripture, those which reason proves inexact must be rejected, lest Scripture be held up to the mockery of unbelievers and their approach to the faith be closed off. In other words, that truth must be the object of critical judgment. It is not, however, merely a question of fact, but one of principle, for the truth of Scripture flows from the prophetic knowledge from which the sacred authors benefited in one form or another. [53] Certainly, what the prophets could say on their own must be distinguished from what they said under the influence of their charism. But granted that, it must be admitted that *"quidquid in sacra Scriptura continetur, verum est"* [54]; to hold the contrary would be heretical. [55] This teaching was repeated, practically without

[49] Our knowledge of these pagan attacks comes mainly from the Christian apologists who refuted them: Origen, *Contra Celsum*, PG 11, 641-1632; Cyril of Alexandria, *Contra Julianum*, PG 76, 509-1064. See the articles by J. Bareille, "Celse," *DTC* 2-2, cols. 2090-2100; L. Vaganay, "Porphyre," *DTC* 12-2, cols. 2555-2590; P. Benoit, "Un adversaire du christianisme au IIIᵉ siècle," *Exégèse et théologie* 2 (Paris: Cerf, 1961), pp. 428-435; J. Viteau, "Julien l'Apostat," *DTC* 8-2, cols. 1959 ff.

[50] A summary of St. Jerome's teaching can be found in the encyclical *Spiritus Paraclitus*, *Ench. B.* 450-453. See G. Courtade in *DBS* 4, col. 527.

[51] ("I readily admit that either the text is corrupt, or the translator did not understand what was intended, or that I failed to understand it.") *Letter* 62, 1, 3, *PL* 33, 277, a long letter to St. Jerome. It should be noted that St. Augustine applied his talents to the questions raised by the apparent contradictions of the gospels in *De consensu evangelistarum*, *PL* 34, 1041-1230.

[52] Iᵃ, q. 68, art. 1.

[53] IIᵃ-IIᵃᵉ, q. 171, art. 6, *in corp*.

[54] *Quodlibet* 12, q. 17, art. 1, ad 1. ("Whatever is contained in sacred Scripture is true.") Once he had laid down this principle, St. Thomas hastened to add that those who translate Scripture are obviously not invested with its infallibility (Ed. R. Spiazzi [Turin-Rome: Marietti, 1949], p. 235).

[55] *In Joannis evangelium* 13, lect. 1 (ed. R. Cai [Turin: Marietti, 1952], p. 324). In this passage the commentary attempts to resolve the chronological problem of the date of the last supper, about which the synoptics and St. John seem to contradict one another.

change, by the theologians of the 16th century. Suarez, for example, states in regard to the inspired author *"quod Spiritus illi specialiter assistat et custodiat illum ab omni errore et falsitate et ab omnibus verbis, quae non expediunt vel decent talem Scripturam."* [56]

## II. FROM THE 17TH TO THE 20TH CENTURY

### 1. *Critical Objections*

A clash between this doctrine, tranquilly held by the theologians, and science, still in its early stages, was not long in coming. The first battlefield was that of the natural sciences. The background of the Galileo affair was a discussion about the inerrancy of Scripture. [57] According to the opinion of his judges, Galileo imputed error to the Bible by stating that the earth revolved around the sun. Do not the expressions employed by the sacred texts impose the contrary opinion? In the 19th century, the antinomy became such that theologians were hard put to find some way to reconcile the less and less hypothetical findings of science with a Scripture that had become embarrassing. The various concordist systems attempted to reconcile them; their chances of success were proportionately less as they were forced to follow the evolution of scientific knowledge. [58]

The conflict then tended to change grounds, for the development of historical science then called inerrancy into question on its own field. The problem of the internal contradictions between the gospels was left behind; it was the documentary value of all the "historical" books that was more and more called into question, at least under the form in which the traditional interpretation usually understood it. The result was a refusal on the part of some critics to admit the inspiration of Scripture, as Renan explained so well: "The most mitigated Catholic doctrines do not allow the admission of any apparent error, any contradiction, in the sacred text, even in matters which

---

[56] ("that the Spirit gives him special assistance and protects him from all error and falsity and from any words which might not be fitting or proper for Scripture.") *De fide. De regulis fidei*, Disp. 5, 3, 3 (cited in *Institutiones biblicae*, n. 26).

[57] The 400th anniversary of Galileo's birth was the occasion for a reexamination of his case. Thus it was shown that his positions in exegesis anticipated those adopted by Leo XIII in the encyclical *Providentissimus*. See the whole issue of the *Revue d'Histoire des Sciences* 17 (1964), 289-408 (including a translation of the letter from Galileo to Christian of Lorraine, reprinted in *BVC* 68 [1966], 13-48); D. Dubarle, "Les principes exégétiques et théologiques de Galilée," *Parole et Mission* 7 (1964), 565-576; A. M. Dubarle, "Les principes exégétiques et théologiques de Galilée concernant les sciences de la nature," *RSPT* 50 (1966), 67-87.

[58] G. Courtade in *DBS* 4, cols. 544 f.

do not concern faith or morals. Now let us suppose that, among the thousand skirmishes which critics and apologists indulge in over details of the allegedly sacred text, by chance and contrary to appearances the apologist is right in one or the other instance. It is impossible that he will win his bet a thousand times, and it suffices that he be wrong once to annihilate the thesis of inspiration." [59] Once again, critical rationalism and traditionalist apologetics, having set out from opposing premises, found themselves in similar positions.

## 2. *Catholic Positions*

Theologians and exegetes who were fully informed of the firm conclusions of modern science could not but feel ill at ease. Basically, Catholic exegesis had reached a dead end, and it had to find a way to extricate itself. The first attempts in this direction proved debatable, if not lamentable, for want of a proper distinction between the question of inspiration and that of inerrancy, and for having employed a vocabulary not devoid of equivocation. Some proposed to limit inspiration only to matters of faith or morals, [60] or to withdraw from it the *obiter dicta* [61] or implicit citations. [62] Fr. Zanecchia spoke of the "relative truth" of Scripture in a perfectly orthodox sense, [63] but Loisy used the same terminology to explain one of the fundamental theses of modernism. [64] The positions taken by ecclesiastical authority aimed to exclude these errors or improper statements of the problem. In the encyclical *Providentissimus*, the main statement devoted to inspiration is actually a restatement of biblical inerrancy, qualified, but no less firm. [65] The decree *Lamentabili* and the encyclical *Pascendi* rejected any restriction to the extent of inspiration, [66] every equivocal theory concerning "relative truth." [67] At the same time, the decrees of the Biblical Commission checked the infatuation for the new critical hypotheses which would have risked

---

[59] E. Renan, *Souvenirs d'enfance et de jeunesse*, 5, 4 *in fine*.

[60] Inspiration "would guarantee the writing free of all error in matters of faith and morals, but it would be admitted that this preservation goes no further; it would therefore have the same limits as the infallibility of the Church" (Msgr. d'Hulst, "La question biblique," *Le Correspondant*, January 1893; see G. Courtade, *art. cit.*, col. 522).

[61] The expression is Newman's; see G. Courtade, *art. cit.*, col. 498.

[62] A. Lemonnyer, "Citations implicites," *DBS* 2, cols. 51-55.

[63] *Scriptor sacer sub divina inspiratione* (Rome: Pustet, 1903), pp. 84-91. On Zanecchia's doctrine, see G. Courtade, *art. cit.*, cols. 323-324.

[64] *Ibid.*, cols. 322-323 (including the essential bibliography).

[65] *Ench. B.* 120-125.

[66] *Ibid.*, 202, 259, 265.

[67] *Ibid.*, 263.

putting in jeopardy the truth of the sacred books. [68] The same warnings can be found afterwards in the encyclical *Spiritus Paraclitus*, which is very severe in its condemnation of the abuse of the theory of literary genres. [69]

### III. 20TH CENTURY DEVELOPMENTS

#### 1. From "Providentissimus" to "Divino afflante Spiritu"

A comparison of the encyclical *Providentissimus* with *Divino afflante Spiritu* shows the progress made during the fifty years that separate them. Leo XIII already discarded the equivocation, held by the conservative apologists, concerning the agreement of the Bible and the natural sciences. He recalled that, in this matter, according to the expression of St. Augustine, "The Holy Spirit 'who spoke by them (the sacred writers), did not intend to teach men these things (that is to say, the essential nature of things of the visible universe), things in no way profitable unto salvation'." [70] The sacred authors speak of these sensible things "according to appearances," as St. Thomas had said. [71] That placed the problem in its proper terms and settled the controversy over concordism. But could the same principle be applied to history, as a phrase of the encyclical seemed to insinuate, [72] according to Fr. Lagrange's opinion? [73] What would a history "according to appearances" be like? [74] The encyclical *Spiritus Paraclitus* decisively rejected such an interpretation, [75] thus cutting short the theory of "historical appearances." [76] The encyclical *Divino afflante Spiritu* approached the problem from another

---

[68] The texts can be found in *Ench. B.* A translation can be found in Robert—Tricot, *Guide to the Bible* I, pp. 755-771. To gauge the exact weight of these documents, see the explanations given by the Secretary of the Biblical Commission on the occasion of a new edition of the *Enchiridion Biblicum* in J. Levie, *The Bible, Word of God in Words of Men*, pp. 186-190. Eng. translation in *Rome and the Study of Scripture*, pp. 175 f.

[69] *Ench. B.* 461.

[70] *Ibid.*, 121. Translation: *Rome and the Study of Scripture*, p. 22.

[71] I$^a$, q. 70, art. 1, ad 3.

[72] "The principles here laid down will apply to cognate sciences, and especially to history" (*Ench. B.* 123; translation: *Rome and the Study of Scripture*, p. 23).

[73] M. J. Lagrange, *La méthode historique*, p. 104. In the following pages Fr. Lagrange cites, following Fr. Cornely, some texts from St. Augustine and St. Jerome which seem to speak in the same sense.

[74] The expression is that of F. von Hummelauer, "Exegetisches zur Inspirationsfrage," *Biblische Studien* 9 (1904), 367-495; cf. G. Courtade, *art. cit.*, DBS 4, cols. 546-547.

[75] *Ench. B.* 457.

[76] This theory had already been considered by the second decree of the Biblical Commission (June 23, 1905), *ibid.*, 161. See the comments of G. Courtade, *art. cit.*, cols. 547-548.

angle. Recalling that the writers of old did not share our conception of expounding facts and did not use the same language, it states clearly: "When some persons reproachfully charge the sacred writers with some historical error or inaccuracy in the recording of facts, on closer examination it turns out to be nothing else than those customary modes of expression and narration peculiar to the ancients, which used to be employed in the mutual dealings of social life and which in fact were sanctioned by common usage. Justice demands that they be no more taxed with error than when they occur in the ordinary intercourse of daily life." [77] The whole question thus returns to a problem of literary criticism properly understood, since it is the variety of "historical" genres that are in question. This overture to critical study, which is explicitly invited to clarify the question when particular difficulties arise, points to the direction theology ought to take in order to extricate itself from the impasses in which it previously found itself.

## 2. After *"Divino afflante Spiritu"*

These general principles did not exclude difficult problems when it came to their application. Nevertheless, writings on the subject after 1943 are more satisfying than those of the beginning of this century. Cardinal Bea, in *Institutiones biblicae*, examined at length the problem of the "sacred authors' assertions," [78] since it is precisely here that the formal element of their teaching is to be sought; he then sought to apply the principle of inerrancy to the various literary genres. [79] More in the classic mold, the *Introductio generalis* of Höpfl-Leloir [80] begins with the "biblical question" and studies the relations of the Bible to the sciences and history, presenting again the three problems of history according to appearances, literary genres in history, and implicit citations. G. Courtade's analysis is much more detailed; he lays down a series of leading principles centered mainly on the literary study of biblical texts. [81] Despite his best efforts, his exposition leaves one with the feeling that it is difficult to find a common ground between the concrete demands of critical science and the abstract statements of theology: their basic agreement risks leaving many points of friction. Fr. Benoit [82] remains closer to Thomistic psychology while attempting to mark off the exact limits

---

[77] *Ench. B.* 560; translation: *Rome and the Study of Scripture,* p. 98.

[78] *Institutiones biblicae,* pp. 75-84.

[79] *Ibid.,* pp. 90-97.

[80] Höpfl—Leloir, *Introductio generalis,* pp. 79-118.

[81] G. Courtade, *art. cit., DBS* 4, cols. 530-558.

[82] P. Benoit, *La Prophétie,* pp. 340-353; Robert—Tricot, *Guide to the Bible* I, pp. 40-52; cf. *RB* 65 (1956), 418-421.

of inerrancy in regard to three elements: the formal object of the writer's judgment, his degree of affirmation, and his presentation of the truth for the reader's assent, considering the literary genre he employs. While this exposition has in practice been adopted by many theologians, [83] it has been criticized by J. Coppens, [84] and more recently by P. Zerafa, [85] who contested the criteria used, and would retain only that of literary genres, since the meaning of the texts has not yet been established by the authentic interpretation of the Church. All of this indicates that, on several points, the question is still under study. [86] Despite the reservations made by P. Zerafa, it can be held that a more careful theological examination of the basic facts involved is capable of clarifying the issue. Indeed, N. Lohfink's effort [87] to link the inerrancy of the Old Testament to its inner unity, such as it was understood by the apostolic Church, shows that this delicate problem appears in a different light when it is viewed from a more distant perspective. That is the path we will endeavor to follow. But, as we have said, in order to eliminate all equivocation, we will deliberately substitute for the current statement of the problem of inerrancy a more exact one: that of the truth of Scripture. [88]

## II. FUNDAMENTAL PRINCIPLES

Rather than begin, as Fr. Benoit does, with the psychology of the sacred author, we will return to consider under two different aspects the definition of Scripture as the word of God addressed to men through the medium of the inspired writers. God speaks to men only to reveal something to them; the truth of Scripture is, therefore, of the same order as that of revelation. God speaks to men only through other men; in Scripture, therefore, his

[83] A. Barucq and H. Cazelles in Robert—Feuillet, *Introduction à la Bible* 1, 2nd ed., pp. 58-68. J. T. Forestell, "The Limitations of Inerrancy," *CBQ* 20 (1958), 9-18.

[84] J. Coppens in *ETL* 32 (1956), 715 ff. (reply of P. Benoit in *RB* 65 [1956], 416-422); "L'inspiration et l'inerrance bibliques," *ETL* 33 [1957], 36-57.

[85] P. Zerafa, "The Limits of Biblical Inerrancy," *Angelicum* 38 (1962), 92-119.

[86] Despite its clarity, the work of M. Adinolfi, *Ispirazione e inerranza*, remains in the beaten track and continues to consider the problem of inerrancy negatively. But "the principal consequence of inspiration" consists rather in "the inexhaustible richness which flows from the reality of God's word to men; inerrancy is only the negative aspect of this truth" (F. Festorazzi in *La scuola cattolica, Supplemento bibliografico* [1963], 126*). In other words, what is needed is a new approach to the problem.

[87] N. Lohfink, "Über die Irrtumlosigkeit und die Einheit der Schrift," *Stimmen der Zeit* 174 (1964), 161-181. Except for reservations on some details, this article received the approbation of J. Coppens, "Comment mieux concevoir et énoncer l'inspiration et l'inerrance des saintes Écritures?" *NRT* 86 (1964), 933-947.

[88] The work of O. Loretz, *Die Warheit der Bibel* (Freiburg i. Br.: Herder, 1964) reached us too late to be taken into consideration here.

teaching reaches us through that of the sacred writers. Thus, in order to clarify the present problem, it is necessary to reflect on two points: the truth of divine revelation, and the teaching of the sacred authors.

## I. THE TRUTH OF REVELATION

### I. *The Formal Object of Revelation*

In our previous discussion of Scripture as word of God, we saw that this qualification confers on it a profound unity of object and of point of view. [89] Basically, God reveals only one thing in Scripture: the mystery of salvation realized in Christ. It is understood that this mystery has various aspects, in the same measure that all the aspects of human experience are involved in it or are in some way connected with it. To reduce it to certain religious and moral truths, separable from cosmic, social, or historical realities, would be to misunderstand the very idea of human salvation such as biblical revelation presents it. But granted that, it remains true that no reality of this world is the object of divine instruction, imparted by means of revelation, except from the particular standpoint of its relation to the mystery of salvation.

In formulating this principle, we by no means intend to return to the defective theories which limited either the field of inspiration or that of inerrancy. Only it must be recognized that divine revelation has its own proper domain, or better (to use scholastic terminology) an *objectum formale quo* which specifies all the material objects that the word of God might touch. [90] The teachings which ought to be sought in Scripture belong all to the same domain. There is no divinely guaranteed truth in it except on those points at which it is related to that domain, since beyond that Scripture contains no positive teaching which requires an assent of faith on our part. We shall see later on how this principle is to be applied to the various branches of human knowledge. It suffices for now to have stated the principle clearly.

---

[89] Above, pp. 83 f.

[90] St. Thomas uses the same criterion to determine what can be "material for prophecy": "Everything whose knowledge might be useful for salvation is material for prophecy, whether past or future, whether eternal, necessary, or contingent. But whatever has no relation to salvation lies outside material for prophecy....By necessary for salvation I mean necessary for the instruction of faith or for the disciplining of morals. Now many things that the sciences have proven can be useful for this purpose; ...and thus we find some of them mentioned in sacred Scripture" (*De veritate*, q. 12, art. 2, *in corp.*). It will be noted here that prophecy and Sacred Scripture are practically identified. But what St. Thomas calls "material for prophecy" is obviously considered in respect to salvation in order to become the object of some teaching in Scripture.

## 2. The Progressive Character of Revelation

The unique object of revelation was not made known to men all at once. It came to light progressively through the joint operation of two factors: meaningful events, in which the word of God manifested itself at work, and prophetic words, which explained the meaning of those events, or found in them signs worthy of credence. Thus is underlined the insertion of revelation in human history, but at the same time, its growth in the course of time as well. The fulness of revelation was given to men in Christ, jointly in his words and his deeds. That explains why the recipients of that revelation understood its content more exactly the closer they were to Christ, either before him, or after, as St. Thomas repeats several times. [91]

Still the growth of revelation was not brought about in the same manner before Christ as after him. Before him, in the Old Testament, the various aspects of his mystery were revealed only inchoatively, emerging momentarily from almost total darkness, and remaining always pointed in the direction of an illumination still to come. There was thus a substantial growth in the articles of faith in the Old Testament, even if in essence the mystery remained basically the same. [92] But once Christ had come down to earth, when he had spoken and acted, accomplished his sacrifice in his death and resurrection, revelation was virtually completed, because no further revelatory act was to be expected on the part of God. It was still necessary that the witnesses chosen by Christ and guided by his Holy Spirit, should, each in his own way, explain the meaning of his words, his acts, his final destiny. It is in this sense that it is possible to speak of an increase of revelation between Pentecost and the death of the last apostle. After that, in ecclesiastical tradition, dogmatic progress no longer affects the essence of revelation; it does no more than explain its content.

The sacred books fall naturally into an arrangement according to the ages in which revelation was in its process of growth, and they record the word of God at the successive levels through which the divine pedagogy passed. [93] That means that their positive content ought to be judged in a dynamic perspective, taking into account their place in time. To dismantle the books of the Old Testament into so many formal propositions to which is attributed the same character of truth as to the letter to the Romans or to the fourth

---

[91] II<sup>a</sup>-II<sup>æ</sup>, q. 174, art. 6, in corp.; cf. q. 1, art. 7, ad 1.

[92] Sens chrétien de l'A.T., pp. 143-150.

[93] St. Thomas excellently noted this relation of growth in faith to the divine pedagogy: "Just as a teacher, who has full command of his subject matter, does not hand it over to his pupil all at once, because he would not be able to grasp it, but gradually, accommodating himself to the other's capacity; in this way they grew in the knowledge of faith through several stages" (II<sup>a</sup>-II<sup>æ</sup>, q. 1, art. 7, ad 2).

gospel would be to forget that Christ, by his words and deeds, accomplished the Old Testament and unveiled the meaning of its law, its history, and its Scriptures. The truth of those texts resides essentially in that accomplishment. It therefore necessarily surpasses the understanding the sacred writers themselves could have had of it. To hold only to the latter would be to mutilate the real content of their message. When the apostolic Church bequeathed the Jewish Bible to future ages, it was not as a fixed letter, but as an accomplished Scripture. [94]

As for the texts of the New Testament, they all express, according to the explicit intention of their authors, the revelation consummated in Jesus Christ. Does that mean that they all express it with the same perfection? In reality the full revelation of the mystery of Christ results from the sum of all the apostolic testimony, each one aiding the understanding of the others. It is therefore possible that certain texts throw only a partial light on that mystery, and that only a comparison of parallel and complementary texts can disclose their true meaning. New Testament doctrine should not then be reduced to a certain critically established letter, which would limit apostolic testimony to the explicit assertions of one or the other author. Even the words of Christ during his earthly life sometimes need some complementary light to be rightly understood. For example, can the question of Christ's knowledge be resolved on the sole basis of the synoptic statement [95] in which Jesus declares he does not know the hour of the end (Mk 13:32 par.)? That statement must indeed be integrated into Christian theology, and it certainly must not be slighted. But the apostolic testimony about Christ in his mortal condition must not be reduced to just that. It cannot be reduced even to the synoptic tradition alone. Whatever problems the Johannine tradition poses, its testimony must be accepted too, and then the nature of the problem is altered. [96] This simple example shows that the truth of each text is to be

[94] This point was admirably stressed by N. Lohfink, "Über die Irrtumlosigkeit und die Einheit der Schrift," *Stimmen der Zeit* 174 (1964), 173-181: Scripture cannot be said to be without error unless it is read as a whole and unless the particular affirmations it contains are reordered in relation to this whole (p. 178). But it does not seem necessary to us to found this principle on the attribution of a sort of scriptural inspiration to the apostolic Church, inasmuch as it was the final author of the Old Testament (cf. above, p. 49). On this point we therefore separate ourselves from J. Coppens, *art. cit.*, NRT 86 (1964), 940, 946.

[95] See the commentary of M. J. Lagrange, *Évangile selon saint Marc*, 4th ed. (Paris: Lecoffre, 1929), pp. 350-351. For patristic comments on this saying, J. Lebreton, *Histoire du dogme de la Trinité* I, pp. 559-590. It was around this text that Loisy reconstructed Jesus' human psychology (*Les évangiles synoptiques* 2 [Ceffonds, 1908], pp. 437-440).

[96] For Loisy the realist saying of Mk 13:32 represents history; the Johannine texts crystallize a later Christian ideology. See his exchange of letters with M. Blondel in *Au cœur de la crise moderniste: Le dossier d'une controverse* (Paris: Aubier, 1960), pp. 81-111.

estimated by considering it within the whole of revelation and of its progressive character.

## II. THE INSPIRED AUTHORS' TEACHING

### 1. *Personal Opinions and Charismatic Teaching*

In the case of the sacred authors, and in that of the prophets as well, charismatic knowledge does not influence all the branches of knowledge in the same way, and does not equally enlighten all the aspects of the mystery of faith. It applies exclusively to the particular message which a certain prophet or writer is to transmit to the people of God in given circumstances. Even in the case of the prophets, St. Thomas lays down as a principle [97] that personal opinions, expressed by a man on his own authority, must be distinguished from the message transmitted under the influence of the prophetic charism. A concrete example will illustrate this distinction: the contradiction between the two successive declarations of Nathan to David (2 S 7:3 and 5 ff.), the first made on his own authority, and the second after receiving a word of God. The case is enlightening, for it cautions us against attributing to the sacred writers a sort of universal infallibility, as if a revealed doctrine could be deduced from any details that reflect the ideas they had in mind. [98] When St. Thomas declared: *Quidquid in sacra Scriptura continetur, verum est,* he obviously understood it within the limits we are describing.

It is therefore important to discover, for each book or part of one, the type of instruction the author actually set forth for the assent of his readers. That requires that one put himself in the author's position and appreciate correctly his didactic intention. Here literary analysis comes into play, for each genre has its own truth, or rather, each genre is suited to transmit teaching of one or the other order. Besides, an author's individual use of any genre whatsoever in a particular case can lead to numerous variations. It is essential, therefore, to establish carefully where the accent lies, the central point around which the material is arranged. A simple comparison of Mt 8:5-13 and Lk 7:1-10 shows, for example, that in these two accounts the point is not whether the centurion implored the healing of his servant himself (Matthew), or whether he had some Jewish elders make his request (Luke). On this particular point the two accounts are irreconcilable. [99]

---

[97] *Quodlibet* 12, q. 26, art. 17, ad 1.

[98] See the examples given by P. Benoit in Robert—Tricot, *Guide to the Bible* 1, p. 47.

[99] It is always possible to attempt a harmonious solution. M. J. Lagrange, *Évangile selon saint Matthieu* (Paris: Lecoffre, 1923), p. 164, preferred that of St. Augustine in *De consensu evangelistarum*, 2, 20 (*PL* 34, 1100-1101). But this attempt to

But the detail in question must not be allowed to hypnotize the attention, because it is a part of a larger whole which constitutes the essential object of the statement; it should not be separated from that whole if its import is to be exactly measured. In brief, when it is stated that divine teaching passes through that of the inspired writers, it must be understood that, through the charism of inspiration, the Word assumes their didactic intention, without however changing the laws of their psychology, nor the conditions of literary expression they received from their milieu.

### 2. Degrees of Affirmation

This leads us to one final point. Scripture is not a collection of abstract principles of a religious nature. As the functional literature of the people of God, it presents alternatively the voice of God speaking to men, and that of man who responds to God in his life of faith. [100] The mystery of salvation, therefore, which is the object of divine instruction, can be presented in two manners: sometimes under the form of a message announced in the name of God; sometimes under the form of a reality experienced, which has its place in human experience, and which gives rise to prayer. This duality must be kept in mind to draw from each text the information it might furnish. And even if this is done, the weight of the inspired affirmation is not always easy to define.

The most simple case is obviously that of an author proposing on his own some teaching in the name of God. Now in that case the degree in which he commits himself can vary. "Whatever the sacred writer states, announces, or insinuates must be considered as stated, announced, or insinuated by the Holy Spirit," the Biblical Commission declared in 1915. [101] P. Benoit rightly observed, "Besides the categorical affirmation, there are other kinds of proposition: probability, possibility, indeed a simple conjecture, or even a doubt." [102] That is an important point, which, in each particular case, can cause the degree of certitude to vary. The situation is even more complex when the author describes a certain human experience (historical, social, or psychological) and on that basis formulates a response of faith or a prayer. Where in that case is the intended teaching to be found? When the author

sort out the details of the event leads one away from the teaching the evangelists intended to impart, even if it is proved that one of them provides a more realistic and precise picture of the past.

[100] Above, pp. 83f.

[101] *Ench. B.* 415.

[102] Robert—Tricot, *Guide to the Bible* I, pp. 44-45. It is to this remark that P. Benoit relates the problem of implicit citations. Cf. A. Moretti, "De scripturarum inerrantia et de hagiographis opinantibus," *Divus Thomas* 3rd s. 36 (1959), 32-68.

of the book of Job describes the anguish that the problem of evil causes a man, in presenting Job and his three friends discussing this problem and holding contradictory positions, what precisely is he teaching? Cardinal Bea, in *Institutiones biblicae*, rightly remarks that alongside positive teachings Scripture also contains doubtful expressions or sentiments which do not constitute teaching in the proper sense. [103] Here again, psychological and literary analysis must necessarily be employed before the dogmatic theologian can make a proper use of the texts.

## III. APPLICATION OF THE PRINCIPLES

The principles we have just formulated remain quite general. Their application to the biblical texts raises a series of questions, the most important of which ought to be noted. Besides the distinction made between the private opinion of the sacred authors, which might be apparent in their works, and their formal teaching, [104] the problems turn around three factors which condition the expression of that teaching: the formal object of revelation, its progressive character, and the variety of language and genres which serve to present it.

### I. THE FORMAL OBJECT OF REVELATION

Since the formal object of revelation defines that of the teaching contained in Scripture, it is proper to inquire in what measure the various branches of learning fall under its influence. About dogma, the revelation of supernatural mysteries, and morals, the revelation of the ways to follow in order to reach and live them, there is no question; they come under it fully. But it is only in rare cases that Scripture treats those matters in their pure state, and it is in this regard that many problems arise; does Scripture also teach metaphysics, the natural sciences, history?

---

[103] This point must be judged concretely in each particular case. For example, there can be no doubt that for the author of Psalm 88 God no longer remembers the dead, and they are deprived of his protecting hand (v. 5; cf. 11-13). This doctrine is obviously false, if it is compared with the whole of revelation. But the grace proper to the psalmist was to express charismatically man's anguish when faced with such a perspective. It would therefore be absurd to draw a theological conclusion from his phrase, as if that were the message he was charged to transmit. Nothing could have been further from his mind!

[104] *Institutiones biblicae*, Nos 77 f.

## 1. *Scripture and Metaphysics*

In whatever concern metaphysics, there must be an agreement on what the word means. If one understands by it an attempt to explain things rationally, developed by means of abstract reflection and directed toward the construction of a coherent system (like those of Plato or Aristotle, of Descartes or Hegel), then the Bible contains none. Only scarcely, if at all, can occasional traces of it be found in the book of Wisdom or in certain letters; from this point of view, the language of revelation and its mental substratum are pre-philosophical. [105] But, if one understands by metaphysics the affirmation of certain realities or of certain values which cannot be perceived by the senses, though knowledge of them throws light on the profound nature of human experience, then Scripture contains it, explicitly or implicitly, [106] and philosophy can find in it the starting point for new and unexpected development. In this sense it is perfectly just to speak of a biblical metaphysics, which permanently marked the thought of the Fathers of the Church and of Christian philosophers. [107]

Let us consider some examples. The concept of God as the Unique, as "He who is, who was, and is to come," as the personal Absolute on whom we are totally dependent, as the One to whom man's religious homage is to be directed, contains a tenet of natural theodicy. Now this concept entered fully into the field of human reflection only through the revelation of the God of the covenant with whom Israel bound its fortunes at Sinai, and who finally manifested himself in his Son. In like manner, the definition of the relation between God and the world in terms of creation provides an essential element of cosmology, both by averting temptations to pantheism, polytheism, or dualism, and by conferring on created beings a sense of religious duty. It is true that the progressive revelation of the intimate nature of God is linked to this affirmation: in the Old Testament God creates by his Word and his Spirit (Ps 33:6), by the action of his Wisdom (Pr 8); in the New, he creates through his Son, who is his visible image (Col 1:15-16) and his word (Jn 1:3). This second level of depth no longer belongs to philosophy; but that does not prohibit the notion of creation from possessing a rational intelligibility, which allowed Christian philosophers to use it to revise Platonic exemplarism and Aristotelian cosmology. [108] In the field of

---

[105] Above, p. 89.

[106] See the examples St. Thomas gives, *De veritate*, q. 12, art. 2.

[107] C. Tresmontant, *La métaphysique du christianisme et la naissance de la philosophie chrétienne* (Paris: Seuil, 1962); *Les idées maîtresses de la métaphysique chrétienne* (Paris: Seuil, 1962).

[108] E. Gilson, *The Spirit of Medieval Philosophy* (Scribner: New York, 1936).

anthropology, [109] the scriptural conception of man strenuously underscores the unity of his being, to the exclusion of all metaphysical dualism; it affirms his character of image of God (Gn 1:27), which is the basis for his dignity and his dominion over the world; it defends the goodness of the sexes, which is the basis for the dignity of marriage (Gn 1:27-28; 2:21-24), etc. All these points clarify natural truths which, once known, fully satisfy human reason. But there was lacking a supernatural revelation to correct their understanding by the darkened mind of sinful humanity (cf. Rm 1:21-22).

This is the sense in which metaphysics ought to be sought in Scripture: not in the form of a particular system defined once for all, but as a concrete perception of certain fundamental realities on which all systems turn, no matter what their nature. This is the approach one must adopt, and not that of technical philosophers, in order to gain a proper appreciation of the *philosophia perennis* inherent in Christian thought. Any philosophy which appropriates its data properly will be Christian.

## 2. *Scripture and Natural Sciences*

The concept of the world which all the biblical authors share seems totally obsolete to us, as much or more so than Aristotle's Physics. This point has been a source of difficulty for a long time. [110] To clarify the matter, it was sufficient to return to sane Augustinian and Thomistic principles: in Scripture God does not teach us the intimate constitution of natural things; the sacred authors speak of them according to the representation which was in use in their age. [111] It is only normal, therefore, that scientific investigation should surpass that archaic representation and reach a more objective view of things, even as to their intimate constitution. The results obtained will never be in conflict with the affirmations of Scripture, provided that the latter are properly understood, and that the scientific hypothesis does not furtively introduce some erroneous metaphysical assertion. For example, the idea of creation, properly understood, leaves untouched the question of how God created, what role he allotted to secondary causes in bringing about the effects of his creative act, through what stages the history of the created world passed, [112] etc. The points on which revelation and the natural sciences

[109] On biblical anthropology, see the brief discussion by R. Guelluy, *La création* (Tournai-Paris: Desclée, 1963), pp. 67-76, which includes a bibliography on the subject; X. Léon-Dufour, "Homme," *VTB*, cols. 441-450. A good integration of the biblical data and theological reflection can be found in R. le Troquer, *Homme, qui suis-je? Éssai d'anthropologie chrétienne* (Paris: Fayard, 1957).

[110] Above, p. 102.

[111] *Ench. B.* 120-122.

[112] See the position taken by the encyclical *Humani Generis* in *Ench. B.* 616.

meet head on are, all things considered, very rare. We might cite the assertion of the unity of the human race and its solidarity "in Adam," which is scarcely intelligible without some biological foundation; on this point, theology founded on Scripture encounters human paleontology.[113] The virginal maternity of Mary, which in any hypothesis is a scientifically unverifiable miracle of grace, is no less a formal assertion of the New Testament.[114]

### 3. Scripture and History

The question becomes much more complex when history is considered. It can be treated only in steps, by first inquiring what is in general the object of historical knowledge, and then what within that domain is the object of a scriptural assertion.

a) *Object and method of historical science.*—The problem we encounter here pertains to scientific method. In fact, during the 19th and early 20th centuries, the rationalist critics' denunciation of historical errors in the Bible was linked to a certain conception of history which apologists did not dream of disputing, and of which some theologians are still unknowing victims. It was thought that history could be given the status of a science by patterning its object and methods after the model of the natural sciences.[115] The historian was consequently required to present a perfectly objective picture of the past, practically, that is, a photograph of events, considered as things

---

[113] *Ibid.*, 617. We ought to note here that the expressions employed by the encyclical must themselves be understood according to their intent and their own genre. When it recalls the essence of a dogma that the Christian must hold, the document does not pretend to say everything there is to be said about that dogma. Two facts make this clear. From the scientific point of view, no distinction is made between monophyletism and monogenism, which suppose quite different conditions, and pose distinct problems for theology. From the point of view of exegesis, the broad assertions of Gn 2—3 and Rm 5 are mentioned in a general way; the question of literary conventions used in Gn 2—3 to speak of the origin of things, and especially of Adam, is not raised. But this question must be considered by the theologian who wants to determine the manner in which Scripture teaches the unity of the human race, which is supposed by the theology of original sin and redemption. There is room, therefore, for positive investigation, which is admittedly difficult, but very important for a proper understanding of the scriptural assertions and of the dogma itself (cf. *Sens chrétien de l'A.T.*, p. 98, note 3). On the scientific aspect of the problem, see E. Boné, "Un siècle d'anthropologie préhistorique. Compatibilité ou incompatibilité du monogénisme," *NRT* 84 (1962), 622-631, 709-734. On the exegetical problem, see J. De Fraine, *The Bible and the Origin of Man* (New York: Desclée, 1960).

[114] On this point, which was recently the object of a controversy, see the qualified position of K. Rahner, *Maria Mutter des Herrn* (Freiburg i. Br.: Herder, 1956), who respects the mystery and avoids raising insoluble questions; *idem, Virginitas in partu,* a technical explanation of the theological problem.

[115] See the classic work of C. V. Langlois and C. Seignobos, *L'histoire et ses méthodes* (Paris: Hachette, 1898).

in themselves, impartially observable and describable with exactness in their separate details.    True history meant exact history.    Criticism of sources was regulated accordingly: mercilessly casting aside all subjective elements which ancient witnesses and narrators could have mixed into their accounts, the historian was supposed to retain only the residue, which in his eyes would constitute the objective fact, reduced perhaps to a skeleton, but at least critically certain.

This was a chimerical and even partially false conception of history, as recent historians have pointed out. [116]  What is in fact an event?  Is it simply a collection of details laid side by side, which could have existed independently of human subjectivity?  Is it not rather what constitutes the unifying principle of those details, that is, finally, a human experience, lived by an individual or a more or less extensive group (at most, by the whole human race), observed by the historian on a scale more or less large according to the breadth of the human group whose reactions he intends to analyze? Undoubtedly there is in this human experience a part consisting of objective elements observable from without and materially verifiable; but their sense and meaning, which is what constitutes their human interest, goes beyond this simple materiality.  By the same token, in historical science, exactness of the details in question is subordinate to the proper significance of the experience of which they are a part; it is the apprehension of the latter that formally constitutes the objective truth of history. [117]  So the subjective cannot be eliminated without in the same act emptying history of its content. It is, moreover, precisely the subjective that confers on history its genuine human interest.  Why, in effect, do we strive to know the past of our race, if not to find some of the possibilities of existence realized there, possibilities which are virtually our own?  What we uncover through history is not

---

[116] R. Aron, *Introduction à la philosophie de l'histoire. Essai sur les limites de l'objectivité historique* (Paris: Gallimard, 1938); Eng. trans. *Introduction to the Philosophy of History* (London: Weidenfeld, 1961); *idem*, "De l'object de l'histoire," *Dimensions de la conscience historique* (Paris: Plon, 1961), pp. 93-123. M. Bloch, *Apologie pour l'histoire, ou Métier d'historien* (Paris: Colin, 1961). H. I. Marrou, *De la connaissance historique*, 4th ed. (Paris: Seuil, 1959); *idem*, "Qu'est-ce que l'histoire?" *L'histoire et ses méthodes*, ed. C. Samaran (Paris: 1961), pp. 1-33. J. Hours, *Valeur de l'histoire* (Paris, 1953). P. Ricoeur, *Histoire et vérité*, 2nd ed. (Paris, 1964), pp. 23-44 (objectivity and subjectivity in history).  A cogent critique of historical positivism was already outlined by M. Blondel, "Histoire et dogme," *Premiers écrits* (Paris: Presses Univ. de France, 1956), pp. 161-200; cf. his letters to Loisy in *Au cœur de la crise moderniste*, pp. 72-113.  But his remarks were made in the midst of a theological controversy, and they came from a philosopher who was only slightly familiar with the use of the historical method.

[117] To complete this definition, we would have to add a study of the consequences of the fact, which have become manifest in further human experience.  Here we have limited ourselves to an examination of the starting point in an attempt to determine its exact nature.

a dead past; it is ourselves, grappling with time just as men of the past did. Here history opens onto metaphysics, not in the sense of allowing us to identify, underlying human evolution, some Idea on the move, which would supply the key to its explanation, [118] but in the sense that it reveals to us man in his concrete condition, facing situations in which he must realize his earthly destiny. [119] It is impossible to write history without at the same time developing a philosophy of history. [120] Those who claim most loudly to do it no less profess faith unconsciously in the system which governs their thought and their life.

The historian's labor over his sources, therefore, cannot take the form of a critical reduction which aims to free them of their subjective elements. It is on the contrary a matter of deeply comprehending those human subjective elements, whose discovery and verification, in those determined circumstances, constitutes the essence of the event, beyond the sensible phenomena which go to make it up. Evidence is therefore more interesting in the measure that its author was more involved in the event he reports. It is, of course, necessary to be careful to interpret it correctly, by taking into account the witness' point of view, by marking its limitations if necessary, and especially by comparing it with that left by other participants. [121] The method sketched out here differs profoundly from that of the natural sciences. First of all, it deals principally with individual facts which are never repeated exactly, and which cannot be totally related to general laws, even when certain psychological or social mechanisms play an obvious role in them. [122] Then too, the

[118] This basic point of the Hegelian system, which applies to the collective future of humanity the Kantian notions of phenomenon and noumenon, was reinterpreted by Marxism according to philosophic materialism, but that did not change its nature. J. Maritain, *On the Philosophy of History* (New York: Scribner, 1957), pp. 19-28, has every reason to denounce this "Hegelian illusion." On the roots of this concept in Kant, see J. Lacroix, "La philosophie kantienne de l'histoire," *Histoire et mystère* (Paris: Casterman, 1962), pp. 29-58.

[119] This approach to the question provided M. Heidegger one of the principal elements of his system, which he expounded in *Sein und Zeit*, 9th ed. (Tübingen: Max Niemeyer, 1960), pp. 372 ff.

[120] The importance of this change in the concept of history has been pointed out by scholars as different in outlook as W. F. Albright, *From the Stone Age to Christianity* (Baltimore: Johns Hopkins, 1946), pp. 48-87, and R. Bultmann, *History and Eschatology* (Edinburgh: Univ. Press, 1957). On this point Bultmann adopts the views of Heidegger's existentialism.

[121] To this should be added a comparison of it with the consequences which appear later, for the seeds of these latter existed in the event, and it is not impossible that some perceptive participant sensed in some measure the hidden presence of these virtualities.

[122] It is in this sense that it is possible to speak of the laws of history. The word "law" takes on another meaning when it is employed in the context of a philosophical reflection on history, for example in J. Maritain, *On the Philosophy of History* (New York: Scribner, 1957), pp. 77-118 ("Typological Formulas or Vectorial Laws").

object to be grasped does not pertain to the order of things which can be measured and reduced to formulas. That object is man himself, not in general as in physiology or metaphysics, but in the particular facts of his individual and social existence which reveal the depth of his being. Historical study, then, requires much psychological intuition, an understanding sympathy with men of the past, whose experience must be relived in order to communicate it to readers of today. Under this last aspect, historical study belongs less to science than to philosophy and to art in the higher sense of that word. But that implies a continual intervention of subjective factors in sorting and selecting data, in order to organize it into a continuous narrative and so render it intelligible. [123]

In such a perspective, what becomes of exactness of material details, of the sensible phenomena which form the external appearance of the facts? It is not a matter of sacrificing them, but of putting them in their proper place. For the important thing in history is the global truth of the whole in which phenomena go together and take on a meaning—in other words, the truth of the human experience in which they figured. Certainly, to remain true, the picture of the whole cannot be reconstructed arbitrarily, at the whim of individual fantasy. [124] But, on the one hand, its focal point might be a more or less extensive human experience (that of an individual, of a restricted group, of a state, of the whole world), and that will considerably modify the significance of the details which come into play. On the other hand, the further one departs from that center, the more the truth of the picture adjusts itself to a progressively larger area of approximation, of summary and conventional phraseology. But how could it be otherwise, since full recovery of all the details is impossible to realize, and still less their restitution in a narration. It is obvious, therefore, that in the account of a witness, just as in that of a professional historian, not all details have the same weight; they do not stand

---

[123] "The historian does not acquire data; he arranges it according to certain values; he finds patterns in it according to certain fundamental choices. Given a compact mass of facts, he extracts the significant and passes over the insignificant; he distinguishes between the important and the accessory, the essential and the accidental, tension and equilibrium, between advancement, accomplishments and decline. All of history is a free choice of perspectives, hypothetical knowledge unceasingly in search of verification. One cannot prevent the intrusion of the historian into history, nor that of option into observation or of experience into knowledge" (J. Bouveresse, "Savoir absolu et théologie de l'histoire," *L'histoire et l'historien* (Recherches et débats du Centre Catholique) 17 [1964], 166 ff.). It is not a question, to be sure, of bending objective history to the subjectivity of the historian; it is a question of applying the latter to the proper understanding of past human experience by means of a flexibility and inner openness that demand great mental discipline (cf. P. Ricoeur, *Histoire et vérité* [Paris: Seuil, 1955], pp. 34 ff.).

[124] Among details there are some which the historian must necessarily retain, but it is not necessarily of these that witnesses kept the most precise recollection.

out with the same degree of affirmation. *True* history must not be confused with *exact* history. [125] On the one hand, it can be true by accomodating itself to the inexactness of details, if the details in question are not central to the event; absolute exactness, for the rest, surpasses human possibility. On the contrary, critical history might gather the exact details without being true, if in recounting a past human experience and making a qualitative judgment about it, it misses the essential point, or imposes on the details an interpretation that contradicts the testimony of the participants. And these are the opposite poles of historical positivism.

b) *The historical import of Scripture.*—In relation to the plan of salvation, unique object of the teaching of Scripture, human history is in a very different situation from that of the natural sciences. On the one hand, the word of God is an event which survives in time, and the signs that accredit it are likewise events. On the other, it was in a series of events that the salvation of mankind was realized, not only because it was consummated in the death and ressurrection of Jesus Christ, but because it comports the progressive institution, in the midst of human societies, of a unique society in which man enters into communion with God. That is why Christian doctrine, contrary to all the mysticisms of evasion which seek a means of escape from history, is built around a mystery which becomes present to us by inserting itself in history: the incarnation of the word of God, "born of the Virgin Mary, crucified under Pontius Pilate, raised from the dead on the third day." This intimate connection between revelation and human historical experience explains why history occupies such an important place in Scripture. [126] It is therefore out of the question to exclude history from its teaching, but it is necessary to see exactly how it is contained therein.

In the first place, Scripture never considers human history except under the aspect of relations between God and men. These relations take place within an historical society: Israel, then the Church. Consequently, the experience of that society, which includes observable aspects very similar to those encountered elsewhere, nevertheless takes on a meaning which is progressively revealed by the word of God. The events which make it up manifest the acts of God in time; it is for this reason that the sacred books record them, not so much to record the part which the people of God took in the general story of mankind, as to bear witness to their practical experience and revelation of the ways of God, who leads men to salvation and unveils

---

[125] "History is essentially the kingdom of the inexact. This discovery is not without worth; it redeems the historian. It redeems him from all his perplexities. The historical method can be no other than an inexact method" (P. Ricœur, *op. cit.*, pp. 79 f.).

[126] Cf. *Sens chrétien de l'A.T.*, pp. 257 f.

the ultimate meaning of his existence. The result of this is that human history becomes sacred history, and it is formally as sacred history that it is the object of teaching in the Bible. [127]

It follows too that the respective importance of all the elements which make up sacred history (personalities, contingencies, concrete details of every kind) cannot be measured by the norms which profane historians use; the sacred historians make their judgment on the basis of the plan of salvation they intend to present. And it would be absurd to put all the episodes which the biblical narrations contain on the same footing, from the adventures of the outlaw David to the death of Christ, as if this simple juxtaposition sufficed to indicate the genre of teaching they contain. In reality, the testimony of the sacred authors has less to do with the materiality of these raw facts than with their relation to the mystery of salvation, with the significance that flows from them. [128] If it is true every historical account aims, on the basis of the evidence, to relive the experience of men of other times, the inspired historians seek to reach a second level of depth. For they see in the former only an outer covering and a support of a spiritual experience, more important than the complex of phenomena that underlie it, since the relation of man with God in the plan of salvation is there concretely revealed. That is the objective reality they strive to manifest. But it is a supernatural objectivity, which by definition is beyond the scope of scientific history!

In order to bring out that presence of the plan of salvation in time, the sacred writers make a judgment—at least implicitly—on the significance of the human facts they relate. Now in more than one instance, it is necessary to examine their account from a distance in order to be aware of that judgment, for the place they allot to sensible details is not always proportionate to their respective importance. For example, the accounts of the adventures of the outlaw David and of the revolt of Jehu are more detailed and often more exact than that of the apparitions of the risen Christ. [129] Does that mean that the teaching imparted in them is more abundant or of better quality?

---

[127] This point is brought out at the conclusion of a study of the historical genre in ancient Israel by J. Hempel, *Geschichten und Geschichte im Alten Testament bis zur persischen Zeit* (Gütersloh: Gütersloher, 1964), pp. 232-236.

[128] *Sens chrétien de l'A.T.*, pp. 273 f.

[129] It is true that the apparitions of the risen Christ were concentrated in a briefer time, and that the record of them has reached us by a number of routes which are apparently independent since they do not always agree in detail. That is sufficient to assure their historical reality as events experienced by a number of witnesses. But in addition, in the gospel accounts, the acts and words of the risen Christ are all full of religious significance, even when their historical detail remains blurred (X. Léon-Dufour, *The Gospels and the Jesus of History* [New York: Desclée, 1968], pp. 256-258). From this point of view their case is profoundly different from the Old Testament facts to which we allude here.

Not at all, for the scope and significance of the episodes in question appear only as part of a larger whole: the life of David, the elect of God, and the drama of Israel, a sinful people. At what level, then, is the positive teaching that the sacred authors intended to impart, and which demands an assent of faith, to be found? Is it at the level of these grand themes, in which shorter episodes play their proportionate part? Or at the level of the details themselves, materially exact in the cases considered here, but void of religious significance outside the larger framework in which they have been placed? There can be no doubt about the reply: details must be examined from the height of the full accounts. Likewise, it would be fallacious to hold that the Edomite document reproduced in Gn 36:9-43 becomes *ipso facto* an object of faith because it is cited by Scripture. Actually its relation to sacred history cannot be understood except in relation to two other facts: David's conquest of Edom (2 S 8:13-14; cf. Nb 24: 17 ff.), a manifestation of the power conferred by God on his chosen one, and the mystery of divine election, which fell to Isarel rather than to its brother nation (cf. Gn 25:19-34; 27-33; 35-36; Ml 1:2; Rm 9:13). This meditation on the meaning of history, which remains at the level of a very incomplete revelation, required a concrete representation from the Edomite past to nourish its development, and it was to fill that need that it settled upon the short account taken from the archives of Edom. Does that mean that it puts emphasis on the details of that account with the intention of transforming them into an object of faith? Not in the least, for it makes use of them, without altering them, for what they can contribute to clarifying what was really the object of the faith of Israel: Israel's election and the religious significance of David's victories. In short, the sacred writers are interested in history as a mystery, no matter what might be the nature of the materials they use to relate its sensible aspect. We will come back to this last point again when we examine the variety of historical genres in the Bible. But the fundamental orientation of the genre must be determined before its religious object can be defined.

These remarks do not mean that historical phenomena as such lie outside the sacred authors' intentions, but that their use of them is subordinate to a more important element. Who will deny, for example, that the mystery of Christ, king of the nations from the moment of his birth, is the essential affirmation to which the tradition of the visit of the Magi to Bethlehem in the account of Mt 2:1-12 is ordered? That mystery is indeed the direct object of Christian faith, whereas the Magi episode in itself pertains to it only indirectly. [130] Still it must be kept in mind that every reflection on the

---

[130] For the exegesis of this chapter, see S. Muñoz Iglesias, "El genero literario del Evangelio de la Infancia en San Mateo," *EstB* n.s. 17 (1958), 243-273; M. M. Bourke, "The Literary Genus of Matthew 1-2," *CBQ* 22 (1960), 160-175;

meaning of history supposes the reality of the facts which are reflected upon. One might, in this particular case, ask what exactly is under consideration: is Mt 2:1-12 a reflection on the infancy of Christ, or on the journey of the Magi? And if the evangelist intended above all to present concretely Christ as king of the nations, does he nonetheless attribute the character of historical fact to the episode he gathered from Christian tradition? But if it is permissible, and even necessary, thus to investigate the exact intentions of the sacred authors, it would be wrong to see in their presentation of sacred history a purely mental construction, destined solely to transmit religious ideas and to illustrate the faith. There are narrations of that sort, Job or Jonah, for example. But such cannot be the case of those which intend to recount the acts of God here below. These latter have a global historical purpose, which cannot be put in doubt without distorting Jewish and Christian faith. [131]

In this matter, non-Catholic exegesis, under the influence of the positivist conception of scientific history and metaphysical prejudices against the supernatural, has often underestimated the requirements of historical knowledge, which, in the biblical context, are always dependent on the faith. [132] There can be no question of falling into step with them, of adopting opinions which *"in discrimen adducunt germanam veritatem historicam et objectivam Scripturae Sacrae,"* as a recent *Monitum* from the Holy Office put it. [133] That would be as dangerous an error as to fall into the opposite excess and to repeat, in the name of a misunderstood faith and of a perfectly objectionable conception of scientific history, the same confusion between true history and exact history whose fallacies we have pointed out above. In appealing to the *"germana veritas historica et objectiva"* of Scripture, the Holy Office ruled out two grave errors: 1) that which would see in the biblical accounts which narrate the history of salvation merely legendary narrations,

X. Léon-Dufour, *op. cit.*, pp. 214-218; A. Vögtle, "Die Genealogie Mt 1,2-16 und die matthäische Kindheitsgeschichte," *BZ* N.F. 8 (1964), 45-58, 239-262; N.F. 9 (1965), 32-49.

[131] For the Old Testament, see *Sens chrétien de l'A.T.*, pp. 258-259. For the gospels, see the remarks of X. Léon-Dufour in Robert—Feuillet, *Introduction to the New Testament*, pp. 304 f.

[132] Typical examples: A. Loisy, *La naissance du christianisme* (Paris: Nourry, 1933), 7f.; C. Guignebert, *Jésus* (Paris: Renaissance du livre, 1933), 46f.: "They were interested only in the myth of salvation which they had substituted for the reality of existence and the preaching of Jesus, and whatever they perhaps allowed to subsist of the earliest tradition, of exact recollections of the Galilean Master, was only whatever their conception of the Lord could accept, with the exception of one or the other inadvertence" (p. 47). It would be difficult to conceive a worse misinterpretation of the interest devoted to the Jesus of history by those who saw in him the Lord of faith. See the remarks of X. Léon-Dufour, "Jésus-Christ et l'historien," *BCE* (1961), 357-360.

[133] "...which endanger the native historical and objective truth of Sacred Scripture." Complete text in *CBQ* 23 (1961), 465; *AER* 145 (1961), 137.

totally dominated by the ideas they transmit, without a real foundation in the human experience they pretend to relate; 2) that which would consider the supernatural realities, in which those accounts find the principle which explains the facts, as totally subjective interpretations of faith, without foundation in the divine world into which faith introduces man. That said, it would be offensive to attribute to the Holy Office a concept of objectivity identical with that of the positivist historians. It is possible that some theologians and apologists have inadvertently fallen into that pitfall.[134] That is no reason to follow in their footsteps.

Let us draw up a provisional conclusion. The history lived by the people of God always carried with it, as a human experience, a supernatural significance which conferred on it its true value. Apprehension of that significance was never a spontaneous perception of human genius, and still less the artificial creation of a faith without objective foundation, but the fruit of a revelation brought by God's messengers. It was to make that knowledge available, with every increasing depth, that the sacred writers recorded the recollection of the corresponding events. Then they tirelessly made use of the account of them, under forms which sufficed for their doctrinal purpose even though they do not correspond to our modern concept

[134] This notion of historical objectivity seemingly underlies a certain number of articles written in recent years in reaction to the extravagances of criticism, for example: A. Romeo, "L'enciclica 'Divino afflante Spiritu' e le 'opiniones novae,'" *Divinitas* 4 (1960), 385-456 (the controversy opened by this article is summarized by J. A. Fitzmyer, "A Recent Scriptural Roman Controversy," *Theological Studies* 22 [1961], 426-444); Card. E. Ruffini, "Literary Genres and Working Hypotheses in Recent Biblical Studies," *AER* 145 (1961), 362-365 (translation of an article which appeared in *L'Osservatore Romano*, August 24, 1961); "The Bible and its Genuine Historical and Objective Truth," *AER* 146 (1962), 361-368; G. T. Kennedy, "The Holy Office Monitum and the Teaching of Scripture," *ibid.* 145 (1961), 145-151 (followed by a controversy in the same review: W. L. Moran, "Father Kennedy's Exegesis of the Monitum," *ibid.*, 146 [1962], 174-180; G. T. Kennedy, "A Reply to Fr. Moran," *ibid.*, 181-191; J. C. Fenton, "Father Moran's Prediction," *ibid.*, 192-201); F. Spadafora, *Razionalismo, esegesi cattolica e magistero* (Rovigo: Padano, 1962). In all of these articles the methodological problem of the formal object of history in general, and of sacred history in particular, was never examined in depth. It was taken for granted, as if it were self-evident. The fact that it is difficult to define and that historical positivism was partially mistaken about it should have called for greater caution. In particular, criticism should have been advanced in regard to the narrow concept of history as science, of which many of our contemporaries are unconsciously victims, inasmuch as they use it as a basis for attacking the veracity of the Bible, or tacitly admit it in their defense of its historicity. Perhaps the difficulty in theology comes from the fact that our ecclesiastical studies are still based on a too abstract human culture, in which the particular problem of historical knowledge is not sufficiently appreciated, and in which familiarity with the particular methods of history does not match the level of metaphysical instruction. Consequently, truth in matters of history is conceived under a form identical to truth in metaphysics or dogma. But truth is not univocal; it is analogous, and is specified by the matter to which it is applied, by the object with which human judgment happens to be dealing.

of history. This last point merits a more detailed examination. Here we will note only that the biblical authors, in order to emphasize the significance of a fact in the plan of salvation, often resorted to literary methods very different from those a modern theologian would employ. If, here and there, whole chapters of theology can be found (Jg 2:10-23; 2 K 17:7-23), more often religious reflection is an integral part of other accounts, themselves displaying a wide variety of forms. This is already enough to indicate that Scripture's teaching in the field of history is surprisingly complex.

## II. THE PROGRESSIVE CHARACTER OF REVELATION

### 1. Faith as Educator

Since Scripture is the book of divine pedagogy, the affirmation of revealed truths increased in it with time. A sufficient foundation for Christian theology cannot, therefore, be found in the texts of the Old Testament, unless one goes beyond the limits imposed on them by their situation in time. Taken literally, they constantly reveal these limits. Christ himself, during his earthly life, left some points of doctrine in semi-darkness. Only his resurrection could fully clarify them, and only under the influence of the Holy Spirit (Jn 14:26; 16:13) could the apostles comprehend them. So it was with the mystery of the kingdom of God in its relations with the Church, or with the mystery of the Messiah "who had to suffer before entering into his glory." To remain in the Old Testament, dogmatic progress is there manifested in a constant maturation of problems for which the word of God provides more and more complete solutions. It is less a matter of adding new truths to those already held, than throwing new light on the truths already held in order to illumine unexpected aspects of them, while waiting for all to become fully clear in Christ.

As long as revelation was thus moving toward its goal, the texts do not limit themselves to disclosing the truths of the faith; they transmit human ignorance as well, and sometimes the anguish it causes. Thus in the problem of individual retribution, which tormented the psalmists (Ps 39:6-7. 11-14; 49; 73), the author of Job and Qoheleth (Qo 7:15; 8:10)—no light for so long on a happy afterlife [135] (Ps 88; Is 38:18-19)! Besides, a change of perspective sometimes contributed to a radical modification in the expression of belief. For example, the dynastic messianism of 2 S 7:12-16 gave way, beginning with Isaiah (Is 9:1-6; 11:1-7), to the expectation of a future king whose temporal glories are described with relish [136] (Zc 9:9-10; cf. Ps 2; 72; 110,

---

[135] See Sens chrétien de l'A.T., pp. 344-346 (including bibliography).
[136] Ibid., pp. 375 f. (including bibliography).

interpreted messianically). Where lies the truth of these texts, which Christ did not accomplish without transforming? Even in those cases where the internal mutation of the scriptures is less apparent, the expression of the mysteries of faith remained for a long time hidden, inchoative. One will search in vain in the Old Testament for a complete doctrine of original sin [137]: the exact meaning of Gn 3 does not become clear until the redemption is accomplished, in Rm 5:1-19 or Rv 12. And so it goes for all dogmas.

It is not a question here of arriving at a theory of relative truth, such as modernist theology proposed, or even such as certain Catholic theologians adopted in an awkward and fumbling formulation. [138]   But one fact must be kept in mind: in the inspired books, doctrine was the object of successive treatments which in their turn covered the problems comprehensively. The diverse aspects of the mystery of salvation appear in them only sketchily at first, progressively better outlined, but never definitively drawn before the New Testament. They are truthful witnesses certainly, for the part of positive teaching they contain; but their truth was proportionate to the measure of light God allotted to their authors, relative to the situation in which the community of salvation found itself in their age, and to the role they were to play in the divine pedagogy. [139]

### 2. Moral Education

The same sort of progress is noticeable when the problem is considered from the point of view of human conduct and the rules that guide it. [140]   The Old Testament is not a collection of edifying stories, in the sense in which popular opinion tends to understand them. As a book of instruction, it shows men as they are and not as they ought to be; it presents their reactions before the word of God, the spiritual drama that is born of their evil heart, and which brings their free will to grips with grace. This type of account does aim to edify, but by recognizing sin as sin, and by manifesting its consequences. In biblical pedagogy, sin itself serves God's purposes by revealing man's

---

[137] A. M. Dubarle, *Le péché originel dans l'Écriture* (Paris: Cerf, 1958).

[138] Above, p. 103, note 61.

[139] Regarding the growth of the articles of faith in time, St. Thomas brilliantly wrote: "Although some among men acted as causes because they were teachers of the faith, the manifestation of the Spirit was nevertheless given to them for the common good, as 1 Co 12 states; and therefore the fathers, who were the founders of faith, were given the measure of understanding of the faith that the people of that time needed to have, either openly or figuratively" (II$^a$-II$^{ae}$, q. 1, art. 7, ad 3).

[140] A. Gelin, "Morale et Ancien Testament," *Problèmes d'Ancien Testament* (Lyon: Vitte, 1952), pp. 71-92. J. Levie, *The Bible, Word of God in Words of Men*, pp. 232-246.

need of grace which only Christ can satisfy. [141] Regarding the personages who cross the stage in Scripture, as much in the New Testament as in the Old, a discernment of spirits must be exercised; for they represent, according to the case, either authentic fidelity or conduct to be avoided.

There is another factor which must be taken into account in order to appreciate the moral instruction contained in the biblical texts. The revelation of the law of perfection came only with Jesus Christ (Mt 5: 48), at the same time that the Holy Spirit was given, making possible the accomplishment of the justice of the Law in us (Rm 8:3-11). Before that, the commandments never appear, therefore, in a state of perfection, since they remain outside man (Rm 7:1-13): to have them "in one's heart" (Dt 6:6) is a grace reserved for the time of the eschatological alliance (Jr 31:33). Even their formulation bears traces of the state of spiritual impotence into which the human race had fallen: some prescriptions of the Mosaic law were given because the Hebrews were unteachable (Mt 19:8), and Christ had to correct them (Mt 5:20-48) in order to accomplish the law and the prophets (Mt 5:17-19). An obvious consequence follows: in the field of morality, as in that of dogma, the positive content of the texts must be sought with the light of a criterion which only the New Testament can supply. [142]

The truth of Scripture will thus be gathered from its totality; it is not to be found in each text taken by itself unless it be taken as part of that totality. Biblical theology, that is, that branch of positive theology which studies the scriptural sources of doctrine, [143] is of its nature historical. It cannot content itself with an appeal to certain *auctoritates* removed from their context. It must follow from one piece to another the development of ideas and themes within revelation.[144] We will return to this point in the final chapter of this work. [145]

### III. VARIETIES OF HUMAN EXPRESSION

#### 1. General Problems

a) *Literary forms and the truth of Scripture.*—While speaking of literary forms in the Bible, we emphasized their close relation to the life and organization of

---

[141] *Sens chrétien de l'A.T.*, pp. 205 f. (cf. below, pp. 263-266).

[142] *Ibid.*, pp. 198-200; cf. N. Lohfink, *art. cit.*, *Stimmen der Zeit* 174 (1964), 177 ff. This fulness of sense which the precepts of the old law take on in the New Testament is well pointed out by J. M. Aubert, *Loi de Dieu, loi des hommes* (Tournai-Paris: Desclée, 1964), pp. 116-150 (especially 141 ff.).

[143] F. J. Cwiekowski, "Biblical Theology as Historical Theology," *CBQ* 24 (1962), 404-411.

[144] *Sens chrétien de l'A.T.*, pp. 439 f.

[145] Below, p. 366.

the people of God. [146] This point raises no difficulties in regard to the truth of Scripture. Quite the contrary: it clarifies the content of the individual texts, and as a consequence, the type of truth which ought to be sought in them, since there is always a correlation between the teaching intended and the author's position in the life of the community, whether in Israel or in the primitive Church. But we have also seen that in every age the human culture of the biblical world conditioned the language and literary forms employed in Scripture. [147] And this touches the question of the truth of Scripture, not in the sense that it becomes relative, but in the sense that its formulation accommodates itself to the mentality and the civilization of the environment in which the sacred books were written.

The encyclical *Divino afflante Spiritu* insisted on this point with eminent clarity: "For of the modes of expression which, among ancient peoples, and especially those of the East, human language used to express its thought, none is excluded from the sacred books, provided the way of speaking adopted in no wise contradicts the holiness and truth of God.... [148] Hence the Catholic commentator, in order to comply with the present needs of biblical studies, in explaining the Sacred Scripture and in demonstrating and proving its immunity from all error, should also make a prudent use of this means, determine, that is, to what extent the manner of expression or the literary mode adopted by the sacred writer may lead to a correct and genuine interpretation.... By this knowledge and exact appreciation of the modes of speaking and writing in use among the ancients can be solved many difficulties, which are raised against the veracity and historical value of the divine scriptures." [149] In these declarations a defensive apologetic attitude is still perceptible, but the principles stated have nonetheless a positive value: in order to appreciate correctly the truth of the sacred books, their literary genre must be taken into account, for each genre has its own kind of truth. [150]

b) *The problem of myth.*—Is the inspired character of the sacred books compatible with any and every genre? It should be noted that the question does not come up in exactly these terms, because the functional character of Scripture and its relation to the religious life of the people of God excludes purely profane genres. [151] Among those which remain, can any be considered

---

[146] Above, pp. 89-93.

[147] Above, pp. 93-100.

[148] *Ench. B.* 559; translation: *Rome and the Study of Scripture*, p. 98.

[149] *Ench. B.* 560; translation: *Rome and the Study of Scripture*, p. 99.

[150] This general principle is not questioned by anyone. See for example the statement of G. T. Kennedy: "Each literary form has a species of truth proper to it and must be considered closely to determine the author's purpose in employing it" (*art. cit., AER* 146 [1962], 189).

[151] Above, p. 98, note 42.

*a priori* unworthy of the word of God? The problem of history aside for the moment, only one of them requires discussion: myth, the religious genre par excellence in all ancient civilizations. [152]

Was Scripture able to make use of myth to express the revelation of the living God? [153] It all depends on how it is defined. If myth is the expression of a doctrine in which the divine mixes with the things of the world and society, in such a way that the origin of the cosmos is rooted in the genealogy of the gods; if its essential point is to narrate an exemplary history of the gods in which our experience of existence finds its ultimate explanation, then biblical thought and literature stand in obvious opposition to it. But if it is a question of a simple literary form in which, in order to speak of God, symbolism plays the same role as abstract language in metaphysics, [154] in which the relations between God and man are presented dramatically, then the Bible gladly makes use of it, for it finds in it a manner of expression well suited to the tastes and needs of the Israelite milieu. The Bible is strong enough in its confession of the one God to describe him freely in anthropomorphic terms (if that is the method of myth!), and even make use of ancient mythological themes, stripped of their error. Faced with polytheistic myths, which proved so seductive to ancient man, it opposes doctrine to doctrine, confuting their erroneous doctrinal content. But in order to do this effectively, in more than one case, it uses the same symbols, to which it gives a new meaning [155] (for example: Ps 18:8-16; 74:12-15; 89:10-11, etc.).

Understood in this limited sense, myth is a literary genre like all the rest; it possesses its own proper truth and is not unworthy of the word of God, since it suggests under a symbolic veil what could not be said so clearly in

---

[152] R. Caillois, *Le mythe et l'homme* (Paris: Gallimard, 1938). M. Eliade, *Traité d'histoire des religions* (Paris: Payot, 1949), pp. 350-372. *Aspects du mythe* (Paris: Gallimard, 1963), pp. 9-32. P. Ricoeur, *Finitude et culpabilité. II. La symbolique du mal* (Paris: Aubier, 1960), pp. 153-162. P. Grimal, "L'homme et le mythe," *Mythologies* I (Paris: 1963), pp. 4-13.

[153] J. Henniger, H. Cazelles, R. Marlé, "Mythe," *DBS* 6, cols. 225-268. J. L. McKenzie, "Myth and the Old Testament," *CBQ* 21 (1959), 265-282 (reprinted in *Myths and Realities* [Milwaukee: Bruce, 1963], pp. 182-200). B. S. Childs, *Myth and Reality in the Old Testament* (London: SCM Press, 1960). A. Anwander, *Zum Problem des Mythos* (Würzburg: Echter, 1964).

[154] On the relation of this symbolic language to Platonic exemplarism, see M. Eliade, *Le mythe de l'éternel retour* (Paris: Gallimard, 1949), pp. 63-65. This aspect of myth is well explained by P. Ricoeur, *La symbolique du mal*, pp. 153 ff.; idem, "Herméneutique des symboles," *Il problema della demitizzazione* (Congress of International Center of Humanistic Studies) (Rome: Ist. di Studi Filosofici, 1961), pp. 51-73.

[155] Some good examples can be found in E. Lipinski, "Yâhveh mâlāk," *Biblica* 44 (1963), 405-460 (especially 434 and 456). Cf. P. Ricoeur in *Herméneutique et tradition*, p. 33.

abstract language. [156] The statements of the magisterium relative to this question (decisions of the Biblical Commission [157] on the first chapters of Genesis, and the encyclical *Humani Generis* [158]) never take the perspective of this reevaluation of myth, which is today common among ethnologists and historians of religion. They take the word in its older meaning, which remains that of common language. [159] From that point of view, it is indeed undeniable that revelation has substituted a totally different sacred history for the divine histories of ancient mythologies. It no longer unfolds in the universe of the gods and primordial time, but within the created world, in cosmic and human time. It is there that the drama of human existence takes place, and it is only to emphasize the religious dimension of that drama that Scripture presents a concrete representation of God that makes him run the risk of mythology without falling into it [160] (cf. Gn 2:8-9; 3:8 ff.; 7:16b, etc.).

## 2. The Problem of History in the Bible [161]

We have seen why and in what way the sacred books necessarily are concerned with history. [162] The result in the two Testaments is an appreciation of the historical genre that has no parallel in other religious literatures, as the encyclical *Divino afflante Spiritu* rightly pointed out. [163] But once these points are granted, the problem of literary forms in which historical testimony is presented remains intact. For in every age and in all civilizations there is no genre as complex as history. It would be naive to imagine that the

---

[156] The mythical expression of religious thought is actually closer to existential experience than its abstract expression, which represents a first effort to remove the myth. Concerning the relation between myth and rational thought, see the excellent study of G. Gusdorf, *Mythe et métaphysique* (Paris: Flammarion, 1953), especially pp. 216-229 and 244-262. The conclusion we have arrived at is substantially identical to that of H. Fries, "Le mythe et la révélation," *Questions théologiques aujourd'hui* I, pp. 49-58. We will not here enter into the discussion raised by Bultmann in regard to the demythologization of the New Testament; suffice it to say that his definition of myth does not agree with the one we have given (cf. R. Marlé, *Bultmann et l'interprétation du Nouveau Testament* [Paris: Aubier, 1956], pp. 41-71). We will return to this question in our treatment of the science of interpretation (below, p. 212; 229, note 187; 349).

[157] *Ench. B.* 325 (and already the encyclical *Providentissimus, ibid.*, 100).

[158] *Ibid.*, 618.

[159] See J. Henniger, *art. cit.*, *DBS* 6, cols. 245-256, where the evolution of the meaning of this term is described; at one time devoid of meaning, it is today given a positive content. See likewise G. Gusdorf, *op. cit.*, pp. 216 f.

[160] H. Duesberg, *Les valeurs chrétiennes de l'Ancien Testament* (Tournai: Casterman, 1960), p. 98.

[161] G. Courtade, *art. cit.*, *DBS* 4, cols. 550-557. A. Bea, *Institutiones biblicae*, Nos 95-97. Höpfl-Leloir, *Introductio generalis*, pp. 101-118.

[162] Above, pp. 118-124.

[163] *Ench. B.* 558 f.

inspired writers accepted in advance the scientific norms to which we are accustomed, either in regard to the objectivity of evidence and sources, or to the impartiality of the account; first of all, because our particular preoccupations cannot be transposed to oriental antiquity, and secondly, because that would be to suppose a theory of scientific history which is highly subject to reservations. [164] Just such a supposition was the starting point for certain 19th century rationalist critics who attempted to empty biblical history of its content. In their determination to combat them, many apologists played their part too well and followed them onto their own battlefield. They classified all the texts as historical or non-historical, and never inquired about the nature and forms of history. [165] That is a simplist position; it confuses rather than clarifies the problem.

a) *Types of history.*—The aim of the historical genre considered in its most general aspect is to preserve live the remembrance of past human experience, either orally or in writing, whether at the level of rudimentary documentation or of masterly syntheses. But there are a thousand ways of doing that, each corresponding to the mentality and degree of culture of a given social group. All the methods applied to that end are admissible from the moment that they are commonly accepted.

A few examples chosen from the great works of western literature will suffice to give an idea of this diversity of methods. They pass, according to the case, from popular legend, in which the reality is dressed in a robe of fiction (Lucretius' history explaining the fall of the last Etruscan king of Rome), to the minute descriptions whose details have all been verified [166] (Fustel de Coulanges, *La cité antique*), from the epic expansions in which the wondrous plays a part (the death of Roland at Roncevaux in the *Chanson de Roland* compared with Eginhard's chronicle) to an account which clarifies the entanglement of human responsibilities (Thucydides' *History of the Peloponnesian War* [167]). At a certain level of civilization and for certain classes of facts, the legend [168] and the epic are therefore normal methods of

---

[164] Above, pp. 115-118.

[165] Above, p. 123, note 134.

[166] There naturally remains a measure of hypothesis in the presentation, because the raw facts had to be interpreted in order to become a part of the final synthesis. But that is the common fate of all historical knowledge.

[167] See R. Aron, "Thucidyde et le récit historique," *Dimensions de la conscience historique* (Paris: Plon, 1961), pp. 126 f.

[168] Legend as a literary genre, therefore, needs revaluation. The contempt the 19th century had for it (and for the myth as well) was a consequence of that pretentious positivism which spread everywhere the reign of its naive conception of history as science. It should only be remarked that the problem of legends is not simple, for they can have several sources. Some of them rise out of history; others are only ancient myths that have degenerated into tales; still others are a mixture of the two. Judgment must be made piece by piece in each particular case.

preserving recollections, as numerous examples from oriental and classical antiquity as well as the Middle Ages show. Between such cases and that of the chronicle written by a firsthand witness of the facts he recounts (the case of Joinville describing the figure of St. Louis), there are a multitude of intermediate forms: moralizing histories which report only one aspect of the facts in order to draw a lesson from them, stories of eponymous heroes which absorb the history of social groups, etiological accounts which explain a fact of civilization (custom, rite, place name, relation between peoples) by succinctly recalling its origin, etc. Besides, in each particular case, a number of factors modify the exactness and the function of the details which fill out the narrations. It is furthermore only rarely that they have an exclusively historical value; usually it is necessary to analyze them from several angles in order to extract their content.

Since these methods of writing existed with full right in ancient literatures, there is no reason why biblical literature ought to reject them. It was sufficient that they should be capable of being adapted to the didactic purpose, always religious, of the sacred authors, permitting them to present a picture of the past that suited their purpose. This statement does not bring those authors' veracity into question, but it leaves open the question of the literary forms they used. [169] That must be closely examined in each particular case.

b) *History in the Old Testament.* [170]—The historical genre in the Old Testament is essentially manifold, according to the nature of the events to be narrated, the materials available to do that, the lessons to be inculcated in those accounts, the literary conventions to be followed.

Here are some examples taken from the Pentateuch. [171] Its narrations do intend to recount a real history: that of the plan of salvation which emerges from the history of Israel. But their constituent material is drawn from sources (oral or written) which range the full length of the degrees noted above. But the inspired writers did not modify the nature and literary form of those sources when they appropriated their content to revelation. Granted that in subordinating and adapting them to their own message, they were guided by the infallible instinct of their charism [172]; but that does not mean

---

[169] Cf. the encyclical *Divino afflante Spiritu*, Ench. B. 559. Well before this text appeared, this principle can be found brilliantly enunciated in a prophetic piece by L. Desnoyers, *Bulletin de Littérature Ecclésiastique* 28 (1927), 132-138.

[170] A. Robert, "Historique (Genre)," *DBS* 4, cols. 7-23. O. Eissfeldt, *The Old Testament. An Introduction*, pp. 47-56 (with a bibliography on the question). J. Hempel, *Geschichten und Geschichte im Alten Testament bis zur persischen Zeit* (Gütersloh: Gütersloher, 1964).

[171] For all of the examples given here, one might consult the commentaries on the books in question, for example, the *ICC* or the Anchor Bible.

[172] See the encyclical *Humani Generis*, Ench. B. 618.

that they have passed on to us accounts that can be immediately utilized in a critical history of Israel. [173] From the legendary epic of the flood biblical historians draw a typical example of a catastrophe which manifests the actualization of the judgment of God in human history. That is a religious reinterpretation which leaves intact all the problems posed by the corresponding Mesopotamian tradition. The eponym Cain, the supposed ancestor of the Cainites, serves to recall the barbarity of the desert in prehistoric times and the fratricidal quarrels which are a general feature of human history (Gn 4:1-16). The story of the eponyms Simeon and Levi (Gn 34) preserves the memory of an obscure episode in which the two corresponding tribes were involved toward the end of the patriarchal age; this is precious historical data, expressed in a literary form which is found less complete in Jg 1:3 ff. The history of Joseph has taken the form of a didactic narration, related to wisdom literature by its moralizing purpose and redactional methods [174]; that must be kept in mind when extracting from it useful elements for a critical history, and that will surely give rise to a discussion in which opinions will differ. [175] Jos 10:12-13 has fortunately preserved a fragment of an epic poem used by the narrator in his account of the battle of Gibeon; that fragment throws light on the exact genre of the prose account (10:10-14) which imitates its procedures. With that example in mind, the grand prose epic of the exodus from Egypt (Ex 5-14), which is obviously a composite, [176] can be better understood: Yahweh is its central hero, and everything is calculated to exalt his victory over Pharaoh, exactly as in the lyric pieces which celebrate that victory in other ways (Ex 15:2-17; Ps 77:14-21; 78:12-31. 43-54; 106:7 ff.; 114; Is 63:8-13, etc.).

All of these texts belong to history from a certain point of view; they even furnish a good documentation, unjustly rejected by a radical criticism which, for the rest, is in decline. But their historical truth is not to be found at the level of anecdotal details placed side by side; it is not to be confused

---

[173] From this point of view, G. Ricciotti, *Storia d'Israele* (Torino: SEI, 1932-1934) is not entirely satisfactory, but extreme reservations must be made concerning certain points and disputable critical preferences in M. Noth, *Geschichte Israels* (Göttingen: Vandenhoeck & Ruprecht, 1954). A more balanced judgment can be found in J. Bright, *A History of Israel* (London: SCM, 1960). On the critical evaluation of evidence, see the excellent remarks of M. J. Lagrange, *La méthode historique*, pp. 183 ff.

[174] G. von Rad, "Josephgeschichte und die ältere Chokma," *VT Supplement* 1 (Leiden, 1953), 120-127 (reprinted in *Gesammelte Studien zum Alten Testament* [Munich: Kaiser, 1958], pp. 272-280).

[175] J. Vergote, *Joseph en Égypte* (Louvain: Publ. Univ., 1959). P. Montet, *L'Égypte et la Bible* (Neuchâtel-Paris: Delachaux, 1959), pp. 15-23. H. Cazelles, "Patriarches," *DBS* 7, cols 114 ff., 137.

[176] A. Clamer, *L'Exode*, pp. 16-18.

with a material exactness that does not go beyond the level of sensible phenomena. To grasp it, two elements must be taken into consideration: the accepted customs of writing proper to each narration, and the didactic intent which relates the event in question to the plan of salvation of which it becomes a part. This is a complex procedure, which excludes any *a priori* definition of the historical genre, but all undue generalization as well. It is not because Simeon and Levi personify collectivities in Gn 34 that the same can be said of Abraham, Isaac, and Jacob [177]; it is not because the etiological account of Jg 2:1-5 is an artificial construction based on the place name Bochim that that in Gn 28:10-19 does not prove an historical connection between the holy place of Bethel and the ancestors of Israel during the patriarchal age; and so on, case by case. From this perspective it becomes easier to state precisely the relation of Gn 3 to history. [178] That account is not in any sense a realistic representation of the sin of original times as seen from an external point of view, but a substantial recollection in which the psychology of temptation is adorned with an abundance of judiciously chosen symbols. Placed at the beginning of human history, this image of the typical sin (the pretension to "know good and evil" without reference to the law of God) lays the premise in wisdom style for a theological reflection for which the New Testament supplies the conclusion: the first use of human freedom, man's first choice before God, was, therefore, a refusal! That is substantially the fact, related to the presence of sin in history, which the account allows us to grasp; but it presents only a conventional representation of that fact, so much more meaningful as it aims to express what the essence of sin is.

The manifold nature of the historical genre should not be restricted to ancient texts only, as if the compositions of a later age were necessarily close to our own manner of writing. That is true of a document like the internal history of David's reign and that of his successors, [179] a masterpiece composed by an eyewitness to the facts, whose theological intentions remain remarkably discrete. But alongside this, narrative forms which employ the miraculous in order to render the supernatural sensible to their readers still persist: the midrash on the exodus contained in Ws 16-19 outdoes in that regard even the older accounts. In addition, the narrative genre tended to develop in the

---

[177] H. Cazelles, *art. cit., DBS* 7, cols. 120-135.

[178] Besides commentaries on Genesis, see G. Lambert, "Le drame du jardin d'Éden," *NRT* 76 (1954), 917-948, 1044-1072. A. M. Dubarle, *Le péché originel dans l'Écriture*, pp. 39-74. L. Ligier, *Péché d'Adam et péché du monde* I (Paris: Aubier, 1960), pp. 171-286. L. Alonso-Schökel, "Motivos sapienciales y de alianza en Gn 2-3, "*Biblica* 43 (1962), 295-316.

[179] J. Delorme in Robert—Feuillet, *Introduction to the Old Testament,* pp. 202-205, 225 ff.

direction of didactic fiction,[180] in which historical realism is lost sight of (Judith, Esther, whatever might have been their traditional starting point). Even in the books of Kings and Chronicles the materials are different, and those who used them did not have the same understanding of their task as historians.[181] Everyone is aware of the chronological problems raised by the books of Ezra and Nehemiah[182]: in ordering the content of his records as he did, did the Chronicler intend to take responsibility for a problem of dates? A comparison of the two books of Maccabees, when possible, leads to a firsthand grasp of the method proper to each of the two authors.[183] But in modern criticism's estimation, neither the apologetic history of the first book of Maccabees, influenced by older biblical accounts and by Greek historiography at once, nor the moving history of the second book, which aims to edify and sometimes recurs to the miraculous, are free of weaknesses. Everything depends upon a correct understanding of the intent of each author within his own limitations and according to the conventions he followed (compare 1 M 4:28-35 with 2 M 11:5-12).

These are only a few examples. They suffice to show that the simple juxtaposition of accounts drawn from the Bible in our classic Bible histories, which were more respectful of a fixed letter than they were careful to understand their real meaning, is a deception which plays into the hands of modern critics.

*c) History in the New Testament.*[184] The social and cultural milieu in which New Testament history took form cannot be likened either to Israel at the time of the judges, nor to that of the Solomonic court, nor to that of the Babylonian captivity, nor finally to any of the milieux in which the books of the Old Testament were born. This means that its historical forms are quite different. The recollections preserved there can be divided into two distinct groups: those which concern Jesus Christ, the central object of

---

[180] A. Lefèvre, *ibid.*, pp. 520 ff. (Judith). H. Lusseau, *ibid.*, pp. 468 ff. (Esther). A. Robert, *art. cit.*, *DBS* 4, cols. 20-22 (Esther). A. Barucq, *Judith, Esther, BJ*, pp. 13-15, 77-80. H. Cazelles, "Note sur la composition du rouleau d'Esther," *Lex tua veritas. Festschrift H. Junker* (Trier: Paulinus, 1961), pp. 17-29. E. Haag, *Studien zum Buche Judith* (Trier: Paulinus, 1963).

[181] J. Delorme in Robert—Feuillet, *Introduction to the Old Testament*, pp. 225 240 (Kings). H. Lusseau, *ibid.*, pp. 495-503 (Chronicles). A. M. Brunet, "Le Chroniste et ses sources," *RB* 62 (1953), 481-508; 63 (1954), 349-386.

[182] An explanation of the problem by R. de Vaux, "Israël," *DBS* 4, cols. 765-769. H. Lusseau in Robert—Feuillet, *Introduction to the Old Testament*, pp. 489-491. V. Pavlovsky, "Die Chronologie der Tätigkeit Esdras," *Biblica* 38 (1957), 275-305, 428-456.

[183] See the introduction of J. Starcky, *Les livres des Maccabées, BJ*, pp. 13-14.

[184] L. Vénard, "Historique (Genre)," *DBS* 4, cols. 23-32, is too summary a treatment, and is in part outdated by more recent studies.

Christian faith, and those which concern the origins of the Church (Acts and occasional allusions in the letters). These two categories pose different problems, for their relation to the mystery of faith is not the same.

Recollections concerning the origin of Christianity are in part preserved in firsthand accounts: the Pauline letters and the "we-sections" of Acts. [185] That does not mean that these passages require no critical examination, for a particular man's point of view does not necessarily express the full complexity of a situation, especially if that man is engaged in a controversy (the case of the letter to the Galatians, for example). As for secondhand information (for example, in Ac 1—15), it requires sympathetic understanding, but possesses no less a very diverse character. [186] The worth of its details therefore varies in the same degree, for the inspired historian's degree of affirmation is ruled by two elements: his specifically religious point of view and the nature of the materials he happens to be using. If the conversion of Cornelius in Ac 10:1—11:18 takes place before the founding of the church at Antioch (11:19-21), the reason is not one of chronology (11:19 is connected to 8:3), but a reason of another kind: Peter and the mother church of Jerusalem retain their precedence when a question arises over the admission of a pagan into the Church without obliging him to pass through Judaism. Luke's intention on this point, so clear from a reading of chap. 15, must be respected.

As for the problem of the gospel narratives, [187] it must be approached dispassionately if its discussion is not to end in deadlock. It is taken for granted that, overall, they intend to preserve the memory of a real historical person, of his deeds and his words, of his meaningful acts and of the final fate that consummated his life. The central point of the apostolic preaching (in St. Paul as well as the Acts) is actually the identity of the Lord of faith and Jesus of Nazareth, known through the tradition of his witnesses. [188] The whole problem is to know how those witnesses, and oral tradition after

---

[185] J. Dupont, *Les sources du livre des Actes* (Bruges-Paris: Desclée de Brouwer, 1960), pp. 73-107.

[186] L. Cerfaux in Robert—Feuillet, *Introduction to the New Testament*, pp. 343-347. L. Trocmé, *Le livre des Actes et l'histoire* (Paris: Presses Univ. de France, 1957), pp. 154-214.

[187] X. Léon-Dufour in Robert-Feuillet, *Introduction to the New Testament*, pp. 319-324; *idem, The Gospels and the Jesus of History*, pp. 210-218. We will not now enter into a detailed discussion of the various genres to which the gospel narratives might belong. That is a problem of literary criticism that would demand too long a discussion. A summary treatment of the question can be found in *The Gospels and the Jesus of History*, pp. 163-166. See also the clarification of A. Bea, "Storicità dei Vangeli Sinottici," *Civiltà Cattolica* 115/2 (1964), 417-436, 526-545.

[188] X. Léon-Dufour, "Jésus-Christ et l'historien," *BCE* (1961), 357-360; *id., The Gospels and the Jesus of History*, pp. 272-276. Thus the modernist approach to the problem, which artificially opposed the Jesus of history to the Jesus of faith, has become outmoded (above, p. 122, note 132).

them, and finally the authors of the gospel syntheses, preserved that memory, under what forms they gave its features literary fixation at dates that probably range the full length of the 1st century. [189] Posing this question does not call into doubt the veracity of the accounts in question; it is just a matter of striving to understand them intelligently, as the recent instruction of the Biblical Commission on the historical truth of the gospels recommends. [190] In sum, the crystallization of memories did not have as its essential purpose to recount the history of Jesus in order to satisfy the curiosity of the faithful, [191] but to nourish their faith by giving them a concrete acquaintance with his person.

Besides, there is no gospel passage in which a didactic intent other than historical cannot be discerned, dogmatic, moral, apologetic, liturgical, etc. It would be strange if that did not leave its mark in some way on their literary texture, for the manner of writing surely goes hand in hand with the intended teaching.   History and doctrine do not exclude one another, they overlap; but it follows that not all accounts depend on the same laws.   It is not a matter of suspecting them of deforming history in order to twist them into ideological theses, nor is there a question of defending at any cost the material exactness of all the details they include.   It is a matter of staking out their rules of composition.   Through such an analysis one will certainly arrive at a better estimation of the limits of the historical knowledge it is possible to have about Jesus.   But what does that matter, as long as that knowledge remains authentic, under the diverse forms which transmit its substance, and as long as, beyond the visible drama in which the apostles were participants and witnesses, the mystery underlying that human experience, so full of meaning, is reached? [192]   Actually there are few passages that pose the same problems.   The visit of the Magi to Bethlehem, the story of the Annunciation,

---

[189] The question of date is important, for the long oral transmission of a tradition evidently influences its literary form and the preciseness of its details.  The narrative of the last supper, which was substantially fixed very early (1 Co 11:23-25 displays a tradition of it which Paul most likely received in the circle in which he was baptized), is one problem; another is that of Matthew's infancy narratives, which belong to the latest redactional layer of the gospel, and which were until then transmitted orally (L. Vaganay, *Le problème synoptique* [Tournai-Paris: Desclée, 1954], pp. 234-237); still different is the problem of the Johannine narratives, which reached their final form quite late, even if traces of the tradition on which they depend can be found earlier (cf. J. A. Bailey, *The Traditions Common to the Gospels of Luke and John* [Leyden: Brill, 1963]).

[190] Text and translation in *AER* 151 (1964), 5-11.

[191] This is the purpose of the apocryphal gospels; they are acknowledged to be of little worth (cf. J. Bonsirven and C. Bigaré in Robert—Feuillet, *Introduction to the New Testament*, pp. 730-739; E. Amann, "Apocryphes du Nouveau Testament," *DBS* 1, cols. 470-488).

[192] X. Léon-Dufour, *The Gospels and the Jesus of History*, pp. 259-270.

that of the baptism of Christ, that of the triple temptation, the healing of Jairus' daughter according to St. Mark and that of the man born blind according to St. John, the account of the last supper, etc., do not fall under the same literary laws. [193] The gospel, even when it aims to impart knowledge of Jesus Christ as a person in human history, is a manifold genre. To understand its import correctly our minds must assume a flexible attitude toward this great variety.

Scripture, therefore, does not teach history as the councils teach dogma or decree canon law: such a statement is only a matter of common sense. Let us beware of carrying over into this particular field methods of reasoning that are suitable for others. To interpret as dogma the historical import of the inspired texts is to expose oneself to dreadful misinterpretations. The geometric mind of the logicians must here give way to a more flexible mentality.

### IV. CONCLUSION

It should be apparent what meaning should be given to the Thomistic adage: *Quidquid in sacra Scriptura continetur, verum est.* In this context, *continetur* does not mean the mere material presence of a proposition in the sacred books, even excluding those which the author obviously does not accept as his own ("There is no God!" says the fool in his heart...). St. Thomas had in mind the formal teachings passed on by the sacred writers under the influence of their charism. That does not reduce either the extent of inspiration or that of inerrancy; but it is an incitement to appreciate properly the extent of formal teachings. These, in fact, are not the result of an analysis of the phrases contained in the texts. They depend on the three factors we have enumerated: the formal object of revelation, which determines the point of view of all biblical assertions; the progress of revelation, which introduces a relative factor into the formulation of doctrine; and the diversity of literary genres, which indicate the intent of each text.

From this point of view, so much more exact than that of the 13th century, or even that of the opening of the 20th, the Renan affair, involving an open clash with the principle of inerrancy, [194] appears founded on a gross misunderstanding. It is true that in Renan's case the misunderstanding was compounded by his implicit adherence to another kind of faith. The acceptance of philosophical ideas then in vogue in Germany accompanied his

---

[193] *Ibid.*, pp. 165 ff., 211 ff.
[194] Above, p. 103, note 59.

approach to a critical study of the Bible. [195] Theology and apologetics are in much better condition for having liberated themselves of the misunderstanding. Freed from false problems and poorly put questions, they can devote themselves to their proper tasks: to expound the content of revelation as it is found in Scripture, and, with the help of Scripture, to stake out the path to faith.

[195] This adhesion to a philosophic *Credo* can constantly be felt in *Souvenirs d'enfance et de jeunesse*, even though Renan attributed his loss of faith to historical criticism alone. But it is a fact that having left the seminary in 1845, Renan began *L'avenir de la science* in 1848-1849 (J. Pommier, *Renan d'après des documents inédits* [Paris: 1943], pp. 73 ff.). Concerning Renan's religious philosophy, see J. Pommier, *La pensée religieuse d'Ernest Renan* (Paris, 1925) (cf. just the chapter on God, pp. 15-22). A similar implicit philosophy underlies Loisy's thought, even when he denies presenting anything but history; see for example his letter to M. Blondel in the collection published by R. Marlé, *Au cœur de la crise moderniste*, p. 84; cf. H. Gouhier, "Tradition et développement à l'époque du modernisme," *Herméneutique et tradition*, pp. 75-104. It can be said that this is always the case, for there is no historian who does not bring his most intimate preferences to bear on his study of the Bible. He cannot reconstruct its unfolding without taking a stand in regard to the message that is bound up with it, and this interior decision governs not only his evaluations, but even his working hypotheses. We will come back to this point when we examine the problem of historical criticism in interpretation (below, pp. 335-338).

# CHAPTER IV

# THE CANON OF SCRIPTURE [1]

The inspiration granted by God to the sacred authors had as its fruit the composition of the books to which first Jewish tradition, and then that of the apostles and the Church, gave the significative name scripture. As for the Greek word canon (or its Latin equivalent regula), in the New Testament [2] it stands for the rule of life (Ga 6:16), and in the ancient Church, the rule of conduct (1 Clem 1:3) handed down by tradition (1 Clem 7:2), the rule of a sacred function (1 Clem 41:3), the rule of faith or of truth, [3] ecclesiastical discipline. [4] These uses make it clear what meaning the canon of scriptures had at first: it meant the rule (of faith and of life) provided by the scriptures; the latter were said to be canonical in the active sense of the word. But at the beginning of the 3rd century, the name canon began to be given also to the normative list of scriptures. [5] Since then they have been called canonical in the passive sense of the word, and the verb to canonize took on the meaning of to inscribe in the canon of Scriptures. This meaning passed into the common language of the Latin west, notably into the conciliar decrees of Trent and Vatican I. By studying concretely the history of the canonical collection of scriptures, we will the better be able to grasp the theological problems this subject raises. Then we will be able to conclude by considering those problems themselves.

---

[1] J. Ruwet in Institutiones biblicae, 6th ed., pp. 109-232 (with a bibliography of works published up to 1951). E. Mangenot, "Canon des livres saints," DTC 2, cols. 1550-1605. H. Höpfl, "Canonicité," DBS 1, cols. 1022-1045. A. Tricot, "The Canon of Scriptures," in Robert—Tricot, Guide to the Bible 1, 2nd ed., pp. 66-128. H. Höpfl—L. Leloir, Introductio generalis, pp. 119-179.

[2] H. W. Beyer, "Κανών," TWNT 3, pp. 600-606.

[3] For example, St. Irenaeus, Adversus Haereses, 4, 35, 4 (PG 7, 1089); the same usage can be found in Polycrate of Ephesus, Clement of Alexandria, Hippolytus, Tertullian (cf. DBS, art. cit., cols. 1022-1024).

[4] Especially in Clement of Alexandria and Origen (ibid., 1024 f.).

[5] Origen, Homilies on Joshua. It is true that we are here dealing with a Latin translation by Rufinus, which might reflect the 5th-century use of the word. In any case, this same usage is formally attested in the 4th century (see the texts cited by H. Höpfl, art. cit., DBS, cols. 1026-1029).

## § I. HISTORY OF THE PROBLEM

### I. FROM THE OPENING OF REVELATION TO ITS CLOSE[6]

It is not a question here of searching the two Testaments for traces of a list of sacred books analogous to what is today the canon of scriptures, but to see how, in Israel and then in the primitive Church, a collection of writings, which furnished a rule of faith and life because they were the word of God, came progressively into being.  The essential point is then to analyze a practice and to strive to perceive all its implications.

#### I. FROM THE BEGINNING TO CHRIST

##### *1. The Sacred Books in Israelite Tradition*

In our treatment of inspiration we saw that the development of Israelite tradition, closely related to that of revelation, was given a form by certain charismatic functions related to the word of God. [7]  Among them we distinguished in general two categories: 1) the prophetic activity, in which man became the direct organ of that word, whatever might have been the nature and extent of the message transmitted; 2) the various traditional activities related to the different aspects of community life: priests, levites, and chanters devoted to worship; priests and lawyers responsible for the law; scribes devoted to civil administration and afterwards at the service of the word of God.  No more need be mentioned to understand in what manner there came little by little into being a collection of normative books (canonical, in the active sense of the term).

The word of Moses the super-prophet, along with a strictly religious message, included a whole rule of life destined for the Israelite community: moral commandments, a law, ritual prescriptions.  That legacy went through a certain development with the passing of time, thanks to the priestly circles which had as their mission to preserve the Mosaic tradition intact and live. At the same time, that tradition took on a written form through various

---

[6] Besides the works cited in note 1 on page 139, see J. P. van Kasteren, "Le Canon juif vers le commencement de notre ère," *RB* 5 (1896), 408-415; 575-594; H. Strack—P. Billerbeck, *Kommentar zum Neuen Testament aus Talmud und Midrasch* 4, pp. 415-451 (which includes a translation of the texts relating to the question). For a Protestant point of view, see F. Michaéli, "A propos du Canon de l'Ancien Testament," *Études théologiques et religieuses* 36 (1961), 61-81.

[7] Above, pp. 50-57.

stages, which space prohibits recounting here [8]: the first dated from the time of Moses himself, with the decalogue [9] engraved on tablets of stone (Ex 34:28; cf. 32:15-16); the final stage is probably to be related to the activity of Ezra (Ezr 7:10.14.25-26). There was always in Israel, therefore, a regulatory tradition whose authority flowed from the word of God, and the writing down of that tradition in fragments or in large blocks resulted in endowing the people with normative books, which were gathered together under the name *Torah*. The Bible makes no direct reference to the exact content of these books, but it contains a sufficient number of allusions which point to their importance (Ex 24:7; Dt 31:9-13.24-27; Jos 8:32-35; 2 K 22:8-10; 23:2). While they all enjoyed the authority of Moses, the unique legislator, it is certain that levitical or priestly scribes collaborated in their composition, both in their legislative sections and in their narrative elements. They were held to be no less sacred, inasmuch as they were the word of God handed down by Moses. That is apparent especially in the fact that the final compilators of the Pentateuch did not hesitate to preserve side by side parallel laws whose details are sometimes contradictory. From the time of Ezra, the collection was complete and definitively fixed. Under the providential pressure of the Persian authorities [10] it was accepted by Jews and Samaritans, and was preserved by the Samaritans even after their schism (probably around the time of Alexander). That was the first canonical collection the literature of Israel possessed.

The word and activity of the prophets too, while inserting itself in a tradition to which it remained subordinate, represented a message received directly from God. The Deuteronomist clearly places the prophets in the line of Moses by underlining the divine source of their authority (Dt 18:15-22). It is for that reason that tradition strove to preserve the memory of the word of God which they had delivered to his people. This it did in various ways: through biographical accounts which sketched some episodes of their lives, through summaries of their preaching more or less faithful to the letter, and finally through a transcription of their sermons themselves (beginning with Amos). The prophets' disciples, and then the groups of followers devoted to their message, cooperated in this work in an extremely variable measure. In any case the result of their work enjoyed the same authority that was attributed to the oral preaching of the divine messengers. This was above all the case for the prophetic collections, whose

---

[8] On this point, one might consult H. Cazelles in *Introduction to the Old Testament*, pp. 118-166; *id.*, "Pentateuque," *DBS* 6, cols. 729-858.

[9] Concerning the primitive decalogue and its later literary developments, see above, pp. 10-11.

[10] H. Cazelles, "La mission d'Esdras," *VT* 4 (1954), 113-140.

internal complexity sometimes reflects a long literary development. By the Hellenistic age, there thus existed the canonical (in the active sense!) books of Jeremiah, Ezekiel, Isaiah and the twelve prophets; but their text or the order of their chapters had not always been definitively fixed. Moreover, the personality of the prophets so dominated the historical syntheses covering the period from the conquest to the captivity (from Joshua to the second book of Kings) that they were for that reason likewise considered prophetical books. In this case, however, the development of traditional material was wholly due to scribes, priestly or lay, who put their professional skill at the service of the authentic religious tradition.

Finally, after the captivity, other collections came to supplement those of the law and the prophets. First came that of the psalms, the norm of community prayer fixed by the circle of chanters; but there is evidence that the Chronicler did not hesitate to attribute to these chanters a sort of prophetic charism (1 Ch 25:1-3). Then came the wisdom books, heirs to an already long tradition, edited by scribes on whom Wisdom conferred a new sort of authority. [11] On this last point, the collection of authoritative writings remained open for a long time. Their great diversity, furthermore, prohibited recourse, when there was a question of adding new books to the collection, to criteria as clear as in the case of the law or the prophets. In some cases the personality of the supposed author facilitated their acceptance (Solomon in the case of the Song of Songs; Daniel, the name of attribution of an apocalypse from the Maccabean age). But the work of the Chronicler was accepted only at the cost of dismemberment (Ezra and Nehemiah separated from the Chronicles). Finally, in the early 2nd century, Ben Sira found Scripture a complex collection in which are included the law, prophecies, discourses, parables (Si 39:1-2). When his grandson translated his book, the collection was composed of three parts: the law, the prophets, and the other writings (Si Prologue: 1.7-9.24-25).

## 2. The Sacred Books in Judaism

Many factors played a part in the formation of that collection. First came the personal authority of Moses and the prophets; but there was also the authority of the tradition which preserved their teaching in an authentic form, since the scribes who transmitted it were beneficiaries of a divine assistance which likened them to the inspired authors. Writings commended by one of these two titles could play the role of rule of faith and conduct in the community. Consequently, they were preserved and used not only within the narrow circles of professional scribes; the liturgy of the synagogue, organized

---

[11] On the charism proper to the scribes, cf. above, p. 54.

gradually after the exile, had its practical needs too. The reading of the law was the first to be introduced (cf. Ne 8:8), accompanied probably by prophetic texts and psalms. Beyond that, it is difficult to assign a date for the entry of each book into synagogal use, which was in practice equivalent to an official "canonization." [12]

What can be said, however, is that usages varied according to places and milieux. It is known, for example, that the tradition of the Sadducees, which in this point agrees with that of the Samaritans, recognized as sacred books only those of the Pentateuch. Among the Qumran sect some late books like Daniel, Tobit and Ben Sira were known, [13] but it is difficult to say what authority they had. Besides, that sect used the book of Henoch, Jubilees and other apocrypha, without counting their own particular books (rules, hymns, etc.): is it certain that some of these did not enjoy an esteem equal to that accorded the scripture? And what of the scroll of psalms that has been found, apparently intended for liturgical use, in which many apocryphal pieces have been mixed with canonical ones? [14] In the lack of certain evidence, therefore, it would be imprudent to speculate upon the Qumran canon. [15] On the contrary, evidence proves a real difference between the usages of Palestinian and Alexandrian Judaism. For the first, Josephus [16] (in 97-98), the 4th book of Ezra [17] (14:37-48), and an opinion of Rabbi Juda

[12] This admission to use in the synagogue usually included a traditional interpretation, since Scripture had to be actualized by preachers for the spiritual profit of the community. It is difficult in the case of the Song of Songs, for example, to dissociate the book's acceptance into the canon, its use in the liturgy of the synagogue and its allegorical interpretation, which is clearly attested by R. Aqiba at the beginning of the second century (Strack—Billerbeck, *op. cit.*, Vol. 4, p. 432) and certainly antedates him (A. Robert—R. Tournay, *Le Cantique des cantiques* [Paris: Lecoffre, 1963], p. 211 f.; P. Grelot, "Le sens du Cantique des cantiques," *RB* 73 [1964], p. 53).

[13] See the collection of Qumran bibliography in J. T. Milik, *Ten Years of Discovery in the Wilderness of Judea* (London: SCM Press, 1959), pp. 20-43. F. M. Cross Jr., *The Ancient Library of Qumran and Modern Studies* (New York: Doubleday, 1958), pp. 23-36.

[14] Awaiting the definitive publication of these texts, see J. A. Sanders, "The Scroll of Psalms (11QPss) from Cave 11: A Preliminary Report," *BASOR* 165 (1962), 11-15; "Psalm 151 in 11QPss," *ZAW* 75 (1963), 73-85; "Two Non-Canonical Psalms of 11 QPss," *ZAW* 66 (1964), 57-75.

[15] I. H. Eybers, "Some Light on the Canon of the Qumran Sect," *New Light on Some Old Testament Problems* (Pretoria: U. of South Africa, 1962), 1-14.

[16] Josephus, *Contra Apion* 1, 8, limits the list to 22, the number of letters in the Hebrew alphabet. He attributes the psalms to David and Proverbs, Ecclesiastes and the Song of Songs to Solomon. He notes that since the time of Artaxerxes (cf. the book of Nehemiah) other books have been written, but they do not enjoy the same authority because of the absence of a prophet. In practice, however, Josephus uses those books as historical documentation.

[17] According to which Ezra dictated 24 books to be published for the reading of all, and 70 "to be set aside and entrusted to the wise." The Apocalypse of Ezra would naturally be one such esoteric book.

the Holy preserved in the Babylonian Talmud [18] agree upon an official list of 24 books (or 22 if Ruth is joined to Judges, and Lamentations to Jeremiah). It was this same list that was sanctioned by the synod of Jamnia (about A. D. 90), but not without long discussions over Ezekiel, Proverbs, Qoheleth, Esther, and the Song of Songs. [19] Hellenistic Judaism, on the other hand, was more receptive toward certain later books, certain of which were not even translations from the Hebrew, but composed directly in Greek (Wisdom and the second book of Maccabees at least). Still it is difficult once again to set down exact limits; it is unknown, in fact, in what measure all these works were read in the synagogue or used as Scripture, [20] and in what measure authority was attributed to certain apocryphal books likewise translated into Greek [21] (Henoch, Jubilees, the Testaments of the Patriarchs, the Assumption of Moses [22]). In brief, while the principle of a fixed list was common to all of Judaism, and the books listed in them had canonical status as the word of God, yet their limits fluctuated. That is not surprising when one considers that since revelation was not yet closed, inspiration could always be accorded an author without the prophetic criterion to discern immediately its presence.

## II. CHRIST AND THE APOSTOLIC CHURCH [23]

### 1. Use of the Older Scriptures

Concerning the use of Scripture, the passage from Judaism to the Church was an unnoticeable transition. There was no discussion over the existence of inspired books or over the extent of their list; no decision was made in this

[18] Cf. bT, *Baba batra* 14b (Strack—Billerbeck, *op. cit.*, Vol. 4, pp. 424-425). This baraita would date from about the year 150. It enumerates the authors who, in the rabbinic opinion, wrote the 24 canonical books.

[19] The texts are cited *ibid.*, pp. 426-433.

[20] Rabbinic Judaism itself made use of some of these works, such as Baruch, Ecclesiasticus, Tobit, Judith, though it never attributed them the character of sacred objects "which soil the hands." This was perhaps the result of a rigorous application of the criterion laid down by Josephus (above, p. 143, note 16), which was itself closely linked to a theory of literary authenticity of the canonical books.

[21] It seems in any case that the Greek compilation of the third book of Ezra, which includes extracts from 2 Ch, Ezr and Ne, and adds to them two legendary chapters whose hero is Zorobabel, preceded the translation of the canonical book of Ezra. On this point, see S. A. Cook's introduction in R. H. Charles, *The Apocrypha of the Old Testament* 1 (Oxford: Clarendon, 1913), pp. 1-19, and especially the study by E. Bayer, *Das dritte Buch Esdras und sein Verhältnis zu den Büchern Esra-Nehemia* (Freiburg i. Br.: Herder, 1911).

[22] The complete rejection of these books was most likely due to a reaction in official circles to Essenism and to Christians who made use of some of them.

[23] To the general works cited in note 1 on page 139, add M. J. Lagrange, *Histoire ancienne du Canon du N.T.* (Paris: Lecoffre, 1933); L. M. Dewailly, "Canon du N.T. et histoire des dogmes," *Vivre et Penser* 1 (= *RB* 50 [1941]), 78-93.

matter either by Christ or by the apostles. Yet it was Christ and his apostles who definitively fixed the canon of the Old Testament for the Christian faith at the same time that they determined its authentic interpretation. [24] But to learn their mind on this point, it is their attitude in practice which must be examined, avoiding too hasty or unjustified inferences.

A certain number of texts cited as Scripture, explicitly or implicitly, are to be found on the lips of Jesus or in the apostolic writings. [25] The books from which they are taken include the major portion of the Old Testament: the law, historian and writing prophets, Daniel (Mt 24:15), Psalms, Proverbs, Job. The absence of certain works accepted by Palestinian Judaism (Ezr, Ne, Qo, Sg, Est) is an accidental fact of no consequence; it puts us on our guard against recurring to the argument from silence to establish the limits of the canon in apostolic times. In fact, apart from citations, there are also cases in which the sacred authors make use of other Old Testament writings, whose phrases they repeat, or whose content they give evidence of being acquainted with. Now apart from the Chronicles [26] and the Song of Songs, [27] these are works which Palestinian Judaism did not retain in its canon, but which were in vogue in the Greek speaking world: Wisdom (Rm 1:19 ff., Heb 8:14), Tobit (Rv 8:2, cf. Tb 12:15), 2 Maccabees (Heb 11:34 ff.), Ben Sira (Jm 1:19), perhaps Judith (1 Co 2:10 cf. Jdt 8:14). What complicates the issue, however, is that allusions and verbal similarities to some apocryphal books can also be found: Heb 11:37 alludes to the Martyrdom of Isaiah, [28] the letter of Jude to the Assumption of Moses (Jude 9) and to the book of Henoch (Jude 14-16).

The usage of the primitive Church is therefore difficult to determine with precision and to interpret rigorously on the basis of the New Testament alone.

[24] This fact led N. Lohfink, "Über die Irrtumlosigkeit und die Einheit der Schrift," *Stimmen der Zeit* 179 (1964), 168-173, to see in the apostolic church the final "inspired author" of the Old Testament. We have stated why it does not seem to us necessary to adopt this view (above, p. 48).

[25] L. Vénard, "Citations de l'A.T. dans le N.T.," *DBS* 2, cols. 23-51. C. H. Dodd, *According to the Scriptures* (London: Nisbet, 1953), pp. 61-110.

[26] The allusion to the death of Zechariah (Mt 23:35 par.) probably refers to 2 Ch 24:20 ff.

[27] The question of allusions to the Song of Songs in the New Testament is not fully clear. In favor of a positive solution, see: A. Feuillet, "Le Cantique des cantiques et l'Apocalypse," *RSR* 52 (1961), 321-353; M. Cambe, "L'influence du Cantique des cantiques sur le Nouveau Testament," *RTh* 70 (1962), 5-26; A. Robert—R. Tournay, *op. cit.*, pp. 25 f. But on the negative side see J. Winandy, "Le Cantique des cantiques et le Nouveau Testament," *RB* 73 (1964), 161-190.

[28] *Ascension of Isaiah* 5 (cf. E. Tisserant, *Ascension d'Isaïe* [Paris, 1909], pp. 128-132). Nevertheless, the episode could have been taken from a Palestinian targum of the prophets, for it figures in the marginal gloss of codex Reuchlin on Is 66:1 (cf. A. Sperber, *The Bible in Aramaic* 3 [Leyden: Brill, 1959-1962], pp. 129 f.).

It would have to have followed that of the Jewish communities in which the gospel was announced: the Palestinian usage in Juda and Galilee, Greek usage in the Diaspora.   To determine its exact limits, it is necessary to recur to the Church of the 2nd century, the heir of an apostolic tradition which it neither censured nor extended. [29]

## 2. The Birth of the New Testament

When one spoke of Scripture in the time of the apostles, he thought only of the Old Testament.   But at the same time that the apostolic tradition was bringing its interpretation of the Old Testament into line with the gospel, it was itself tending toward written form, thanks to texts of a practical nature which responded to the vital needs of the churches. [30]   Consequently, the same process which had in the past ended in the formation of canonical collections is repeated with the same result.   First, whatever could lay direct claim to the authority of the apostles was prized as a rule of faith and practical life. [31]   The letters of St. Paul were read publicly to the brethren (1 Th 5:27) and passed from one church to another (2 Co 1:1; Col 4:16); there is no doubt that once the circumstances that had motivated their sending had ceased to exist, they were preserved with no loss of authority.   As for the gospel collections, no matter who collaborated in their writing in the exercise of their offices, they have no other purpose than to set down the content of the witness and the teaching handed down from the apostles, in order to assure a sound basis for the faith of Christians (cf. Lk 1:1-4).

But it must be noted that the criterion of apostolic origin was not understood, in that age, as strictly as modern literary criticism understands it when it studies questions of authenticity; apostolicity of doctrine and tradition counted more than the direct participation of the apostles in the composition of written works.   The fathers of the 2nd century were conscious of possessing the witness of Peter in the gospel according to Mark, and the first letter of St. Peter itself reveals the name of its editor, Silas (1 P 5:12). Proof that there existed then a principle of critical discernment is perhaps to be found in the restricted number of works preserved as canonical.   Thus there surely existed, at a very ancient date, a number of specifically Christian

---

[29] We are here applying to the problem of the canon the principle established above concerning the relation of ecclesiastical tradition to apostolic tradition (cf. above, chap. I, pp. 22-26).

[30] Cf. above, pp. 89-93: Scripture as Functional Literature.

[31] Above, p. 58.   The apostolic criterion therefore requires acceptance of the inspiration and "canonicity" of letters that have been lost (1 Co 5:9).   The canon recognized by the church of the second century on the basis of extant texts did not therefore necessarily coincide with primitive "canonical" literature.

hymns to which the letters allude (Col 3:16; Ep 5:19) or from which they borrow (Ep 5:14, etc.; cf. Lk 1:46-55; 1:68-79; 2:29-32; Rv 5:9-10, etc.). But apart from a few fragments cited on occasion, it seems that they were never recognized as canonical writings, so that they were eventually lost. Similarly, the Pauline letters allow a glimpse of a quite important prophetic authority. Certain critics think that the *Didaché* could have been compiled in the 1st century [32]; but it never appeared in the canon of scriptures. On the other hand, an analysis of the second letter of Peter [33] reveals that its writer regarded the age of the apostles from a certain distance; he even knows of a collection of Pauline letters (3:16). But the book was nonetheless admitted into the canon. If the use of a false name were solely responsible, why was it not the same for the Letter of Barnabas, for example, which is hardly a later work? [34]

In spite of a great number of obscure points, it seems, therefore, that the criterion of apostolicity, founded upon a direct or mediate relation of works to the person of the apostles, or at least upon an exact preservation of their tradition, and regulated by the authorities in charge of the churches, served as the basis for the formation of the collection. The first formal traces of an assimilation of the apostolic writings to the scriptures, furthermore, are provided by the New Testament itself: 1 Tm 5:18 cites Dt 25:4 and Mt 10:10 side by side, while 2 P 3:16 reserves to the authorities in charge the authentic interpretation of the Pauline letters "just as... the rest of scripture." No more could be expected from an age in which the tradition of the founding apostles was still so close that the churches could discover it without recourse to their writings. [35] At least it is established that they were carefully verified, whatever might have been their exact literary relation to the person of the apostles. What was expected of them was perhaps not to furnish material for an ecclesiastical tradition, which was still nourished directly by the apostolic tradition, though the exchange of texts allowed the various testimonies to enrich each other mutually. But that very attachment to the apostolic tradition, sole mediator of the one gospel, demanded a religious respect for the books which allow one to come in contact with it at its source.

[32] This is the position of J. P. Audet, *La Didachè, Instruction des apôtres* (Paris: Gabalda, 1958).

[33] On the problem of literary authenticity posed by the Second Letter of Peter, see ch. II, p. 36, note 4.

[34] See the state of the question in J. Quasten, *Patrology. I. The Beginnings of Patristic Literature*, p. 89; and the cautious conclusion of P. Prigent, *L'épître de Barnabé I-XVI et ses sources* (Paris: Lecoffre, 1961), pp. 219 ff.

[35] See 1 Clem 42; 44:1-3; St. Ignatius of Antioch, *Ad Romanos* 4:3. Cf. R. M. Grant, "Scripture and Tradition in St. Ignatius of Antioch," *CBQ* 25 (1963), 322-335.

## II. THE SACRED BOOKS IN ECCLESIASTICAL TRADITION

### 1. THE PRINCIPLE OF THE CANON OF SCRIPTURES

#### *1. The Historical Situation in the 2nd Century*

From all we have just said it is apparent that attachment to the apostolic rule of faith and life never failed to manifest itself in the churches, [36] either while the apostles lived or after their death, no matter what might have been the means for coming in contact with that rule: writings which attest it directly, sacramentary usages jealously preserved thanks to the apostolic succession of the local ministers, the traditional interpretation of the older scriptures in Christian preaching, particular traditions handed down by word of mouth. When St. Irenaeus, at the end of the 2nd century, appealed to the rule of truth, it was of all this that he was thinking, for it never entered his mind to separate living tradition from Scripture. [37]   Now attachment to apostolic tradition was at that time a crucial problem.   In fact, intellectual movements foreign to the apostolic rule were then striving to incorporate some of its elements into radically different syntheses, and their literature liked to pass itself off under the name of the apostles.   Thus rising gnosticism made use of gospels [38] which it attributed to Thomas, Philip, etc.   It also circulated apocryphal letters and acts [39] which pertained to the same propaganda literature.   Marcion, [40] for his part, made use of a restricted list of apostolic writings for his system: an expurgated gospel of St. Luke and some of the letters of St. Paul.   Less radical movements such as Docetism and Judeo-Christianity also had their particular gospels. [41]   And even where

[36] This is the "trust" mentioned in the pastoral letters: 1 Tm 6:20; 2 Tm 1:12.14; 2:2; 3:14; Tt 2:1.   Cf. the excursus of C. Spicq, *Les épîtres pastorales*, pp. 327 ff.

[37] Above, ch. I, pp. 23 f., 29.

[38] The recent discoveries at Nag-Hamadi have restored the texts of some of them.   The *Gospel of Truth*, a witness of Valentinian gnosticism, carries no author's name (cf. J. E. Ménard, *L'Évangile de vérité* [Paris: Letouzey et Ané, 1962]).   On the Gospel of Thomas see the commentaries of J. Doresse (Paris: Plon, 1959); R. Kasser (Neuchâtel-Paris: Delachaux, 1961).   On the Gospel of Philip see R. Mc L. Wilson, *The Gospel of Philip* (London: Mowbray, 1962); C. J. de Catanzaro, "The Gospel according to Philip," *JTS* n.s. 13 (1962), 35-71; J. E. Ménard, *L'Évangile selon Philippe* (Montreal: U. of Montreal, 1964).   Several works fragmentarily cited by the Fathers are probably to be classed in the same category: the Gospel of the Egyptians, the Traditions of Matthias, etc. (cf. E. Amann, "Apocryphes du N.T.," *DBS* 1, cols. 478-480).

[39] Especially worthy of note are the Acts of Judas-Thomas (*ibid.*, cols. 501-504).

[40] *Ibid.*, col. 481 (where there is a reference to A. Harnack, *Marcion: Das Evangelium vom fremden Gott* [Leipzig: Hinrichs, 1924]).

[41] These are gospels similar in type to that of the synoptics; a few citations of them are extant: the Gospel according to the Hebrews, the Gospel of the Ebionites

heretical speculation was not openly apparent, a popular literature had no qualms about developing, under legendary form, the story of the infancy of Christ, or that of his passion and resurrection. [42] It must be added that the oral traditions passed on within the churches, even under the name of ministers who had known the apostles, are not always trustworthy material: Papias of Hierapolis cites some that are obviously erroneous, [43] and it was to them that St. Irenaeus owed his millenarist tendencies. [44] Besides, how could their origin be verified in each particular case? But it was important to have an indisputable rule of faith at hand. In the eyes of the great bishops who were defending orthodoxy, St. Irenaeus for example, apostolic succession is the certain sign of a continous tradition possessing the assistance of the Holy Spirit. [45] But to that a concrete criterion is added, that of the scriptures. That is not to say that from that age the Church set down the complete and exclusive list of them by an authoritative act. Rather she took care, by conforming to the practice of the apostolic and sub-apostolic generations, to allow no heretical or suspect work to be introduced among those which represented the authentic tradition of the apostles. It was in this sense that the Church laid down the principle of a canon of scriptures: not as a novelty unknown in the previous age, but as a vigilant preservation of its legacy.

## 2. The Fixation of the Canon and its Significance

O. Cullman made an effort to determine the meaning of this fact. [46] In his opinion, "by establishing the principle of a canon, the Church implicitly

(or of the Twelve), the Gospel called of the Nazareens. Concerning their number and structure, see E. Amann, *art. cit.*, cols. 471-475. Also to be noted is the abundant pseudo-Clementine literature (*ibid.*, cols. 514-518).

[42] *Ibid.*, cols. 481-488. On the gospel of Peter, which is earlier than St. Justin (*ibid.*, cols. 476 f.), cf. L. Vaganay, *L'Évangile de Pierre* (Paris: Gabalda, 1930). This literature has recently been augmented by the Greek text of the Protevangelium of James (M. Testuz, *Papyrus Bodmer V, Nativité de Marie* [Cologny-Genève: Bodmer, 1958]) and of the Gospel of Gamaliel (M. A. van Oudenrijn, *Gamaliel, Äthiopische Texte zur Pilatusliteratur* [Freiburg i Br.: Herder, 1959]). The majority of the apocryphal Acts, letters and apocalypses belong to this edifying fictional literature (*DBS, art. cit.*, cols. 488 ff.). Summary bibliographies, more recent than that of E. Amman, are provided by J. Bonsirven—C. Bigaré in Robert—Feuillet, *Introduction to the New Testament*, pp. 724-725; J. Quasten, *op. cit.*, Vol. I, pp. 106-157.

[43] See Eusebius of Caesarea, *Ecclesiastical History*, 3, 39, 7-14.

[44] *Ibid.*, 3, 39, 13; cf. J. Quasten, *op. cit.*, vol. I, p. 289.

[45] J. Quasten, *op. cit.*, pp. 300-301. Cf. M. J. Congar, *Tradition and Traditions*, pp. 26-35. H. Holstein, *La tradition dans l'Église*, pp. 61-88.

[46] O. Cullmann, *La tradition* (Neuchâtel-Paris, 1953) (reproduced in part in *Catholiques et protestants, Confrontations théologiques* [Paris: Seuil, 1963], pp. 15-45). On this point Cullmann occupies a special position among Protestant theologians.

admitted that from that moment on tradition was no longer a criterion of truth. It put a leash on apostolic tradition.... It certainly did not wish thereby to put an end to the continued evolution of tradition. But through an act of humility, so to speak, it submitted the further self-development of that tradition to the higher criterion of the apostolic tradition codified in the sacred scriptures." [47]  Concerning the value of criterion accorded the scriptures, inasmuch as they are authorized (and inspired) witnesses of apostolic tradition, this position is correct. Ecclesiastical tradition does, in fact, ceaselessly seek there for the essential means of assuring its own fidelity. But in the devaluation of tradition itself, which is no longer "a criterion of truth," there is an obvious misunderstanding. [48]

If one considers the various ecclesiastical traditions which have come into being over the centuries, especially those of a disciplinary or practical nature, it is evident that they vary considerably in value; so much so that the Church has never pretended to canonize them as if they were revealed. But if one considers tradition as the essential bearer of divine revelation, it is the assistance of the Holy Spirit working through the functional charisms of the Church that is finally called into question. [49]  The outcome is to establish a sort of opposition between this tradition, which if left to itself would lead spontaneously to all sorts of deviations, and Scripture, which would detach itself from tradition in order to regulate it. By the same token, the apostolic heritage would be reduced to just the explicit statements of the New Testament. The idea that ecclesiastical tradition could integrally preserve that heritage in a richer and fuller form, either in its oral traditions, or better in its sacramentary, theological, exegetical usage, etc.,—this idea is out of the question. A barrier is effectively placed between the tradition of the apostles and that of the Church; but it is Mr. Cullman who puts it there. For it is not at all apparent that the ecclesiastical writers of the 2nd and 3rd centuries ever dreamed of anything of the kind. Correcting the weak points of this theory, one might therefore say that by laying down the principle of a canon, the Church was interested not in expelling from its living tradition that part of the apostolic tradition which was not explicitly attested in Scripture, but in putting a protective hedge around the books which put it in direct contact with apostolic tradition, for the purpose of realizing the potential of its content according to the practices of its living tradition. Scripture provides a norm, but living tradition provides a principle for understanding Scripture.

A description of the positions of other contemporaries, from K. Barth to G. Ebeling, can be found in P. Lengsfeld, *Tradition, Écriture et Église*, pp. 85-99.

[47] O. Cullmann, *op. cit.*, p. 44.

[48] See the critique of M. J. Congar, *op. cit.*, pp. 38-42.

[49] Above, ch. I, p. 23 ff.; ch. II, p. 60.

It is impossible to split the two, impossible to separate the principle of a canon from the traditional interpretation, which alone is capable of revealing the richness of the text.

## II. THE LIMITS OF THE CANON

While the principle of the canon of scriptures was a constant and universal element in ecclesiastical tradition, its practical application varied. Without retracing in detail its complex history, [50] we ought to note here its salient points, which were to determine future conciliar decisions.

### *1. The Canon of the Old Testament*

There was never any problem over the canonicity of the books recognized by the Jewish doctors at the synod of Jamnia (90-100 A. D.); there is no need, therefore, to insist on them. The question of the books accepted by Alexandrian Judaism is more complicated. Some of them, we have seen, were already cited in the New Testament. The intervention of the tradition of the ancient Church is also helpful, for it attests indirectly the apostolic usage which it preserved. From the end of the 1st century, Clement of Rome mentions Judith and the parts of Esther found only in the Greek Bible, [51] and he borrows frequently from the book of Wisdom. [52] In the 2nd century, St. Polycarp furnishes the oldest known citation of Tobit. [53] There is little to be drawn from Pseudo-Barnabas, [54] who cites as Scripture the Book of Henoch (16:5) and the Apocalypse of Ezra (12:1). In his *Dialogue with Trypho*, St. Justin [55] protests against the Jewish doctors who in substituting new Greek versions for the Septuagint suppressed from the Scriptures

---

[50] On this point one might consult the treatments cited on page 139, note 1. A good résumé of the question (sometimes a bit partial) can be found in R. Cornely— A. Merk, *Manuel d'introduction aux saintes Écritures* (Paris: Lethielleux, 130), pp. 27-85.

[51] St. Clement of Rome, *Epistle to the Corinthians* 55, 4-6 (in *Ancient Christian Writers* 1, pp. 42-43).

[52] *Ibid.*, 3,4 and 27,5. The allusion in 7,5 is more doubtful. It is true that besides canonical texts Clement also cites fragments which cannot be identified (cf. 8,3), and he alludes to Jewish traditions not included in Scripture (Noah, preacher of repentance in 7,6 and herald of regeneration in 9,4).

[53] *Epistle of Polycarp* 10,2 citing Tb 4:10 and 12:9 (in *Ancient Christian Writers* 6, p. 80).

[54] On the problem of the citations in the Epistle of Barnabas, see P. Prigent, *L'épître de Barnabé I-XVI et ses sources*, which contains a systematic study of the *Testimonia* and midrashic traditions used in its composition.

[55] *Dialogue with Trypho*.

some messianic passages (71:1-2); unfortunately, the examples he gives (72:1.4; 73:1; 120:5) prove very little, since they are not to be found in the canonical books. [56] The evidence provided by Hermas in favor of Ben Sira and Wisdom would carry more weight if he had not also cited as Scripture the apocryphal Books of Eldad and Medad. [57] In short, around the year 150, writers had a tendency to expand the Greek Jewish canon because of their mistaken opinion about the origin of certain books; in particular, the reaction against the pseudepigraphous works which passed under great names had not yet arisen.

The situation becomes clearer with the authors who were engaged in combating heresy. For example, the canon of the Muratorian fragment, which concerns principally the New Testament, cites in that context the Wisdom of Solomon. [58] St. Irenaeus [59] made use of Wisdom, [60] Baruch (under the name of Jeremiah [61]) and the Greek fragments of Daniel. [62] These last reappear in Hippolytus, [63] as well as Tobit [64] and the Maccabees [65]; elsewhere, Hippolytus cites Wisdom [66] and Baruch. [67] Tertullian [68] adds Ben Sira to

---

[56] The citation of Pseudo-Esdras in 72,1 appears again in Lactantius (4,18,22). The text attributed to Jeremiah in 72,4 speaks of the Lord's descent into hell; St. Irenaeus cites it under the name of Jeremiah (*Adversus Haereses* 4, 22, 1; *Proof of the Apostolic Preaching* 78) and of Isaiah (*Adversus Haereses* 3, 20, 4). The amplification of Ps 95 cited in 73,1 has no support before Justin. As for the legend of the martyrdom of Isaiah cited in 120,5, it belongs to Jewish tradition, and the Letter to the Hebrews had already mentioned it in passing (above, p. 145, note 28).

[57] Hermas, *The Pastor* 7,4 (= Vision 3,4). Concerning this apocryphal book, cf. M. R. James, *Lost Apocrypha of the Old Testament* (London: SPCK, 1920), pp. 38 ff.

[58] *Ench. B.* 6. Cf. G. Bardy, "Muratori (Canon de)," *DBS* 5, cols. 1399-1408. This mention of Wisdom "written by the friends of Solomon in his honor" is out of harmony with the context.

[59] Concerning St. Irenaeus' scriptural canon, see the discussion published by Migne, *PG* 7, 245-249 (on the Old Testament).

[60] Cf. Eusebius, *Ecclesiastical History* 5,26. Text of the letter: *PG* 16, 47-86.

[61] Ba 3:28 in *Adversus Haereses* 4, 20, 4; Ba 3:29-4:1 in *Proof of the Apostolic Preaching* 97; Ba 4:36-5 in *Adversus Haereses* 5, 35, 1.

[62] Greek fragments of Daniel in *Adversus Haereses* 4, 5, 2 and 4, 26, 3. But it must be added that Irenaeus also uses the Fourth Book of Ezra in *Adversus Haereses* 3, 21, 2 (cf. 4 Ezr 4, 14).

[63] *Commentary on Daniel.*

[64] Tb 3:24 in the *Commentary on Daniel* 1, 28.

[65] There are a dozen citations of the Maccabees in the same work.

[66] Citations of Wisdom in *Proof against the Jews* 9-10. Cf. the translation of P. Nautin, "Notes sur le catalogue des œuvres d'Hippolyte," *RSR* 38 (1947), 350-351.

[67] Citations of Baruch in *Contra Noetum* 2 and 5 (*PG* 10, 805-806 and 809-810).

[68] For the biblical citations in the works of Tertullian, see the list of references in *CCL*, vol. 2, pp. 457 ff.

these, but he also cites Henoch. [69] Clement of Alexandria used all the books of the Greek Bible, and Origen even went to the trouble of solving the doubts of Julius Africanus in regard to those books which were not included in the Jewish Palestinian canon. [70] Variations of detail do not lessen the importance of this substantial agreement between Asia Minor (represented by Irenaeus, who originated there), Rome (Clement and Hippolytus), Africa (Tertullian, to be followed by Cyprian) and Alexandria (Clement and Origen). The principal difficulty encountered concerns the pseudepigraphous works, whose pseudonym won them unmerited respect in more than one case. [71]

The western Church always held these fundamental positions. If problems arose in the East, the reason was their closer contact to Palestinian Judaism, which had decided upon a restricted list of canonical books at the synod of Jamnia. Melito of Sardis [72] (about 170) explicitly depends on the Palestinian tradition in his *Extracts for Onesimus* (only the book of Esther is missing). Origen was aware of the Jewish canon of 22 books, [73] but does not feel bound by it. [74] But from the 4th century, a distinction begins to be made between the books included in that canon and those "which are not listed in the canon, but which the fathers suggest be read by those who join the faith," according to the expression of St. Athanasius. [75] That was the origin of the

[69] See the references in F. Martin, *Le livre d'Hénoch* (Paris: Letouzey et Ané, 1906), pp. cxxv f. Tertullian writes explicitly: "Since Enoch also speaks of the Lord in the same book, we must not reject any of it that concerns us. And we read that any writing which is designed to edify is divinely inspired. That is likely the reason the Jews reject it; they reject anything that smacks of Christ." (*De cultu feminarum* I, 3, *CCL* I, pp. 341 f). Witness to Christ is therefore considered the criterion of canonicity, which always supposes inspiration. But the error about its literary authenticity undoubtedly accounts in part for the favor it enjoyed.

[70] See *PG* 11, 49. 52 f. 60 f. 80.

[71] Especially it seems that the Third Book of Ezra (above, p. 144, note 21) was universally used as canonical in the Greek East, and even in the West before St. Jerome (who made some reservations). It is therefore not irrelevant to raise the question of its canonicity; cf. T. Denter, *Die Stellung der Bücher Esdras im Kanon des Alten Testaments* (Marienstatt: Dissert. U. of Fribourg, 1962).

[72] Eusebius, *Ecclesiastical History* 4, 26, 13. In this list, Ezra is named separately and must stand for the books of Ezra and Nehemiah. Conversely, the phrase concerning Solomon apparently mentions two titles which it takes as equivalents (Σολομῶνος Παροιμίαι ἥ καὶ Σοφία).

[73] See his prologue to Psalm 1 (*PG* 12, 1084) and Eusebius, *Ecclesiastical History* 6, 25, 1-2.

[74] Even the canon given by Eusebius, who renders the Hebrew titles alongside the Greek, attributes the Letter of Jeremiah (= Ba 6) to Jeremiah and names the Maccabees separately. Cf. J. P. van Casteren, "L'Ancien Testament d'Origène," *RB* 10 (1901), 413-423.

[75] St. Athanasius, *Festal Letter* 39 (*Ench. P.* 791; *PG* 26, 1176 f., cf. 1436 f.). Baruch figures in the first category; the second includes Ws, Si, Jdt, Tb and Est which are thus dissociated from the Jewish canon. Despite this position in principle, Athanasius uses the deuterocanonical books and explicitly cites Tobit as Scripture (*Apologia adversus Arianos*, *PG* 25, 268).

distinction between protocanonical and deuterocanonical books. It obviously coincides with the distinction St. Cyril of Jerusalem made between the books received by all and the doubtful books. [76] In practice, however, the Alexandrian and Palestinian writers made use of the deuterocanonical books, as did many other eastern writers. But in Syria and Cappadocia the influence of the Hebrew canon is more marked; it apparently underlies the list sanctioned by the Council of Laodicea in Phrygia [77] (363?). It was under the influence of the same canon that Rufinus of Aquilaea separated from the canonical books the "ecclesiastical" books, which were unsuited to establish the authority of faith, [78] while St. Jerome transferred them to an appendix of his Latin translation [79] in the name of *Veritas hebraica*. It is true that in the same age Pope Innocent I cited the complete canon in his letter to Exuperius of Toulouse [80] (405) and that the African councils officially sanctioned it. [81]

It is somewhat difficult, therefore, to verify the position of the authentic tradition. But the disagreements can be explained by the side influence of Judaism, whose effect was to throw suspicion on the deuterocanonical books.

---

[76] *Catechesis* 4, 35 f. (*PG* 33, 497 ff.; *Ench. B.* 8-9) holds to the Hebrew canon without following its order, while Baruch and the letter of Jeremiah are joined to the book of the prophet. Elsewhere, however, Cyril attributes Wisdom to Solomon and cites Ecclesiasticus and the Greek fragments of Daniel.

[77] The date of the council is disputed. Cf. E. Amann, "Laodicée (Concile de)," *DTC* 8/2, cols. 2613-2619. The canon of the Old Testament was perhaps arrived at by eliminating certain books (Jdt, Tb, Si, Ws) from the Greek Bible, because in it Baruch and Jeremiah's letter are appended to the book of the prophet along with Lamentations. For that reason the question of the Greek fragments of Esther and Daniel remains unsettled. For the rest, canons 59 and 60 of the council (which include this list of the sacred books) are unknown in the oldest eastern canonical collections (for example, the *Apostolic Canons* of John the Scholastic in the 6th century). Their authenticity and origin are for that reason disputed (cf. E. Amann, *art. cit.*, cols. 2616 f.).

[78] Rufinus of Aquilea, *A Commentary on the Apostles' Creed*, *PL* 21, 373 f. (*Ancient Christian Writers* 20, pp. 73 f.). We note here the position of St. Athanasius, which is in opposition to that of the churches of the West. But that does not hinder Rufinus from defending the Greek fragments of Daniel against St. Jerome in another place (*Apologia* 2, 32,37; *PL* 21, 611 and 615 f.) and in another from citing Baruch and Wisdom among the "prophetic" writings.

[79] Until 390 St. Jerome cited all the books of the Greek Bible without distinction. But from the moment that he undertook to retranslate the whole Old Testament from the Hebrew, he adopted the view of the Jews of his time, as he explains in the *Prologus galeatus* (*PL* 28, 547-558): Ws, Si, Jdt and Tb are placed among the apocryphal works (along with the Pastor of Hermas!); 1M exists in Hebrew, but 2M is Greek. Baruch is not mentioned (see also the prologues to Tb and Jdt: *PL* 29, 23-26 and 37-40). At the end of the commentary on Daniel the Greek fragments are rapidly annotated, but are treated as *fabulae* (*PL* 25, 580-584).

[80] Text in *Ench. B.* 21.

[81] Text of the canons of Hippo (393) and Carthage (397 and 419) in *Ench. B.* 16-19.

The constant practice of the Church, on the contrary, was favorable to them. During the following centuries some of the positions taken in the 4th century continued to carry a certain weight with theologians. In the West, despite the authority of a decree attributed to Pope Gelasius, [82] the prestige of St. Jerome led some to grant the deuterocanonical books less authority, [83] or to doubt their canonicity. [84]  In the East, St. John Damascene [85] and others rejected them, despite the decision of the Council *In Trullo* (692) which ratified the complete canon of the African councils. [86]  But it should be noted, however, that these were private opinions, which were not to be supported by any decision of a general council, and which did not prevent the books in question from enjoying broad esteem.

## 2. The Canon of the New Testament [87]

At the beginning of the post-apostolic age, one of the burning questions which faced the Church was to distinguish authentic apostolic books from those which were not, in order to gather the former into as complete a collection as possible.  For the gospels this operation took place rapidly. Already at the end of the 2nd century St. Irenaeus recognized the fourfold

[82] *Ench. B.* 26.

[83] Hugh of St. Victor, *De scripturis et scriptoribus sacris* 6 (*PL* 175, 15. 16. 20); *Eruditio didascalica* 6, 2 (*PL* 176, 784).  On the problem of the canon in the 12th century cf. C. Spicq, *Esquisse d'une histoire de l'exégèse latine au moyen-âge* (Paris: Vrin, 1944), pp. 105-107.

[84] This is the position of Nicholas of Lyra (C. Spicq, *op. cit.*, pp. 152 f.), which he explains in the prefaces to the commentary on Tobit and Esther.  That does not prevent him from explaining the deuterocanonical books as well as the protocanonical (except for the Greek fragments of Esther).  The position of St. Thomas is completely different; he formally distinguished the question of literary authenticity from that of canonicity and held that the Church had with its authority sanctioned the canonicity of certain "apocryphal" (in the literary sense of the word) works. Cf. C. Spicq, *op. cit.*, pp. 149-152; P. Synave, "Le Canon scripturaire de saint Thomas," *RB* 34 (1925), 522-533.

[85] St. John Damascene, *De fide orthodoxa* 4, 17, attributes a real utility to Ws and Si, but excludes them from the canon (*PG* 94, 1179-1180); but he happens to have used Baruch as Scripture (*De imaginibus* 1, 16; *PG* 94, 1245) and he quotes a text of Leontius Byzantinus which cites Wisdom under the name of Solomon (*ibid.*, 1273).

[86] G. Fritz, "Quinisexte (Concile)," *DTC* 13/2, col. 1583.  It is true that canon 2 of this council gives global approval to a whole series of ancient conciliar canons, among which are those of Laodicea of Phrygia (above, p. 154, note 77) and those of Carthage.  But the scriptural canons of these councils contradict one another as far as the deuterocanonical works are concerned.  It should be noted that Photius (*Nomocanon* 3, 2; *PG* 104, 589-592) presents three scriptural canons side by side: that of the apostles, which declares Ws and Si useful but excludes them, that of Laodicea and that of Carthage.  This is evidence of hesitation in the oriental tradition.

[87] See the works cited above, p. 144, note 23.  P. Battifol, "L'Eglise naissante: Le canon du Nouveau Testament," *RB* 12 (1903), 10-26.

gospel, [88] and that position was practically never questioned. There existed certain other gospels, some of heretical origin, and others doctrinally unobjectionable. But even those who cite fragments of them (Origen, St. Jerome) did not consider them Scripture. The case of the other apostolic writings was quite different. When their literary authenticity was assured beyond all possible doubt, their authority was likewise solidly established. But when their authenticity seemed doubtful, it became difficult to distinguish them from other edifying, useful, and orthodox works, like the Letter of Clement of Rome or the letters of St. Ignatius of Antioch. Some, more credulous than critical, ascribed undue merit to some pseudepigraphous works, such as the Letter of Pseudo-Barnabas, the Apocalypse of Peter, and even the Pastor of Hermas. [89] Others, on the contrary, called into doubt the canonicity of works accepted elsewhere. In the West, the canon of the Muratorian fragment [90] (about 180) does not mention the letter to the Hebrews, nor the letters of James and Peter. But these three books are certainly cited in the work of St. Irenaeus. [91] Hippolytus of Rome surely used all the catholic letters; but if he refers to the letter to the Hebrews, he does not attribute it to St. Paul, [92] which creates a difficulty for its canonical authority. For the same reason it was in the same period excluded from the African canon, [93] and it is probable that the second letter of Peter is in the same situation. Some time passed before Rome and Carthage, probably under the influence of Alexandria, accepted these books. That was an accomplished fact by the end of the 4th century, as is evident from the decisions of the African

---

[88] St. Irenaeus, *Adversus Haereses* 3, 11, 8. Though its beginning is mutilated, the canon of the Muratorian fragment certainly included also the four gospels, and it is well established that at about the same time Tatian composed his *Diatessaron* based on them.

[89] St. Irenaeus cites the Pastor of Hermas as Scripture (*Adversus Haereses* 4, 20, 2), a position that the canon of the Muratorian fragment strongly rejects. But this latter document states that some admit the Apocalypse of Peter. Clement of Alexandria admits the Apocalypse of Peter and the Letter of Barnabas; as for his acceptance of the Letter to the Hebrews, it is due to a theory of Pauline authenticity which hardly had Origen's favor and which was not shared by the West (Eusebius, *Ecclesiastical History* 6, 14, 1).

[90] Above, p. 152, note 58.

[91] Above, p. 152, note 59 (concerning St. Irenaeus' canon).

[92] Hippolytus' opinion on the Letter to the Hebrews is recorded by Photius in his *Bibliotheca*, both with respect to codex 121 (*PG* 103, 463) and in a later allusion (*PG* 103, 1104). Cf. the introduction to the works of Hippolytus in *PG* 10, 349.

[93] Tertullian attributes the Letter to Barnabas (*De pudicitia* 20, 2; in *CCL* 2, p. 1324). St. Cyprian, on the other hand, says that St. Paul wrote to seven churches (*Exhortatio ad martyrium* 11; *PL* 4, 668), which excludes the Letter to the Hebrews. Neither Tertullian nor Cyprian cites the two short Johannine Letters, but given their brevity, nothing can be concluded from that—all the more so since 2Jn was cited by the bishop Aurelius at the Council of Carthage of 256 (*PL* 3, 1072).

councils [94] and the letter of Innocent I to Exuperius of Toulouse. [95] The non-Pauline origin of the letter to the Hebrews, which was widely held, [96] and the occasional attribution of 2 Jn and 3 Jn to another John, [97] did not weaken that position, despite the reserves of St. Jerome, [98] who was influenced by the opinions dominant in the East.

In the East in fact, the letter to the Hebrews was retained, notwithstanding the literary difficulties to which Origen had already called attention. [99] But the problems of the catholic letters and of Revelation were not resolved so easily. With the exception of Alexandria, where a letter of St. Athanasius (367) enumerates 27 books, all apostolic and canonical, [100] the various churches wavered not a little. Eusebius of Caesarea [101] lists among the books "accepted by all" only the gospels, the 14 Pauline letters, 1 Peter, 1 John, and "if it seems right," Revelation; the other catholic letters [102] are "controversial" books; as for Revelation, Eusebius inclines rather to class it among the "spurious" books. [103] This doubt about Revelation had its origin in the

[94] The Councils of Hippo (393) and of Carthage (397 and 419); cf. *Ench. B.* 16-18.

[95] *Ench. B.* 21 f.

[96] St. Augustine echoes the doubts expressed on this point in his age (*De civitate Dei* 16, 22), but it is his judgment that this literary question does not settle the problem of canonicity (*De peccatorum remissione et meritis* 1, 27, 50; *PL* 44, 137). It should be noted that the list of the Council of Carthage (389) mentions the thirteen letters of St. Paul and then adds: "one by the same to the Hebrews" (which seems to indicate a recent addition to the Pauline *corpus*). For a summary of opinions in the West, see C. Spicq, *L'épître aux Hébreux* I, pp. 177-189.

[97] St. Damasus' list (in a Roman document from about 382) includes the following: "one letter by the apostle John, two letters by some other John." Might we not see in this the influence of St. Jerome who echoed the views of the East? Cf. M. J. Lagrange, *Histoire ancienne du Canon du N.T.*, p. 150.

[98] His doubts about the authenticity of the Letter to the Hebrews: *De viris illustribus* 5 (*PL* 23, 617-618); *Letter to Dardanus* 129, 3 (*PL* 22, 1103-1104). Concerning the short letters of John: *De viris illustribus* 9 and 18 (*PL* 23, 623 f. 637). Concerning the First of Peter: *ibid.*, 1 (col. 609); *Letter* 120, 11 (*PL* 22, 1102). Concerning James and Jude: *ibid.*, 2 and 4 (*PL* 23, 609. 615).

[99] Cf. Eusebius, *Ecclesiastical History* 6, 25, 11. On the question of the canonicity of the letter in eastern churches, see the references gathered by C. Spicq, *L'épître aux Hébreux*, pp. 169-176.

[100] St. Athanasius, *Festal Letter* 39 (*PG* 26, 1437 f.; *Ench. P.* 791); cf. *Ench. B.* 14-15.

[101] Eusebius, *Ecclesiastical History* 3, 25.

[102] The phrases he uses indicate that Eusebius does not accept the literary authencity of the letters in question, and perhaps not even of the First Letter of John (τὴν φερομένην Ἰωάννου προτέραν). As for the brief Johannine letters, he states explicitly: "whether they were written by the evangelist or by someone of the same name"(*Ecclesiastical History* 3, 25, 3).

[103] In this category Revelation of John is joined by the Acts of Paul, the Pastor of Hermas, the Apocalypse of Peter, the Letter of Barnabas, and the Didache (compare 3, 3). It should be noted that these are orthodox works which Eusebius explicitly distinguishes from those which are to be proscribed.

opinion of Dionysius of Alexandria, who attributed it to an author other than the apostle John.[104]   Doubt was rather general in Syria and Asia Minor, from St. Cyril of Jerusalem[105] to St. Gregory Nazianzen[106] and from codex *Sinaiticus* to the Antiochan writers[107] (St. John Chrysostom, Theodoret). Similarly, the group of Catholic letters was often reduced to 1 Peter and 1 John, to which some added the letter of James.   Again, it is probable that problems of literary authenticity posed by the letter of Jude, 2 Peter and the short letters of John contributed to the uncertainty about their canonicity. Some time passed before opinion in the East overcame its doubts, and even then some opponents remained.[108]   Thus the New Testament too has its deuterocanonical books, which, furthermore, are not the same ones in East and West.   Since apostolic authority appeared to be connected to a book's literary origin, any critical observation which called their composition by an apostle into doubt automatically put their canonicity in doubt.

### III. ECCLESIASTICAL DECISIONS

There was no formal decision of the Church at the basis of the process of the formation of the canon of Scripture.   It all rested on the more or less rapidly acquired recognition of a normative practice which ecclesiastical tradition owed, in the final analysis, to the apostolic tradition itself.   It is true that in the course of the centuries some provincial councils or local authorities had laid down precise rules in this regard.   But it was not before the *Decree for the Jacobites* promulgated at the Council of Florence (1441) that a general council took a position on the question.[109]   And not even that put an end to the

[104] Dionysius attributes to the apostle John only the Gospel and the First Letter (Eusebius, *Ecclesiastical History* 7, 25, 7).

[105] See St. Cyril of Jerusalem's list in *Ench. B*. 10.   But in this list the seven catholic letters are included as well as the fourteen of St. Paul.

[106] It is true that the metrical canon attributed to St. Gregory Nazianzen (the text is quoted in M. J. Lagrange, *Histoire ancienne du Canon du N.T.*, p. 116) is of doubtful authenticity.   But an allusion to the dispute over Revelation can also be found in the *Epistula iambica ad Seleucum* of Amphilochius of Iconium (*PG* 37, 1593); cf. M. J. Lagrange, *op. cit.*, pp. 118-120.

[107] *Ibid.*, pp. 156-158.

[108] Thus Revelation, which was accepted by Andreas of Cesarea, Leontius Byzantinus and St. John Damascene (*De fide orthodoxa* 4, 17; *PG* 94, 1179-1180 with the complete canon), was thrown in doubt by Nicephorus' *Stichometria*. Photius, *Nomocanon* 3,2 (*PG* 104, 589) presents contradictory lists: the canon of the apostles and that of Laodicea, which exclude the book, and the canon of Carthage, which accepts it (cf. p. 155, note 84).   In the 14th century Nicephorus Callistus possessed a complete canon identical to that of the Latins.

[109] Text in *Ench. B*. 47.

controversies. As late as the 16th century, Erasmus [110] accorded the deutero-canonical books of the New Testament a reduced authority (Heb, Jm, 2 P, 2-3 Jn, Jude, Rv), and Cajetan [111] applied to the two Testaments the rules drawn up by St. Jerome, which meant suspecting the canonicity of the books excluded by the Palestinian Jews and of the letters whose author was not certain (Heb, Jm, 2-3 Jn and Jude).

The controversy took a new turn with the Protestant reformers. The doubts thrown on the literary authenticity of some books of the New Testament by the humanists perhaps had some influence on them. But it was above all the rejection of any other normative authority but Scripture itself that rendered the solution to the problem so difficult. If it is impossible to refer to ecclesiastical tradition, or to any magisterium whatsoever, in order to settle the doctrinal question of the canon of Scriptures, what criterion can be invoked? And if it is true that the books admitted by everyone since Christian antiquity have in their favor that public consensus of which Calvin spoke, [112] what can be said of the deuterocanonical books? For those of the Old Testament, Luther adopted a compromise solution: he consigned them to an appendix to the Bible under the name apocrypha. [113] That is the position taken by the various confessions of faith of the 16th century: "While one cannot refer to these books to establish dogmas, they may be read in order to find examples and to mould morals." [114] In the New Testament likewise, a variable list of deuterocanonical books was set apart and was accorded less authority (Heb, Jm, Jude, Rv for Luther, and in addition 2 P and 2-3 Jn for other reformers). Nevertheless, later, aided by the anti-Catholic climate, opposition to these books became more pronounced. Following the Calvinists and Presbyterians, the Bible Society of London excluded the "apocrypha" from its editions of the Bible in 1826, against the will of the Lutheran churches. [115] On the Catholic side, the decisions of Trent [116] were

[110] See his edition of the New Testament (Basel, 1516).

[111] Thomas de Vio Cardinal Cajetan, *Epistulae Pauli et aliorum apostolorum...juxta sensum litteralem enarratae*, Prooemium in epistulam ad Hebraeos.

[112] See S. de Dietrich, *Le renouveau biblique* (Neuchâtel-Paris: Delachaux, 1947), p. 37.

[113] Cf. *Institutiones biblicae*, p. 144.

[114] The Gallican Confession of 1559, art. 6.

[115] In the Greek church, Patriarch Cyril Loukaris attempted to introduce this abbreviated canon under the influence of Protestantism, but he met with strong resistance. Conversely, the Sacred Synod of the Russian church excluded the deuterocanonical books of the Old Testament in the 19th century. On this question, see M. Jugie, *Histoire du Canon de l'Ancien Testament dans l'Église grecque et russe* (Paris: Beauchesne, 1909).

[116] *Ench. B.* 57-60.

upheld and renewed at Vatican I,[117] in order to cut short any distinction between proto- and deuterocanonical books.[118] It ought to be noted that in present-day Protestantism the deuterocanonical works of the New Testament are frequently treated as equals of the other books, but those of the Old Testament are not. They are always called "apocrypha," while the Catholic apocrypha are called "pseudepigrapha."

## § II. QUESTIONS RELATED TO THE CANON

### I. DISCERNMENT OF CANONICITY

The problem to be examined here is twofold: 1) How can one recognize the books to which divine inspiration has given canonical value (in the active sense of the word)? 2) To whom does it fall to perform that discernment? The history of the canon of scriptures has furnished us the essential elements for a reply. It is now a matter of gathering them together and relating them, on the one hand, to the doctrine of inspiration (chap. II), and, on the other, to that of the relations between Scripture and Tradition in the Church (chap. I).

Neither Christian antiquity nor the Middle Ages ever carried on a discussion on this subject. It is only since the 16th century that the Protestant movement, by rejecting every other dogmatic authority but Scripture itself, and by reducing ecclesiastical tradition to merely human testimony, useful in proportion to its submission to Scripture, but devoid of normative value, has brought up the question. How can the principle of canonicity, which accredits Scripture, be based on Scripture? In place of external criteria related to the authority of the Church and its tradition, it is necessary to substitute internal criteria capable of imposing themselves on every believer and upon the Church itself.

In practice, Protestant theology has approached the problem from quite different directions. Luther[119] appealed to the testimony the scriptures

---

[117] *Ibid.*, 77.

[118] This quite unfortunate distinction entered common usage after Sixtus of Siena, who used it in his *Bibliotheca sancta*. It might be noted that the same author doubted the canonicity of the Greek fragments of Esther, following St. Jerome, although the Council of Trent had defined the limits of the canon according to the content of the Vulgate. But it is a fact that in the Vulgate St. Jerome rightly placed those fragments translated from the Greek in an appendix!

[119] A brief summary can be found in S. de Dietrich, *Le renouveau biblique*, pp. 36-38. In fact, in order to reject the deuterocanonical books of the New Testament, Luther recurred rather to the criterion of apostolic inauthenticity, for if there is one letter whose theme is Christological, it is the Letter to the Hebrews. See also

rendered to Christ and his redemptive work, and it was this principle that led him to distinguish several degrees of authority among the sacred books. Furthermore, he probably invoked the principle of lack of apostolic authenticity to reject the deuterocanonical books of the New Testament. Calvin [120] spoke of a sovereign decision of God which provoked a public consensus in the primitive Church. After them, the various confessions of faith, [121] without denying these relatively objective criteria, stressed more and more the role of the Holy Spirit, who testifies to himself in the hearts of believers and gives them an interior persuasion of the divine character of the scriptures. This view is forcefully reaffirmed in our day in the theology of Karl Barth, [122] for whom the absolute character of the word of God occupies a fundamental place. Nevertheless, since the 19th century, a new search for objective criteria has appeared. Renouncing any adventure in the world of principles, several historians have attempted to establish the way in which the scriptures became canonical at the Church's beginning. Zahn [123] proposed the role of edification which the apostolic writings, read in the Christian assemblies, played very early in the churches. Harnack [124] pointed to ecclesiastical charisms, which caused the books to be written under their influence to be considered inspired. There is no reason to condemn these efforts, for they generally put their finger on some exact factor which Catholic theology ought to integrate into its synthesis. Closer yet to traditional doctrine are the views of O. Cullman, [125] who sees in the fixation of the canon an act of the Church, which by this recognition of the scriptures expressed its submission to the word of God. Even more recently, M. Lods has spoken of a sort of religious

E. Mangenot, "Canon des Écritures," *DTC* 2/2, cols. 1556 f. Luther's position has recently been adopted by P. Althaus, *Die christliche Wahrheit: Lehrbuch der Dogmatik*, 4th ed. (Gütersloh: Bertelsmann, 1958), pp. 158 ff. (cf. P. Lengsfeld, *Tradition, Écriture et Église*, pp. 92-95).

[120] S. de Dietrich, *op. cit.*, pp. 39 f.; E. Mangenot, *art. cit.*, cols. 1557 f. (cf. A. Baudrillart, "Calvin," *ibid.*, cols. 1399 f.).

[121] See the quotations cited by S. de Dietrich, *op. cit.*, pp. 35 f.

[122] The word of God cannot be recognized by anyone at all without the testimony which the Holy Spirit renders to himself; cf. H. Bouillard, *Karl Barth, Genèse et évolution de la théologie dialectique* (Paris: Aubier, 1957), pp. 122-126. For that matter, this principle is perfectly true when it is applied to the Christian's personal faith, taken as adherence to the word of God. But it cannot be generalized and applied to the discernment of the canonical Scriptures. The problem is not solved by affirming with force: "The Bible presents itself as the canon. It is that because it has imposed itself, and still imposes itself as such on the Church" (Quoted by P. Lengsfeld, *Tradition, Écriture et Église*, p. 85).

[123] T. Zahn, *Forschungen zur Geschichte des neutestamentlichen Canons*, 8 Vols. (Erlangen: Deichert, 1881-1929); cf. H. Höpfl, "Canonicité," *DBS* 2, cols. 1038 f.

[124] H. Höpfl, *art. cit.*, cols. 1040-f.

[125] O. Cullmann, *La tradition* (Neuchâtel-Paris: Delachaux, 1953), pp. 41-52 (in *Catholiques et protestants, Confrontations théologiques* [Paris: Seuil, 1963], pp. 30-41).

intuition granted to the Church of the 2nd century to enable it to discern the writings which bore authentic divine revelation. [126]   Our own discussion of the problem will examine in order the question of the criteria of canonicity and then that of the subject capable of making that discernment.

## I. THE CRITERIA OF CANONICITY

Since it is a question here of recognizing the books to which inspiration has given the value of word of God, two elements might be involved: on the one hand, the personality of their authors, and on the other, the content or form of their testimony.   We shall see that these two elements did in fact play some role in the process of canonization of the scriptures.   But the different situations of the two Testaments in this regard oblige us to treat them separately.

### 1. The Books of the Old Testament

Our examination of the problem of inspiration led us to conclude that the prophetic charism conferred the authority of word of God upon every message transmitted by God's messenger in the exercise of his mission, either orally or in writing. [127]   It follows that every writing originating directly from a prophet possessed canonical status (in the active sense of the term), and it was for this reason that writings of such nature formed the core of collections of scriptures: the authority of Moses guaranteed the law handed down by him (whether it was written or preserved orally), and the authority of the prophets covered collections of their pronouncements.

But that was only a starting point for the scriptures.   For independently of the texts set down to be retained as they were, the message delivered by the divine messengers was also preserved in a living tradition which was shaped by charismatic functions. [128]   There the message grew, developed, and ended finally in manifold collections: from legislative codes, which gathered elements of public law, to codes of cultic law, from accounts relating the history of God's design to the biographies of the prophets, from chants employed in community prayer to sapiential and theological works.   In all of these cases the responsibility of the prophets was no longer involved at the literary

---

[126] M. Lods, "Tradition et Canon des Écritures," *Études théologiques et religieuses* 36 (1961), p. 58.   Taking the point of view of a historian, Lods admits elsewhere that certain objective criteria played a role in the process of formation of the Canon.

[127] Above, pp. 52 f., 55 f.

[128] Above, pp. 59-61.

level, but the tradition founded upon it continued to play an essential role, both as to the origin of the works and as to the source of their authority. And that, first, in a negative way, for any work which swerved from that tradition by that very fact cut itself off from the grand current of divine revelation: was this criterion of discernment not applied to the prophets themselves (Dt 13:2-6)? And in a positive way as well, for every authentic element of tradition and every legitimate development grafted onto it possessed of itself a normative value for faith and religious life; the books in which these elements were set down also tended spontaneously to acquire authority as witnesses of the word of God transmitted by the prophets.

Here, however, a new problem arose. Even if the authors of the works in question exercised charismatic functions in the people of God (as priests, chanters, scribes, etc.), it could not be taken for granted that their writings had *ipso facto* the same worth as word of God which the writings of the prophets had. There was a place in the community for a religious literature entirely faithful to tradition, but distinct from Scripture. No examples have come down from ancient times, but after the exile, and especially with the advent of the Hellenistic age, works of this kind multiplied. [129] How could it be determined whether their authors benefited from the charism of inspiration? In form and content, nothing distinguishes the opinions of Ben Sira from those preserved in the collection of *Pirqe Aboth*, nor the more recent biblical psalms from the psalms of Solomon or from the hymns of Qumran, nor the story of Tobit from that of Joseph and Asenath, and so on. The indirect criterion of prophetic approbation could have influenced works of that sort passed down from Israelite antiquity (for example, Deuteronomic literature), but to whom could one appeal when there were no longer any prophets? It is understandable why Palestinian Judaism, according to Josephus, decided to limit its canon to the age in which prophetism came to an end. [130] That explains too why the latest category of canonical works caused some discussion and retained unsettled boundaries. The employment of books in the community, in worship in particular, constituted a quite uncertain criterion: it was not the same in Palestine and in the Greek language Diaspora; it even varied

[129] A simple example: the Elephantine paschal papyrus, which is closely related to the final layer of priestly legislation preserved in the Pentateuch, was certainly sent to this community of the Egyptian Diaspora by someone who held authority within Judaism. Moreover, he intended to provide an authentic legal decision concerning the feast of Azymes; cf. P. Grelot, *VT* 4 (1954), 349-384; 5 (1955), 250-265; 6 (1956), 174-189.

[130] Flavius Josephus, *Contra Apion* I, 8. According to this text the Palestinian canon of 22 books was closed under Artaxerxes, that is, with Ezra and Nehemiah. "From Artaxerxes to our days, all the happenings have been recounted, but the same value is not accorded them as the earlier ones, because there has not been a continuous succession of prophets."

according to milieux and currents of thought! [131]  And finally, if it is true that the assistance of the Holy Spirit in some way guided the community in its recognition of the word of God, still there was no authority with the necessary competence to decide doubtful or disputed cases. [132]  The position taken by the synod of Jamnia (90-100 A. D.) reflects only the opinion of the doctors of the time, whose Pharisaic leanings are strongly marked; their opinion could by no means be imposed on the Church.  It cannot even be said that they represented exactly the Palestinian tradition of the time of Christ, for in their reaction against Essenism and Christianity they were forced to exclude from the scriptures certain works which up to then had been held in high esteem.

To settle this difficult problem, therefore, there remains no other solution than to question the mind and practice of the apostolic Church: what books, under the authority of the apostles, did it regard as inspired Scripture? Unfortunately, the explicit testimony of the New Testament is not sufficient to supply an answer, since it contains no official list.  It can only be presumed that its habitual use of the Greek Bible implied a use of the works translated or composed in that language.  We have already pointed out some indications in the New Testament itself. [133]  Furthermore, the heritage of the apostolic Church preserved in the communities of the following century attests a broader canon than that of Jamnia. [134]  It is true that in that same age certain elements of Jewish tradition preserved in the Targums or Midrashim and apocryphal works, such as Henoch or the Testaments of the Patriarchs, were also used for the edification of Christians.  But this excess at least shows that the criteria laid down by the Palestinian doctors were not considered binding. An examination of the content of a work surely played a part, since it was always required that it be in conformity with divine revelation and render testimony to Jesus Christ. [135]  As for an examination of their origin, it caused

---

[131] In this respect the sectarian narrowness of certain currents of thought would be an obstacle to the charism of biblical inspiration, even if these currents should serve as vehicles of positive values, as was the case with Essenism or Pharisaism. But it is not excluded that a message addressed by God to all of Israel be colored by its author's tendencies (1M is the work of a partisan of the Hasmoneans) or be written within a particular community (Esther in the eastern Diaspora, Wisdom in the Alexandrian community).

[132] The Spirit's assistance to the community is effected through functional charisms (cf. above, pp. 53 f.).  In the present case, leaving aside prophecy properly so called, no charism of this type carries with it an absolute certainty of inerrancy. Cf. H. Höpfl, art. cit., cols. 1032 f.

[133] Above, pp. 144 f.

[134] Above, pp. 151 ff.

[135] Cf. the reasons alleged by St. Justin (p. 151, note 55) and Tertullian (p. 153, note 69).

more problems than it solved, in the measure that those works abusively presented themselves under grand prophetic names (Isaiah, Ezra, Henoch, the patriarchs, Moses, etc.) We can conclude that an examination of internal criteria did not provide sufficient evidence of inspiration and canonicity.

## 2. The Books of the New Testament

All things being equal, the writing of the New Testament caused an analogous problem. [136] The authority of the apostles as depositories of revelation made their testimony and the practices they established the rule of Christian faith and life. That was the case no matter how that testimony and those practices were preserved in the churches: whether in a manifold living tradition, or in writings which verified their content. In any case, apostolicity was the criterion of canonicity (in the active sense). An important consequence followed: every writing emanating directly from an apostle, and composed in the exercise of his ecclesiastical functions, was covered by the apostolic charism; it was an authentic presentation of the word of the Lord working in his Church. [137] By that very fact it took its place alongside the books of the Old Testament in the category of scriptures. [138]

But the same cannot be said of that part of Christian literature whose authors did not belong to the apostolic group. It was not enough that these authors possessed a functional charism which placed them under the influence of the Holy Spirit (as prophets, teachers, pastors, evangelists, etc.) to make their literary compositions inspired in the full sense. On this point Harnack did not correctly estimate the role of charisms in the primitive Church. Admittedly, there were cases in which the redaction of a work, while leaving the redactor a wide margin of freedom, was performed under the control or with the approbation of one of the apostles; thus Silas writing 1 Peter. In this case, the apostle's authority continued to cover the book and provided a sufficient criterion for discernment. This principle could be extended, in a certain measure, to the case of the gospels which take care to present the preaching of an apostle after the latter's death (Mark presenting the preaching of Peter, or John's disciples giving his work its definitive form). But there remain all the other cases in which the most authentic apostolic tradition was expressed by writers acting in their own name: so Luke, who made use of

[136] Besides the works of Lagrange and Dewailly (p. 144, note 23), see W. S. Reilly, "Le Canon du Nouveau Testament et le critère de la canonicité," *RB* 30 (1921), 195-205 and H. Höpfl, *art. cit.*, cols. 1034-1037.

[137] Above, pp. 61 f.

[138] This is already the position of the author of the Second Letter of Peter regarding the letters of Paul (2P 3:16).

previous works and interviewed witnesses of the past; or the author of the letter to the Hebrews, who composed his exhortatory discourse in a very original manner (13:22); or the author of Revelation, if that prophet John was other than the apostle; and the redactors of some of the letters, who formulated apostolic material (the pastoral letters or those of James and Jude), even, if necessary, pseudonymously (the case of 2 Peter). How could these works be distinguished from other literature which was edifying, perfectly orthodox, but which was not equally esteemed?

It is just for this reason that the list of canonical works (in the active sense) lacked precise limits in the 2nd and 3rd centuries. On the one hand, for the edification of the faithful, quite legitimate use was made of works which had their origin in ecclesiastical tradition, and which preserved the apostolic legacy in forms very similar to those of the New Testament, with rules of composition very close to those of the inspired texts—including a literary imitation of the latter, their anthological style, even their authoritative language and false inscription: thus the Gospel of the Hebrews, the Letter of Barnabas, the *Didaché*, etc. The danger, therefore, was that propaganda works, suspect or frankly heretical, should gain entrance into the churches under grand names. As a reaction to that danger, on the other hand, there was a tendency to connect the apostolicity of writings to the proof of their literary authenticity. And that led to doubts about their authority whenever such authenticity was contested for reasons of internal criticism or external tradition. Such was the case for the letter to the Hebrews and 2 Peter in the West, for Revelation and some catholic letters in the East. These opposite dangers show the insufficiency of objective criteria when applied alone. Since the inspiration of authors is an unverifiable fact, the real problem is to discern which works the churches of the 2nd century received as normative, if not from the apostolic generation itself, at least from that which knew the apostles, because there could have been an interval between the oral transmission of the apostolic preaching and its written record (the classic case of the gospel of Mark). That is a question of fact, difficult to settle; that is why it received different solutions in different times and in different churches.

## II. WHO CAN PERFORM THIS DISCERNMENT?

Scripture alone, therefore, does not supply all the necessary elements to establish the canon. Whether it is a question of the books of the Old Testament used in the churches, or of those of the New Testament composed for the Christian churches, we are forced to turn to ancient ecclesiastical tradition as the heir of apostolic tradition. On this fundamental point Catholic theology finds itself in accord with a good number of contemporary Protestants, such as O. Cullman and M. Lods. The differences begin when it comes to interpreting the act of the Church in laying down the principle of a canon, and even more, of estimating the proper value of ecclesiastical tradition in this field and the part that its authorities played. Here the divergent positions reflect the differing ecclesiologies on which they depend. When we discussed Scripture and Tradition above, we saw that neither ecclesiastical tradition nor the magisterium which forms it can be regarded as merely human recording mechanisms. [139] And that not only because the obedience of faith subjects them to the word of God transmitted by the apostles, but because the Holy Spirit continues to act in the Church through his charisms, and especially through those which have to do with the offices of teaching and ruling. [140] After having inspired the apostles to announce the revelation brought by Christ, and then inspired the sacred authors to set down in writing what the scriptures have preserved, the Spirit has always assisted, and continues to assist the Church in safeguarding that revelation in its entirety. It is at this precise point that the authentic recognition of the inspired books and the formulation of the canon find their explanation.

Protestant theology cannot be faulted when it appeals to the witness of the Holy Spirit to explain this fundamental fact. But it must be determined who is the subject who receives that witness. It is neither the individual believer, nor yet the Church of one determined age (in practice, that of the 2nd century). It is the post-apostolic Church in all the centuries of its history, which is shaped by charismatic offices and governed by a magisterium, which in matters of faith has the benefit of infallibility in order to preserve (not to modify or amplify!) the revealed data. [141] It is true that in the matter of the canon of Scripture ecclesiastical tradition went through variations in detail. But before drawing an argument from that fact, the reason for it should be taken into consideration. When certain authors or certain churches abusively treated some of the apocrypha as Scripture, the reason was always a misunderstanding concerning their origin and literary authenticity. When, on the contrary, the deuterocanonical books of the two Testaments were rejected, the reason was never in order to return to ancient usage, but was the critical difficulties that were raised in their regard: exclusion from the Jewish

---

[139] Above, pp. 24 f.; cf. Y. Congar, *Tradition and Traditions*, pp. 38-42; 417-424.

[140] Thus we would complete the suggestion put forward by M. Lods, *art. cit.*, p. 157, note 7, in order to define the manner in which this intuition of the church's faith operates and can be verified.

[141] P. Lengsfeld, *op. cit.*, pp. 117-123.

Palestinian canon, questionable literary authenticity, etc. In short, recourse to internal criteria would introduce a disruptive element into common usage, so much so that attachment to that usage led men such as Origen, St. Augustine, and St. Thomas Aquinas to separate the critical questions related to the problem from that of canonicity. [142] These facts must be kept in mind to grasp the real spirit of authentic ecclesiastical tradition, both eastern and western, in the patristic and Middle Ages.

When the Protestant reform put forward the well- known difficulties in order to exclude the deuterocanonical books from the Bible, it is understandable that the Council of Trent should have rejected those objections and retained the common usage sanctioned long ago by the African councils and by Roman documents from the same period (the letter of Innocent I to Exuperius of Toulouse). The Council introduced nothing new. The authority it invoked made no pretense of substituting itself for ancient ecclesiastical tradition, and still less for apostolic authority. It merely performed its normal function, with the assistance of the Holy Spirit, in settling definitively an obscure or contested point of ecclesiastical tradition. Its decree, moreover, is very clear on this point: *"Si quis autem libros ipsos integros cum omnibus suis partibus, prout in ecclesia catholica legi consueverunt et in veteri latina editione habentur, pro sacris et canonicis non susceperit,* etc." [143] The First Vatican Council did no more than repeat these terms. [144]

## II. THE EXTENSION OF CANONICITY

We can take as our starting point here the definition of the Council of Trent and analyze its meaning. All of the sacred books which make up the Latin Vulgate are received as canonical *cum omnibus suis partibus*. No distinction is made between varying degrees or varying modes of canonicity, for the latter is independent both of the personality of the sacred authors and of the more or less rich or edifying quality of their message. It attests no more than that divine inspiration cooperated in the composition of all the books in question. In speaking of the Latin Vulgate, the Council obviously did not canonize that version as such. It recognized it as "authentic" in all the public acts of the

---

[142] St. Augustine's position in regard to the Letter to the Hebrews: *De peccatorum meritis et remissione* I, 50 (*PL* 44, 137). On St. Thomas' position, cf. C. Spicq, *Esquisse...*, p. 146.

[143] *Ench. B.* 60. "If anyone refuses to accept these whole books and every part of them just as they have been accustomed to be read in the Catholic Church, and which appear in the ancient Latin Vulgate version, as sacred and canonical...."

[144] *Ibid.*, 57.

ecclesiastical ministry [145] (in the Latin church, to be sure). But the encyclical *Divino afflante Spiritu* made quite clear that "authentic" is to be understood in a juridical sense: the Latin Vulgate contains no doctrinal error and is in conformity with the normative interpretation of Scripture which is part of the tradition of the Church. [146] All the versions of Scripture which date from after the apostolic age are in the same situation as regards canonicity. Since canonicity is linked to inspiration, it can apply only to the original texts written by the inspired writers. Hence the necessity of returning to the original texts, beyond the translations, which are secondary witnesses of them, and to reconstitute the text through critical study. [147] There remain, however, three questions to be examined: 1) that of lost works which were in use in Judaism or the apostolic Church; 2) that of the Greek version of the Old Testament; 3) that of the deuterocanonical books of the Old Testament whose original Semitic text is lost.

### I. LOST WORKS

We said a few words about this problem when speaking of inspiration. [148] It will be sufficient here to recall the essentials of what we have already said. On the one hand, every book written by a prophet or an apostle in the exercise of his office must be considered inspired, and therefore as canonical. On the other, every book considered as word of God by a prophet, an apostle or an inspired author ought also to be held as such. In the first case, inspiration is established by the charismatic office of the author; in the second, by the testimony (at least implicit) of another inspired person. We gave some examples of this above. Outside these cases, it is impossible to prove the fact of inspiration, since no other charismatic function carries with it inspiration as a necessary consequence, except prophecy understood in the sense of Heb 1:1, and the apostolate in the strict sense. Anything beyond this is pure speculation; its only interest is in reminding us that our present Bible is the residue of an inspired literature which was certainly more extensive. It is superfluous to imagine that a disposition of providence rightly caused the disappearance of all the works which were not to become part of the canon, and only those. [149] As a matter of fact, the canonical literature of the people of God, in spite of vigilant care, has experienced accidents of transmission

[145] *Ibid.*, 61.
[146] *Ibid.*, 549.
[147] *Ibid.*, 548.
[148] Above, pp. 76 f..
[149] This is Calvin's view on the writings of the New Testament; cf. S. de Dietrich, *Le renouveau biblique*, p. 39.

due to all sorts of causes. But it is useless to split hairs further over books which we no longer have.

## II. THE SEPTUAGINT AND THE CANON OF SCRIPTURE [150]

### *1. History of the Question*

*a) Belief in the inspiration of the Septuagint in Christian antiquity.*—Belief in the inspiration of the Septuagint was born in Alexandrian Judaism. The *Letter of Aristeas* recounts the legend of the 72 elders called together by Ptolemy II Philadelphos to translate the Pentateuch, but limits itself to a discrete suggestion on the question of its inspiration. [151] However, at the same time that the New Testament was being formed, Philo of Alexandria states it explicitly: "Those who read the two texts, both the Hebrew and the translation... call not simply translators, but hierophants and prophets, those men who were able to follow, with transparent expressions, the so pure thought of Moses." [152] Now rabbinic Judaism preserved a partial echo of this doctrine, as an opinion of Rabbi Juda the Prince, the compiler of the Mishna, attests: "The Holy One put his counsel in the heart of each of them, and they were of one mind; nevertheless, they wrote:... (there follow 13 passages in which the LXX altered the Hebrew text)." [153]

That explains why the apostolic Church of Greek language, while retaining a real liberty in its manner of citing the texts, made use of the Greek Bible the same way that Palestinian Judaism used the original Hebrew, that is, as an inspired text. It is probable that the reaction of the synod of Jamnia (90-100) against the Septuagint, and against the deuterocanonical books it contained, was in part motivated by the place they held in Christian theology and apologetics. Having reduced the canon to the 22 books recognized in Palestine, they decided to undertake a new Greek version more faithful to the original Hebrew. [154] An echo of this controversy between Jews

[150] For a detailed treatment of this question, see P. Grelot, "Sur l'inspiration et la canonicité de la Septante," *Sciences ecclésiastiques* 17 (1964), 386-418.

[151] A Pelletier, *Lettre d'Aristée à Philocrate* (Sources chrétiennes 89) (Paris: Cerf, 1962), p. 78. The author then traces the development of this legend through the ages, and presents in French translation the principal relevant texts.

[152] Philo of Alexandria, *Life of Moses* 2, 37. See the other texts of Philo in A. Pelletier, *op. cit.*, pp. 78-81.

[153] *bT*, *Megillah* 9a. Text in L. Goldschmidt, *Der babylonische Talmud* 3, pp. 564 f.

[154] B. J. Roberts, *The Old Testament Text and Versions* (Cardiff: Univ. Press, 1951), p. 122, makes note of this polemical anti-Christian character in the version of Aquila. His dependence upon Aqiba is minutely examined by D. Barthélemy, *Les devanciers d'Aquila*, *VT* Supplement 10 (Leyden: Brill, 1963), pp. 3-30.

and Christians can be found in St. Justin, who accuses his interlocutor Trypho of having falsified the text of Scripture by changing certain messianic passages, which he himself cites according to the Greek text. [155] Granted that in recounting the legend popularized by the *Letter of Aristeas*, he does not mention the inspiration of its translators, [156] but on the other hand he extends that miraculous origin to "the books containing the prophecies." [157] After him the inspiration of the 70 (or 72) ancients is positively attested by St. Irenaeus, the *Cohortatio ad Graecos* (which complicates the legend still more), Clement of Alexandria, St. Cyril of Jerusalem, and others, [158]—which amounts to recognizing the Greek version of the Old Testament as canonical. The fathers who are the least explicit at least admit its incontestable authority, a certain indication of a disposition of providence which watched over its preparation. [159] Even St. Jerome, who devoted his energies to discredit the later amplifications of the legend of the Septuagint, [160] who made a clear distinction between the charism of the prophets and that of translators, [161] and who attempted to bring the Church back to the *Veritas hebraica*, admits nonetheless that the Greek translators, "*Spiritu sancto pleni, ea quae vera fuerant transtulerunt.*" [162] His contemporary St. Augustine is still more assertive. [163] The only problem that was raised in this regard in Christian antiquity concerned which books were translated by Ptolemy's ancients; St. Jerome thought they were limited to the Pentateuch alone. [164] But even this discussion remains speculative, since in practice all the Greek-language fathers made use of the Septuagint as a canonical text in its own right. Origen, in his letter to Julius Africanus, is very precise: The Bible of the Church is the Greek Bible. [165] In the West, furthermore, the Latin Vulgate

[155] St. Justin, *Dialogue with Trypho* 71, 1-2; cf. D. Barthélemy, *op. cit.*, pp. 203 f.

[156] St. Justin, *Apologia* I, 31, 1-2.

[157] *Ibid.*, 31, 2.

[158] See *Sciences ecclésiastiques* 17 (1964), pp. 391 f.; texts in A. Pelletier, *Lettre d'Aristée à Philocrate*, pp. 81-86.

[159] Thus St. Hilary, *Tractatus in Psalmos* 2, 3 (*PL* 9, 262-264; A. Pelletier, *op. cit.*, p. 85). Likewise St. John Chrysostom, *In Matthaeum* 5, 2 (*PG* 57, 56-57).

[160] St. Jerome, *Comm. in Ezechielem* 33, 23 (*PL* 25, 323).

[161] *Praefatio in Pentateuchum* (*PL* 28, 152).

[162] ("Filled with the Holy Spirit, they translated whatever was true.") *Praefatio in librum Paralipomenon juxta LXX interpretes* (*PL* 29, 402) It must be conceded that this quote antedates his undertaking a new Latin version from the Hebrew.

[163] St. Augustine, *The City of God* 18, 42-43 (*PL* 41, 602-604); *De doctrina christiana* 2, 15 (*PL* 34, 46). Texts quoted by A. Pelletier, *op. cit.*, pp. 91-93.

[164] St. Jerome, *Comm. in Michaeam* 2, 9 (*PL* 25, 1171). It should be noted that in this passage of Micah Jerome underlines the differences between the *Veritas hebraica* and the Septuagint, but he nonetheless comments on the two texts to show that they apply to Christ and to the Church.

[165] Origen, *Letter to Julius Africanus* 4 (*PG* 11, 57-60).

172

of that time, that is, the *Vetus Latina* in all its forms, was a translation of the Greek text, and the preference of St. Jerome for the *Veritas hebraica* could not but have seemed the interest of an isolated scholar.

b) *The acceptance of the Septuagint in the Latin West.*—In the Greek Orient, the authority of the Septuagint remained intact through the centuries. Just one practical measure was taken in regard to the book of Daniel: since its translation was defective, Theodotion's version was substituted for it in current usage. [166] In the Latin West, on the contrary, the situation underwent profound change. From the age of the decline of Latin, the authority of St. Jerome as translator took firm hold; as a consequence, his version supplanted the *Vetus latina* as the Vulgate, and to his version writers turned to find a *Veritas hebraica* [167] to which very few had direct access. With that, the Septuagint appeared as only one more Greek version among the many gathered by Origen in the columns of the Hexapla. In the 12th century, Rupert of Deutz manifests a certain diffidence toward it [168]; Hugh of St. Victor, who followed St. Jerome in rejecting the amplifications added to the Letter of Aristeas, cites the versions of Aquila, Symmachus and Theodotion alongside that of the Septuagint. [169] That was only a beginning, for in the 16th century a growing number of scholars rejected the Letter of Aristeas itself as apocryphal (Scaliger, Louis Vivès). [170] Then the Septuagint became no more than an anonymous work completed gradually by numerous authors. In these circumstances, how could the theologians maintain its inspiration, when such a name as Cajetan hesitated over that of the deutero-canonical books, whose literary authenticity did not seem certain to him? [171]

This reversal of opinion gained more and more ground. Granted that Bossuet [172] in the 17th century still defended the historicity of the account of Aristeas, within the limits set down by St. Jerome, against Richard Simon, [173] who considered it a legend. But by the 18th century the process

[166] See the critical edition of the two texts in J. Ziegler, *Susanna, Daniel, Bel et Draco* (Göttingen: Vandenhoek & Ruprecht, 1954). P. Kahle, *The Cairo Geniza* (Oxford: Blackwell, 1959), pp. 252 f., remarks that this operation was due to the influence of Origen and therefore to a critical concern.

[167] This is already the case with St. Bede; cf. C. Spicq, *Esquisse d'une histoire de l'exégèse au moyen-âge*, p. 31.

[168] Rupert of Deutz, *De divinis officiis* 17 (*PL* 170, 280 f.).

[169] Hugh of St. Victor, *De scripturis et scriptoribus inspiratis* 9 (*PL* 175, 17). Concerning the opposition to the Septuagint during the 12th century, see C. Spicq, *op. cit.*, p. 107.

[170] J. Scaliger, *Ad Chronicum Eusebii*, cited in *PL* 27, 483. L. Vives, *In Augustini "De civitate Dei"* 18, 42 (Basel, 1522).

[171] Above, p. 159.

[172] J. B. Bossuet, *Praefatio in Proverbiis* in *Œuvres complètes*, ed. Vivès 1, p. 449.

[173] Richard Simon, *Histoire critique du Vieux Testament* (Rotterdam: Leers, 1685), pp. 186 f.

had reached its conclusion. Not only did Dom Calmet reject the legend of the Septuagint, but he found arguments to deny the ancient Greek version's inspiration: "For the Holy Spirit cannot contradict himself, by speaking in one way in Hebrew and another way in Greek; he cannot fall into error, as those translators obviously fell in many passages of their translation." [174] Though the reasoning is somewhat sophistic, founded upon a quite inexact notion of inerrancy, it won general acceptance: Dom Calmet's opinion was common among the theologians of the 19th and 20th centuries, who took little care to consult the ancient tradition of the Greek church, [175] of which many of them seem actually to have been unaware.

*c) Toward a return to the position of the fathers.*—Since 1950 the situation has changed in the opposite direction. Modern exegesis has undertaken to dispel certain equivocations which encumbered the discussion of the problem since the Middle Ages, and even since antiquity. It makes a distinction between the questions of literary authenticity and canonicity; it considers scriptural inspiration a charism shared by a great number of men, sometimes absolutely unknown; it no longer considers the doctrinal inerrancy of a text and the exactness of a translation as equivalent or intrinsically related notions. Thus, returning to the practice of the ancient Church, Fr. Benoit [176] in 1951 and Fr. Auvray [177] in 1952 invited theologians to reconsider the whole question. They did not win unanimous following. Shortly before them, J. Schildenberger [178] expressed himself hardly in favor of the hypothesis, but since then the new edition of Höpfl-Leloir's *Introductio generalis* formally excludes it. [179] A. Barucq and H. Cazelles in *Introduction to the Old*

[174] A. Calmet, *Dissertation pour servir de prolégomènes de l'Écriture sainte* 1/2 (Paris: 1720), p. 81. For the rest, this *Dissertation sur la version des septante interprètes* (pp. 74-93) manifests an excellent understanding of Jewish and patristic evidence.
[175] Belief in the inspiration of the Septuagint "has never been more than a personal opinion in the Church.... It has never been taught by the Church. Only a few fathers held it, based on their belief in the legend of the separate cells.... St. Jerome strongly opposed it, and St. Chrysostom did not speak of it" (E. Mangenot, "Inspiration," *DB* 5, col. 1629). It would be useless to enumerate all the authors who share this sentiment. Their agreement is well summed up by R. Cornely—A. Merk, *Manuel d'introduction à toutes les saintes Écritures* 1 (Paris: Lethielleux, 1930), pp. 185 f.
[176] P. Benoit, "La Septante est-elle inspirée?" *Vom Wort des Leben, Festschrift für Max Meinerz* (Münster: Aschendorff, 1951) (reprinted in *Exégèse et théologie 1*, pp. 3-12). This article has since been completed by a more detailed examination of patristic evidence: "L'inspiration des Septante d'après les Pères," *L'homme devant Dieu* 1 (Paris: Montaigne, 1964), pp. 169-187.
[177] P. Auvray, "Comment se pose le problème de l'inspiration des Septante," *RB* 61 (1952), 321-336.
[178] J. Schildenberger, *Vom Geheimnis des Gotteswortes*, pp. 476 f.
[179] Höpfl—L. Leloir, *Introductio generalis in sacram Scripturam*, 6th ed. (Rome-Naples: M. D'Auria, 1958), p. 58 : "Versions... cannot be called inspired, except equivalently or mediately," which holds for the Septuagint as well.

*Testament* set forth objectively the arguments in its favor, but in the end they reserve judgment. [180] Everyone agrees that, although the Septuagint does not always adhere to the original text, it nevertheless represents substantially the word of God which the original contains; that it is an authoritative, faithful, and even privileged witness to the tradition in which revelation was preserved before the time of Christ, not without a certain assistance of the Holy Spirit. [181] Are there sound reasons to confer on it still greater authority by seeing in it the word of God in the strict sense?

## 2. Examination of the Question

*a) The difficulties.*—The principal difficulties raised against the inspiration and canonicity of the Septuagint have long been known. The first is the legendary character of the account of Pseudo-Aristeas. Already St. Jerome reacted against the supplementary passages attested by the *Cohortatio ad Graecos;* there can be no doubt that if he had known modern critical conclusions, he would have rejected the whole story of the 72 ancients, translators of the Pentateuch. Once this fundamental story has been discredited, do not all the theological conclusions which Philo and the fathers of the Church drew from it fall along with it? There is, secondly, the fact put forward by Dom Calmet [182]: the errors, mistranslations, false translations, and meaningless translations made by the translators. While their overall fidelity to revealed doctrine is not in doubt, it must be admitted that in more than one case they were mistaken in rendering into Greek the meaning of individual texts. This defect is so apparent that the Eastern Church officially substituted Theodotion's version of the book of Daniel for that of the Septuagint. How can that be reconciled with the inerrancy of the sacred authors? At most, the Septuagint might be accorded the same sort of juridical authenticity that the Council of Trent extended to the Latin Vulgate. [183] Finally, a closer look at the whole question will make it apparent that the inspiration of the Septuagint is a useless hypothesis. Certainly, the notion of a certain divine assistance watching over the production of this version, in view of its importance in the primitive Church, can be maintained. But it is important here to distinguish the various charisms of the Spirit. As St. Jerome remarked: the charism of the prophet is one thing, that of the

[180] A. Robert—A. Feuillet, *Interpreting the Scriptures,* pp. 27 f.

[181] "It cannot be denied that divine providence guarded lest they should translate the sacred books so badly into Greek that their translation could not be called a trustworthy font of revelation" (A. Vaccari in *Institutiones biblicae,* p. 351).

[182] Above, p. 173, note 174.

[183] Above, p 169, note 145.

translator, another.[184]   And St. John Chrysostom, still more clearly, said that God inspired Moses and Ezra to compose and restore the Pentateuch, sent the prophets, and disposed (ᾠκονόμησεν) translators.[185]   Such a functional charism suffices in the present case, and it would be useless to add the scriptural charism.

*b) Positive arguments for inspiration.*—The above arguments are only apparently convincing, for the opposing thesis can present much stronger ones.

In the first place must be considered the eminent place the Septuagint occupied in the history of revelation.   We have seen[186] that revelation is expressed in a specific language which, while making use of the Hebrew and Greek thought structures, in some manner recasts them in order to make them bearers of the word of God.   For the Hebrew, this operation undoubtedly took place within the very recipients of that word, the prophets in the broad sense of the term.   And for the Greek?   In the New Testament age, apostolic preaching found at its disposition a linguistic instrument already prepared.   That enabled them to announce the gospel in Greek by resorting liberally to scriptural formulas in current use in Judaism of that time. Whence came those expressions, if not from the Alexandrian translators of the Old Testament?[187]   As early as the 1st century before Christ, the author of Wisdom already made use of the product of their labor.   How can one fail to see in that the effect of a positive intervention of the Holy Spirit? From this point of view alone it would be legitimate to speak of an inspiration of those translators, and stand by the expression of St. Clement of Alexandria, who saw in their work a "prophecy in Greek" proclaimed for Greeks.[188]

Secondly, it must be recalled that the Septuagint is not a simple translation.   In more than one case it adapts the original text; it interprets it in the light of living tradition; it gives it a charismatic interpretation which deepens the data of revelation.   Now when the New Testament appropriated the text of the Bible in order to read in it the outline of the mystery of Christ, it assumed it in the form of its expression in Greek, which is richer than the original Hebrew.[189]   Thus, for example, in Is 7:14, the mystery of the virginal conception is already outlined, and the richer Septuagint text appears in the

---

[184] Above, p. 171, note 161.
[185] St. John Chrysostom, *Homilies on the Letter to the Hebrews* 8, 4 (*PG* 63, 74 f.).
[186] Above, pp. 86 ff.
[187] J. Coste, "La première expérience de traduction biblique, La Septante," *LMD* 53 (1958), 56-88.
[188] Clement of Alexandria, *Stromata* 1, 22 (*PG* 8, 894 f.).
[189] P. Benoit, in the first article cited on page 173, note 176, gives three examples: Is 7:14, Ps 16:8-11, and Gn 12:3.

citation of Ps 16:8-11 in Ac 2:25-31 and 13:35-37, in that of Gn 12:3 and 22:18 in Ac 3:25 and Ga 3:8-9, and in that of Am 9:11-12 in Ac 15:16-17. [190] In these cases the translators of the Greek Bible appear as the instruments of God, entrusted with setting down in written form the progress of revelation as a positive preparation for the gospel. There is no reason to restrict this role only to the passages which the authors of the New Testament cited explicitly. It is proper rather to consider those translators as real authors who, in transferring the word of God from Hebrew to Greek, in more or less large measure reshaped it. [191] Once again, scriptural inspiration is highly fitting for the exercise of such a function.

We have just mentioned reshaped texts. In some cases it would be better to speak simply of creation. The Septuagint, in fact, contains texts which are not found (or are no longer found) in the original Hebrew. The most important of these are obviously the books or parts of them which have been called deuterocanonical. Must it then be admitted that for these texts some original inspired text definitively escaped the Church's grasp? [192] Besides these long sections, there are other additions of less importance, scattered here and there (for example, in Pr 4:27; 6:8; 7:1; 8:21; 9:10; 9:18; 10:4, etc.). Rather than exclude them a priori from the canon of Scripture, should we not second the remark of St. Ambrose [193]: it is not without utility (non otiose) that the translators made additions to the Hebrew text? Should it be necessary, on the other hand, according to the ironic reflection of Origen, [194] for the Church to ask the Jews for an uncontaminated text in order to correct its Bible?

This collection of convergent arguments invites at least admission of great probability for the thesis of the inspiration and canonicity of the Septuagint. To advance from probability to certitude, it is necessary, as in all questions relative to the canon, to resort to ancient ecclesiastical tradition, as the heir of apostolic tradition, for its attitude toward the Septuagint. Now the ancient Church sought in the Septuagint the basis of its theological language; it took advantage of the doctrinal progress evident in it; it employed as Scripture all the books, parts of books and minor additions included in it; it unanimously spoke of it as a canonical text, and often as an inspired text. The reaction

[190] E. Haenchen, Die Apostelgeschichte (Göttingen: Vandenhoeck & Ruprecht, 1961), p. 394. An echo of the Septuagint is to be found in Ac 15:14 according to J. Dupont, "Laos ex ethnon (Act 15,14)," NTS 3 (1956-1957), 47-50.

[191] J. Coste, "Le texte grec d'Isaïe 25, 1-5," RB 63 (1954), 35-66. Cf. I. L. Seeligmann, The Septuagint Version of Isaiah: A Discussion of its Problems (Leiden: Brill, 1948), pp. 95-121.

[192] This question will be treated below, pp. 178 ff.

[193] St. Ambrose, Hexaemeron 3, 5, 20 (PL 14, 165).

[194] Origen, Letter to Julius Africanus 4 (PG 11, 57-60).

of St. Jerome in favor of the *Veritas hebraica* cannot blot out the attachment of all Christian antiquity to the *Veritas graeca.*

c) *Conclusion.*—In spite of a long eclipse, whose reasons we have examined, there is a good case for returning to the traditional position which incorporates the Septuagint as such in the canon of sacred books, without prejudice to the peculiar value which the Hebrew original retains. In this case, the authors of this version, working in the name of the community to which they belonged, benefited from a suitable functional charism: the charism of translator, distinct from that of prophecy, as St. John Chrysostom and St. Jerome justly pointed out [195]; the charism of scribes as well, authorized witnesses to living tradition. But since their labor produced books which the Church, and the authors of the New Testament already, employed as the word of God, it must be admitted that that functional charism received moreover the prolongation of the scriptural charism, as in the case of all the inspired scribes. [196] The Septuagint, therefore, is not just one version of the Old Testament among many. It will be noted that this view is in no way opposed to the definition of the Council of Trent. That definition was directed entirely against the shortened canon of the first reformers, and did not touch the question of the Greek Bible. By sanctioning the canon of the ancient African synods, it adopted Origen's position, and we have already noted his clear position on the point in question. Nothing, therefore, would prevent the extraordinary magisterium of the Church from completing that definition, if it sees fit, by recognizing that the Old Testament is inspired and canonical under its two forms, Hebrew and Greek. [197]

[195] This distinction is to be found already in St. Irenaeus: "For one and the same Spirit of God, who through the prophets foretold the circumstances of the Lord's coming, through the elders rightly interpreted what had been rightly prophesied; and the same announced through the apostles that the fulness of the time of adoption had arrived..." *Adversus haereses* 3, 21, 4 (*PG* 7, 950; the original Greek of the passage has been lost).

[196] This conclusion poses a problem for the Book of Ezra, since the Greek Ezra which appears in the Septuagint does not agree with the Hebrew Ezra of the Jewish canon, but with the composite text of 3 Ezr (above, p. 144, note 21); on this subject, see the bibliography given on p. 143, note 71. The list set down at Trent was directed against the mutilated canon of the Protestants, and not against the ancient canon of the Greek churches; it cannot therefore be used to settle the question under consideration.

[197] This general judgment leaves untouched the question of the primitive text of the Septuagint. P. Kahle, *The Cairo Geniza*, pp. 249-252, argued from the disagreement between the New Testament and the Septuagint to deny the existence of a uniform Greek translation before the New Testament. But that is rather a question of the diverse recensions the Greek translation underwent in the Jewish world. On this question, see D. Barthélemy, *Les devanciers d'Aquila* (Leyden: Brill, 1963). It should be noted that the same problem comes up for the Hebrew text of the Old Testament, of which there were likewise diverse recensions. Our conclusion is in accord with that of D. Barthélemy in his conference at the Journées Bibliques in Louvain, 1963 (cf. *ETL* 39 [1963], pp. 829 f.).

*d) Solution to difficulties.*—The difficulties mentioned above will now appear to carry very little weight. The legendary character of the Letter of Aristeas and the later expansions added to it leave the basic problem untouched. In fact, it was not that legend which gave rise to a belief in the authority and inspiration of the Greek version; it was rather the belief that created the legend, to provide it a concrete expression and a literary support. Every Catholic theologian knows that it was the same for the belief in the assumption of the Virgin Mary: the legendary account of the *Transitus Mariae* is not the foundation of faith, but the result of it. There is no difficulty in dropping the legend and preserving the faith. The critical exorcism begun by St. Jerome, and completed by the scholars of the 16th century with respect to Ptolemy's ancients, constitutes, from this point of view, a useful pruning which serves to clarify the problem. But there is no reason to draw unjustified conclusions from it. Secondly, the objection which Dom Calmet drew from errors of translation rests on a sophism, for it did not take into account the truth of the Greek text from a doctrinal point of view, but judges its exactness in relation to the Hebrew original which underlies it. And that overlooks the fact that scriptural inspiration does not have as its aim to render authors perfect and infallible in every respect, but to make them authorized witnesses of the word of God through the message they put into writing. The doctrinal value of their text is, therefore, compatible with any imperfections imaginable, including false interpretations of the Hebrew and the phrases which transliterate the Hebrew without giving it any sense. As for the pretended uselessness of the hypothesis, it has been pointed out in passing what must be thought of it. The fault of the 19th-century theologians was to have too narrow a concept of scriptural inspiration, which consequently was hardly adaptable to the various situations of the inspired authors. The concept we have worked out above fits without difficulty the undertaking of the Greek translators of the Hebrew Bible.

### III. DEUTEROCANONICAL BOOKS WHOSE SEMITIC ORIGINAL IS LOST

#### *1. The Problem*

It is a fact that many deuterocanonical books and passages of the Old Testament exist only in firsthand or secondhand versions, among which the Septuagint is the oldest. In many cases it is supposed that the original was written in Hebrew: the first book of Maccabees, Baruch and the letter of Jeremiah (except probably [198] Ba 4:5—5:9), Ben Sira, the additions to

---

[198] O. C. Whitehouse, "The Book of Baruch" in R. H. Charles, *The Apocrypha and Pseudepigrapha of the Old Testament* I (Oxford: Clarendon, 1913), pp. 572 ff.

Daniel [199] (but not those of Esther [200]). But St. Jerome made the Latin translation of Judith and Tobit from an Aramaic text (the original or a targum?), and from the caves of Qumran have come fragments of Tobit in Hebrew and in Aramaic (which is the original?). The Greek version is usually literal enough to be a substantial representation of the primitive text. Nevertheless, there are two quite different recensions of Tobit [201]: on the one side, codex *Sinaiticus*, the *Vetus Latina*, the unpublished Qumran fragments, and the late Aramaic retranslation published by Neubauer [202]; on the other, codex *Alexandrinus* and *Vaticanus*; the Vulgate makes still other minor additions, whose origin raises further problems. The situation of Ben Sira [203] is still more complicated: the Greek and Syriac versions, which were both based on the Hebrew, do not agree; the Hebrew fragments recovered from the Cairo Geniza contain another type of text; the *Vetus Latina*, which was apparently translated from the Greek, presents still other variants and additions.

The problem is the following: for all of these books, where is the inspired and canonical text to be found? In theory there are three possibilities: 1) Either the original Semitic text was the only one inspired; in this case, it is hopelessly lost, unless some fragments of it might be found in the Cairo Geniza or at Qumran. And if direct contact with it is impossible, how can it be recognized, since the versions present substantially divergent texts? 2) Or the Greek version is the only one inspired, as the inspired adaptation of an originally profane book. The case of the second book of Maccabees,

fragments found in cave 2 at Qumran are too restricted to allow a fruitful comparison (published by M. Baillet, *Les petites grottes de Qumran* [Oxford: Clarendon, 1962], pp. 75 ff.).

[199] W. H. Bennett in R. H. Charles, *op. cit.*, pp. 627 ff., and T. Witton Davies, *ibid.*, pp. 641 f., 655 f. There is scarcely any doubt except for the connecting passage Dn 3:46-50, which fills a real void in the Massoretic Aramaic text.

[200] A. Lefèvre in Robert—Feuillet, *Introduction to the Old Testament*, p. 551, is right in writing: "These are not properly speaking supplements, but there are two different editions of Esther." There are besides two quite different recensions of this Greek edition, and as J. A. F. Gregg remarks in R. H. Charles, *op. cit.*, p. 669, there might be in the pieces preserved the trace of several hands.

[201] D. C. Simpson in Charles, *op. cit.*, pp. 174-182 (before the discoveries at Qumran).

[202] A. Neubauer, *The Book of Tobit: A Chaldee Text* (Oxford: Clarendon, 1868) (which reproduces the Latin version of the *Itala*).

[203] W. O. E. Oesterley, *Ecclesiasticus* (Cambridge Bible, 1922). W. O. E. Oesterley—G. H. Box in Charles, *op. cit.*, p. 268-517. This commentary took into account the Hebrew fragments discovered at the beginning of this century. New fragments have been published since then: J. Marcus in *JQR* n.s. 21 (1930-1931), 223-240; E. Vogt in *Biblica* 40 (1959), 1060-1062; 41 (1960), 184-190 (following the Hebrew published by J. Schirman); a more careful edition by A. di Lella, "The Recently Identified Leaves of Sirach in Hebrew," *Biblica* 45 (1964) 153-167. The

an abridgement of the work of Jason of Cyrene, might suggest something of this sort [204]; the only problem then would be the textual criticism of the Greek text.    3) Or both the Semitic original and its Greek version are equally inspired and canonical.


## 2. Examination of the Solutions

a) *Only the Semitic original is inspired.*—This hypothesis contradicts all the observations we made in our discussion of the problem of the inspiration of the Septuagint.  Besides, it leads to insoluble problems, since the texts we possess are contradictory.  Even admitting that in the case of Tobit the evidence provided by the Qumran fragments clearly indicates that the text of *Alexandrinus* is secondary, [205] what about Ben Sira?  Having taken such liberties with the original text, are its translations really trustworthy witnesses of the word of God?  And if it should turn out that the Cairo Geniza fragments, far from being a retranslation, preserve a substantially authentic recension of the text, [206] does it follow that the Church will have to substitute it for what was so long its Bible, to go back to a line of reasoning that Origen had already criticized?  It is decidedly better to visualize the whole matter differently.

b) *Only the Septuagint is inspired.*—The preceding difficulty disappears when the position explained above on the inspiration and canonicity of the Septuagint is adopted.  Nothing seemingly remains to be resolved but problems of textual criticism, for example, to choose one of the two recensions of Tobit.  For Ben Sira, the matter seems clear: "The Hebrew text of Ecclesiasticus was never canonical, neither in the Christian Church nor in the Jewish community... There was never any canonical text but the Greek text and the Latin version." [207]  Concerning this last, it is certainly a matter of equivalent canonicity, which in reality belongs to the original Greek it

---

[204] On the problem of Second Maccabees, see J. Starcky, *Les livres des Maccabées*, *BJ* (Paris, 1961), pp. 17 ff.  It is not so certain that the religious character of the work can be attributed to the abbreviator alone, since he himself seems explicitly to say the opposite (2M 2:19-23).  It would seem better, therefore, to leave the question open.

[205] Is it certain that as often as there are two different recensions of the same work they cannot be equally inspired and canonical?  Ex 20:1-17 and Dt 5:6-22 present two different recensions of the dialogue which are equally authoritative.

[206] There should be no haste to reach a conclusion, for the problem is complex.  See the conclusions of A. di Lella, "Qumran and the Geniza Fragments of Sirach," *CBQ* 24 (1962), pp. 266 ff.; "Authenticity of the Geniza Fragments of Sirach," *Biblica* 44 (1963), 171-200.

[207] H. Duesberg—P. Auvray, *L'Ecclésiastique, BJ*, pp. 21 f.

represents. But can we be content with this restrictive solution? The foreword which the translator of Ben Sira added to this grandfather's work clearly insists on its benefit for "those who, domiciled abroad, wish to study how to fit themselves and their manners for living according to the Law" (34-35); he seems to liken it to "the Law and the Prophets and the others that followed them" (1-2), and if he translates it, the reason was to add it to that collection (27 ff.). All of this hardly leads us to the hypothesis of a non-inspired original. That is still less likely of the additions to Daniel, although these do not pertain to the Palestinian Jewish canon. In making the word of God available to the Greek language world, would the translators have added for its edification profane material rendered sacred only by the use they made of it? There are even stronger reasons to reject the mixed theory, which would hold as the only canonical books, on the one hand, the Hebrew originals of the rabbinic Bible, and on the other, the Greek text of the supplements which are not included in the rabbinic Bible. Would not inspiration be a capricious phenomenon, sometimes standing by translators when they leave the canonical original, sometimes abandoning them when they return to it?

*c) The double inspired text.*—It is better in the final analysis to adopt for the deuterocanonical books translated from Hebrew or Aramaic the same solution as for the rest of the Septuagint. The translators intended to make available for their readers texts which they themselves more or less clearly considered sacred, and which in fact were sacred. Their work was itself carried out under the influence of inspiration. The text of these books is thus inspired and canonical at both the successive stages of its writing. [208] It is therefore proper to employ the Greek text of Ben Sira and all the other books as the word of God. In this view, there is not even any reason not to consider the translator's foreword to Ben Sira as an inspired text. [209] But, in return, the Semitic originals cannot be neglected, as if they were sources

---

[208] Some pages back we brought up the problem of the Third Book of Ezra. It is beyond doubt that the Hebrew sources used in this book belong with full right to the canon, for they are found also in 2 Ch, Ezr and Ne. There remains the case of the legend of Zorobabel (3 Ezr 3:1-4:6) which is translated from a Semitic original (cf. E. Bayer, *Das dritte Buch Esdras*, p. 137). But the text held as canonical by Palestinian Judaism was that of Ezra-Nehemiah, and not that of 3 Ezra.

[209] This is the opinion of C. Spicq, *L'Écclésiastique*, BPC (Paris, 1946), p. 150. P. Auvray, "Notes sur le Prologue de l'Ecclésiastique" *Mélanges A. Robert* (Paris: Bloud & Gay, 1958), pp. 281-287, is much more reserved about the prologue, despite his attachment to the canonicity of the book in its Greek form. That could be taken as illogical, since the prologue testifies in favor of the normative authority of the original, while at the same time it specifies the purpose of its Greek translation (not without underlining the importance and difficulty of passing from one language to another, Prol. 15-26).

for the sacred books and not an integral part of them. And as modern manuscript discoveries succeed in restoring fragments of them in varying length, these fragments have full right to a place in our Bible. The Church could very well, after an examination, pass explicit judgment recognizing their origin, their value, and their authority, without prejudicing the canonicity of the Septuagint. That would not be an innovation, but a recuperation, and such an eventuality cannot be excluded *a priori*.

## IV. CONCLUSION

The last three questions considered (the Septuagint, lost books, and the deuterocanonical books) have led us to adopt a notion of the inspired book that is at once complex and flexible. But at the level of the Hebrew originals, does not literary criticism discern already the successive contributions of authors, editors, glossators, all equally inspired? Now it is the case to add the Greek translators and adaptors to the list. Scriptural inspiration remains, let it be noted, a personal charism at all these levels, positively directed to the production of a book which will set down in writing the word of God. Only this production is not the private action of an isolated man. It belongs to a living tradition in which the word of God is preserved, handed on, explained, in which its meaning and content undergo substantial progress. Tradition's real fidelity to the word on which it is based does not consist in the material transmission of a dead text. It implies an ever deepening understanding of the word, an adaptation of its message to the needs of new times and new environments, thanks to the charisms which put certain men at the service of the whole community. But in this framework, it happens that scriptural inspiration as such is a prolongation of the various functional charims, since God wills that the material elaborated in living tradition enter in its turn into the Book which serves as norm for the faith. The relations between Scripture and Tradition, [210] between the scriptural charism and the functional charisms, [211] thus cooperated intimately in the formation of the canonical collection that Judaism bequeathed to the Church under two forms and in two languages.

[210] Cf. ch. I, pp.26-32.
[211] Cf. ch. II, pp. 61-64.

# PART II

# THE INTERPRETATION OF SCRIPTURE

# CHAPTER V

# HISTORY OF THE PROBLEM
# OF BIBLICAL INTERPRETATION


Up to this point, we have studied the Bible in itself to obtain a proper idea
of its nature, its limits, its place in the economy of salvation, and its relation
to divine revelation and to the Church. We now proceed to an examination
of the problem of its interpretation. In the course of the preceding chapters
two elements have already provided us a direct preparation. First, we have
seen that Scripture must never be separated from ecclesiastical tradition,
because the word of God is there found in its fulness (chap. I). Secondly,
the fact that the word of God is transmitted in Scripture in a human language
allowed us to determine the many factors which condition its expression of
divine truth (chap. III). Now it remains for us to draw the consequences
of these observations. The problem of interpretation, however, did not
arise just in our times. And its history has more than documentary interest:
it constitutes the best of introductions to a systematic study by the very
fact that it gradually puts all the factors in order. [1] In retracing that history,
we will devote more space to its most recent period (from the 16th century
to our own day) because it provides an understanding of contemporary
problems.


## § I. THE SOURCES OF CHRISTIAN EXEGESIS


If, in the course of the centuries, the interpretation of Scripture has been
the occasion of disputes over method in the Church, this fact was always
conditioned by a certain factor passed down by apostolic tradition and, by
that token, discernible within some of the inspired texts themselves. Not
that the New Testament provides an authentic interpretation destined

---

[1] A. Vaccari, "Historia exegeseos," *Institutiones biblicae*, 6th ed., pp. 510-567.
J. Bonsirven, G. Bardy, M. Jugie, C. Spicq, A. Robert, L. Vaganay, "Interprétation
(Histoire de l')," *DBS* 4, cols. 561-646. G. Ebeling, "Hermeneutik," *RGG*, cols. 242-
262. In these three treatments will be found a more complete bibliography on the
subject. Shorter treatments in A. Robert—A. Tricot, *Guide to the Bible* I, pp. 679-731;
H. Höpfl—L. Leloir, *Introductio generalis*, 6th ed., pp. 504-539; A. Robert—
A. Feuillet, *Introduction à la Bible* I, pp. 171-202; G. Auzou, *La Parole de Dieu*,
2nd ed. (Paris: l'Orante, 1960), pp. 217-391.

to be authoritative for every page of the Old Testament, nor that the meaning and content of its own texts never cause any problem. If that were so, there would be no further problem. But the apostolic Church, heir to the Old Testament through the intermediary of Judaism, and herald of the gospel, laid the foundations of an exegetical method dominated by the fact of Christ, the supreme revelation of the mystery of salvation and of the mystery of God.

## I. THE LEGACY OF THE OLD TESTAMENT AND OF JUDAISM

### I. INTERPRETATION OF SCRIPTURE IN THE OLD TESTAMENT

Already in the Old Testament, the problem of the meaning of the word of God was raised and received practical solutions. When, in fact, the word of God took the form of a particular message destined for certain men of a given age—whether it was the priestly Torah, a prophetical oracle, or a sapiential discourse—its meaning was, as a rule, devoid of ambiguity, even though its implications were not necessarily discernible at first glance, given the mysterious depths the word of God always conceals. But when that same message was once set down in writing and continued to impart the word of God to all following generations, it became necessary to add to it an interpretation which would point up its permanent validity in the midst of changing circumstances. Such an authorized interpretation belonged properly to tradition to make. [2]

The first traces of such interpretation can be found in the biblical texts themselves. Thus Deuteronomic law appears in more than one case to be a collection of legal decisions grafted on to the ancient code of the covenant, [3] and the final redactional layer of the Pentateuch seems to have had as its purpose to harmonize the sometimes contrary legal decisions. [4] It is apparently for a similar reason that the canonical texts of the prophets include inspired glosses, which explain the meaning of the ancient oracles by clarifying them through other scriptures (thus Is 11:10-16 [5] grafted

[2] Cf. chap. I, p. 10.

[3] S. R. Driver, *Deuteronomium, ICC* (1895), pp. iii-x (terminology of parallel passages). It is not a matter, however, of mere interpretation of the law, as is stressed by G. von Rad, *Old Testament Theology* (Edinburgh : Oliver and Boyd, 1962), I, pp. 226-231.

[4] P. Grelot, "La dernière étape de la rédaction sacerdotale," *VT* 6 (1956), 174-189. H. Cazelles in Robert—Feuillet, *Introduction to the Old Testament*, pp. 162 f.; idem, "Pentateuque," *DBS* 7, cols. 844-855.

[5] Commentators have long recognized this fact: A. Condamin, "Le livre d'Isaïe," *EB* (1905), 97 f.; B. Duhm, *Das Buch Jesaja*, 4th ed. (Göttingen: Vandenhoeck & Ruprecht, 1922), pp. 109 f.; G. B. Gray, *The Book of Isaiah, ICC* (1912),

to Is 11:1). The phenomenon is even more clear when the sacred authors systematically use the expressions of their predecessors to transmit their own message. This stylistic procedure, which has been called anthological, [6] indirectly reveals the type of exegesis its users employed. It is frequent in the postexilic psalms: thus Ps 51:9.12 ff. is based on Ezk 36:25-27, etc.; it is found also in the later prophetic texts: thus Zc 11:4-17 and 13:7-9 rework Ezk 34. It even happens that a particular author informs his readers in what manner he actualizes the scriptures: thus Dn 9 interprets Jr 25:11-12 eschatologically.

All of these texts are evidence of a charismatic exegesis, produced not only in the light of faith, but under the influence of functional charisms which always accompanied scriptural inspiration in the sacred authors. [7] From this point of view, they provide a normative interpretation of the scriptures they explain. But at the same time they reveal concretely the spirit and methods of a very ancient mode of interpretation, which is at the source of Jewish exegesis. To describe it, we might resort to the generic term *midrash*. [8] A midrash is a study, an investigation into the meaning of the sacred text, not the meaning that former people for whom it was first written could have understood, but the meaning it has now, and the light it casts on the vital problems of the present. To uncover that meaning, one must know how to make the text speak, to discover behind its words the aspect of the mystery of faith they illumine, to comprehend its import as part of a revelation which forms a whole and which progresses with time. By comparing the texts one with another, by reading them in a new historical or theological perspective, the exegete discovers an undoubtedly deeper meaning in them. For example, after there was no longer a king in Jerusalem, the royal psalms preserved in the liturgy served to sing in advance the glories of the future Messiah. This is an example of enlarging exegesis, which shows the evolution of messianic concepts since the time of the composition of these psalms. [9] To perform this practical operation, through which the word of God exercised its normative role in the community, all

---

pp. 222-228; A. Feuillet, "Isaïe," *DBS* 4, col. 675; V. Herntrich, *Der Prophet Jesaja,* *ATD* (1957), pp. 216-219.

[6] A. Robert, "Littéraires (Genres)," *DBS* 5, col. 411; "Le genre littéraire du Cantique des cantiques," *Vivre et penser* 3 (= *RB* 53 [1944]), 199 ff.

[7] Above, pp. 50-55.

[8] R. Bloch, "Midrash," *DBS* 5, cols. 1263 ff. (cf. Robert—Feuillet, *Introduction à la Bible* 1, pp. 173 ff.). It would be better to reserve the name midrash for this exegetical method, rather than to extend it to literary compositions which make use of its results, as was done, for example, by R. Bloch, "Ézéchiel XVI: exemple parfait du procédé midrashique dans la Bible," *CS* 9 (1955), 193-223.

[9] *Sens chrétien de l'A.T.*, pp. 335, 375 f.

the means provided by Jewish culture, even those borrowed from neighboring cultures, were employed. They became more pronounced in intertestamentary Judaism.

## II. JEWISH EXEGESIS IN THE AGE OF THE NEW TESTAMENT

Many currents can be distinguished in Jewish exegesis at the time of the New Testament. That of the Essenes has become directly accessible to us through the discoveries at Qumran. [10] That of Alexandrian Judaism, attested in the Septuagint, [11] the book of Wisdom and a whole Greek language literature, took, with Philo, [12] a peculiar turn which linked it to the expression of a philosophy. The rabbinic compilations completed since the 2nd century of our era provide information on the Pharisaic current, whose tradition goes back much further. [13] That of the Sadducees is the most difficult to investigate for lack of firsthand documents.

Jewish doctors divided their exegesis into two classes: those explanations which supported legally binding rules belonged to the *halakah*; the others, which were intended to nourish faith and hope, to edify, to aid in prayer, etc., belonged to *haggadah*. This was an entirely practical classification, obviously the work of juridical minds. Both *halakôt* and *haggadôt* are found in the exegesis of the Qumran community, though these technical terms are not used to describe them. But another particular form of interpretation is found there too, the *pesher*. [14] This form involved a deciphering of scriptural texts as if they were visions or dreams (cf. Dn 2; 4; 5; 7), in order to read in them a hidden prediction of present or future events. This procedure is

---

[10] F. F. Bruce, *Biblical Exegesis in the Qumran Texts* (Den Haag: van Kerlen, 1959).

[11] Concerning the importance of the Septuagint as the authorized (and inspired) witness of Alexandrian interpretation, cf. above, chap. IV, pp. 175 ff..

[12] Concerning Philo's exegesis, see especially J. Daniélou, *Philon d'Alexandrie* (Paris: Fayard, 1958), pp. 119-142.

[13] J. Bonsirven, *Exégèse rabbinique et exégèse paulinienne* (Paris: Beauchesne, 1939), pp. 7-259. J. W. Doeve, *Jewish Hermeneutics in the Synoptic Gospels and Acts* (Assen: Van Gorcum, 1954), pp. 52-90.

[14] A. Dupont-Sommer, *Les écrits esséniens découverts près de la mer Morte* (Paris: Payot, 1959), pp. 267-290, 319 ff. J. Carmignac, *Les textes de Qumrân traduits et annotés* 2 (Paris: Letouzey et Ané, 1963), pp. 46 ff. It has been suggested that this method shows the influence of Egyptian literature: F. Daumas, "Littérature prophétique et exégétique égyptienne et commentaires esséniens," *A la rencontre de Dieu. Mémorial A. Gelin* (Le Puy—Paris: Mappus, 1961), pp. 203-221. But the comparison with certain rabbinic methods is convincing: L. H. Silberman, "Unriddling the Riddle. A Study in the Structure and Language of the Habakkuk Pesher," *RQ* 3 (1961), 323-335; A. Finkel, "The Pesher of Dreams and Scriptures," *RQ* 4 (1963), 357-370.

based on the conviction that present times are the last days, and that all of Scripture has a certain relation with the eschatological crisis that is about to close out history. That was already the basic premise of Dn 9, a charismatic exegesis of the 70 weeks of Jr 25:11-12. The Essenes' violent eschatological bent explains the large place this type of exegesis took in that community, but it left its traces in rabbinic literature as well.

It is impossible here to analyze in detail the various aspects of Jewish interpretation. It will suffice to say that two elements, closely related in practice, but very different in nature, must be distinguished. The first, which is properly theological, defines its spirit. It is faith in the absolute and actual value of Scripture as the word of God. Inspired down to its very letters, [15] all of Scripture is related to a single object, which is of the religious order: the relation between God and men, undertaken long ago by divine initiative, defined in terms of covenant, experienced by Israel in the course of the centuries in the concrete arena of its institutions and its history, moving toward a final consummation which the prophecies announce in advance. Moreover, light for all of the problems which face the people of God can be found there. It is this profound conviction which led interpreters to actualize the texts, whether in preaching in the synagogue or in scholarly discussions. Nevertheless, theological principles did not suffice to guarantee success in interpreting. To them had to be added exegetical techniques, which were necessarily bound to some cultural element: simple exegesis, based on the obvious meaning of the text; philological exegesis, which speculated on its linguistic details; logical exegesis, which based its reasoning on the content of the text. The Palestinian doctors of the 2nd century attempted to codify these rules of exegesis, [16] which had already been in use for a long time; but the Qumran texts provide earlier examples which are completely parallel. [17] The letter of Scripture is thus enriched, sometimes in several directions, through procedures which dismay us because they typically reflect the mentality of the time. In Hellenistic Judaism, the exegesis practiced still depended in large measure on its Palestinian sources, but it adapted itself to the spirit of Alexandrian culture.

---

[15] Concerning this concept of inspiration in ancient Judaism, see above, chap. II, p. 41, note 28.

[16] A detailed analysis of these methods may be found in the work of J. Bonsirven, *Exégèse rabbinique et exégèse paulinienne.*

[17] Cf. G. Vermès, *Scripture and Tradition in Judaism: Haggadic Studies* (Leyden: Brill, 1961), pp. 11-66. On the possible influence of Essene exegesis on the rabbinic midrash, see N. H. Glatzer, "Hillel the Elder in the Light of the Dead Sea Scrolls" in K. Stendahl, *The Scrolls and the New Testament* (New York: Harper, 1957), pp. 236 ff.

In Philo,[18] it is even united to philosophic reflection and systematically resorts to allegory to develop the sacred texts. Thus Jewish tradition in its interpretation closely associated the authentic heritage of the Old Testament to the most insignificant peculiarities of Palestinian and Alexandrian culture. The same was to happen in Christian exegesis.

## II. CHRIST AND SCRIPTURE

### I. THE ACCOMPLISHMENT OF SCRIPTURE

The attitude of Christ toward Scripture is obviously of incomparable value, since it opened the way to Christian exegesis. In various ways, he more than once appealed to the authority of Scripture, "which cannot be rejected" (Jn 10:35). Thus he used it to justify his ways of acting (Mk 11:17 par.) and his teachings (Mk 12:29-31 par.), and he accused his adversaries of misunderstanding its true sense (Mt 9:13; 12:3; 22:29; Jn 5:39). But that meaning took a new turn with him; he came, in fact, to "complete [19] Scripture," that is to say, to reveal its definitive meaning and to bring it in every way to its perfection. His doctrine fulfils the law and the prophets (Mt 5:17); his life fulfils the texts which outlined the shape of the mystery of salvation (Mk 14:49 par.). While the charismatic exegesis of the inspired scribes in the Old Testament already tended continually to enlarge the meaning of the ancient texts in view of a revelation which increased, Jesus' exegesis brought that tendency to its completion. Moreover, far from feeling bound by interpretations which his contemporaries held as traditional, he handled the most venerable texts with a liberty that scandalized the scribes (Mk 2:23-28; Mt 15:12), and he presented his personal interpretations "with authority" (Mk 1:22). Thus by his words and deeds he less explained the meaning of the scriptures than revealed it; that is the reason his listeners were struck by the quality of newness that shone from everything he said and did (Mk 1:27). It is only from this perspective that the manner in which he occasionally practiced the anthological style can be understood. In using the words of Scripture to express his gospel, he charged them with a new and original content: the revelation of the kingdom of God and of himself.

---

[18] The old work of C. Siegfried, *Philo von Alexandrien als Ausleger des Alten Testaments* (Jena: Dufft, 1875) remains basic; but it needs to be supplemented at a number of points. Cf. E. Stein, *Die allegorische Exegese des Philo aus Alexandria* (Giessen: Töpelmann, 1929); I. Heinemann, *Philons griechische und jüdische Bildung* (Breslau: Marcus, 1932); *Alt jüdische Allegoristik* (Breslau: Marcus, 1936).

[19] Cf. above, p. 14, note 30. On Jesus' attitude toward the Old Testament, see C. Larcher, *L'actualité chrétienne de l'Ancien Testament d'après le Nouveau Testament* (Paris: Cerf, 1962), pp. 45-255; E. Stauffer, "Jesus und seine Bibel," *Abraham unser Vater. Festschrift O. Michel* (Leyden: Brill, 1963), pp. 440-449.

## II. CHRIST AND EXEGETICAL METHODS [20]

Since Christ lived in Palestine and shared its culture, he could be expected to make use of the exegetical methods familiar to his contemporaries. In fact, those methods hardly appeared in his usual manner of preaching, but he occasionally employed them expertly. In the discussion on divorce, he firmly established on Genesis [21] the new *halakah* he substituted for the tolerance of the Mosaic law and subsequent tradition (Mt 19:1-9). In the discussion on the resurrection (Mt 22:23-32), a haggadic theme, he appealed with much subtleness to the Pentateuch for a convincing proof against the Sadducees. [22] There is no lack of the rabbinic type of argumentation in the gospel of St. John, [23] but it is always in discussions with the scribes, not in his personal teaching, which apparently abhorred this classic method.

Finally, since the Qumran texts have drawn attention to that peculiar actualization of Scripture called the *pesher*, it has become clear that that method, familiar to all apocalyptic milieux, was also employed by Christ. He thus applied the scriptures not only to the judgment of Jerusalem announced for an indetermined future (Mt 24:15), but also to the facts of his own life: the failure of his preaching (Mt 13:13-15), his passion (Mt 26:31. 54, etc.; Jn 13:18), and resurrection (Lk 24:44-46). The lessons in biblical interpretation the apostles received after the resurrection (Lk 24:27.32.45) fit into this framework: the real consummation of the mystery of salvation in a historical event retrospectively clarified all the texts which in one way or another traced its features (cf. also Mk 12:19 par.).

It is apparent that the exegetical methods in use in Palestinian Judaism occupied a certain place in the preaching of Christ. Nevertheless, two remarks must be made: 1) While he surely employed them, Jesus displayed a remarkable reserve in the use of the practical methods which at that time

---

[20] Some examples can be found in D. Daube, *The New Testament and Rabbinic Judaism* (London: Athlone, 1956); J. W. Doeve, *Jewish Hermeneutics in the Synoptic Gospels*, pp. 91 ff.

[21] An interesting parallel can be found in the Zadokite Document, IV, 21 - V, 1, which reflects the Qumran *halakah* (cf. C. Rabin, *The Zadokite Documents* 1 [Oxford: Clarendon, 1958], pp. 17 f.). For a comparison with rabbinic tradition, see D. Daube, *op. cit.*, pp. 71-86.

[22] F. Dreyfus, "L'argumentation scripturaire de Jésus en faveur de la résurrection des morts," *RB* 68 (1959), 213-224. For the Sadducees, the scriptural argument had to be taken from the Pentateuch, the only canonical book.

[23] For a comparison of the fourth gospel with rabbinic Judaism, see C. H. Dodd. *The Interpretation of the Fourth Gospel* (Cambridge: Univ. Press, 1953), pp. 74-96, It should be noted, however, that the number of formal citations of Scripture in the fourth gospel is quite restricted. See the detailed study of F. M. Braun, *Jean le théologien. II. Les grandes traditions d'Israël* (Paris: Gabalda, 1964) especially the first two chapters.

served to enrich the content of the text. Disdaining subtleties, he went directly to the heart of Scripture to grasp its essence. 2) He always made those methods secondary to a deeper and more solid principle of interpretation: the gospel message he had received from his Father and was to communicate to the world. The Jewish doctors knew how to use Scripture to clarify Scripture. Christ clarified it by projecting on it the light of his person and his gospel.

## III. EXEGESIS IN THE APOSTOLIC CHURCH

### I. INTERPRETATION OF THE OLD TESTAMENT [24]

Continuing in the line of the principles laid down by Christ, and prolonging the interpretations given by him, the apostolic Church gradually developed an interpretation of the scriptures that reshaped its Jewish predecessor from top to bottom.    Not, to be sure, in the matter of exegetical methods: on this point, Christian preaching undoubtedly appeared much less burdened when compared with rabbinic or Essene writings, but it instinctively turned to the methods employed in the Jewish *midrash*.    Even though it had broken with the "tradition of the ancients," it still searched the Scriptures for *halakôt* (1 Co 5:13; 9:9; 2 Co 13:1; 1 Tm 5:18-19).    It even more willingly practiced the *haggadah*, especially in moral exhortations (for example, 1 Co 10:1-10).    In the field of apologetics, the application of texts to the passion and resurrection of Christ is very similar to the method of the Qumran *pesher* (for example, Ac 2:15-21.24-35; 3:21-23; 4:25-28, etc.).    And the Pauline letters contain argumentations of a rabbinic flavor. [25]    A use of certain Alexandrian methods can be noted in the letter to the Hebrews; they can perhaps be explained by a side influence of Philo. [26]    To be sure,

---

[24] Besides the works of J. Bonsirven (p. 188, note 13), D. Daube and J. W. Doeve (p. 191, note 20), see C. H. Dodd, *According to the Scriptures* (London: Nisbet, 1953); K. Stendahl, *The School of St. Matthew and its Use of the Old Testament* (Uppsala: Almquist, 1954), pp. 39 ff.; L. Cerfaux, "Simples réflexions à propos de l'exégèse apostolique," and "L'exégèse de l'Ancien Testament dans le Nouveau," *Recueil L. Cerfaux* 2, pp. 189-217; B. Lindars, *New Testament Apologetic* (London: SCM Press, 1961); K. H. Schelkle, "Hermeneutische Zeugnisse im Neuen Testament," *BZ* n.F. 6 (1962), 161-177; C. Larcher, *L'actualité chrétienne de l'Ancien Testament*, pp. 255-513; C. F. D. Moule, *The Birth of the New Testament* (London: A. & C. Black, 1962), pp. 53-85. Cf. Robert—Feuillet, *Introduction à la Bible* 1, pp. 178-184; *Sens chrétien de l'A.T.*, pp. 4-27.

[25] Examples provided by J. Bonsirven, *op. cit.*, pp. 295 ff. For a systematic study of Pauline exegesis, see E. E. Ellis, *Paul's Use of the Old Testament* (Edinburgh: Oliver & Boyd, 1957); a comparison with contemporary Jewish exegesis, *ibid.*, pp. 38 ff.

[26] On this question, see C. Spicq, *L'épître aux Hébreux* 1, pp. 53-64. Still it should be noted that the letter's symbolic and typological exegesis is very different

in all these cases the technical vocabulary of Jewish exegesis is reduced to a few less characteristic phrases. But there is at least one case in which St. Paul explicitly announces that he is allegorizing [27] (Ga 4:24), and that transports us fully into Hellenistic culture.

Nevertheless, this is not the essence of Christian exegesis. It is to be found rather in the conviction that all of Scripture applies to Christ; it testifies to him in anticipation of salvation realized in him. The Christian apologetic use of Scripture in the discourses of Acts and elsewhere, [28] addressed to the Jews who recognized it as the word of God, aimed to show that the various formulations of salvation provided by the Old Testament attain their full richness, their "completion," in the death and resurrection of Christ, in the experience of salvation and of the Holy Spirit, which the Lord was then granting his Church. To support this exercise in interpretation, the history and institutions of the Old Testament too received an interpretation which discovered in them figures of Christ to come: the technical terms *typos* and *antitypos* (which were used in contrary senses [29] by St. Paul and 1 Peter on the one hand, and the letter to the Hebrews on the other) were used to define the relation between the two Testaments. Given this fact, it hardly matters that the form of argumentation was sometimes borrowed from rabbinic or Alexandrian culture. In this regard, it is true, the methods used cannot be considered normative for Christian exegesis of every age. But the manner in which the apostolic Church sought in the sacred texts the single object of faith of which all of Scripture speaks gave Christian exegesis a permanent direction: the real sense of the Old Testament is the testimony it renders to Christ, no matter what methods are used to bring that meaning to light. This is unquestionably an enlarging exegesis, since, hardly even asking what the sacred author's contemporaries might have understood by the texts, it makes explicit their mysterious content, which was hidden beneath their words. [30] And the reason is that Scripture can no longer be read as the Jews read it, now that Christ has completed

---

from Philo's allegory. As for the argumentation of chap. 7 on Gn 14, it is rather of the rabbinic type.

[27] R. M. Grant, *The Letter and the Spirit* (London: SPCK, 1957), pp. 48 f., 121 ff. E. E. Ellis, *op. cit.*, pp. 51-54, stresses that this allegory has a typological base that is in no way Greek.

[28] J. Dupont, "L'utilisation apologétique de l'Ancien Testament dans les discours des Actes," *ETL* 29 (1953), 289-327 (cf. the works of C. H. Dodd and B. Lindars cited above, p. 192, note 24).

[29] *Sens chrétien de l'A. T.*, pp. 25-27, 215 f., 294 ff.; cf. L. Goppelt, *Typos. Die typologische Deutung des A.T.s im Neuen* (Gütersloh: Bertelsmann, 1939).

[30] In the case of the Letter to the Hebrews, the fact has been studied by J. van der Ploeg, "L'exégèse de l'A.T. dans l'épître aux Hébreux," *RB* 56 (1947), 114-131 (cf. C. Spicq, *op. cit.*, pp. 330-350).

it and, at the same time, revealed its implications. [31]   Thus when the book
of Revelation employs prophetic texts to express its message of hope, it
places them in a wholly different eschatological perspective, which transforms their meaning. [32]   The exegesis underlying this reading of the prophets
shows how they ought now to be actualized.

## II. INTERPRETATION OF THE WORDS AND DEEDS OF CHRIST

It goes without saying that to be able to relate the scriptures to Jesus Christ,
the apostolic Church preserved a living memory of what he had done and
taught (Ac 1:1).   That is precisely the object of the gospel tradition. [33]
But that tradition did not pass on to the faithful raw facts, viewed only under
their phenomenal aspect.   Since the mystery of Christ reached its consummation through his final entry into glory, all previous history was viewed
and interpreted in the light of the resurrection, with the fixed intention
of extracting from it certain essential facts which give it present value.
Every gospel passage thus incorporates with its historical substratum a
didactic content, which becomes richer with time, and which can vary
somewhat from one gospel to another.   It is not only in the fourth gospel
that the acts of Christ are "signs," relating to the revelation of his mystery
and to the life of the Christian communities; they are already implicitly such
in the synoptics.

The transmission of the words of Christ took place in somewhat different
circumstances.   Undoubtedly 1st-century Judaism had a method of oral
tradition which favored the preservation of this manifold material, [34] but
its influence on the New Testament should not be exaggerated.   The
apostolic Church did not, in fact, have as its single interest the preservation
of the *ipsissima verba* of Christ with the material fidelity of a recording.
It desired to find in the words of the Master spiritual nourishment, exactly
as in the scriptures, and even more so since Christ alone provides the key
to those scriptures.   It is only to be expected then that the Church should

---

[31] Cf. the allegory of Moses' veil developed by St. Paul in 2Co 3:12-18.

[32] J. Cambier, "Les images de l'Ancien Testament dans l'Apocalypse de saint Jean," *NRT* 77 (1955), 113-122; A. Vanhoye, "L'utilisation d'Ézéchiel dans l'Apocalypse," *Biblica* 43 (1962), 436-476.

[33] Above, pp. 15 ff.   A more detailed treatment of the question under discussion can be found in X. Léon-Dufour, *The Gospels and the Jesus of History* (New York: Desclée, 1968).

[34] B. Gerhardsson, *Memory and Manuscript. Oral Tradition and Written Transmission in Rabbinic Judaism and Early Christianity* (Uppsala: Gleerup, 1961) provides interesting examples, but he likens the two cases excessively.   See the critical remarks of W. D. Davies, *The Setting of the Sermon on the Mount* (Cambridge: Univ. Press, 1964), pp. 464-480.

exploit their full richness, exactly as it did for the other sacred texts. Is it only by chance that 1 Tm 5:18 cites Dt 25:4 and Lk 10:7 side by side to establish the practical rule announced in 5:17? The resurrection, followed by the profusion of the Holy Spirit, projected a new light on all the teachings of Christ. It was proper, therefore, to profit by them by rereading his words and searching their depths, under the influence of the Spirit who revealed their meaning to the apostles (Jn 14:26; 16:13-15). Thus traditional transmission went hand in hand with an actualization of the material transmitted, which became material to be interpreted. This inspired exegesis most certainly took place in a climate of total fidelity which guaranteed its result. This fact is especially confirmed when a saying of Jesus provides the basis for a rule of conduct which is substituted for a Jewish *halakah*: thus in the case of the prohibition of divorce (Mt 5:32; 1 Co 7:10 ff.). But a comparison of parallel texts in more than one instance reveals either real doctrinal progress or practical applications which differ in intent or accent (compare Mt 18:12-14 with Lk 15:3-7; Lk 14:16-24 with Mt 22:1-11). And once again, the effort to comprehend the traditional material in depth was pushed to its maximum in the gospel according to St. John.

In short, the history of Jesus was everywhere treated as the sacred history par excellence, and the words of Jesus as the divine word par excellence. That implies two things at once: a respect matching that which Judaism and the Church paid to the scriptures, and secondly, a constantly renewed reflection on the inexhaustible import of his life and words.

## § II. CHRISTIAN EXEGESIS IN PRACTICE

The legacy of the apostolic Church in the field of interpretation, therefore, includes two elements which differ in nature. First, there is a theological element. The whole Old Testament is related to Christ and to the mystery of salvation realized by him: its history and institutions as a preparation and prefiguration, the texts themselves as a foreannouncement of his work, his person, his gospel. Its details can be understood only in this total perspective, and Christ appears as the unique key that explains everything. As for the tradition which centered on him, the meaning of the deeds and words preserved in it and later set down in writing remains open to reflection and deeper understanding, since the comparison of each recollection and each text with the whole body of apostolic teachings might provide an insight into unsuspected riches. That is the fundamental principle of exegesis. Secondly, in practice, a cultural element accompanies this basic principle: the use of the exegetical methods common in Judaism of that age, whether in Palestine or in Alexandria. Thus it required no effort to pass from Jewish *midrash* to Christian *midrash*; the originality of the gospel injected new blood into the traditional interpretation of the scriptures. From this foundation, Christian exegesis went on to develop on its own, not without experiencing the repercussions of a cultural evolution from which the Church could not escape.

## I. THE PATRISTIC AGE [35]

### I. PROBLEMS AND METHODS

In the 2nd century, the writings left by the apostolic age joined those of the Old Testament in the collection of scriptures. [36]   There then appeared no division between living tradition, which was conscious of owing all its content to apostolic teaching, and Scripture, which made that teaching directly attainable, both because it was its immediate fruit, and because its interpretation as "accomplished Scripture" was itself of apostolic origin. The result was an intimate connection between Scripture and Tradition in ecclesiastical teaching. [37]   On the one hand, the depositaries of ecclesiastical tradition always took great care to base their preaching upon Scripture, so as to put the faithful in contact with the word of God itself. But on the other hand, the meaning given the scriptural texts was in practice drawn from a tradition which explained the biblical writings on the basis of the apostolic revelation it preserved intact.

It was in this spirit that preaching and the liturgy, apologetics and learned theology turned to Scripture as to their source. The principles of interpretation set forth in the New Testament were plainly at the basis of all exegesis. When treating texts of the Old Testament, [38] that exegesis aimed to go beyond the letter to arrive at the spirit, that is, the mystery of Christ veiled beneath imperfect formulas, either by giving the doctrinal language of Israel the fulness of meaning which the New Testament gave them, or by applying the principle of types in order to discover Christ behind the history and institutions of long ago. Its approach to texts of apostolic origin was obviously different. But that did not hinder it, here too, from

---

[35] A general treatment of patristic exegesis by G. Bardy, "Commentaires patristiques de l'Écriture," *DBS* 2, cols. 73-103.

[36] Above, chap. IV, pp. 146-151.

[37] Above, chap. I, pp. 22-26.

[38] *Sens chrétien de l'A.T.*, pp. 28-45.

striving to use one to illumine others, to discover the hidden meaning of the least acts of Christ, to extract the potential content of his least words, etc. In brief, the methods the apostolic age had begun were applied systematically, for the purpose of nourishing the faith of the people and of building up a theology. These two concerns went together in the pastoral activity of the Church and expanded into a science of interpretation. This is not surprising, for according to the expression of St. Augustine, the fulness and end of all the divine scriptures is none other than life in charity. [39]

All of this could not be done, however, without making use of the practical means provided by the culture of the time. The Jewish *midrash* lost ground as time went on, [40] now that the Church was planted in the Greco-Roman world; if a lasting influence of it can be noted in the churches of Syria, the reason is to be found in a cultural affinity arising from the common use of Semitic languages. But the Hellenistic world, notably at Alexandria, provided a method of explaining texts from which biblical exegesis could benefit, just as Christian theology used the language of Greek philosophy to make its message accessible to educated minds. [41] That explains the fact that with Origen allegory became a common method; thanks to it Christian instruction found a basis and support in all the inspired texts. [42] Philo had provided a model of this method when he applied his philosophical doctrine to the Bible. The fathers profoundly transformed the allegorical method: with them it no longer aimed to lead minds from sensible realities to their intelligible meaning, at the risk of losing contact with the terrestrial world and history, but to lead them beyond figurative realities to the Reality prefigured, from the preparatory economy to the historical realization of Salvation and then to its consummation beyond time. [43]

---

[39] *De doctrina christiana* I, 35 (*PL* 34, 34).

[40] But see J. Daniélou, *Théologie du judéo-christianisme* (Tournai-Paris: Desclée, 1958), pp. 102-129; Eng. trans. *Theology of Jewish Christianity* (Chicago: Regnery, 1964).

[41] A synthetic study of the second and third centuries in J. Daniélou, *Message évangélique et culture hellénistique* (Tournai-Paris: Desclée, 1961), pp. 183-275.

[42] H. de Lubac, *Histoire et esprit: L'intelligence de l'Écriture d'après Origène* (Paris: Aubier, 1950); R. P. C. Hanson, *Allegory and Event: A Study of the Source and Significance of Origen's Interpretation of Scripture* (London: SCM Press, 1959); J. H. Waszink, "Allegorese," *Encyclopedia für Antike und Christentum* I, 272-293; R. M. Grant, *The Letter and the Spirit*, pp. 85-114 (which includes an important appendix on the terminology of Greek exegesis, pp. 120-142). The sources of Origen's exegesis have been examined by J. Daniélou, *Origène* (Paris: La Table Ronde, 1948), pp. 145-198.

[43] This fact is forcefully stated by H. de Lubac, "A propos de l'allégorie chrétienne," *RSR* 50 (1959), 6-43, against the misleading comparisons made by J. Pépin, *Mythe et allégorie: Les origines grecques et les contestations chrétiennes* (Paris: Montaigne, 1958).

This originality of Christian allegory obviously had its source in the theology of the New Testament. It does not matter that the systematic exploitation of the texts by means of this logic of symbols bears the mark of a certain age and environment. Besides, not all the Greek fathers made use of it in the same degree or in the same manner. At Antioch, which was less Platonic and more open to Aristotelian philosophy, the preference was for the *theoria* [44] over allegory; the former, in principle, had more respect for the proper value of the letter and of history, while still attempting to surpass it. [45] The Latin West, which arrived later at theology and exegesis, was the heir of these methods. It did, however, adapt them to its less speculative and more juridical mind. [46] St. Jerome even laid the foundations of a sort of critical science [47] which was to counter, at least theoretically, the abuses of allegory. But on the other hand, the analytic methods held in esteem by the grammarians and rhetoricians of decadent Latinity were widely employed to explain Scripture, as can be confirmed by an examination of the works of St. Augustine [48] and even more those of St. Gregory the Great. [49]

## II. THE DOCTRINE OF THE SENSES OF SCRIPTURE

Christian exegesis (which was not formally distinguishable from theology itself) could not fail, during its development under the influence of these

[44] A. Vaccari, "La θεωρία nella scuola esegetica d'Antiochia," *Biblica* 1 (1920), 4-36 (cf. *Biblica* 15 [1934], 94-101); P. Ternant, "La θεωρία d'Antioche dans le cadre des sens de l'Écriture," *Biblica* 34 (1953), 135-158, 354-383, 456-486.

[45] On the relations between Alexandrian and Antiochean exegesis, see J. Guillet, "Les exégèses d'Alexandrie et d'Antioche: conflit ou malentendu?" *RSR* 38 (1947), 257 ff. The exegetical methods of various fathers have been the object of monographs during recent decades: R. Devreesse, "La méthode exégétique de Théodore de Mopsueste," *RB* 55 (1946), 207-241 (reprinted in *Essai sur Théodore de Mopsueste* [Vatican City, 1948], pp. 53-93); A. Kerrigan, *St. Cyril of Alexandria Interpreter of the Old Testament* (Rome: Pont. Biblical Inst., 1952).

[46] O. Kuss, "Zur Hermeneutik Tertullians," *Neutestamentliche Aufsätze (Festschrift J. Schmid)* (Ratisbon: Pustet, 1963), pp. 138-160.

[47] A. Penna, *Principi e caratteri dell'esegesi di S. Gerolamo* (Rome: Pont. Biblical Inst., 1950).

[48] M. Pontet, *L'exégèse de saint Augustin prédicateur* (Paris: Aubier, 1944); G. Strauss, *Schriftgebrauch, Schriftauslegung und Schriftbeweiss bei Augustin* (Tübingen, 1959). Augustine's cultural milieu has been analyzed by H. I. Marrou, *Saint Augustin et la fin de la culture antique* (Paris: De Bouard, 1949). One will note, for example, in *De doctrina christiana* 3 (*PL* 34, 65-90), a continual confusion between two quite different questions: that of biblical prefigurations and that of figures of speech.

[49] On St. Gregory and the culture of his age see H. de Lubac, *Exégèse médiévale* 2/1, pp. 53 ff.

diverse factors, to attempt to formulate its own method. It found a formulation in the doctrine of the senses of Scripture. Whatever relations to Philo might be found in it, [50] the doctrine was wholly original. But why speak of the senses of Scripture, in the plural? For two related reasons. First, the texts of the two Testaments can be read at the level of their simple letter, of the history they recount, of the physical world in which that history unfolded; but faith teaches us to go beyond this literal, historical, physical sense, to reach the mystery of Christ which is hidden beneath it, and this religious understanding of Scripture constitutes its spiritual sense. Secondly, the allegorical interpretation of the texts ordained by this fundamental principle can take several directions, according to the several aspects of the mystery of Christ. Sometimes it will lead from representative history to contemplation of Christ and his Church in their historical reality, and that is allegory pure and simple. Sometimes it extracts from it a spiritual doctrine apt to direct Christian life: tropology. Sometimes, surpassing even the ecclesial economy, it evokes the heavenly and eschatological realities which constitute the object of Christian hope: anagoge.

It goes without saying that this threefold manner of surpassing the letter and history concerns above all the texts of the Old Testament. Nevertheless, New Testament texts as well are capable of signifying something other than their literal sense denotes, since their historical element is itself meaningful with relation to the sacramental system, the Christian's spiritual life, and the object of Christian hope. Here too, then, several senses will be found in Scripture. It should be apparent that the doctrine of scriptural senses is quite complex, without considering that there have been several formulations of the same doctrine, [51] and that it has not always been explained as clearly as one would like. It attempts to unite in a logical synthesis the doctrinal principles drawn from the New Testament, the practical aims of exegesis in ecclesiastical life, and the methods of interpretation borrowed from contemporary culture.

---

[50] H. de Lubac, *Histoire et esprit*, pp. 150 ff.
[51] The question of the patristic origins of this doctrine is taken up in detail by H. de Lubac, *Exégèse médiévale* I, pp. 171-219.

## II. THE LATIN MIDDLE AGES [52]

### I. THE PATRISTIC HERITAGE IN MONASTIC THEOLOGY

In the early Middle Ages in the West, [53] the doctrine of the four senses of Scripture constituted at once a method of exegesis and a practical outline for explaining doctrine, since the two were never separated. [54] The allegorical interpretation that originated with Origen, St. Augustine, and St. Gregory the Great was then the general rule. That does not mean that the literal and historical sense of Scripture was neglected, since it was the foundation of all the others. [55] But no one could be content with just that. What monastic theology actually sought in the *lectio divina* [56] was not knowledge of a forever lost past, nor satisfaction of an avid curiosity for knowledge. It was rather nourishment for a faith which, taking the sacred texts and the facts they recounted as its starting point, desired to experience the mystery of Christ and the Church, in order to grow in Christian living and contemplate in advance the eternity toward which it was directed. [57] The method employed to realize these aims naturally corresponded to the culture of the times, the heir of both the grammarians and the fathers. [58] That method was literalist to excess; it analyzed the sacred texts without a sense of perspective, attentive only to their stylistic figures of speech. [59] But at the same time,

[52] C. Spicq, *Esquisse d'une histoire de l'exégèse latine au moyen âge* (Paris: Vrin, 1944). B. Smalley, *The Study of the Bible in the Middle Ages* (Oxford: Blackwell, 1952). These two works contain a more systematic analysis of exegetical methods than the monumental work of H. de Lubac, *Exégèse médiévale, Les quatre sens de l'Écriture* (Paris, Aubier, Part 1, 1959; Part 2, Vol. 1, 1961; Vol. 2, 1964). But the latter stresses better the interdependence of exegesis and theology.

[53] From this point on, we will follow the history of the problem only in the theology of the West. It would nevertheless be interesting to see how the heritage of the Greek fathers developed in the Byzantine Middle Ages and down to our own day. M. Jugie, "Interprétation," *DBS* 4, cols. 591-608, outlines this history down to the 15th century, and adds a brief account of the non-Byzantine orientals.

[54] This is precisely the subject of H. de Lubac's work, *Exégèse médiévale*, which, however, points out the existence of various formulas (Part I, pp. 139-169).

[55] *Ibid.*, pp. 425-487.

[56] J. Leclercq, *Initiation aux auteurs monastiques du moyen âge: L'amour des lettres et le désir de Dieu* (Paris: Cerf, 1957), pp. 70 ff.

[57] Hence the chapter headings chosen by H. de Lubac, *op. cit.*, pp. 489 ff., "L'allégorie, sens de la foi"; "La tropologie mystique"; "Anagogie et eschatologie."

[58] A typical example is Rabanus Maurus, *De clericorum institutione* 3 (*PL* 107: 379-420): from the principles of Christian exegesis (384-391) depends the theory of the liberal arts (391-405), knowledge of which enables one to expound the doctrine of Scripture (405-420). Concerning the culture of the age: J. Leclercq, *op. cit.*, pp. 40-52; concerning its exegetical method: C. Spicq, *op. cit.*, pp. 19-25.

[59] St. Bede the Venerable, *De schematibus et tropis sacrae Scripturae* (*PL* 90, 179-187).

it delighted in an abundance of symbols, which provided it the means to enrich the letter of Scripture. A close relation was thus established between allegorical exegesis and symbolic theology, a relation that was to blossom in the 12th century. [60]

## II. EXEGESIS AND SCHOLASTIC THEOLOGY

The situation changed when, alongside the monastic *lectio*, the scholastic *lectio* began to develop; the latter was concerned with the *quaestiones* which the explanation of the *Sacra Pagina* occasioned at every turn. [61] This theological interest led Hugo of St. Victor to formulate a well reasoned exegetical method. [62] A short time later the masters of the 13th century introduced into theology Aristotelian dialectic with its rigorous demands. That changed the whole approach to exegesis. [63] In his running commentary on Scripture, which remained his habitual occupation, the theologian prepared material which was apt to fit into a more systematic synthesis. He then arranged his doctrine in *summas* in which the *quaestiones* followed in logical sequence. For each of them, after having presented the opposing opinions, he had to find in Scripture an *auctoritas* which really supported the solution he adopted. From then on, the use of allegory lost its interest, for to serve as a proof a text must be credible. Thus can be explained the importance given to the *sensus litteralis* by St. Thomas, [64] for example. The realities of the Old Testament still possessed the value of signs in relation to the mystery of Christ in all its aspects, but that spiritual or mystical sense could not furnish proofs to theologians, for it contains nothing that cannot be found clearly stated somewhere in the literal sense of Scripture. [65] Only the text (the letter) is demonstrative. The only important thing is to understand its meaning well. For if it is true that it relates a history that took

---

[60] On this flowering of symbolism, see M. D. Chenu, *La théologie au XIIe siècle* (Paris: Vrin, 1957); H. de Lubac, *op. cit.*, Part 2, Vol. 2, pp. 125-262.

[61] On this evolution of theological method, see A. Forest in Fliche—Martin, *Histoire de l'Église* 13, pp. 149 ff.

[62] An outline can be found in *De scripturis et scriptoribus sacris* (PL 175, 9-28); a more lengthy treatment in *Eruditio didascalia* 4-6 (PL 176, 777-812).

[63] M. D. Chenu, *Introduction à l'étude de saint Thomas d'Aquin* (Paris: Vrin, 1954), pp. 199-225.

[64] *Quodlibet* 7, q. 6, art. 14-16, and again in *Super epistolam ad Galatas lectura*, cap. 4, lect. 7 (ed. Cai, Turin, 1953, Vol. 1, pp. 620 ff.) and in Iª, q. 1, art. 10. Cf. C. Spicq, *op. cit.*, pp. 202-288; H. de Lubac, *op. cit.*, Part 2, Vol. 2, pp. 263-325. T. F. Torrance, "Scientific Hermeneutics according to St. Thomas", *JTS* n.s. 13 (1962), 259-289, judges this exegesis from too modern a point of view.

[65] Iª, q. 1, art. 10, ad 1; cf. *Quodlibet* 7, q. 6, art. 14, ad 4, and *In Sententias*, prol., q. 1, art. 5.

place here below long ago, it is no less true that its sole object is the mystery of Christ, announced and prefigured in the Old Testament, become a fact of human experience since his first coming, sacramentally present during the time of the Church, tending toward its final consummation at the end of the ages. The letter of Scripture always concerns one aspect or the other of this mystery, whose revelation it records in writing.

In relation to the classical doctrine of the four senses of Scripture, the change in approach was considerable. A more strict definition of the *sensus litteralis* forbade any further confusion between figures of speech and biblical prefigurations; a firmly established principle of grammar decreed that the literal sense could be either proper or figurative, according to the case. [66] This was, however, not yet the modern concept of the literal sense. It was not, in fact, literary analysis alone that St. Thomas used to establish the meaning of the biblical texts, but first of all he resorted to ecclesiastical tradition, within which he intended to put himself before all else. Moreover, he applied Old Testament texts, which we would read in relation to the religion of Israel, directly to the mystery of Christ; this fact stands out, for example, in his commentary on the Psalms. In other words, the *sensus litteralis* as he understood it implies a fulness which only the believer can discover in it with the light of all of revelation. [67] For several centuries, exegesis followed this method without examining it closely. Entirely subordinate to theology, it strove to improve its analyses in the measure in which contact with Jewish exegesis [68] and the demands of theology itself permitted. But quite often its performance had the air of a school exercise about it. The manual of theology had decidedly taken over the principal place in university teaching, [69] and more than once the scriptural proof was reduced to an artificial allegory. [70]

---

[66] *Quodlibet* 7, q. 6, art. 15, ad 1; Iᵃ, q. 1, art. 10, ad 3. Article 9, while examining the problem of metaphors in Scripture, goes beyond that subject and in fact treats the use of symbols in religious language.

[67] "Exegesis develops the literal sense more than it explains it," notes C. Spicq, *op. cit.*, p. 223; but he takes a modern point of view in speaking of "literal sense."

[68] This concern is noticeable, for example, in Nicholas of Lyra (cf. C. Spicq, *op. cit.*, pp. 335 ff.; F. Vernet, "Lyre (Nicolas de)," *DTC* 9/1, cols. 1410-1422; H. de Lubac, *op. cit.*, Part 2, Vol. 2, pp. 344 ff.), even if his allegorical applications of Scripture sometimes reveal concordism at its worst, the distant heritage of Joachim of Fiore.

[69] H. de Lubac, *ibid.*, pp. 370 ff. There should be no need to point out that with Wycliffe, and later with Luther, the determination to return to Scripture is to be explained in the first place as a reaction against this decadent scholasticism. On this point see P. de Voogt, "Wiclef et la 'Scriptura sola'," *ETL* 39 (1963), 50-86.

[70] H. de Lubac, *op. cit.*, pp. 386 ff.

## III. FROM THE RENAISSANCE TO MODERN TIMES

### I. THE ARRIVAL OF CRITICISM

After the fall of the Roman Empire, the preservation of the Greco-Roman heritage and then the development of medieval culture were accomplished in the climate of faith and under the shield of theology. The study of Scripture naturally profited from that fact. But with the Renaissance, the cultural development of the West began to break away from the direction of the Church. The result for the state of exegesis was a complete transformation.

### 1. *Textual, Literary and Historical Criticism*

When it preserved the works of classical antiquity, the Middle Ages had christianized their values and incorporated them into its civilization. It was in the Christian perspective that grammarians and philosophers of the day explained them. But the 16th-century humanists, breaking with the traditional commentaries, introduced a new approach to the texts in order to rediscover living antiquity in its original freshness. To their search for, and publication of, manuscripts, they joined a profound knowledge of ancient languages and of more objective methods of literary analysis. Besides, a general interest in resurrecting the past brought about a progressive refinement of historical criticism, which reached its climax in history's 19th-century pretension to the dignity of an exact science.

All these facts had their repercussions on biblical studies. [71] The Bible too became an object of textual criticism, and has remained so without interruption from the 16th century to our own day. [72] Literary criticism broke with the scholastic method, which decided *a priori* the meaning of the sacred texts, and set about to discover that meaning in its native state. [73] That is no easy task when one is dealing with such ancient works. To pass judgment on them, the only materials for comparison until the mid-19th century were the works of classical antiquity. Since then the recovery of

[71] The names of Erasmus and Lefèvre d'Étaples come first to mind (cf. R. Aubenas in Fliche—Martin, *Histoire de l'Église* 15, pp. 240-246, 252-255; L. Willaert, *ibid.*, Vol. 18/1, pp. 227-230).

[72] After the rabbinic Bible of Bomberg at Venice came the polyglot Bibles of Alcala (1520), Antwerp (1569-1572), Paris (1645), and London (1657). Since these efforts at textual criticism caused no difficulty for hermeneutics, we have not insisted on them here.

[73] But it should be noted, in the case of Lefèvre d'Étaples as well as that of Erasmus, that this search for the literal sense of Scripture remained profoundly traditional in its spirit; cf. H. de Lubac, *op. cit.*, pp. 411-422, 434-453. Scripture always has as its sole object the mystery of Jesus Christ.

oriental literatures (Egyptian, Assyro-Babylonian, Cananaean) removed the Bible from its isolation and provided material for a fruitful comparison. Given these new perspectives, the allure of the search for the literal sense naturally changed. Finally, the effort undertaken by historians to resurrect the past on the basis of critically examined documentation also reached the two Testaments. Their texts were pared down with the same meticulous care in order to reconstruct a scientific biblical history. On this point, archeological research, methodically undertaken since 1850, has produced precious results which serve as a check on the results obtained from a criticism of the text. In itself, all this effort was not directed against theology; nevertheless, right from its beginning, it developed independently of it, with its own methods and no intention of serving it. Traditionalist theologians, who felt no need for this critical study, quickly took offense at such autonomy when it was applied to the sacred books. Already in the 17th century, Richard Simon, [74] who can be considered the father of modern exegesis, aroused the ire of Bossuet, who obtained the condemnation of his books. In the 18th century, separation widened proportionally as the critics insisted on their freedom to call into question the traditional interpretations held by the theologians. [75]

## 2. Philosophical Criticism

To make matters worse, this perfectly legitimate undertaking was shortly taken up by thinkers who joined to it a philosophical criticism com-

---

[74] On Richard Simon, see the well documented work of J. Steinmann, *Richard Simon et les origines de l'exégèse biblique* (Paris: Desclée de Brouwer, 1960). H. J. Kraus, *Geschichte der historisch-kritischen Erforschung des Alten Testaments von der Reformation bis zur Gegenwart* (Neukirchen: Erziehungsverein, 1956), pp. 60-64, renders merited homage to this precursor.

[75] Montesquieu's derision of theologians is apparent in this passage from the *Persian Letters:*
"Father," I asked him, "what are those large volumes that cover all this side of the library?"
"Those," he replied, "are the works of the interpreters of Scripture."
"There have been a great number of them!" I rejoined. "Scripture must have been very obscure in bygone days and very clear today. Is anything still in doubt? Could there be any disputed points left?"
"Oh, to be sure, there certainly are," he replied. "There are just about as many as there are lines."
"What?" I said. "What did all these authors accomplish then?"
"These authors," he explained, "did not search the Scriptures for what is to be believed, but what they themselves believed. They did not consider the Bible a book which contains the dogmas they should have accepted, but a work which could lend authority to their personal ideas—that is why they corrupted all its meanings and tortured its every passage. It is a country into which men of every sect march and come to loot; it is a battlefield on which warring nations wage many battles, where attacks are launched, and all sorts of skirmishes take place." (Letter 134)

pletely detached from the faith, [76] in the name of which they presumed to stand in sovereign judgment over theology, the content of the Bible, and religion itself. Its fundamental principles were already laid down by Spinoza in the 17th century in his *Tractatus Theologico-Politicus*. [77] In the 18th century, deist rationalism seized on them, [78] and thence proceeded in the 19th century a whole series of systems which mutually influenced one another, from Hegelian idealism to the evolutionism of Spencer, from Auguste Comte's positivism to the sociologism of Durkheim, etc. In this context, the positivist concept of history as science [79] held sway, and it quite naturally applied its canons to the Bible. Excluding *a priori* any explanation of facts or ideas that involved supernatural causality, it attempted to reduce them critically according to its underlying philosophy. In practice, though, this reduction took various forms, for each historian chose from among Christian values and strove to save at any cost those which fit into his own system of thought.

Exegesis had to accommodate itself to this pre-established situation in order to function. Literary analysis, historical criticism, the conclusions of sociology and the history of religions, and finally those of archeology, all supplied positive elements which individuals attempted to interpret and unify into a synthetic presentation. The theories thus constructed claimed to be independent of any preconception and of any faith. In fact they were no less dominated by a ruling principle which was not in this case scientific, but philosophical. The hypothetical reconstructions of biblical history to which they led changed according to the personal preference of the one who organized the available material. After the Jesus of Reimarus (whose papers were published by Lessing) came that of the *Vicaire savoyard*, full of religious sentiment. That of Strauss was followed by that of Renan, which is less arbitrary, since Renan was acquainted with oriental archeology and Palestinian geography. [80] In the 20th century came portraits of Jesus by

---

[76] This current of thought had distant roots in 16th-century Italy and in the freethinkers against whom Pascal and Bossuet wrote; but we will here examine only the application of its principles to the Bible. For its history see P. Hazard, *La crise de la conscience européenne (1680-1715)* (Paris: Fayard, 1961) and *La pensée européenne au XVIIIe siècle de Montesquieu à Lessing* (Paris: Fayard, 1963).

[77] B. de Spinoza, *Chief Works* (New York: Dover, 1951). In chap. 7 Spinoza poses as a principle that the critical examination of Scripture is sufficient unto itself; in chap. 15 he establishes a radical separation between philosophy and theology.

[78] Concerning this general problem see E. Préclin—E. Jarry in Fliche—Martin, *Histoire de l'Église* 19, pp. 701-746 (on the loss of faith between 1648 and 1789, and the apologetics which combatted it).

[79] On this particular problem, see above, p. 115.

[80] Add to that "a live taste for the ideal of the gospel and for the character of the founder of Christianity" which he himself says he tried to project in his *Life of Jesus* (E. Renan, *Souvenirs d'enfance et de jeunesse* 5, 5). But this affective attitude naturally supposes a radical reduction of Jesus to human limits.

Couchoud [81] and Guignebert, [82] so different one from the other. In such circumstances, is it surprising that theologians mistrusted a so often conjectural criticism, which its practitioners linked to a world view foreign to the faith, if not openly hostile to it? Despite that, they were forced to take notice of the new conception of literal sense which that criticism presented. Their concern thus took a new direction: from God, author of Scripture, it turned to the human authors to whom we owe the sacred texts; without knowing what those authors intended to write, and actually wrote, how can one pretend to understand the meaning of the biblical texts? So also in theology, the notion of literal sense became that of modern culture. We will return to this point later. [83]

## II. THE PROTESTANT CRISIS AND "SCRIPTURE ALONE" [84]

### 1. The Reform Tradition

Alongside of this cultural evolution, the Protestant revolt introduced a new principle of interpretation of Scripture into Christian theo-

[81] P. L. Couchoud, Le mystère de Jésus (Paris: Rieder, 1924), resurrected the thesis of myths which deny the very existence of Jesus.

[82] C. Guignebert, Jésus (Paris: Michel, 1947) indeed intended to rid himself of "the hypnosis of ancestral prejudices" which he still detected in Renan. With a total absence of sympathy for the subject he treated, he reconstructed the personality of Jesus in his own manner, and then naively confessed: "I do not deceive myself about the poverty, or the incoherency, or, for that matter, the uncertainty of this brief sketch of the psychology of Jesus, whose elements I have drawn from the opinion our evangelists had formed of him. These elements, let us not forget, are already interpretations which might be prejudiced, recollections which might not be exact, traditional accounts which might not have anything to do with reality. Nevertheless, as I see in all that nothing particularly glorious for Christ, nor anything superhuman, I would willingly admit that Ur-Markus and the Logia have preserved for us at least a reflection of the image of the man Jesus" (op. cit., p. 215).

[83] Below, pp. 273 f.

[84] For the history of Protestant exegesis, see R. Cornely—A. Merk, Manuel d'introduction à toutes les saintes Écritures I (Paris: Lethielleux, 1930), pp. 363-374; A. Robert and A. Vaganay, "Interprétation," DBS 4, cols. 627-634 and 637-646 (includes a bibliography); A. Vincent and A. Vaganay in Robert—Tricot, Guide to the Bible I, pp. 707-729 (these treatments have a decidedly marked critical character); G. Ebeling, "Hermeneutik," RGG 3, cols. 251-258 (a methodical presentation of tendencies and authors with a rich bibliography); A. Bea, " 'Religionswissenschaftliche' oder 'theologische' Exegese? Zur Geschichte der neueren biblischen Hermeneutik," Biblica 40 (1959), 322-341 (a good summary). For Old Testament exegesis: H. J. Kraus, Geschichte der historisch-kritischen Forschung des Alten Testaments von der Reformation bis zur Gegenwart (Neukirchen: Erziehungsverein, 1956); E. G. Kraeling, The Old Testament since the Reformation (London, 1955) (excellent treatments of the subject from the standpoint of Protestant theology). For New Testament exegesis: A. Schweitzer, Geschichte der Leben-Jesu-Forschung, 5th ed. (Tübingen: Mohr, 1933); Geschichte der paulinischen Forschung (Tübingen: Mohr, 1933); S. Neill, The Interpretation of the New Testament, 1861-1961 (London: Oxford U. Press, 1964).

logy. [85]  The authority of the Church as the living rule of faith was rejected, and the meaning of the sacred books was no longer sought in ecclesiastical tradition expressed through a magisterium.  As a consequence, it became necessary to construct the whole edifice of the faith and Christian reflection on the basis of Scripture alone, eliminating from it all the purely human additions that antiquity or especially the Middle Ages might have added to its explicit statements.  By attempting thus to regain apostolic Christianity in its pure state, Protestantism posed for itself a difficult problem of interpretation. If Scripture is required to be its own interpreter, [86] still the activity of the preacher and theologian who expound its texts cannot be passed over in silence; they need a method to insure that their view is correct.  But what can serve this purpose, if the symbiosis of Scripture and Tradition which had persisted up to the great scholastics is discarded?  The earliest reformers required that the word of God be read with faith, in the light of the Holy Spirit; still it is necessary that this light manifest itself in some unmistakable way. [87]  Furthermore, Reform exegesis soon had to come to grips with the critical movement born in the Renaissance.  Then it was constrained, just as Catholic theology was, to declare itself for or against the new methods of literary or historical criticism, for or against the philosophical reinterpretations of revelation detached from traditional doctrine.

In the face of these problems, Protestant exegesis divided into opposing currents.  An ultraconservative faction, which found a theological basis in the theory of verbal inspiration, [88] was opposed in principle not only to the philosophical criticism imbued with modern rationalism, but even to literary and historical criticism, which seemed to them disrespectful to the word of God.  This excessively literalist faction lived on in the fundamentalist current, which is open to ancient history and archeology only in the measure that they seem to prove that "the Bible is right."  This right wing considerably hardened the position of the early reformers, which was resolutely theological, attached to the dogmas clearly attested in Scripture, oriented toward an existential interpretation which was attentive to the life

[85] See above, chap. I, pp. 20 ff.  On the problem posed by the Reformation, see G. H. Tavard, *Écriture ou Église? La crise de la Réforme* (Paris: Cerf, 1963) (especially chaps. VI and VII).

[86] That is the real meaning of the principle: *Scriptura sola*.  But this submission of the Church to Scripture does not preclude that, for the simple faithful, Scripture is to be read in the Church.

[87] Concerning this aspect of Calvin's doctrine, see G. H. Tavard, *op. cit.*, pp. 145-161.  It should be noted that while rejecting the Catholic concept of tradition, Calvin and several other reformers remained very attentive to the patristic exegesis of Scripture, which remained for them a valuable possession of the Church.

[88] Above, p. 41, note 29.

values included in the sacred texts, still to some extent mindful of the example of the ancient fathers, but not at all closed to a sane use of the methods introduced by the humanists. [89] This original position was preserved by the "orthodox" Lutherans and Calvinists, for whom the fathers of the Reform hold a place similar to that which modern Thomists attribute to the *Doctor communis*. [90] A good number of Anglican exegetes retained that position as well, joining this real religious sense to a renewed interest in patristic tradition when the Oxford movement restored it to a place of honor. The newly born critical movement did not find a poor reception in such an environment (for example, in the 17th century, from L. Cappelle and J. Cocceius, [91] and in the 18th, from J.D. Michaelis [92]).

## 2. Liberal Protestantism

On the opposing side, since the end of the 16th century a left wing (Harmensen and the Socinians) moved toward rationalist anti-dogmatism. [93] In the 17th century H. Grotius [94] added a more demanding concern for historical criticism. In the 18th, theologians of this tendency (J. G. Semler, J. G. Herder [95]) underwent the strong influence of the *Aufklärung*. It was undoubtedly such men as these who laid the foundations in the first decades of the 19th century for modern criticism of the Old Testament [96] (Eichhorn, De Wette, Vatke, Ewald), but their practical aim in doing so was to exclude it from Christian theology. [97] And that aim was not without its influence on Schleiermacher's theology. [98] A history of the religion of Israel, crowned by a history of Christian origins, tended to take the place of the theology of biblical revelation. The movement of ideas that agitated the ancient world

---

[89] On the exegesis of the first reformers see H. J. Kraus, *op. cit.*, pp. 5-27; E. G. Kraeling, *op. cit.*, pp. 7-32; a bibliography on the subject in G. Ebeling, *art. cit.*, cols. 259 f.; E. de Moreau in Fliche—Martin, *Histoire de l'Église* 16, pp. 85 ff., 94-97, 107 f., 201; H. Strohl, "La méthode exégétique des réformateurs," *Le problème biblique dans le protestantisme* (Paris: P.U.F., 1955), pp. 87-104 (which shows as little understanding of patristic and medieval exegesis as many Catholic polemicists do of that of the reformers).

[90] A typical quotation in G. H. Tavard, *op. cit.*, pp. 143 f.

[91] H. J. Kraus, *op. cit.*, pp. 43-46, 49 ff.

[93] *Ibid.*, pp. 87-93.

[93] *Ibid.*, p. 37 ff.

[94] *Ibid.*, pp. 46-48; his *Adnotationes ad Vetus et Novum Testamentum* date from 1641-1647, 40 years before R. Simon's, *Histoire critique du Vieux Testament*.

[95] *Ibid.*, pp. 93-119. Kraus stresses the relationship of ideas between Herder and Lessing. On this latter, see E. Préclin—E. Jarry in Fliche—Martin, *Histoire de l'Église* 19, p. 738.

[96] H. J. Kraus, *op. cit.*, pp. 121-175, 179-190.

[97] *Ibid.*, pp. 175-179.

[98] E. G. Kraeling, *op. cit.*, pp. 59-68 (with an overall presentation of the place of the Old Testament in Protestant theology in the 19th-century, pp. 69 ff.).

continued to be considered the supreme manifestation of the religious aspirations of man, but the tendency was to impose on it a reinterpretation in accord with modern philosophies.

Liberal Protestantism, the fruit of these conflicting influences, held sway in exegesis up to the time of the First World War, [99] using the services of a criticism continually more sure of itself, bold in its hypotheses, and the more dogmatic as it believed itself founded upon incontestable scientific principles. The results were systems in which the positive acquisitions of a sound analysis of the texts stood side by side with the most conjectural of evolutionary schemes. Thus it was with the criticism of the Pentateuch which Wellhausen [100] incorporated into a presentation of Israelite history in which religion follows an evolutionary process, from polytheism to monolatry to monotheism. And the same was the case with the history of Christian origins, in which the person of Christ, a moral preacher for some (Harnack), the herald of the eschatological catastrophe for others (J. Weiss), became an object of speculation in a primitive church dependent on Greco-oriental syncretism. [101] When it reached this point, liberal Protestantism was hardly distinguishable from the rationalist criticism that surrounded it, even if a touch of pietism can be noted in some of its proponents. The radical separation between criticism and theology, which was largely prepared by the thought of Ritschl and then of Troeltsch, [102] was then complete, to the great detriment of the faith and, in the end, of criticism.

### 3. *The Return to Biblical Theology* [103]

At about the time of the First World War a reaction against this dominant current could be detected from several directions at once. In the field of historical criticism itself, the great advance of archeology [104] put a brake on

[99] A good synthesis in J. Levie, *The Bible, Word of God in Words of Men,* pp. 21-39.

[100] H. J. Kraus, *op. cit.,* pp. 235-249; H. Cazelles in Robert—Feuillet, *Introduction to the Old Testament,* pp. 84-93.

[101] A presentation and discussion of these systems can be found in F. M. Braun, *Où en est le problème de Jésus?* (Paris: Gabalda, 1932), pp. 29-136; L. de Grandmaison, *Jésus-Christ* (Paris: Beauchesne, 1928), pp. 178-218.

[102] E. G. Kraeling, *op. cit.,* pp. 99-125. Concerning Ritschl and Troeltsch, see the articles in *RGG* 5, 1114-1117 and Vol. 6, 1044-1047.

[103] A brief treatment in J. Levie, *op. cit.,* pp. 119-128. The evolution of the problem is excellently treated by R. Marlé, *Le problème théologique de l'herméneutique: Les grands axes de la recherche contemporaine* (Paris: L'Orante, 1963).

[104] J. Levie, *op. cit.,* pp. 11-113, provides a concise bibliography that is constantly growing. The contributions of archeology to the exegesis of the Old Testament are presented by S. H. Hooke in H. W. Robinson, *Record and Revelation* (Oxford: Clarendon, 1938), pp. 348-373; W. F. Albright in H. H. Rowley, *The Old Testament and Modern Study* (Oxford: Clarendon, 1951), pp. 1-47. To form an idea of what

adventurous hypotheses by unearthing the Bible's solid roots in constantly better known oriental antiquity. At the same time, the transmission of recollections through oral tradition was reevaluated in a much more positive sense.[105] In the domain of theology, Protestant orthodoxy found new vigor with Karl Barth and his dialectical theology.[106] In his commentary on the letter to the Romans (1921), Barth introduced a method of interpretation which, without ignoring critical studies, was avowedly dogmatic: what it sought in the texts, beyond historical contingencies, was the absolute of the word of God. The movement gained ground steadily. Having caused criticism itself to temper its pretensions and to be aware of its own limits, it went on to bring about a revival of biblical theology, which the school of the history of religions had consigned to the category of the outmoded.[107] The first to benefit was the theology of the New Testament; the evidence is G. Kittel's monumental *Theologisches Wörterbuch zum Neuen Testament*.[108] But exegesis returned also to the theology of the Old Testament, discarding a common prejudice among the liberal critics which Harnack clearly defined.[109] What is more, the relation between the two Testaments became the object of studies and discussions in which, without abandoning criticism, theologians resumed the best tradition of Luther and Calvin.[110]

influence it has had, one might compare, on the one hand, J. Wellhausen, *Prolegomena zur Geschichte Israels* (Berlin: Reimer, 1886) or A. Loisy, *La religion d'Israël* (Paris: Nourry, 1933) with, on the other hand, W. F. Albright, *Archaeology and the Religion of Israel* (Baltimore: Hopkins, 1946); idem, *From the Stone Age to Christianity* (Baltimore: Hopkins, 1946); M. Noth, *Geschichte Israels* (Göttingen: Vandenhoeck & Ruprecht, 1954); J. Bright, *A History of Israel* (Philadelphia: Westminster, 1959) (cf. G. E. Wright, "Archaeology and Old Testament Studies," *JBL* 77 [1958], 39-51).

[105] The sometimes excessive works of the Scandinavian school ought to be mentioned here, following J. Pedersen, *Israel, Its Life and Culture*, 2 Vols. (Copenhagen: Poul—Branner, 1926-1940); cf. E. Nielsen, *Oral Tradition, A Modern Problem in Old Testament Introduction* (London: SCM Press, 1954). Likewise, for the gospels: B. Gerhardsson, *Memory and Manuscript* (Uppsala: Gleerup, 1961).

[106] See in K. Barth, *Dogmatics I. The Doctrine of the Word of God.* On the exegesis of K. Barth, cf. J. Hamer, *Karl Barth* (Westminster: Newman, 1962), pp. 107-131; H. Bouillard, *Karl Barth: Parole de Dieu et existence humaine* 2 (Paris: Aubier, 1957), pp. 41-45.

[107] C. Colpe, *Die religionsgeschichtliche Schule. Darstellung und Kritik ihres Bildes vom gnostichen Erlösermythen* (Göttingen, 1961).

[108] See the works cited by R. Schnackenburg, *New Testament Theology Today* (New York: Herder, 1963), especially pp. 29-43, who discusses the state of the problem without distinguishing the works of Catholics from those of Protestants.

[109] H. J. Kraus, *op. cit.*, pp. 350 ff.; E. G. Kraeling, *op. cit.*, pp. 147 ff.; cf. *Sens chrétien de l'A.T.*, p. 76 (where the successive reactions of Kautzsch [1903], Eissfeldt [1921], and Hempel [1932] are pointed out).

[110] See the bibliographies gathered by C. Westermann, *Probleme alttestamentlicher Hermeneutik* (Munich: Kaiser, 1960) and S. Amsler, *L'Ancien Testament dans l'Église* (Neuchâtel-Paris: Delachaux, 1960).

And that is not all, for exegetical method itself underwent serious adjustments as new concerns arose. Documentary criticism now centered its attention on an aspect of the biblical books which the preceding age had left relatively neglected: their concrete relation to the sociological environment in which they were produced. At the same time it helped to determine their literary forms in relation to the faith, religious life, practical needs, and culture of that environment. This *Gattungsgeschichte*, undertaken for the Old Testament by Gunkel and Gressmann, [111] became for the New Testament exegetes *Formgeschichte* (form criticism), which was applied first to the gospels. [112] This new current did not indeed liberate itself all at once from the historical skepticism to which the hypercriticism of liberal Protestantism had arrived. Obvious remnants of it can be seen in Dibelius, and still more in Bultmann. [113] But at least an effort was made to reach, beyond the texts, the faith which those texts were designed to transmit, for the purpose of allowing Christian faith of today to nourish itself through contact with that of the primitive Church. [114]

For R. Bultmann, however, the *formgeschichtliche Methode* is only a part of a larger undertaking, both exegetical and theological which aims to rethink the whole of the science of interpretation. [115] God's message expressed in Scripture, and more precisely by the New Testament which

[111] H. Cazelles, "L'école de l'histoire des formes et le Pentateuque," *BCE* 7 (1954), 31-42. Besides, Gunkel and Gressmann are representatives of the *religionsgeschichtliche Schule* (cf. H. J. Kraus, *op. cit.*, pp. 295-334); that is the root of their hostility to dogmatism, which is hardly favorable to biblical theology (*ibid.*, p. 333).

[112] A concise treatment with bibliography by X. Léon-Dufour in Robert— Feuillet, *Introduction to the New Testament*, pp. 288 ff.

[113] Here again Form Criticism preserves the heritage of the history of religions school. See, for example, M. Dibelius, "Jungfrauensohn und Krippenkind," *Botschaft und Geschichte* I (Tübingen: Mohr, 1953), pp. 1-78; "Evangelienkritik und Christologie," *ibid.*, pp. 293-358. R. Bultmann, *Primitive Christianity in its Contemporary Setting* (Cleveland: Meridian pap., 1956) (especially chap. V: Primitive Christianity as a Syncretist Phenomenon). But with V. Taylor, *The Formation of the Gospel Tradition* (London: Macmillan, 1933) the position is already quite different.

[114] This aim of Form Criticism, which intended to extricate itself from the impasse in which liberal exegesis found itself, was clearly stated by O. Cullmann as early as 1925: "Les récentes études sur la formation de la tradition évangélique," *RHPR* 5 (1925), 579.

[115] See the translation of the most important of Bultmann's articles in W. Kegley, *The Theology of Rudolf Bultmann* (London: SCM Press, 1966). The systematic treatment of A. Malet, *Mythos et logos, La pensée de Rudolf Bultmann* (Geneva: Labor et Fides, 1962) received the complete approbation of the Master. Critical studies from the standpoint of Catholic theology: L. Malevez, *Le message chrétien et le mythe* (Paris: Desclée de Brouwer, 1954); R. Marlé, *Bultmann et l'interprétation du Nouveau Testament* (Paris: Aubier, 1956) (summarized in *Le problème théologique de l'herméneutique*, pp. 34-78); G. Hasenhüttl, *Der Glaubensvollzug. Eine Begegnung mit Rudolf Bultmann aus katholischen Glaubensverständnis* (Essen: Wingen, 1963).

announces the gospel of salvation to man, was transmitted by the biblical authors according to the consciousness of it which their own faith gave them, but they performed their task in a language that necessarily resorts to the categories of myth, in the sense that it expresses in terms of this world the reality of salvation which is a pure act of God and does not belong to this world. In order to understand that message, therefore, it must be transposed into a language that is intelligible to us by demythologizing it, that is, by translating the mythical language in which it is expressed to uncover what, beneath this covering, is the only thing that interests us: our Christian existence as men called to salvation, into which we enter by a decision of faith. Critical studies give us an understanding of the conditions in which the primitive mythologizing of the message took place [116]; but it cannot take the place of the exegete's decision of faith through which he recognizes in this message the very word of God. Once he has entered the faith, the exegete is able to realize conjointly an existentialist interpretation of Scripture, which reveals its demythologized message, and a Christian interpretation of human existence, understood in the perspective of salvation already announced. Theology is nothing other than this twofold interpretation of Scripture and existence. [117]

Since the Second World War, Bultmann's undertaking has gradually gained ground within Protestantism, while at the same time undergoing a quite profound transformation at the hands of some of the Master of Marburg's disciples, either as a reaction against his critical radicalism, [118] or as a further elaboration of the theology of the word of God. [119] But his undertaking has also been the object of numerous objections, sometimes violent ones. To the flat rejection of conservative theologians was added the voice

[116] In this Bultmann's debt to liberal criticism and the school of the history of religions is apparent. Its application dominates his *Theology of the New Testament* (New York: Scribner's Sons, 1951).

[117] It is to be noted that in Bultmann's approach the Old Testament plays only a negative role and does not fit well into theology. Cf. E. G. Kraeling, *op. cit.*, pp. 227-238; *Sens chrétien de l'A.T.*, p. 423, note 1; below, p. 266.

[118] J. M. Robinson, *A New Quest of the Historical Jesus* (London: SCM Press, 1959) surveys the movement and provides a bibliography; cf. H. Anderson, *Jesus and Christian Origins: A Commentary on Modern Viewpoints* (New York: Oxford U.P., 1964).

[119] That is the case with G. Ebeling, *Das Wesen des christlichen Glaubens* (Tübingen: Mohr, 1959); *idem, Word and Faith* (Philadelphia: Fortress, 1963). Cf. R. Marlé, "Foi et Parole: La théologie de Gerhard Ebeling," *RSR* 53 (1962), 5-31 (the theological problem of hermeneutics, pp. 79-102). On the post-Bultmann movement, see R. E. Brown, "After Bultmann, What? An Introduction to the Post-Bultmannians," *CBQ* 26 (1964), 1-30; J. Cahill, "Rudolf Bultmann and Post-Bultmann Tendencies," *CBQ* 26 (1964), 153-178; J. M. Robinson, *The Bultmann School of Biblical Interpretation: New Directions?* (New York: Harper, 1965).

of K. Barth in the name of dialectic theology,[120] that of O. Cullmann, whose conception of Christian theology as comprehension of the history of salvation led him to consider favorably philosophical and historical exegesis,[121] and many others.[122] Despite their very different approaches, both Bultmann and his critics pose an identical task for biblical exegesis today: 1) the development of a method of interpretation that, while remaining under the guidance of faith, incorporates critical study into its work[123]; 2) the construction of a theology,[124] that is, an understanding of Scripture which presents its content systematically without losing sight of its pastoral importance. Biblical theology too is experiencing a renaissance in contemporary Protestantism.[125]

### III. THE PROBLEM OF EXEGESIS IN CATHOLIC THEOLOGY

From the 16th century to our own day, the evolution of the problem of interpretation in Catholicism was largely determined by the existence of Protestant exegesis and of a current of faithless criticism. Several periods

[120] Concerning this debate, see the strictly Bultmannian point of view of A. Malet, *op. cit.*, pp. 347-389; L. Malevez, "Exégèse biblique et philosophie. Deux conceptions opposées de leurs rapports: R. Bultmann et K. Barth," *NRT* 78 (1956), 897-914, 1027-1042.

[121] O. Cullmann, "La nécessité et la fonction de l'exégèse philologique et historique de la Bible," *Le problème biblique dans le protestantisme*, pp. 131-147. Cullmann's exegetical and theological principles are objectively set forth by J. Frisque, *Oscar Cullmann: Une théologie de l'histoire du salut* (Paris: Casterman, 1960), pp. 13-63 (on his opposition to Bultmann, pp. 57-63). On the debate between Cullmann and Bultmann, see L. Bini, *L'intervento di Oscar Cullmann nella discussione bultmanniana* (Rome: Pont. Univ. Greg., 1961).

[122] To be noted, from the philosophical viewpoint, is the critique of K. Jaspers, published in French translation along with Bultmann's reply in *Études théologiques et religieuses* 29 (1954), 21-90. Contributions to the discussion that arose over *Entmythologisierung* have been collected in the volumes entitled *Kerygma und Mythos* (Hamburh: Reich, 1948 ff.).

[123] This problem of the relationship of criticism to faith is itself a difficult one. Cf. M. Goguel, "La critique et la foi," *Le problème biblique dans le protestantisme*, pp. 11-44; J. C. Rylaarsdam, "The Problem of Faith and History in Biblical Interpretation," *JBL* 77 (1958), 26-32.

[124] On this point, note the similar conclusions of E. G. Kraeling, *op. cit.*, pp. 250-284, and H. J. Kraus, *op. cit.*, pp. 441-444. Cf. J. Muilenburg, "Preface to Hermeneutics," *JBL* 76 (1957), 18-26; N. F. S. Ferré, "Notes by a Theologian on Biblical Hermeneutics," *JBL* 78 (1959), 105-114. The search for a middle way between rationalist liberalism and false pietism is likewise to be found in the work of A. Mickelsen, *Interpreting the Bible* (Grand Rapids: Eerdmans, 1963).

[125] On the state of this question in recent years, see the article (of Bultmannian tendency) by E. Fuchs, "Das hermeneutische Problem" in E. Dinkler, *Zeit und Geschichte* (Tübingen: Mohr, 1964), pp. 357-366.

should be distinguished; the encyclicals *Providentissimus* (1893) and *Divino afflante Spiritu* (1943) conveniently mark off their limits.

## *1. Counter-Reform Theology*

In patristic antiquity and the early Middle Ages, exegesis and theology were one; they were still organically connected at the height of scholasticism in the 13th century. The Counter Reformation perpetuated their distinction, and soon their practical separation, for three centuries. The humanism of the Renaissance did, indeed, after the Council of Trent, favor an immediate and fruitful revitalization of exegesis, [126] by providing interpreters of Scripture a deeper knowledge of biblical languages, and by renovating the methods of analysis applied to the sacred texts. Some excellent theological commentaries resulted, nourished by patristic elements, but resolutely constructive, especially for the books of the New Testament (such as those of Maldonatus, Toletus, Serier, Estius, etc.). But in the course of the 17th century this progress was cut short. Despite a development of positive theology, whose necessity Melchior Cano had shown in his treatise *De locis theologicis*, [127] the place allotted exegesis in post-Tridentine scholasticism did not permit it any real growth.

Scripture then no longer occupied the place in theology it had held through the 13th century. It was no longer the *Sacra doctrina*, whose content theology strove to expound even while it was arranging its declarations logically in a *Summa*. Granted that the break with the contrived allegories which reigned in the 15th century marked an incontestable progress. But positive theology itself was made subordinate to scholastic theology; the medieval *summa* (the *Sentences* of Peter Lombard or the *Summa* of St. Thomas) became the theology manual that was explained, developed, and retained as point of reference. Scripture became no more than the first of theological sources from which arguments were drawn to justify doctrine. Since Protestantism brandished the principle of "Scripture alone," Catholic theology emphasized the authority of Tradition and the

---

[126] L. Willaert, "La restauration catholique" in Fliche—Martin, *Histoire de l'Église* 18/1, pp. 242-246, rightfully links this progress to that of patristic studies (pp. 246 ff.).

[127] M. Cano, *De locis theologicis* (Salamanca, 1523); in Migne, *Theologiae cursus completus* 1, pp. 57-716; cf. L. Willaert, *op. cit.*, pp. 238 f. (includes bibliography). In itself, the recourse to theological sources favors positive theology, and biblical exegesis should be the first to benefit; a case in point is Maldonatus, who freed himself from the manual and organized the matter of his course in his own way (*ibid.*, p. 239). But the methods of scholasticism finally triumphed, with adjustments to meet the climate of controversy.

magisterium, which were forcefully defended by the Council of Trent. In these circumstances, the biblical commentary tended to take on a utilitarian bent; the exegete was to prepare the material which the theologian could use in his demonstrations. As a matter of fact, dogmatic theology was marked by the method of controversy, and everything was presented under the form of theses to defend—against the heretics of the past, against Luther and Calvin, then against Baius and Jansen, and finally against rationalism, which soon became the apologists' principal anxiety. Having been transformed into a simple servant of dogma and apologetics, [128] exegesis was entrusted with the thankless task of supplying scriptural arguments, against the Protestants, to prove the points they denied, and against unbelievers, arguments from reason to prove the necessity of believing the Scriptures.

The consequences of this situation were in the long run disastrous. At the very moment when criticism was developing, the traditionalist theologians considered it only one more danger. In a defensive reaction they barred the way to this novelty, as is exemplified in Bossuet's opposition to Richard Simon. [129] Thus recalled to beaten paths, commentators of the Bible [130] put their erudition, often substantial, at the service of a conservatism in which the dogmatic tradition of the Church is scarcely distinguishable from opinions accepted without question or from routine mental procedures. When modern thought raised new problems, generally poorly put, but nonetheless real, they felt themselves obliged to defend the "traditional" position, for example, in the question of the Pentateuch. [131] Shackled by a false concept of inerrancy, they resorted to concordist systems in an attempt to save the scientific truth of Scripture. [132] They were above all opposed to applying to Scripture the methods of historical criticism which were applied to all other human documents. Finally, occupied in the work of contro-

---

[128] This situation coincided with the triumph of the theory of two sources, in which Scripture and Tradition lost the organic relationship that antiquity and the Middle Ages had recognized; cf. above, pp. 196-203.

[129] Above, p. 204.

[130] Concerning the works this conservative exegesis produced, see the discussion of R. Cornely, *Introductio in utriusque Testamenti libros sacros* I (Paris: 1894), pp. 535-616. A. Vaccari in *Institutiones biblicae*, pp. 551-561, gives a mere enumeration of names and works. For some idea of the erudition of the authors in question, it is sufficient to recall the names of A. Calmet in the 18th-century, and F. Vigouroux, the editor of the *Dictionnaire de la Bible*, which made generous use of the early finds of archeology.

[131] E. Mangenot, *L'authenticité mosaïque du Pentateuque* (Paris: Letouzey, 1907) presents a synthesis of the positions of this conservative current from a strictly apologetic standpoint.

[132] Above, pp. 102 ff.

versy, exegetes scarcely had the time to construct an authentic theology based on Scripture, much less to set forth its spiritual riches; theology and spirituality were none of their business. Unfortunately, professional theologians, experienced in the dialectic exercises of the schools, seldom versed in knowledge of the fathers, had usually little awareness of the problems of exegesis; since they were ignorant of critical methods, the Bible posed no problem for them. They were heirs of a doctrinal tradition which they were dedicated to maintain, but because they saw with the eyes of centuries past, they had an *a priori* conception of interpretation. The Thomistic classification of the senses of Scripture provided them the outline for their interpretation, as can be seen, for example, in the exposition of Patrizi,[133] an excellent work of its kind. Within its limits, this is not a false method, but the modern notion of literal sense, the one employed in biblical criticism, remained beyond its grasp, for St. Thomas' approach to the problem was worked out from another point of view and belonged to another culture.

Our purpose is not merely to darken the picture, but to recognize the extreme weakness of Catholic exegesis in the 18th and 19th centuries. The best theologians of the time were in no way competent biblicists, not even Newman.[134] He was familiar with Scripture from his childhood,[135] and enriched his preaching and his theology with it as Origen or St. Bernard might have done. His understanding of the modern world, his great knowledge of the fathers and St. Thomas, and his keen mind enabled him to grasp the real problems and to foresee their solution. But he had no experience of critical questions. When the discussion on inspiration and inerrancy became acute, his contribution,[136] prepared long beforehand, made some useful points, but did not provide the happy formulation which would have extricated theology from its deadlock. If he appears today a precursor, it is less for a particular theory of interpretation than for his manner of practicing exegesis.[137] While not losing sight of the historical problems posed by the literal sense of Scripture, he was able to reach beyond them and find in the

---

[133] F. X. Patrizi, *Institutio de interpretatione Bibliorum* (Rome, 1876).

[134] J. Seynaeve, "Newman (Doctrine scripturaire du Cardinal)," *DBS* 6, cols. 427-474; *Cardinal Newman's Doctrine on Holy Scripture according to his Published Works and Previously Unedited Manuscripts* (Oxford: Blackwell, 1953).

[135] Witness the statement which opens chap. 1 of the *Apologia pro vita sua:* "I was brought up from a child to take great delight in reading the Bible."

[136] Two articles published in brochure: *Essays on Controversial Points Variously Illustrated* (London, 1884). J. Seynaeve has published some *Inspiration Papers* which date from 1861-1863, which show that Newman was already preoccupied with this problem 25 years earlier (cf. *art. cit.*, cols. 129-132).

[137] *Ibid.*, cols. 447 ff.

biblical texts the essential source of his doctrine and spirituality, thus escaping the progressive emaciation that was everywhere overtaking commentaries of the sacred text. Meanwhile, the biblical question came to a head. A ringing article by Msgr. d'Hulst (January, 1893) made the discussion a public matter.[138] Leo XIII took a stand shortly thereafter with the encyclical *Providentissimus*,[139] with the intention of reaffirming the traditional doctrine of the Church on Sacred Scripture. While this document marked an unquestionable advance over the theological wavering of the past, its positions in regard to biblical criticism remained prudent and reserved, because in its view the questions were obviously not mature.

## 2. The Rebirth of Catholic Exegesis

During the ten years following the encyclical, the controversy[140] became more lively than ever, for a new factor intervened. A. Loisy fell into step with the criticism then in fashion in liberal Protestantism. He not only adopted its technical methods, but also made its conclusions his own, even going so far as to advocate a complete reinterpretation of Catholic dogmas on the basis of what he believed to be historical science.[141] Fortunately, some Catholic exegetes then saw more clearly what their calling demanded of them; but taking note of the danger of Loisy's position, they publicly disassociated themselves from it. Their principal exponent was Fr. Lagrange.[142] Thanks to his solid theological formation, he was able to develop within the framework of sound Thomism a concept of inspiration which was flexible enough to adapt itself to the requirements of scientific work.[143] On the other hand, recognizing the advantage theology and apologetics could derive from criticism, he heartily adopted the historical method for use in studying the sacred books.[144] Finally, he traced the line of separation between the

[138] G. Courtade, "Inspiration et inerrance," *DBS* 4, col. 522.

[139] *Ench. B.*, 81-134.

[140] See the documentation assembled by A. Houtin, *La question biblique chez les catholiques en France au XIXᵉ siècle* (Paris: Nourry, 1902); *La question biblique au XXᵉ siècle*, 2nd ed. (Paris: Nourry, 1906) (a partial presentation, from a modernist viewpoint).

[141] A. Loisy, *L'Évangile et l'Église* (Paris, 1902). Concerning the reactions this book occasioned, a rich documentation has been published and utilized in recent years: R. Marlé, *Au cœur de la crise moderniste: Le dossier inédit d'une controverse* (Paris: Aubier, 1960); E. Poulat, *Histoire, dogme et critique dans la crise moderniste* (Paris, 1962); J. Steinmann, *Friedrich von Hügel* (Paris: Aubier, 1962).

[142] While awaiting the appearance of the life of Fr. Lagrange written by Fr. Vincent, see F. M. Braun, *The Work of Père Lagrange* (Milwaukee: Bruce, 1963).

[143] Above, p. 44.

[144] *La méthode historique, surtout à propos de l'Ancien Testament* (Paris, 1904).

doctrinal tradition of the Church, within which the exegete works, and the critical opinions admitted long ago by the fathers and theologians, in regard to which the exegete remains free in his judgments and choices. This search for a new approach met with violent opposition from a conservative element which sought to implicate the biblical criticism of which Fr. Lagrange was the pioneer in the condemnation of modernism. [145]  As a matter of fact, since the encyclical *Pascendi* and the decree *Lamentabili* (1907) remained on a purely theological and philosophical level, they dealt with exegetical questions only indirectly [146]; they limited themselves to opposing an intemperate criticism which would overstep its limits and destroy the historical foundation of Christian faith, or bind its fate to a false concept of inspiration and inerrancy. The path blazed by Fr. Lagrange therefore remained open.

Nevertheless, the antimodernist reaction did not allow it to bear fruit immediately. The prudential decrees of the Biblical Commission [147] between 1908 and 1915 maintained strictly conservative positions; without completely closing the door to future evolution, they invited exegetes at least to reconsider from the foundation up the problems raised by modern criticism before proposing new solutions. In the encyclical *Spiritus Paraclitus* [148] (1917) in which Benedict XV praised the exegetical method of St. Jerome, a precursor of criticism, severe warnings against the abuses that can be made of it are still to be found. Such mistrust is not surprising when one considers to what point the exegesis of liberal Protestantism, under the influence of the *religionsgeschichtliche Schule*, [149] had arrived: the most extreme of evolutionary theories were given free rein to explain the historical process followed by Israelite religion and primitive Christianity. Since the end of the First World War, the *formgeschichtliche Methode* began to show a new interest in extricating itself from this position, but the strongly negative positions adopted by some of its exponents in matters of historical criticism were no longer considered decisive.

---

[145] L. H. Vincent, "Le Père Lagrange," *RB* 47 (1938), 343-350.

[146] *Ench. B.*, 190-282.

[147] Texts in *Ench. B.* according to their date of appearance; English translation in Robert—Tricot, *Guide to the Bible*, pp. 759 ff. On the occasion of a new edition of the *Enchiridion Biblicum* in 1955, the exact force of these decrees was explained in two officious clarifications by A. Miller (cf. *Rome and the Study of Scripture*, p. 175; *CBQ* 18 [1956], 24-25) and A. Kleinhans (cf. *Antonianum* 30 [1955], 64 ff.). Cf. J. Levie, *The Bible, Word of God in Words of Men*, pp. 186-190; J. Dupont, "A propos du nouvel Enchiridion Biblicum," *RB* 64 (1955), 414-419; E. Vogt, "De decretis Commissionis biblicae distinguendis," *Biblica* 36 (1955), 564 ff.

[148] *Ench. B.*, 444-495.

[149] As an example, see the work of C. Clemen, *Religionsgeschichtliche Erklärung des Neuen Testaments* (Giessen: Töpelmann, 1909); cf. the work cited above, p. 210, note 107.

Despite everything, the exegetical movement begun by Fr. Lagrange bore its first fruits between 1910 and 1940, for in the same circles that had opposed the new hypotheses biblical criticism was now taken seriously.[150] Worthwhile articles and commentaries began to appear, marked by a loyal attachment to Catholic orthodoxy joined to a sane and constructive criticism. These works, however, were too often marred by apologetical preoccupations, since they felt the need to keep their distance from liberal criticism, the modernism of Loisy, and even from *Formgeschichte*.[151] Besides, they did not immediately result in theological syntheses from which theologians could draw material for reflection that would revitalize their own work. Consequently, despite a rebirth of biblical studies in Catholicism, the rift between exegesis and theology was still far from being bridged.

### 3. *The Encyclical "Divino afflante Spiritu"*

The use of criticism could always count on opponents in certain traditionalist circles. In 1941, one of them published a violent pamphlet[152] which extolled a method characterized by two traits: strict conservatism in all questions of authenticity, historicity, literary genre, etc. raised by modern commentators, and a generalized theory of allegory to expose what was called the spiritual sense of the sacred books.[153] After a letter from the Biblical

[150] J. Levie, *op. cit.*, pp. 122-132, summarizes this work without hiding the malaise exegesis then experienced in Catholic circles.

[151] As examples we could cite here the commentaries of Fr. Lagrange on the four gospels and the work of L. de Grandmaison, *Jesus-Christ* (New York: Sheed Ward, 1961), which dominated apologetics and the exegesis of the gospels between the two wars. For the rest, it should be noted that in general concern for theology is more marked among exegetes than concern for critical exegesis among the dogmaticians. This gaping chasm is undoubtedly explained by the difference between the abstract method of scholastic theology and the historical method of modern exegesis.

[152] J. Levie, *op. cit.*, pp. 133 f.

[153] This exegesis invites comparison with that of P. Claudel, who set forth his principles in *Introduction au Livre de Ruth* (Paris: Desclée de Brouwer, 1938), pp. 18-121, and repeated them in passing in many other books. Actually, what one finds in the poet's work are a mass of violent attacks against "those ruinous products of critical investigation" (*Présence et prophétie* [Fribourg, 1942], p. 208). But it could be asked whether conservative commentaries received any better treatment, beginning with Fillion's *Bible*: "It is not famous, but at least it is orthodox. No matter how silly and annoying the commentary, it at least allows a basic understanding of the text..." (Jacques Rivière and Paul Claudel, *Correspondance* [Paris: Plon, 1926], p. 43). In fact, Claudel explicitly paid homage to "the holy and magnificent task" of historical exegesis dedicated to the literal sense: "It is to this that the respected Père Lagrange and his disciples have consecrated themselves, and the benefit has been inestimable" (*Introduction au Livre du Ruth*, p. 25). What Claudel really desired without finding it was a theological and spiritual commentary of Scripture that would renew that of the fathers of the Church, after the manner of Newman's sermons, whose reading he recommended to J. Rivière ("Whatever you can find of Newman," *op. cit.*, p. 42).

Commission to the bishops of Italy, [154] Pope Pius XII clarified the issue in the encyclical *Divino afflante Spiritu* [155] (1943). After recounting the fruitful work accomplished in the Church during the previous 40 years, and honoring the pioneers who had made it possible, the Pope laid down clearly the principles of Catholic interpretation. A sane theology of inspiration, a development of that of Fr. Lagrange, enabled him to take a positive attitude toward critical investigation: exegetes were invited to make use of it prudently to determine the literal sense of the biblical texts, that is, the sense the inspired authors intended to give to their works. [156] It will be noted that this notion of the literal sense is no longer that defined by St. Thomas; it is that of criticism itself, which thus gained official entry into Catholic theology.

But the literal sense cannot be determined *a priori*; to attain it, the exegete must carefully determine the literary genres employed by the sacred authors, especially in the field of history, since these genres depended on multiple human factors which can be properly appreciated only through a knowledge of the ancient Orient. Such critical work, however, is only a first step in exegesis; for while it eliminates many false problems, it is not the interpreter's final goal. What he must seek to expose above all else is the doctrine contained in the texts; by that token, exegesis opens directly onto theology and is at the service of the care of souls, from which theology cannot be separated. The organic unity of theology and exegesis, which was spontaneously realized in patristic antiquity and in the Middle Ages, should therefore be reestablished in a new way, by integrating the positive contribution of a well-understood and sanely practiced criticism. Thus defined, the science of interpretation will be adapted to modern culture, just as Origen's methods were to Alexandrian culture, and will respond to the demands of the doctrine of inspiration itself.

This *Magna Charta*, the way for which was paved by 40 years of hidden labor, at last permitted Catholic exegesis to come out of its ghetto and to meet Protestant exegesis and critical study outside the faith on equal ground. Freed from the utilitarian preoccupations which defensive apologetics had imposed on it, it could thenceforth devote itself to more serene research, openly critical in its methods, but solidly anchored in the faith and directed toward a theological study of Scripture. [157] It was in this spirit that the Biblical Commission, supplementing the encyclical of 1943 on a particular

---

[154] *Ench. B.*, 522-533.

[155] *Ibid.*, 538-569; J. Levie, *op. cit.*, pp. 139-190.

[156] *Ench. B.*, 550, 558.

[157] Cf. R. Schnackenburg, "Der Weg der katholischen Exegese," *BZ* n. F. 2 (1958), 161-176.

point, drew up its *Instruction on the Historical Truth of the Gospels* (April 21, 1964), in which the positive aspects of the *Formgeschichte* are openly acknowledged and prudently commended.[158] The path thus indicated coincides in large measure with that which Protestant interpretation has taken in recent decades.[159] Besides, the situation has drastically changed during the past 20 years.[160] There still exists, to be sure, on the Protestant side as well as on the Catholic, an anticritical or conservative current, bound on the one side to fundamentalism, and on the other to a self-enclosed scholasticism[161]; but the works produced by this shortsighted and theologically unsound conservatism have been negligible. On the contrary, the exegetes of both persuasions who employ biblical criticism have manifested a like concern for going beyond criticism to make a contribution to theology and the pastoral activity of the Church. This convergence of points of view has made worthwhile discussion of common problems possible; the critical considerations and theological investigations of the two currents enrich each other mutually, even when they point up some fundamental disagreement. The dialogue undertaken at this level makes it possible to take up in new circumstances the dogmatic controversies opened in the 16th century, by approaching them from the angle of exegesis. That is an indication that on both sides exegesis and theology are on their way to reassuming their respective roles. And this introduces us to an examination of the present state of the problem.

## IV. THE PRESENT STATE OF THE PROBLEM

### I. THEOLOGICAL FACTORS

Since we had adopted the approach of a dogmatic treatise, we ought first of all to summarize the theological factors involved in the problem of Christian interpretation of Scripture. The latter deals with an inspired text which contains the revelation imparted by God to his Church for the salvation of men. As a result, it *ipso facto* falls within the limits of theology. More than one non-believer has manifested his uneasiness, fearing that the theologian unjustly dictates to the exegete critical conclusions which should never be judged in advance. As a matter of fact, it has happened that

---

[158] Text in *Ench. S.* 3999 and *Biblica* 45 (1964), 466-471.

[159] Above, pp. 209-213.

[160] Cf. J. L. McKenzie, "Problems of Hermeneutics in Roman Catholic Exegesis," *JBL* 77 (1958), 197-204.

[161] Above, chap. IV, p. 123, note 134.

theologians, and even ecclesiastical authorities, have acted (or appear to have acted) in such fashion in ages past. No matter what justification there might have been for such actions, they can only be deplored, because they have no necessary connection with Christian theology rightly understood. Let us see then what doctrinal points must be considered in this question.

## 1. The Theology of Revelation

Theology [162] affirms both revelation's transcendent origin and its immersion in human history, its profound unity in the mystery of Christ and the stratification of its successive layers, the substantial identity of its assertions in every age and the reality of its progress during the course of the ages. [163] Theology, therefore, favors the systematic study of the history of revelation, in which it recognizes the tangible evidence of divine pedagogy. [164] But to make such a study properly, certain conditions must be met. In the first place, the historian must not unjustly pass judgments on matters that lie outside his competence. It is not easy for him to avoid the temptation. When, for example, a non-believing historian, confusing all doctrinal development with the natural evolution of human affairs, [165] identifies the progress of ideas in the two Testaments with a series of syncretist phenomena, in which the activity of certain religious personalities is combined with the individual spirit of Israelite society or primitive Christianity, he leaves the domain of history behind and enters that of the philosophy of religion. And in his presentation of the past, the objective historical reality is, in fact, forced into the mold of his personal religious (or anti-religious) preference. As a matter of fact, it is impossible that the historian's work, given the

---

[162] For a general treatment of the question, see R. Latourelle, *Theology of Revelation* (Staten Island: Alba, 1967), who recounts the history of the problem and in conclusion outlines a constructive synthesis.

[163] *Sens chrétien de l'A.T.*, pp. 145-151. See the explanation given by St. Thomas, II$^a$ II$^{ae}$, q. 1, art. 7: "Whether the articles of faith increase with the passing of time."

[164] *Sens chrétien de l'A.T.*, pp. 196-209, 275-286.

[165] On the difference between development and evolution, see M. Blondel's letter to F. von Hügel in *Au cœur de la crise moderniste*, pp. 129 f. In it Blondel states himself directly opposed to the views of Loisy. Although Newman in *An Essay on the Development of Christian Doctrine* took the viewpoint of an accomplished revelation whose content leaves room for dogmatic development in the Church, his ideas are susceptible of a more general application which involves revelation itself; cf. the study of J. Guitton, *La notion de développement et son application à la religion chez J. H. Newman* (Paris, 1933). But there is a difference: as M. Nédoncelle remarks, "the dispensation confided the Jews has a quite different character from Christianity: the first calls for growth, the latter, an elucidation" (*Œuvres philosophiques de Newman* [Paris: Aubier, 1945], p. 143). In this matter it is the notion of economy, which Newman borrowed from the Greek fathers, that serves to explain the facts (*ibid.*, pp. 139-143). On these points Newman refuted Loisy's sophisms in advance.

fact that he deals with the domain in which the essential values of existence come into play, should not be colored one way or another by an element that does not pertain to the science of history. Still, it is important that the historian be clearly aware of this for the sake of his own scientific honesty. Theology can demand that much of the unbeliever as well as one of the faithful. [166]

In the second place, addressing itself to the Christian exegete, theology pleads with him not to stop short at critical study. As necessary as it might be, criticism ought to be integrated into a larger whole. The sacred books owe their inner unity to the mystery of Christ which is their unique object; it is important therefore to uncover it, from the Old Testament onward, in the signs which organically connect the facts, institutions and texts to it. [167] Is not a seed judged by the tree that grows from it, and the tree by its fruits? In like manner, the end of the law, which is Christ (Rm 10:4), shows what riches were hidden within it from the beginning, since it is He who determined all its development.

Moreover, since revelation forms a coherent whole whose cornerstone is Christ, it follows that every text must be placed within this whole context if its meaning and implication is to be gauged accurately, especially when it is a question of an obscure or difficult text. The analogy of faith [168] thus plays a regulatory role in exegesis in two ways: negatively, by closing off access to paths that lead nowhere; positively, by giving direction to research, allowing the exegete to put into their proper context and suitably clarify the texts he is to analyze.

## 2. *The Theology of Inspiration*

The theology of inspiration, freed from the false problems which still encumbered it at the beginning of this century, makes it possible to take the measure of criticism's place in relation to the religious understaking of Scripture.

---

[166] Here we touch upon a crucial point, which obviously reaches its peak in the case of the history of Christ. It underlies the entire work of X. Léon-Dufour, *The Gospels and the Jesus of History* (New York: Desclée, 1968), an example of an objective historical study whose final implications, without ceasing to belong to the science of history, are nevertheless determined by the author's decision of faith. See our review of the book in *BCE* (1963), 217-221; in *Catéchèse* (1964), 239-244. We will return to this point later, below, pp. 339 ff.

[167] It is this strictly theological work that we have attempted to do, on the basis of a critical exegesis, in *Sens chrétien de l'A.T.*

[168] J. B. Franzelin, *De divina traditione et scriptura* (Rome: S. C. de Prop. Fide, 1896), pp. 200-210. A concise treatment in *Institutiones biblicae*, pp. 481 ff. (A. Fernández). This principle was repeated by Leo XIII (cf. *Ench. B.*, 109 and 143) in a rather negative context, that of the problem of inerrancy.

If God, in making use of the sacred authors as free and intelligent instruments, respected their literary personality,[169] it is not only permitted, but necessary, to analyze carefully every facet of the sacred books which reflect their peculiarities; otherwise, an essential element for understanding the content of those books would be lacking. The divine teaching contained in Scripture passed through the didactic intent of the sacred authors in order to reach us.[170] That fact makes literary and historical criticism the indispensable aid to theology when the latter strives to grasp its proper object as contained in Scripture. It is true that in some cases there can be a real difference between the sense which the inspired authors consciously gave their texts and the meaning those same texts have acquired in the perspective of the fulness of revelation; this fact is especially noticeable in the Old Testament, in which no point of doctrine is ever expressed fully. But even here, the theology of inspiration can easily enough explain that partial deficiency, which in no case can be likened to the teaching of error. It lays down as a principle that each sacred author expressed the divine truth according to the measure of light God allotted him, in relation to his particular mission and to his times.[171]

### 3. The Theology of the Church

The theology of the Church enters into exegesis for another reason. God did not deposit his revelation in Scripture so that each man should have to search there for it on his own with the assistance of the Holy Spirit. He made Scripture a constituent element of the Church, so that it could accomplish its mission of announcing the gospel to men. It is through the Church that the word of God deposited in Scripture becomes live and arouses in hearts the submission of faith. Thus the Church has a role to play in the explanation of the sacred texts, to the end that men find in them the single object of their testimony, the gospel of which the Church is custodian. It would, therefore, be misleading to oppose the one authority to the other, that which Scripture possesses as the word of God, and the interpretative authority which the Church possesses as the Body of Christ assisted by the Holy Spirit, as if Scripture and the Church were two separate entities, foreign to one another, or as if their relation were inconceivable in any other terms but those of subordination.[172] In reality, the same Holy Spirit

---

[169] Above, pp. 69 ff., note 94.
[170] Above, pp. 110 f.
[171] Above, pp. 108 ff.
[172] Contrary to medieval theology, the decadent scholasticism of the 15th-century accentuated the dissociation of Scripture from the Church considered in its present

who inspired the sacred authors continues to work in the Church through his diverse charisms, especially those related to the offices of teaching and pastoral responsibility. [173] That is why the Church is in basic accord with Scripture; it possesses its sense as if by instinct, in such a way that it could not modify it or forfeit any part whatsoever of its content. [174] The manifestation of the word of God throughout the time of the Church is the result of concrete interaction, to which Scripture and ecclesiastical tradition expressed through a magisterium are equally necessary. [175]

It should, however, be noted that the Church's mission thus defined has to do with the doctrinal interpretation and spiritual understanding of the biblical texts; it does not concern the clarification of critical problems which arise in regard to them, since the faith is not involved in them. Such matters are not a part of the apostolic heritage. [176] Those who down through history have attempted to find solutions for them have done so at their own risk, on no one's authority but their own. In such matters opinions have varied from one century to another and from one exegete to another, [177] for hypotheses are in order when it is a question of searching for the truth

life. This fact explains why the Church-Scripture problem could present itself in Luther's eyes in the form of a dilemma (cf. G. H. Tavard, *Écriture ou Église: La crise de la Réforme*, pp. 73-99). In this context Luther chose Scripture and subordinated the Church to it, for the word of God "is incomparably above the Church; and in this word the Church has no power to found, to rule or to do anything at all, but it is she, a simple creature, who must be founded, ruled and made" (quoted *ibid.*, p. 130). Hence Melanchthon's definition: the Church "signifies the holy union of those who participate together in the communion of the same Gospel or of the same doctrine and of the same Holy Spirit, who renews, sanctifies and governs hearts" (*ibid.*, p. 135). The institutional Church as such seems no longer to be animated and governed by the Holy Spirit. It is possible that in the theology of the late Middle Ages the abuse of juridicism led to conceiving the role of the Church and its relationship to Scripture in terms of power rather than of mission, and that Luther's position can be explained in part as an excessive reaction against this genuinely criticizable situation. But the result is still the same: an actual dissolution of the notion of Church.

[173] Above, pp. 59 ff.

[174] This is one of the principal points of K. Rahner's study, *Inspiration in the Bible* (above, p. 45).

[175] Here again we come across a fact noted in chap. I, above, pp. 28-32. It has been studied at length by C. Journet, *Le message révélé*, chaps. III to V. See also P. Lengsfeld, *Tradition, Écriture et Église*, pp. 200-228.

[176] That is why it would be fallacious, for example, to intend to solve the question of the author of the Psalms or of Is 40 ff. on the sole basis of Mk 1:2 f. (who elsewhere also cites Ml 3:1 under the name of Isaiah!) and of Mk 12:36 f. The evangelist and Christ himself expressed themselves within the framework of the ideas of the time without intending either to confirm or correct them; but their intention is obviously not to pass on to the Church some doctrine relative to the literary authenticity of Ps 110 or of Isaiah! It is important to retain a sane and clear idea of the apostolic testimony, of its object and its content.

[177] See the encyclical *Divino afflante Spiritu*, in Ench. B., 555, 564-565.

instead of defining it dogmatically. [178] Moreover, these critical problems have been the occasion of a growing awakening for which modern discoveries are principally responsible, having brought to the fore historical and literary facts which neither antiquity nor the Middle Ages even suspected. In the task undertaken, therefore, the exegete's duty is to remain loyal to the faith in his work by conforming to the doctrinal teaching of the Church, and the Church in turn will support his efforts and request that he resolutely persevere in them. [179] It might occasionally happen that the Church should intervene in critical questions, whenever the faith or its proper understanding are in some way involved—either because under the cover of criticism there is danger of transforming its content, or because the hypotheses proposed to resolve certain new problems have not yet been given a balanced formulation. In the first case, the warnings or condemnations pronounced obviously do not affect criticism itself, but the abuse made of it; in the second, it is a matter of a prudent intervention whose aim is not to thwart or limit further work, but to give it proper direction, even at the risk of putting off until later the solution of questions which are not yet mature. [180] Between 1900 and 1910, the encyclical *Pascendi* was of the first type, [181] the replies of the Biblical Commission, of the second.

## 4. Scripture and Christian Life

The three theological considerations we have just noted should not be viewed abstractly, but in relation to the goal to which the corresponding realities are ordered: revelation, Scripture, and even the Church exist only for the

[178] The necessity of investigation in critical questions is explicitly mentioned, *ibid.*, 563. The position taken on this point by Cardinal E. Ruffini, "Literary Genres and Working Hypotheses," *AER* 145 (1961), 362-365 manifests a strange confusion between the dogmatic and critical points of view, and it completely ignores the role of hypothesis in the historical sciences.

[179] Encyclical *Divino afflante Spiritu* (*Ench. B.*, 561 and 564), repeated in the opening of the "Instruction on the historical truth of the gospels" (April 21, 1964); *CBQ* 26 (1964), 299-312.

[180] Cf. the officious clarifications provided by the Biblical Commission concerning the force of its decrees, above, p. 218, note 147. A still clearer example is provided by the decree of the Holy Office on the *Comma johannea* (1897, *Ench B.*, 135), which was practically revoked by a later official interpretation (1927, *Ench. B.*, 136); cf. A. Feuillet in Robert—Feuillet, *Introduction to the New Testament*, pp. 683-685. On this question, see the clarifications of C. Journet, *Le message révélé*, pp. 147-150.

[181] Of the same type are the passages of the encyclical *Humani Generis* which treat of the Bible (*Ench. B.*, 611-620). Yet it should be noted that this encyclical was obviously not drawn up by trained exegetes, for the formulation of the problems in which the Bible is involved suffers from real deficiencies, not, to be sure, from the point of view of the doctrine it presents, but from that of exegetical method. In this regard, more exactness, and at the same time more nuances, would have been desirable, especially as concerns the use or evaluation of Genesis texts.

salvation of men, to allow them to enter already here below into that life of the new man which constitutes Christian existence. The interpretation of Scripture in the Church is directed toward the same end. Consequently, it is not enough to say that exegesis ought to go beyond criticism and open onto theology. It must at the same time enter into the pastoral activity of the Church, whose role is to announce the gospel to men and thus bring them into contact with the living God. Theology is not abstract knowledge, sufficient unto itself and able to be constructed independently of time, but an understanding of the mystery of faith which Christian living brings to life. It is only right, then, that the theological interpretation of the sacred text, which completes critical investigation, should itself be subordinate to an existential interpretation, which transfers its riches to the life of the Christian people. [182] Considering just the theological factors involved in the problem of interpretation, we are already beginning to see the outline of a complex method whose inner workings we will examine further on.

## II. CULTURAL FACTORS

We have already noted several times that this theological element of Christian exegesis, which is independent of time and space, is always mixed with a cultural element, which varies like all the facts of civilization. That the interpretation of the inspired texts could successively borrow its practical methods from Jewish rabbinical culture, from Alexandrian allegory, from Latin rhetoric, from the formal logic of medieval Aristotelianism, etc.,—this is evidence that its roots were sunk in the human cultures of the past. A similar implantation must be realized today, one which responds to the legitimate demands of our culture and gives proper esteem to the technical means it offers us. Perhaps the contact of the gospel with Indian or Chinese culture would raise other problems, even in our own age, when the inter-dependance of civilizations has made certain elements of western culture quite universal. Be that as it may, it is certain that our contemporaries do not spontaneously approach the Bible with the same mental attitude as the men of antiquity or of the Middle Ages, putting aside all questions of faith. In recounting the history of exegesis from the 16th century to our own day, we have seen the characteristics of this mentality become progressively clearer; it has its strong and weak points, but in any case it determines the concrete problems of contemporary interpretation.

---

[182] A. Bea, " 'Religionswissenschaftliche' oder 'theologische' Exegese," *Biblica* 40 (1959), 339, stresses the existential character of revelation; but he strives to distinguish the proper field of exegesis, biblical theology, of moral and ascetical theology and of preaching. Should not their necessary relations be pointed out at the same time?

## 1. Scientific Thought

Men have always desired to understand objectively the secret of sensible things, and it would be naive to attribute to the ancients a credulity they never possessed. Nevertheless, it is undeniable that the rise of the sciences has since the 16th century profoundly modified conceptions of the universe and of man considered in their actual state and their centuries-old progress. The modern world is untiring in its investigations into cosmic, biological, psycho-physical, and social phenomena, not only to know them better, but to ponder them and obtain mastery over them. On this point, ancient thought had other points of reference.

Let us take an example from cosmology. In the pagan world, the three-storied universe (heaven, earth, lower regions), bound with cyclic time to the law of eternal return, was intimately related to the mythical world, and the concept of human existence was closely bound both to that cosmology and to that mythology. In biblical revelation, the reduction of all things to the state of creatures subject to man (Gn 1:28-29) radically demythologized cosmic realities and gave a religious foundation to man's mastery over things; at the same time, the theology of the plan of salvation provided an insight into the true nature of the temporal and historical dimension of human existence. But despite this revolutionary idea, the vision of a three-storied world was carried over in the expression of doctrine even into the New Testament: it is enough to recall Christ's descent into Hades (Ac 2:24; Ep 4:9) and his ascent into heaven! Thus the original language of revelation, which passed into Christian catechesis, has its roots in a pre-scientific notion of the universe,—not in the sense that it transformed doctrine into a true myth, parallel to those which were current in the pagan world of the time, [183] but in the sense that it used that notion to formulate certain symbols for use in speaking of the living God, considered in himself and in his relations with men. The result is that there is a difference of key between the Bible and modern minds, which extends not only to the domain of conscious ideas, but to the substructure of the mind; the different language of the two is evidence of that difference. [184]

It is the task of interpretation to build a bridge between these two worlds, to make intelligible to modern men a message that was long ago

[183] It is surprising to see the place R. Bultmann accords these elements of New Testament language, since he compares it to that of contemporary gnosticism and qualifies it "mythic." Cf. R. Marlé, *Bultmann et l'interprétation du Nouveau Testament,* pp. 49-56.

[184] For that matter, the difficulty of a dialogue carried on in these conditions does not concern only the Bible, but everything that concerns the faith; cf. R. Russo, "Cent années d'un dialogue difficile entre la science et la foi," *Science et foi* (Paris, 1962), pp. 239-266.

expressed in other categories of thought, to translate it for them without betraying it or losing any of it, to find in the older categories the points of contact which will enable it to attach itself to their minds, not as a foreign body might subsist by reason of habit alone, but as a completely assimilated vital element. To accomplish this difficult task, it is obviously important not to make an absolute of the modern spirit, remaining blind to its limits and imperfections. For example, scientific and technical thought patterns cannot be applied to everything. They are incapable of themselves of surmounting the threshold of the inner life of man, and even less that of transcendent realities. Access to these guarded worlds can be made only through the means of symbolism, phenomenology, and philosophic abstraction, each of which has its own logic and its own language. Refusal to adopt such means would be to mutilate the human spirit. But the greatest discord that exists between the Bible and a good number of our contemporaries arises precisely from the fact that certain of their mental processes suffer from a grave deficiency [185] which the interpreter of the Bible must strive to overcome. This point having been made, it remains no less true that the problem of interpretation is quite different than it was for St. Augustine or St. Thomas. Bultmann has attempted to clarify the problem by defining his task as that of demythologization. [186] The term is somewhat unfortunate because of its ambiguity; the method so described requires even greater reservation, for it sacrifices some essential points of scriptural evidence. [187]

[185] In certain cases it would be possible to speak of a real atrophy. Recall with what lyric terms the communist press greeted the flight of the first cosmonaut, a real "ascension" of man, in the course of which no God was encountered in the heavens. Such ignorance would be laughable were it not evidence of a certain materialist mentality that is drunk of technical knowledge and closed to anything that smacks of the spiritual.

[186] See the articles and works mentioned on p. 211, note 115.

[187] One might give words any meaning he likes on condition that he define them. Moreover, the definition settled upon must not, under the appearance of objectivity, covertly introduce into the discussion the conclusion one intended to prove when he adopted it. Bultmann's concept of myth actually depends on several *a priori* principles which he never questions. 1) A positivist concept of Science, the scientific mind and historical method, according to which the whole content of the New Testament is immediately classified, evaluated and separated into two distinct categories: the mythical, to which the modern mind is considered non-receptive, and the non-mythical, to which the message of Scripture must necessarily be reduced. 2) A strictly Lutheran concept of faith, conceived as the pure acceptance of the word through which God assures me that he has saved me, to the exclusion of any possible knowledge of what God is in himself, of the acts by which he accomplishes man's salvation, of his presence in the world and to the mind of man. Whatever does not fit into this limited concept of faith belongs to the order of myth, not in the sense that it is devoid of meaning, but in the sense that it is the mythical expression of the experience of faith taken in its purely existential state. This positivist position should logically lead Bultmann to radical agnosticism; he avoids this by a "decision of faith" which in reality proceeds from pure fideism, and in which the knowledge of faith

But the problem is a real one, and the exegete must face it squarely if he intends to fulfill his task as a theologian and meet his pastoral responsibilities.

## 2. The Critical Mind

The rise of critical study in the West since the Renaissance has also left its mark on the minds of our contemporaries, more or less deeply according to the degree of culture attained by the individual, but certainly in some degree, since even primary education is calculated to awaken the child's critical mind. The resulting mentality indeed risks falling into widespread rationalism, [188] naively boastful of its own capabilities; this fault is to the true critical spirit what superstitious credulity is to faith. Be that as it may, modern persons before the Bible will spontaneously tend not to accept the content of the sacred texts without a rational examination, without asking certain crucial questions about them: Is it an authentic work of such and such an author? Is it historical? Whence comes the text? etc. The manner of putting these questions might reveal a disconcerting ignorance, a symptom of superficial culture; for example, a book is either authentic, or it is the work of a forger; an account is either historical, or it is a legend without interest or worth, etc. The positivist notion of history, [189] which in our day has come under attack from historians themselves, continues to influence a great number of them, [190] and even more the great mass of readers for whom the questions involved are too complex to be grasped. That does not make the questions raised any less real. Those who attempt to solve them dogmatically, basing themselves on what they consider the tradition of the Church, would launch apologetics on a vicious circle. Is it possible, in laying a foundation for faith, to draw an argument from the critical positions imposed by that same faith? The defensive apologetics of the 18th and 19th centuries always pretended to prove rationally the conservative positions it was defending, thus admitting indirectly that faith itself needs to be certain of its reasonableness in order to be an authentic human act.

As a matter of fact, this apologetics put exegesis in a dangerous position. The interpreter of Scripture ought certainly to purify his heart to keep it

---

is emptied of its content; cf. L. Malevez, *Le message chrétien et le mythe: La théologie de Rudolf Bultmann* (Paris: Desclée de Brouwer, 1954), pp. 152-157. However, F. Refoulé, "La vague bultmanienne," *RSPT* 48 (1964), 253-259, prefers in this matter to insist on Bultmann's dependence on Kierkegaard.

[188] Above, pp. 204 ff.

[189] Above, p. 115.

[190] Notably on R. Bultmann himself, whose radicalism derives entirely from liberal criticism which rests upon "objective" history (cf. pp. 208 ff): because the gospels testify to faith in the paschal message, they cannot possibly provide objective knowledge of the Jesus of history.

prepared to receive the word of God; but he should at the same time employ his intellectual faculties to the utmost, not only to understand that word, but also to be aware of the conditions in which it reaches him—and that is the object of critical study. Willingly or not, our contemporaries, confronted with biblical history and with texts which speak of it, find themselves faced with human realities which they cannot brush aside, and which present them with a basic question, the same one Christ presented to his disciples: "Who do you say I am?" That is the right moment for the Christian exegete to enter boldly into the picture and play his proper role! He ought, then, to take seriously modern man's desire not to believe blindly, but to know the why of things. And he himself should bring to his study of the Bible a keen intellect which shows his profound comprehension of the problems it poses. He should at every instant employ a rigorous method to discern the truth of Scripture in the concrete circumstances in which it has come down to us, defining its nature exactly and not confusing it with the particular opinions of exegetes of long ago on disputed points! In a word, he ought to perform his work with real intellectual honesty. His theological study of the texts will lose nothing for it, and the value of his witness to Christ will gain all.

We will undertake later to specify the manner in which criticism (literary, historical, philosophical) is related to theology and the pastoral activity of the Church. [191] For now it suffices to note its necessity. It is not a matter of simple tactical opportunism or of a concession to the misfortunes of our times. It is a matter of a normal demand of human reason, which is in full harmony with the truly human character of the sacred books and the history they recount. It is furthermore fortunate that modern culture puts at our disposal an instrument for work which, precisely in this matter, appears more perfect, and much more adapted to its object, than were Alexandrian allegory or Aristotelian logic joined to the rules of the ancient and medieval grammarians.

## 3. *Reflection on the Meaning of Existence*

There is, finally, an aspect of contemporary thought with which the science of interpretation must remain in close contact: it is reflection on the meaning of existence. Whether believers or atheists, men of today put this question to themselves from two different perspectives, which they find difficult to reconcile with one another. Man exists in the individual and in society. The individual is thrown upon history, and he asks, in these circumstances,

[191] Below, pp. 361-368.

what the meaning of his destiny is.   But history in its turn is not an object in itself: it is the record of human society, whose sense and goal pose a problem which no reflecting mind can avoid.   The philosophical systems which consider the questions waver between two positions.   Some (notably those influenced by Hegel and Marx) extol History, whose secret they claim to have solved, and it is in relation to it that they give a meaning to the existence of individuals. [192]   Others (from Nietzsche to the existentialists), who have no such faith in the meaning of history, search for something to justify the existence of individuals considered in their concrete historical circumstances. [193]

Questions thus raised—the meaning of history and the meaning of existence—are fundamental.   And it is precisely to these questions that the revelation contained in Scripture provides an answer.   That answer does indeed surpass the limits of simple philosophic reflection, but it supplies the framework in which such reflection can gain its true balance without renouncing any of its own accomplishments.   When the exegete deciphers the message of Scripture to make it accessible to other men, therefore, he should never lose sight of its historical and existential character, for it is only at that price that he will be able to reveal the lasting relevancy of the biblical revolution.   A theological exegesis which would conceive the truth of Scripture in an atemporal form, similar to the Platonic ideas, would constitute a real act of treason. [194]   For the word of God which I strive to discover in the Bible in reality reveals to me the mystery of my existence in the world and in history, by the fact that it places me, along with the world and history, in the presence of God.   In return, the same problems of my existence in the world and in history predispose me to discover the authentic meaning of the word of God spoken through Scripture, and thus to escape the temptation

---

[192] *Sens chrétien de l'A.T.*, pp. 85 f.   On this point Hegel and Marx themselves depend upon the philosophy of the enlightenment, in which reflection on history took shape with the works of J. G. Herder, *Ideen zur Philosophie der Geschichte der Menschheit* and *Auch eine Philosophie der Geschichte*.   This reflection was in reality a copy of the Christian theology of history and of biblical eschatology (cf. H. J. Kraus, *Geschichte der historisch-kritischen Erforschung des A.T.s*, pp. 111-116).   The same dependence in different dress is obvious in the Hegelian system (he frankly admitted it) and in Marxist eschatology (he staunchly denied it).   Is not the success of all these secular philosophies due in large measure to the fact that since the 18th century the Christian theology of history has suffered the same eclipse as biblical exegesis?   Cf. *Sens chrétien de l'A.T.*, pp. 74 f.

[193] Actually, concern for historicity played no part in reflection upon existence until Heidegger (*Sein und Zeit*, 1927).

[194] This was not the case, it should be noted, either in patristic antiquity or in the Middle Ages, whatever might have been the importance of Platonian or Aristotelian terms in theological expression.   Is it so certain that the same could and can be said of modern scholasticism?

to abstract speculation in which the statements of the Bible would be organized into an intellectual system with no connection with the real life of men. By laying down the principle of existentialist exegesis, in which biblical interpretation and the search for the meaning of existence mutually affect one another, Bultmann undoubtedly touched the heart of the matter. [195] That does not mean that his manner of conceiving existentialist exegesis can be accepted without reservation, especially as regards his use of Heidegger's thought to define Christian existence, [196] and his reduction of the biblical message to an appeal to the decision of faith to the exclusion of any objective revelation of supernatural realities. [197] But these serious reservations on his system of interpretation should not be a hindrance to holding firmly with him that biblical exegesis should really be existentialist, [198] as much out of fidelity to Scripture as attention to the demands of the man of today. It would not be right, under the pretext of opposing the mutilation Bultmann has inflicted on traditional Christian doctrine, to inflict the inverse mutilation on it by hiding under a bushel one of its essential elements.

[195] R. Marlé, *Bultmann et l'interprétation du N.T.*, pp. 73-97.

[196] Bultmann claims at the outset to have built his theology on Heidegger's philosophy; he used Heidegger because in his view "Heidegger did no more than rediscover New Testament ontology" understood according to the Protestant tradition (A. Malet, *Mythos et Logos, La pensée de Rudolf Bultmann*, p. 307). It is certainly interesting to ascertain Heidegger's dependence upon Lutheran theology. But the full agreement and complete fidelity of his ontology with the New Testament message can still be called into question, for such agreement and fidelity are certain only in the interpretation proposed by Bultmann. These remarks are not intended to deny the Christian influence which underlies Heidegger's thought, and which extends from Augustine to Kierkegaard (cf. A. D. Sertillange, *Le christianisme et les philosophies* 2 [Paris: Aubier, 1941], pp. 540 f.). But it is another question whether Heidegger's ontology corresponds in every point to the demands of Christian faith.

[197] For Bultmann the cross and resurrection of Christ constitute the message of salvation only in the sense that by the cross of Christ God signified to men his decision to save them from sin and death, thus inviting them to a decision of faith which opens the way to eschatological existence for them. But this meaning of the cross and resurrection for human existence is bereft of any ontological support. For to relate the value of the cross to the incarnation of Christ, or to understand his resurrection as a reality which affected his body, would be to mythologize the message of the cross (A. Malet, *op. cit.*, pp. 141-171). This basic position is closely related to a number of decisive critical choices which prolong the radicalism of the old liberal school, but Bultmann never questions them, because in his eyes they represent Science. Once again we might be permitted to raise some doubts. It could be asked, for example, whether this critical radicalism might not proceed from the thought of the "natural man" which Bultmann rightly intends to persecute even among theologians. And if that is the case, his whole case collapses. Concerning the objectivity of the knowledge of faith and the possibility of an objective theology, see the remarks by J. Cahill, "Bultmann and Post-Bultmann Tendencies," *CBQ* 26 (1964), 171-175.

[198] This is the conclusion of H. Bouillard, "Bultmann et la théologie catholique," *BCE* (1961), 455 f. (reprinted in *Logique de la foi* [Paris: Aubier, 1964], pp. 141 ff.) and of G. Hasenhüttl, *op. cit.*, p. 208, note 1; the latter attempts to outline an integration of Bultmann's accomplishment and Catholic theology.

# CHAPTER VI

# THE SIGNIFICANCE OF BIBLICAL REALITIES

The history of the problem of interpretation enabled us to point out the factors which bear on its present position. Following that, it would be logical to continue on to an exposition of the method suited to resolve it, while making allowance for the legitimate demands of reason as much as for those of faith. We will come to that, however, only after a quite long digression. For among the elements of the problem there is one which controls in some fashion every consideration of scriptural texts: it is the way in which Christian faith understands the realities of which the texts speak, whether it is a question of the person of Jesus Christ, or the history of the Old Testament, or Christian institutions. A preliminary examination of this point will clear the way for a consideration of exegesis, which we will study in detail in the following chapter.

## § I. STATEMENT OF THE PROBLEM

### I. THE DOCTRINE OF THE SENSES OF SCRIPTURE [1]

#### I. FROM THE PATRISTIC AGE TO ST. THOMAS AQUINAS

In the patristic age, theology and preaching developed in the form of exegesis; they were based on Sacred Scripture read in the light of living tradition. [2] To accomplish this operation, Christian exegesis formulated its rules in the doctrine of the senses of Scripture. Whatever might be the significance of its original double formulation, which has been noted by Fr. de Lubac, [3] this doctrine was set during the high Middle Ages in the

---

[1] This problem is treated in all general introductions to Sacred Scripture. The classical treatment of F. X. Patrizi, *Institutio de interpretatione Bibliorum* (Rome: Marini, 1876) influenced all those that followed it until the encyclical *Divino afflante Spiritu* (1943), even if an evolution in treatment had begun to appear. Recent treatments: A. Fernández in *Institutiones biblicae*, pp. 366-393; H. Höpfl—L. Leloir, *Introductio generalis*, pp. 407-450; J. Schildenberger, *Vom Geheimnis des Gotteswortes*, pp. 87-105 (the literal sense), 392-470 (the spiritual sense).

[2] Above, chap. I, pp. 29-33; chap. V, p. 198.

[3] H. de Lubac, *Exégèse médiévale. Les quatre sens de l' Écriture*, Part I, pp. 119-169.

fourfold classification that is summarized in the famous couplet cited by Nicholas of Lyra:

*Littera gesta docet, quid credas allegoria,*
*Moralis quid agas, quo tendas* (var. *quid speres) anagogia.* [4]

As a matter of fact, what was thus presented as a principle of exegesis was more properly a practical classification of the sacred disciplines, all referred to Scripture as to their necessary foundation [5]: sacred history *(gesta)*, dogma *(quid credas)*, moral theology *(quid agas)*, mystical theology *(quo tendas)*. It is not surprising, then, that in the scholastic age (12th-13th centuries), the break up of these disciplines [6] and the subsequent effort to confer the status of a science on theology [7] overthrew the formula which had ruled exegesis until then; in a new system of thought, it had to undergo internal renovation.

A change, as a matter of fact, can be noted in St. Thomas [8]: the basic distinction he makes is between the *sensus litteralis* and the *sensus spiritualis*. Despite the use of Pauline vocabulary, this distinction by no means coincides with that of the letter and the spirit as St. Paul understood them. [9] The *sensus litteralis* is the meaning of the sacred texts, in which God speaks to us through words; the *sensus spiritualis* is the meaning of the things of which those texts speak. The first is the material of exegesis properly so called, which serves as the foundation of theology [10]; the second is nothing but a

---

[4] "The letter tells you what took place; allegory, what to believe; the moral, what you ought to do, and anagoge, to hope." *Ibid.*, pp. 23 f. In fact, this couplet appears for the first time from the pen of the Dominican Aage of Denmark (Augustine of Dacia) in the 13th century. Cf. F. Chatillon, "Vocabulaire et prosodie du distique attribué à Augustin de Dacie sur les quatre sens de l'Écriture," *L'homme devant Dieu (Mélanges H. de Lubac)* (Paris: Montaigne, 1964), Vol. 1, pp. 17-28.

[5] H. de Lubac, *op. cit.*, Part I, pp. 426-681, studies in detail this presentation of medieval theology on the basis of Scripture.

[6] *Ibid.*, Part II, Vol. 1, pp. 418-429: the break up began to occur in the Victorine school itself in the course of the 12th century, that is, just when scholastic theology was taking shape.

[7] For this point we refer the reader to the study of M. D. Chenu, *La théologie comme science au XIII*e *siècle* (Paris: Vrin, 1957).

[8] H. de Lubac, *op. cit.*, Part II, Vol. 2, pp. 272-302, points out both the traditional character of Thomistic doctrine and the new elements which determined its presentation. Likewise C. Spicq, *Esquisse d'une histoire de l'exégèse latine au moyen âge*, pp. 273-288.

[9] Furthermore, St. Thomas does not cite St. Paul to explain the use of the word *spiritualis;* he refers to Pseudo-Dionysius: "Thus it is that the sense which is gathered from figures is called spiritual" (Quodl. 7, q. 6, art. 2 *in corp.*). And it is abundantly clear that his *sensus litteralis* is not the "letter that kills."

[10] Theology has its own structure inasmuch as it is a methodical system of knowledge based on the principles of the faith; but it has no other aim than to apply the doctrine found in Scripture with the aid of traditional interpretation. The separation of disciplines leaves intact the vital bonds that connect them.

theological reflection on the history, persons, institutions, etc., which are mentioned in the course of the scriptural texts. By that fact, allegory, tropology (or moral), and anagoge become simply the three ways of applying the spiritual sense; they define the three possible relations of biblical realities to the mystery of faith, which is present in human history through Christ and his Church, which underlies Christian life, and which will be consummated in eternity. This methodical reclassification responded so well to the needs of theological labor that it in turn became classic and found a place in post-Tridentine tracts on the science of interpretation.

## II. FROM ST. THOMAS TO THE PRESENT

Does that mean that the history of the problem stopped there? Not at all, for the modern reader of the *Summa* finds the Thomistic notion of the *sensus litteralis* quite ambiguous. St. Thomas centered his attention on the teaching which God, the principal author of Scripture,[11] imparts to us through the biblical texts; he gives scant attention to the sacred writers, the instrumental authors used by God to transmit his word to us. Consequently, in a number of cases, especially in the Old Testament, he does not hesitate to enrich the text by projecting on it the light of the whole of revelation, so that its *sensus litteralis* goes far beyond what a modern interpreter would call its literal sense.[12] For in the modern view, the literal sense is defined by the didactic intention of the human author, which is always accessible to critical study; this is the way the encyclical *Divino afflante Spiritu* defined it.[13] What relation is there, then, between this restricted literal sense and the fulness of teaching which St. Thomas attributed to God, the principal author?

The problem, therefore, has continued to evolve as critical study has progressed. Since Christian antiquity it was held that Scripture had four senses. To the question: *Utrum sacra Scriptura sub una littera habeat plures sensus*, St. Thomas replied: It has two senses, one of which has three species. Now the question is: Must we speak of the senses or of the sense of Scripture? For while the Thomistic teaching still carries weight with

---

[11] "The literal sense is that which the author intended; but the author of sacred Scripture is God, who in his mind comprehends all things at once" (Iᵃ, q. 1, art. 10 *in corp.*). "...Scripture whose author is the Holy Spirit, and man the instrument" (*Quodl.* 7, q. 6, art. 3 *in corp.*).

[12] Hence the evaluation of a contemporary exegete: "The danger (of the theological exegesis practiced in the time of St. Thomas) is to attribute to the biblical text ideas that are more recent and especially too precise. Exegesis develops the literal sense more than it explains it" (C. Spicq, *op. cit.*, p. 223).

[13] "The exegete, just as he must search out and expound the literal meaning of the words intended and expressed by the sacred writer..." (*Ench. B.*, 552).

theologians, critical scholars in practice recognize only the literal sense; the three spiritual senses are on the way to retaining only an historical interest. What place, in fact, do modern commentators of Scripture give them? Theologians and exegetes could without great difficulty agree to abandon them to liturgists, preachers, and spiritual writers after stating the reservations and warnings that are justified by the excesses of those who tend to allegorize without restraint [14]; that is practically the position that *Divino afflante Spiritu* took. [15] It must be admitted that this position would have astonished the fathers and medieval writers. The evolution of vocabulary is not the only contributing factor to this state of affairs. Much more responsible is the break up of disciplines accomplished around the 12th century and accentuated since the Renaissance, which reached its ultimate consequences in partitioning exegesis into three separate spheres which have no apparent vital link between them: criticism, theology, and the pastoral care of souls.

In short, it is difficult to see how the ancient doctrine of the senses of Scripture, even after its Thomistic recasting, can be organically related to modern critical study of the Bible. The latter appears as a foreign body when put into the context of traditional theology. Conversely, to the modern mind patristic and medieval exegesis seems a web of artificial constructions, founded upon obsolete methods, an integral part of an antiquated culture, and even Thomistic exegesis seems to merit a word of caution, for it does not possess the strict objectivity that modern criticism demands. Such a separation is dangerous for theology. But to avoid it, it is not sufficient to patch onto the traditional doctrine elements which are foreign to it; what is needed is a basic reexamination of the whole problem. To accomplish this, the Thomistic formulation will be of service by providing a perfectly adequate general outline. Accordingly, we will first treat the question of the significance of things in Scripture. This is a purely theological matter; criticism will be of help only indirectly. The subject nevertheless dominates the whole field of exegesis when it is exercised under the influence of faith. In the following chapter we will treat the question of the meaning of biblical texts, a mixed field in which criticism and theology work hand in hand.

[14] We might mention P. Claudel's publication of *Introduction au 'Livre de Ruth'*— *Texte intégral de l'Ouvrage de l'abbé Tardif de Moidrey* (1938), the book which had introduced biblical exegesis to Léon Bloy.

[15] *Ench. B.*, 552 f.

## II. WHAT IS MEANT BY THE SIGNIFICANCE OF THINGS?

### I. VALUE AND LIMITS OF THE THOMISTIC POSITION

Nothing in human history, from the creation to the final judgment, escapes the realization of the divine plan whose unfolding constitutes sacred history. From this point of view, therefore, it must be admitted that nothing is devoid of meaning, no matter how obscure and enigmatic it may sometimes seem. [16] But in speaking here of the significance of things in the Bible, we are taking a more restricted point of view: that of supernatural revelation. This, we have said, is brought about conjointly by the word of inspired men and the intervention of certain significative realities. [17] In this perspective, all the things which pertain to the life of the people of God possess a meaning in relation to the unique object of revelation: the mystery of God manifested in the mystery of Christ. Those which concern the very person of Christ are its essential sign and direct manifestation at the level of human experience. Those which precede his coming are related to it as preparation, instruction and prefiguration. Those of the time of the Church translate sacramentally its presence and activity here below. We are here faced with a theological factor which in some way controls all Christian interpretation of the Scriptures. St. Thomas, summarizing the elements provided by previous tradition, has clearly outlined this factor in three texts which complement one another: *Quodlibet* 7, q. 6 [18]; *Commentary on the Letter to the Galatians*, [19] on 4:24a; *Summa theologica*, [20] I³, q. 1, art. 9-10. These texts can serve as a starting point for our discussion, provided their content is used with discernment.

[16] It goes without saying that profane history has its own coherence, whose laws and internal dynamism philosophy can and should examine. But that does not mean that the meaning uncovered at this level can be sufficient unto itself, for profane history is subordinate to a further end which is of another order, and it cannot reach it unless the grace of Christ intervenes in it (cf. *Sens chrétien de l'A.T.*, pp. 102-112).

[17] Above, pp. 3-7.

[18] We are using the edition of the *Quaestiones quodlibetales* prepared by R. Spiazzi (Turin-Rome: Marietti, 1949), pp. 145-148. The date of this *Quodlibet* is disputed: between 1255 and 1257 for some, in 1265-1267 for Mandonnet and Grabmann (H. de Lubac, *op. cit.*, p. 273), leans toward the first solution.

[19] We are using the edition of R. Cai, *Super epistolas S. Pauli Lectura* (Turin-Rome: Marietti, 1953), pp. 620 f. (nn. 253 f.). The commentary dates from 1260-1261 according to Mandonnet, from 1266-1267 according to Synave and Glorieux.

[20] The composition of this first question: in 1266 according to Walz (*DTC* 15, col. 639), in 1268 according to Synave, "La doctrine de saint Thomas d'Aquin sur le sens littéral des Écritures," *RB* 35 (1926), 57 f.

The terminology of these texts actually proves somewhat unfortunate when it is transferred to the perspective of present-day exegesis and theology. Without ignoring the word allegory, which was consecrated by long use, [21] St. Thomas prefers the words spiritual, or mystical, or figurative (= *figuralis* [22]), of which the allegorical or typical sense is one of the three subdivisions. In the present-day vocabulary the word "spiritual" would implicitly call to mind the spirit of Scripture which St. Paul distinguished from the letter (2 Co 3:6); but the Pauline meaning concerns the texts as well as the realities in the Bible. The word *figuralis*, by evoking biblical figures of speech, gives a too restrictive meaning to the meaning of biblical realities; we will have occasion to point out its insufficiency. The word "mystical" would be the best, since it intends to indicate only the relation of things to the mystery of Christ [23]; unfortunately, it has been given so many different meanings that it would be difficult to give it only that meaning, which is not in great use today. We will therefore refrain from adopting any particular term to designate the significance of things in the Bible.

To this superficial matter, a deeper critical observation might be added. When St. Thomas speaks of the spiritual sense, he places himself exclusively in the perspective of his theological synthesis, which has as its object God, Christ, and our life in him; he asks only what the Bible reveals to us about them, either through its texts, or through the realities of which the texts speak. But this narrow point of view does not embrace everything that contemporary exegetes would include under the expressions "the significance of things, the meaning of history." For between the realities in the Bible and the mystery of salvation in Christ there are all sorts of conceivable relationships, and all of them should be taken into consideration. The Old Testament is not only a prefiguration of Christ, but a historical preparation and an instruction as well; these two aspects of the question are not included in the Thomistic definition of the spiritual sense. Moreover, when St. Thomas considers the three subdivisions of the spiritual sense (allegorical, moral, and anagogic), he applies their definition univocally to the realities of the two Testaments, although their relation to the mystery of Christ differs profoundly in the two instances. Thus he sees in the Old Testament the figure of the New, and in the New, that of the heavenly

---

[21] *Ad Galatas*, n. 253. On the traditional use of the word *allegory*, which is due finally to St. Paul, see H. de Lubac, *op. cit.*, Part I, pp. 373-396.

[22] This term is not to be found in the three classical places cited above. But it is used in the articles of the *Summa* in which St. Thomas interprets figuratively the institutions of the Old Testament (I[a] II[ae], q. 101, art. 2; q. 104, art. 2).

[23] H. de Lubac, *op. cit.*, Part I, pp. 498-511.

realities, and even in the person of Christ, that of his Church. [24] This formal identification introduces a real equivocation into the notion of figure, which is already sufficiently complex. St. Thomas can therefore provide us a guideline only in the measure that we take account of his deficiencies.

## II. SIGNIFICANCE OF THINGS AND MEANING OF HISTORY

A modern man who is acquainted with the history of religions and the methods of phenomenology finds nothing perplexing in the fact that everything in the two Testaments has a significance. As we have seen above, [25] no matter what the particular case may be, religious understanding and the vocabulary used to express it are always based upon man's sense experience; a symbolic value is conferred upon things which are sensibly apprehended. This point, furthermore, did not escape St. Thomas, who on this cites the fundamental principle of Dionysius' symbolism: "*Visibilia solent esse figurae invisibilium,*" [26] and in this way justifies the use of symbols in scriptural language. [27] From this general point of view, the meaning of each thing is its intelligible relation to the mysterious Reality which is the object of religious experience. But within this universally applicable fact there also exists in the Bible a particular symbolism whose basis is no longer the data of common experience used in various religions, but the specific experience linked to the historical realization of the plan of salvation. [28] The previously known analogy between heaven and earth, between time and eternity, is not abolished, but it is given a new value, for the revelation of the living God is henceforth accomplished through the medium of events in which his

---

[24] "The Old Testament was a figure of the New; the Old and the New together are a figure of heavenly things" (*Quodl.* 7, art. 2 *in corps.*). "The true body of Christ and its actions are a figure of the mystical body of Christ and the things which occur in it" (*ibid.*, ad 2). This generic application of the notion of figure can be explained by the fact that St. Thomas envisages only the unfolding of time which in successive stages passes from the Old Testament to Christ, from Christ to the Church, from the Church to eternal life. Nevertheless, the figurative representation of eternal life by the two Testaments is considered in the exemplarist perspective of Pseudo-Dionysius, who is explicitly cited in *Quodlibet* 7 (q. 6, art. 2, *in corp.*) and in the commentary on the letter to the Galatians (n. 254).

[25] Above, pp. 85 f.

[26] *Quodl.* 7, q. 6, art. 2, *in corp.*

[27] I[a], q. 1, art. 9. Three citations of Pseudo-Dionysius are to be found in this article (*in corp.*, ad 2, ad 3). Platonian exemplarism, on which Pseudo-Dionysius is closely dependent, is no more than a philosophical elaboration of the symbolism which underlies all the cults of oriental and Greek antiquity (cf. *Sens chrétien de l'A.T.*, pp. 210 ff.). It is therefore not surprising that through it St. Thomas assimilated an element familiar to historians of religions.

[28] Above, pp. 86-88.

people, illuminated by his word, recognize his sovereign intervention for the salvation of men. This integration of history into the domain of religious symbolism [29] and the consequent reinterpretation of all religious symbolism in terms of the history of salvation are ideas found only in the Bible. Only there does the sovereign master of all things make use of the very course of events directed by his providence to reveal his will. It is in this precise perspective that the significance of things in the Bible ought to be understood. The things in question are not abstract objects, but human realities, related to social groups, to their institutions, to their life; they have a meaning only because they are part of a history *(cursus rerum)* in which the plan of salvation gradually unfolds in time. [30] Since Christ is the cornerstone and key to that plan, he is by that fact the universal principle of intelligibility to whom everything is directed.

Given this fact, it is obvious that the relation of all things to Christ will be qualitatively different according to the stage of the plane of salvation that is considered: the time of the incarnation, the preparatory time during which Christ was expected, the time of the Church which followed his first coming. The problem of the meaning of things ought, therefore, to be studied at these three separate levels.

## § II. CHRIST AT THE CENTER OF HISTORY [31]

### I. HISTORY AS A MEANS OF REVELATION

#### I. SIGNIFICANCE OF THE WORD BECOME FLESH

##### *1. The Problem of the Relation of Christ to Time*

At the point of contact between the two Testaments there is a privileged history which is of unique value, that of Jesus himself. Whoever considers

---

[29] M. Éliade, *Le mythe de l'éternel retour* (Paris: Gallimard, 1949), pp. 152-166; Eng. trans. *The Myth of the Eternal Return* (New York: Pantheon, 1954).

[30] *Quodl.* 7, q. 6, art. 3, *in corp.*: "The spiritual sense of Sacred Scripture results from this, that things traversing their course signify something else, which is perceived through the spiritual sense. But things in their course are so ordered that that sense can be learned from them, because it is his alone who governs things in his providence, and that is God alone. For just as man can employ certain words or certain figures of speech to signify something, so God employs the very course of things which are subject to his providence to signify something else...Hence in no science built up through human effort can there strictly speaking be found anything but a literal sense, but only in Scripture..." This text is clearly very far from the exemplarism of Pseudo-Dionysius.

[31] In the perspective of a theology of the history of salvation, which J. C. K. von Hofmann undertook in the 19th century, O. Cullmann has examined this

revelation and the history of salvation in their entirety and tries to situate the time of Jesus in relation to the two Testaments is bound to remain somewhat perplexed. The divergence on this precise point which divides the theologians of the school of Bultmann has been pointed out. [32] According to Bultmann [33] and H. Conzelmann, [34] the passage from the ancient world to the new world was accomplished between the death of Jesus and the paschal experience of the apostles; as a result of this radical discontinuity, Jesus the Jew belongs to the Old Testament, while the New knows him only as Christ the Lord. For G. Bornkamm [35] and J. M. Robinson, [36] on the other hand, the change took place between the preaching of John the Baptist, who prepared the Jews for the future kingdom, and that of Jesus, who announced the kingdom already present; Jesus is found on the Christian slope of biblical revelation. Actually, in both of these views the time of Christ is not determined with reference to the mystery of his person, which seems to be of no interest, but with reference to his message of salvation, which alone is important for men. Is Jesus already the herald when he proclaims the gospel of the kingdom of God, or must his death first intervene so that his message becomes effective? One is tempted to reply, "So what?," since in any case Christ's temporality no longer retains the meaning given it by a theology of the incarnation which views it with full realism. Willingly or not, such a concept implies a notion of time in which only the existential aspect is considered, the punctual, without duration, without possibility

problem in detail in *Christ and Time*, 3rd ed. (London: SCM, 1962). The sympathetic treatment of J. Frisque, *Oscar Cullmann: Une théologie de l'histoire du salut* (Tournai-Paris: Casterman, 1960) (especially, pp. 69-105), nevertheless contains some serious reservations (cf. pp. 236 ff.), much less forceful than those of J. Barr, *Biblical Words for Time* (London: SCM Press, 1962) (criticism of semantic foundations, pp. 47-81; of philosophical and theological positions, pp. 133-152). A much better approach to the problem is that of H. Urs von Balthasar, *A Theology of History* (New York: Sheed & Ward) and *Das Ganze im Fragment* (Einsiedeln, 1963); J. Mouroux, *The Mystery of Time* (New York: Desclée, 1964). In the 3rd edition of *Christ and Time*, pp. XVII-XXX, O. Cullmann replied to his various critics, notably R. Bultmann. But on this point read the apt remarks of L. Malevez, "Les dimensions de l'histoire du salut," *NRT* 86 (1964), 561-578.

[32] Summary treatment of the question by X. Léon-Dufour, *Les évangiles et l'histoire de Jésus* (Paris: Seuil, 1963), p. 491.

[33] This position is evidently related to the radical reduction of the preaching of Jesus which Bultmann effects in his *Theology of the New Testament* 1 (New York: Scribner, 1955), pp. 3-32, on the basis of an equally radical criticism of the gospel texts; cf. "Der Mensch zwischen den Zeiten," *Glauben und Verstehen* 3, pp. 35-54.

[34] Besides the article cited by X. Léon-Dufour (*ZTK* 54 [1957], 7 ff.), see *The Theology of St. Luke* (London: Faber & Faber, 1960), pp. 185 ff.

[35] G. Bornkamm, *Jesus von Nazareth* (Stuttgart: Kohlhammer, 1957), p. 46; Eng. trans. *Jesus of Nazareth* (London: Hodder & Stoughton, 1960).

[36] J. M. Robinson, *A New Quest of the Historical Jesus* (London: SCM Press, 1959).

of being rendered objective—the time in which man's decision when confronted with the word of God is made. [37]    But does Jesus really belong to that time?

## 2. Christ at the Juncture of the Two Testaments

J. Mouroux, basing himself on the gospels without the distortion due to the Bultmann approach, has much more accurately analyzed the concrete relation of Christ to time. [38]    Let us take the viewpoint of St. John's prologue: in the person of Christ, the Word has burst into human time; he assumed the condition of human history in order to transform its meaning radically. If he was sent by God among men, it was no longer as a prophet, but as the Son, living in a unique relationship with the Father; as such, he appeared here below as the temporal epiphany of the invisible Father, whose activity and very being he manifested beneath a veil.   To comprehend with such depth the meaning of his person, it is indeed not enough to consider the years of his public life which came to a close at the moment of the cross. [39]    Also to be taken into consideration is the time that preceded those years, as well as that in which Jesus reestablished contact with his disciples in his resurrected glory. [40]    Is not the object of the message of salvation, of the gospel, as the evangelist of the Word puts it, "something...that we have heard, and we have seen with our own eyes; that we have watched and touched with our hands: the Word, who is life" (1 Jn 1:1-2)?   If the eternal existence of the Word in the bosom of the Father radically escapes our grasp, from the moment

[37] J. Mouroux, The Mystery of Time, pp. 131-136.

[38] Ibid., pp. 85-182.

[39] At this point in our discussion we encounter that reduction of the history of Jesus which Bultmann inherited from liberal criticism.   Jesus pertains to the science of history only during the years that his life was attested by direct witnesses; even their testimony must be stripped of whatever pertains to subjective beliefs. Whatever in the gospels concerns the experience of the resurrection belongs to that order; whatever speaks of the infancy of Jesus is a legendary or mythical interpretation of the faith (cf. A. Malet, Mythos et Logos: La pensée de Rudolf Bultmann, p. 151). There remain the years of the public life; from the account of them can be eliminated a priori whatever agrees with the later faith of the primitive Church.   For it is understood that Jesus is not properly speaking the founder of that faith or the one who evoked it, but solely its object mythically represented in categories of thought in which it is believed can be detected Judeo-Hellenistic syncretism.   Given such premises, the question of Jesus' consciousness of sonship in his relations with the heavenly Father is rejected as devoid of meaning, without even asking whether faith in the incarnation, whatever might have been the development of its formulation in the apostolic Church, might not have found its starting point and its roots in human history.   Such a method is as foreign to historical science as it is to theology, for it introduces a prejudice into the one as well as the other.

[40] H. Urs von Balthasar, A Theology of History, pp. 81-90.

that he became flesh to dwell among us, on the contrary, he entered the domain of human experience, so that his witnesses could "see his glory" (Jn 1:14), and the vision of that glory was not given them fully until he appeared to them resurrected.

This is the paradox of the incarnation: for as long as this assumption of the human temporal condition by the eternal Word of God lasted, the manifestation of the divine glory on the face of Christ (2 Co 4:6) went through alternations. Sometimes it pierced through the veil of the flesh, which was the sign of its presence here below, as the Second Letter of Peter explicitly notes in regard to the transfiguration (2 P 1:17-18); sometimes the veil so thickened as to conceal it completely from the sight of men, as at the moment of the agony and the cross (cf. Heb 5:7-8). These correlative aspects of "Jesus' pilgrimage in time" (to quote the phrase of J. Mouroux [41]), contrary but inseparable, had their definitive meaning revealed in the light of the resurrection, when that temporal condition was accomplished by being transformed (cf. Heb 5:9-10). Thus, from his entrance into the world until his return to glory, Christ was the Sacrament par excellence [42] "of eternal salvation of which he became for all who obey him the source" (Heb 5:9), and of the Father whose glory reposed in him from his conception (Heb 5:5-6). On this point the penetrating reflections of the letter to the Hebrews echo the texts in which the fourth gospel summarized the earthly mission of Christ (cf. Jn 16:28; 17:1-5). It is perfectly true that between the cross and the resurrection there appeared a breach, not on the plane of profane history, which retained its experiential continuity, but on that of sacred history, on which the plan of salvation is realized. At the moment when Christ passed from the ancient world to the world to come (to use the language of Jewish apocalypse), time was in some way unbalanced: that of the Church took the place of the time in which the Jewish community had lived, since sinful humanity and the regime of the law, which Christ had assumed during his earthly life, died with him on the cross. From the moment of the incarnation, however, the new humanity with its regenerated time was already present in him within the heart of the old world, in the form of the preparatory economy. The resurrection only fully manifested the lordship

---

[41] J. Mouroux, *op. cit.*, pp. 136-144, shows that these two aspects, which are distinct in the synoptics, are joined in the fourth gospel: in Jn 12:23-32 the agony and the transfiguration are superimposed, and the elevation of Jesus on the cross is also his glorification, as if the glory of the resurrection absorbed in advance the humiliation of the passion.

[42] R. Thibaut, *Le sens de l'homme Dieu* (Paris: Desclée de Brouwer, 1942); E. H. Schillebeeckx, *Christ: The Sacrament of the Encounter with God* (New York: Sheed & Ward, 1963); P. T. Camelot, "Le Christ sacrement de Dieu," *L'homme devant Dieu (Mélanges H. de Lubac)* (Paris: Montaigne, 1964), Vol. 3, pp. 355-364.

of the Son of man until then hidden under the form of a servant which he willed to assume (Ph 2:6-11; cf. Heb 2:6-9). Thus the time of Jesus pertains neither to the Old Testament nor to the New; it constitutes the hinge between them. [43]

## II. REVELATION WRITTEN IN EVENTS

If Christ contained in himself the totality of revelation, nothing which came in contact with his person can be devoid of significance: not only his words, but his life, his history. The way, however, in which this history actually performs a revelatory function must be made clear. There is a danger that under the word "history" we might include quite different things. In our previous reflections on the nature of history as a science, we remarked that its object was constitued less by the external details which always go to make up a fact, than by the experience itself which gives those details their concrete unity and their human significance. [44] In the case of Christ, the external details of history have very often fallen into oblivion; we need only mention topographical and chronological indications, which are sorely lacking in the gospels. But that is not what is really important; much more important were the human experiences in which these secondary elements actually played a very subordinate role. In speaking here of human experience, we have in mind first of all that of Christ himself: purposeful acts which revealed his mission of salvation and his intimate mystery; the events of his destiny as man, bearing the marks of our terrestrial condition and nevertheless working our salvation. But for these acts and these events to play an efficacious role as means of revelation, they had also to enter the experience of Christ's contemporaries and witnesses. After having been for them the manifestation of the mystery of Christ, they became the same for us through the medium of their testimony. For one will search the gospels in vain for that famous neutral testimony which would give us the facts of Christ's life in their raw state, before their interpretation by Christian faith. In reporting the facts, the evangelists also give us their meaning, because the person whom those facts concern was at the center of their faith.

What were some of the purposeful acts of Christ? At the age of 12 he remained behind in the temple; he preached the gospel of the kingdom, received sinners and forgave sin, drove the money changers from the temple; he ate with men as a sign of fraternal communion, condemned the hypocritical

---

[43] X. Léon-Dufour, *op. cit.*, pp. 491 f. (French ed.).
[44] Above, pp. 115-118.

scribes and Pharisees, cursed the sterile fig tree; he healed the sick, calmed the tempest, raised the dead, drove Satan from the possessed; he prayed to his Father, begged him to remove the chalice from him, but accepted his will; he chose the twelve, sent them on a mission, conferred on them certain powers, ordered them to repeat "in memory of him" what he did at the last supper. And while it is true that most of these acts, accompanied by words which explained them, took place before the cross, some of them are explicitly placed during the time of the apparitions which followed the resurrection. Thus the risen Christ could transcend the level of historical phenomena, because he had entered the "world to come"; through the experience of the apostles he nevertheless reintroduced himself in another manner to perfect his work here below. [45] In their account of all these significant acts, the evangelists did not content themselves to relate the meaning their immediate witnesses gave them right at the moment; they were only too aware of the incomprehension Jesus suffered until his death, even on the part of his own (cf. Mk 4:13; 7:18; 8:17.33; 9:32, etc.). It was in the light of his resurrection that they understood his deep purpose; the experience they had in the Church led them to perceive its far off goal, beyond even what Christ had explicitly revealed about it in the beginning.

[45] X. Léon-Dufour, *op. cit.*, pp. 254-258, shows how this paradoxical reintroduction of the resurrection, a pure object of faith, into the historical experience of a certain number of men poses for every historian an inevitable question concerning the person of Jesus—a question whose answer is reserved to faith. H. Duméry, *La foi n'est pas un cri*, p. 78, is likewise right in protesting against historians who "break the bond between Jesus and the risen one" by removing the latter from history. But it cannot be said that his treatment of the question (pp. 78-89) is entirely satisfactory. In particular, faith in the resurrection of Jesus (the necessary condition for the apparitions, which assuredly touch upon an objective reality of the supernatural order) cannot be founded on prior faith in his messianity. For while Judaism professed both expectation of the resurrection and expectation of the Messiah, it did not do so by joining the two. The events, therefore, cannot be reconstructed thus: during Jesus' lifetime the apostles "considered him the Messiah; after his execution they were upset, downcast, disconcerted; later they recalled some of the master's words about suffering, certain verses of Isaiah, as well as certain psalms on the deliverance of the just from the bonds of death; at length they "saw" and believed, or, following the plan of Jn 11:40 (if you believe, you will see), they believed and they saw—that is plausible, coherent, in agreement with the texts" (*op. cit.*, pp. 84 ff.). As a matter of fact, neither the alleged verses of Isaiah nor the psalms of deliverance were read by the Jews as messianic texts. In appropriating them Jesus certainly prepared his disciples to understand the meaning of his death as a prior condition for his resurrection and messianic glorification. But it does violence to the gospel texts to place this understanding of his death in the light of the Scriptures before his apparitions: all the texts relate this clarification of the faith to the experience of the apparitions. It was only then that the disciples could apply to Jesus as the Messiah the psalms on suffering or Is 53, and transfer to the plane of the "world to come" and of the resurrection the texts relating to the glorious Messiah. Likewise in the case of St. Paul (to whom the author alludes, *op. cit.*, p. 85) it was the apparition on the road to Damascus that determined the recasting of beliefs whose result we know from his letters. The whole of the author's analysis, therefore, stands in need of correction.

With even greater reason did the evangelists employ this key of interpretation to show in the events of his life something other than diverse
facts [46] arranged in the usual succession of human affairs. For it is true
that Jesus, in the particular circumstances in which his life unfolded, participated fully in our common condition. But he assumed it in such a way
that his situation was unique: in relation to the Father, as the "well beloved
son"; in relation to men, as the eschatological savior. It is from this point of
view that the evangelists present his experiences as man, similar to those of
others from many standpoints, but at the same time without any equivalent:
Jesus, conceived of the Holy Spirit by a virgin mother, was born at Bethlehem
as the Davidic messiah; his growing years allowed him to assimilate the
whole religious tradition of Judaism, which fashioned his mind and his
sensibility [47]; at the time of his baptism he had a mystical experience parallel,
but not identical, to prophetic vocation; he experienced the spiritual struggle
with Satan, which remained in the background during his whole public
ministry; he saw his preaching both accepted and rejected by men; he was
misunderstood at Nazareth, persecuted by his enemies who besieged him,
and finally betrayed, arrested on the order of the Jewish authorities, judged,
crucified under Pontius Pilate; but his privileged witnesses saw him again
afterward in the glory of his resurrection and received the Spirit he had
promised. The evangelists never recount these facts without in one way
or another revealing their significance, because they were not interested in
them except by reason of that significance. That is why they sometimes
explain them with the aid of the Scriptures, and sometimes compare them
with statements Jesus made. And in every case they examine them in
the light of the resurrection, which alone dissipated their enigmatic, disconcerting, even scandalous character.

This is the way the gospels present to us the meaningful history whose
hero is Jesus. It remains to be seen what reality it reveals, what leap into
the invisible it makes possible for him who believes.

---

[46] Profane history is not ignorant of the punishment of Jesus under the procurator
Pontius Pilate, if only through the allusion to it in Tacitus, *Annals* 15, 44. But Tacitus
rightly sees in it a different meaning, relative to the "detestable superstition" that
was born in Judea and reached Rome before Nero's time. This negative value
judgment constitutes for him a subjective interpretation of the fact, which must be
related to a certain pagan and Roman concept of existence. It is no more unprejudiced
than the value judgment of the apostolic writings.

[47] When it is stated that Jesus recapitulates the Old Testament in himself,
this should not be considered a mere impractical idealization, because through his
Jewish education the Old Testament determined the particular form of his thought
and religious life. Thus the biblical figures and promises, by becoming of the
substance of his human life, were brought to their accomplishment. But the accomplishment naturally surpasses in every way the preludes and sketches which bore
his mark (cf. H. Urs von Balthasar, *op. cit.*, pp. 49-57).

## II. THE MYSTERY REVEALED IN JESUS CHRIST

### I. FROM THE HISTORY OF CHRIST TO THE MYSTERY OF CHRIST

#### *1. The Mystery of Christ the Head*

The place of Jesus' history at the center of time, at the juncture of the preparatory economy and the sacramental economy, at the point where the age of the sinful world oppressed by the inheritance of Adam was transformed into a new age immersed in divine eternity, makes it the key to all that went before and all that follows it, or (as H. Urs von Balthasar has said) the norm of history. [48] In relation to what preceded it, in the age of promises and expectation, it is that eschatological reality which from the beginning exercised a mysterious attraction on the course of things. [49] While the mystery it concealed waited centuries before issuing in an event, it was nonetheless at the basis of the Old Testament, of the time of the old economy, and even of the creation (Col 1:16): all of that takes its meaning from that mystery, for it was all directed to it as to its archetype. [50] As for the age which follows Christ, that of the Church, which tends to the second coming and the transfiguration of earthly time, the history of Jesus reveals its meaning in advance as its concrete exemplar and as a promise to be fulfilled. [51] Here too the hidden mystery insinuates its presence under sacramental signs, in expectation of being unveiled fully when "the world as we know it passes away" (1 Co 7:31).

What then is this mystery of which Jesus' history, from his conception to his resurrection, constitutes the visible representation? It is the full realization of the religious relationship between God and men in the new Adam, their head. While members of fallen humanity, their destiny burdened by the consequences of the sin which enslaved them since the beginning of history, they are nonetheless called to enter into intimate union with God in Jesus Christ his Son. Christ reveals this by living it among men: struggling, suffering, dying like and with them, he is no less the Son in whom the Father is well pleased; his death itself is a passing from this world to the Father, it is the way to eternal glory. Thus the mystery concerns first and foremost the person of the Word made flesh: it first manifested itself in the time of pilgrimage in which all the race of Adam lives, since it is there that the Son of

---

[48] *Ibid.*, pp. 79 ff.
[49] J. Mouroux, *op. cit.*, pp. 101 ff.
[50] *Ibid.*, pp. 170-176. *Sens chrétien de l'A.T.*, pp. 139-165.
[51] J. Mouroux, *op. cit.*, pp. 176-182.

God assumed our wounded nature; then it was completed beyond time, in that new kind of duration into which the risen Christ has conducted our glorified nature.

But through the person of Christ, the intimate nature of God himself becomes perceptible to men. [52] When the Son, the Word and Wisdom of God, visibly manifested himself in the flesh, he made known the Father whom no one can see (Jn 1:18): who has seen him has seen the Father (Jn 14: 9), for the Father is in him and he in the Father (Jn 10:38), the Father and he are one (Jn 10:30). Since he has the fulness of the Spirit in himself (Mt 3: 16 par.), he reveals him as a person when he promises his coming as an eschatological gift (Jn 14:16.26; 16:13 ff.; Ac 1:8). The words of Jesus assuredly play a major role in this revelation. But what those words express is in no wise a speculation on God, of the kind which the rationalist critics gratuitously attribute to primitive Christianity in regard to the incarnation or the trinity. It is the content of a spiritual experience, unique in its kind, which is perceptible every time Jesus speaks of the Father with such astonishing familiarity. [53] That is where the secret of his personality lies, the profound source of all his human activity. That is why that activity, by the interior attitude it supposes as well as by the acts it involved, is the concrete expression of that experience at the level of the most commonplace history.

## 2. The Mystery of Christian Existence

The mystery of Christ has also another aspect which concerns us directly. Man cannot come in contact with the word of God in Christ without seeing himself in his true existential condition, wavering between tragic despair and the hope of salvation. One of the most outstanding features of the fourth

---

[52] See on this point the reflections of Y. Congar, "Dum visibiliter Deum cognoscimus... Méditation théologique," *LMD* 59 (1959), 131-161 (reprinted in *Les voies du Dieu vivant* [Paris: Cerf, 1962], pp. 79-107).

[53] We would here refer the reader to the exhaustive study by W. Marchel, *Abba, Père! La prière du Christ et des chrétiens* (Rome: Pont. Bibl. Inst., 1963). It is curious to note how some critics, who are alien to authentic Christian faith, are quick to explain its origins with the aid of a pattern fixed once for all, universally applicable in the history of religions. The idea that there could have been a spiritual experience of a particular type in Christ, and not just a sublime one among all others, but irreducible to any other, is excluded *a priori*. The texts which might lead to that conclusion *must* be explained otherwise, as a pure product of Helleno-Christian syncretism. The texts resist, but one must persist, for the hypothesis is absolutely necessary in order to reconcile the presentation of the history of primitive Christianity with the refusal of faith in Christ the Son of God. We might admit that the hypothesis is not absurd and that it merits serious consideration. But let us recognize at the same time that it cannot claim more scientific objectivity than the contrary hypothesis, which is held by Christian faith. And finally the choice between the two does not pertain to science, but to belief, no matter for which part one settles (cf. below, pp. 339 ff.).

gospel is its presentation of the spiritual drama which, for Jesus' contemporaries as for every man, plays about his person. [54] When Christ appeared here below, man was constrained to make a choice that was to determine his existential situation: the obedience of faith would allow him to enter into regenerated existence, in which Christ already lives in communion with the Father; refusal to believe would plunge him into the fallen existence he received at his birth. He was then drawn into a basic struggle in which his eternal destiny was at stake: between darkness and light, between life and death. St. Paul would add, between the old man born of Adam and the new man recreated in Jesus Christ. This is a revelation of the existentialist order, and R. Bultmann cannot be faulted for having so forcefully emphasized it. [55] The synoptics were not unaware of it (cf. especially Lk 2:34 ff.). In St. John's gospel it becomes in some way the motive for Jesus' appearance in history: God sent his son into the world so that the world might be saved through him, and whoever believes in him actually participates in salvation; but whoever does not believe is already judged (Jn 3:16-21). But it would be wrong to reduce to this unveiling of the most basic human drama the content of the revelation brought by Christ, as if the figurative or real references to salvation and to grace contained in the New Testament were human constructions without any ground in real being, destined to translate mythically the Christian experience of faith. [56] The existentialist and the ontological are not mutually exclusive: they overlap.

[54] P. Grelot, "Le problème de la foi dans le IV<sup>e</sup> évangile," *BVC* 52 (1963), 60-71; cf. M. Bonningues, *La foi dans l'évangile de saint Jean* (Bruxelles: La Pensée catholique, 1955), pp. 70 ff.

[55] The conclusions of his commentary on the fourth gospel on this point are summarized in his *Theology of the New Testament*, Vol. 2, pp. 75 ff.: Faith as Eschatological Existence. A similar insistence on the decision of faith and on the existential drama which plays about it will be noted in the work of R. Guardini, *The Lord* (London: Longmans, 1956), pp. 208-215, 292-298. But it is found already in the *Tractatus in Joannem* of St. Augustine, for example, 12, 12-14 (*PL* 35, 1490-1492), 27, 7-11 (*PL* 35, 1618-1621), etc.

[56] In order to find in the fourth gospel a demythologization of the salvation event as the primitive kerygma preached it, Bultmann was led to deny the realism of the incarnation which the Johannine accounts suppose, and to interpret the miraculous or supernatural features which they contain as pure symbols, which John superimposed upon the accounts he received from tradition (*Theology of the New Testament* 2, pp. 40-49; cf. A. Malet, *Mythos et Logos*, pp. 164-169). But this result of exegetical analysis was present from the start in the existentialist postulate which governed its execution. If it is taken for granted at the start that all ontological realism proceeds from the natural reason at work in Greek philosophy, but remains foreign to the eschatological existence into which the decision of faith transports us, it is difficult to see what might remain of the intended teaching of the fourth gospel. But what is the meaning of this superimposition and this confusion of three heterogeneous distinctions: between the ontological and the existentialist, between Greek speculation and the biblical message, between the works of the old man and Christian existence?

By his mere presence in the world, Christ revealed the world to itself
in the state sin had placed it. In the light of his glance, and especially at the
foot of the cross, were manifested both the depth of the mystery of sin and
its power, man's radical impotence before that force that held him in its
sway, and his absolute need of an unmerited grace. [57] But it would be too
little thus to see in Christ the word of God because his cross, by revealing
sin, was the occasion for the announcement of the message of grace. He is
the Word become flesh in person. As such, he brought into the world
that new humanity in which those who believe could thenceforth participate.
It would not only wrest them from the sinful existence of a condemned
world, but it would transport them with it into life with the Father, it would
make them participants in his sacrifice and his glory. His relation to them
is that of the head to the members, of the model in relation to its more or
less similar imitations, of the source of salvation (Heb 5:9) in relation to the
saved. His actions, too, and the events of his life have a revelatory value
which directly concerns their life as redeemed. His acts manifest concretely
the diverse aspects of the grace he brings to man; the events of his life display
the new existence already fully experienced by him who is its originator and
its source. There is a whole network of connections between them and
the various aspects of Christian existence, both at the level of life in the
Church, where it operates under sacramental signs, and at the level of its
consummation beyond time. [58]

Let us consider first the events of Jesus' life. His failures, the perse-
cutions he suffered, and finally his passion determine the value of suffering
and death in the economy of salvation. Consequently, a similar experience
can be foreseen, in participation with his, in the life of his Church (cf. Rv 12:
13-17), of those who serve him (Rv 11:7-9; Mt 10:24 ff.; Jn 15:20 ff.), of all
those who believe in him (2 Tm 3:12); so one must carry the cross with
him to obtain salvation (Mt 16:24 ff. par.), and the very meaning of baptism
is to make us die in his death (Rm 6:4), in order to put an end to the sinful
existence of "the old man" which we had inherited from Adam (Col 3:3).
Similarly, the resurrection of Christ reveals not only the goal toward which
the Church's hope tends (Rm 8:19-23), but also the mysterious action that

---

[57] In this will be noted the thought of St. Paul in Rm 5:12-21 and 7:14-25.

[58] The significance of the history of Christ for us is excellently expressed by
St. Thomas in *Quodlibet* 7, q. 6, art. 2, ad 5: "The true body of Christ and its actions
are a figure of the mystical body of Christ and the things which occur in it, in such
wise that we should take from him, namely Christ, an example of how to live. Our
future glory was also foretold us in Christ; hence whatever is said of Christ the Head
can be explained allegorically, by referring them to his mystical body, morally, by
referring them to our acts which must be reformed according to him, and anagogically,
inasmuch as the way to glory is shown us in Christ." Cf. J. Schildenberger, *Vom
Geheimnis des Gotteswortes*, pp. 440-446.

takes place in him who believes in the call of the Son of God (Jn 5:25), when he rises spiritually to lead his new life (Rm 6:4-5). The same principle of interpretation can be applied to all the events which made up the human experience of Christ. That of his baptism, for example, which forecast his baptism in death (Lk 12:50), fully manifests the mysterious life into which our own baptism introduces us: the Father makes us his adopted sons (Rm 8:14-16), and we receive the Holy Spirit (Rm 5:5; 8:15). Likewise, in the transfiguration we see the transformation God desires to work on our mortal flesh, since by conferring his Spirit on it he plants in it the seed of its final glory [59] (cf. Rm 8:23; 2 Co 1:22). Therefore, the facts themselves of Jesus's life speak, and it is important to examine them with the greatest care in order to understand in what the life of which he is the principle consists. [60]

As for the deeds of Christ as a pilgrim, they began in a veiled way what he now accomplishes from his throne of glory. To show that he was realizing the eschatological event announced in the Scriptures (Mt 11:4-5), he worked symbolic miracles which showed his victory over the evils humanity suffers in its present condition: the healing of paralytics (Jn 5:21) and the blind (Jn 9:5), the raising of the dead (Jn 11:24). But this same victory is prolonged into the time of the Church, thanks to the same efficacious word which is at work in sacramental signs [61]: is not baptism a healing, an illumination, and a resurrection (Ep 5:14), in expectation of what will come to pass after the final resurrection (Rv 19:4-6; cf. Jn 5:28 ff.), perfect healing (Rv 22:2) and eternal illumination (Rv 21:23 ff.)? Similarly, the miraculous meal of the multiplied loaves, at which the crowds were invited to Christ's table, symbolically announced the eucharistic meal instituted at the last supper and continued in the Church (1 Co 11:26), in expectation of the heavenly banquet which will consummate beyond time the same mystery of communion (Rv 3:20; 19:19). The list of examples could go on and on.

[59] Recall the importance of the transfiguration in the spiritual theology of oriental Christians; cf. V. Lossky, *Essai sur la théologie mystique de l'église d'orient* (Paris: Aubier, 1944), pp. 145 ff., 218 ff. See likewise the excellent conclusions of A. M. Ramsey, *The Glory of God and Transfiguration of Christ* (London, 1949), pp. 128-143.

[60] On the relation of the mystery of the incarnation to Christian anthropology, see the profound remarks of K. Rahner, "On the Theology of the Incarnation" in *Theological Investigations* (Baltimore: Helicon, 1961 ff.), Vol. 4, pp. 105-120.

[61] R. Bultmann stresses extremely well the symbolic character of the miracles—or more exactly, of the signs—worked by Jesus, but solely in order to see in them the image of his task as revealer, which brings grace and truth to men (*Theology of the New Testament* 2, pp. 44 f.). All sacramental symbolism is emptied in principle, for it is understood that "No specifically ecclesiological interest can be detected. There is no interest in cult or organization" in the Johannine writings (*ibid.*, p. 91). Still within Protestant theology, an opposite view can be found in O. Cullmann *Les sacrements dans l'évangile johannique* (Paris: Presses Univ. Fr., 1951).

## II. CHRISTIAN REFLECTION ON THE HISTORY OF CHRIST

The work of reflection to bring to light this meaning of the acts of Jesus and the facts of his life was undertaken right from the birth of the Church. The proclamation of the gospel in the age of the apostles already laid the foundations for such reflection. The written gospels, each in its own way, carried on the search in the line of their particular preoccupations; it is implied in the Pauline letters, though in them it centers on a few essential facts which constitute the mystery of salvation. Furthermore, the contemplation of this mystery is not the only matter involved, for every meditation on the faith ought to end in practical decisions; Christ's conduct provides the Christian a model on which he ought to pattern his existence. If Christ "became poor for your sake, to make you rich out of his poverty," that is an example of generosity which ought to be imitated unceasingly (2 Co 8:9; cf. Ph 2:5 ff.). In thus proposing the various aspects of the mystery of Christ on the basis of his history, the New Testament opened the way to theology.

Much, however, remained to be done later, both as regards arranging its conclusions systematically, and discovering the manifold implications of each act of Jesus, of every event recorded in the gospel. It is to this that theology, liturgy, and preaching have, with varying results, devoted themselves down through the ages. Their various approaches have not always led them to give equal emphasis to what we have called existentialist revelation and ontological revelation, which were intimately connected in the concrete reality of Christ. Theology has sometimes surrendered to the temptation to separate them through methodical abstraction; it has drawn from Scripture an ontology of the trinity, the incarnation, the economy of grace, without relating them closely enough to a consideration of Christian existence, its drama, its risk, all things in which homiletics could not but be interested. Perhaps a philosophy of essences inherited from Greece has weighed too heavily on the speculations of the Christian *gnosis*—that is, of theology raised to the status of science. Conversely, the form of religious experience proper to Luther and the existentialism dependent on Kierkegaard today influence in another way the theology of Bultmann and his school, which tends to empty the mystery of Christ of its realist content, [62] provided that the decision of

---

[62] That was already the case with liberal demythization and with that of the history of religions school, whom Bultmann accuses of having reached the point of suppressing all Christology (cf. A. Malet, *Mythos et Logos*, pp. 137-141). His own project of demythologization rightly aims to avoid this pitfall through the existentialist interpretation based on the decision of faith. But what remains of Christology so reinterpreted? Unless paradoxically the decision of faith has implications which surpass the clear consciousness of him who makes it: "If one looks to Jesus, to his cross and death, and really believes that there the living God has said his last word,

faith remains intact. Both reins must be kept firmly in hand in order to comprehend how Christ is the living norm of history, of which he is the center, and the norm of each of our individual existences, inserted in the Church but directed to eternal life.

These several preoccupations are easily evident in the doctrine of the senses of Scripture as it has come down from the patristic age and the early Middle Ages. On the basis of the history of Jesus Christ, from his birth to his resurrection, Christian interpreters strove to understand three things: the ecclesial reality under all its aspects (allegory); its heavenly consummation, which is already actual for Christ the Head and his Church (cf. Ga 4:26) but still to come for the faithful at large (anagoge); and finally Christian existence, governed by a moral norm but also conducted by a mystical experience founded on the decision of faith and informed by charity (tropology). Such an interpretation of the gospel content has not lost its actuality. It is independent of the exegetical methods applied to the details which fill out those facts. If in this matter allegorizing has often gone to excess, in accord with the cultural inclinations inherited from the ancient world, it is still true that its basic principle is actually faith in the Word made flesh, thanks to which man's historical experience is transformed into an experience of faith and expands into theology.

## § III. THE SIGNIFICANCE OF THINGS BEFORE CHRIST

### I. NATURE OF THE PROBLEM

#### I. THE AGE OF PREPARATION

Now we will consider the meaning of the realities which preceded the coming of Christ here below. The age of preparation includes several stages. The first, that of the origin, [63] determined once for all the lasting characteristics of human temporality, such as we know it from experience (cf. Gn 1-3; Ws 2:23-24; Mt 19:4-8; Rm 5:12 ff.). If this temporality is ambiguous, the reason is that it depends upon two opposing principles: on the one hand, the finality it received from its creator; on the other, the

decisive, irrevocable and hence comprehensive; if he really believes that there God redeems him from the imprisonment and tyranny of the existentials of his blocked, guilty and doomed existence: he believes something that can only be true and real, if Jesus is what the faith of Christianity confesses. Whether he knows it consciously or not, he believes in the incarnation of the Word of God" (K. Rahner, *art. cit.*, p. 118).

[63] *Sens chrétien de l'A.T.*, pp. 97-99.

fallen state in which it found itself after the entrance of sin into the world. The second stage, that of the primitive economy, [64] was likened by medieval theology to the law of nature, [65] not in the sense that there then existed a human nature, in the Greek sense of the term, which was self-sufficient in its own order, but in the sense that men, through their conscience subject to divine influence, could know God through his works (Rm 1:19-21) and accomplish "naturally" the prescriptions of his law (Rm 2:14-15). Finally, with Abraham began the stage of the ancient economy or Old Testament, which was explicitly directed toward the salvation accomplished and revealed in Christ.

To determine what, in this temporal outline, has a signification in relation to Christ, we must return to the principle stated above [66]: realities *(res)* receive their meaning from their place in a history *(cursus rerum)* which tends to the coming of Christ. But just what must be included under the word "history?" For human history can be considered from two quite different aspects. 1) Whatever concerns the relations of men with the world and the relations of men among themselves constitutes profane history: the history of races and nations, of science and technology, of societies and civilizations, of languages and cultures. 2) Whatever concerns the relations of men with God constitutes sacred history, properly so called. These two aspects are closely related, [67] first of all because the problem of relations with God is intimately intertwined with the rest of human life. And furthermore, profane history finds its ultimate goal and its justification only in sacred history, to which it is positively ordered; it consequently also depends upon the only mediator through whom the human race in any circumstances obtains its salvation, Jesus Christ. These two aspects of human history, however, are not related to Christ in the same way. Sacred history attained full reality in his first coming; it has as its center of gravity his incarnation, which joined God to man. Profane history, on the other hand, continues to unfold in ambiguity until his second coming; only then will he definitively select its positive elements and transform them in eternal life.

Our attempt to illumine the meaning of human realities during the age of preparation adopts the perspective of the first coming of Christ. The "Christological" significance of the profane aspects of this part of history should not indeed be neglected. But that significance will not become fully apparent until the following part of our reflection, in which we will consider

---

[64] *Ibid.*, pp. 115-121.
[65] Cf. the title of the work of Hugh of St. Victor: *De sacramentis Legis naturalis et scriptae (PL* 176, 17-42).
[66] Above, pp. 241 ff.
[67] *Sens chrétien de l'A.T.*, pp. 102-112.

the meaning of the realities in the New Testament. What interests us here is what properly constituted sacred history before Christ. In this regard, the first three stages of the plan of salvation do not present the same problem. That of the origin determines the relation of human temporality and whatever was to flow from it through the ages of God; it therefore belongs fully to sacred history, no matter in what form it might be expressed. [68] That of the primitive economy brings to the fore the general characteristics which in every age mark the permanent relation between human temporality and sacred history, whatever might be the particular events in which those characteristics appear. [69] As for the ancient economy, while it still assumes these same general characteristics, it incorporates them in a series of singular events which have a specific significance because they directly prepare for the coming of Christ.

## II. THE MYSTERY OF CHRIST AND THE MEANING OF HISTORY

All of history which preceded Christ, therefore, everything which it gathered in its course to make it a part of sacred history, has some significance in relation to Christ. Let us clarify this vague principle at two points.

When we say "in relation to Christ," we do not intend only Christ the Head considered in his individual life, which began in time at his incarnation until his cross and was consummated beyond time after his entrance into glory. We have in mind the mystery of Christ in all its breadth, which includes its historical extension, which is realized here below in the Church and will be consummated on the last day in the glory of the resurrection. That is the reality to which all history before the first coming of Christ is related.

And how is the meaning of this history to be defined? The Thomistic doctrine of the senses of Scripture reduced it to just one function, that of prefiguring Christ; this, as we have seen, [70] is a too narrow view of the

---

[68] What pertains to sacred history in this is not the external representation of original humanity, but its spiritual drama at the moment that the historical process was set in motion. On the first point the Bible employs conventional representations which leave the field completely open for scientific investigation. On the second, it subordinates its imagery to a conception of God, man, their relations, of sin, which is related to the whole of revelation and whose agreement with our own spiritual experience can easily be discovered.

[69] *Sens chrétien de l'A.T.*, pp. 115 ff. Here too the presentation of human history is drawn up according to the conventional methods corresponding to Israel's cultural level. The anecdotal material of Gn 4-11, whose source are popular traditions, have a representative value that has to do with the theology of history. It is in this order of ideas that they "state the principal truths which are fundamental for our salvation" (encyclical *Humani Generis*, *Ench. B.*, 618).

[70] Above, p. 240.

situation. The relation of history and all it contains to Christ, its ultimate goal, can actually be viewed in three different ways. 1) The sacred history which preceded Christ constituted the preparation for his coming; from this point of view, the advent of Christ appears as the accomplishment of time (Mk 1:15). 2) Within this scheme was realized a divine pedagogy whose practical means was the law (Ga 3:24); from this point of view, Christ brought an end to the pedagogy (Ga 3:25) by accomplishing the law (Mt 5:17). 3) Finally, the arrival of salvation in Christ was promised to men, not only by prophetic statements, but also by concrete realities which were its prefiguration; from this point of view, Christ realized here below the accomplishment of the divine promises in word and in deed. These are the three points we will examine in succession.

Awareness of this meaning of the realities involved in the dynamic action of sacred history was gained only progressively. Before Abraham and outside the people of the old alliance it was not completely unknown; but man's religious instinct, blunted by the deficiency of a wounded conscience, had no more than an ambiguous, and on some points very vague, notion of it. [71] In the Old Testament, it became the object of a continuous revelation whose successive stages can be indicated; but that was still only an incomplete manifestation of it. Full revelation came only with Jesus Christ; his history and his words, therefore, such as the apostles understood and recounted them, must serve as the basis for explaining it. The positive elements provided by the Old Testament (or even those of the history of religions) must consequently be integrated in a synthetic view which surpasses them, if a complete theological exposition of them is to be achieved.

## II. HISTORICAL PREPARATION FOR CHRIST [72]

Only a superficial understanding of the historical preparation for Christ will be gained if it is reduced to the sequence of external events which preceded his advent here below and the genealogy which ends with his birth in the flesh. The course of history in which this double preparation for his first coming was realized also fulfilled another function: within it

---

[71] An analysis of the myths and rites of ancient religions makes this apparent: the phenomena of nature, of family and social life, are the object of a constant but often equivocal sacralization; historical events as such, on the contrary, seem impossible to sacralize (cf. *Sens chrétien de l'A.T.*, pp. 113 ff.). It should be noted that the conciliar declaration of Vatican II (session III) on non-Christian religions evaluates quite positively these presentiments of revelation which appear in some measure everywhere (Hinduism and Buddhism are explicitly mentioned).

[72] J. Mouroux, *op. cit.*, pp. 170-176.

was revealed the temporal human state, such as Christ was to assume as a son of Adam (Lk 3:38) and under the particular form which it took for him as a son of David and of Abraham (Mt 1:1).

## I. ADAM'S HISTORICAL HERITAGE

By temporality [73] we mean the existential condition of man in time, as an individual, or as a society whose becoming constitutes history. The opposing characteristics of this present condition have not escaped the attention of philosophers. But a complete solution to the enigma requires recourse to the mystery of the beginning considered in two ways: as a vocation to existence addressed by God to man, and as a dramatization of existence through the entrance of death and sin into the world. [74] In the creator's intention, man's time has a well-defined meaning: it is a time for glorifying and serving God, a time for love, joy, and life. This is not an abstract speculation, artificially tacked onto reality. It is written on the heart of man, who has within him an innate sense of God and a deep desire to be united to him, an insatiable thirst to live and to love, a dream of the well-being of paradise. Yet the concrete condition man experiences at every instant apparently contradicts these basic needs. Man's time, marked by the presence of evil and a propensity to reject God, seems a time for struggle, a time for adversity, a time for dying. Is man then an absurd being? [75]

Chapters 1-11 of Genesis, meditated in passing by the wisemen of Israel, and then reread in the light of Christ by the authors of the New Testament, are the theological source in which is revealed, not this temporality itself, of which we already have an idea from our long experience, but the meaning it takes on in the perspective of the history of salvation. It is because the human condition is that of a sinful race that it implies the contradictions that put the dialectic of history in motion [76]: the antagonism of the sexes (cf. Gn

---

[73] J. Mouroux, *op. cit.*, pp. 58-81. The terminology used here obviously derives from that of Heidegger (in *Sein und Zeit*, Eng. tran. *Being and Time* [London: SCM Press, 1962]). The use that J. Mouroux makes of it shows that he has a good grasp of the problem we are about to examine, but it does not imply an adherence to all of Heidegger's views nor a theological use of his philosophy similar to that of R. Bultmann. On Bultmann and Heidegger, see A. Malet, *Mythos et Logos*, pp. 277-311, and above, p. 233, note 196.

[74] J. Mouroux, *op. cit.*, p. 81, speaks admirably of original sin as an inversion of time.

[75] The atheistic existentialism of Sartre deliberately assumes the position of this radical absurdity, and strives to give a meaning to man's existence through the commitment which follows this basic acceptance of despair.

[76] To recognize that human history has a dialectic structure, that its process is made up of a series of clashes, belongs to common sense, and not to philosophical theories. The difficulty consists in qualifying that fact, in recognizing its significance.

3:16b), of classes and social groups, of nations and cultures; the struggle of man against hostile nature (Gn 3:17-18; 7:11 ff.), which he nevertheless feels called to master (Gn 1:28; 2:20a); the division of each individual against himself in the interior struggle of his torn conscience (Rm 7:15-20).

In becoming man, Christ willed to assume the common condition· Born of a woman (Ga 4:24), a son of Adam through the mediation of his ancestors (cf. Lk 2:23-38), he fully assumed that heritage which made him one with all sinful men. That is why man's long historical experience, deposited layer on layer over the ages, marked by the contradiction of the thrust of the creator's plan and the scars of sin, shaped, on the one hand, the human abasement of His ego, and on the other, the social environment, contact with which was to determine His own destiny. In this view, without losing anything of his unique situation as Son of God, he recapitulated in himself the existential experience of all humanity, to which he was like in everything except sin (Heb 4:15). That is why he experienced, as all other men, human time as a time for struggle, adversity, and death. [77] Thus the preparation for the drama of the cross was not accomplished only during the years of his public life, but throughout human history from the events of the beginning. From this it follows that that history, even down to its most ordinary characteristics, always contained eschatological significance in relation to Christ who was its goal.

## II. HISTORICAL HERITAGE FROM ABRAHAM AND DAVID [78]

Within this history God set apart a certain period of time in order to disclose visibly within it his plan of salvation, the Old Testament. Its unfolding presents the same general traits that are found everywhere else, since the human group which it concerns came from the same ancestory as all the others, and experienced the same temporal condition. But it was different in this, that within it was realized a series of divine elections [79] which set apart the remnant through whom salvation was to reach men: the election of Abraham

---

By hypostatizing History and making the dialectic a law of nature as such, Hegel and Marx perverted the whole state of the problem. The historical dialectic is the iron law under which fallen humanity struggles, one of the principal aspects of his sinful condition. The problem of salvation is to find a way to escape from it, and there is no other way than that revealed in Jesus Christ.

[77] See the remarks of J. Mouroux, *op. cit.*, pp. 144-148, on the carnal temporality of Christ.

[78] *Ibid.*, pp. 89-96.

[79] On this important theme of election, see *Sens chrétien de l'A.T.*, pp. 135-136 (bibliography, p. 135, note 4). On the election of a remnant as a general law of the divine plan realized in salvation history, see Rm 9:6-29; 11:1-10.

and the patriarchs (cf. Is 41:8), of the people of Israel (Is 41:9), of the tribe Juda and of Jerusalem (Ps 78:67 ff.), of David and his line (Ps 78:70). The result of this unique disposition of providence was that within human history there arose a particular history, which the finality of the plan of salvation influenced directly—its social, political, cultural, and religious history, which encompasses all the aspects of human experience; a history intimately entwined in the convulsive events of all sorts which shook the Middle East for those two thousand years. This experience had the effect of conferring some original characteristics upon the remnant of sinful humanity, set apart for the work of salvation, the descendants of Abraham, the people of Israel, the Jewish community. Their human condition remained the same as it was elsewhere, but once integrated in this series of singular events which tended toward an *eschaton*, salvation, it thereby took on a new meaning which could not be found elsewhere. The meaning of human temporality was no longer understood with reference only to its origin, which determined its contradictory traits, but with reference also to that goal, which exercised a constant influence on its development.

That goal was Christ. As a descendant of David (Rm 1:3) and of Abraham (Ga 3:16) in an unbroken line (Mt 1:1-6), he assumed the heritage of Adam with the particular modifications it received in Judaism. In him the law of election and setting apart, which was already fully at work in the Old Testament, found its supreme application. For the race of Abraham and the people of Israel, despite the plan of salvation revealed to them, remained at the level of sinful humanity. But the election of Christ fell to the unique Just Man[80] who by himself constituted the remnant set apart for the salvation of men. Thus in his person the mysterious meaning of the previous elections and segregations was revealed, the meaning of that singular history which tended to him though its participants were not fully aware of it. Having received from his mother the heritage of Abraham, of Israel, of David, of a whole national and religious tradition, [81] he recapitulated the whole history of the Old Testament; it was in this precise form that he experienced human temporality in order to incorporate it into the mystery of salvation through the incarnation and the cross, the resurrection and the Church. To become man, he became a Jew. To extend salvation to all of humanity, he grafted the Church, his Body, onto the trunk of Israel (Rm 11:17-24).

---

[80] In Ac 3:14 Jesus is given the characteristic title of "Holy and Just" (cf. V. Taylor, *The Names of Jesus* [London: MacMillan, 1954], pp. 80-83; L. Sabourin, *The Names and Titles of Jesus* [New York: MacMillan, 1967], pp. 52-55).

[81] H. Urs von Balthasar, *op. cit.*, pp. 49 ff.; L. Deiss, *Marie, fille de Sion* (Bruges-Paris: Desclée de Brouwer, 1959), pp. 65 f.

### III. CHRIST AND THE CONSUMMATION OF TIME

We are now able to see how the history which preceded Christ, while it receives its meaning from him, nonetheless reveals a whole aspect of his mystery. An understanding of that history makes comprehensible, on the one hand, his tragic destiny as a son of Adam, and on the other, his personal character as a son of David and of Abraham, chosen for the salvation of men, but rejected by his own people. His entrance into history marked the fulness of time (cf. Ga 4:4) in one special sense: the *eschaton* broke into the very midst of human temporality. [82] Time was then also consummated (Mk 1:15) in another sense: all the material content of that temporality, set from the beginning in its general characteristics, and then developed at length in the course of the ages, then became concentrated in the person of Christ, who assumed it in full. It is true that in a certain sense the course of profane history continues its expansive movement around him in the whole human race, headed toward the day when it will be assimilated in full; but to what practical goal, and with what result, so long as it is marked with the ambiguity which permanently characterizes the human temporal condition? From this point of view, sacred history's historical unfolding, which passes from Adam to Christ through a series of successive elections, appears as a progressive reduction of the horizon [83]: from all of humanity to Israel alone, from the whole Israelite people to its remnant, and finally to Christ alone, who in fact constitutes that remnant. But this narrowing of perspective was rightly destined to dissipate the ambiguity of time: thanks to it, a new human temporality could arise in Christ, a temporality freed from time's defects and in the end transfigured. This time too is now on the march toward the last day, progressively extending itself to the whole race of Adam and integrating all its redeemed values. That is the meaning of the time of the Church, which we will examine further on.

## III. PREPARATORY INSTRUCTION FOR CHRIST'S COMING

Now we come to the heart of the psychological and spiritual problem which faces man throughout his history. St. Paul introduces us to it by his reflection

---

[82] The *eschaton* is there because in Jesus the eternal burst into the temporal: the paradox of the incarnation which is a stumbling block for the theology of Bultmann (J. Mouroux, *op. cit.*, p. 134). Consequently, his evaluation of Christ's temporality and its eschatological significance differs radically from our own.

[83] O. Cullmann, *Christ et le temps*, pp. 81-82; cf. J. Frisque, *Oscar Cullmann: Une théologie de l'histoire du salut*, pp. 88-103.

on the meaning of the Old Testament considered as the time of the law: "Before faith came, we were allowed no freedom by the Law; we were being looked after till faith was revealed. The Law was to be our guardian until the Christ came and we could be justified by faith" (Ga 3:23-24). In what does this pedagogy, [84] which is a second meaning of sacred history, consist?

## I. THE SITUATION OF SINFUL MAN

When St. Paul employs the image of guardian or tutor, he does not give it all the positive meaning which immediately comes to mind, and which, as we shall see, can be given it from another point of view. The Law-guardian holds man beneath a rod in order to enable him one day to be saved by Christ, and rightly so, for man had need of the rod. Let us return to his existential situation as we described it above. In whatever way it might be viewed—the relation of man with the world, with other men, with himself—that situation has a dramatic character which flows from its basic component, the position of sinful humanity before God. In the spontaneous intuitions of the human conscience, this basic problem of existence is more experienced than reflected upon, more felt than defined. How then did its real nature become clear? Here we come to the second function of the Old Testament, that of a concrete instruction, which disposed men to recognize their savior Jesus Christ. The instruments used in this instruction were, on the one hand, divine law, and on the other, man's historical experience. [85]

### *1. Law and the Revelation of Sin*

The Law is the rule of life given to man by the word of God. Before the Old Testament and outside of it, it cannot be said that men were completely ignorant of it. The creative word of God wrote it in their being, [86] and it was manifested to them through conscience, which, despite its hesitations and obscurities, "can be said to 'be' the Law" (Rm 2:14). It is in the Old Testament, though, that the existence and content of that divine Law were clearly revealed [87]: the Law is there the object of a revealed teaching which, while including the acquisitions of conscience, makes them clearer and goes beyond them. To the fundamental moral and religious precepts which constitute

[84] G. Bertram, "παιδεύω," *TWNT* 5, pp. 618 ff.; L. Cerfaux, *Christ in the Theology of St. Paul* (New York: Herder, 1959), pp. 222-229.

[85] *Sens chrétien de l'A.T.*, pp. 196-209, 275-277.

[86] Cf. E. Hamel, *Loi naturelle et loi du Christ* (Bruges-Paris: Desclée de Brouwer, 1964).

[87] *Sens chrétien de l'A.T.*, pp. 172-179.

the "natural law," it adds two important elements which are bound up with the particular terms of the Sinaitic alliance: thanks to its highly structured legislation, it endeavors to transfer the requirements of the moral commandments to Israel's civil institutions, and the requirements of the religious commandments to its cultic institutions. In these two points, therefore, the divine Law takes the form of a positive law, adapted to the closed society which then constituted the people of God. This manifestation of the divine will to Israel already possessed an instructive value in itself, and the Deuteronomist delights in emphasizing it (Dt 4:5-8; cf. Ps 119 passim). But the essence of the divine pedagogy is to be found elsewhere.

While the Law contains an ideal of justice and sanctity, the men to whom it was given remained basically sinners. Its precepts, therefore, could be holy, just, and good in themselves (Rm 7:12), and could truly have proceeded from the Spirit of God (cf. Rm 7:14); they still could not change the state of those to whom they were given. Their first effect was to make men realize their true situation before God. In this we are repeating the reflections of St. Paul on the meaning of the Law in the plan of salvation. [88] The Law was given "to specify crimes" (Ga 3:19), that is, "to multiply the opportunities of falling" (Rm 5:20); "it tells us what is sinful" (Rm 3:20), but was powerless to overcome it. When it makes man aware of evil and cupidity, it discloses that that cupidity actually has possesssion of him (Rm 7:7); he realizes that sin dwells in him (Rm 7:17.20) as a tyrannical power which holds him enslaved (Rm 7:14), since sin seizes the occasion of the precept to seduce him and lead him to death (Rm 7:11). In a word, man sees himself powerless before this sin, which rules him and makes him act in spite of himself (Rm 7:17-20). Thus the Law reveals his existential condition as a real spiritual alienation, which makes him the slave of sin (Rm 6:17).

## 2. Revelation of the Judgment of God

This first revelation in the existential order entails a second, for there is an absolute contradiction between sin and the holiness of God. By the very action of sin, which dominates him, and the voluntary assent he gives it, man finds himself in a state of hostility in relation to God. That is why, by revealing the human "mystery of iniquity" (cf. 2 Th 2:7), the Law at the same time reveals that terrible reality which is the Judgment of God. [89]

---

[88] L. Cerfaux, The Christian in the Theology of St. Paul (London: Chapman, 1967), pp. 432-441. C. Larcher, L'actualité chrétienne de l'Ancien Testament (Paris: Cerf, 1962), pp. 255-264.

[89] Sens chrétien de l'A.T., pp. 270 ff., 307 ff.

By engendering sin, it brought down anger [90] (Rm 4:15); it gave sinners over to the curse (Ga 3:10), so that in itself it is a letter which brings death (2 Co 3: 6). That explains all the tragic aspects of the condition which is the lot of the whole human race (Rm 1:18). Since their forefather (cf. Gn 3:14-19), they are as a group under the sentence of divine judgment; in all its depressing aspects their historical experience is the concrete manifestation of that judgment, for they are by nature "under God's anger" [91] (Ep 2:3). The human conscience already instinctively felt this, but in a vague and groping way. The Old Testament clearly revealed it at the moment when, in the treaty of alliance, it linked earthly evils to the inobservance of the Law (Ex 23:20-33; Dt 28; cf. 27:11-26). By means of the Law, therefore, man's existential situation was revealed as a situation of judgment, not only for Israel, which was directly concerned in the Sinaitic economy, but for the whole human race descendent from Adam: death, the supreme punishment for sin, reigned here below from Adam to Moses (Rm 5:14); even before Abraham Genesis presents the type of judgment in the typical catastrophe of the flood (Gn 6—9); finally, the sacred books identify numerous divine judgments in the history of all the peoples around Israel, who through this means pay the debt of their sins.

Thus the economy of the Law, and even to some extent the primitive economy in which conscience served as the Law, confronted man with a problem he could not solve; they put his existence under the sentence of a judgment he could not escape, and under a curse he was radically incapable of lifting. By that very fact they revealed to him his need of salvation by grace; they showed him the hollow in his existence to be filled by Christ. Once again, this is a revelation of the existentialist order, which R. Bultmann cannot be reproached for having strongly emphasized: reduced to the elements described here, the Old Testament is actually the history of a failure, that of the Sinaitic economy, and by that very failure it renders testimony to Christ by inviting men to turn to the grace that will save them. [92] Reservations must certainly be made in regard to the notion of faith and of salvation

---

[90] J. Fichtner—G. Stählin, "'Οργή," *TWNT* 5, pp. 392-410 (O.T.), 419-448 (N.T.).

[91] On the interpretation of this expression in theological tradition, cf. J. Mehlmann, *Natura filii irae* (Rome: Pont. Bibl. Inst., 1957).

[92] Cf. A. Malet, *Mythos et Logos*, pp. 246 f. The essential article is "The Significance of the Old Testament for the Christian Faith" in B. W. Anderson (ed.), *The Old Testament and Christian Faith* (London: SCM Press, 1964), pp. 8-35 (followed by a series of studies which discuss this position, and to which might be added H. Schulte, "Rudolf Bultmanns Stellung zum Alten Testament und ihre Bedeutung für den Religionsunterricht" in E. Dinkler (ed.), *Zeit und Geschichte. Dankesgabe an R. Bultmann* [Tübingen: Mohr, 1964], pp. 719-727).

which underlies Bultmann's theology, [93] but the theme it here develops is basically a classic one. Commenting on Ga 3:22, St. Thomas wrote [94]: "In a general way, the Law served God's promises in two ways. First, it manifested sins: 'All the Law does is to tell us what is sinful' (Rm 3:20). Secondly, it manifested human weakness, since man can avoid sin only through a grace which the Law did not give. [95] And just as the awareness of sickness and the impotence of the sick person constrain him to call the doctor, so awareness of sin and of his own impotence led man to search for Christ." That was basically the object of the divine pedagogy. [96]

## II. CHRIST, THE END OF THE LAW (Rm 10:4)

### 1. Christ Terminates the Pedagogy of the Law

Once Christ had come, the work of the guardian or tutor came to an end (Ga 3:25). How is this to be understood? First of all, in the sense that with Christ was terminated not only the reign of sin over the world, but also the economy of the Law which was bound to it. [97] The mystery of sin and of judgment, which the Old Testament had begun to disclose, was fully revealed in the drama which unfolded around Christ. The fourth gospel is here the best guide to theological reflection. The Jewish leaders, by their incredulity and their willful blindness (Jn 12:37-41; cf. 9:41), represent the sinful world [98] which cannot receive Christ because it is bound to its darkness (Jn 3:19 ff.), which cannot hear his word because its father is the devil (Jn 8:43 ff.). The death of Christ is this world's supreme crime against God, the height of sin in which it will perish (Jn 8:21-24; 15:22; 16:9), the final manifestation of the power of Satan (Jn 13:2; 14:30). But at the moment when the sin of the world is culminated by the death of Christ on the cross, the judgment of the world is inserted in the fiber of time: "Now sentence is being passed on this world; now the prince of this world is to be overthrown" (Jn 12:31; cf. 15:11). This judgment does not signify only the victory

---

[93] A. Malet, op. cit., pp. 205 ff.: a totally negative concept of grace and salvation, correlative to the rejection of the theology of the incarnation which we pointed out above (p. 251, note 56).

[94] Super epistulam ad Galatas, lect. 2 (ed. Cai, Turin: Marietti, 1953, No. 174, p. 604).

[95] Cf. Super epistulam ad Romanos, lect. 2 (ibid., Nos. 297-298, p. 52).

[96] Other traditional texts are cited in Sens chrétien de l'A.T., pp. 205-206 (reference is also made to the patristic collections of D. Petau, De lege et gratia, and L. Thomassin, De adventu Christi).

[97] L. Cerfaux, The Christian in the Theology of St. Paul, pp. 441 ff.

[98] E. K. Lee, The Religious Thought of St. John (London: SPCK, 1951), pp. 121 ff.

of Christ over Satan, but also the condemnation of everything Satan brought with him: in Johannine terms, the evil world and the Jewish establishment which became its instrument; in Pauline terms, the old man descended from Adam, a prisoner of his flesh, dominated by sin and death. In a word, when Christ died, taking on himself the curse of the Law (Ga 3:13), sinful humanity's sinful condition came to an end by virtue of the judgment of God. Consequently, all the divine judgments disclosed by Scripture over the course of the preceding ages, and all those to be accomplished afterward, until the figure of this condemned world passes away, receive their meaning from the moment of Christ's death. As for the economy of the Law, [99] since its role had ceased (Ep 2:14), it also died with this world with which it was correlative.

For Christ died only "to pass from this world to the Father" (Jn 13:1), as his resurrection clearly revealed to his disciples. By that act he became the principle of a new humanity (Ep 2:15-17; 2 Co 5:17). Eschatological existence, which he had inaugurated but kept hidden under the condition of a slave until his death on the cross (Ph 2:7 ff.), was now withdrawn from that temporary servitude. [100] And he furthermore communicated it to those who believe in him: they rose with him to undertake a new life (Rm 6:4-11) which has its source in the Holy Spirit. [101] This spirit, promised by Christ (Jn 14:16.26; 16:13 ff.), was then given to men (Ac 2:38), and he planted the love of God in their hearts [102] (Rm 5:5). Thus was dissolved the contradiction in which their sinful existence shuddered. Held to the observation of the Law, but incapable of accomplishing it, they had been in a way forced to despair. But the spirit freed them from the law of sin and of death (Rm 8:2), so that now the justice of the Law could be accomplished in them (8:4). Since the Old Testament, this absolutely new eschatological existence had been the object of a promise (cf. Jr 31:33 ff.; Ezk 36:25-28). The promise was now kept, and there is no longer any condemnation for those who are in Christ Jesus (Rm 8:1): they are saved from the judgment by their faith in him (Jn 3:18); they escape the curse and receive the blessing promised to Abraham (Ga 3:9.14). They are no longer subject to the peda-

---

[99] L. Cerfaux, *Christ in the Theology of St. Paul*, pp. 147-151; C. Larcher, *Actualité chrétienne de l'Ancien Testament*, pp. 264-277.

[100] J. Mouroux, *The Mystery of Time*, pp. 148-156.

[101] L. Cerfaux, *The Christian in the Theology of St. Paul*, pp. 443 ff., analyzes the themes connected with the gift of the Spirit in Christian life.

[102] R. Bultmann disputes this interpretation of Rm 5:5; he understands "the love of God" as "the love by which he pardons us," which brings us back to the negative concept of grace and salvation we mentioned above (cf. A. Malet, *op. cit.*, p. 231); it is through the Spirit that this act of the love of God, signified in Christ, becomes efficacious for us.

gogy of the Law (Ga 5:18; cf. 3:25), because if they allow themselves to be led by the Spirit and bear his fruits, there is no longer any Law against them (Ga 5:22).

## 2. Christ Brings the Law to its Accomplishment

Does that mean that the Law, as an expression of the will of God for men, has lost its meaning? The reply requires some distinctions. For those who live according to the Spirit, there remains only one Law, that of love. [103] Charity, which is the fulness of the Law (Rm 13:10), is the commandment which encompasses in itself the whole Law and the prophets (Mt 22:40). And that is the commandment of Christ (Jn 13:34; 15:12.17; I Jn 2:8). But this commandment is no longer outside man once he has entered into eschatological existence. The Spirit has planted it in his heart (Rm 5:5; cf. Jr 31:31); he then lives "under the Law of Christ" [104] (I Co 9:21; cf. Ga 6:2). Thus Christ, at the very moment that he put an end to the reign of the Law in its provisional and void aspects, did not properly speaking abolish the Law, but completed it [105] (Mt 5:17); he revealed all of its positive content, transformed it and incorporated it into the gospel. But then it was no longer a question of a reality of the old alliance. The Law so understood rightly belongs to the new: it is the rule of action for life in Christ; it is the fruit of the Holy Spirit in the reborn man. [106] In the measure, therefore, that the Old Testament, and even the age of the primitive economy, knew it as such, in them the Law signified the anticipated presence of the economy of grace. [107] At the heart of the divine pedagogy which revealed to man his sinful condition and his state of judgment, the Holy Spirit was at work inclining docile hearts toward the Law of love.

---

[103] Bultmann's position on this point is governed by a concept of the Law as a norm of "objective morality" (A. Malet, *op. cit.*, pp. 223 ff.) which is that of Greece and not of the Old Testament, which is explicitly cited by Christ (Mt 22:34-40 par.). The antinomies: natural man—new man, Law—grace, the Greek concept of man—the existentialist concept, are in his position perfectly interchangeable, and stand in opposition just as good and evil. Such a view of things is not acceptable, for it deforms the real relation of the two Testaments. On love as Jesus' preeminent commandment, cf. R. Schnackenburg, *The Moral Teaching of the New Testament* (New York: Herder, 1965), pp. 90 ff., 316-328.

[104] C. H. Dodd, "Ἔννομος χριστοῦ : I Cor 9,19-22," *Studia paulina in honorem J. De Zwaan* (Haarlem: Bohn, 1953), pp. 96-110.

[105] On this accomplishment of the Law, see the qualified solution of C. Larcher, *op. cit.*, pp. 231-255, 272-284.

[106] L. Cerfaux, "Condition chrétienne et liberté selon saint Paul," *Recueil L. Cerfaux* 3, pp. 293 ff.; C. H. Dodd, *Gospel and Law* (Cambridge: Univ. Press, 1951), pp. 64-83.

[107] *Sens chrétien de l'A.T.*, p. 204, note 2. On the presence of the grace of Christ in the Old Testament, cf. *ibid.*, pp. 151-164.

## IV. PREFIGURATION OF CHRIST

If the salvation brought by Christ was the object of man's expectation, the reason was that it had been promised by God as the solution for the problem of existence which we have examined above. In the Old Testament, the history of Israel, and behind it all of human history, appears then as united by its tendency to a final event (an *eschaton*) which determines the meaning of all its components because it constitutes its ultimate end. [108] Here we do not intend to examine directly the content of the divine promises which point in advance to that *eschaton*. [109] Rather our task is to see how the realities involved in the historical experience before Christ have a meaning in relation to him, how they anticipate his appearance, not certainly fully and directly, but in a symbolic way, in figures.

### I. THE NOTION OF FIGURE IN THE NEW TESTAMENT

In the New Testament the notion of figure is used in two different contexts. St. Paul [110] defines it in relation to its function in the unfolding of sacred history. In relation to the mystery of Christ, who is the goal of that history, the persons and events which precede his coming have a prophetic meaning. Adam was the figure (τύπος) of Christ who was to come (Rm 5:4), considered in his role as head (cf. 1 Co 15:45-49). The events of the exodus and the desert were "warnings (τύποι) for us"; they happened "as a warning (τυπικῶς)" (1 Co 10:6.10). A figure *(typos)* is therefore a symbol which announces some eschatological reality, written in the texture of sacred history. What corresponds to it in the New Testament, especially at the level of the Christian experience which brings man a participation in salvation, can be termed *antitypos*; thus baptism according to 1 P 3:21.

Upon this eschatological symbolism, which is a specific element of biblical revelation, the letter to the Hebrews [111] superimposes a typology which is similar to the religious symbolism common to all of oriental and classical antiquity. This symbolism regarded the things of this world, caught up in the flow of time, as imperfect reflections of an ideal on high,

---

[108] *Ibid.*, pp. 291 f.

[109] *Ibid.*, pp. 329 ff.

[110] S. Amsler, *L'Ancien Testament dans l'Église* (Neuchâtel-Paris: Delachaux, 1960), pp. 55-60; "La typologie de l'Ancien Testament chez saint Paul," *RTP* 2 s. 37 (1949), 113-128 (a summary of the same author's theology thesis).

[111] *Sens chrétien de l'A.T.*, pp. 215 f., 296; C. K. Barrett, "The Eschatology of the Epistle to the Hebrews," *The Background of the New Testament and its Eschatology* (Cambridge: Univ. Press, 1956), pp. 363-393.

outside and above time. This divine unchangeable world, through the mythical history it had known in primordial times, had fixed forever the characteristics of all things; the worship and religious institutions of society did no more than imitate this supreme archetype. [112] Biblical revelation is not above using symbols of this type to speak of God and divine things. But except for the creative act, which is presented differently, [113] it radically suppresses all divine primordial history and substitutes for it its own conception of sacred history directed toward a final act of God, the *eschaton*. [114] And this is the context in which the Letter to the Hebrews' notion of figure must be placed. [115] The mystery of Christ who came at the end of time, inaugurated on earth and consummated in heaven, is the divine model to which all sacred history is related. It is the heavenly reality (τὰ ἐπουράνια : 6:4; 8:5; 9:23; 11:16; 12:22), the real reality (τὰ ἀληθινά : 8:2; 9:24), and therefore the archetype (τύπος :8:5), or better the *teleo*-type, [116] for in the Old Testament that model was still a future reality (ὁ μέλλων : 6:5; 9:11; 10:1; 13:14), which was to arrive at the end of preparatory times. In relation to it, therefore, the history and institutions of the Old Testament constituted a symbol (παραβολή : 9:9; 11:19), a shadow (σκία : 8:5; 10:1), a copy (ὑπόδειγμα : 8:5; 9:23), a reproduction (ἀντίτυπος : 9:24). Conversely, in the Church we encounter a faithful image of it which contains its reality (εἰκών : 10:1). In this approach, then, typology is radically transformed by an eschatological symbolism identical to that of St. Paul.

The insertion of the mystery of Christ into human history and the presence of figurative things in the history that prepared for his coming are evidently essential to the biblical notion of figure, which as such is unique in ancient religions. [117] The Old Testament laid the foundations for it, first by its finalist conception of history, and then by its use of past history to represent the object of eschatological promises. [118] Is this, as R. Bultmann has proposed, [119] only a particular application of the law of recurrence which determines the eternal return of things, the return in this case occurring

[112] *Sens chrétien de l'A.T.*, pp. 210-211, 287-290.

[113] P. van Imschoot, *Theology of the Old Testament* I, pp. 89-98; see pp. 90-92 on the traces of a mythical representation of creation as a primordial combat between God and the forces of chaos.

[114] *Sens chrétien de l'A.T.*, pp. 291-294.

[115] For a comparison of this doctrine with Philo's exemplarism, see C. Spicq, *L'épître aux Hébreux* I, pp. 72-75, 346 f.

[116] *Sens chrétien de l'A.T.*, p. 292, note 2.

[117] *Ibid.*, pp. 214 f.

[118] *Ibid.*, pp. 363 ff.

[119] R. Bultmann, "Ursprung und Sinn der Typologie als hermeneutischer Methode," *TLZ* 75 (1950), 205-212 (= *Glauben und Verstehen* I, pp. 315 ff.).

just once at the end of a unique cycle? [120]   Such a view unjustly minimizes the originality of biblical typology; it would make it just one "mythical" expression of faith among many.   In fact, this originality does not arise only from the single cycle, which Bultmann rightly noted, but from the connection which the Old Testament established between the historical experience of Israel and the development of its faith.   Here we arrive at the positive aspect of the divine pedagogy, [121] which not only disposed men's hearts toward Christ their Savior, but also gave them a certain anticipatory knowledge of his mystery. [122]   We shall make this clear in regard to the three areas in which the principle of figures is applied: creation and the fall, the history of Israel, and worship before Christ.

### II. CHRIST AND THE MYSTERY OF OUR ORIGIN

#### *1. The Two Adams*

The biblical presentation of our origin reveals first of all the meaning of the human condition in its actual state and in its primordial cause.   The image of paradise represents concretely the end for which man was, and remains, created and was placed in the world; his expulsion from paradise opposes to that end the situation he finds himself in because of sin.   Adam thus incorporates all of humanity: at the same time that he represents the historical origin of the human race in his quality of eponym, he is the typical man that all of us are.   He incarnates the two opposing aspects of our temporality.   For that reason his relation to Christ is twofold. [123]   By his fall and the condition that followed it, he determined the wounded temporal condition Christ was to assume, and he manifested negatively what his redemptive action was to imply.   This is the point St. Paul develops in Rm 5:12-19: the prefiguration of Christ is in this case to be understood antithetically. But the blissful condition in which Adam was presented before his fall sketches positively the characteristics of the eschatological existence into which Christ was to enter and conduct us by his resurrection.   God's

---

[120] This reduction of eschatology to the cyclic recurrence of the great years was previously proposed by R. Berthelot, "L'astrobiologie et la pensée de l'Asie," *Revue de métaphysique et de morale* (1935), 194 ff.   See the remarks of H. de Lubac, *Catholicisme*, pp. 110 ff.

[121] H. de Lubac, *op. cit.*, pp. 190-198, employs for this viewpoint (which was that of Clement of Alexandria) the idea of pedagogy, the diverse context of which in the only text in which St. Paul mentions it explicitly we have pointed out. Cf. *Sens chrétien de l'A.T.*, pp. 278-286 (on the theological education of Israel).

[122] *Sens chrétien de l'A.T.*, pp. 246 f., 322-326.

[123] L. Cerfaux, *Christ in the Theology of St. Paul*, pp. 230-246; O. Cullmann, *The Christology of the New Testament* (London: SCM Press, 1959), pp. 137-151.

plan from creation to eternal life retains its unity. And the familiarity with God, the joy of paradise, the unity in love, the mastery over the world, which the story of the beginning attributes to the first couple from which the human race sprung, are in fact realized in Christ the Head in his glory (Heb 2:6 ff.; 1 Co 15:25 and Ep 1:22 citing Ps 8), who will enable his members to participate in them after their trial on earth (Rv 2:7; 21:4; 22:3.14).

All of this leads to the conclusion that, in creating man, God had Christ in mind. Since as Word and Wisdom he is the image of the invisible God, everything was created in him, by him, and for him (Col 1:15-16). He was therefore the model according to which "God created man in the image of himself" (Gn 1:26 f.). By the incarnation the model himself became man as a son of Adam; he manifested in the midst of time the archetype which existed before its beginning (cf. Heb 1:2-3). Thus the divinity of the Word assures the absolute primacy of Christ, in the order of creation as well as in that of redemption; Adam, because he bore the image of God, sketched concretely the characteristics of Christ to come. This reflection on the relation of Adam to Christ makes explicit a thought which was already current in the Old Testament. [124] Even before the development of prophetic eschatology, the description of the primitive paradise which opens the Yahwistic sacred history (Gn 2) defined in some manner the basic aim of the plan of creation; it thus hovers in the background of those texts of the Pentateuch which describe the divine promises and the hope of Israel in their most ancient form (for example, Gn 27:27-29; 49:25-26; Ex 23:25-26; Lv 26:3-12; Dt 6:3, etc.). The prophets later systematically introduced it into their description of the *eschaton* which would restore man to paradise regained (Ho 2:20.23 ff.; Is 7:15; 11:6-9; 51:3; 65:17-25; 25:7; Ezk 37:35; 47:8-12; Jl 4:18; Zc 14:6-9, etc.).

## 2. Originality of the Biblical Concept

It might be asked whether this transferal of original perfection to the end of time does not follow the more general principle, of which oriental mythologies furnish a number of examples: *Urzeit wird Endzeit*. [125] Could this be merely the particular form which the law of cyclic return took in Israel, just as in Hesiod's description of the expectation of the Great Year, which figures in the Pythagorean primitive degradation of time? As a matter of

---

[124] *Sens chrétien de l'A.T.*, pp. 386 ff. For an analysis of the literary themes of paradise, see H. Gressmann, *Der Messias* (Göttingen: Vandenhoeck & Ruprecht, 1929), pp. 149-181; S. Mowinckel, *He That Cometh* (Oxford: Blackwell, 1956), pp. 81, 112, 146, 182, etc.

[125] Above, p. 270, note 119.

fact, the imagery employed is practically the same in both cases. [126] But that is not surprising, since the paradise myth (taking the word myth in a technical sense which is not depreciatory, and does not include the idea of a divine primordial history) is no more than the reverse side of our existential experience, which is beset by evils of all sorts despite our deep-seated desire for happiness. [127] Ancient thought was confronted with this problem just as modern philosophers are. It is not in this point that biblical revelation's mode of expression differs from that of similar mythologies.

To discover the difference, the literary context in which this imagery is placed must be examined. Let us take two typical examples. In the Gilgamesh epic, [128] that imagery serves to present a pessimistic view of existence: the hero's quest for life is hopeless, for the tree of life escapes him; his voyage to paradise does not prevent him from dying. In Pythagorean speculation, on the other hand, the expectation of the return of the golden age is bound to a mechanism of cosmic cycles governed by astrological fatalism [129]; the coming of the Great Year thus takes on the character of necessity, and totally excludes the activity of human free will. This wavering of ancient thought between despair and the dream world lacks the two elements which determine the paradise imagery in the Bible: the fact of a history of salvation whose unfolding is controlled by God, and the fact of a divine promise made known to man in time, which gives a positive foundation for hope in paradise regained. The Old Testament therefore completely transformed the paradise myth. The meaning of the imagery in which it is presented, however, was only partially unveiled; it was not completely

---

[126] Thus in the vision of the terrestrial paradise with which the whole of the 28th canto of his Purgatory is concerned, Dante could write of the pagan poets: "Those men of yore who sang the golden time and all its happy state—maybe indeed They on Parnassus dreamed of this fair clime" (vv. 139-141, trans. D. L. Sayers, *Purgatory* [London: Penguin Classics, 1955], p. 293).

[127] On paradise symbolism, see G. van der Leeuw, "Urzeit und Endzeit," *Eranos Jahrbuch* 17 (1949), 11-51; E. Cothenet, "Paradis," *DBS* 6, cols. 1177-1220.

[128] On this important work of oriental antiquity, see the exhaustive bibliography by L. de Meyer in *Gilgameš et sa légende*, ed. P. Garelli (Paris: Klincksieck, 1960), pp. 1-30. There are numerous translations, among which might be noted: E. Ebeling in *AOT* (Berlin-Leipzig: de Gruyter, 1926); G. Contenau (Paris: Artisan du Livre, 1939); A. Heidel, *The Gilgamesh Epic and Old Testament Parallels* (Chicago: Univ. Press, 1949); S. N. Kramer—E. A. Speiser in *ANET* (Princeton: Princeton Univ. Press, 1955); A. Schott—W. von Soden (Stuttgart: Reclan, 1958); F. M. de Liagre Böhl, *Het Gilgamsj-Epos, National Heldendicht van Babylonie* (Amsterdam, 1958). Cf. F. M. de Liagre Böhl, "Das Problem ewigen Lebens im Zyklus und Epos des Gilgamesch" in *Opera minora* (Groningen: Wolters, 1953), pp. 234-262.

[129] On this question, see the texts of Cicero, *De natura deorum*, 2, 20; *De republica* 6, 22. 24; J. Carcopino, *Virgile et le mystère de la quatrième églogue* (Paris, 1930); P. Boyancé, *La religion de Virgile* (Paris: Univ. Press, 1963), pp. 124-132 (who on this point stresses Virgil's dependence upon Cicero, Varro, and Nigidius Figulus).

revealed until the hour when Christ, having assumed the human condition even unto death on the cross, passed from this world to his Father. The risen state he then entered changed the nature of his relation to the universe, and the transfigured universe constitutes the real paradise into which he would henceforth gather to himself those who die in faith in him (Lk 23:43). The typology of Adam, whose foundations we have examined, thus extends to the whole paradise imagery.

### III. CHRIST AND THE HISTORICAL EXPERIENCE OF ISRAEL

*1. Outline of the Problem*

We have just seen that the fact of the history of salvation and that of the divine promises which are points of attraction in its development constitute two essential and coordinate factors in biblical revelation. This brings up the question of the role of Israel's historical experience in biblical revelation, from the call of Abraham to the time of the apostles. It would be insufficient to see in it just the exterior framework in which that revelation was announced by certain divine messengers; it was a determining element in its very development. The influence it exerted on the evolution of ideas in Israel and on the formation of biblical language cannot escape anyone's notice; but opinions differ when it comes to estimating the importance of this fact. [130]

Without taking into account the interpretations proposed by liberal Protestantism, the history of religions school, and Catholic modernism, let us take an example from a more recent period. If, from the standpoint of Lutheran theology, the object of revelation were reduced to a proclamation of the message of grace, and the faith to an existential attitude of openness to that message, one could be tempted to attribute the progressive elaboration of beliefs and of the language which expresses them to a simple natural process. Since the unique absolute element of the experience of faith becomes awareness of the message of grace, its notional expression would then be a pure creation of the human mind, completely relative to the circumstances in which it was formulated. The historical reminiscences contained in it would show how, in its formulation in a language, faith transformed history into myth. Considered in itself, how can human history actually reveal the mystery of God? Properly speaking, God does not intervene in it at all, he does not manifest himself through it; there as elsewhere, he remains beyond man's comprehension. This will be recognized

---

[130] We here leave aside the evaluations of rationalist historians, for whom the evolution of religious ideas cannot have a different character in Israel and the rest of the world.

as the position of R. Bultmann, [131] who, while he is in reaction against the theology of history of Protestant liberalism, nonetheless depends upon it for whatever concerns the interpretation of the notional expressions the experience of faith assumes. This view is not shared by all present-day Protestant theologians. A good number of them, on the contrary, insist on the properly revelatory character of the history of salvation whose presence they recognize in the Bible. This is particularly the case with O. Cullmann, in whose view this history of salvation with Christ as its center rightly constitutes the essential object of biblical revelation. [132] As for Catholic theology, without ignoring the importance of linguistic criticism to which Bultmann has justly called attention, [133] it rejects his reduction of revelation and of faith to their existentialist dimensions alone.

The word of God does not have as its sole object to give man an assurance in regard to his salvation. The faith which accepts it implies, both in the Old Testament and in the New, a real knowledge [134] of the mystery of salvation, understood as an experienced and conscious relation with God into which man is thus introduced. In the New Testament this knowledge is based on the perfect symbol, Jesus Christ. Before that it remained in an imperfect state, but its positive aspects should not be underestimated: as the

---

[131] A. Malet, *Mythos et Logos,* pp. 87 f. The idea of a direct manifestation of God in history is disputed by other Protestant theologians too; cf. G. Widmer, "Événement chrétien et théologie de l'histoire," *RTP* 3 s. 13 (1963), 138-151, who prefers to speak of an *ethic* or of a *spirituality* rather than a *theology* of history.

[132] See on this point the reservations formulated from the viewpoint of a Catholic theologian by J. Frisque, *op. cit.,* pp. 230-259, and especially by L. Malevez, "Les dimensions de l'histoire," *NRT* 86 (1964), 561-578, who points out the validity of some of Bultmann's criticisms of O. Cullmann.

[133] Below, pp. 348-351.

[134] For Bultmann any pretense of theology to speak of God reduces him to the state of an object, which amounts to ignoring his transcendence. Even the traditional *via negationis* falls short in its project: "From nature and history man has only a negative concept of God. His knowledge is a non-knowing" (A. Malet, *op. cit.,* p. 88). "We cannot say of God how he is in himself, but only what he does for us" (cited *ibid.,* p. 106). For the object of the word of God as a message addressed to man is exclusively the grace of pardon and of salvation. The relation of Christian faith to Jesus Christ has to do with that alone: "There is not alongside of God another divine person, as though the Jewish faith in the one God were made complete by faith in a second divine person; nor does the Christian faith give assent to metaphysical speculations about the deity of Christ and his natures. Rather, faith in Christ is nothing else but faith in God's deed in Christ." ("The Significance of the Old Testament for the Christian Faith" in B. W. Anderson, *The Old Testament and Christian Faith* [London: SCM Press, 1964], pp. 28 f.). This radical agnosticism can be explained as a reaction against Greek rationalism, whose presence Bultmann finds in every orthodox theology (A. Malet, *op. cit.,* pp. 21-27) and to which he opposes the existentialism of biblical thought which considers man's historical situation. This is not the place to discuss this problem in depth; it is sufficient to point out the exact point where Bultmann and Catholicism differ (cf. F. Refoulé, "La vague bultmannienne," *RSPT* 48 [1964], 263-270).

letter to the Hebrews says, the men of the Old Testament "died in faith, before receiving any of the things that had been promised, but they saw them in the far distance and welcomed them" (Heb 11:13). How then did God arouse this knowledge in their hearts? How did he progressively instruct them? Through two related means: his word, and the concrete signs whose meaning that word gradually unveiled. At this point, we find ourselves once again before the role of Israel's historical experience in revelation. [135]

By an absolutely special divine dispensation, Israel was at once a nation of this world, equal to all others, and the people of God, segregated for the work of salvation. As a consequence, its historical experience is both similar to all others and situated in another order. Its temporal destiny does not escape any of the laws which govern the unfolding of human affairs; it is nevertheless through it that God's plan moved toward its goal. Its constituent elements, therefore, can be strangely similar to those found in many other histories; they nevertheless have a meaning which transcends the order of profane affairs. It was a unique fact in human history, and the reason is easy to understand: only the train of events in which, since the Old Testament, the history of salvation was realized, and in which man's call to faith was written, could reveal the mystery of salvation toward which that faith was directed. All during its unfolding, it bore the mark of the Event par excellence which constituted its ultimate goal, the fact of Christ, "put to death for our sins and raised to life to justify us" (Rm 4:25). In the midst of earthly realities, Israel's history sketched concretely the characteristics of that goal, and this figurative anticipation allowed those who believed to have an obscure anticipatory knowledge of it and to adhere to it by faith. [136] To grasp the revelatory function of history in all its realism, therefore, it is important to understand properly the relation between historical experience and the experience of faith in the very heart of the Old Testament. This is the basis on which biblical prefiguration can be correctly understood.

### 2. An Examination of the Scriptural Evidence

a) The Old Testament.—From the earliest stage of revelation, the message of the prophets taught Israel to recognize in its history the perceptible sign of the acts of God here below. The persons who played a role of national importance in it, the events that took place in it, the institutions which were

---

[135] Sens chrétien de l'A.T., pp. 251-286. Likewise S. Amsler, L'Ancien Testament dans l'Église, pp. 161-163.

[136] Sens chrétien de l'A.T., pp. 322-326.

developed, were not the occasional products of a series of fortunate chance happenings; God providentially arranged them in order to accomplish his plan, and at the same time gradually unveil his secret intentions. It was therefore by recognizing their meaning that Israel's faith clearly realized it own object. [137] At this first stage of revelation, however, their interpretation was still rudimentary: if God saved his people in order to lead them into Canaan, if he sent them leaders such as Moses, Joshua and David, if he provided them with institutions destined to shape their national life, was this not due to the fact that his reign and the salvation of men were to be realized through the medium of the material success of Israel? This was an ambiguous notion, and the following age was to strip away its delusions. Israel soon learned through its own experience the nature of the human evil over which the plan of salvation must triumph.

It learned first of all by experiencing sin. Despite all the gifts it had received, Israel was unfaithful to God; the sinful condition of man was thus revealed, as the preaching of the prophets never tired of repeating. It was necessary too that God's judgment be equally manifested in Israel's history; the prophets therefore announced the national catastrophe that would mark its coming. Salvation would not arrive until after the accomplishment of that judgment, not as the harmonious blossoming of an auspiciously begun history, but as an unmerited grace conferred by God on a sinful people. [138] This is precisely the object of the prophetic promises: God's design cannot be hindered by the perverse will of men; but its realization was postponed to an indetermined future—it would constitute the eschatological conclusion of history. To the revelation of human sin and divine judgment, the essential object of the divine pedagogy, [139] was thus added a more complete and profound revelation of the mystery of salvation itself. In this new perspective, the significance of past historical experience became presently important, for it was that experience which provided a means of representing concretely the *eschaton*. What God had once done imperfectly and partially in the history of his people he would fully accomplish at the end of time. Final salvation thus took on the characteristics of an idealized past, as if Israel's history were in some way to begin all over again on a new level: a new exodus, new alliance, new law, new promised land,

---

[137] *Ibid.*, pp. 267-272. Naturally this awareness was reached only through the word of God.

[138] *Ibid.*, pp. 336-339; on the promise of grace, see pp. 356-358. It will be noted that here our evaluation agrees with that of R. Bultmann, *The Old Testament and Christian Faith*, pp. 22-29. The promise of grace does constitute the heart of prophetic eschatology, and its realization is at the core of the gospel message. But the disagreement begins when the notion of grace is defined and an attempt is made to evaluate its constituent elements.

[139] Above, pp. 263-266.

new Jerusalem, new king, etc. The essential element in those great revelatory experiences is then repeated in figurative language in these prophecies;
the inspired images of the history of Israel took their place alongside those of
paradise regained. [140]

   b) *The New Testament.*—The integration of history into the experience
of faith was therefore an accomplished fact well before the advent of Christ.
Nevertheless, the meaning of that history was not completely clarified,
because the key that would unlock the ambiguity of the divine promises
written in the train of events, or announced in prophetic oracles, was still
lacking. [141]   The coming of Christ, as the realization of the promised and
expected salvation, thus retained its unforeseeable and original character;
but when he appeared, he appeared as the accomplishment of all those
promises. Consequently, he explained himself in light of them at the same
time that he explained their true content. [142]   Nor is it surprising that the
New Testament, while underlining the absolute originality of Christ, systematically constructed its Christology and soteriology upon the eschatological
oracles of the prophets and the historical prefigurations which had served as
their basis.   The typological interpretation of the history of Israel, that is,
the understanding of its full revelatory value, thus constituted an essential
part of the apostolic message.   Only the manner in which salvation was
accomplished in Jesus Christ, in turn, made it possible to judge correctly
the content of the prefigurations and to relate them to one another.   The life
of Christ is the point in which the passage from the old world to the future
world was made, from the painful existence bound to the mystery of sin to
the eschatological existence freed from the grasp of death, from the pilgrim
temporality to the transfigured temporality.   Both of these successive states
through which the Son of God willed to pass are outlined, though in different
ways, in the historical experience of Israel.

   The first shows us Christ participating in all the degrading conditions
of our earthly life in order to announce to men the gospel of the kingdom
of God.   In this respect, the Word accomplished in person a truly prophetic
mission, which classical eschatology had to a certain point foreseen (cf. Is 42:
1-6; 49:1-6; 61:1-2 cited in Lk 4:18 ff.), and which crowns the series of
similar missions fulfilled by other divine messengers. [143]   When he presented

[140] *Sens chrétien de l'A.T.*, pp. 363-388.
[141] *Ibid.*, pp. 389-398.
[142] *Ibid.*, pp. 398-403; S. Amsler, *op. cit.*, pp. 121-134.
[143] "The Lord is a prophet, and the Lord is the Word of God, and no prophet
prophesies without the Word of God; the Word of God is with prophets, and the
Word of God is a prophet.   Past times merited prophets inspired and possessed
by the Word of God; we merited the Word of God as prophet" (St. Augustine,
*Tractatus in Johannem* 24, 7).

himself among men as a prophet, a legislator, a master of wisdom, [144] it could therefore be said that these traits had been long ago positively outlined by all the bearers of the word of God, Moses and his successors (cf. Ac 3:22). Furthermore, by assuming the lot of human temporality, Christ also entered upon the way that would necessarily [145] lead to his passion and cross. But neither was this perspective missing from classic eschatology and the past experience of the people of God. The mystery of the suffering of the just, already linked to that of redemption by the prophet of the servant of Yahweh [146] (Is 52:13—53:12), received its full meaning when the just man par excellence, having become one with his sinful brethren, died on the cross to expiate their transgressions. It became clear in that moment that the cross cast its shadow over the world every time that in the past a just man unjustly suffered the rigors of the human condition. Abel put to death (Heb 12:24), Isaac on the pyre (Heb 11:17-19), Moses rejected (Ac 7:37), the prophets persecuted (Lk 11:47-51; Ac 7:52), the psalmists pouring out their anguish (Ps 22; cf. Mt 27:42 ff.): these are so many piercing sketches of the passion of Christ, or better, anticipated participations in his cross. [147] The accomplishment of Christ's mission in the midst of human temporality was therefore preceded by a great number of clues, until then unintelligible, whose sense was then made clearly apparent. [148]

The case is different for Jesus' entry into his glory, the source and model of the eschatological existence to which men are now called. In this case, the mystery of salvation breaks through the limits of human temporality in which the history of Israel remained enclosed. [149] But there is a proportional relation between the aspects of that history which were long ago understood as experiences of salvation [150]—imperfect as those experiences

[144] H. Duesberg, *Jésus prophète et docteur de la Loi* (Maredsous, 1955); F. Gils, *Jésus prophète d'après les évangiles synoptiques* (Louvain: Publ. Univ., 1957); O. Cullmann, *Christology of the New Testament*, pp. 13-50.

[145] This necessity is understood in relation to the will of God and to the plan of salvation, as the use of the formula in the New Testament shows; cf. W. Grundmann, "Δεῖ," *TWNT* 2, pp. 21-25.

[146] *Sens chrétien de l'A.T.*, pp. 377, 483 f. On Jesus, the Servant of Yahweh, see O. Cullmann, *The Christology of the New Testament*, pp. 51-82.

[147] *Sens chrétien de l'A.T.*, pp. 313, 316, 462 ff.

[148] These indications are not to be found only in the prophecy of the suffering servant. According to Lk 24:27 they are to be sought in "all the prophets," and according to Lk 24:44 in "the Law of Moses, in the Prophets and in the Psalms." But it is true that in these two places the prophecy concerns the whole of the mystery of Christ, and not just the cross.

[149] Prophetic eschatology tended to surpass these limits when it presented the *eschaton* as a return to paradise. But the surpassing becomes complete only in the apocalypse of Daniel with the personage of the Son of Man; cf. *Sens chrétien de l'A.T.*, pp. 380 ff. On the use of this biblical symbol in the New Testament, cf. O. Cullmann, *op. cit.*, pp. 137-192.

[150] *Sens chrétien de l'A.T.*, pp. 310-315.

might have been—and the true salvation Christ inaugurated with his resurrection, and which he presently communicates to men under sacramental signs, and whose fulness is the object of Christian hope. In this sense, then, it is still proper to speak of a figurative history, since the experiences of Israel, without abandoning the temporal plane directly accessible to human knowledge, positively outlined the characteristics of the new condition into which Christ wills to conduct us. They were admittedly imperfect figures, faint shadows of that mysterious Reality into which the old world was transfigured; they were nonetheless symbols full of meaning, thanks to which biblical revelation can properly speak of things that no human eye has seen [151] (1 Co 2:9). The risen Christ is that glorious Messiah whose mark was already borne by the kings of Israel (Ac 2:30-36). The Church is that City on high (Ga 5:26; cf. Rv 21:2 ff.) whose future role was obscurely announced by the terrestrial Jerusalem (Heb 12:22). We are called to that true place of divine rest of which the promised land was an image, at once promising and disappointing (Heb 4:1-11); and through the sacraments of Christian initiation we experience a salvation which was prefigured in the first exodus (1 Co 10:1-11).

## 3. The Place of Typology in Revelation

The typological interpretation of the history of Israel is therefore something entirely different from a superficial, arbitrary comparison between the details of the two Testaments. It pertains to what is most essential in revelation. In the Old Testament, the historical experience of the people of God determined the form of its spiritual experience and of its knowledge of faith; that is why it was integrated into the religious symbolism which from that time on provided revelation its language. [152] In the New Testament, once there appeared in history the Sign par excellence who fully revealed the mystery of salvation and the mystery of God, Jesus Christ, knowledge of faith and spiritual experience paradoxically retained the same form. At the same time, the religious symbols which had their origin in the historical experience of Israel manifested their figurative content.

---

[151] Failure to recognize this point is the principal criticism made of Bultmann by A. Richardson, "Is the Old Testament the Propaedeutic to Christian Faith?" in *The Old Testament and Christian Faith*, pp. 45 f.: "If one suppose that God's action in history is mere mythology, the New Testament view of history will have been set aside in favour of a view of the nature of the historical which took its origin in the rationalism of the Enlightenment. And it will have to be admitted that typology must be discarded along with allegorical interpretation, since there are no knowable historical correspondances upon which it can be founded."

[152] Above, pp. 86-89.

This fact can be better understood when it is examined on the level of Christ himself. Having come at the end of a preparatory history, all of whose legacy he intended to assume, he allowed the ancient signs to mold his human personality as son of Abraham and son of David, his attitudes, his psychology, his language. [153] It is for this reason that in the concrete circumstances of his own historical experience, crowned by the cross and resurrection, he could bring to their accomplishment all the figurative signs of which he alone had a perfect understanding. For us who participate in the mystery of Christ by our faith and Christian life, their meaning now appears in its fulness. [154] Where the Jews read an obscure and enigmatic portent of an *eschaton*, which they expected without fully understanding it, we recognize the imperfect but definitively unveiled announcement of the salvation realized by Christ.

## IV. CHRIST AND ISRAEL'S WORSHIP

In our examination of the experience of the people of the Old Testament, we have until now said nothing of its religious rites. [155] As an expression of the relation between God and men, they have a special importance in the problem we are considering. The salvation accomplished in Jesus Christ has for its first object to seal definitively this relation by providing its norm. Israel's cult, therefore, is related to the mystery of Christ much more directly than its temporal history, whose importance we have pointed out above. Following the development of revelation, we will now consider how this mystery was intimated in advance.

### 1. The Old Testament Evidence

The cult of Israel in large measure borrowed its rites and its language from surrounding religions, not, however, without judicious selection. [156] It thus integrated into revelation a body of symbolic material which was developed in what we have called the primitive economy, or law of nature: sacred times linked to cosmic or seasonal cycles, offerings and sacrifices related to social and economic activities, rites of purification or expiation, sanctuaries and sacred objects of various types, a functional priesthood, etc. The

---

[153] Above, pp. 259 f.

[154] *Sens chrétien de l'A.T.*, pp. 392-403.

[155] *Ibid.*, pp. 227-242. In that chapter devoted to the Law of the Old Testament cultic institutions are treated together with civil institutions, while here we have related the latter to the historical experience of Israel.

[156] *Ibid.*, pp. 183-189 (with a brief bibliography).

existence of such borrowing takes nothing away from the originality of Israelite cult, which was situated in another ideological world. The nature of the religious relation which it expressed indelibly marked the particular historical experience which set Israel apart as a worshiping community, "a kingdom of priests, a consecrated nation" (Ex 19:6): the exodus, the Sinaitic covenant, the promise of the Holy Land. Consequently, the cultic symbols of older origin were reinterpreted in the context of sacred history, [157] which continued its course, and in which Israelite cult took its place. The seasonal feasts (Ex 23:14-17) became commemorations of the exodus (Ex 12:25 ff.), of the covenant at Sinai (the meaning of Pentecost, which is attested in ancient Jewish tradition), of the wandering in the desert (Lv 23:42 ff.); the offering of the first fruits recalled the gift of the promised land (Dt 26:1-11); circumcision became the sign of belonging to the people of the alliance (Gn 17:1-14), and the sabbath, the celebration of God the creator (Gn 2:1-3; Ex 31:12 ff.). If it is kept in mind that the events thus commemorated in worship gradually took on an eschatological meaning until they became in the prophetic oracles the signs of final salvation, it becomes clear that this figurative significance must also have colored the rites which in some manner celebrated or recalled them. Could the ray of hope which the memory of the exodus brought fail to attach itself to the paschal meal which commemorated it yearly? [158]

Moreover, from the moment when prophetic eschatology began to take shape, it tended to incorporate all the elements of Israelite cult in its description of salvation, or better, to represent the life of redeemed Israel and reconciled humanity in essentially cultic terms. How could it have been otherwise? Once God had put an end to the wars between peoples which constituted the most outstanding feature of their historical experience, would not the unique purpose of their existence be that for which God set Israel apart as a worshiping community, the performance of his service and, through this means, the consecration of all earthly activity? In Ezk 40-48 the *eschaton* takes on the aspect of a perpetual liturgy, of which Jerusalem, as the place of the divine presence here below, is the center (48:35). Other texts describe the procession of peoples who come to render homage to God in the new sanctuary (Is 2:1-4; 60); there they participate in the eschatological banquet, which is celebrated in the joy of paradise (Is 25:6-8). Deutero-Zechariah explicitly relates the same image to the context of the feast of

---

[157] *Ibid.*, pp. 293 f., 318 f.

[158] On the expectation of the Messiah and of the new exodus in the paschal night, see the exhaustive study of R. LeDéaut, *La nuit pascale: Essai sur la signification de la pâque juive à partir du Targum d'Exode XII* 42 (Rome: Pont. Bibl. Inst., 1963).

Tents, thus giving it its eschatological significance. [159]   This entrance of
the liturgy into the language of prophecy necessarily had its repercussions
on the spirit in which those feasts were celebrated: as imperfect as Jewish
cult still was, it was no longer only a commemoration of the past; it called
to mind and stressed the salvation toward which the history of Israel, and
that of all humanity, tended.   It constituted the sketch and the introduction
of the mystery of God with men, whose realization was hoped for at the end
of the preparatory age; thus the meaning of the symbols which eschatology
had borrowed from the historical experience of Israel became more precise.

### 2. New Testament Evidence

From the point of view of Christian theology, nothing could be clearer.
Since Christ is the sole mediator for all men of all times, it was in him and
through him that Israel praised its God, sought to be purified from its sins,
and to enter into communion with him.   The symbols of its cult were, of
course, in themselves deficient and inefficacious, incapable of producing
those effects (cf. Heb 9:9-10; 10:1-4).   But they nonetheless contained
a positive significance in relation to the only efficacious cultic act which,
when it was realized in time, was to seal forever the union of men with God. [160]
In fact, when Christ appeared here below, the essentially religious purpose
of his mission was unmistakable, not only because his own attitudes showed
that such were the intimate dispositions of his soul (cf. Heb 10:5 ff.), but
also because his preaching and all his acts were centered on just one question:
the relation of men to God.   It was in this specific domain that he exercised
his mediation.   If he brought men salvation in every respect, it was as the
fruit of their conversion to the kingdom of God into which he wanted above
all to incorporate them.   It is true that his personal relation with the Father
was beyond normal classifications, and as a result the religious level at
which Israelite cult was situated remained far below it.   But that relationship
was no less the religious attitude of a man before God, and of a man whose
thought, attitudes and deeds had been shaped by Jewish cult.   Just as the

---

[159] J. Daniélou, "Le symbolisme eschatologique de la fête des Tabernacles,"
*Irenikon* 35 (1958), 19-40.

[160] *Sens chrétien de l'A.T.*, pp. 163 f.   It is to men's faith in the future Christ
that St. Thomas relates the significance they gave their rites: "After the sin the
incarnation of Christ was explicitly believed, not only as regards the incarnation,
but also as regards the passion and resurrection through which the human race is
freed from sin and death; otherwise they would not have prefigured the passion through
certain sacrifices both before the Law and under the Law" (II\a II\ae, q. 2, art. 7,
*in corps.*).   The only qualification to be made concerns the explicit character of this
faith in the *majores* who assured the *minores* "a certain veiled knowledge."   Even the
prophets never had more than a veiled understanding of Christ (cf. *ibid.*, p. 149).

historical legacy of Israel, so too its cultic legacy was fully assumed by Christ when he sealed with his blood the covenant which saves all of humanity. It was in the context of that cult that he considered his own life an act of religious homage offered to the Father, and his death, an expiatory sacrifice and a covenant sacrifice (Mt 26:28), thanks to which the eschatological Passover would be accomplished (Lk 22:15-16).

Thus the figurative meaning of all the Jewish rites was fully revealed in the unique act of the new cult, which realized that to which the ancient cult tended and was not able to reach.   Everything in the old pointed figuratively to the new, just as the new, in its turn, informs and renders efficacious the worship of the Church.  This explains why the letter to the Hebrews, in its typological interpretation of the liturgical institutions of Israel, presented Christ as the only high priest of men, [161] whose death and resurrection constituted the real sacrifice, both of expiation and of alliance, offered in the heavenly sanctuary (Heb 8:1-10:18).  In the perspective that is thus opened, it becomes possible to search every Old Testament rite for a figurative meaning, which will differ from case to case, and will have more or less importance for understanding the mystery of Christ; the authors of the New Testament provide occasional examples (cf. 1 Co 5:7 ff.; 1 P 1:19; Rv 5:6; Rm 12:1; Heb 13:10-15; Ga 5:1-2, etc.).  Even before the Old Testament, it is possible to find a certain figurative meaning, and therefore a positive religious value, in the rites carried out in the context of the law of nature; for, as St. Thomas said, [162] "Since before the law there were some men who were endowed with the prophetic spirit, it must be admitted that they were led by a divine instinct, as if by some private law, to a manner of adoring God which both aptly expressed their interior submission and aptly signified the mysteries of Christ, which were prefigured also by other aspects of their history."   In short, by his sacrifice Christ accomplished all the liturgical prefigurations which preceded him, because from him the religion of the human race, whose head and mediator he is, takes its meaning.

---

[161] On Christ the high priest, cf. O. Cullmann, *The Christology of the New Testament*, pp. 83-107; C. Spicq, *L'épître aux Hébreux* I, pp. 291-300.

[162] "Because before the Law there were some outstanding men who had the prophetic spirit, it is to be believed that out of a divine extinct, as if from some private law, they were led to some particular way of worshipping God which would both be in accord with interior worship, and would also serve to signify the mysteries of Christ, which were prefigured likewise by others of their deeds." (Iᵃ IIᵃᵉ, q. 103, art. 1, *in corp.*).   Several problems deserve to be studied in this perspective: that of the value of non-Christian religions, that of the salvation of non-believers.

## V. DISCERNMENT AND SYSTEMATIC STUDY OF BIBLICAL FIGURES [163]

### *1. Prefiguration and Biblical Criticism*

An understanding of the biblical notion of figure presupposes what we have written above on the historical preparation for Christ and the divine pedagogy in view of his coming. Within that preparation and parallel to that pedagogy, it is a matter of discerning in the history previous to Christ a revelation of a symbolic character which, in conjunction with the word of God, brought about a maturation of faith in those who benefited from it. The difficulties raised in this matter come either from the superficial idea some have of it, or from the absence of a trustworthy method for discerning authentic figures. In particular, the existence of an allegorical exegesis which has used and abused the principle of typology has contributed a great deal to the scorn many moderns, who are accustomed to a critical reading of the texts, have for typology. [164] There has been here a misunderstanding which requires clarification.

The fathers, and already some of the New Testament authors, made use of biblical texts by allegorizing them (cf. Ga 4:24), that is, by giving all their details particular meanings related to some aspect of the mystery of Christ. This Christian allegory undoubtedly had typology as its foundation and starting point, [165] since it intended to show the relation of preparatory history to its *eschaton*, Christ. But despite this original character, which formally distinguished it from the hellenistic allegory, [166] it could not help but lead to confusion between two operations which are closely related yet very different: the theological interpretation of biblical realities in the light of Christ and his mystery, and the exegesis of the texts in which these realities are mentioned. The Thomistic distinction between the *sensus litteralis* and

---

[163] Cf. P. Grelot, "Les figures bibliques," *NRT* 84 (1962), 568-575 and 687-695 (the same material in *Sens chrétien de l'A.T.*, pp. 216-219 and 299-303).

[164] Critizing the proof from Scripture adduced by the authors of the New Testament as manifesting a notion of prophecy which reduces it to a prediction of future events, Bultmann writes: "Such a proof from Scripture is, as a matter of fact, impossible. The alleged prophecies of the Old Testament, taken in their own meaning, are in some instances not prophecies at all; in other instances they are not directed toward Jesus or the Christian Church, but simply portray the Israelite-Jewish hope for the future. Most of the passages must be understood—e.g. with the aid of the allegorical method—contrary to their original sense in order to yield a suitable prediction..." (*The Old Testament and Christian Faith*, p. 33). Much could be said both about this notion of prophecy (which was that of 19th-century apologetics), and about the implicit confusion between typology and allegory.

[165] This is pointed out, for the authors of the New Testament, by S. Amsler, *op. cit.*, pp. 164-172, who, however, sees in allegory an error in method.

[166] H. de Lubac, "A propos de l'allégorie chrétienne," *RSR* 50 (1959), 5-43; *Exégèse médiévale*, Part I, pp. 373-396.

the *sensus spiritualis* is an aid to arriving at a more correct view of the problem. [167] But the extensive use of the allegorical method nonetheless had introduced a troublesome element into the investigation of biblical figures, because it led interpreters to consider the details of texts separate from the corresponding realities, and to interpret them independently of their context. [168] But the discernment of authentic figures requires a wider point of view, for the realities in question acquire their figurative meaning only when they are inserted in a living experience, either historical or cultic, in which their details become organic wholes. To atomize these organic groupings makes the results of investigation dubious, and puts that investigation out of contact with a critical study of the text which requires the same broad view. The distinction between the theological study of figures and allegorical exegesis therefore clarifies the discussion, and restores to theology the critical support which allegory had withdrawn from it.

Let us take a first example from among historical prefigurations. The reason that the exodus from Egypt, from the call of Moses to the crossing of the Red Sea, could acquire the value of a sign is that it forms a whole. It became for Israel the experience of an act of God, revealed God as a Savior, and as such, prefigured the definitive salvation accomplished by Jesus Christ. This event, as is the case with any event, is not therefore just a collection of details laid side by side, to which particular meanings can be given, either by the faith of Israel or by Christian faith. The event does indeed reach its climax in one or the other of them, which determines or manifests the meaning of the others: the celebration of the Passover, or the crossing of the Red Sea, for example. But when the sacred authors, in vastly different ways, call the event to mind, they are deeply conscious of the unity of the whole, and on the meaning of the whole depends the interpretation they incorporate into their narrative or their poems. A critical reading of the biblical texts, which rightly exposes this religious interpretation of history without which the raw facts would be without interest, is therefore the first guide to follow in searching for real prefigurations. It provides the proper orientation, sometimes reveals the completely relative character of certain details, and in every case discloses the reason that a historical experience could take on the meaning of an experience of faith. This is especially noticeable when the recollection of a past even passes into a profession of faith (Ex 13:14-15; Dt 26:5-9), is transformed into prayer (Ps 105; Is 63:8-14,

---

[167] Above, p. 236.

[168] As we said above (p. 195 f.), the exegesis of every age includes a variable cultural element. That of the patristic age used Alexandrian allegorizing for this purpose (cf. *Sens chrétien de l'A.T.*, p. 221, note 4). In this we note the limits that the culture of their age imposed upon them.

etc.), or provides a traditional representation of the *eschaton* (Is 43:16-21). Literal exegesis is therefore the necessary basis for all investigation into typology.

The same principle is to be applied to liturgical realities. Here too the minute details acquire a meaning as a group which expresses the life of faith. Their figurative sense appears only as a part of this whole significance, and it would be beside the point to search for a meaning for each one of them taken separately, whether it be in regard to the temple utensils, the various rites, the prohibitions laid down by the holiness code, etc. In this matter, critical study must take account of the findings of the history of religions, in order to relate Israelite cult to the general field of religious phenomenology, while still recognizing its distinctive characteristics. This is a complex undertaking that leads to a proper evaluation of the rationale of sacred objects and times, of liturgical functions and rites, in the twofold context of the Old Testament and the law of nature. The objective examination can subsequently be undertaken with reasonable hope of success. In the field of history, and that of worship as well, therefore, biblical criticism provides a first foundation with which theology cannot dispense.

### 2. Correspondence of the Two Experiences of Faith

The second foundation for the study of biblical figures is a comparative study of the two experiences of faith which characterize the two Testaments. The two, as a matter of fact, are in complete conformity with one another on the existential plane: as regards acceptance of the word of God, openness to his grace, expectation of the salvation promised by him, conscious entry into a sacred history in which the plan of salvation is realized. This shows that in the two Testaments faith has a fundamentally identical structure. But its two realizations nonetheless have different features, both as regards the signs which serve as its foundation, and those through which it is expressed: the history of Israel and its liturgical institutions on the one hand, and the person of Christ and the life of the Church on the other. From the Old to the New Testament, "the signs change, the faith remains the same."[169] This unparalleled paradox has important consequences in the matter of prefiguration. A comparison of these two experiences of faith reveals the similarity of the situations their respective signs occupy. The role provisionally filled by Moses, or David, or the temple, or the paschal lamb, or the suffering just men of bygone times, etc., is now filled by Christ considered in the diverse aspects of his mystery. The position occupied for

---

[169] "The sacraments were changed, not the faith. The signs which stood for something were changed, not the things that were signified" (St. Augustine, *Sermo* 19 [*PL* 38, 133]).

a time by the Israelite nation, as a political society centered in Jerusalem, or as a worshiping community centered in the temple, is today held by the Church, the Body of Christ. What the experience of the exodus from Egypt was long ago for Israel, or the manna and water in the desert, or the entry into the promised land, or the victory over surrounding enemies, or the covenant at Sinai, or communion with God in liturgical meals,—all these have their parallel in Christian experience, which draws all its efficacy from the mystery of Christ. By using systematically the conclusions of critical study, therefore, comparison of the two experiences of faith furnishes the necessary criterion for discerning authentic figures. The error of rampant allegorizing was precisely in neglecting such study, if not for the outstanding realities for which the New Testament already supplied the key, at least for a multitude of details which were artificially compared with one another. [170]

It might be objected that the New Testament occasionally finds figures of Christ and of salvation outside the context of the ancient economy, in the context of the primitive economy and human origins. Is that not evidence that the experience of faith proper to Israel was not necessary to the existence of figures? The difficulty is more apparent than real. For while it is true that historical experiences or cultic realities connected with the law of nature are involved there [171] (the history of Noah, the sacrifice of Abel or that of Melchizedek), their interpretation is always related to the revelation which specifies the ancient economy. For example, the history of Noah represents the typical experience of salvation, patterned after the covenant, which men underwent, and continued to undergo, under the economy of nature. From this point of view, the biblical tradition presents a universalist view of the plan of God which goes beyond the narrow framework of the people of Israel, and which chapters 1-11 of Genesis present in literary form. But this experience of salvation would remain incomprehensible, and would even have passed unnoticed, if it were not for the revelation of the ancient economy. The proof is that the literary material used here by Genesis, although borrowed from Mesopotamian traditions, is reinterpreted in a sense completely unknown to those traditions. And it was this sense upon which the figurative interpretation was developed in the New Testament and then used extensively in Christian tradition [172] (cf. 1 P 4:20 ff.; 2 P 2:5).

---

[170] *Sens chrétien de l'A.T.*, pp. 239 ff.

[171] When in this respect we speak of *historical* experiences, the expression must be understood with respect to the literary forms of Gn 4-11, in which the representative value of the accounts goes beyond the anecdotal material used. Each story represents a certain human experience, previous to the ancient economy and broader than it. It is as such that it is the object of a religious interpretation.

[172] On the typology of the flood in patristic tradition, see J. Daniélou, *Sacramentum futuri* (Paris: Beauchesne, 1950), pp. 55-94.

The study of biblical figures is a delicate and complex operation. To execute it correctly, it is not enough to consult the New Testament without weighing the material it presents, because the use of rabbinic methods and allegorizing sometimes play a part in its presentation along with theological reflection on biblical realities. These cultural elements included in New Testament exegesis do not have the same worth as the doctrinal assertions which express apostolic revelation. On the other hand, there is no indication that the authors of the New Testament furnished a complete list of the prefigurations included in the Old. The principles they give are clear, but the applications they make of them remain occasional and limited. [173] It is, therefore, legitimate to systematize the operation they introduced, so long as it is done with method and rigor. But a detailed study of this point would take us beyond the limits of our discussion.

### 3. Diverse Applications of Typology

One point remains to be clarified. The notion of figure is not univocal, for the *eschaton* toward which all sacred history before Christ tends has many aspects, closely related, but distinct: that of Christ the Head, and that of the Church, his Body; that of the pilgrim state in which Christ passed his earthly life and in which the Church lives its sacramental history in expectation of the final day, and that of eternity, into which Christ entered by his resurrection, and into which his members will follow him at the time of the restoration of the universe (Ac 3:21). The figurative meaning of biblical realities is determined by their relation to a certain determined aspect of this manifold mystery, or to several of its aspects. Many types of figures can therefore be distinguished, corresponding to the various aspects of the mystery of Christ. Traditional theology and exegesis recognized this when they distinguished, beneath the literal or historical sense of Scripture, an allegorical sense, an anagogic, and a tropologic. [174] The allegory corresponds to the prefigurations which sketch the mystery of Christ and of the Church in their pilgrim state (the earthly life of Christ, the terrestrial history of the Church). The anagoge sought in Scripture a figure of that mystery in its consummation beyond time—in the present for the risen Christ, after the parousia for all his members.

As for tropology, its practical orientation set it apart, since it sought above all concrete examples in biblical history which would provide the Christian people a rule of life. While still organically related to allegory

[173] *Sens chrétien de l'A.T.*, p. 220.
[174] Above, p. 199.

and anagoge, it was situated on the fringe of prefigurations properly so called, very near to moral exemplarism. For example, reflection on the sufferings of Israel in the desert is based on typology both in 1 Co 10:5-11 and in Heb 3:7-4:11. But can it be said that the moral lessons that are drawn in these passages in themselves go beyond those drawn in Ps 95:7-11, which is cited in the letter to the Hebrews? The same mystery of human obstinacy which was manifest long ago among the Israelites in the desert was manifest also among lukewarm Christians; but can it be said that the first case was the figure of the second? The punishment of those at fault certainly takes on a new aspect, because beyond the promise of the holy land has now appeared that of genuine divine peace (Heb 4:5-11). But this new perspective opened to us by Christ colors the motive of the spiritual drama more than it changes its nature and rules. The historical experiences in question were part of that divine pedagogy which prepared hearts to turn toward Christ the savior, rather than occasions which led to the maturation of Israel's faith by figuratively sketching the salvation expected from him. It seems better, therefore, to include classical tropology under the study of the divine pedagogy, rather than under that of prefigurations. Their close ties with allegory and anagoge prove only that there are analogous links between the pedagogic significance of biblical history and its figurative significance.

## § IV. THE SIGNIFICANCE OF THINGS AFTER CHRIST

### I. CHRIST AND THE AGE OF THE CHURCH

#### I. THE PASSAGE FROM THE OLD TESTAMENT TO THE NEW

##### *1. The Turning Point in Salvation History*

Christ is the center of sacred history. Before him, everything tended to him in such a way that the mystery of salvation reached maturity in his person. From him the same mystery unfolds to extend the economy of grace, which his coming inaugurated, to all mankind. [175] The preparatory age thus received its meaning from a future event: the *eschaton*, which was gradually revealed through the prophetic promises. The age of the Church receives its meaning from a past event, the first coming of Christ, and while it too remains directed toward a final fulness, this latter is already made present by the resurrection of Christ.

---

[175] Above, pp. 249 ff.

The passage from one Testament to the other, therefore, entailed a radical transformation, both in sacred history and in the community which lived it. To the preparation for salvation [176] succeeded its permanent actualization in the Church. Since the pedagogy of the Law [177] came to an end when the cross of Christ fully revealed sin and grace, judgment and salvation, mankind is now presented directly with the fulness of the gospel. When it is announced to them, they must take a stand, either for or against Christ. From the age of prefigurations, [178] of sketches, of shadows, mankind has passed to that of the long awaited reality. Granted that when Christ entered the glory of the Father he kept the direct perception of this reality hidden from us, but it is no less present here below in a group of signs (εἰκών, Heb 10:1) which contain its substance and render it accessible to us under a sacramental veil. [179] Furthermore, the end of the Old Testament did not entail the disappearance of the visible society which was the guardian of the plan of salvation, but rather its transformation. Under the old covenant, the extension of the people of God was quite restricted: the Israelite nation as a worshiping community. Today this provisional limitation no longer holds; the people of God appears as the Body of Christ, that is, the visible extension of his person in time. [180] It is in this sense that the Church is the accomplishment of the various figures with which ancient Israel was rich: it is the Israel of God (Ga 5:16), the people of the new alliance (1 P 2:9 ff.) the true worshiping community, the Jerusalem on high, the mother of the redeemed (Ga 4:26) and the spouse of Christ (Rv 21).

The mystery of the cross and the resurrection thus marks the moment when human time, so to speak, was transformed. Yet if that fact is traced to its roots, that transformation was made possible only by the incarnation of the Son of God. It was only through the mediation of his individual body, the tangible proof of a human nature subject to the common condition of the sons of Adam, that Christ was able to assume all humanity and conduct them into the mystery of his cross and resurrection, making them his Body of which we are members, his spouse whose sons we are (cf. Ep 5:29-32).

[176] Above, pp. 258-262.

[177] Above, pp. 262-269.

[178] Above, pp. 269-290.

[179] On the meaning of εἰκών in Heb 10:1, see C. Spicq, *L'épître aux Hébreux 2*, p. 302: "εἰκών must be given the derived meaning of: the figure in which the reality of a thing is expressed, its 'essence' (G. Kittel, *TWNT* 2, p. 393), its form."

[180] On the origin of the idea of the Body of Christ in Pauline theology, see L. Cerfaux, *La théologie de l'Église suivant saint Paul*, pp. 201-218, 247-260; P. Benoit, "Corps, tête et plérôme dans les épîtres de la captivité," *RB* 65 (1956), 5-44 (reprinted in *Exégèse et théologie 2*, pp. 107-153); L. Ouelette, "L'Église, corps du Christ," *L'Église dans la Bible* (Bruges-Paris: Desclée de Brouwer, 1962), pp. 85-93.

That is why faith in salvation itself falls to ruin when the realism of the incarnation is called into question, [181] for if the cross has any meaning at all, the reason is that it concerns the very Son of God. This fact leads our reflection to the moment of the incarnation and to the woman (Ga 4:4) in whom it was accomplished, for there we come to grips with the crucial point of the economy of salvation.

### 2. The Place of Mary in Salvation History [182]

Does Mary, of whom Christ was born (Mt 1:16), belong to the Old Testament or to the New? Does she belong to the Israel subject to the Law, or to the Israel recipient of grace? We must beware of giving a hasty reply to this question. For on the one hand, Mary does belong to the age of preparation, though it is her mission to bring it to its conclusion. The race of Adam, the line descended from Abraham and David, was concentrated in her for the birth of Christ, the mediator of salvation. [183] It was through her that the human temporal condition was transmitted to him with all the traits the history of sinful humanity had conferred upon it. [184] In the exercise of her maternal role, she was not a passive instrument, designed just to provide Christ his human body. Just as he experienced a real growth "in wisdom, in stature, and in favor" (Lk 2:52) before becoming an adult Jew, she exercised in his regard the usual educatory function of a mother. Thus it was thanks to her that the branch of David truly blossomed [185] from the history which prepared for and preceded his coming.

But on the other hand, the manner in which the evangelists speak of Mary shows that, contrary to St. John the Baptist, for example, they do not regard her as an Old Testament personage. She received the first call to faith which explicitly had for its object the person of Christ, the Davidic

---

[181] See above, p. 251, note 56, and 254, note 62 (on the christology of R. Bultmann).

[182] The limited scope of our theological investigation dispenses us with presenting a detailed bibliography on the virgin Mary; we intend only to evaluate her exact position with regard to the two Testaments. We will, however, indicate a few studies which adhere to the biblical texts: F. M. Braun, *La mère des fidèles: Essai de théologie johannique* (Tournai-Paris: Casterman, 1954); R. Laurentin, *Structure et théologie de Luc I-II* (Paris: Gabalda, 1957); J. Galot, *Marie dans l'évangile* (Paris: Desclée de Brouwer, 1958); L. Deiss, *Marie, fille de Sion* (Paris: Desclée de Brouwer, 1959); M. Thurian, *Marie, mère du Seigneur, figure de l'Église* (Taizé: Presses de Taizé, 1962).

[183] Above, pp. 258-262.

[184] Above, p. 248.

[185] "Ask no longer why the Lord was born so late. He was not only to be the dew from heaven and the gift from on high, he was also to be the "fruit of the earth" (Is 4:2) and "to bud forth" from the earth (Is 45:8). He was not to rush upon the world like a bolt, he had to germinate slowly in the sun like a plant" (Card. Faulhaber, quoted by H. de Lubac, *Catholicisme*, p. 346).

Messiah and Son of God (Lk 1:31-37), and she was the first to respond to the call (Lk 1:45) with perfect obedience (Lk 1:38); with her, therefore, the faith of the Church had its beginning. [186]  Her faith undoubtedly increased; the gospel narratives discretely mark off the stages of that growth up to the cross (Jn 19:25 ff.).  But the final mention of Mary in Scripture (Ac 1:14) shows her entering the age of the Church right at its beginning; the resurrection of her son had brought the development of her faith to perfection.  Moreover, because of her pivotal situation with regard to Christ, the unique link which joined her to him, God inaugurated for her the economy of grace to which believers are called in the Church—from the moment of the annunciation she was already full of grace (Lk 1:28), as later will be all those who believe (Ep 1:6).  In her can thus be glimpsed a mystery of life with God (Lk 1:28) which a modest reserve keeps hidden from our view, but which bestows a profound meaning upon the outstanding traits of her spiritual personality: her responsiveness to the call of God (Lk 1:38) and her virginal state. [187]  This last is the more important, for it is the essential condition of the mystery of the incarnation.  She conceived by the Holy Spirit alone (Mt 1:20; Lk 1:35), and for that reason the son of Mary (Mk 6:3) would clearly appear as the Son of the Most High (Lk 1:32). Thus, although in the eyes of men Joseph took her to himself (Mt 1:20), she actually knew no other husband (Lk 1:34) but God himself.  She thus realized in her soul and in her flesh that condition of virgin-spouse to which the faithful are called (2 Co 11:2) and which defines the mystery of the Church itself (cf. Rv 21:2).

All of this, at length, can be understood only in the perspective of Mary's maternity; it was to fulfill her role of mother that she gained access to the faith; it was because the incarnation of the Son of God was accomplished in her that she is "the most blessed of all women" (Lk 1:42); it was because she was set apart to become the "mother of the Lord" (Lk 1:43) that she was, even before the incarnation, "highly favored" (Lk 1:28.30). Consequently, without ceasing to belong to the ancient people of God, since Christ was to inherit through her the throne of David [188] (Lk 1:32 ff.), she belongs fully to the new humanity which chapter 12 of Revelation describes in expressive terms. [189]  In this passage, the woman who brings into the

---

[186] On Mary's faith, see E. Schillebeeckx, *Marie, mère de la rédemption* (Paris: Cerf, 1963), pp. 18-44; Eng. trans. *Mary, Mother of the Redemption* (New York: Sheed & Ward, 1964).

[187] L. Legrand, *La virginité dans la Bible* (Paris: Cerf, 1964), pp. 107-127.

[188] L. Deiss, *Marie, fille de Sion*, pp. 39-67.

[189] On the difficulties posed by this chapter of Revelation, see F. M. Braun, *La mère des fidèles*, pp. 134-176; B. J. Le Frois, *The Woman Clothed with the Sun* (Rome: Orbis Catholicus, 1954); L. Cerfaux, "La vision de la Femme et du Dragon de l'Apocalypse en relation avec le protévangile," *ETL* 32 (1956), 21-23 (= *Recuei.*

world "the male child who was to rule all the nations" (Rv 12:5) represents primarily the new Jerusalem announced in prophetic eschatology (Is 66:7 ff.). The manner in which the divine protection allows her and her son to escape the schemes of the dragon (Rv 12:6.14-16) shows that she is at the same time the antitype of Eve, victim of the serpent of old, just as Christ is the antitype of Adam in Rm 5:12-21. But to accomplish this birth that brought Christ the Head into the world, the new humanity concentrated its being in Mary, daughter of Sion, inheritor of the whole Old Testament. [190] Jesus is her own Son; he received from her his body. The transformation of the old Israel into the new Israel was, therefore, through the grace of God, accomplished in the person of Mary to make way for the birth of Christ the Head. By the same act was inaugurated in her a mystery of maternity which will never cease its spiritual activity in the Church (Ga 4:26 ff.), as a result of which the Body of Christ grows in the measure that the Church gives birth to new sons. [191]

There thus exists between Mary and the Church a special relation which has no equivalent elsewhere. [192] In any attempt to define the meaning

L. Cerfaux 3, pp. 237-251); A. M. Dubarle, "La Femme couronnée d'étoiles (Apoc. 12)" in *Mélanges bibliques rédigés en l'honneur d'André Robert* (Paris: Bloud & Gay), pp. 512-518; A. Feuillet, "Le Messie et sa mère d'après le chap. XII de l'Apocalypse" in *Études johanniques* (Bruges-Paris: Desclée de Brouwer, 1962), pp. 272-310 (reprint from *RB* 68 [1959], 55-86); A. Kassing, *Die Kirche und Maria, Ihr Verhältnis im 12. Kapitel der Apokalypse* (Würzburg: Patmos, 1958). On the exegesis of this chapter in past ages, see P. Prigent, *Apocalypse 12: Histoire de l'exégèse* (Tübingen: Mohr, 1959). On the present state of the problem, see A. Feuillet, *L'Apocalypse* (Bruges-Paris: Desclée de Brouwer, 1962), pp. 91-98. The question naturally is treated in all commentaries on the book.

[190] On Mary, the symbolic personification of Israel, see the provocative remarks of P. Benoit, "Et toi-même, un glaive te transpercera l'âme (Luc 2,35)," *CBQ* 25 (1963), 251-261.

[191] "The Church is a virgin. You might ask me: if she is a virgin, how does she give birth to sons?... I reply: she is a virgin and she gives birth. She imitates Mary, who gave birth to the Lord. Did not the holy virgin Mary give birth, and did she not remain a virgin? Thus the Church gives birth and she is a virgin. And if you consider it well, she gives birth to Christ: for those who are baptized are the members of Christ. 'You are,' says the Apostle, 'the Body of Christ and his members' (1 Co 12:27). If therefore she gives birth to the members of Christ, she is utterly like Mary" (St. Augustine, sermon published by G. Morin, *Miscellanea Agostiniana*, I, 1).

[192] H. de Lubac, *Méditation sur l'Église* (Paris: Aubier, 1953), pp. 241-285. The collective volumes: *Marie et l'Église, Études mariales*, I-III (Paris: Lethielleux, 1951-1953); H. Rahner, *Our Lady and the Church* (New York: Pantheon, 1961); Y. Congar, "Marie et l'Église dans la pensée patristique," *RSPT* 38 (1954), 3-38 (in reference to A. Müller, *Ecclesia-Maria, Die Einheit Marias und der Kirche* [Freiburg, 1955]; J. Galot, "Marie et l'Église," *NRT* 81 (1959), 113-131. A clear treatment and an abundant bibliography will be found in G. Philips, "Marie et l'Église, Un thème théologique renouvelé" in H. du Manoir, *Maria, Études sur la sainte Vierge* 7 (Paris: Beauchesne, 1964), pp. 363-419. This aspect of the mystery of Mary is fortunately emphasized in the dogmatic constitution *Lumen Gentium* of Vatican II (Nos. 53 and 60-65).

of the realities scattered throughout sacred history, Mary cannot be treated like any other personage, neither in the New Testament, nor *a fortiori* in the Old; her significance is unique.[193] Not only was she the first member of the Church in point of time, but the position she occupies and the role she plays make her the perfect model of the mystery of the Church, in the realm of faith as in that of grace, both as virgin and as mother. It would be insufficient to call her the figure of the Church,[194] if the word figure is given the same meaning it has for the personages and realities of the Old Testament. She is something greater and better than a figure. Next to Christ, in her humble position, she in some way personifies the Church, and it is not unintentional that the fourth gospel depicts her at the foot of the cross becoming by the will of Christ the mother of the beloved disciple who represents all Christians.[195] Because she is the mother of Christ, because her maternal suffering associated her with the passion of her son (cf. Lk 2:35), by virtue of the will of Christ she concretely personifies and signifies the maternity of the Church at its source, which is precisely the fruit of the cross. In a word, in Mary the mystery of the Church is positively revealed in its most perfect form.[196] It can therefore be concluded that this same mystery in turn clarifies that of God's grace in Mary, which is only briefly alluded to in the New Testament.[197]

[193] It is therefore understandable why the conciliar fathers should have hesitated on the place to give to the schema on the virgin Mary in relation to the schema on the Church: inclusion or separate treatment? (cf. R. Laurentin, *L'enjeu du concile. II. Bilan de la deuxième session* (Paris: Seuil, 1964), p. 100-101).

[194] This is a traditional expression in Latin theology, but in another sense, as this text of Pseudo-Augustine commenting on Rv 12:4 shows: "None of you is unaware that the dragon is the devil. The woman signifies the virgin Mary, who being spotless bore our spotless Head, and who also in herself represented a figure of holy Church: just as she bearing a son remained a virgin, so too the latter bears his members in every age without losing her virginity" (*PL* 39, 661).

[195] Besides the works cited on p. 000, note 0, see finally A. Feuillet, "Les adieux du Christ à sa mère (Jn 19:25-27) et la maternité spirituelle de Marie," *NRT* 86 (1964), 469-489.

[196] "Mary... is the prototype of the Church, as the idea of the Church is originally realized in her person and in the most perfect manner. Since she herself belongs to the Church and at the same time forms the head-member as root and heart, the idea of the Church as a supernatural principle assisting Christ receives all its full, concrete, and living figure" (M. J. Scheeben, *Mariology* [St. Louis: Herder, 1946], p. 217). Cf. O. Semmelroth, *Urbild der Kirche* (Würzburg: Echter, 1950); C. Journet, *L'Église du Verbe incarné* 2 (Paris, 1951), pp. 382-453. The idea is not unknown in Protestant theology; cf. M. Thurian, *Marie, mère du Seigneur, figure de l'Église* (Taizé: Presses de Taizé, 1962), pp. 175-259.

[197] Cf. below, pp. 381 ff.

## II. THE CHURCH AND TIME [198]

### 1. The Church in its Pilgrim State

The present condition of the Church constitutes a real paradox, just as that of Christ during his earthly life. On the one hand, as the Body of Christ, it is an eschatological reality. Associated with the risen Lord from whom it receives its being, it is even now the Jerusalem on high (Ga 4:26 ff.) which will be manifest on the last day with the new heaven and the new earth (Rv 21), the heavenly Jerusalem which is the city of the living God (Heb 12:22), the holy and immaculate spouse of Christ (Ep 5:27). As such, its mode of existence is no longer that of ancient humanity, subject to the suffering of the human condition determined by sin. It possesses the eschatological existence inaugurated by the resurrection by Christ; it lives in a redeemed temporal condition which is a return to that of paradise of old. But on the other hand, this mystery of grace remains in fact hidden beneath bewildering external appearances; for until the day when the figure of this world will pass away, it lives in the midst of the old temporal condition subject to the consequences of sin. As the people of God, the Church must lead a pilgrim existence until the parousia, and that implicates it intimately with fallen humanity, and makes it a partaker of its earthly condition. Its meta-historical reality, which will be revealed at the time of the parousia, until then subsists in the murkiness of history. [199]

It is perhaps at the level of individuals that this paradoxical situation appears most clearly. [200] In them the two temporal states coexist and clash. By their faith in the gospel and by their baptism, they have become members of the new humanity (Ep 4:24); they participate in eschatological existence, they live in the redeemed temporal condition of the sons of God (1 Jn 3:1). Nevertheless, the new existence they have received cannot yet be fully manifested (1 Jn 3:2); it remains the object of hope (Rm 8:23 ff.). For now, the suffering of the old temporal condition remains with them: the law of the flesh which inclines them to evil (Rm 7:14-24), subjection to suffering and death. Their eschatological existence, unlike that of Christ during his earthly life, is not only subject to temporary bondage, which contributes to the death of the old man and the renovation of the new (2 Co 5:16); they

---

[198] O. Cullmann, *Christ and Time*, pp. 211 ff., satisfactorily completed (and occasionally corrected) by J. Mouroux, *The Mystery of Time*, pp. 186-241.

[199] Hence the coexistence of two types of eschatology, futuristic and realized, in the New Testament; cf. W. G. Kümmel, "Futuristic and Realised Eschatology in the Earliest Stages of Christianity," *Journal of Religion* 43 (1963), 303-314.

[200] J. Mouroux, *op. cit.*, pp. 252-270.

are at grips with a spiritual struggle whose outcome is forever in doubt (cf. 1 Co 10:12 ff.; Jm 1:13 ff.). Now the visible presence of the Church in history is assured only by this people of redeemed sinners, established only precariously in the new temporal condition. The very signs of the grace of Christ here below are confided to their fragile hands, in such wise that the external appearances of the Church are even more deceptive than were those of Christ to the eyes of his contemporaries. The eschatological reality is hidden beneath a bewildering veil.

## 2. The Church and Profane History

Despite this bondage, the presence of the Church in human history manages to manifest the meaning of that history, not only at the level of sacred history on which the return of men to God is realized, but also at that of the human history which serves as its substructure. [201] The relation of the one to the other is admittedly different in the two Testaments. In the Old, the identification of the people of God with a secular community, the Israelite nation, resulted in the total integration of that community's profane history in sacred history strictly so called, so that by that fact the former acquired a revelatory significance. [202] In the New, the distinction Christ established between the salvation community and human communities of this world, between the domain of God and that of Caesar (Mt 22:21), put an end to that identification. Profane history and its component realities no longer in themselves reveal anything about the mystery of salvation [203]; their meaning can no longer be sought in that direction. But at the same time, their real relation to this mystery is made quite clear. Profane history remains ordered to sacred history as to its ultimate goal; what all creation is eagerly awaiting is the final revelation of the sons of God at the eschatological resurrection (Rm 8:9 ff.). The relations of men to one another and to the world have as a consequence of sin suffered a radical disturbance which only the grace of the redemption can heal. The enmity between man and nature and the contrasts within society, which give rise to the dialectic structure of history, [204] can be overcome only in Christ the Savior. This mediation of Christ is presently exercised by the Church, and it is through it that the relation of the Church to the profane world is determined. The world subsists in its

---

[201] H. Urs von Balthasar, *A Theology of History*, pp. 130 ff.

[202] Above, pp. 269 ff.

[203] Call to mind the positions taken by M. I. Montuclard, "La médiation de l'Église et la médiation de l'Histoire," *Jeunesse de l'Église* 7 (1947), 9-36, and especially in *Les événements et la foi* (see an incisive criticism of these positions in G. Fessard, *De l'actualité historique* [Bruges-Paris: Desclée de Brouwer, 1960], Vol. 2, pp. 27-71).

[204] Above, p. 259, note 76.

own order, but it cannot attain its own ends except by being incorporated in the new humanity and entering eschatological existence.

Just as all the individuals who compose the human race, therefore, profane history is torn between two temporal conditions: that of fallen man and that of redeemed man. For that very reason all of its values remain fragile and ambiguous, its technical conquests and mastery of the earth, its empire building and efforts to unite mankind, its cultural exchange and tendency toward cultural universality, etc. Left to the internal logic of the fallen world, these values prove self-destructive, these efforts are repaid with failure, or even turn to man's harm. But these same values and efforts, when undertaken by the new humanity which is the Body of Christ, regain their providential destination and their deep significance, such as the Creator intended them. This cannot be brought about, however, except through the free response of men to the grace of Christ and the call of his gospel. As long as the present world lasts, as long as the Church remains in its pilgrim condition, men's response remains uncertain, conditional, always in doubt. It is therefore absolutely impossible to predict whether profane history is heading toward success or failure, to a Christian assumption of its values in a final transformation of the earth, or toward the annihilation of its values in a catastrophe which will manifest the judgment of God. [205]

---

[205] It is perhaps precisely at this point that Teilhard de Chardin's optimistic outlook, founded on faith in God the creator who cannot help but succeed in his designs, and in Christ the redeemer who cannot fail in the fulfillment of the world, appears most vulnerable, or at least the most one-sided. The idea of history's natural tendency toward human "planetisation" is right: "But why should we not assume... that the parousiac spark can, of physical and organic necessity, only be kindled between Heaven and a Mankind which has biologically reached a certain critical evolutionary point of collective maturity?" (*The Future of Man* [New York: Harper & Row, 1964], p. 267). Nor has the dialectic of life and death, viewed in the light of the cross and resurrection of Christ, been overlooked in this prospect of the final assumption of the cosmos by "Christ the evolver": "I admit as a basic principle that the completion of the world cannot be accomplished except through a death, a 'night,' a return, an excentration and a sort of depersonalization of its monads. The aggregation of a monad to Christ presupposes in it a sort of internal disaggregation, that is, an alteration of its whole being, the condition of its re-creation and integration in the Pleroma" (text published in *Archives de philosophie* 24 [1961], p. 135). "Before passing into the Beyond, the World and its elements must attain what may be called their point of annihilation.' And it is precisely to this critical point that we must ultimately be brought by the effort consciously to further, within and around ourselves, the movement of universal convergence" (*The Future of Man*, p. 56).

But if that points up the close cohesion of the creative design manifested by universal evolution and the redeeming act accomplished by grace in the Church, one thing remains uncertain: what finally will be the attitude of human society, when it reaches its highest point of concentration (and thus its biological maturity), toward this necessity of dying with Christ in order to live in him? Will it be one of concurrence or of refusal? And by the same token, will the parousia of Christ, when he comes to transfigure the world, mean a loss of itself in ecstasy for the collectivity so concentrated, or a catastrophic death in final impenitence? In any case,

In the midst of this ambiguous world the Church is the only true sign of hope, for within it human time is already secretly transfigured, history has reached its goal. It remains, then, to see what meaning, in this context, the realities which make up the Church take on.

## II. THE MEANING OF ECCLESIAL REALITIES

As we have already said, [206] ecclesial realities take their meaning from Christ the Head, but that very fact makes them significant. St. Thomas, treating this question in the framework of the four senses of Scripture, rightly pointed out that their significance may lie in only two directions, that of the individual Christian life, for which they furnish a rule of action, and that of other-worldly hope, of which they present a sketch and a foretaste: "What is said of the Church in the literal sense cannot be explained allegorically, unless perhaps what is said of the primitive Church be so interpreted in order to apply it to the later condition of the Church: but such things are open to a moral and anagogic interpretation." [207] In fact, it would be even better to say that in the primitive Church considered at the New Testament stage, the mystery of the Church is manifest at its source just as it would be for all times. For the Church of today, the apostolic Church is not a figure but a norm; then, as now, we find the same ecclesial realities with an identical meaning.

### I. THE SIGNIFICANT REALITIES

The study of ecclesial realities covers the whole field of theology. An exhaustive treatment of the question is therefore out of the question here. But it will be useful to point out that in the New Testament, just as in the

---

transfiguration will occur for the Church, the remnant of sinful humanity, even if its members must undergo the same corporal death as Christ in order so to enter into glory; and from this standpoint the creative design will have attained its purpose—by the way of the cross. But it would be presumptuous to imagine a sort of disappearance of sin, which would open the way to a final transformation without any uprooting or shock, as if humanity at large were rendered capable of a free response to the grace which attracts it. For it, just as for each of its members, everything will remain uncertain and ambiguous up to the last day. Concerning these problems, see the clarification of P. Smulders, *La vision de Teilhard de Chardin* (Bruges-Paris: Desclée de Brouwer, 1964), pp. 126 ff., who cites the texts in which Teilhard mentions the possibility of a final failure (cf. pp. 151-157). Likewise E. Rideau, *La pensée du Père Teilhard de Chardin* (Paris: Seuil, 1965), pp. 351-355 (and notes 132 to 151 of the same chapter); Eng. trans. *The Thought of Teilhard de Chardin* (New York: Harper).

[206] Above, pp. 250-254.

[207] *Quodl.* 7, q. 6, art. 2, ad 2.

Old, the significance of these realities is founded on their relation to the history of salvation: they are not just *res* in general, but *res cursum suum peragentes*. [208] The Church is a historical reality, and it is as such that it signifies something. In its history, however, two quite different aspects must be distinguished: a sacramental aspect and an experiential aspect. [209]

## 1. Sacramental History [210]

The Church has as its principal mission to signify in time the presence and action of the glorious Christ, and thus to insert a metahistorical reality into human history. [211] For the glorious Christ remained in contact with his disciples only during the forty days which preceded his ascension [212]; but in that time he revealed what sort of activity he would not cease to exercise in his Church through the Holy Spirit he was to send. It is clear, then, in what sense it is possible to speak of history in this matter: not in the sense that something new and original happens here below, but in the sense that certain purposeful acts performed by the Church in time express for men the very acts of Christ in glory. [213] These acts can be divided into two classes. The first pertain to the announcement of the revelation imparted in Jesus Christ: the proclamation of the gospel, which is "the power of God saving all who have faith" (Rm 1:16); the working of signs, which, as a continuation of those worked by Christ long ago (Mt 11:5), accompany the word and testify in its favor before men (Mk 16:17.20). The second category pertains to the sanctification of men by the active word of Christ and the operation of the Holy Spirit: the sacraments, and in general all the rites similar to them, especially the rite which signifies the sacrifice of Christ by reproducing the actions of the last supper. [214]

This whole group of acts accomplished by the Church are an unfolding within it of Christ in glory, the sacrament par excellence, so that in their respect one could speak of a sacramental history in which is achieved not only the consecration of men to God, but even of the created realities which the Church employs in its worship. From this standpoint, the persons who play a role in it have no significance by reason of their individuality, of

---

[208] Above, pp. 241 f.

[209] Cf. A. Feuillet, "Le temps de l'Église selon saint Jean," *Études johanniques*, pp. 152-174.

[210] J. Mouroux, *The Mystery of Time*, pp. 224-232.

[211] E. Schillebeeckx, *Christ: The Sacrament of the Encounter with God*, pp. 47 ff.

[212] H. Urs von Balthasar, *op. cit.*, pp. 81-90.

[213] J. Daniélou, *Essai sur le mystère de l'histoire* (Paris: Seuil, 1953), pp. 84 ff. J. Geffré, "Les sacrements et le temps," *LMD* 65 (1961), 96-108.

[214] E. Schillebeeckx, *op. cit.*, pp. 54-63.

their comportment, or of their personal action, but only by reason of their ecclesial function, since it is by reason of the latter that they represent the presence and action of Christ. Thus Peter and the eleven, to whom Paul was added, independently of the apostolic office which is absolutely intransmissible, signify for the Church of all times the existence of a sacramental hierarchy within which the ecclesial ministry acquires significance.

## 2. Experiential History

The twofold mission of which we have just spoken, however, is accomplished by the Church in a world subject to the law of time, which pursues its own course about it. [215] For this reason, the life of the Church is made up of particular events which coincide with those of profane history and become of a piece with them. A close examination quickly reveals that those events in some way prolong those of Christ's earthly life, which were likewise immersed in the real world. Christ was sent into the world to announce the gospel, to bring salvation to the men in it, to found in it the kingdom of God; but when this mission encountered the perverse will of men, it took on the nature of a conflict with the world which logically led to the passion and the cross. The Church carries on the same mission and meets the same opposition. [216]

*a) The Church's mission.*—The mission of the Church follows a law of growth [217] whose stages are virtually marked out in the book of the Acts. The testimony rendered with the assistance of the Holy Spirit was to spread, beginning with Jerusalem, to the ends of the earth (Ac 1:8), symbolized by the capital of the pagan world (Ac 28:17-31); the gospel was to be proclaimed to all peoples (Mt 24:14; cf. 28:19) in every language, as indicated in the symbolic experience of Pentecost (Ac 2:11). In this regard, the Church's break with its Jewish origin has a significance which the texts vie with one another in emphasizing (cf. Ac 15:8 f. 14-17; Rm 15:8-12, etc.). The actual development of the Church over the ages is only a practical realization of the growth already present in principle from the moment of the cross (cf. Rv 5:9 ff.; Ep 2:14 ff.). At the same time, this movement toward an actual catholicity progressively effects the consecration to God of societies and civilizations, which is one of the aspects of the Church's sacramental

[215] On this relation of the Church to history, see J. Daniélou, *op. cit.*, pp. 193-200 (christology and history).

[216] J. Mouroux, *op. cit.*, pp. 199-210.

[217] *Ibid.*, pp. 232-237.

history. [218]   Moreover, since that movement coincides with the tendency of mankind to an internal unity, it provides it the means to reach its goal; by allowing itself to be absorbed in a process superior to profane history, to the end that the new humanity, in which all races, nations and languages meet (Ep 3:15), be established in Christ.  In short, it is through the organic growth of the Body of Christ that profane history, in all its aspects, can regain progress toward its specific goal.  The catholicity of the Church, while formally distinct from the universality of temporal society, places the leaven in a world which the wound of sin had divided against itself. [219]

   b) *Conflict of Church and world.* [220]—Nevertheless, the Church's mission, like that of Christ, cannot avoid conflict with the world.  The new city of God was established with only the remnant of ancient humanity, whether Jewish or pagan, which responded to the proclamation of the gospel. Consequently, a separation of a new type takes place in humanity: no longer between Jews and pagan nations, but within Judaism and the pagan nations themselves, between believers and unbelievers.  Already in the apostolic age the division appeared in the Jewish communities, only a remnant of which entered the new Israel (Rm 11; Ac 18:5-8).  It appeared likewise in the pagan world (Ac 14:1-5), so that the gospel appeared everywhere as the sign of contradiction which lays bare secret thoughts (cf. Lk 2:34 ff.). This open manifestation of the world's sin [221] became even more apparent when the opposition to the gospel was taken over by the temporal authorities who governed the pagan world.  Then over against the new Jerusalem, the city of the living God, rose up the city of evil, Babylon, whose activity is inspired by the diabolic dragon (Rv 13—18).  The old man and the new man at war within each one of us (cf. Rm 7), therefore, clash visibly on the stage of history, not in a political struggle in which the Church would fight on its enemies' chosen battlefield, but in a spiritual struggle [222] in which the Church's victory is assured by the same means Christ employed in his passion, the testimony of blood (cf. Ac 4:24-30; Rv 12:10 ff.).  Thus the meaning of the opposition and persecution encountered by preachers of the

---

[218] H. Urs von Balthasar, *op. cit.*, pp. 90-107.

[219] That is why the dream of human unity did not appear in pagan cultures, but within the Christian world.  Originally a theological conclusion, it has become laicized since the Renaissance, especially in the philosophy of the Enlightenment, in Hegel and the Marxist current; cf. Y. Congar, "Unité de l'humanité et vocation des peuples," *Sainte Église, Études et approches ecclésiologiques* (Paris: Cerf, 1963), pp. 173-180.

[220] H. Urs von Balthasar, *op. cit.*, pp. 134-140.

[221] Above, p. 263 f.

[222] Cf. L. Cerfaux, "Le conflit entre Dieu et le souverain divinisé dans l'Apocalypse de Jean," *Recueil L. Cerfaux* 3, pp. 225-236.

gospel and the faithful appears clearly, ever since the age of the apostles, in the wake of the passion and cross.

The experiental history of the Church, such as it flows from its relation with temporal society, therefore, will always present a twofold aspect: on the one hand, as the accomplishment of a mission of consecration and salvation, and on the other, as a struggle with a hostile force. [223] It cannot be excluded that in the accomplishment of this mission the members of the Church and its authorities might allow themselves to be taken in by the spirit of the world to which they are sent, since they are themselves weak sinners, and thus make the Church's position ambiguous. [224] The apostolic age did not yet display the symptoms of a crisis of this kind, in which members of the Church give in to Christ's second temptation (Lk 4:6) and compromise the purity of the gifts of the Spirit. Still it was not completely free of Satan's mischief in its midst. The same dangers of doctrinal and moral perversion which long before beset the people of the old alliance likewise lie in wait for those of the new. Referring to pertinent examples recounted in Scripture or Jewish tradition, the pastoral letters, that of Jude, the second of St. Peter, and the letters to the churches which open the book of Revelation ring with the sound of the battle which must be conducted against false doctors. [225] The significance of this battle is clear: instead of genuinely converting to the gospel message, the evil world sought to assimilate only what it found acceptable in it; rather than break with its sinful existence to enter eschatological existence, it dreamed of integrating the live forces of newborn Christianity with the old dreams so dear to paganism (cf. Ac 8: 18 ff.: the episode of Simon the magician, whom the fathers regarded as the creator of the false gnosis). All the future dramas in which the Church had to confront either political powers profoundly marked with the spirit of this world, or the cultural circles in which it was expressed, were thus foreshadowed from the moment when the apostolic Church came into contact with the Roman Empire permeated with Hellenistic civilization.

Parallel with this revelation of the world's sin, which adds nothing to what the cross had revealed, but which shows its permanent presence, the revelation of the judgment of the world continues apace, and the New

---

[223] Here we note again the duality pointed out above in regard to the relation of profane history to sacred history (above, pp. 297 ff.). Cf. A. Feuillet, *L'Apocalypse*, pp. 62-65.

[224] This will be the danger inherent in Christianity's various situations, quite similar to that which menaced the Jewish institution of old.

[225] See the commentaries on these books, for example: C. Spicq, *Les épîtres pastorales*, pp. lii-lxxii; J. Chaine, *Les épîtres catholiques*, pp. 58-80, 120 ff., 280-286; K. H. Schelkle, *Die Petrusbriefe. Der Judasbrief* (Herders theologischer Kommentar zum N.T.), pp. 230-239; E. B. Allo, *Saint Jean, L'Apocalypse*, pp. 57 ff.

Testament presents occasional evidence of it. In roundabout ways, Matthew and Luke seem to be aware of the divine judgment which has fallen on Judaism, [226] which rejected the call of Christ (Mt 22:7; Lk 21:20.24; cf. 19:43), while Revelation awaits the first signs of the judgment which cannot fail to strike the persecutor, the Roman Empire [227] (Rv 9:14 ff.; 16:12-16 seems to allude to the menace of the Parths [228]).

In brief, the New Testament furnishes a vision of history in which, in one way or another, everything takes on the nature of a sign in relation to certain general symbols which will remain in the background of all times to come. For this reason it can be said that all of profane history flows into sacred history and becomes progressively a part of it, in proportion as more and more of human society comes in contact with the gospel. The realization of the Church's mission in the world, considered in its positive results, would present much the same picture, but only in relation to an aspect of profane history in which the original plan of the Creator remained in some manner visible beneath the defiguration which sin inflicted on it. It is the whole negative aspect of the same profane history—incapable of integration into the sacramental history of the Church, since from the beginning it constitutes its sacrilegious counterpart—which now cooperates despite itself in the economy of salvation, just as in the time of Christ's earthly life Jewish incredulity, the opposition of the constituted authorities, and finally the betrayal of Judas, unwitting instruments of the monstrous venture of Satan against him who came to establish the kingdom of God here below, paradoxically accomplished the work of redemption. As long as the history of the Church continues to unfold, the whole sum of earthly things thus constitutes an enormous mass of significant realities whose hidden meaning remains to be disclosed.

## II. THE MYSTERY SIGNIFIED

To illumine ecclesial realities, and more generally the realities of human history in their relation to the Church, the New Testament casts a double light on them: that which comes from Christ, for the Church is nothing else

---

[226] Admittedly this literary recasting of the words of Jesus, intended to stress their historical accomplishment, is disputed by critics. We accept, on this point, the position of A. Wikenhauser, *New Testament Introduction* (New York: Herder, 1963), pp. 186 and 212 ff.

[227] On the difficult question of historical allusions in Revelation, see the discussion of the problem by A. Feuillet, *op. cit.*, pp. 36-52.

[228] While E. B. Allo is skeptical about the historical interpretation of the first of these two passages (*L'Apocalypse*, pp. 133 ff.), he comes out positively for the second (*ibid.*, p. 258).

but "Jesus Christ spread out and communicated," [229] and that which comes from the Old Testament, for the mystery of the people of God in history had already been realized in Israel as a foreshadowing, at the level of a figurative experience. With the aid of this double light, the mystery of the Church, the sacrament of Christ and of salvation, and the mystery of human history, now reduced to the norm of Christ, [230] appeared in bold relief. For us who are still involved with earthly life, the significance of all these things is to be sought in two directions: that of the end toward which our Christian existence is moving (the anagoge of the medieval theologians), and that of this existence itself (which the same theologians called tropology). In other terminology, we might speak of an eschatological meaning and an existential application.

## *1. Anagogic or Eschatological Sense*

*a) Christian life and the mystery of heaven.*—By his return to the Father, his resurrection and entry into the transfigured universe and paradise regained, Christ revealed the goal toward which Christian existence tends. [231] This goal, however, is not yet the object of direct apprehension. While through baptism man "tastes the gift from heaven, and receives a share of the Holy Spirit, and appreciates the good message of God and the powers of the world to come" [232] (Heb 6:4 ff.), this experience [233] takes place in the obscurity of faith. "We must be content to hope that we shall be saved— our salvation is not in sight, we should not have to be hoping for it if it were—but... we must hope to be saved since we are not saved yet—it is something we must wait for with patience" (Rm 8:24 ff.). How then can we speak of this world which is inaccessible to our senses, where Christ has already gone, and where we aspire to "stay with the Lord for ever" (1 Th 4:17; 5:10)? First, because the reception of the Holy Spirit constitutes its beginning and pledge (Rm 8:23; 2 Co 1:22; 5:8; Ep 1:14). But also because already here below our communion with God takes concrete form in the life of the Church, in such a way that on this tangible basis we can picture "the things that no eye has seen and no ear has heard, things beyond the mind of man, all that God has prepared for those who love him" (1 Co 2:9).

[229] J. B. Bossuet, *Œuvres oratoires*, ed. Lebarcq-Urbain-Levesque, Vol. 6, p. 508.

[230] H. Urs von Balthasar, *op. cit.*

[231] Above, pp. 252 f. On the eschatological tension of faith in Christ, cf. L. M. Dewailly, "Le temps et la fin du temps selon saint Paul," *LMD* 65 (1961), 133-143.

[232] On this text see C. Spicq, *L'épître aux Hébreux* 2, pp. 150 ff.

[233] The themes of Christian experience are excellently analyzed by J. Mouroux, *The Christian Experience* (New York: Sheed & Ward, 1954).

The new universe portrayed in Revelation (Rv 21:5) is not a product of pure imagination, a mythical representation devoid of realistic content.[234] Whether it is considered a present reality into which Christ has already entered (which is the anagogic sense), or as a future reality into which we will enter after our death and resurrection (which is the eschatological sense), it possesses a structure of which the Church in its terrestrial state constitutes the living sacrament.

The anagogic or eschatological significance of the Church is indicated by the book of Revelation when, although it applies to the heavenly city of God the various figures taken from the Old Testament (Jerusalem, the holy land, paradise, the twelve tribes), it makes its foundation the twelve apostles of Jesus Christ, the founders of the Church as a terrestrial society (Rv 21:14; cf. Ep 2:20). In this view, the Church's experience, figuratively sketched in the Old Testament, should be considered the foretaste and promise of the experience of heaven. In essence that experience will be nothing other than a life with God (Rv 21:3), a face to face vision of God (1 Co 13:12; 1 Jn 3:2), a transformation of man into the image of Christ (1 Co 15:45-53), life with Christ (Ph 1:23). But it should not be pictured as a solitary contemplation or beatitude: it will be, and already is, the assembly of the elect around Christ (1 Th 4:15-17; Mt 24:31; Rv 7; 22:3 ff.), as can be gathered from the earthly structure of the Church, its projection in time. Sacramental life too should be understood as the reflection[235] (εἰκών, Heb 10:1) of that ultra-terrestrial and supra-temporal mystery in which it already permits the faithful to participate. The eucharistic service is not only a memorial of the passion (1 Co 11:26), or more exactly of the Lord's sacrifice, which began with the shedding of his blood but was consummated by his ascension into heaven (Heb 9:11 ff. 24); it is also the proclamation of his return (1 Co 11:26; cf. Heb 9:28). Inasmuch as it is a meal with the risen Lord, it commences in a veiled manner the eschatological banquet of heaven[236] (Rv 3:20; 19:9). Likewise, the fact that in baptism we have risen with Christ to enter a new life (Rm 6:1-11; Jn 5:25) commences in the

---

[234] Once again we come across the problem raised by Bultmann with regard to "mythic" language which expresses the experience of faith. For Bultmann faith is not knowledge of supernatural realities, but a pure existential attitude from which flows a revelation to man of his own existence. The idea of a knowledge through signs, translated in symbolic language, seems to be rejected as a side product of Greek philosophy. This is not the place to discuss this viewpoint, in which 19th-century rationalism is curiously wed to Lutheran fideism. It is sufficient that we mark off our distance from it.

[235] On the meaning of this term, see above, p. 291, note 179.

[236] This sacramental presence of eternity in time is pointed out in similar fashion by O. Casel, "Hodie," *LMD* 65 (1961), 127-132, and J. Guitton, "L'éternité dans le temps," *ibid.*, pp. 144-154.

midst of time the mystery of our corporal resurrection, which is the object of our hope (Rm 8:23).

While the return of Christ, therefore, and also the resurrection of the body, and eternal life remain beyond the capacity of our imagination and intellect, it is still possible to affirm something positive about them, because our Christian life in practice teaches us something about the final act of human history. Seeing what the grace of God does in the Church now, we understand something of the goal toward which it tends. The very language of the New Testament indicates this interdependence of Christian existence and eschatology [237]; sometimes in fact, it actualizes eschatology to describe Christian life (Jn 5:25 compared with 5:28 f.); on other occasions it takes the same figures from the Old Testament to characterize indiscriminately the life of the Church in time and its consummation beyond time.

*b) Christian life and the mystery of final judgment.*—Eschatological significance is not limited to just the suffering and somber aspect of the Church's history. It goes deeper, for the revelation of the world's sin and of the judgment of God, begun in the Old Testament and consummated at the moment of the cross, [238] continues its course around the proclamation of the gospel, only to be consummated on the last day. [239] The mystery of iniquity which is presently at work in the world (2 Th 2:7) is also inevitably tending toward a sort of parousia (2 Th 2:3 f. 8-11). Based on the Church's actual experience of this diabolical action, therefore, it is possible to depict the moment when it will reach its climax (cf. Rv 13; 17), for between the antichrists to the final Antichrist [240] there is no break in continuity (cf. 1 Jn 2:18 ff.). We are already in the last times in which the perverse world launches its last attack on Christ (1 Jn 2:18; 1 Tm 4:1), the battle which Revelation describes in scriptural images (Rv 19:19; 20:7 ff.).

Consequently, the mystery of God's judgment, also presently at work, is similarly moving toward its final act. The representation of this

---

[237] This is the perspective required to overcome the opposition between consequent eschatology and realized eschatology, which some exegetes of the New Testament stress to excess (cf. A. Feuillet in Robert—Feuillet, *Introduction to the New Testament*, pp. 758-761).

[238] Above, pp. 250 f. and 263 f.

[239] On the complex of problems raised here, cf. B. Rigaux, *L'Antéchrist et l'opposition au royaume messianique dans l'Ancien et le Nouveau Testament* (Paris: Gembloux, 1932); *idem, Les épîtres aux Thessaloniciens,* pp. 247-280; R. Schnackenburg, *Die Johannesbriefe,* pp. 127-132.

[240] The term *antichrist* is found only in the letters of John, but it is there cited (1 Jn 2:18) as a well-known term. John is apparently actualizing a traditional apocalyptic representation. Cf. J. Bonsirven, *Épîtres de saint Jean* (Paris, 1935), pp. 134 ff.; J. Chaine, *Les épîtres catholiques,* pp. 166 ff.; R. Schnackenburg, *op. cit., in loco.*

denouement of human history, as the history of the sinful world, has long
been the subject of prophetic and apocalyptic literature; it cannot be claimed
that the New Testament offers anything really new on the subject, except
in one respect: it rearranges all the classic images around the person of Jesus
Christ, the glorious Messiah and son of man. The final judgment, the solemn
manifestation of a sentence passed at the moment of Christ's death (Jn 12:31),
will actually be nothing else but the total integration of all the particular
judgments passed in the course of history, either upon individual sinners
(for example 1 Co 11:30 ff.), or upon the human societies opposed to the
plan of God. But this theme, if the matter is studied thoroughly, is not
proper to the New Testament; it extends in perfect homogeneity from Genesis
(Gn 3:14-19; 6:5-7, etc.) to Revelation (Rv 6; 8—9; 14:6-20; 16; 18). It
does not strictly belong to Christian anagoge or eschatology, for which it
serves rather as a prelude. It applies to the whole of humanity this fundamental principle, that in a world held captive by sin, existence can only be
existence for death. Upon this principle, which is firmly rooted in the Old
Testament (cf. Gn 3:19; Ws 2:23 ff.), the New Testament makes only one
correction: Christ, by his cross, has radically changed the meaning of death
for those who through faith acquire eschatological existence. As a result,
the same corporal death becomes for some the means of victory (Rv 12:10 ff.)
whose reality will be manifested in their resurrection (Rv 20:4-6), while for
others it opens the way to second death (Rv 20:14 ff.).

c) The value and content of symbols in Christian eschatology.—To describe
the language with which Scripture announces the mystery of the ultimate
consummation of things, both for individuals and for all of mankind, more
than one critic has been tempted to call it mythical, since in this case, as in
that of the origin of things, the object described lies beyond the grasp of
our sensible apprehension, which is bound to the limits of our life in time. [241]
Actually, the word myth could in this case be given a perfectly acceptable
technical sense, [242] but it would remain ambiguous. The problem is not only
whether the language in question is realistic or symbolic, but from what source
the symbols which make it up were drawn. No symbolic language is a pure
product of the human imagination; at its origin there is always some existential
experience refracted through the prism of the imagination of a man or group

[241] This use of the word *myth* (above, p. 273) goes far beyond the use R. Bultmann,
whose position we have repeatedly discussed, makes of it. For a historical treatment
of the question, see P. Barthel, *Interprétation du langage mythique et théologie biblique*
(Leyden: Brill, 1963), pp. 15-67.

[242] A meaning given it basically by P. Ricœur, *Finitude et culpabilité. II. La
symbolique du mal*, pp. 153-165. But see the discussion between Ricœur and
G. Fessard, "Image, symbole et historicité" in E. Castelli (ed.), *Demitizzazione
e immagine* (Padua: CEDAM, 1962), pp. 43-79.

of men. [243] What is the significance of this experience, and of the symbolic imagination which provides its means of expression: these are the real questions on which the significance of the language itself depends. [244] In the present case, the existential experience in which the symbols are rooted, while belonging to the domain of common human experience, imply a practical experience of life with God, the life which Christ himself lived and which he made accessible to men, opening for them the way to eschatological existence—in the Old Testament, under the veil of a figurative history and cult; in the New, under the sacramental system in which the ultra—terrestrial reality is made present. [245] The source of the symbolic language, by a special disposition of divine providence, is therefore intimately linked to the revelation of salvation which God dispensed to his people. This language is not an accidental wrapping which human faith took on because of the contingencies of history; it is its normative expression, full of meaning and valid for all times by the very fact of its implantation in history. [246] The experience of Israel, now transfigured into the experience of the Church, is itself indicative of the invisible mystery toward which our faith and hope are directed.

## 2. Existential or Tropological Application

The tropology of the medieval exegetes is not coterminous with the field of morality in the strict sense this word received in counter-reform theology. It includes everything that concerns Christian existence, in the life of individuals as well as that of groups, "the Christian anthropology and spirituality which flows from dogma." [247] That is why Fr. de Lubac may legitimately speak in this regard of "mystical tropology," [248] since as a matter of fact it is a question of the Christian's internal experience of the mystery of Christ in the Church. Actually, this reflection on the significance of the ecclesial realities attested by the New Testament is something quite different from the anagogic or eschatological theology of which we have spoken. [249] It

---

[243] G. Gusdorf, *Mythe et métaphysique*, pp. 203-239.

[244] Despite its quite summary evaluations of Catholic theology, see the statement of the problem by G. Durand, *L'imagination symbolique* (Paris, 1964) (with bibliography); cf. S. Breton, "Présence et représentation, Essai sur l'imaginaire" in *Demitizzazione e immagine*, pp. 287-305.

[245] J. Daniélou, *Essai sur le mystère de l'histoire*, pp. 127-141.

[246] It should be noted that Bultmann's mythic reduction of language and his denial of any revelatory significance in history go hand in hand.

[247] H. de Lubac, *Exégèse médiévale, Les quatre sens de l'Écriture*, Part I, pp. 555 ff.

[248] *Ibid.*, chap. IX, pp. 549 ff.

[249] Cf. above, pp. 305 ff.

supposes that one recognizes in the person of Christ, and more especially in his cross and resurrection, the existentialist revelation [250] which definitely clarified the meaning of human life; that having chosen Christ by a decision of faith, one has himself already entered eschatological existence, presently experienced in the Church and directed toward its final fulness.   In this context, the daily problem is to renew this fundamental decision, in order to die in truth in Jesus Christ to live with him the life of the new man. New Testament realities, those of sacramental history as well as those of experiential history, clarify this problem and manifest all its dimensions. From the moment when the existentialist revelation imparted in Jesus Christ conferred a meaning on the experiences spoken of in Scripture, it has become possible to find multiple existential applications for each of them.

Although these applications have diverse aspects, they have a center of gravity: the decision which sinful man must make in regard to Jesus Christ. The apprehension of sin, of judgment and the danger of damnation, on the one hand, and of grace and the good news of salvation, on the other, present man with a choice which determines his position in relation to God, and consequently, his destiny.   To believe or to refuse to believe, to convert or to remain attached to evil, to love in response to the love of God or to close oneself to love: this alternative recurs at every moment in the life of all those who have met Jesus Christ, either during his lifetime, or through the proc-lamation of the gospel message.   It is useless to go into further detail in this regard.   Only it should be kept in mind that this summary of man's spiritual drama does not exhaust the content of the message announced in Scripture, [251] for the nature and importance of that drama can be truly measured only by relating their realism to the mystery of the incarnation, to the mystery of the living God revealed in the incarnation of his Son, and to the mystery of the Holy Spirit in the Church which the Christian sacraments bring to life.   It is this point which distinguishes the existential applications of Scripture, included in the prolongation of the mystical tropology of medieval theologians, from the existentialist interpretation proposed by Bultmann.   But since we have already discussed this matter above, we need not insist on it further.

---

[250] Above, pp. 250-254.
[251] Above, p. 251.

## § V. CONCLUSION: THE MEANING OF THINGS AND MEANING OF THE TEXTS

This chapter began with a classic theological question, that of the senses of Scripture. On this point, tracts on the science of interpretation are usually content to explain the doctrine of St. Thomas while attempting to adapt it to the perspectives opened by biblical criticism. [252] It seemed to us that this approach was insufficient. In the Bible, in fact, the meaning of things and the meaning of the text cannot be separated from one another, but they cannot be treated in the same way. The texts present realities which constitute the object of revelation; but these realities, because they are a part of salvation history, are themselves meaningful: it is through them that we perceive the mystery into which the life of faith conducts us. Thus the interpretation of biblical texts leads to an interpretation of the realities of which they speak, and this last is nothing else but theology. St. Thomas' *sensus rerum* does not, therefore, directly depend on what modern interpreters call exegesis, and it is understandable that St. Thomas could write that the meaning of things has no demonstrative value in theology. But that does not lessen the value of Sacred Scripture, for the spiritual sense contains nothing necessary to the faith which Scripture does not somewhere teach in its literal sense. [253] In truth, this spiritual sense is a part of theological reflection itself. It issues from the relation established by the comparison of texts between the various realities which constitute either the foundation or the object of faith. The whole of the present chapter, then, is a sort of theological synthesis whose center is Christ, and which, beginning with him extends in the form of sacred history: from the creation to Christ through the Old Testament, and from Christ to the eschatological consummation of things through the age of the Church.

Does this mean that this sort of discussion has no place in a treatment of the science of interpretation? It would be an error to think so, for the meaning of biblical texts can be properly understood only within a larger perspective, that of revelation and faith. Granted, there can be no question of determining that meaning *a priori* without recourse to the methods of exegesis. But exegesis is not an independent undertaking, limited to rational means, which can develop in a closed environment. The texts to be interpreted are the word of God; they reveal the mystery of God and of

---

[252] That is what we did in our treatment of "The Catholic Interpretation of the Sacred Books" in Robert—Feuillet, *Interpreting the Scriptures*, pp. 202-208.

[253] Ia, q. 1, art. 10, *in corp.*

salvation.  While human reason should apply all its energies to understand them, it ought to do so within the act of faith which opens it to the word of God which reveals the mystery.  When we turn now to the problems proper to exegesis, we will constantly come across the doctrinal factors synthesized in this chapter; they will always be present in the background, even when methodical procedure requires us to abstract from them for the moment.

# CHAPTER VII

# BIBLICAL HERMENEUTICS

In our historical account of the problem of interpretation in chapter V, the present state of the problem gradually became clear.[1] The classic doctrine of the senses of Scripture, even under the form St. Thomas gave it, was evidently not developed with this situation in mind. So it is not surprising that there exists a gap between its conclusions, which are presented in the majority of theological tracts *De sacra Scriptura*, and the practical requisites of contemporary exegesis. Nevertheless, by clearly distinguishing the sense of biblical texts *(sensus litteralis)* from the sense of the things of which Scripture speaks *(sensus rerum* or *sensus spiritualis)*, St. Thomas achieved a first clarification whose importance we have pointed out. In our analysis of the content of this *sensus rerum* in chapter VI, we outlined a theological synthesis, which took on the same form as salvation history, centered on the person of Jesus Christ. There remains the *sensus litteralis*, the proper field of an exegesis organically related to theology. It is within this limited field that the whole question of the science of biblical interpretation must be treated. But on this point the doctrine of St. Thomas is too elementary to satisfy the needs of modern exegesis and theology. Moreover, before treating the method of interpretation as such, we must first examine the fundamental question of the *sensus litteralis* itself: what is to be said of it now that critical usage has accustomed us to a certain notion of literal sense which the encyclical *Divino afflante Spiritu* fully adopted?[2]

## § I. THE SENSE OF SCRIPTURAL TEXTS

### I. THE THEOLOGICAL PROBLEM OF THE SENSE OF BIBLICAL TEXTS

#### I. STATEMENT OF THE PROBLEM

The definition of the *sensus litteralis* of Scripture has varied down through the ages to keep pace with the cultural evolution whose repercussions

---

[1] Above, pp. 221-233.
[2] Above, p. 237, note 13.

necessarily influenced theology. We can dispense with a discussion of those early medieval texts in which the literal sense was restricted to what we today would call the proper sense, the metaphorical sense having been classed under the *sensus figuralis* and more or less placed in the category of the spiritual senses of Scripture. [3] In the Thomistic classification, the notion of *sensus litteralis*, which can be proper or metaphorical according to the case, completely overcame this confusion. [4] Nevertheless, St. Thomas accorded the *sensus litteralis* of Scripture a greater extension than modern criticism gives the literal sense; he included in it all the instruction which God, the primary author of Scripture, gives us through the letter of the text; he was unconcerned whether this instruction pertained explicitly to the didactic intent of the sacred writers, the instrumental authors whom God moved to formulate his own word. [5] It is precisely this point that modern criticism emphasizes, and it is on the basis of the human author's intention that the literal sense of the text is defined. The *sensus litteralis* defined by St. Thomas and in constant use by theologians who follow him thus poses an important problem: Did the divine didactic intention and that of his human instrument perfectly coincide, or can there be a difference between them? On the one hand, it is certain that a text cannot have a meaning contrary to the intention of the man who wrote it; a sane theology of inspiration even necessitates the admission that the instruction given by God in the biblical texts necessarily passed through the didactic intention of the sacred authors. [6] But must it be concluded that that teaching is limited to their explicit intention?

To this question, critical science can provide no answer. Its field is limited by definition to an investigation of the sense which results from the author's intention, such as a rational analysis of his writing allows one to comprehend it, taking into account the milieu, the age, and the circumstances in which it was written. In the context of such an analysis, there is a place for a study of the mental mechanism at work in the author's subconscious; it is thus possible to bring to light certain ideological implications in the

---

[3] C. Spicq, *Esquisse d'une histoire de l'exégèse latine au moyen âge*, pp. 20-21, 27. See also Hugh of St. Victor, *Eruditio didascalica* (*PL* 176, 801).

[4] Above, p. 202. On this point, cf. P. Synave, "La doctrine de saint Thomas d'Aquin sur le sens littéral," *RB* 35 (1926), 48-61.

[5] Certain allusions, however, show indirectly that St. Thomas distinguished the two levels and considered it possible that they might differ. He writes, for example, in *De potentia:* "If those who explain Sacred Scripture adapt some things to its letter which its author did not understand, there is no doubt that the Holy Spirit, who is the principal author of divine Scripture, understood it. Hence any truth which can be adapted to divine Scripture while safeguarding the meaning of the letter is its meaning" (*De Potentia*, q. 4, art. 1).

[6] Above, p. 110.

text which do not appear at first sight. But this study remains at the level of psychology, which contributes no special light in understanding and defining the intentions of God. Theology views the matter differently. For it the Bible is one book, which possesses an internal unity, and whose whole concerns an all-embracing object: the revelation of the mystery of salvation of men in Jesus Christ, and, through the dispensation of this salvation (which the Greek fathers called the economy), the revelation of the mystery of God (or theology). The particular message which each biblical author consciously brought to the people of God is positively ordered to this total revelation; the effect of inspiration is to predispose its ultimate goal just as it does its language. But the author himself does not necessarily have clear consciousness of the fulness of revelation to which he contributes in a fragmentary way. His act of writing takes place in a providential disposition which certainly does not totally escape him, but of which he necessarily has only a limited view.

This fact is clear in the Old Testament. No sacred writer then possessed a full knowledge of the economy of salvation he was testifying, since Christ had not yet come. Certainly, the only purpose of his work was to manifest or to set down in writing the revelation of this mystery, which he apprehended through his faith and, according to the case, through his prophetic charism; but it was only within the limits of his explicit knowledge that he possessed it. As long as Christ had not entered into man's historical experience, this knowledge necessarily remained in an inchoative state; the author was radically incapable of presenting a perfect expression of the full richness of a mystery of which he had only a glimpse. His work, one could say, lends itself to two successive readings. At the level of his clear and distinct consciousness, it already possesses an undeniable doctrinal aim; it already supplies positive information on the mystery of our salvation in Christ, in the measure that that mystery was revealed when the author composed it. [7] But reread in the light of Christ's advent and of the gospel announced to the world, it acquires a new depth; its ambiguities disappear, its insufficiencies are filled, its limits are broken, for the aspects of the mystery it aimed to present without being able to do so adequately now appear in all their fulness. And it is perfectly legitimate to give this fulness of meaning to a text which formerly provided only an inchoative expression of doctrine: this is only to trace the development of revelation, in which a given text occupies a determined place, like a station along the way from its source to its final destination.

---

[7] Concerning the revelation of the mystery of Christ in the Old Testament, see *Sens chrétien de l'A.T.*, pp. 125-141.

Even in the New Testament, a similar phenomenon can be detected. In the first place, while it is true that the mystery of salvation is fully revealed at this final stage of sacred history, it is still necessary to allow for a certain development in time. In particular, the earthly life of Christ and his apparitions after the resurrection, the starting point for the age of the Church, constitute clearly distinct stages in New Testament revelation. Since this is so, it is to be expected that the words pronounced by Christ before his death should take on a deeper meaning when they pass from one stage to the other. Even within the apostolic Church, while it is true that the fulness of the mystery of Christ was already revealed in substance since his resurrection, that does not mean that each of the apostles perfectly discerned all its implications, nor that each of the sacred authors perfectly manifests all its aspects in each of his texts. Every text, therefore, when it is placed within the whole of apostolic tradition and of the Scriptures which are evidence of it, is susceptible of an illumination which will reveal rich implications which were hardly perceptible at a first reading. This supplementary light is not foreign to the text's deep purpose, but it does go beyond the explicit intent of its author.

## II. QUESTIONS OF TERMINOLOGY

The terminology used to designate this deepening of the literal sense is not yet definitively fixed. Taking his cue from a passage of the encyclical *Providentissimus*, Fr. Lagrange wrote in 1900: "These words (of the encyclical) seem to allude to a sort of supraliteral sense which can be determined only by a competent authority. Given belief in the inspiration of the Scriptures, it must be admitted that they contain more than the obvious and purely literal sense." [8] In 1927 Fr. A. Fernández preferred to speak of a *sensus plenior ac profundior*, [9] which lies beneath the *sensus litteralis*. Since then the problem has centered on this Latin expression *(sensus plenior)*, usually called the fuller sense in English, and a growing number of exegetes and theologians make use of it to explain the corresponding doctrine. [10] It cannot be said, however, that it has received universal approval. [11] In 1950

---

[8] M. J. Lagrange, "L'interprétation de la sainte Écriture par l'Église," *RB* 9 (1900), 141.

[9] *Institutiones biblicae*, 2nd ed. (Rome: P.I.B., 1927), p. 306.

[10] A bibliography can be found in the works of J. Coppens, *Les harmonies des deux Testaments: Essai sur les divers sens des Écritures et sur l'unité de la révélation* (Tournai-Paris: Casterman, 1949) and R. E. Brown, *The 'Sensus Plenior' of Sacred Scripture* (Baltimore: St. Mary, 1955) (complemented by "The 'Sensus Plenior' in the Last Ten Years," *CBQ* 25 [1963], 262-285). Cf. *Sens chrétien de l'A.T.*, pp. 449 ff.

[11] It might be added that the very definition of the fuller sense is the object of discussion among those who admit its existence. Concerning the exposition by

G. Courtade [12] questioned the existence of a fuller sense; while still admitting that the literal sense of biblical texts might acquire, in the framework of the whole of revelation, a meaning which surpasses their author's intent, he based his objection on the doctrine of inspiration. Other opposing voices have been heard, all of which repeat a similar thesis: as R. E. Brown [13] noted in regard to C. H. Giblin, J. L. McKenzie, T. Barrosse, and B. Vawter, it would be better to speak of a "fuller understanding" of the literal sense than a "fuller sense," and the theological meaning of Scripture is to be found precisely here. In this view, B. Vawter sees in the theory of a fuller sense only a residue of the patristic doctrine of the four senses, which needlessly complicates the question. [14] On the contrary, Dom Charlier regards it a fortunate revival of the ancient distinction between literal sense and spiritual sense. [15]

These discussions about terminology go deeper than mere terminology. The question is whether the fulness of meaning which theology and Christian pastoral use legitimately attribute to a biblical text was objectively given it at the moment of its composition by an inspired author. If one replies in the affirmative, he must explain how this could happen without the author's knowledge; if he replies negatively, he must explain how the meaning in question can still be considered objective, as distinguished from arbitrary accommodations of which Jewish and Christian interpreters have provided numerous examples. It is our position that the fuller sense is a real and objective sense of Scripture. Not only is it not foreign to the literal sense as criticism defines it, neither is it, properly speaking, a distinct sense: it is the same literal sense grasped at a second level of depth. Since it owes its existence to the Holy Spirit, the principal author of whom every sacred

P. Sansegondo, *Exposicion historico-critica del hoy llamado 'Sensus plenior' de la Sagrada Escritura* (Avila: Revista Studium, 1963), see the remarks of J. J. O'Rourke in *CBQ* 26 (1964), 501 ff., who refers to his own article, "Marginal Notes on the Sensus Plenior," *CBQ* 21 (1959), 64-71.

[12] G. Courtade, "Les Écritures ont-elles un sens plénier?," *RSR* 41 (1950), 481-499. Likewise, R. Bierberg, "Does Sacred Scripture Have a Sensus Plenior?," *CBQ* 10 (1948), 181-195; C. Spicq, "L'Écriture et saint Thomas," *Bulletin Thomiste* 8 (1947-1953), 210-221, who nevertheless speaks "of the depth or the density of the literal sense" (p. 217).

[13] In *CBQ* 25 (1963), 273-281. Cf. C. H. Giblin, " 'As it is Written!...' — A Basic Problem in Noematics and its Relevance to Biblical Theology," *CBQ* 20 (1958), 327-354, 477-498; J. L. McKenzie, *The Two-Edged Sword* (Milwaukee: Bruce, 1956), pp. 295-308; *idem,* "Problems of Hermeneutics in Roman Catholic Exegesis," *JBL* 77 (1958), 197-204; T. Barrosse, "The Senses of Scripture and the Liturgical Pericopes," *CBQ* 21 (1959), 1-23; B. Vawter, *The Conscience of Israel* (New York: Sheed & Ward, 1961), pp. 289-295.

[14] B. Vawter, "The Fuller Sense, Some Considerations," *CBQ* 26 (1964), p. 96.

[15] C. Charlier, "Méthode historique et lecture spirituelle des Écritures," *BVC* 18 (1957), p. 26.

writer is an instrument, it would be possible to call it a spiritual sense. [16]
This distinction of literal and spiritual sense, however, which is quite different
from the terminology of St. Thomas, is not exactly the same as the Pauline
distinction between the letter and the spirit. Besides the fact that Paul had
only the Old Testament in mind, he conceived the letter in a disparaging
way, as an understanding of Scripture which excludes all reference to Christ
who is its key; but the modern notion of literal sense is indifferent to the
judgment an exegete might make in this regard. As for the *sensus litteralis*
of St. Thomas, the foundation of Christian theology, it always implies the
fulness of meaning which biblical texts acquire in relation to the mystery
of Christ; while including our literal sense, therefore, it would correspond
to what we call the fuller sense. So it does not seem opportune to translate
*sensus litteralis* by literal sense, if ambiguity is to be avoided. It would
be better to speak of the literary sense, that is, the meaning of the text (of
the letter) as opposed to the significance of the realities of which the text
speaks. This literary sense thus contains two levels, closely related one to
the other: that of the literal sense, which is the goal of critical study, and that
of the fuller sense, which makes use of the results of criticism, but surpasses
them.

## II. THE PASSAGE FROM LITERAL SENSE TO FULLER SENSE

The literal sense poses no special problem, since the sacred author's didactic
intention suffices to define it: once that intention is objectively determined
and its literary expression is properly appreciated, the literal sense is
established. It need only be remarked that the intention in question is
always of the doctrinal order; its aim, and therefore the formal object of
the resulting text, in every case have to do with the mystery of man's salvation,
finally revealed as the mystery of Christ. [17] The literal sense so defined
constitutes a meeting place not only for exegetes of the various Christian
confessions, but for all who take an interest in the Bible, whether believers
or not. We will return to this question when we take up the question of the
methodology for determining the literal sense. [18] The problem of the fuller
sense, on the contrary, is much more complex. We will attempt to define
it as precisely as possible for each of the Testaments, and following that,
to determine what place it occupies in the traditional interpretation of
Scripture.

[16] The spiritual sense of Scripture is one of the points on which terminology
fluctuates the most; cf. *Sens chrétien de l'A.T.*, p. 444 (bibliography in note 6).
  [17] Above, pp. 106 f.
  [18] Below, pp. 361 f.

### I. THE FULLER SENSE IN THE OLD TESTAMENT

We treated this question at length in an earlier work, *Sens chrétien de l'Ancien Testament*. [19]   We will content ourselves here with a summary of our conclusions.

### *1. Existence of the Fuller Sense*

The present question can be properly treated only if a soundly established principle of Christian doctrine is kept in mind: the people of the Old Testament, although they lived before the coming of Christ, already lived in the mystery of Christ; although Christ had not yet manifested himself in history, their faith gave them a rudimentary knowledge of his mystery, in proportion to the participation in it allotted them. [20]   Consequently, those among them whom a special charism led to set down divine revelation in writing wrote nothing except in the perspective of this mystery, which even then constituted its unique object.   It can therefore be said that all their writings really point to this mystery, [21] though they could never provide more than an imperfect and provisional formulation of it, according to the partial knowledge they had of it.

Is it possible to clarify somewhat, with the aid of the results of exegesis, the manner in which the texts in question point to the mystery of Christ? Yes, but by distinguishing two categories of texts.   On the one hand, the eschatological promises of the prophets have as their object the full realization of the plan of salvation at the end of sacred history, even if, in their description of the future, the *eschaton* properly so called cannot be clearly distinguished from more proximate events which carry history toward it.   Thus in second Isaiah the postexilic restauration is constantly superimposed upon eschatological salvation.   In such cases the literal sense of the text points directly to the mystery of Christ to come; it furnishes a theology in anticipation of it which differs only in depth and precision.   Then there are all the other texts. In their literal sense they concern directly the life of the people of God such as the institutions of the old alliance made it: law and practical wisdom which flowed from it, history in which is established a relation between God and his people that frequently becomes a drama, prayer and liturgical life in which that relation finds its concrete expression.   All these texts are related to the mystery of Christ only indirectly, in the measure that it was actually experienced by Israel, and can be perceived by way of the implications

[19] *Sens chrétien de l'A. T.*, pp. 449-455, 458-499.
[20] *Ibid.*, pp. 125-159.
[21] Above, pp. 83-85.

of a faith which "before receiving any of the things that had been promised...
saw them in the far distance and welcomed them" (Heb 11:13).

Such is the fuller sense that an analysis of the Old Testament reveals.
Beyond the clear ideas which the sacred authors had of the mystery of God
with men, such as they experienced it and expected its consummation at
the end of time, their works contain information on the reality of salvation
that was later made manifest in Jesus Christ. Consequently, beneath their
imperfect, and sometimes even elementary formulations, it is legitimate to
search out its presence, thus enriching the words and concepts they used by
projecting on them the fulness of meaning which the whole of revelation
entails.

### 2. The Fuller Sense and the Inspired Authors' Consciousness [22]

Were the inspired authors conscious of the fuller sense which we find in
their writings after the fact? If by consciousness we mean clear and distinct
knowledge, obviously not; otherwise there would be no distinction between
the literal sense and the fuller sense. But does the knowledge of faith refer
completely to clear and distinct ideas? Do those faithless critics who,
when they analyze the biblical texts retrace the history of religious ideas in
Israel, possess the secret of Israel's faith? The life of faith is a personal
relation between man and God in Jesus Christ. The real knowledge that
it implies (to use the terminology of Newman [23]) is proportionately deep;
the very richness of its object causes it always to surpass the notions and
words that serve to express it. [24] In the Old Testament, as St. Thomas rightly
noted, it has an implicit content [25] which is confusedly perceived in the shadow
of a living experience that is richer than its notional expression. That is
precisely where the fuller sense of biblical texts is found. And that is the
reason it must be regarded as an objective sense, although it cannot be
attained through a mere analysis of the concepts which are signified by their
words. In his article on the fulness of meaning of the sacred books, Fr. Benoit

[22] *Sens chrétien de l'A.T.*, pp. 452-455.

[23] J. H. Newman, *A Grammar of Assent*, chap. IV.

[24] This is precisely the fact noted in the encyclical *Providentissimus*, in the
passage commented upon by Fr. Lagrange, who spoke in this regard of a supra-literal
sense: "For the language of the Bible is employed to express, under the inspiration
of the Holy Spirit, many things which are beyond the power and scope of the reason
of man—that is to say, divine mysteries and all that is related to them. There is
sometimes in such passages a fullness and a hidden depth of meaning which the
letter hardly expresses and which the laws of interpretation hardly warrant" (*RB* 9
(1900), 141; text in *Ench. B.*, 108).

[25] Cf. II^a II^ae, q. 1, art. 7, *in corp.* (increase of the articles of faith
"*quoad explicationem*").

preferred to emphasize the sacred writers' lack of consciousness of the activity God caused them to undertake as part of a total revelation whose outcome they evidently could not have known.[26] He nevertheless noted "in the primary literal sense, that is, in the consciousness of the sacred writer, a certain implicit content, like an obscure halo in which the author glimpses, in a confused manner in which the intuitions of the heart play a great role, the mysterious implications of his message."[27] It is this point which we prefer to emphasize, so that the fuller sense is organically linked to the psychology of the sacred writers, and its use does not seem like one of those artifices of exegesis which modern critics, using the criteria they employ in their own work, often denounce in the writings of the fathers of the Church.

### 3. Investigation into the Fuller Sense

Investigation into the fuller sense supposes the prior understanding of the literal sense, but it is carried on in another way. To determine the literal sense of the biblical texts, Scripture is read in the order of time; the historical and ideological outlook which limits each author's message is everywhere taken into account. Although the goal toward which the Old Testament tends as preparation, pedagogy and prefiguration of the mystery of Christ[28] is known, and although this global view of God's plan makes possible a more exact evaluation of the texts and an exclusion of certain false interpretations,[29] the literal sense is prohibited by principle from resorting to this source to determine the meaning of the passage under analysis and its author's didactic intent. It is possible to find in the Old Testament texts whose meaning deepened considerably in the course of time, both in the use that later authors made of them, and in the interpretation they occasionally gave them.[30] But this growth in meaning, which accompanies the development of revelation, never reached the fulness which only Christ can give to sacred Scripture. Conversely, the search for the fuller sense supposes a regressive reading of the Bible, one that begins with the New Testament and goes back in order of time. When read with Jesus Christ as their starting point, the

---

[26] P. Benoit, "La plénitude de sens des livres saints," *RB* 69 (1960), 174 ff.

[27] *Ibid.*, p. 172. The fact is pointed out with more accuracy, for the authors of both Testaments, by J. Schildenberger: By reason of divine inspiration "the human author has in the depths of his spirit a deep, illuminating, silent understanding of the subject in question, which does not have to rise fully to his clear consciousness, but which determines his compositional concepts and consequently his words, and is thus expressed in them" (*Vom Geheimnis des Gotteswortes*, p. 84).

[28] Above, pp. 257 f.

[29] Above, pp. 108, 124-126.

[30] *Sens chrétien de l'A.T.*, pp. 458 ff.; cf. P. Benoit, *RB* 69 (1960), 184 ff.

texts take on their definitive dimensions. Then it becomes clear what aspects of the mystery of salvation are there sketched in groping and imperfect expressions. And as a consequence the object toward which they pointed in a certain manner, but which necessarily surpassed their conceptual affirmation, becomes fully apparent.

There need never be any fear that this regressive reading will contradict the conclusions of critical study. On the contrary, the two mesh perfectly, since the aspect of the mystery of Christ sketched in any text whatsoever is to be found precisely in the prolongation of the teaching its author purposely wrote into it. The relation of the literal sense to the fuller sense is basically no different than that of Old Testament faith to Christian faith. These two actualizations of the same attitude of faith, defined as obedience to the word of God, have the same structure in different circumstances; that is why, despite the transformation brought about by Christ, they retain a perfect continuity. And the religious concepts used to express them are in a similar situation with relation to Christ, thus assuring manifold points of agreement between them. The search for the fuller sense rightly makes use of these points of agreement; they are the basis for finding indications of the mystery of Christ in the Old Testament. [31] Thus it reaches what St. Paul called the spirit of Scripture, [32] without losing contact with what modern interpreters call the literal sense. [33] The whole aim of patristic and medieval exegesis was nothing but this. [34] From a critical point of view, their methods are open to criticism; it is quite possible that in a number of cases the relation of the mystery of Christ to the texts of the Old Testament was established with the aid of artificial methods and was uncritical. As such they cannot be examples for us. But we ought to have a just esteem of the profound purpose that moved them, and without abandoning our critical requirements, we ought to assume their goals as our own, so that our exegesis might similarly contribute to theology and the care of souls as our faith demands.

## II. THE FULLER SENSE IN THE NEW TESTAMENT

The problem of the fuller sense must be treated differently for the texts of the New Testament. For all of them explicitly deal with the mystery of

[31] Some examples are given in *Sens chrétien de l'A.T.*, pp. 126-141, 460 ff.

[32] On the opposition Γράμμα/Πνεῦμα, see G. Schrenk, *TWNT* I, pp. 765-768.

[33] This problem was already raised by Lefèvre d'Étaples and was given the same solution. See the two typical texts quoted by H. de Lubac, *Exégèse médiévale*, Part II, Vol. 2, pp. 412 ff. (on the literal sense which is no other than the Jewish letter, and that which coincides with the spiritual sense).

[34] H. de Lubac, *Histoire et esprit: L'intelligence de l'Écriture d'après Origène* (Paris: Aubier, 1950), pp. 267-294; *Exégèse médiévale*, Part I, pp. 355-363; M. Pontet, *L'exégèse de saint Augustin prédicateur* (Paris: Aubier, 1944), pp. 149-194.

Christ fully manifested in human history as the accomplishment of the salvation promised long before. There can no longer be any question of a gap between the didactic intent of the authors and the definitive content of their works, as in the Old Testament. Fr. Benoit, who developed his theory of the fuller sense on the basis of the Old Testament, does not apply it to the New. [35] Two facts lead us, however, to believe that in the texts of the latter there are rich implications of which the sacred authors were not completely conscious [36]: 1) the internal development of revelation between the birth of Christ until the end of the apostolic age; 2) the close connection between the various aspects of salvation, finally viewed in its fulness.

### *1. The Internal Development of Revelation*

In New Testament revelation, time still plays a pivotal role. It is, in fact, through a series of historical experiences that the mystery of salvation was manifested in all its dimensions. In this regard, two points must be distinguished.

*a) The two periods of the manifestation of Christ.*—First of all, considering Christ as the bearer of revelation, a clear distinction must be made between the time when he participated in the history of the present world, and the time when he appeared in glory to his disciples. [37] The first period already evidences a real development in the revelation given by Christ, both in word and in deed. It was not for nothing that Jesus first led a hidden life, then announced the gospel of the kingdom of God, then witnessed his ministry opposed and rejected, and was finally arrested and put to death. These events had their effect on his words and deeds; both remained enigmatic for those who first witnessed them (Lk 2:50; Mk 8:17; 9:11.33), for their intent seemed to change in proportion to the unfolding of the drama which ended in the cross. But there was a second period. When Christ manifested himself to his own in the glory of his resurrection, he was not content to open their minds to the understanding of the Scriptures (Lk 24:45). All the words he pronounced before his death, and all the acts he had previously performed at the same time acquired their definitive meaning in relation to the mystery of salvation then consummated. It was not a question of imposing on them an interpretation foreign to their obvious meaning, as if faith in the risen Christ had become the basis of an ideological system to

---

[35] "La plénitude de sens des livres saints," *RB* 69 (1960), 184 ff.

[36] In this we agree with the position of R. E. Brown, "The 'Sensus Plenior' in the Last Ten Years," *CBQ* 25 (1963), 271-274.

[37] Above, pp. 242-246.

which the legacy of Jesus was, for better or worse, adapted. [38] In reality, the acts and words of Christ included a mysterious content until then grasped in the shadow of an imperfect faith, but then revealed in its full richness. The gospel texts thus do not lend themselves to two different readings, that of the historian, who attempts to follow the passage of time from Jesus' conception to his death, and that of the theologian, who, guided by the sacred writers themselves, reconstructs it on the basis of the resurrection.

  *b) The experience of the apostolic Church.*—That is not all, for the time of the resurrection was only the starting point of the Church. Even within the age of the Church, the apostolic body went through a series of significant experiences, [39] through which revelation became more explicit: the experience of the Holy Spirit, who "leads to the complete truth" (Jn 16:13) and calls to mind the words of Christ (Jn 14:26) to give the apostles a full understanding of them; the experience of ecclesiastical and sacramental life, which concretely manifested the content of the grace of redemption; the experience of opposition and persecution, which showed the permanence of the drama of the cross in the life of the Church (cf. Ac 4:24-30; 5:41); the experience of rejection of the gospel by Judaism, which provoked the evangelization of the pagan world until the Church detached itself completely from the synagogue; the experience of conflict with the totalitarian pagan empire, which produced a recognition of the real situation of the Church in a sinful world. In proportion as this history unfolded, the mysterious significance contained in the words and acts of Christ gradually emerged. That is why the gospel syntheses preserved for us give evidence of a theological reflection in which the words of Christ and recollections of his life take on a fulness of meaning which they did not originally possess. [40]

  It is true that in the cases we have just considered, the passage from the literal sense to the fuller sense is a part (at least in principle) of the didactic intent of the final authors to whom we owe the New Testament books. But

---

[38] Concerning this opposition between the 'gospel of Christ' and the 'gospel about Christ,' common to rationalist criticism (Guignebert), liberal Protestantism (Harnack), modernism (Loisy) and R. Bultmann, see X. Léon-Dufour, *The Gospels and the Jesus of History*, pp. 53 f. A similar effort to overcome this approach to the problem will be noted in H. Anderson, *Jesus and Christian Origins* (New York: Oxford, U.P., 1964).

  [39] Above, pp. 300-304.

  [40] It is in this sense that a distinction can be made with P. Henry, "La Bible et la théologie" in Robert—Tricot, *Initiation biblique*³, pp. 967 ff., between the meaning of the spoken word and the meaning of the written word, even if certain qualifications must be made concerning this formulation of the question. The problem is only touched in passing by R. Thibaut, *Le sens des paroles du Christ* (Paris: Desclée, 1940); see pp. 48 f., 94 f.

we have no assurance that they performed this operation for all the words and all the acts of Christ in a complete and systematic way. On the basis of the examples they themselves have provided, and as a prolongation of their explicit testimony, there is, therefore, room for theological research which the exegete cannot afford to neglect.

## 2. The Internal Coherence of the Mystery of Salvation

It must be noted, finally, that the object of Christian faith, as it is revealed in the New Testament, is not made up of a collection of unrelated truths strung up one next to the other like pearls on a necklace. The person of Christ is at the center of the mystery of salvation, and all the aspects of that mystery are organically related to him. This fact not only relates them one to another; it gives them intimate links and points of agreement. Thus it is, for example, between the eternal life Christ entered by his resurrection, and its communication to men in the Church under sacramental signs; between the collective experience of the Church community immersed in the history of the present world, and the experience of the individual Christian which is only a participation in it; between the acts of Christ during his earthly life, and the communication of salvation in the Church; between the mystery of the Church, which is the new humanity saved by grace, and the mystery of Mary in whom this eschatological reality is manifested as in its prototype. [41]

Since this is so, how can the scriptural texts which touch any one of these points fail to cast a light also on all the others connected with it? And how can it be denied that this light belongs to the objective sense of Scripture, even though the sacred authors did not explicitly have it in mind? Here again, it is not a case of adding elements foreign to their texts, or *a fortiori* opposed to them; it is a matter of investigating their implications, their virtual content, using as a guide what theology calls the analogy of faith. [42] Too often this principle is used only as a negative criterion, which prohibits attributing to a sacred text a meaning that is not in harmony with the whole of revelation. [43] In fact, this principle ought to be applied also in a positive role. [44] It would then enable one to go beyond the explicit intentions of the sacred authors, who were limited by the outlook of their age, influenced by the practical problems they had to face, interested in particular aspects of

[41] On this last point, cf. above, pp. 292-295.

[42] J. Levie, *The Bible, Word of God in Words of Men*, pp. 247-252.

[43] This is the viewpoint taken by the encyclical *Providentissimus*, Ench. B., 109.

[44] This point is admitted in principle by A. Fernández, *Institutiones biblicae*, 3rd ed., pp. 481-483, but no practical consequence is drawn from it.

the mystery of Christ. Beginning with occasional texts, whose object is often restricted, the fuller sense aims to attain the totality of a religious thought whose various components make up a coherent whole. Respect for the literal sense established through critical study does not forbid— quite the contrary—seeking out its manifold implications. The resulting fuller sense may thus take on one of any number of forms, given the multiple connections of every aspect of the mystery of salvation.

The operations we have been describing cannot but be baffling to critics outside the faith. For them, the study of New Testament texts has as its unique goal to retrace the religious ideas in primitive Christianity; there is no question, then, of leaving the field of the literal sense. But for anyone who has experienced the faith, this approach is highly questionable. Not that the literal sense of the texts does not lend itself to retracing this history of religious ideas. But the truth found in Scripture is not situated simply at the level of ideas developed in human groups, in this case, the Christian communities of the apostolic age. Since the object of that truth is the personal relation with Christ the Lord which every believer may live in the Church, it dominates the field of human ideas, since it defines their purpose and shapes their real content. [45] Consequently, only from the standpoint of the faith is one in a position to gather the whole truth contained in Scripture. This was the attitude of Christian exegesis in every age; it took great care to read the texts as the word of God, and not as simple human documents. And the passage from literal sense to fuller sense was always made spontaneously, for the New Testament as well as for the Old. On this point, our age is returning to the practice of the Middle Ages and patristic antiquity. [46]

### III. THE FULLER SENSE AND THE TRADITIONAL INTERPRETATION OF SCRIPTURE

The time has come to step back a bit from the problem we have been considering in order to relate it to the question we treated in chapter I: the relation

---

[45] Non-believing criticism, whose concern is this history of ideas, might in all good faith think that it respects their integrity in the measure that it is a neutral observer in their regard. But that is an illusion, for this supposed neutrality in fact includes a negative value judgment which holds them to be non-credible. By that token their import and their existential content become difficult to perceive, for these are genuinely observable only from within, through participation in the act of faith which gives them meaning. Not that the non-believer is condemned to a radical lack of understanding: he might bring to his study a sympathetic understanding which more or less makes up for his lack of explicit faith by allowing him to imagine what faith would be for him if he had it. But the less the measure of such sympathy, the more his capacity for understanding diminishes.

[46] This is well noted by J. Schildenberger, *Vom Geheimnis des Gotteswortes*, pp. 80-86, in the section he devotes to the fulness of meaning of Sacred Scripture.

of Scripture to ecclesiastical tradition considered as ways of access to the word of God. For the Christian, let us recall, the only source of the faith is the apostolic tradition. [47] Considered in its totality, it contains the entire message of salvation, the whole gospel, and for that reason includes also an authentic interpretation of the scriptures and the tradition which preceded it. Through the inspired texts of the New Testament this apostolic tradition remains directly accessible; but this does not mean that the texts in question explicitly present all of its content. While they are authentic witnesses of the legacy of the apostles, they are no less occasional, fragmentary, limited. [48] How then can the Church still find the fulness of the deposit by which it must continue to live?

To resolve this thorny question, it must first be recalled that Scripture is not an isolated reality, standing over against the Church, which should be pictured as an assembly of believers. What Christ bequeathed to men was not first of all Scripture, the literary crystallization of a message he had confided to his apostles; rather it was his Church, founded upon the apostles and animated by the Holy Spirit. This Church did not change in nature when it passed from the age in which the apostles founded and organized it to that in which it had to continue its course in history without them. In ecclesiastical tradition, the apostolic deposit continued to be transmitted faithfully, thanks to the structure given it from the beginning. Scripture is one of these essential structures, [49] just as are the ministry, which assures the permanent presence of the apostolate among men, and the sacraments, through which the grace of salvation is still dispensed. Ministry, sacraments and Scripture play different roles in ecclesiastical tradition, but it is their combination which makes up the Church and assures it the permanent effectiveness of the apostolic tradition. To attain this in its entirety, it is therefore necessary to consult all three, while respecting the proper role of each. As for the books of the Old Testament, the apostles handed them on to the Church as an accomplished Scripture, whose meaning was definitively fixed by the gospel message. The key to them consequently is to be sought within the legacy of the apostles: in the New Testament, but also in the life of the Church in which the ministry and the sacraments have a special function. Regarding the books of the New Testament, they acquire their full meaning when related to the same life of the Church, since this life is no other than the activation, continually directed by the Holy Spirit, of the same guarantee of the Holy Spirit.

[47] Above, pp. 21 f.
[48] Above, p. 19.
[49] Above, p. 45, note 50 (references to K. Rahner and P. Lengsfeld).

It is true that these inspired books necessarily play a principal role in ecclesial life. It is on the basis of them that the gospel is to be proclaimed; the ministry and the sacraments are to be understood according to the evidence they present. But their proper interpretation, in turn, is possible only within living tradition and in fidelity to its authentic content. Thus the problem of interpretation is inseparable from that of the relation between Scripture and Tradition. [50]  If the apostolic deposit is not preserved in living tradition like dormant capital, if it grows and unfolds in the measure that the Church's experience enables it to uncover its rich implications, its understanding of Scripture is deepened by that very fact. The reason for the development of dogma is that the Church lives the word of God announced by the apostles; at the same time and for the same reason, the virtual content of the texts which fixed this word of God in writing gradually becomes explicit. Scripture is the norm of faith for the Church; but it is through the living tradition of the Church that its full sense is revealed in order to constitute that same norm. For that reason, the interpretation of the sacred text escapes the grasp of an exegesis dominated by cultural factors or particular theological currents. All of an interpreter's work, whether it be that of a critic solicitous for the literal sense of the text, or that of a theologian in search of its implicit riches, has no value unless it reaches that understanding of the word of God which only the whole ecclesial body possesses.

In brief, bringing to light the fuller sense of biblical texts is an ordinary function of the whole life of the Church, which is obliged to announce the gospel on the basis of Scripture, and in the same act to draw from the texts whatever is hidden in them in one way or another. The various organs which compose the body of the Church play a role in this operation that fits their nature, from the body of the faithful through exegetes and theologians to the magisterium; the assistance of the Holy Spirit is present at each of these levels to insure an infallible interpretation of an infallible Scripture. [51]  This is the sense in which the principle of the sufficiency of Scripture ought to be understood; in this sense it has the unanimous support of the fathers and medieval theologians. [52]  It stands in opposition to the

---

[50] Cf. P. Lengsfeld, *Tradition, Écriture et Église dans le dialogue œcuménique*, pp. 200-228.

[51] This is the perspective in which oriental theology views the relations between Scripture and Tradition, as Msgr. Edelby reiterated in the 94th General Congregation of Vatican II (full text in *La documentation catholique* 61, n. 1435, cols. 1414-1416); he concluded: "While the Council does not have to take a position on the question of the *sensus plenior* of Scripture, it should affirm the necessity of a "spiritual" reading, that is, in the Spirit, of Sacred Scripture."

[52] Above, pp. 22-32.

"Scripture alone" of the Protestant reformers, and to the theory of the two sources developed by post-Tridentine theology. Resurrected in an age when biblical criticism has distinctly clarified the notion of the literal sense, it ought to foster the reestablishment of organic unity between the three operations applied to the biblical text[53]: critical analysis, theological use, and pastoral application.

## III. RELATED PROBLEMS

### I. THE PLURALITY OF LITERAL SENSES [54]

Sixteenth-century theology passed on to our own day an academic question which has ever since been the cause of numerous discussions, that of the plurality of literal senses. An opinion attributed to St. Augustine and St. Thomas favors the existence of multiple literal senses in some passages of Scripture. [55] The first defender of this thesis seems to have been Melchior Cano. [56] The looseness of the terminology of the fathers (and even, in a more restricted way, of St. Thomas) in speaking of the problems of interpretation is the principal cause of this controversy. What we have already said concerning the *sensus litteralis* (literary sense) of Scripture according to St. Thomas enables us to set the matter straight. The *sensus litteralis* has two levels: that of the literal sense in the modern sense, and that of the fuller sense. At the first level, the inspired author's didactic intention necessarily excludes any plurality which would render the text ambiguous, unless it be a case of intentional ambiguity, either for the purpose of expressing thought in enigmatic language, or in order to enrich the text with overtones (thus in the fourth gospel Christ sometimes uses double meaning words [57]). But such cases are not beyond the reach of critical analysis.

---

[53] On the fundamental unity of the duties of exegete, theologian and pastor, as interpreters of the Word of God for the Christian people, see our article, "La Parole de Dieu est-elle accessible à l'homme d'aujourd'hui?," *LMD* 80 (1964), 190 ff.

[54] Cf. *Institutiones biblicae*, pp. 370-377.

[55] An explanation of the problem and a discussion of the texts cited can be found in G. M. Perrella, "Il pensiero di S. Agostino e S. Tomaso circa il numero del senso letterale nella S. Scrittura," *Biblica* 26 (1945), 277-302.

[56] Melchior Cano, *De locis theologicis* 2, 11, ad 7 (Migne, *Theologiae cursus completus* 1, 129).

[57] Just one example: does the use of the word ὑψόω in Jn 3:14, 8:28, 12:32.34 concern the elevation on the cross or the ascension into glory? The first interpretation, to the exclusion of the other, is held by M. J. Lagrange, *Évangile selon saint Jean*, p. 81; J. H. Bernard, *The Gospel according to St. John, ICC*, Vol. 1, pp. 112-115; E. Hoskyns—F. N. Davey, *The Fourth Gospel* (London: Faber, 1947), pp. 217-218. The second interpretation is that of C. H. Dodd, *The Interpretation of the Fourth*

There remains the possibility of a plurality in the passage from the literal to the fuller sense. The text of *De potentia* cited in support of the thesis of plurality actually makes a distinction between the intention of the human author and that of the Holy Spirit who is the principal author of Scripture. [58] The plurality of the *sensus litteralis* is limited to just this case, which we have studied in detail. It is true that with the literal sense as a base the fuller sense can develop in several directions, whose connection does not nullify their real diversity. Take the case of the Song of Songs, whose interpretation is so bitterly disputed. The existence of two literal meanings, corresponding to two stages of a work's composition or editing, can be admitted from the Old Testament onward. [59] Poems which originally celebrated human love were given an allegoric interpretation by a later editor, under the influence of the matrimonial allegory elaborated by the prophets; at that stage, what was celebrated was the love of God for the eschatological community, his spouse. In the New Testament, the reality of the eschatological marriage was revealed in all its complexity. For that reason the Song could be legitimately applied to all the aspects of the mystery manifested in Christ: to the Church-spouse, to the virgin Mary, the prototype of the Church, to every soul that personally participated in the marriage of Christ and his Church, etc. In fact, these various interpretations have rightfully found their way into traditional Christian exegesis. [60] The adaptation of details which they reached might be disputed, but the principle behind them is beyond dispute, as is consequently their basic pertinence to the objective fuller sense of the book. Beneath the ancient theory which held for a plurality of the *sensus litteralis* was therefore hidden the intuition, as yet poorly defined, of a fact which today's theological exegesis has rightly emphasized: the existence of the fuller sense beneath the outer cover of the letter.

*Gospel* (Cambridge: Univ. Press, 1953), pp. 306 f., 375 f. As a matter of fact, the close connection between the elevation on the cross and elevation into glory is one of the characteristic features of the gospel of St. John, which the double meaning of the word fittingly intends to stress (cf. R. Bultmann, *Das Evangelium des Johannes*, p. 110, note 2). Concerning the ambiguities of Johannine terminology, see O. Cullmann, "Der johannische Gebrauch doppeldeutiger Ausdrücke als Schlüssel zum Verständnis des vierten Evangelium," *TZ* 4 (1948), 360-372.

[58] Text cited above, p. 314, note 5. A detailed discussion in G. M. Perrella, *art. cit.*, pp. 292-299. The same remark by J. M. Vosté in *RB* 36 (1927), 112, who distinguishes the "strict literal sense" and the sense willed by the Holy Spirit in Scripture.

[59] P. Grelot, "Le sens du Cantique des cantiques d'après deux commentaires récents," *RB* 73 (1964), 42-56.

[60] G. Gerleman, "Das Hoheslied," *Biblischer Kommentar Altes Testament*, XVIII/2, pp. 43-47. G. Pouget—J. Guitton, *Le Cantique des cantiques* (Paris: Lecoffre-Gabalda, 1948), pp. 125-137 (these interpretations are based on the various spiritual meanings of the Song, the theory of the spiritual sense having been outlined on pp. 114-124).

## II. THE CONSEQUENT SENSE [61]

Since the Middle Ages, various theologians have spoken of a consequent sense, when a conclusion was drawn from a proposition which is formally found in Scripture through use of a second proposition supplied by reason. It should be noted that this theory is of the essence of the scholastic method, which was accustomed to syllogistic argumentation in which propositions drawn from Scripture usually were laid down as the major. The patristic practice of theologizing with Scripture as a base would hardly fit into this rigid form, in which everything takes the form of a syllogism; it consisted less in deducing theological assertions from Scripture than in contemplating the mysteries of the faith in the texts which expressed them in one way or another. In fact, the formal dialectic systematically practiced by scholasticism has no value in theology unless its procedures rest on a foundation which surpasses them: the knowledge that comes from faith, whose laws are not those of Aristotelian logic. This fact alone is enough to cast serious doubts on the notion of a consequent sense.

But there are besides this two decisive arguments against it. The first takes the form of a dilemma. Either the conclusion reached through reasoning is really included in the scriptural major—and then it rightfully belongs, if not to the literal sense of the text, at least to its fuller sense—, or it is not really included in Scripture—and then it has no more value than that of human reflection, which does not involve Scripture's authority, and does not really belong to its meaning. Such was the case, for example, when Bossuet pretended to draw from Scripture a complete theory of political philosophy on the rights and duties of the absolute monarchy. [62] The second argument questions the very validity of the reasoning patterned after the example given above. In a minor of the rational order used as a middle term, do the words really have the same meaning and the same content as the scriptural major? In Scripture the language employed to express doctrine has a specific content determined by the formal object of revelation. [63] Take an example: "Christ is a king; but every king possesses judiciary power; therefore, Christ possesses judiciary power." Beneath its airtight appearance, this series of propositions is sophistic, for the word "king" does not have the same value in the minor from reason, where it refers to royalty of this world,

---

[61] *Institutiones biblicae*, pp. 385 f.; H. Höpfl—L. Leloir, *Introductio generalis*, pp. 431 f.   J. Coppens, *Les harmonies des deux Testaments*, pp. 72-78, points out that this statement of the problem "leads us into a more theological than scriptural field" (p. 72), and he assigns the consequent senses to the fuller sense (p. 78).

[62] J. B. Bossuet, *Politique tirée de l'Écriture sainte*, in *Œuvres complètes* (ed. Lachat), Vol. 23, pp. 477-649; Vol. 24, pp. 1-259.

[63] Above, pp. 86 ff.

and in the scriptural major, where it refers to a royalty of another kind (compare Jn 18:37 with 1 P 2:13 ff. or Rm 13:1-7). Thus the consequent sense finds its way into the classification of scriptural senses only as a result of a misunderstanding; it is therefore advisable to exclude it entirely.

### III. THE ACCOMMODATED SENSE

The accommodation of scriptural texts to objects or situations to which they did not originally refer has always been practiced in Christian exegesis, which in this regard merely followed the example of Jewish exegesis. [64] The use of Scripture in preaching, its use in the liturgy, and even, in some cases, its use in theology have involved adaptations of the type which modern critics regard with a mixture of pity and anger. It was one of the basic procedures of the Alexandrian *allegoria*, as well as the Antiochean *theôria*, and medieval spiritual exegesis passed the tradition down to our own day. But this procedure poses a delicate problem: can the accommodated sense be called a biblical sense? Should it not rather be attributed to the ingenuity of those who employ it? A distinction between various cases must be made.

### *1. Simple Verbal Accommodation*

The adaptation of a text is sometimes made without any concern for its original meaning, by playing on the words which, taken from their context, are bent to the meaning one wants to give them. For example, the *Rorate coeli desuper* cites Is 16:1 according to the Vulgate and applies it to the mission of Christ by the Father: "Send forth, O Lord, the Lamb, the ruler of the earth, from Petra of the desert, to the mount of the daughter of Sion." But that text originally had nothing to do with a messianic oracle concerning the lamb of God. [65] Similar cases can be found in the liturgy, [66] and even

---

[64] Above, pp. 188 f., 192 f., 196 ff.

[65] In fact, the text is scarcely certain, and its meaning very uncertain. See G. B. Gray, *Isaiah I-XXVII* in *ICC*, p. 287; A. Condamin, *Le livre d'Isaïe* (Paris: Lecoffre), pp. 115 f.; A. Bentzen, *Jesaja fortolket*, Vol. 1, p. 128. P. Claudel reacted angrily against this literal interpretation in *Présence et prophétie* (Fribourg, 1942), pp. 183 f. (text quoted in *Sens chrétien de l'A.T.*, p. 455). It is true that in *L'Évangile d'Isaïe* (Paris, 1951), p. 66, Claudel confesses that his first symbolic interpretation of Is 16 did not completely satisfy him. But the considerations he substitutes for it are just as arbitrary, and the christological interpretation of "the Lamb, the ruler of the earth" in particular is not questioned.

[66] The Introit of the Mass of the Sunday during the octave of Christmas, which uses Ws 18:14-15, is often cited. It is true that the mission of the destructive word of God during the night of the exodus has nothing to do with the mission of Christ into the world and his birth in the night. But still, in both cases, God sends his Word, the executor of his work on earth. There is, therefore, a real foundation for the adaptation of the text.

more in patristic and medieval commentaries, and even in spiritual writers of more recent times, like St. John of the Cross. [67] In one sense, there is no reason to take exception to this practice, if it is merely a question of finding lyrical and figurative language to express Christian doctrine or prayer in biblical style. The language of Scripture came spontaneously to the mind of St. Bernard when he preached, and he would hardly have paused to reflect whether the use he made of it belonged to the literal sense or was merely a verbal accommodation. His thought quite simply lived on the Bible, and he used it with the liberty of a child in his father's home. [68] Likewise, there can be no objection when the liturgy employs a style full of biblical reminiscences whose value varies greatly. But the result of this operation sometimes has nothing to do with the objective meaning of Scripture. So it is understandable that the encyclical *Divino afflante Spiritu* took a firm stand against a theory of a spiritual exegesis that tended to generalize this practice and presented it as the authentic traditional interpretation, as opposed to the critical approach which is strongly documented. [69]

## 2. Accommodation with a Theological Basis

But the adaptation of a text can also be based on more solid foundations: the figurative signification of the realities of which the text speaks, if it is a passage borrowed from the Old Testament, or the real relation which exists between the various aspects of the mystery of Christ, if it is a passage taken from the New. In such a case, what is called accommodation is in reality nothing but an application of the fuller sense, as we will explain when we discuss the rules for its use. It is true that in some such cases the application of the details of the text to a new object can be effected only with difficulty. Some of them strongly risk being arranged arbitrarily in order to retain at any cost a meaning in the new context in which they are placed. St. Paul himself furnishes examples of such a practice, especially when he resorts to rabbinical or hellenistic techniques to give Scripture his own meaning. In Ga 4:21-31, the "allegory" [70] of the two wives and the two sons

[67] An example is given in *Sens chrétien de l'A.T.*, p. 455. The saint's exegesis has been studied in detail by J. Vilnet, *Bible et mystique chez saint Jean de la Croix* (Bruges-Paris: Desclée de Brouwer, 1949), especially pp. 84-92, 163-172, 176-179 (on the use of accommodation).

[68] P. Dumontier, *Saint Bernard et la Bible* (Paris: Desclée, 1953). Concerning this "exegesis by recollection," see J. Leclercq, *L'amour des Lettres et le désir de Dieu. Initiation aux auteurs monastiques du moyen âge* (Paris: Cerf, 1957), p. 76.

[69] Above, p. 219. See *Ench. B.*, 553; cf. 522-525 (Letter to the bishops of Italy occasioned by the appearance of Dain Cohenel's pamphlet).

[70] Above, p. 193, note 27.

of Abraham is not completely without a foundation in the fuller sense of the texts he cites. In the perspective opened by Is 54:1 ff. (cited in Ga 4:27), the respective situation of Sarah and Hagar, of Isaac and Ishmael, in fact, correctly represents the relative position of the two alliances and of those who belonged to them: slavery and liberty. But in order to embellish this theme, St. Paul accommodated the two accounts, of Gn 16 and Gn 21, by giving their details significations which could well be termed arbitrary He left behind the objective sense of the texts, and made use of practical. procedures to make his thought understood with the aid of scriptural symbols, which is very much in keeping with the cultural customs of his time and environment. In the same way, his use of Dt 25:4 to justify the rights of preachers (1 Co 9:9-10) is a form of *a fortiori* reasoning which could claim the support of certain rabbinic rules, [71] but this accommodation of the legal text could not pass as the revelation of a fuller sense, for its foundation is even more tenuous than that of the allegory we considered above.

These two facts show that a great amount of discernment is required in the search in the New Testament for rules of interpretation that will aid in uncovering the fuller sense of the Old. The practical methods which the authors of the apostolic age owed to their culture cannot be canonized, for these methods do not depend on the doctrine which determines the intimate relationship of the two Testaments. Even more prudence is required regarding the accommodating exegesis which can be found in ecclesiastical tradition. We have admitted that their general purpose is related to what we have here called the search for the fuller sense. [72] It would, therefore, be absurd to reject them all in the name of a criticism which seeks only the literal sense [73]; they ought to be examined for profound intuitions which might profitably complement the results of critical study. But, while admitting that soundly based accommodation thus has a right to a place in preaching, and even in theological works, it is important to avoid attributing to it any demonstrative value, and to use it with prudence. On this point, the culture of our times is more demanding than that of the patristic and Middle Ages; symbolic expression of thought is less in vogue, and the critical mind plays a larger role. [74] The science of interpretation must adapt itself to this situation, not only in theology, but in pastoral practice as well.

---

[71] Above, p. 188, note 13.
[72] Above, pp. 326 ff.
[73] Cf. *Sens chrétien de l'A.T.*, p. 216, note 3.
[74] The assertion of critical reason, provided it does not yield to the temptation of rationalism, is in itself a progression. The same cannot be said of the retreat from the symbolic expression of thought, which indicates a real impoverishment of the mind. Concerning this latter point, the median level of contemporary culture reveals considerable backwardness in regard to psychological research, which has rediscovered the value and the laws of symbolic thought. One need only mention

# § II. THE DISCOVERY AND USE OF THE LITERAL SENSE

## I. THE THEOLOGICAL STATUS OF BIBLICAL CRITICISM [75]

Since the literal sense of Scripture was determined by the formal intention of the inspired authors, and by all the historical and cultural elements which conditioned its realization, in principle it is accessible to any reader who studies the texts intelligently with the aid of adequate methods. In other words, it corresponds exactly with the field of criticism. A critical mentality was never completely absent from the efforts made by Jewish and Christian interpreters of Scripture, but its degree of precision obviously varied with time, circumstances, and individuals. It cannot be denied that the modern Western world since the 16th century has carried it forward considerably, perfecting its methods and awakening minds to a concern for exactness which neither antiquity nor the Middle Ages possessed in the same degree. [76] Contemporary exegesis cannot be content merely to take stock of this progress and adapt its efforts to it [77]; it ought to make a maximum use of the possibilities it offers. It is not our direct concern here to discuss critical methods; that is the task of technical introductions to Sacred Scripture. But it is our purpose to discuss their place in theology, since they should in any case be organically related to that understanding of the word of God which only faith can provide.

### I. FALSE STATEMENTS OF THE PROBLEM

In our historical summary of the problem of interpretation since the 16th century, we saw that the introduction of critical methods was the occasion

the work of G. Bachelard, which is void of any religious reference, and the studies devoted to the problem of myth by R. Caillois, M. Éliade, G. Gusdorf, P. Ricœur, etc. A collection of studies of symbolic thought and language can be found in *Polarité du symbole* (Bruges-Paris: Desclée de Brouwer, 1960). In the perspective opened by all these works the study of scriptural symbolism ought to be developed with a view to incorporating it into literal exegesis and preparing the way for utilization of the fuller sense. Thus scriptural accommodation will receive the regulating principle it needs.

[75] On the overall problem of criticism, see A. Durand, art. "Critique biblique," *DAFC* I, cols. 760-819 (1911); E. Mangenot, art. "Critique," *DTC* 3, cols. 2330-2337 (1911); H. Höpfl, art. "Critique biblique," *DBS* 2, cols. 175-240 (1928). Treatments which date from after the encyclical *Divino afflante Spiritu* take noticeably more exact and sound positions on a number of points: A. Fernández in *Institutiones biblicae*, 3rd ed., pp. 393-460; J. Schildenberger, *Vom Geheimnis des Gotteswortes*, chaps. IV to VII; H. Cazelles—P. Grelot in Robert—Feuillet, *Interpreting the Scriptures*, pp. 67-164.

[76] Above, pp. 203 ff.

[77] Above, pp. 230 ff.

of numerous conflicts, not only between believers and unbelievers, but also between exegetes and theologians who were equally anxious to pay full respect to Scripture. [78] To understand this difficulty, no better example could be cited than the problem which the introduction of logic into theology posed in the 12th century, [79] and then in the 13th century, the adoption of Aristotelian philosophy. [80] In both cases it was a question of determining in what measure and under what conditions the use of certain methods which depended on reason could be beneficial in the study of the word of God or in the explanation of its content. [81] In theology, St. Thomas reached a balanced solution by allowing reason a real autonomy in its domain, provided it accepted the clarification and occasionally the correction offered by the light of faith. [82] In exegesis the solution was not so quickly arrived at. Two factors contributed to confuse the situation.

In the first place, criticism developed, especially since the 18th century, in a climate opposed in principle to the very idea of revelation and to the authority of a faith, a theology and a Church which could in some way impose themselves upon human reason. [83] Rationalist philosophy thus took over biblical criticism and made it an instrument in its attack on all dogmatism. Consequently, the so called independent exegesis sought to clear its own path, formulating literary and historical hypotheses which unashamedly contradicted the basic tenets of Christian faith. Was this fact due solely to the birth pangs of a still new science? The reason goes deeper: a rationalist inspired critical philosophy actually imposed its postulates upon the positive study of the texts and the facts. This mentality still lingers today in large segments of Western thought. Certainly it makes the Bible, the historical process it records, the religious current it represents, the object of attentive study, simply because of their place in the history of religions and in human history. But a fundamental principle, tacitly admitted before any discussion, holds that in any hypothesis the values that appear in the course of one's

---

[78] Above, pp. 214-219.

[79] Abelard's position on this point was violently attacked by St. Bernard. Concerning Abelard, see the remarks of A. Forest in Fliche—Martin, *Histoire de l'Église* 13, pp. 96-105; cf. 148 ff.

[80] The dispute over Aristotelianism in the 13th century is described in its critical phase, as it concerned Siger of Brabant, by F. van Steenberghen in Fliche—Martin, *Histoire de l'Église*, 13, pp. 265-285, 301-305. Cf. M. D. Chenu, *Toward Understanding Thomas* (Chicago: Regnery, 1964).

[81] This concept of theology as the effort to understand Scripture was that of Abelard: "...that our mind might the more easily understand the meaning of the divine page" (*Introductio ad theologiam, Praefatio, PL* 178, 979).

[82] The status of philosophy in Thomistic thought has been explained many times. See, for example, E. Gilson, *The Philosophy of St. Thomas Aquinas*, 2nd ed. (St. Louis: Herder, 1937), pp. 9-30.

[83] Above, pp. 204 ff.

study were the product of human factors, neither more or less transcendent than in any other religious current. *A priori*, everything must be able to be, and is, explained by the interaction of natural causes which had their effect throughout their evolution. As a result, the aim of critical research is not only to discover the material facts which mark out that long and considerably complex history, but to explain their connection, from the age of the patriarchs to primitive Christianity, without resorting to the supernatural causes which faith acknowledges in it. [84]    The evidence must be criticized in this perspective. Wherever the evidence is too meager, working hypotheses supply for the silence, but never abandon the same perspective, which in some way defines the scientific study of the Bible. The influence this view has exercised, and continues to exercise, on the exegesis of liberal Protestantism is well known. [85]    Bultmann, in fact, accepts the same postulates, even if he attempts to avoid their consequences through his existentialist interpretation. [86]

The reaction of Catholic theologians to this situation was not always limited to a firm rejection of the rationalist critics' religious negations. It more than once included in its condemnation of the latter the very methods which the critics employed. As seen from within the Church, the Bible is not a book like other books: it is the word of God, whose interpretation belongs to the Church alone. To understand it properly, therefore, it is not sufficient to preserve a sort of general faith in the revelation its text contains. It is essential to consult the Church's tradition, and more particularly its ordinary and extraordinary magisterium, for a correct interpretation of the texts. And this principle is valid not only for their theological interpretation, which is explicitly a concern of the Church's teaching; it applies also to critical questions in which it is unthinkable to admit that the whole Church was in error for so many centuries,—concerning the literary authenticity of the books, for example, their literary genre or their historical accuracy. In all of these questions the new opinions put forward only within the past two centuries cannot prevail over a long tradition. The problems to which they are related are too closely connected to dogma to rule out an appeal to dogmatic authorities to dispose of them *a priori*. Exegesis, as a specialized discipline, is only a servant to theology. It can claim no liberty whatsoever contrary to the tasks assigned to it by the doctrinal magisterium of the Church. And its proper function is to defend

[84] This basic postulate, founded on a critical examination of the idea of the supernatural, dominates, for example, all of Renan's word. Cf. J. Pommier, *La pensée religieuse de Renan* (Paris, 1925), pp. 33-47.

[85] Above, pp. 208 f.

[86] Above, pp. 210 f.

the firm foundations of the traditional positions and the truth of Scripture, such as the magisterium understands them. It is quite possible that this position was never presented so bluntly as we have presented it. It nevertheless underlies numerous books and articles which, brandishing the official documents of the Church, threw suspicion on the work of exegetes who intended to undertake critical studies without preconceived notions. [87]

Obviously, no dialogue is possible between the rationalists of the first position and the theologians of the second. They resemble one another in their dogmatism, which makes two opposite demands on critical study, the one as excessive as the other. We have already considered what the doctrine of revelation, that of inspiration, and that of the Church can legitimately require of exegetes in the performance of their work. [88] These points need not be repeated here. But it will be useful to insist on a point which the encyclical *Divino afflante Spiritu* stated forcefully: while it is true that the Church and its magisterium have the duty of guarding the deposit of faith contained in Scripture, there are very few texts whose interpretation has been determined by authority, or whose meaning is attested by unanimous ecclesiastical tradition. [89] And it should be added that even when a council has solemnly defined the relation of a text to a particular dogma, for example, that of Rm 5:12 to the dogma of original sin, [90] it has not by that fact defined the exact mode of that relation, nor solved all the problems the text in question might raise. Such a definition must be understood according to its purpose and within the limits of the question in which it intervened. [91]

---

[87] Such a view was especially evident between 1900 and 1910 when a group of conservative exegetes sought to obtain the condemnation of Fr. Lagrange, whose program was set forth in his book on the historical method; cf. above, p. 218, note 145. Despite the principles laid down by the encyclical *Divino afflante Spiritu*, other examples can be found in the past decade; but these polemics are practically devoid of interest (cf. p. 123, note 134).

[88] Above, pp. 221-227.

[89] *Ench. B.*, 565.

[90] Cf. *Ench. S.*, 1512, 1514. The Council nevertheless refused to add to its decrees a condemnation of those who denied that Paul speaks of original sin in Rm 5 (*Acta*, ed. Ehses, p. 217).

[91] Concerning this question, see the studies of S. Lyonnet, "Le sens de ἐφ'ᾧ en Rom 5, 12 et l'exégèse des Pères grecs," *Biblica* 36 (1955), 436-456; "Le péché originel et l'exégèse de Rom 5,12-14" in J. Huby—S. Lyonnet, *Épître aux Romains* (Paris: Beauchesne, 1957), pp. 521-557; "Le péché originel en Rom 5,12: L'exégèse des Pères grecs et les décrets du concile de Trente," *Biblica* 41 (1960), 325-355; cf. "Le sens de πειράζειν en Sap 2,24 et la doctrine du péché originel," *Biblica* 39 (1958), 34-36. The accepted exegesis of the post-Tridentine age often understood the decree of the Council as a canonization of the interpretation given by the Latin Vulgate: "*in quo* omnes peccaverunt," an indefensible translation that modern commentators have rightly abandoned.

## II. CORRECT STATEMENT OF THE PROBLEM

### *1. The Role of Criticism*

Human reason has a role to play both in the approach to faith and in the understanding of faith. It is in terms of this role that the place of biblical criticism in the Church ought to be judged. It is indeed important to measure its limits and its possibilities, but within these limits it should be given its full due. [92]

What are these limits? Rather than considering the technical difficulties of the tasks to be undertaken, a more basic question ought to be asked: in what measure can one speak of a perfectly objective human judgment when religious questions are at stake, and more particularly when it is a question of the Bible, which is centered on the person of Christ, who presented himself as the unique revelation of God and the only way of salvation? There can be no doubt about the reply. By the very fact that the meaning of human existence is at stake, no critic can possibly remain an impartial and disinterested observer, attentive to objective phenomena which do not concern him. As a man he must necessarily feel involved; he cannot avoid making a personal choice when faced with the revelation of his own existence which the Bible claims to offer him. To believe or not to believe: this is a choice that cannot be evaded. It would be useless to protest against this practical necessity of human conduct. The problem of existence is of such a nature that it cannot be resolved by purely rational means; every person resolves it for himself in a free act by which he commits himself completely, in an act of faith in which rational motivation joins the "reasons of the heart" [93] to justify the concept of life on which his choice falls. In other words, the choice which must be made is not between belief and unbelief, but between several kinds of belief, [94] among which must be included irreligion, ration-

---

[92] See the excellent treatment given this question already by M. J. Lagrange, "L'inspiration et les exigences de la critique," *RB* 5 (1896), 496-518; *La méthode historique*, pp. 1-34 (critical exegesis and ecclesiastical dogma).

[93] Pascal's terminology is adopted here purposely, for "we know truth not only through reason, but through the heart as well" (*Pensées*, ed. Lafuma, 110); but "the heart has reasons of which reason has no idea. That is evident in a thousand ways" (*ibid.*, 423). The *heart* for Pascal does not designate the superficial and infra-rational sensibility, but the deep area of the conscience where existential options are made. It is the heart which has access to concrete knowledge of God through the decision of faith. ("It is the heart which senses God, and not reason. That is what faith is: God sensed by the heart, not by reason," *ibid.*, 424.) It is the heart too which chooses between two loves, love of God and love of self (*ibid.*, 423 *in fine*). It is therefore the place where human liberty comes into play, not blindly, but for motives superior to those of the intellect in act.

[94] The vocabulary employed here is obviously not that of F. Jeanson, *La foi d'un incroyant* (Paris, 1963), who reserves the term belief for an inferior type of irra-

alism [95] and atheism. It is useless to imagine that anyone can escape this issue. Catholic criticism and rationalist or atheistic criticism are in this respect in the same position. Their study of the Bible takes its place within the psychological complex of their most intimate choices, and nothing can remove them completely from it. In order to remain coherent with the rest of their thought and their life, their study is inevitably colored by the personal position they have taken in regard to the biblical fact, in regard to Christ. It is no surprise, therefore, that the Christian exegete organically integrates criticism in a theology which systematizes the content of his faith. The unbelieving exegete similarly relates it to a system of thought which expresses another type of belief, based on another scale of values.

If such is the position of criticism, it is inevitable that there should be some doubt whether exegetical work can be properly done at all. There are two indispensable conditions. 1) No exegete should be under the illusion that his work is absolutely objective; he should be sane enough to be aware of the connection between his work and his subjective beliefs. That demands of him not only real interior sincerity, but likewise a rigorous critical self-examination, which is the more difficult as it reaches the depths where existential decisions are made. In the absence of such vigilance, his beliefs will inevitably sway his judgment, not by providing that prior understanding of the problems which is indeed indispensable, [96] but by prejudicing their

tional avowals, which he consequently opposes to faith. We here understand belief as the act of believing in the universality of cases, and we reserve the word *faith* to designate adherence to the word of God which is the Christian's act of belief. It is taken for granted that independently of this distinction everyone who believes holds beliefs of an inferior type which reason can legitimately subject to criticism; but these are not the monopoly of those who believe in God and in Christ. They constitute what Blondel, in *L'Action,* classified under the name of superstition.

[95] It is begging the question to consider rationalism as such a completely rational system of thought under the pretext that it affirms the exclusive and unlimited power of human reason. This very affirmation is not founded, as such, upon any rational demonstration; the conviction it expresses is the result of a choice, the manifestation of a belief. The moral qualification of this belief is not presently in question; that depends in each particular case upon a secret of conscience which only God can know. Its intellectual qualification, on the other hand, should be subjected to a rigorous examination. For the followers of that system can legitimately be accused of not applying to themselves the critical rules to which they subject the faith of others, since they never question the non-rational postulate on which their view of the world and of man, as well as their evaluation of different systems of thought, actually rest.

[96] This is one of the principal elements in the interpretation of the Bible advocated by R. Bultmann: "Every interpretation of a text requires a previous understanding *(Vorverständnis)* of what can be found in it" (R. Marlé, *Bultmann et l'interprétation du Nouveau Testament,* p. 86). In other words, the relation of exegetical analysis to the exegete's existential situation determines the manner in which he questions the biblical text and solicits a response. Concerning the debate between Bultmann and Karl Barth over this "prior understanding," see the summary account by R. Marlé, *Le problème théologique de l'herméneutique,* pp. 67-78. Karl Barth's protest against

solution before having weighed all the evidence, at the risk even of twisting that evidence. In this matter, non-confessional exegetes are no less threatened by the dangers of subjectivism and partiality, which they are quick to denounce in others, than are their Christian counterparts; they are just more a prey to the illusion. 2) The personal beliefs of the exegete must imply the absolute necessity of a critical study of biblical texts and assertions. If that is not the case, then the act of faith loses its truly human dignity and is reduced to credulity and superstition. [97] The position of the Catholic faith on this point is perfectly clear. Since it is not only an *obsequium rationis*, but an *obsequium rationale*, [98] it demands verification, in proportion to the means available, of the rational consistency of the foundations on which it rests. It is a conscious submission to God, a conscious acceptance of the word of God. Such consciousness can only be the result of a thorough examination carried out in the full light of intellect and conscience. Not that the truth of the message in which one believes can ever be proved from reason, nor that a moral necessity for believing can be rationally established; but it must be possible to verify rationally the facts surrounding the manifestation of the word of God, that the signs by which its presence is recognized are open to critical examination, that the encounter which is faith, far from contradicting reason, brings it to fruition and peace.

## 2. The Role of Criticism in Theology

Biblical criticism has its place precisely in this context of verification, which opens the way to a genuine understanding of the word of God. As such, it would seem to be a necessary preamble to faith itself. [99] The exegete need not any more abstract from his faith in order to devote his attention to critical study than the theologian must in order to reflect philosophically on the

the intrusion of a philosophical proposition which predetermines the results of analysis of the text ought indeed to be heeded, for exegesis cannot determine in advance the content of the word of God. Likewise strong reservations must be made in regard to the existentialist system which governs Bultmann's whole method of interpretation. But it is no less true that exegesis' point of departure is the relation of Scripture to man's life in the concrete; it is on the basis of his experience of existence that man can discover its real content. If the reading of Scripture forces him to the decisive choice of faith (or of a refusal to believe), the reason is that in its light he realizes that existence itself forces him to it. Thus he finds within himself the source of a "prior understanding" of Scripture, in which the interior operations of grace and the illumination of the Holy Spirit certainly play a part.

[97] It will be noted in this regard that the integral biblicism of various sects displays a basic hostility to biblical criticism in the same measure in which it is based on illuminism.

[98] *Ench. S.*, 3009.

[99] *Ibid.*, 3019.

human problems related to revelation. His faith, in turn, is no more a hindrance in his research than it is to a theologian in his philosophical reflections. The fact is that every correct use of reason has its place within the faith, whether its object be the general facts of human experience which are the material of philosophy, or the singular historical fact which determined forever the content of Scripture. It is true that the light of faith occasionally corrects the spontaneous inclinations of reason, thus saving it from the blindness to which our sinful world is prone. But in such cases reason itself, interiorly illumined by the Holy Spirit to whom it remains docile, can verify the soundness of this correction which tends to rectify its congenital weakness. [100] The case of exegesis is no different from any other. The theological status of biblical criticism therefore is not the cause of even a shadow of difficulty, provided the problems it deals with are properly stated. This condition has not always been fulfilled in the past three centuries, neither on the side of the critics, nor on that of the theologians. Hence the conflicts which by now are well known. [101] But these difficulties can today be considered overcome. [102]

[100] Such recognition is obviously not possible unless reason allows itself to be guided by the "heart" (in Pascal's sense of the word), which adheres to God and in that free act recognizes the truth he communicates. It must not be thought, therefore, that it can ever become the object of purely rational proof.

[101] Above, pp. 335-339. The ecclesiastical documents of that time must, of course, be understood in relation to the actual situation, which explains their apparently negative character, or at least their caution in regard to criticism. For within the Church as well as in the Bible, the import of a text must be judged within its context.

[102] It would be interesting to see how the relation of criticism to theology was understood in Protestantism over the last few centuries with reference to the reform principle of "Scripture alone." On the one hand, "orthodox" Protestantism's fundamentalism was opposed to criticism, in which it saw an effort of corrupt reason, a lack of submission to the word of God. On the other side, the liberal wing found in it the very key to Scripture, even to the point of making theology depend upon it, thus subjecting it to the whim of the hypothesis in vogue. During the past 50 years exegetes and theologians have attempted in various ways to overcome this contradiction, while respecting the autonomy of the two fields and recognizing that there might exist a certain tension between criticism and faith (cf. M. Goguel, "La critique et la foi" in Le problème biblique dans le Protestantisme [Paris, 1955], pp. 11-44). Karl Barth, without rejecting the historico-critical method, gave it only a relative value, making it a simple preparation for that understanding of the word of God which only faith can provide once it has recognized in Scripture the revelation of Jesus Christ (cf. R. Marlé, Le problème théologique de l'herméneutique, pp. 27-33). With Bultmann the rift between criticism and faith is in one sense more accentuated. On the one hand, criticism appears as a requisite of the modern mind to which the word of God is to be announced; but its very radicalism, the heritage of the age of liberalism, seems bound to destroy all the dogmatic constructions of Christian tradition. In these circumstances faith escapes suffocation only by a leap into paradox without any rational support: the heritage of Kierkegaard, who outdid Luther himself. On that basis, theology is built on two axes: that of demythologization, which is the accomplishment of criticism, and that of the existentialist interpretation, which limits the content of theology to the very act of faith (R. Marlé, op. cit., pp. 53 ff.). More recently G. Ebeling, with his theology of the Word of God, has continued along the

Theologians, of course, since they are interested in divine truth made known through revelation, will always regard criticism as a handmaid of theology, just as they do philosophy. But they should immediately add that they have an absolute need of this handmaid, which enjoys perfect autonomy in its own field: the discernment of the literal sense of Scripture and the study of the history in which it took form. While its organic relation to theology acts as a balancing factor in critical study, and lights its way if need be, the results of its analysis can in no instance be arbitrarily dictated from without, to the detriment of the evidence furnished by the texts. Quite the contrary; what theology expects from criticism is to establish through its own means the original meaning of the texts in question, by placing them in a social, cultural and religious context that has long since disappeared. It ought in this sense to do its utmost: *Quantum potes, tantum aude!* The best service it could possibly render is not to defend, and much less to pretend to prove, dogmas, but to enable the believer and the theologian of today to grasp the authentic history of revelation, exactly as it unfolded in the past, so that in that context the root of dogmas will become apparent. Once that is done, the theologian's work begins.

path opened up by Bultmann (see the collection of his writings *Wort und Glaube* [Tübingen: Mohr, 1960], Eng. trans. *Word and Faith* [London: SCM Press, 1963], to which we refer here; cf. R. Marlé, "Foi et parole: La théologie de Gerhard Ebeling," *RSR* 53 [1962], 5-31). Scripture having been conceived forthwith not as the word of God, but as a witness of the word of God, the same which resounds in man at the moment when the decision of faith is made, its interpretation, guided by the historico-critical method, becomes the very act of theology, which is identified with biblical hermeneutics—not through a reduction which would revive the spirit of liberal theology, but through an application of the existentialist interpretation in which the *explanation* of Scripture becomes identical with its concrete *application* to man's life, and in which, consequently, theology becomes identical with preaching ("Word of God and Hermeneutics" in *Word and Faith*, pp. 305-332; cf. "The Significance of the Critical Method for Church and Theology in Protestantism," *ibid.*, pp. 17-61). This effort to re-establish the unity of exegesis, theology and preaching around Scripture should be noted: while it is worked out from the Bultmannian viewpoint, it harkens back in its own way to the practice of the age of the Fathers. Exegetes influenced by the theology of Barth naturally use quite different means to give theological justification to their use of the historico-critical method. Among them, O. Cullmann thinks it possible to overcome the duality of critical effort and theological exegesis through recourse to an "objective" exegesis (cf. "Les problèmes posés par la méthode exégétique de l'école de Karl Barth," *RHPR* 8 [1928], 72) which synthesizes the two approaches because it draws from the texts that "history of salvation" which is the very object of revelation (cf. "La nécessité et la fonction de l'exégèse philologique et historique de la Bible" in *Le problème biblique dans le protestantisme*, pp. 136-140). Hence the role of philological and historical interpretation at the basis of theology itself (*ibid.*, pp. 140-147; cf. J. Frisque, *Oscar Cullmann: Une théologie de l'histoire du salut*, pp. 28-35, 52-56). The objectivity Cullmann seeks in the texts is therefore that of the mystery of salvation which the incarnation of the Son of God made present in human history. It will be noted that Catholic theology presents points of agreement sometimes with K. Barth's position, sometimes with that of Cullmann, sometimes with that of Bultmann and Ebeling, without being identical with any of them.

In a sense, this objective is exactly the same for the Christian exegete and the rationalist historian, even if after their common quest they pass differing judgments upon what they have drawn from the texts, the one acknowledging the history of divine revelation in the process in which the other sees only the history of a religious ideal elaborated by a particular human group. [103] This same diversity does not destroy a fundamental agreement, for divine revelation came to us precisely through the mediation of the ideas, language, customs and the history of that human group whose outstanding figure was Jesus Christ. This agreement is important, for it allows the critics, whether believers or not, to criticize each other's work, to check on the exactness of their methods and the objectivity of their conclusions. In all the branches of historical study, does not the truth result from a dialogue among historians? There will always be a certain tension in biblical criticism between the investigation that is carried on in the shadow of Christian faith and investigation that is unrelated to it. [104] How could it be otherwise, when basically different notions of existence and of religion influence the judgments made concerning past events and guide the formation of the working hypotheses employed to bring those events back to life? [105] Everything depends, then, on instituting a true dialogue between the two, so that no one will be satisfied with false certainties too easily obtained. Theology itself has nothing to lose and nothing to fear from such a dialogue. Since it is certain a priori that the conclusions of critical study when properly conducted cannot contradict the genuine content of faith, [106] it cannot but await them with confidence to incorporate them into its work, even if it must on occasion correct certain views handed down from the past centuries when it finds them poorly founded or lacking in exactness. Is not such questioning and trial a condition of all life and progress?

Seen in this light, biblical criticism is therefore one of the Church's indispensable duties. [107] Though it is rational in its purpose and its methods,

---

[103] The objective is a fortiori the same for Christian exegetes of the various confessions; but then it is the theological interpretations that differ.

[104] Moreover, two quite different cases should be distinguished. On the one hand, there is the tension between Christian and Jewish interpretations of biblical history and the fact of Christ; on the other, the tension between rationalist and Christian interpretations of the same facts. The dialogue in the two cases has neither the same basis nor the same perspective. One might compare, from early times, St. Justin's Dialogue with Trypho with Origen's Contra Celsum, which already represent these two types of controversy.

[105] This point is rightly stressed by J. Levie, "Interprétation scripturaire, en exégèse—en théologie" in Sacra Pagina (Brussels Congress) (Paris-Gembloux: Duculot, 1959), Vol. I, p. 105.

[106] Ench. S., 3019.

[107] P. G. Duncker, "Biblical Criticism," CBQ 25 (1963), 22-33.

it is nonetheless assumed by the faith of the person who practices it. From that it follows that it belongs to those works of wisdom which already in the Old Testament were held in high esteem (Pr 8:12; Si 39:1-3). As an integral part of the Christian science of interpretation, it is included in the teaching charisms enumerated in the New Testament, provided only that it is subordinate to a higher goal: the theological interpretation of Scripture, to which we will return again.

## II. THE DIVISIONS OF CRITICAL STUDY

The tasks which fall to criticism are of several kinds. One concerns the text itself of the sacred books, which are to be the object of exegesis: textual criticism. Two others, closely related, concern the positive study of their content: literary and historical criticism. The last sets in motion reflection on this content, without however going beyond the limits of rational inquiry: philosophical criticism.

### I. TEXTUAL CRITICISM [108]

Only the inspired text is, as such, the word of God. Beyond its traditional interpretations and translations, the exegete ought therefore, as far as possible, to return to the original text if he desires to present its exact sense, just as the sacred authors expressed it to their contemporaries. Our study of the canon of Scriptures showed that in the Old Testament the original inspired text can pose complex problems. Not only did some books receive their definitive form only after a long process in which several authors, glossators and editors had a hand, but the possibility that some books had several equally canonical forms cannot be excluded [109] (the question comes up, for

---

[108] A. Vaccari in *Institutiones biblicae*, 6th ed., pp. 233-362; L. Dennefeld, "Critique textuelle de l'A.T.," *DBS* 2, cols. 240-256; H. J. Vogels, "Critique textuelle du N.T.," *ibid.*, cols. 256-274. The matter has in large part been reshaped during the last thirty years. See the recent works by H. J. Vogels, *Handbuch der Textkritik des Neuen Testaments* (Bonn: Hanstein, 1955); F. Kenyon, *Our Bible and the Ancient Manuscripts* (London: Eyre & Spottiswoode, 1958); M. Noth, *Die Welt des Alten Testaments*, 3rd ed. (Berlin: Töpelmann, 1957), pp. 237-290. For the New Testament, M. J. Lagrange, *Critique textuelle du Nouveau Testament. I. Critique rationnelle* (Paris, 1934); L. Vaganay, *Initiation à la critique textuelle du Nouveau Testament* (Paris: Bloud & Gay, 1934), is complemented by J. Duplacy, *Où en est la critique textuelle du Nouveau Testament?* (Paris: Gabalda, 1959), and B. M. Metzger, *The Text of the New Testament: Its Transmission, Corruption and Restoration* (Oxford: Clarendon, 1964). The situation of the Old Testament is presently quite fluctuant on account of the gradual publication of the Qumran texts.

[109] Above, p. 180, note 205.

example, regarding the two recensions of Tobit). And finally, the canonicity of all the books of Palestinian origin must be considered at two levels: that of the Semitic original and that of the Greek translation (or adaptation). [110] In other words, the notion of original text must not be taken too strictly, for the fortunes of that text in Israelite and Jewish tradition belong in some measure to the process of formation which is completely covered by the charism of inspiration. [111] The study of this process, therefore, does not belong only to textual criticism, inasmuch as it endeavors to eliminate the parasitic elements added to the text secondarily, and to correct the errors which arose accidentally in its transmission, as is the case for the books of the New Testament. It puts the exegete in contact with the progressive development of the meaning of the text, within revelation still in the process of growth.

This delicate (and controversial) point aside, textual criticism follows the general rules which scholars since the Renaissance have gradually formulated for establishing the critical text of works transmitted through a manuscript tradition. [112] On the basis of copies, translations, citations, etc., the goal is to establish the primitive text, by eliminating secondary glosses, by choosing among variant readings, by correcting any errors that occur. This is a difficult task, and it is made particularly complex by the great number of biblical manuscripts. Still, this is the only way to attain the word of God in its own terms, for the additions of copyists, the misunderstandings and errors of translators (except in the case of the Septuagint [113]) are void of scriptural authority. For this reason the arguments which medieval theologians drew up on the basis of the Latin Vulgate are of value only in the proportion that this translation faithfully represents the Hebrew and Greek originals [114]; and in it can be found obvious mistranslations (1 Co 15:51) and interpretations which inject the faith of the Church into the text (Jb 19:25-27). Today's theology cannot be content with such readings.

[110] Above, pp. 170-178.

[111] We do not believe, however, that this principle is to be applied up to the composition of the texts recognized as canonical (in the active sense of the word) in the apostolic Church, as was suggested by N. Lohfink, "Über die Irrtumlosigkeit und die Einheit der Schrift," *Stimmen der Zeit* 174 (1964), 168-173 (cf. above, p. ooo).

[112] P. Collomp, *La critique des textes* (Paris: Les Belles Lettres, 1931). Of a more general nature: R. Devreesse, *Introduction à l'étude des manuscrits grecs* (Paris: Klincksieck, 1954), (pp. 101-175 are devoted to the Bible); A. Dain, *Les manuscrits*, 2nd ed. (Paris: Les Belles Lettres, 1964).

[113] Above, p. 178.

[114] It should be noted that the medieval reference to the Latin Vulgate rested upon confidence in St. Jerome as a faithful translator. It did not exclude recourse to other versions, Greek for example, nor use of the critical labor accomplished by Origen in his *Hexapla*.

Will this effort to recover the primitive text ever achieve its goal? It is certainly doubtful. Two facts nevertheless make constructive theological work possible on the basis of Scripture, even though the original text partially escapes its grasp. For one thing, the passages that textual criticism finds questionable constitute a minimal part of the Bible, and nowhere do they concern essential doctrines. And secondly, even when copyists or translators made material errors, either in transmitting the text or rendering it in another language, they let themselves be guided by living tradition, which itself owed its doctrine to Scripture, or at least referred to it in order to "guard the deposit"; consequently, their errors suppose a general fidelity to Scripture, even when its letter is not fully respected. In our days, however, theology has reached such a technical level that it must necessarily base its work on a critically established text of the Bible, both the Hebrew and the Greek parts of it. Is this not precisely what Origen and St. Jerome, within the limits of the science of their day, undertook to do? [115]

## II. LITERARY CRITICISM [116]

Once the text is critically established, it is a question of understanding it. That can only be done fully within the faith, which alone gives access to the word of God. But faith does not dispense from the effort of analysis which the sacred books require, just as any other human work. In our study of the consequences of inspiration, we concluded that the word of God was translated into a language and borrowed the literary forms which correspond to the personality of the various inspired authors, to their didactic purposes, to the historical and cultural milieux in which they lived, etc. [117] These are all elements which literary criticism must correctly appreciate in order to arrive at a proper understanding of the message transmitted. It is true that such criticism never attains anything but the ideas of the author

[115] It should not be forgotten that on the Jewish side the Massoretic text of the Hebrew Bible was the result of considerable work of textual criticism, whose origins go far back into the past. Cf. D. Barthélemy, "Les *tiqquné sopherim* et la critique textuelle de l'Ancien Testament" in *VTS* 9 (Bonn Congress) (Leyden: Brill, 1963), pp. 285-304; G. E. Weil, "La nouvelle édition de la Massorah (BHK iv) et l'histoire de la Massorah," *ibid.*, pp. 266-284; *Initiation à la Massorah* (Leyden: Brill, 1964), pp. 29 ff. The Qumran texts now furnish a point of comparison which makes possible a more exact evaluation of this work; but the outcome of this comparative study is not yet certain. A provisional evaluation and a bibliography can be found in P. W. Skehan, "The Qumran Manuscripts and Textual Criticism," *VTS* 4 (Strasbourg Congress) (Leyden: Brill, 1957), pp. 148-160; M. Mansoor, "The Massoretic Text in the Light of Qumran," *VTS* 9, pp. 305-321.

[116] Besides the general works cited on p. 335, note 75, cf. Robert—Feuillet, *Interpreting the Scriptures*, pp. 126-153.

[117] Above, pp. 93-100.

whom God made his instrument. In order to see the concrete evidence of a supernatural word of which they are the human translation, it is evidently necessary to go beyond this result by an appeal to faith. It is no less true that the divine word really passes through those ideas and through that language, which are open to the efforts of any and all to understand and appreciate properly. Christ, the word of God, was himself thus open to the observation and judgment of his contemporaries, and beyond them, to that of all men. So the literary study of the sacred books would seem to be another occasion for a dialogue, both necessary and, in the final analysis, productive, between Christian and non-Christian critics, who are equally desirous of explaining the content of their text.

## *1. Linguistic Criticism*

Linguistic study is the first step in literary criticism. It must be regretted that it is often conceived in too superficial a fashion. It naturally includes the analysis of the stylistic elements [118] which give the expression of thought its variety and its richness: metaphor, synecdoche, metonymy, hyperbole, pleonasm, understatement, euphemism, ellipsis, irony, etc. Neither ancient nor medieval rhetoric was ignorant of these elementary procedures which can be found in any language. But the modern study of the phenomenon of language goes much deeper. Language, [119] as a social phenomenon, makes communication between minds possible. [120] It always takes the form of a particular language which reflects one of the possible forms of the human mind. Every language, as we have already said, [121] displays a certain mental structure, whose categories and working processes can in no instance be held to be universal and absolute. When revelation used Hebrew and Greek in succession and at a certain stage of their internal evolution as its instrument of expression, it reshaped them somewhat so that they would not betray the message entrusted to the sacred authors. [122] But it did not with that suppress their peculiarities; on the contrary, it adopted them,

[118] J. Schildenberger, *op. cit.*, pp. 92-96. A small collection of these figures of speech can be found in C. Lavergne, *L'expression biblique* (Paris, 1947).

[119] E. Sapir, *Language: An Introduction to the Study of Speech* (London, Conn., 1949). Concerning the scientific study of language since the 19th-century, see M. Leroy, *Les grands courants de la linguistique moderne* (Paris, 1963).

[120] This aspect of language is closely connected to general semantics and to philosophical semantics; cf. P. Guiraud, *La sémantique*, 3rd ed. (Paris, 1962), pp. 87-104. On the role of language as an instrument of communication, see G. Gusdorf, *La Parole* (Paris, 1963), pp. 45 ff. (a precise treatment of the philosophical problem). J. A. Hutchinson, *Language and Faith: Studies in Sign, Symbol, and Meaning* (Philadelphia, 1963), pp. 44-72, studies the question in the context of biblical exegesis.

[121] Above, pp. 94 f.

[122] Above, pp. 86-89.

it cast itself into them, so to speak, fully respecting the personality of their human owners. To have a true understanding of the divine message, therefore, it is essential to study critically the linguistic instrument to which it is bound, to know in detail the mental categories to which its words and phrases correspond, to mark the various cultural levels which imposed their conventions on it; in a word, to understand everything which conditioned that singular expression of human thought which God chose as the vehicle of his own word.

Only this linguistic criticism makes possible the avoidance of two opposing dangers. On the one hand, if one were content to gather the words and phrases of the Bible and introduce them into theology without weighing carefully their intent and their meaning, he would end by confusing the absolute of the word of God with the manifold relativity of its human expression, which is accurate, but necessarily limited, destined for a worldwide audience, but necessarily colored by a restricted environment and culture. [123] On the other hand, if one were to judge that language by the standards of modern man, shaped by his scientific and technical civilization, he would tend to misunderstand its distinctive merits, to see in it only a transitory garb of which the biblical message can easily be stripped in order to become accessible to our contemporaries. Such is in fact the purpose of the demythologization which underlies R. Bultmann's whole system of interpretation. [124] If one agrees to call mythical any expression of transcendent and divine realities in a language used to speak of the things of this world, [125] and if one considers this mythical language a purely human

[123] That is the danger inherent in fundamentalism, to which Catholic theologians are not immune, especially when they conceive their work under the form of logical deductions founded upon credible texts. From a Protestant viewpoint, the problem is considered by G. Ebeling, "Word of God and Hermeneutics" in *Word and Faith*, pp. 312-313, who is not content to reject the simple definition "Scripture is the Word of God" and substitute milder expressions ("Scripture contains the word of God" or "witnesses the word of God"), but introduces as an essential element the proclamation of the word of God in the Church.

[124] Above, pp. 211 f. This danger is not peculiar to Bultmannian protes- for an tantism. It appears also in Catholicism, in pastors of souls whom concern "adapted" preaching leads to neglect the value proper to scriptural language in the revelation of the mystery of God. They thus arrive at a "demythization" of which they seem unaware. Bultmann's two clearest statements of his program ("New Testament and Mythology," 1941, and "On Demythization," 1952) can be found in English translation by R. H. Fuller, in *Kerygma and Myth* 1 (London: SPCK, 1953), pp. 1-44 and 191-211. On the opposition between "mythic thought" and "scientific thought," see pp. 188-192.

[125] It should be noted that for Bultmann this effort at expression denotes the intention to lay hold of transcendence itself: "Myth objectifies the hereafter in the here and now, and by that very fact into a controllable reality" (cited by A. Malet, *Mythos et Logos*, p. 48). In this definition the relation of myth to cult is obviously involved, and it is not just a problem of terminology.

creation to which the word of God remains foreign, if one empties symbolic reasoning, which enables us to speak of God in human and terrestrial analogies, of its realism, [126] he would certainly be obliged to strip Scripture of those chance wrappings which no longer correspond to our view of the world and of existence, and retain only its digestible kernel. Let us not misjudge the pertinence of the problem that is thus raised. But the manner in which it is stated is so objectionable that a correct solution cannot be expected. Bultmann's own demythologization misunderstands the real nature of biblical language and its relation to revelation just as much as that of the liberal school and that of the *religionsgeschichtliche Schule*, [127] which Bultmann explicitly rejected. [128] As we have seen above, [129] we are here dealing with a specific religious language, fashioned in the course of an historical experience in which faith taught its adherents to recognize the concrete experience of the acts of God on earth, whose crowning act was the sending of his own Son into the world. Linguistic criticism ought to lead to the discovery, beyond the peculiarities of a certain age, culture, and mentality, of the relation of the language in question to the revelatory experience which gave it its real content.

There is no reason, therefore, to demythologize Scripture; but it is important to understand its language, [130] in order to understand its message and to recast it in the languages of today. Familiarity with the authors who were God's instruments in transmitting his word does, of course, require effort. But that is no more than is required in any human relations. Speech is always an expression of an inner experience occasioned and developed through contact with some reality; it gives the listener an interpretation of that reality which is determined by the mental structure of the person who experienced it; it invites the listener to relive the same inner experience and to come in contact with the same reality. [131]  To

---

[126] Above, pp. 85 f.

[127] Our remarks agree with those of P. Barthel, *Interprétation du langage mythique et théologie biblique* (Leyden: Brill, 1963), pp. 89-101.

[128] Bultmann's position in this regard is excellently explained by A. Malet, *op. cit.*, pp. 137-141.

[129] Above, pp. 86 ff.

[130] According to Bultmann the demythologization is not a critical elimination of myth (like liberal demythization), but an interpretation which expresses its meaning. But this meaning is sought out in a purely existentialist perspective exclusive of any ontology (cf. above, p. 251). For the discussion generated by Bultmann's program, see the philosophical conferences published by E. Castelli, *Il problema della demitiz-zazione* (Padua: CEDAM, 1961) and *Demitizzazione e immagine* (Padua: CEDAM, 1962).

[131] L. Alonso-Schökel, "Hermeneutics in the Light of Language and Literature," *CBQ* 25 (1963), 371-386.

understand another's language is to accept this invitation, setting aside when necessary the mentality acquired through personal experience in order to reproduce in one's self the same mentality from which another's language springs. So understood, linguistic ciriticism is not a surgical operation whose purpose is to remove from the Bible its decadent elements. It is an active and intelligent penetration into the inner experience which found live expression in the sacred author's language. For anyone who approaches Scripture with faith, that inner experience goes beyond the merely human; by virtue of the charism of inspiration, [132] it implies a direct contact with God, a personal approach to the word of God, or better yet, an activity of that word, which thus gained the possibility of being expressed in human terms.

### 2. Literary Form Criticism [133]

The language of the sacred authors, however, does not exist in a vacuum. It is specified by the various literary genres they use. Even in books that are rich in doctrine like the gospels and letters, no phrase can be fully understood outside its context, not only grammatical and logical, but psychological and sociological as well. In the end, there exists no work that does not follow the laws of a determined form, one fixed in its essential lines by conventions of the society for which the author wrote. It is perhaps in this matter that modern literary criticism has made its most spectacular progress over the atomistic analysis practiced in antiquity and the Middle Ages.

When we considered the problem of literary genres in the sacred books, [134] we saw that there were two questions closely intertwined: as the functional literature of the people of God, the Bible always uses forms of expression that are related to the various aspects of its religious life in community; as literature produced in a determined time and circumstances, it necessarily adapts these forms to the cultural level of the people for whom it is written, and that level went through a considerable evolution from the age of the

---

[132] Above, pp. 68-73.

[133] J. Schildenberger, *op. cit.*, pp. 96-102, 172-391, analyzes at length the literary genres of the Bible. Cf. A. Fernández, *Institutiones biblicae*, 3rd ed., pp. 419-460; in Robert—Feuillet, *Introduction to the Old Testament*, pp. 000-000; A. Robert, "Littéraires (Genres)," *DBS* 5, cols. 405-421; *Questioni bibliche alla luce dell'enciclica 'Divino afflante Spiritu'* (Rome: Pont. Bibl. Inst., 1949). Scientific introductions naturally devote an important place to this problem. See, for example, A. Bentzen, *Introduction to the Old Testament* (Copenhagen: Gads, 1948), Vol. 1, pp. 102-264; O. Eissfeldt, *The Old Testament. An Introduction* (Oxford: Blackwell, 1965), pp. 9-153.

[134] Above, pp. 89-93 and 97-100.

ancient oral traditions to the end of the 1st century of our era. These two aspects of the problem must be kept in mind when undertaking a literary criticism of biblical texts. The first has considerable importance, because it shows the constant relation of these texts to the community in which they were composed. By making this point its principal preoccupation, the method called *Formgeschichte* has not only furthered literary criticism, [135] but has furnished a precious instrument of analysis for theologians, to whom this aspect of sacred literature is of particular interest. It is certainly to be regretted that some literary critics were influenced by principles which, all things considered, were not intrinsically related to their work: the sociological theory of the creative community (of religious ideas as well as of literary works), an artificial opposition between the demands of faith and respect for the objectivity of history, etc. We have already stated our position in this regard. [136] But given such corrections, it goes without saying that this method ought to be incorporated into literary criticism, according to its own place and function. [137]

And this brings us to the second aspect of the problem, the relation of the texts to the various cultural levels through which the people of God passed. How could the sacred authors have avoided adapting their modes of expression to the mentality and customs of their contemporaries? The recuperation of ancient oriental literatures and the parallel discoveries provided by ethnology furnish in this matter the information without which the study of the texts could make only groping progress, without concrete and exact points of reference. It is understandable that the encyclical *Divino afflante Spiritu* emphasized this indispensable comparative method, which throws light on the characteristics of biblical literature while underlining its originality and distinctive merits. [138] This is particularly

---

[135] K. Koch, *Was ist Formgeschichte? Neue Wege der Bibel-exegese* (Neukirchen: Neukirchener, 1964), p. xiii, writes quite correctly: "*Formgeschichte* brought to light, in a way that had not been suspected before, the bond between literature and life, between the text and the history of the people of God." This book is a good general presentation of the problem, but all the examples analyzed in detail are taken from the Old Testament.

[136] Above, pp. 91, 211.

[137] See the Biblical Commissions's instruction on the historical truth of the gospels: "In appropriate cases the interpreter is free to seek out what sound elements there are in "the Method of Form-history," and these he can duly make use of to gain a fuller understanding of the Gospels" (*CBQ* 26 (1964), 306). Form-historical studies are obviously not limited to the gospels. For the epistles of St. Paul, see B. Rigaux, *Saint Paul et ses lettres* (Bruges-Paris: Desclée de Brouwer, 1962), pp. 163-199.

[138] *Ench. B.*, 558-560. This passage merits to be quoted in full: "What is the literal sense of a passage is not always as obvious in the speeches and writings of the ancient authors of the East, as it is in the works of our own time. For what they wished to express is not to be determined by the rules of grammar and philology

noticeable in the matter of history, since the forms used to preserve the memory of the past can vary almost indefinitely according to ages and and milieux. But history aside, all the literary genres employed in Sacred Scripture have benefited from this outside source of light, from law to the wisdom writings, from the love songs preserved in the Song of Songs to the religious poetry of the psalms, from the letters of St. Paul to the revelation literature found in the apocalypses. In short, an objective approach to the meaning of the texts, an understanding of the forms of expression used by the sacred authors, an exact determination of their didactic intent, all of these have become much easier for us than they were for the fathers, the medieval writers, and even 19th century critics. Theology can only rejoice, for exegesis through these means provides a sound basis for its work.

## III. HISTORICAL CRITICISM

It is only for reasons of clarity that we have here separated our discussion of literary criticism from that of historical criticism, for the two methods are intimately related and the use of one goes hand in hand with the other. Under the name of historical criticism two clearly distinct questions are often treated together: that of the historical context in which each book was composed, and that of the material any of them might furnish for the use of historians.

### 1. Historical Origin of the Sacred Books

To make a proper literary criticism of any works, it is important to know in what circumstances, in what milieu, they were composed. The problems alone, nor solely by the context; the interpreter must, as it were, go back wholly in spirit to those remote centuries of the East and with the aid of history, archeology, ethnology, and other sciences, accurately determine what modes of writing, so to speak, the authors of that ancient period would be likely to use, and in fact did use. For the ancient peoples of the East, in order to express their ideas, did not always employ those forms or kinds of speech which we use today; but rather those used by the men of their times and countries. What those exactly were the commentator cannot determine as it were in advance, but only after a careful examination of the ancient literature of the East" (*ibid.*, 558). After this very clear statement it is difficult to understand how Cardinal Ruffini could write in *L'Osservatore Romano* of August 24, 1961: "How can one suppose that for 19 centuries the Church presented the divine Book to her sons without discerning its literary genre, which is the key to its exact interpretation? Such an assertion becomes even more absurd when it is recalled that a good number of these hypercritics not only propose new applications of the theory of literary genres to the inspired books, but postpone their definitive clarification to the future when—thanks to history, archeology, ethnology and the other sciences— the modes of speaking and writing of the ancients, especially of the East, will be better known." It sounds as if the author intended to correct the positions of the encyclical, whose expressions he explicitly uses.

of authorship, date, literary authenticity, etc., must be resolved by positive methods which exclude any dogmatic or antidogmatic prejudice. In this field, Jewish tradition and that of the ancient Church had preoccupations quite different from our own. It is very possible that they have preserved interesting information, which ought to be accepted and appreciated for what it is worth. But it still must be interpreted critically, for these traditions did not have our concern for thoroughness and accuracy; they were content with broad views and outlines where we would prefer precise distinctions. To accept without question the positions they have passed on to us in matters that do not jeopardize the faith would not be proof of one's authentic traditional mind; often it would mean canonizing the opinion of a rudimentary historical criticism which is totally insufficient in modern eyes. Theology would therefore find no profit in them. On the other hand, it cannot but gain from a better reconstruction of the literary history of the Bible. Not only do the texts become clearer when their historical context and their authors are known, but the ways of the divine pedagogy are understood proportionally better as a detailed knowledge of the stages of the development of revelation is gained.

Two examples will help to make this point clear. Judaism passed on to us the notion that the Pentateuch was a finished work during the time of Moses. [139] But the activity of God in the Old Testament is undeniably better manifested in the history of its formation as critical study has today revealed it to us, even if the modern explanation still includes a measure of hypothesis. The tradition which owes its beginning to Moses did not remain fixed in the midst of a history in which nothing stirred; it developed organically, adapting itself to the needs of changing times in order to continue to play its role within the people of God. Similarly, the life and thought of the apostolic community in their relation to the gospel received from Christ are more clearly manifested through the history of the formation of the gospels, [140] from the stage of oral preaching to the final edition of our four short books, than in the conservative view which considered them as independent works, hardly even rooted in the milieu which produced them. The degree of hypothesis which remains in this reconstruction of the past corresponds to the degree of approximation which every historical work includes; it stimulates research without endangering the faith in the least.

---

[139] Concerning the question of the Pentateuch, we refer the reader to the very complete article by H. Cazelles, "Pentateuque," *DBS* 7, cols. 687-858.

[140] Statement of the problem by X. Léon-Dufour in Robert—Feuillet, *Introduction to the New Testament*, pp. 141-154, 252-324; by J. Huby, *L'Évangile et les évangiles*, 2nd ed. (Paris: Beauchesne, 1954), pp. 1-98. This formation process is excellently outlined by the Biblical Commission's instruction of April 21, 1964 (cf. *CBQ* 26 [1964], 307 ff.).

It goes without saying that one must proceed with caution in this delicate field, for important matters are at stake. But prudence does not justify mental laziness, and even less blindness to the real problems that arise. Only the conscientious and loyal work of Catholic critics can make possible a discussion among equals with historians who do not share their faith. [141]

## 2. Reconstruction of Biblical History

Historical criticism has also another task: on the basis of the evidence provided by the Bible and that which extra-biblical sources and archeology add to it, it is charged with reconstructing the history of the two Testaments with as much precision as modern methods permit. [142]  Christian faith is, of course, certain of the historical foundations on which it rests, whether it be a question of the history that preceded Christ, that of Christ himself, or that of the primitive Church.  It is certain that the scriptural evidence gives it a true and faithful knowledge of its history.  But this general certainty leaves untouched a multitude of questions of detail, for the historical truth of Scripture needs to be understood properly.  We have seen above the general approach to be taken to it, and how it differs from the scientific exactness for which modern historians strive. [143]  It is from this point of view that the texts ought to be studied critically in order to bring to light their exact meaning.  For there are a thousand ways of representing the human experiences which bear the mark of God's work here below; all of them are true, if they are understood properly.  But it cannot be expected that all of them present the same external description of the facts [144]; their diversity must be respected if they are to be understood properly.

Once this principle is admitted, a vast field of investigation opens up. For while it is true that the very demands of faith introduced into the literature of Israel and of primitive Christianity an interest in history which can scarcely be found in other religious literatures, [145] their recording of the past was

---

[141] An indicative detail: at the beginning of this century introductory manuals written by Catholics treated critical questions in an almost dogmatic way; they opposed a "Catholic thesis" to the theories proposed by rationalist or Protestant adversaries. At present there is a clearer distinction of approach to doctrinal problems and those which are the object of critical research.  And the discussions in this latter field have taken on a tone of serenity which they should never have lost.  Critical choices no longer depend upon an exegete's confessional allegiance.

[142] Concise treatment in Robert—Feuillet, *Interpreting the Scriptures*, pp. 154-164.

[143] Above, pp. 115-124.

[144] Above, pp. 129-137.  The equivocal notion of "fact" is justly criticized by J. Hours, *Valeur de l'histoire* (Paris, 1954), p. 1, note 1, and pp. 55-59.

[145] Cf. *Divino afflante Spiritu*, in *Ench. B.*, 558 f.

always conditioned by cultural conventions very remote from our own. The documentation must be interpreted according to its own conventions, if it is to be allowed to deliver its own message. This rule is as valid for the books of the Old Testament as it is for the gospels, which in any case give us a very imperfect acquaintance with the life of Christ. Measuring the limits of our knowledge, realizing what problems remain to be solved, attempting to unify a piecemeal documentation by resorting to hypotheses [146] —all of these undertakings can enter into exegesis without questioning the foundations or the certainty of faith. Just as it would be unreasonable to introduce into such criticism prejudices inspired by rational positivism, so it would be absurd to shackle progress in the name of an erroneous theology of the word of God and a false concept of inerrancy.

The self criticism which contemporary historians have undertaken in regard to their methods, and the passing of a narrow concept of history as science which misunderstood the human reality it set out to study, [147] have made a great contribution toward clarification of the situation. The historian's approach to a past which can never be fully captured has become both more prudent and more humble, more careful in constructing hypotheses, and more respectful of its sources than was the case at the beginning of this century. But even granted this, there remains much to be done before the history of the two Testaments is scientifically reconstructed in all its details, not only as regards political and social facts, but as regards ideas and religious life. And how can the value of this last aspect of critical studies for theology escape anyone? [148] Is it not the history of revelation itself which thus is clarified, in proportion as the points of its insertion in time and place are more precisely identified? It is therefore a fundamental task of Catholic exegetes to undertake historical criticism; its importance cannot be overemphasized. No appeal to the light of faith can modify its basic rules, because by unfolding in a truly human history, the economy of salvation assumed the condition of all earthly things. In order that reflection on the biblical message might uncover the signs of its presence in the world, it must be able to rest on this positive study, carried out with as much care as for any other event of human history. The stakes are such as to leave no room for mediocrity.

---

[146] On the role played by faith and unbelief in the elaboration of these working hypotheses, see above, p. 344 f.

[147] Above, pp. 115 ff. and J. Hours, *op. cit.*, pp. 43-80.

[148] P. Brunner, "Die grossen Taten Gottes und die historisch-kritische Vernunft: Einsich und Glaube," *Festschrift G. Söhngen* (Freiburg: Herder, 1962), pp. 54-74.

IV. PHILOSOPHICAL CRITICISM

*1. The Problem* [149]

A positive study of the religious phenomenon presented in the Bible cannot be conceived without a parallel reflection which seeks to discover its profound significance and finally to pass judgment on it. We have said above that, in the final analysis, the judgment which underlies all critical studies is of the nature of a belief, since it manifests the exegete's personal choice in regard to the problem of religion. [150] It does not matter that this choice, whether it settles on the Christian faith or not, implies a whole rational process which, as such, belongs to the domain of philosophy. Current works on biblical criticism frequently omit all mention of it, as if literary and historical criticism were self-sufficient without this complement which gives them meaning, or better, which inspires and guides their every step. This deficiency can be explained historically, but nothing can justify it. Is it not, as a matter of fact, precisely at this level that the dialogue between the believing exegete and the skeptical historian takes places, when they study, each in his own way, the religion of the two Testaments? Philosophic reflection on the history of revelation and its contents has always had a place in Christian thought, but until modern times it was rarely carried out independently and within the context of exegesis. Elements of it can be found in the works of theologians, and especially of the apologists, from the *Apologies* of St. Justin [151] to the *Paedagogus* of Clement of Alexandria, [152] from the *Contra Celsum* of Origen [153] to the *City of God*, [154] without overlooking the references found here and there in the *Summa contra Gentiles*.

Since the 17th century, the problem has taken a different form with the development of rationalist inspired criticism, which sought to reduce the origins of the Judeo-Christian religious phenomenon to purely natural causes. [155] From Spinoza to Lessing, from Hegel to contemporary Marxists, from the sociologists to Freud and atheistic existentialism, this attempt has

[149] Cf. *Sens chrétien de l'A.T.*, pp. 414-418.
[150] Above, pp. 339 ff.
[151] St. Justin, *Apology* I, 20-25 (concurrent criticism of Christianity and mythology in the light of philosophy), 50-56; *Apology* II, 7-13 (the revealing Word and the pagan philosophers from Plato to the Stoics).
[152] J. Quasten, *Patrology* (Utrecht: Spectrum, 1953), Vol. 2, pp. 9-12; J. Daniélou, *Message évangélique et culture hellénistique* (Paris: Desclée, 1961), pp. 291-296.
[153] J. Quasten, *op. cit.*, Vol. 2, pp. 52 ff.; H. de Lubac, *Histoire et esprit*, pp. 30 ff.
[154] The first ten books of the *City of God* contain a discussion of the relative value of paganism and biblical revelation in assuring the prosperity of human society and preparing for man's eternal happiness. The following books are a meditation on the meaning of history understood as the parallel development of the two Cities on earth.
[155] Above, pp. 204 ff.

taken quite different forms. Evidently it cannot be said that philosophical criticism of the phenomenon of religion in general, and of the biblical phenomenon in particular, has developed in a very coherent manner. The method used by Bergson in *Les deux sources de la morale et de la religion* does not satisfy all the requirements of Catholic theology. [156] That of Blondel in *L'Action*, while satisfactory from that point of view, incorporates insufficiencies in regard to the history of religions and exegesis, despite some excellent remarks in *Histoire et dogme*. [157] Newman's approach, developed in *Grammar of Assent*, [158] is a good example of the direction reflection ought to take, but Newman was not a trained exegete, and his purpose was to mark out the way of faith rather than to provide a technical explanation of philosophical criticism of the Bible. In general, the defensive attitude taken by the magisterium and Catholic theologians in regard to independent criticism, liberal Protestantism, modernism, and presently to Bultmann's system has not facilitated this important undertaking, which demands equal competence in exegesis, philosophy and theology. The recent attempt of H. Duméry, [159] who strove to take all these factors into account without leaving the level of philosophy, met with outright rejection [160] without bringing the basic problem any nearer to a solution. [161] We cannot be expected, therefore, to provide

---

[156] Furthermore, Bergson did not treat the problem as a Christian philosopher. He merely inquired whether, in the moral and religious fact which is the culmination of the human conscience, it is not possible to discern the mark of the same *élan vital* that is at the source of the dynamism observable in creative evolution. Hence his attention to the "two sources" of morality (closed and open morality) and of religion (static and dynamic religion). But this observation led him to recognize the pivotal position of the fact of the Bible, and more particularly of Christ, as the historical manifestation of the spiritual dynamism on account of which the universe seems to be a *deus ex machina*. The outcome of this philosophical investigation naturally placed Bergson face to face with the problem of faith in Christ. On this latter point, see H. Gouhier, *Bergson et le Christ des évangiles* (Paris: Fayard, 1961).

[157] To this should be added the correspondence between Blondel and Loisy and Von Hügel; cf. R. Marlé, *Au cœur de la crise moderniste: Le dossier d'une controverse* (Paris: Aubier, 1960).

[158] J. H. Newman, *Grammar of Assent*, chap. X (natural and revealed religion), nn. 6-8: the Jews, the relation of Christianity to Judaism, the personal place of Christ.

[159] H. Duméry, *Critique et religion: Recherches sur la méthode en philosophie de la religion* (Paris, 1957); *Philosophie de la religion: Essais sur la signification du christianisme* (Paris, 1957); *La foi n'est pas un cri* (Paris, 1957).

[160] Placed on the index of forbidden books June 17, 1958.

[161] From the Catholic viewpoint, see the critiques of L. Malevez, *Transcendance de Dieu et création des valeurs* (Bruges-Paris: Desclée de Brouwer, 1958); J. Mouroux in *RSPT* 43 (1959), 95-102 (cf. 44 [1960], 89-95); A. Léonard in *RSPT* 43 (1959), 283-300; R. Marlé in *RSR* 50 (1959), 225-241. From the Protestant viewpoint, see P. Barthel, *Interprétation du langage mythique et théologie biblique*, pp. 199-285. H. Duméry explained his position and replied to his critics in the 2nd edition of *La foi n'est pas un cri*, followed by *Foi et institution* (Paris, 1959). Criticism of his position is accompanied by a constructive effort in H. van Luijk, *Philosophie du fait chrétien* (Bruges-Paris: Desclée de Brouwer, 1965).

the solution here; at most we will attempt to clarify some of its essential
elements.

## 2. The Stages of Philosophical Criticism

When the phenomenon of the Bible, considered in its historical reality and
in its religious content, is subjected to philosophical criticism, it should not
be dissociated from all the evidence provided by the history of religions.
In fact, contrary to the practice of the 19th century, the scientific study of the
phenomenon of religion is today no longer content to remain descriptive and
comparative; the criticism that accompanies it is no longer considered just an
operation of analysis and explanation capable of dispelling the mystery of
*homo religiosus*. The use of phenomenology has introduced a new dimension
into it [162]: beyond the facts and religious customs considered in their material
reality, an attempt is made to understand their significance [163] and thus
to "decipher their essense" (to use the terminology of Husserl [164]), while
respecting the unique character of this aspect of human experience. This
attempt at interpretation, in which concern for objectivity is accompanied by
understanding sympathy, undoubtedly proceeds from the general characteristics which are common to all religious movements, including the Bible,
since it aims to understand *homo religiosus* as he is in his universality. But it
is equally attentive to the distinctive traits which make each movement
irreducible to the others, so that the particular significance of each will
emerge. In this perspective, certain aspects of Judeo-Christian religion take
on increased interest, in the very measure that they differ from the whole
of religious experience. For example, the idea of the one God did not appear
in it as the result of a philosophical process; it emerged from an experience
which culminates in the intimate relation of Christ with Him whom he called

[162] A general treatment, under the direction of G. Berger, in *Encyclopédie
française* 39, 32-40 (outline of a phenomenology of religion). Among the works
oriented in this direction we might note those of G. van der Leeuw, *La religion dans
son essence et ses manifestations* (Paris: Payot, 1955); M. Éliade, *Traité d'histoire des
religions: Morphologie du sacré* (Paris: Payot, 1949); C. J. Bleeker, *Grondlijnen tot een
phaenomenologie van der godsdienst* (Groningen, 1943); *The Sacred Bridge: Researches
into the Nature and Structure of Religion* (Leyden: Brill, 1963), pp. 1-35 (methodological tract on the phenomenology of religion). H. Duméry, *Phénoménologie et
religion* (Paris, 1958), joins phenomenology to his own philosophical critique (cf. *La
foi n'est pas un cri*, 2nd ed., pp. 378-387).

[163] See the very clear exposition by G. Berger, *Encyclopédie française* 39, 32, 2.

[164] The phenomenology of religion's debt to Husserl is explicitly acknowledged
by M. Scheler, *Vom Ewigen im Menschen* (1921); G. van der Leeuw, *op. cit.*, pp. 665-
671, adopts Husserl's terminology *(épochè)* to distinguish the phenomenology of
the history of religions and of philosophy properly so called; cf. C. J. Bleeker, *The
Sacred Bridge*, pp. 3 ff.

his Father. In it revelation did not come only through the intermediacy of certain inspired persons; it is bound to a history whose meaning it manifests—which led G. van der Leeuw to remark that it substitutes a "history-myth" for myth. [165]

Such a phenomenology, when applied to the ancient oriental religions, naturally attempts to decipher the symbols which constitute the thread of their language and rites, to interpret the myths which express the existential experience of man in his relations with the world and with the divine. This preoccupation makes it apt to comprehend what, from these two points of view, makes biblical religion similar to the cults which surrounded it, and what makes it different from them: its break with mythology understood as a divine history, but its adoption of mythical language to speak of the activity of God in the world [166]; its use of the usual symbolism in the expression of its faith and worship, but its reinterpretation of those symbols on the basis of an historical experience in which faith discovered the realization of the history of salvation, [167] etc. The interpretation of symbols, to which P. Ricoeur has called attention with his masterful study of the symbolism of evil, [168] thus provides an approach which leads right to the heart of biblical religion, to the message of salvation in which man finds the solution to the problem of his existence, which is likewise what religious myths seek in their own way. Contrary to Bultmann's demythologization, which belittles "mythical" language at the same time that it gives it an existentialist interpretation, this interpretation of symbols intends to respect the modes of expression used in religious language without diminishing the experience it translates. It must certainly be concerned with the non-religious elements which influence the formation of that language (social, economic, political conditions, etc.) but what it is most interested in is the unique experience in which it is rooted, beyond all the influences which might be discovered in it. It thus furnishes a solid basis for that linguistic criticism whose importance we stressed above. [169]

The roots of language in the thought and life of man make it easy to understand why biblical linguistic criticism is inseparable from philosophical

---

[165] "In the midst of history, God unveils the meaning of the world as salvation" (*op. cit.*, p. 563). This remark agrees with that of M. Éliade, *Le mythe de l'éternel retour*, pp. 152 ff., on "history considered as theophany" in biblical revelation.

[166] Above, pp. 127-129.

[167] Above, pp. 85-89.

[168] P. Ricœur, *Philosophie de la volonté. II. Finitude et culpabilité: La symbolique du mal* (Paris: Aubier, 1960); "Herméneutique des symboles et réflexion philosophique" in *Il problema della demitizzazione*, pp. 51-73. P. Ricœur's method has received the approval of P. Barthel, *Interprétation du langage mythique et théologie biblique*, pp. 286-381.

[169] Above, pp. 346-349.

reflection on the religious phenomenon presented in Scripture. And an exegete's judgment on this language always reflects his personal philosophical and religious position. It would therefore be subject to all the dangers of subjectivism if phenomenology did not provide an objective basis, thus making it possible to overcome the opposition between rational dogmatism, which would impose its preconceived views on the history of religions and exegesis, and a narrow theology, too little concerned with the proper place of rational criticism. Does that mean that the undertaking is easy? It would be all the more surprising if it were, as investigation into the significance of the Bible ought finally to lead to a value judgment. But the closer one comes to that end, the more personal factors interfere with an objective treatment of the facts. Not that absolutely no value judgment on the Bible is possible on a strictly rational level: Bergson, Blondel and H. Duméry all intended to remain on that level. But every judgment of this type necessarily borders on the profound choices by which every man finds the scale of values to which he relates everything else. [170] In brief, at this level philosophical reflection reaches a critical point: the domain of the rational, without for all that losing its own autonomy, opens onto the domain of the existential in which free will joins the intellectual faculties in directing a man's progress. For the Christian this reflection joins the adhesion of faith, and enables him to prove its rational soundness.

It is not out of place here to note the way in which the whole of critical investigation enters into relation with this fact which surpasses it, that is, each man's choice in regard to biblical revelation, to Jesus Christ. For if faith, or lack of it, is necessarily related to philosophical criticism, and if this latter is implicitly present in all the operations of literary and historical criticism, it is clear that biblical exegesis is inconceivable without dialogue, without discussion, even without confrontation, between believers and non-believers. This realization brings us to an examination of the place criticism occupies in the Church.

## III. THE PLACE OF CRITICAL INVESTIGATION

### I. CRITICISM AND APOLOGETICS

Christian apologetics always has a defensive aspect and a constructive aspect in which Scripture occupies a considerable place. There was a time when the defensive aspect became predominant, at the same time that the positions defended were a mixture of truths of the faith and conservative critical

---

[170] See the profound critique of H. van Luijk, *op. cit.*, pp. 289 ff.

positions. [171] That age has happily passed. The return to a sane theology of inspiration and a correct notion of inerrancy removed those obstacles. That does not mean that a sane interpretation of Scripture need never be defended against unfounded, slanted, dangerous or simply daring critical hypotheses. But that can properly be done in the context of a dialogue between exegetes of all persuasions: Catholic, Protestant, nonconfessional. Using the same methods and applying them to the same documents, they are bound to explain the basis of their choices and justify them with rational arguments. And what is apologetics, if not the formation of this dialogue, not only at the level of technical research on the texts or on the history of the two Testaments, but at that of the reflection which prolongs that research, posing as it does such basic problems. [172]

In this context, the Christian apologist shows how his critical study of Scripture, carried on with great care proportional to what is at stake, is organically related to his faith. If he occasionally denounces the false conclusions and sophistic reasoning of his colleagues, he takes it for granted that they will not fail to show him his own errors of method or judgment, for he is no less demanding than they are when he is forced to resort to hypotheses to account for the texts and facts he studies. But he is always concerned with going beyond the raw facts in order to investigate their meaning, and finally to pass judgment in their regard. Raising the discussion to the level of philosophical criticism, he does not reject without good reason the explanations which rationalists might oppose to his own; he shows, on the contrary, that the objective study of biblical data forces on every man a decisive choice whose object is Christ. [173] For his own part, he undertakes to give an account of the reasons for his choice, of the signs by which he recognizes, in the religious current whose center is Christ, the authentic revelation of the living God and the realization of human salvation. In a certain sense his explanation is a profession of faith. But at the same time, it demonstrates how faith incorporates all of the observable data, how it is

---

[171] Above, pp. 213 ff.

[172] Such apologetics is not the exclusive possession of Christian exegetes. Not only Jewish exegesis, but also rationalist criticism in all its forms, are apologetics in their own way, for they are linked to the personal choices of their followers and usually aim to demonstrate that they are well founded.

[173] "The historian encounters Jesus of Nazareth as a question posed to himself, and this question demands a response from him. Is Jesus, despite the depth and sublimity of his religious and moral preaching, only a person to be classed among the prophets of the last days, the self-proclaimed messiahs who rose in those days, or not? Investigation halts at this point, and faith begins—or doesn't begin at all. Who has ears to hear, let him hear!" (X. Léon-Dufour, Les évangiles et l'histoire de Jésus, p. 451, quoting E. Sjöberg, Der verborgene Messchensohn [Lund: Gleerup, 1955], p. 246).

in positive accord with literary and historical criticism, how it boldly makes use of phenomenology to surpass its conclusions.

In short, starting from the common ground where all historians meet, the apologist elaborates a constructive argument which in some way indicates the way to belief. He well knows that his reasoning can bring his colleague only to the threshold of faith, since the revelation of God in Jesus Christ is never acknowledged except by a free act which involves the whole man. At least he insists on showing that his own commitment is as reasonable as the contrary commitment, that he has reasons to think that it is more reasonable, [174] and that in any case he would refuse to commit himself if he had to wager on a mere probability. Knowing that the problem of faith rests in the final analysis on a plane above the rational, that of the internal struggle between man and divine grace, [175] he strives at least to eliminate the illusory motives which would pervert that struggle, and to present the contrary motives which lead man to the obedience of faith. If anyone presents him as an objection all the human traits of the Bible and of the history it recounts, he admits them without difficulty. If an argument is made on the basis of the history of religions, he meets it without hesitation. In his eyes it is precisely from such standpoints that the real problem arises. For the more an historian strives to account for the fact of the Bible centered on the person of Jesus Christ, the more he seeks to clarify its meaning, the more he realizes that he cannot remain in the position of a disinterested observer in its regard. The object of his study involves himself, and the judgment he makes on it unfailingly rests on principles that lie beyond the competence of history.

There should be nothing astonishing about such a connection between apologetics and biblical criticism. The object of Christian faith is not ideas but a fact, or better, a person: Jesus Christ, in whom it acknowledges the Son of God who "has come in the flesh" (1 Jn 4:2), made manifest in human history and actually present in his Church. All the investigations which Christ, and the sequence of events which surround him, occasion, therefore, properly belong to the reflection which can lead man to believe. Or better, the very object of apologetics is made up of these investigations and reflections, which are intimately linked to one another and cannot be separated. The classic distinction between external apologetics, dedicated to objective

---

[174] "Reason would never submit itself if it did not judge that there are occasions when it ought to submit. It is therefore right that it should submit when it judges that it ought to submit" (Pascal, *Pensées*, ed. Lafuma, n. 274).

[175] "No one can come to me unless he is drawn by the Father who sent me. . . . It is written in the prophets: 'They will all be taught by God,' and to hear the teaching of the Father, and learn from it, is to come to me" (Jn 6:44-45). Cf. *Ench. S.*, 3010. Concerning this action of grace which "inclines the hearts" of those who believe, see the reflections of Pascal, *Pensées*, nn. 380-382.

and historical proofs, and internal apologetics, whose object is the immanent in man, appears artificial from the moment that philosophical criticism establishes an intrinsic link between the facts and the problem of existence which every man faces in the depths of his own being.  In short, the apologist cannot regard biblical criticism as a mere auxiliary science whose duty it is to supply him with sound arguments, but which remains foreign to his proper work.  And the exegete cannot ignore the fact that his situation puts him at the heart of the problem of apologetics. [176]  In this matter, partitions need to be removed and prejudices abandoned.  The logic of the matter will see to that itself.

## II. CRITICISM AND THEOLOGY

### 1. An Historical Preparation for the Study of Theology

The relation of biblical criticism to theology is twofold.  From one point of view, it can be considered a preparation for the systematic study of theological problems, whether they be dogmatic, moral, sacramental or spiritual. In present practice, a distant offspring of medieval scholasticism, minds are prepared for this study by a purely philosophical preparation, in which they acquire the speculative instrument which they are then supposed to use in elaborating the material provided by revelation.  The system is in itself unassailable: since the function of theology is to establish the link between revelation and the human problems which every age poses, it is obvious that such a philosophical formation is necessary.  The question is not what form it ought to take today in order to fulfill its purpose and respond to the concrete needs of the contemporary Church, while still providing an acquaintance with the language used by the fathers and theologians of the past.  Everyone knows that it is not easy to satisfy all these demands at once.  But there is another aspect of the matter which should never be forgotten.  Revelation is not a collection of abstract truths; its object is salvation history whose center is Christ, and whose source is the word of God of which Scripture alone is an immediately accessible direct witness.  And while it is true that this history and these books posed no problem in the age in which critical methods were still in their infancy, the same is not true today.  How can anyone be a good theologian if he is unaware of the problems posed by the Bible, the discussions it gives rise to, and the manner in which they can be solved in the light of faith?

---

[176] The place of biblical criticism in the problem of apologetics has been well explained by H. Bouillard, "Le sens de l'apologétique," 35 (1961), 311-326 (reprinted in *Logique de la foi* [Paris, 1964], pp. 15-38).

To enter into theology, therefore, a philosophical preparation is no longer sufficient. An historical and scriptural preparation must be added to provide a proper introduction to critical problems and methods. For if it is necessary to know well the man to whom the revealed message is to be announced and explained, it is no less necessary to be acquainted with the human aspect of the facts which lie at the origin of that message. Since the mystery of salvation was revealed in history and through the means of history, it is essential to learn to approach that history correctly in order to understand revelation at its source. In other words, the historical reading of the Bible (which necessarily includes a doctrinal aspect, but also supposes an elementary introduction to criticism) logically precedes its theological reading, and it is impossible to see how it can be dispensed with. In order to do this, there is no need to put faith aside temporarily; faith itself demands this attention to the facts on which it is founded, and this reasoned contact with the inspired texts which remain its supreme norm. Neither is there any need to set aside ecclesiastical tradition, in which these texts manifested all their implications as that tradition interpreted them; but on the other hand, placing oneself in living tradition does not dispense from the effort of familiarizing oneself with the rules of a literal reading. We here encounter in a new form the principle which Hugh of St. Victor stated so well [177]: before devoting oneself to allegory (that is, to a theological and spiritual commentary), one must be familiar with the letter and history. Only the study of the letter and of history is today carried out with better instruments than in the Middle Ages. It could therefore be hoped that a reform of the ecclesiastical *ratio studiorum* would preface theological studies with this twofold introduction, philosophical and biblical, which would be a positive preparation for later systematic study. Similarly, an effort should be made at every level of Christian teaching to prepare the faithful, considering their cultural level, to read Sacred Scripture with understanding.

---

[177] "Read Scripture, and first learn what it materially narrates... For it is my conviction that you cannot become perfectly adept at allegory (that is, in theology and spirituality explained on the basis of Scripture), unless you first become so in history" (*Eruditio didascalica*, PL 179, 790). Hugh of St. Victor visualizes three steps in the study of the *sacra doctrina*. The first consists in this initiation into the letter that relates history, carried out, of course, in a spirit of faith. Then would follow a synthetic exposition of the material gathered in the earlier stage: that is the *De sacramentis christianae fidei*. Thus armed, the exegete could then undertake allegory systematically, that is, a theological and spiritual commentary specially adapted to practical pastoral needs (cf. *Sens chrétien de l'A.T.*, pp. 54-57).

## 2. Criticism and Biblical Theology [178]

Within theology itself criticism retains a very important role. Since its proper field is the literal sense of biblical texts, its task is to clarify them in relation to their age, the level of revelation they represent, the current of thought to which they belong, the personality of their authors. This task, despite the measure of uncertainty or approximation involved in some of its details, is of prime importance for theology. It enables the theologian to follow step by step the progress of revelation and the development of the divine pedagogy in history. It puts him in contact with the realities of the faith at the very point when they emerge from shadow, and makes him a spectator of their progressive unveiling. Just as positive theology studies the development of dogmas from the teaching of the apostles, so biblical theology, founded on the results of criticism, studies their previous development. [179] It thus shows the various themes of the gospel message emerging and deepening in the Old Testament, grouping themselves around Christ who gives them their full meaning, unfolding in the apostolic writings which forever fixed the foundations of Christian theology. [180] In this perspective the Scripture proof of the scholastic theologians is completely transformed; but it acquires a force and richness of content which the accumulations of diverse citations, torn from their historical and literary context, never had. [181] Not only is the objective content of each text fully respected, but their organic relation to the whole raises the value of their assertion to its maximum.

[178] The relation between exegesis and dogmatic theology has been the object of numerous studies during the last two decades. We will cite only some of the most representative: J. Michl, "Dogmatischer Schriftbeweis und Exegese," *BZ* N.F. 2 (1958), 1-14; J. Levie, "Exégèse critique et interprétation théologique: apports et limites de la preuve d'Écriture sainte en théologie," *The Bible, Word of God in Words of Men*, pp. 273-297 (represents two articles which appeared in *Mélanges J. Lebreton* (Paris, 1951), Vol. 1, pp. 237-252, and *NRT* 71 (1949), 1009-1029); *idem*, "Interprétation scripturaire: en exégèse—en théologie" in *Sacra pagina* (Bruxelles-Louvain Congress), Vol. 1, pp. 100-118; A. Descamps, "Réflexions sur la méthode en théologie biblique," *ibid.*, pp. 132-157 (the proper roles of rational criticism and faith). Articles by several authors, both theologians and exegetes, have been brought together by H. Vorgrimler, *Exegese und Dogmatik* (Mayence, 1962). H. Haag, "Zum Verhältnis Exegese—Dogmatik," *Theologischer Quartalschrift* 142 (1962), 1-22; J. Blenkinsopp, "Biblical and Dogmatic Theology," *CBQ* 26 (1964), 70-85; B. Prete, "Il 'senso biblico' in teologia," *Rivista Biblica* 12 (1964), 2-25.

[179] F. J. Cwiekowski, "Biblical Theology as Historical Theology," *CBQ* 24 (1962), 404-411. On the notion of biblical theology, see the older studies by C. Spicq, "L'avènement de la théologie biblique," *RSPT* 35 (1951), 561-574; F. M. Braun, "La théologie biblique," *RTh* 61 (1953), 221-253.

[180] J. Guillet, *Themes of the Bible* (Notre Dame: Fides, 1964), studies some of these themes. A systematic collection of them can be found in X. Léon-Dufour, *Dictionary of Biblical Theology* (New York: Desclée, 1967).

[181] L. Alonso-Schökel, "Argument d'Écriture et théologie biblique dans l'enseignement théologique," *NRT* 81 (1959), 337-354.

It should be noted, however, that biblical theology conceived in this way is enclosed within strict limits: those of the literal sense of the texts, of the explicit didactic intent of the inspired authors, of the particular problem in light of which they expressed their message. It is of course aware that the message in question is the word of God destined for all men, capable of casting light on the problems of all ages. But its purpose is not to discern what light this word contained in the sacred texts throws on today's problems, nor to relate what implications ecclesiastical tradition might have discovered in them down through the ages. Biblical theology is content to examine revelation at the moment it appeared in time, to explore an event, many of whose elements have been lost today. It is certainly not to be confused with the simple history of religious ideas in Israel and primitive Christianity. Its object "is neither the words, nor even the thought of the inspired writers, but the reality of which they speak" [182]; for that reason it is truly a theology. [183] But it is not the same thing thus to examine revealed realities with the eyes of this or that author, taking into account his particular view, and to contemplate them in their fulness with the whole tradition of the Church in order to put the life of modern man in their light. So while the theologian requires of criticism and biblical theology the starting point for his work, he must go beyond the bare facts. We will come back to this point later in regard to the question of the fuller sense.

### III. CRITICISM AND APOSTOLATE

If the limits of criticism are already apparent in theology, they are even more so in the various aspects of pastoral care, the liturgy, preaching, catechetics, etc. An objective knowledge of sacred history just as it unfolded in the concrete can certainly not be neglected; neither can a knowledge of the message of salvation in the form in which it was formulated by the inspired authors and developed in time. The insertion of the revelation of the living God in a real human history, which is verifiable, accessible to the critic's instruments of investigation, is an essential element of Christian faith which it would be dangerous to leave in obscurity. But it is one thing to know that the word of God was really pronounced in the past, that it took this or that form, that it became flesh in Christ; it is quite another to want to hear it pronounced now, as the word of the risen Lord addressed to the Church of today. The literal sense of the biblical texts fills the first of these two needs,

---

[182] C. Spicq, "L'avènement de la théologie biblique," *RSPT* 35 (1951), 567 ff.

[183] This surpassing of the point of view proper to the historian of religions in contemporary Protestantism is likewise emphasized by A. Bea, " 'Religionswissenschaftliche' oder 'theologische exegese?'," *Biblica* 40 (1959), 322-341.

but to satisfy the second, only the fuller sense will suffice. The fact that the fuller sense is nothing but the literal sense understood at a second level of depth shows that criticism cannot be dispensed with; but to reach this second level it is necessary to go beyond criticism. The methodological problem posed by the fuller sense thus stands out sharply at the threshold of theology, and even more at the entrance into the domain of the apostolate. For that reason we will now proceed to examine it in detail.

## § III. THE DISCOVERY AND USE OF THE FULLER SENSE

Since the literal sense is essentially discovered through rational criticism, it is a field common to all who read the Bible. The fact that the Catholic exegete's study of it is "informed" by faith in Christ does not modify either its basic structure or its methodological rules; we did not therefore have to occupy ourselves with it directly. Conversely, the domain of the fuller sense belongs by right only to faith. While it presupposes the discovery of the literal sense of the biblical texts, it takes its stand beyond its limits. It would not be correct to conclude that the practice of spiritual exegesis [184] (the expression we have adopted to designate the investigation of the fuller sense) can be left to the uncontrolled and anarchic initiative of commentators. It is true that in this matter the intuitions of faith control the whole thinking process, since basically it is a matter of contemplating the fulness of the mystery of Christ in some one of its aspects contained in deficient or incomplete formulations, in sketches or hints, to which the sacred authors did not consciously give such a meaning. But why should these intuitions escape all precise control?

We have said several times that the ancient use of allegory, from the patristic age to the 13th century, had no other goal than what we have in mind here. [185] But that does not mean that its actual use, which does not meet our critical demands, its use and abuse of an often artificial symbolism, can be regarded as satisfactory. In the measure that it was bound to cultural levels or forms that have today fallen from use, it has likewise become outmoded. It would be just as harmful to reject its suggestions in a body, under the pretext that they belong to a pre-critical age, as it would be absurd to attribute to all of them the same worth: they must be subjected to a critical examination

---

[184] For the justification of this term, see above, p. 318. It has practically the same meaning given it by L. Bouyer, "Liturgie et exégèse spirituelle," *LMD* 7 (1946), 27-50.

[185] Above, pp. 326 ff.

and a judicious culling.   But that supposes that there are precise rules for spiritual exegesis—not purely rational rules as in the case of criticism, but rules determined by the exercise of theological reasoning methodically applied to the knowledge of faith.   After we have clarified this point, we will be in a position to inquire in what fields the search for the fuller sense has a place.

## I. DISCOVERY OF THE FULLER SENSE

We have seen that the problem of the fuller sense differs for the texts of the Old Testament and for those of the New.   We must then provide for a different treatment in the two cases.

### 1. THE FULLER SENSE IN THE OLD TESTAMENT

We will not repeat in detail all we have said about this point in *Sens chrétien de l'Ancien Testament,* illustrating it with numerous examples. [186]   It will be sufficient to repeat the essential conclusions at which we arrived.

#### *1. Rules Based on the Relation of the Two Testaments*

The formulation of the mystery of Christ in the Old Testament, as it is announced in the eschatological oracles of the prophets, or as the people of God experienced it in the framework of their history and institutions, is necessarily limited and rudimentary.   But sometimes it appears in a language which the New Testament could adopt just as it was, simply giving it a richness of meaning which did not appear until then.   Sometimes it is conditioned by the symbolic history and institutions whose meaning was to be revealed by the advent of Christ.   In the first case, access to the fuller sense is gained simply by a deepening of the formulas used by the sacred authors; in the second, besides that, it demands recourse to the study of biblical figures.

*a) The Deepening of rudimentary formulas.* [187]—The first case is the more simple.   To give expression to life with God in Israel's history and worship, or to the promise of eschatological life with God, the sacred authors employ a vocabulary which is not essentially marked by the concrete conditions of the old alliance.   They did not as yet have a clear idea of the richness of that life with God, which only the coming of Christ and then the mission of the

---

[186] *Sens chrétien de l'A.T.,* pp. 458-495.
[187] *Ibid.,* pp. 460-470, 481-487.

Spirit to the Church were to manifest.   But the expressions they employ do not intrinsically suffer from this limitation of perspective.   Since the mystery they describe is of its nature inexhaustible, their meaning grew in proportion as its revelation moved toward completion.

Let us consider a few examples.   The notion of adoptive sonship conferred by God, not to all men by natural right, but to the people who received his alliance (Ex 4:22) and to all its individual members (Is 1:2), is already stated in an original way in the literal sense of the Old Testament. [188] The essence of this affiliation, however, was manifested only in the Church, through the gift of the Spirit who makes us participate in Jesus' own sonship (Rm 8:14-17).   Once this revelation of the mystery of grace was complete, the texts which sketched it in the Old Testament could then be read in its light, and thus take on their full meaning.   Likewise, the sonship of the king of Israel and of the Messiah (2 S 7:14; Ps 2:7; 89:27) took on heightened meaning when Christ was revealed to men as "the beloved Son" of God (Mk 1:10 par.; 12:6; Mt 11:27 par.).   Consequently, the Christian understanding of the prophetic texts or psalms which spoke of it ordinarily gave the expressions in question their strongest possible meaning; those expressions became the vehicle of Christian Christology (Ac 13:33; Heb 1:5).

The promise of an interior purification and a change of man's heart through the gift of the divine Spirit [189] in Ezk 36:25 ff. was already a very pure eschatological pronouncement; the allusion to the rite of cleansing with the water of purification (36:25) had already to be understood in a metaphorical sense, since it was God himself who undertook to perform it.   The author of Psalm 51 uses exactly the same terms when he begs God to let him benefit personally from the same cleansing (Ps 51:4.9.12-13).   But once the promise was fulfilled in the New Testament, it became clear that purification, won by the blood of Christ, was performed by means of the rite of baptism (Ep 5: 26), and was accompanied by the gift of the Holy Spirit who pours charity into men's hearts (Rm 5:5).   After that, the promise of Ezk 36 and the prayer of Ps 51 could be reread, and their words given the fulness of meaning which the New Testament revealed in them.   This is no more than a deepening of their literal sense.

Psalm 22 and others of the same class express the prayer of the suffering just in the typical Old Testament outlook. [190]   The 4th Servant Song (Is 52:13—53:12) considerably extended their meaning by linking the suffering of the Just par excellence to the salvation of sinners. [191]   The doctrine

[188] *Ibid.*, p. 462.
[189] *Ibid.*, pp. 357 ff., 462.
[190] *Ibid.*, pp. 462 ff.
[191] *Ibid.*, pp. 483 ff.

of these texts therefore comes close to the mystery of redemption, both as a problem posed by human suffering (psalms), and as an act of God using that same suffering for his own purposes (Is 52—53). Christ made these texts his own, both by living himself the drama of the suffering Servant (Mk 10:45; Lk 22:37), and by praying the Psalms of the persecuted just during his passion (Mk 15:34 par.; cf. Jn 13:18). This application of texts to his personal situation, which is without parallel, showed that they are to be read as the advance expression of the mystery of redemption as he in fact realized it; his dignity as Son of God explained the redeeming value of his suffering and death (Is 53), and his membership in the race of Adam was the cause of his unmerited fate. Thus, no matter what the historical conditions of their composition, these texts received their full sense in the context of the passion, the central object of the gospel and of Christian liturgy.

No trace of the theology of the Trinity can be found in the Old Testament [192]; the revelation of the Son and the Spirit as divine persons is bound to their missions in history on the day of the incarnation and that of Pentecost. If it appears that in one text or another the Word of God, his Wisdom, or his Spirit are somewhat hypostatized, the formulas used do not go beyond the limits of mere poetic personification. Nevertheless, behind this theology of the Word, of Wisdom, and of the Spirit, there is something more than mere speculation on the divine attributes, or a conventional presentation using anthropomorphic terms. In the chiaroscuro of their faith and their prophetic or sapiential charism, the sacred authors were in real contact with the divine persons who were to be the object of a mission in history: the Word was present wherever the Word or Wisdom of God was at work, and the Holy Spirit was the primary source of whatever pertained to the Spirit of Yahweh. It is therefore no betrayal of the inspired authors' deep purpose to look deeper, in the light of the New Testament, into their thought and its expression than they did. This is the justification patristic theology had for its use of their texts as witnesses to the doctrine of the Trinity; it did not hesitate to apply Ps 33:6 to the part taken by the Word and the Spirit in the act of creation. This is an excellent theological exegesis; the fuller sense is drawn from the literal sense with respect for its essential intent. Similarly Pr 8:1—9:6, Si 24, Ws 7:22—8:1 were read by the fathers as applying to Christ as Wisdom, preexistent with the Father (cf. Jn 1:18) and finally manifested in human history. [193]

These few examples show how it is possible to pass from the literal sense to the fuller sense. It is indispensable in the first place that the original intent

---

[192] *Ibid.*, pp. 466-469.

[193] A list of examples of this type can be found in the study by J. van der Ploeg, "L'exégèse de l'Ancien Testament dans l'épître aux Hébreux," *RB* 56 (1947), 114-131.

of the text never be lost from view.  The object with which this literal sense deals, the aspect of the mystery of God with men which it treats in an historical or eschatological perspective, determines the aspect of the mystery of Christ that a spiritual interpretation can contemplate in that text.  The usual indication of this continuity between the literal sense and the fuller sense is the identity of the technical terminology which accompanied the development of revelation from one Testament to the other.  When the New Testament uses words and expressions from the Old (and even whole passages) to express its doctrine, it reveals the fuller sense of the texts in which that specific terminology is found.  Not that the mere use of a concordance suffices to illumine the texts of the Old Testament and determine their Christian meaning; the fathers and medieval commentators often abused such artificial comparisons in which a consideration of the context was entirely lacking.  The identity of vocabulary must be accompanied by a thematic continuity of theological thought; thus can be avoided the presentation of a pretended fuller sense which is really only an accommodation. [194]

The spiritual interpretations proposed by the fathers or supposed by the liturgy must always be examined critically, on the basis of the principle stated above, to test their worth.  On this basis, for example, only with reservations can one accept the application to the Virgin Mary of the Old Testament texts which speak of Wisdom, [195] in its role as born of God (Pr 8:22 ff.) or as mother of men (Si 24:18 in the Latin); the fuller sense of these texts concerns Christ, the Wisdom of God, and the poetic use of feminine personification does not strictly speaking suffice to see in them a hint of the mystery of Mary, even if the legitimacy of an accommodation of this type, which has become traditional, is admitted. [196]  This example shows that it is not possible to

[194] Without going back to the Middle Ages, the biblical commentaries of P. Claudel contain hundreds of these verbal comparisons which are devoid of real worth, but which were suggested through the immoderate use of a Latin concordance. Some detailed allegorizations, however, can be grafted onto a correct use of the fuller sense, and they must be taken for what they are worth.  For example, the citation of Is 25:8 and Ho 13:14 in 1 Co 15:54-55 respects the fuller sense of the two texts when it applies them to Christ's triumph over death.  But the commentary that follows, "Now the sting of death is sin" (15:56), is no more than a quite artificial adaptation.

[195] "Scripture tells us that the Holy Virgin was brought forth before the hills, that she is the cause, the term, and as it were the image of all creation, and that it was with eyes fixed on her that the demiurge prepared, realized, and set in motion all things" (P. Claudel, L'épée et le miroir, p. 215).  But elsewhere the same author applies these texts to the Church: "I, wisdom, says the Church, dwell in counsel and am present in learned thoughts, etc." (Un poète regarde la Croix, p. 106).

[196] "Mary is properly the Throne of Wisdom, of the uncreated Wisdom manifested in creation as her Son, who is also the Son of the Father.  And hence she is the historical source of eschatological Wisdom, created in time in order in it to espouse its eternal realization in the Word-Son" (L. Bouyer, Le trône de la Sagesse

speak of the fuller sense indiscriminately, but that the development of criteria is very necessary.

*b) Recourse to the study of biblical figures.* [197]—It is only rarely that the passage from the literal sense to the fuller sense can be made by such simple enrichment of the terminology used in the texts. In most cases, the language of the Old Testament is strongly marked by the particular conditions which then influenced the expression of revelation and of the life of faith, that of an historical experience which encompassed the whole temporal aspect of Israel's life, and that of the political and religious institutions which constituted the provisional social structure of the people of God. Even in the prophets' eschatological promises, the concrete description of final salvation projects to the end of history a complex of symbols which owe their expressive content to the same historical experience and significant institutions. [198] With even more reason are these same elements found in legislative, historical and liturgical texts. Wherever they appear, determining the fuller sense of a text cannot be done except through an accompanying passage from figurative realities to the Reality prefigured. The problem of the meaning of realities in the Bible then becomes one with that of the meaning of the text; the two must be solved together, in such a way that spiritual exegesis (in the sense we have defined it) is at the same time typological exegesis. [199] The key to the fuller sense of the text is therefore the systematic study of biblical figures, the rules for which we have already discussed. [200]

Once again, a few examples will clarify the point. Contrary to the Suffering Servant prophecy, the texts relating to royal messianism cannot be

[Paris: Cerf, 1957], p. 282). For a proper use of the texts regarding Wisdom, one might refer to the well-known books of B. H. Suso, *Le livre de la Sagesse éternelle,* and of St. Louis Mary De Montfort, *L'amour de la Sagesse éternelle.* However, adaptations of some of these texts can be found in the second author. For example: Mary "gives (to her faithful servants) to eat of the most exquisite meats of the table of God; for she gives them to eat of the bread of life, which she herself has formed. My dear children, she says, under the name of Divine Wisdom, be filled with my generations; that is to say, with Jesus, the fruit of life, Whom I have brought into the world for you. Come, she repeats to them in another place, eat my bread, which is Jesus, and drink the wine of His love, which I have mixed for you..." (*True Devotion to the Blessed Virgin Mary* [Bay Shore, N.Y.: Montfort Publ., 1950], pp. 153 f.). The use of Pr 8 and Si 24 in the liturgy of the Blessed Virgin explains these adaptations but it cannot be denied that they are often the cause of uneasiness in modern readers, who are more accustomed to a literal reading of the biblical texts.

[197] *Sens chrétien de l'A.T.*, pp. 470-481, 487-495.

[198] *Ibid.*, pp. 364 ff.

[199] J. Gribomont, "Sens plénier, sens typique, sens littéral," *Problèmes et méthode d'exégèse théologique* (Louvain, 1950), pp. 21-31; R. E. Brown, *The Sensus Plenior of Sacred Scripture,* pp. 114 ff.; J. Schildenberger, "Vollsinn und typischer Sinn im Alten Testament," *Bibel und Liturgie* 24 (1956-1957), 255-259.

[200] Above, pp. 285 ff.

fully understood without recourse to a study of the figures involved. [201] When
these latter attribute royal status to the mediator of salvation, they do so with
the historical experience of Israel in mind, even if the perfection they attribute
to him implies an exaggeration of the actual state of affairs in the old order.
Now the accomplishment of these promises by Christ did not take place on
the level of this world's history, to which Christ's kingship did not pertain
(Jn 18:36), but outside history in the world to come, which Christ entered
by his resurrection. Consequently, the fuller sense of the texts which point
in advance to his messianic reign does not become apparent unless the
expressions related to the past experience of Israelite royalty, to its glories
and battles, to its duties and exercise, undergo a symbolic transformation.
The New Testament offers several examples of this: the quotation of Ps 2 in
Ac 13:33 and Rv 19:15, that of Is 11:4 in 2 Th 2:8 and Rv 19: 15, etc. In
these instances, the images of temporal power are transferred to the new
world in which Christ was enthroned by his resurrection and in which he
will manifest his power by his return.

The same operation is necessary for texts in which Jerusalem and its
temple play a role as signs of the divine presence in the world, [202] either in the
context of historical experience (Ps 46; 48; 87; 122), or in the context of
eschatological hope (Is 54; 60—62; Tb 13:9-17). The New Testament has
shown that these imperfect and temporary signs were to be replaced by a
definitive sign, the body of Christ (Jn 3:21) of which the Church our mother
is the complement (cf. Ga 4:26 ff.). As a consequence, the spiritual exegesis
of these texts demands the substitution for the figurative realities mentioned
in them of the realities which correspond to them in the present order, for
the passage from the literal sense to the fuller sense is identical with the
transformation of signs which the coming of Christ effected in human faith.
In this case, some might be tempted to speak of demythologization, as if
Christian interpretation were limited to relieving prophetic language of the
elements which the experience of the cross has shown to be unreal. This
would be to underestimate the realistic content which is proper to symbolic
language, especially when this language is not based on the general laws of
analogy, but on the revelatory significance enclosed by God himself in the
historical experience of Israel. In this particular case, the typological interpretation incorporated in spiritual exegesis does no more than carry to its
limit the linguistic criticism incorporated in exegesis of the literal sense. [203]

Attainment of the fuller sense of the biblical texts, in the case of eschatological oracles, and still more in all the others, poses some delicate problems.

---

[201] *Sens chrétien de l'A.T.*, pp. 487 ff.; cf. 375 ff.
[202] *Ibid.*, pp. 490-492.
[203] Above, pp. 348-351.

The interpretation of these unique biblical figures is subject to strict laws. Whether it is a question of historical experiences (the exodus, the alliance, the conquest of the promised land) or of institutions (the Davidic kingship, Jerusalem, the temple), they must be considered in their organic unity if their figurative content is to become apparent. [204] The texts which speak of these things treat them in some detail, sometimes more, as in the historical books and laws, sometimes less, as in eschatological prophecies and some psalms. How are all these details to be handled? Must they be passed over in silence when exposing the fuller sense, or, on the contrary, must a particular objective significance be found for all of them?

Here the occasion for a prolongation of the fuller sense by a freer accommodation presents itself, an accommodation which is less certain exegetically the further it wanders from the pole which gives those details their meaning. If by virtue of the figurative principle the text treats the mystery of Christ and Christian realities in symbolic language, it is tempting to see in these symbols a whole chain of metaphors all of equal value—in short, to interpret the text in question as an allegory. This, as a matter of fact, was the origin of the scriptural allegorizing in Alexandrian and medieval exegesis, in times when the cultural atmosphere favored just such a development. [205] There can be no question, however, of a revival of that practice. Literal exegesis necessarily exercises a preponderant influence upon the spiritual exegesis we have in mind. [206] It forbids seeking close correspondence between the mystery of Christ on the one hand, and all the details of Israelite history and institutions on the other, both because the reality represented symbolically is for various reasons not an exact copy of its prefiguration, and because in presenting these latter, the sacred authors did not give all the elements the same value. Consequently, the details found in the biblical texts do not all have the same signifying value in relation to whatever is the object of the fuller sense. It is therefore necessary to practice a differential exegesis in their regard, one that throws some of them into relief and leaves others in the background. [207] Thus the new spiritual exegesis will avoid the pitfalls of allegorizing.

---

[204] Above, pp. 285 ff.

[205] H. de Lubac, *Exégèse médiévale*, Part II, Vol. 2, pp. 85-94, emphasizes that the allegorists had no illusion about the value of the meaning they proposed: "Seeking understanding, they seized the occasion of a text rather than pretending strictly to explain that text as such. They merely proposed to the reader the fruit of meditation" (pp. 85 ff.).

[206] In this our conclusion agrees with that of K. H. Schelkle, "Über alte und neue Auslegung," *BZ* N.F. 1 (1957), 161-177.

[207] *Sens chrétien de l'A.T.*, p. 315.

## 2. Rules Founded on the Complexity of the Mystery of Christ

When showing how the mystery of Christ can be discovered under the rudimentary expressions of the Old Testament, we have until now considered it as a whole, without considering its internal complexity. This introduces a new element of interpretation into investigation of the fuller sense, for the relation of a text to the mystery of Christ can be understood in various ways. This mystery has two levels, that of Christ the Head, who first assumed the human temporal condition unto the death on the cross and only afterwards entered into the glory of the new world, and that of the Church, his Body, which is formed in history before experiencing final transfiguration in eternal life. Add to that that at this second level the problem of salvation can be considered from two different standpoints, that of the ecclesial community as such, and that of the individuals who participate in it. [208] To which of these aspects of the mystery of Christ will the interpreter appeal when explaining the fuller sense of the Old Testament texts? According to the nature of the experience they describe or the hope they entertain, they lend themselves to comparison now with one, now with another, sometimes with several at once. For this reason, the fuller sense will vary, and on occasion become multiple. [209] In our earlier study of the meaning of the history of Christ [210] and the meaning of realities after Christ, [211] we prepared the elements which must be applied in this investigation into the fuller sense.

Once again, some examples. In its announcement of the eschatological revelation of the glory of God, [212] Is 40:5 interpreted the historic theophany of Sinai [213] (Ex 24:16 ff.) figuratively. The accomplishment of this promise took place in two distinctly different moments. At the time of his advent into the world, Christ had already manifested the glory of God on earth (Jn 1:14), but beneath a veil, whether through his miracles (Jn 2:17; 11:40), or secretly at the transfiguration (Lk 9:32; 2 P 1:16-18). Once he had attained the full glorification of his body by his return to the Father and his resurrection (Jn 17:5), he was to reveal this glory in its fulness at his second coming; then all flesh will see it without its brilliance tarnished by the blindness of disbelief. The fuller sense of Is 40:5, therefore, must be undestood at two levels, which correspond to the two comings of Christ. Nor should the middle viewpoint, which corresponds to the individual Christian life, be forgotten; the glory of God is revealed there too, and he who contemplates it in faith reflects it in

---

[208] *Ibid.*, p. 496.
[209] Above, pp. 330 f.
[210] Above, pp. 249-255, 296-299.
[211] Above, pp. 299-310.
[212] *Sens chrétien de l'A.T.*, pp. 481 ff.
[213] *Ibid.*, pp. 370 ff.

himself as in a mirror (2 Co 3:18). It is interesting to note that medieval exegesis related these three explanations of the sense suggested by the text to allegory (the first coming of Christ), anagoge (the resurrection and second coming) and tropology (Christian life). This shows that the theory of the four senses of Scripture was not without foundation in reality, since we have come to the same conclusions in our renewed spiritual exegesis.

The experience of the exodus which Israel underwent long ago prefigured that of salvation in the New Testament. [214] But the latter took various forms. By passing from this world to the Father (Jn 13:1), Christ accomplished his personal exodus (Lk 9:31), the type of what after him all the redeemed are to experience. The Christian people in their march toward divine repose accomplishes it after him by participating in his mystery (Heb 4:1-11); the concrete expression of this for the individual is the sacramental experience (cf. 1 Co 10:1-4). In this perspective, what approach is to be made to the biblical texts which deal with the first exodus or announce eschatological salvation under the traits of an exodus undertaken anew? First, by examining their precise relation to the significant experience of long ago, in order to discover the aspect of Christian salvation they symbolically describe. The rite of the paschal lamb (Ex 12) will thus direct one's thought to the liturgical commemoration of Jesus' Passover, the foundation of Christian deliverance (1 Co 5:7-8), while the canticle of Moses (Ex 15) will be seen to sing the great deliverance in which the saints in heaven participate fully (Rv 15:3) and of which baptism already provides the pledge (cf. the use of Ex 15 in the liturgy of the night of the Passover).

The problem of the fuller interpretation thus varies according to the texts to be examined, and it is essential to refer to the conclusions of literal exegesis to judge them properly. The plurality of applications, however, of which we have just given two examples, is possible only for those texts which in some way were related to an experience of salvation undergone or hoped for by the people of the Old Testament. It is only within the economy of salvation realized in Christ that these close relations, which allow Old Testament themes to evolve without losing their organic unity, can be found. But there are also many texts which refer to another sort of experience: that of divine judgment, [215] which affects all sinners without exception. The judgment of God does not change at all in nature, whether it concerns the men of the Old Testament or those of the New; the signs of its presence are always and everywhere the same, both in the present history of the world and in its final consummation. Consequently, the texts which refer to

[214] *Ibid.*, pp. 492 ff.
[215] *Ibid.*, pp. 479 ff.; cf. 364-369.

judgment retain their permanent actuality in the context of Christian tropology (cf. 1 Co 10:5-11; Heb 3:7—4:10), with the proviso that the ancient doctrine of individual retribution be expanded in the light of Christ's cross and resurrection. [216]

These examples show that the method of determining the fuller sense must vary according to the character of the texts under examination. The general outlines that we have sketched should not be taken as practical guides, which can be applied mechanically in every case. The fuller sense, it should be repeated, is only a second level of depth within the literal sense; it can therefore be reached only by a proper appreciation of the positive elements of the latter, giving each element its due. Under such rules the spiritual sense can be developed correctly. And the principles on which it rests will provide criteria to pass judgment on the interpretations of the Old Testament presented to us by patristic and medieval exegesis.

## II. THE FULLER SENSE IN THE NEW TESTAMENT

The methodological rules we are now going to examine flow from the principles which establish the existence of the fuller sense in the New Testament. [217] The application of these rules will show in what way the theological and spiritual reading of these texts can be carried out.

### 1. Basic Rules

a) *Rules founded on the historical development of revelation.*—In relation to the period which preceded Christ, the total content of the New Testament constitutes the *eschaton*. But this *eschaton* itself went through internal development; it unfolded in three stages which differ in nature, and the three constitute so many stages in the revelation of God and of salvation. The first stage was that of Christ as a pilgrim: his acts, his words, his whole life, by taking place in human history, afforded it a seminal revelation whose content was to become apparent after the resurrection and Pentecost. The second stage is that of the Church: while Christ the Head has already reached the end of time, the Church, his Body, is still immersed in the temporal condition

---

[216] When we visualize the *result* of the judgment, and especially the reward of the just, we find ourselves in the presence of the problem of *salvation*. The promises of the Old Testament in this regard were at first formulated in terms of earthly life before passing to the meta-historical plane (*Sens chrétien de l'A.T.*, pp. 339 ff.). Consequently, the texts which contain them require recourse to the dialectic of figures in every instance in which they employ this "figurative" language.

[217] Above, pp. 326-331.

of the pilgrim. [218]   The revelation of God and of salvation takes on a sacramental form, both through the gospel message, which informs men of all times of the word of Christ, and through the sacramental system, which is the sign of the actual presence of Christ here below and of the permanent action of the Spirit in the Church. [219]   This stage will itself one day come to an end, to give way to an ultra-temporal state of things in which the Church will join its Head in glory.   Then the unveiling of the mystery of God and of salvation will become complete, since instead of seeing God dimly as in a mirror, men will see him face to face, just as he is (1 Co 13:12; 1 Jn 3:2). Between these three stages of eschatological history, there are relations and likenesses which play an important role in revelation.   The realities which at any of these stages manifest the plan of salvation in the course of its realization have a prophetic meaning in relation to the stage or stages that follow.

In the opening stage, the words and deeds of Christ in his pilgrim state inaugurated and signified under the form of an historical event the mystery of salvation which is actually rendered present in the Church under a sacramental form [220]; at the same time, his fate as a man partaking of our pilgrim temporal condition inaugurated and signified the manner in which the economy of salvation is realized for men in the age of the Church. [221]   Consequently, the texts which preserve his words for us and which describe for us his deeds and his destiny do not acquire the fulness of their meaning unless they are compared with the whole of Christian experience.   Those texts regulate Christian experience, but in return it explains them.   For example, the mission of the twelve in Galilee during the public life was a forecast of their universal mission after the resurrection (compare Mt 10:5 and 28:18-20); likewise the advice given them then (Mk 6:6-13; Lk 9:1-6) should be understood as the prescription for Christian missionaries of all times (that is already the sense given them in Mt 10 and in Lk 10:1-20). In the same way, the texts which refer to the role of the twelve and of Peter in the community founded by Christ not only show the place the testimony of the apostles was to occupy in the early stages of the Church considered as the formulator of the gospel; they also sketch the characteristics that Church was to retain forever.   The apostolate continues to play its role through the intermediary of set structures, the seeds of which it contained within itself from the beginning, and which their depositors themselves erected.   It is, therefore, legitimate to seek from these texts instructions on the essential institutions of the present Church, even though the texts

---

[218] Above, pp. 296-299.
[219] Above, pp. 300 f.
[220] Above, pp. 246 f., 253.
[221] Above, pp. 247 f., 252 f.

treat these institutions only from the standpoint of the office of the apostles. [222] The passage from their literal sense to their fuller sense is made by making explicit a virtual content which only the experience of the Church could have brought out.

The same law is at work *a fortiori* when it is a matter of finding expressions to speak of the final consummation of the plan of salvation. This future beyond time is the immediate concern of a whole eschatological literature which made it its specific object, and which to this end borrowed the representations of it provided by the prophetic and apocalyptic texts of the Old Testament, subjecting them to the necessary reinterpretation. [223] But to succeed in such an operation, Christian eschatology must also forge its own language, the fundamental elements of which are supplied by the terrestrial life of Christ and the experience of the Church. The fact of "being with" Christ was a crucial experience for the twelve (Mk 3:14; Lk 22:28; Jn 15:27) which was the concrete sign of their entrance into the kingdom of God; this experience thereafter made it possible to understand in what eternal life will consist (Ph 1:23), and that gives a new content to the old images used in Jewish apocalyptic literature [224] (Lk 23:43; 1 Th 4:14-17). The form which this intimacy with Christ will take is illumined also by the eucharistic experience (Rv 3:20), [225] the meal with the risen Christ (cf. Lk 24:29 ff. 41-43; Ac 10:41); as a result, the ancient images of the eschatological banquet [226] (cf. Mt 8:11; Lk 14:15) take on, in this perspective, a significance unknown before then (Lk 22:30). Thus, in the texts whose literal sense concerns the time of Christ and of the Church, it is normal also to look for light on the eschatological consummation of things; a realistic presentation of the latter is hardly possible except on this basis.

---

[222] This is the use Vatican Council I, session IV, made of them in its constitution on the Church; cf. *Ench. S.*, 3050, 3053. It applied them to the successors of Peter in chaps. II-IV, especially 3066 (citing Pope Hormisdas and 3070). The same usage can be found in the work of Vatican II on the college of bishops, the successor of the apostolic college: *Lumen gentium*, 18-27.

[223] Especially is that the case in Revelation of St. John (cf. L. Cerfaux—J. Cambier, *L'apocalypse de saint Jean lue aux chrétiens* [Paris: Cerf, 1955], who systematically stress these reinterpretations of the texts).

[224] B. Rigaux, *Les épîtres aux Thessaloniciens* (Paris-Gembloux: Gabalda/Duculot, 1956), pp. 550 ff.

[225] For the relation of this text to the liturgy of the Eucharist, see P. Prigent, *Apocalypse et liturgie* (Neuchâtel-Paris: Niestlé Delachaux, 1964), who translates: "I will take the Supper with him" (p. 35).

[226] The image of the banquet serves also as the starting point of a parable on the kingdom of God (Lk 14:16-24; Mt 22:1-13). Comparing Luke's version with that of Matthew, one notes that the notion of kingdom becomes more precise and richer, while the parable is allegorized to the point of becoming "an outline of the plan of redemption" (J. Jeremias, *The Parables of Jesus* [London: SCM, rev. 1963], p. 69; cf. pp. 67 ff. and 176 ff.). Finally, a certain eucharistic resonance can be noted in it, thanks to the insertion of Mt 22:10-13 (compare 1 Co 11:28-32).

*b) Rules founded on the internal coherence of revelation.*—In all the cases we have just examined, the search for the fuller sense went hand in hand with that for the meaning of things, such as we defined it in chapter VI. [227] But there is also another fact which must be taken into consideration. Since all the aspects of the mystery of Christ are perfectly coherent among themselves and mutually illumine one another, texts which refer to some one of them acquire the fulness of their meaning only when they are placed in the vast whole to which they belong. This general principle can be applied in several different ways.

First of all, certain religious realities situated on the same level of the history of salvation are so connected that the theological interpretation of one necessarily affects the others. The principal case that we have in mind here is that of the mystery of Mary and that of the Church, such as we outlined it above. [228] Since Mary is, on the level of faith as well as that of grace, the type of the mystery of the Church and its perfect realization, texts which refer to Mary cast light on the theology of the Church, and vice versa. Consequently, it is only natural to compare the ones with the others (Lk 1—2; Jn 2:1-11; 19:25-27; Rv 12:1-17) to obtain a comprehensive view of Mary which bares the implications of each of these texts. In this view, the parallel situation of Mary and the Church as the new Eve of the humanity redeemed by Christ becomes clearly apparent, [229] and the fact that the mother of the Messiah is preserved from all the wiles of the dragon (Rv 12:6.13-16), that is, from sin and death, [230] gives an insight into the mystery of grace which Christ communi-

---

[227] Above, pp. 299-309.

[228] Above, pp. 291-296.

[229] On the roots of this theme in the New Testament, see F. M. Braun, "La mère de Jésus dans l'œuvre de saint Jean," *RTh* 58 (1950), 429-479; *La mère des fidèles*, pp. 88-96 (who sees in Rv 12 an exegesis of Gn 3:15 according to the fuller sense); L. Cerfaux, "La vision de la femme et du dragon de l'Apocalypse en relation avec le Protévangile," *ETL* 32 (1956), 21-33 (reprinted in *Recueil L. Cerfaux*, Vol. 3, pp. 237-251); A. M. Dubarle, "Les fondements bibliques du titre marial de Nouvelle Ève" in *Mélanges J. Lebreton* (Paris, 1951), Vol. 1, pp. 49-64; J. Galot, *Marie dans l'Évangile* (Bruges-Paris: Desclée de Brouwer, 1958), pp. 148 ff., 186 ff.; M. E. Boismard, *Du baptême à Cana* (Paris: Cerf, 1956), pp. 133-159. On the theme in patristic writings, see the summary survey by L. Deiss, *Marie, Fille de Sion*, pp. 245-254. For a more developed theological elaboration, see M. J. Scheeben, *Mariology*, pp. 211 ff.; G. Philips, "La Nouvelle Ève dans la théologie contemporaine," *La Nouvelle Ève* (Paris, 1956), Vol. 3, pp. 101 ff.; M. J. Nicolas, "La doctrine mariale et la théologie de la femme," *Maria, Études sur la Vierge*, under the direction of H. du Manoir (Paris, 1964), Vol. 7, pp. 343-362.

[230] The dragon is none other than the devil, the seducer (20:10), who is at work on earth through the beast and false prophets to lead men to sin and turn them against God and his Christ (cf. chap. 13). The eschatological judgment assigns the same lot to the devil, the beast and false prophets (20:10), Death and Hades (20:14), and casts them into the second death. Thus Sin and Death (personified as in Rm 5:12 ff.) are always outlined behind the personage of the dragon, as was already the case in Gn 3.

cated to his mother, just as to his Church. The result is that the meaning of κεχαριτωμένη in Lk 1:28 emerges explicitly, and it appears as the scriptural foundation for the dogmas of the immaculate conception and the assumption. [231] Thus Marian theology rests on a specifically biblical basis, not so much through the logical deduction of certain conclusions from revealed premises, as through contemplation of the mystery of Mary in that of the Church. [232]

Secondly, it must be recalled that when it comes to determining New Testament revelation, the teachings of the apostles complement one another. [233] As a consequence, for any point of doctrine whatsoever, each of them should be clarified by the parallel texts which concern the same object. For example, while the literal exegesis of each gospel aims to uncover the specific characteristics of the theology of its author, a full understanding of the mystery of Christ to which his text testifies can be obtained only by a second undertaking. When the Christ of Paul and John, for example, is projected on the synoptics, new insights appear, written, as it were, on their watermark. Thus the theological and spiritual explanation of texts, while based on their critical explanation, goes far beyond those limits. [234] To take just one example, the mission entrusted to Peter to strengthen his brothers in the faith might be understood as referring only to the time of trial which the passion of Christ was for the apostles (cf. Lk 22:31a). But the comparison of this text with Mt 16:19 and Jn 21:15-17, which were not written from that standpoint, suggests considering the Lucan text as a veiled hint of a permanent duty for the time of trial, which for the Church will go on forever. [235]

Finally, to bring to light the riches of both Testaments, it is helpful to refer to the experience of life in the Church, which can function much as a developer for photographic film. When early in this book we examined the relations between Scripture and ecclesiastical tradition, we emphasized the fact that these two modes of transmitting the apostolic deposit are neither

[231] M. J. Scheeben, op. cit., does not separate Mary and the Church in order to treat her immaculate conception and assumption from a biblical standpoint. It will be noted that the new liturgy of the feast of the Assumption chose precisely Rv 12 as introit for the Mass.

[232] E. Schillebeeckx in H. Vorgrimmler, Exegese und Dogmatik, p. 110. There should be no need to stress the importance of this remark, both for theological method, and for the necessary relation of Marian theology to Scripture.

[233] Above, pp. 16-18; cf. J. Levie, The Bible, Word of God in Words of Men, pp. 270 f.

[234] This principle is valid for all texts. It explains why older commentaries, which were less attentive than we are to literary and historical criticism, are often richer in content than modern commentaries. For an example, see the article by J. Bonsirven, "Pour une intelligence plus profonde de saint Jean" in Mélanges J. Lebreton, Vol. I, pp. 176-196, who cites St. Cyril and St. Augustine as models.

[235] Ench. S., 3070.

independent of one another nor in any way subordinate one to the other. It is through their union that the Church of all ages reaches the tradition of the apostles and of the gospel in its entirety.[236] In some respects, the Scripture handed down from the primitive Church does constitute the norm of tradition, because it is a direct witness of the apostolic deposit. But its obscurities and its occasional or fragmentary nature pose a problem of interpretation that it is impossible to solve without referring to living tradition, which in this regard performs a normative function. Consequently, the true content of certain texts really appeared only through the agency of the later faith and practice of the Church, which insisted on retaining it while explaining whatever there was of the hidden or enigmatic in its content. In this regard we might cite the relation of Christian penance, understood as a sacrament, with the texts of Mt 16:19 and 18:18, of Jn 20:23, Jm 5:15 ff., and 1 Jn 5:16. The continual existence of a sacramental practice, whose forms varied considerably in the course of the ages, clarifies these vague passages and discloses their fuller sense, which criticism alone might never have been able to elucidate completely.[237]

It is, finally, to the totality of the two Testaments that the principles we have laid down are to be applied. The Old Testament cannot add anything essential to the message of the New, but the authors of the New Testament did not always explicitly take up the points treated by the Scripture they had before them. The apostolic Church was usually content to pass on to the following generations an authentic interpretation of this Scripture. Consequently, the fulness of Christian doctrine results from the reciprocal clarification which the two Testaments bring to one another when they are received and interpreted in the context of ecclesiastical tradition. For example, to construct the Christian theology of man's earthly state, it is necessary to combine the doctrine of the Old Testament (the theology of creation and sin) with that of the New Testament (the theology of sin and redemption), without forgetting that the latter manifests a distinction between the order of temporal things and that of grace which leaves intact the subordination of the former to the latter.[238] The exact meaning of Gn 1:26, as an expression of the relation between man and nature in the design of God, cannot be reduced either to a purely Christological interpretation (cf. Heb 2:6-8, where Ps 8:5-7, a parallel to Gn 1:26, is cited) which would absorb the whole natural order in that of grace, or to an affirmation of man's power over nature that overlooks

---

[236] Above, pp. 29-33.

[237] Cf. the use of texts made by the Council of Trent in *Ench. S.*, 1679, 1684, 1692.

[238] See, for example, R. Guelluy, *La création* (*Le mystère chrétien*, Théologie dogmatique, 4) (Tournai-Paris: Desclée, 1963), which includes a bibliography on the question.

the necessity of the redemption worked by Christ alone. The fuller sense of this text, as of all others, requires its comparison with the testimony of all of Scripture as the Church in its living tradition has understood it. Any system of interpretation that ignores this norm displays ignorance of the true nature of Scripture and its exact relation to the Church.

## 2. Application of the Basic Rules

Like the spiritual exegesis of the Old Testament, [239] the literal or fuller interpretation of the New Testament puts its texts in relation to the various aspects of the mystery of salvation realized in Christ: the dispensation of grace in the Church on earth, the heavenly consummation of the mystery beyond time, the individual participation of men in this eschatological existence which God offers them in the Church. If the conclusions of exegesis are classed according to this practical outline, they agree with the classic notions which medieval exegesis classified under the names of allegory, anagoge and tropology. This brings one to the realization that investigation of the fuller sense, which is closely related to reflection on the meaning of biblical realities, is no other than a renewal of traditional exegesis with the introduction into it of the methodic exactness demanded by a critical study of the literal sense.

That does not mean that all New Testament texts are open to all these applications at once. This must be determined in each particular case according to the conclusions of an objective criticism. Thus the account of the baptism of Christ, which is basically Christological, cannot be separated from the "baptism in the Holy Spirit" received by the apostles on Pentecost (Ac 1:5; 2:1-4); in the context of the history of Christ, it contains a veiled announcement of it (the Middle Ages would have said that it signifies it *secundum allegoriam*). But neither can it be separated from Christian baptism, the individual participation in the "baptism in the Holy Spirit"; it is, so to speak, its prototype, since the manifestation of the Spirit is in the account of Christ's baptism related to the divine sonship of Christ (compare Rm 8:14-17). Here the Middle Ages would have spoken of an interpretation of the gospel passage *secundum tropologiam*. Finally, the relation of the life of the baptized person to eternal life, of which the possession of the Spirit constitutes the first-fruits (Rm 8:23), leads one to read this trinitarian theophany *secundum anagogiam*, by taking it as a concrete representation of the heavenly life of which Christ has made us coheirs (Rm 8:17). It is quite obvious that these three readings of the text do not constitute three different

---

[239] Above, pp. 376-378.

senses; they merely make explicit three aspects of the doctrine included in the literal sense. [240]

## II. USE OF THE FULLER SENSE

### I. THE FULLER SENSE AND APOLOGETICS

In our earlier examination [241] of the place criticism ought to occupy in apologetics, we put ourselves in the perspective of the dialogue between the Christian and the unbeliever, for whom biblical history and religion are merely human matters among all others. In such apologetics there is no place for the fuller sense of Scripture, because to recognize its existence, it is necessary to believe in the divine origin of Scripture and of the revelation it brings to us. But there is one class of non-Christians who fulfill this condition, not indeed for the whole of the two Testaments, but for the Old: the Jews, whose canon of Scripture is substantially identical with that of the apostolic Church. [242] And what was true in the time of the apostles remains so today: for them, the essential sign of the arrival of salvation in Jesus Christ is to be found in the conformity of his message, of his life, of the grace he offered, with the scriptures which announced God's eschatological reign. The apology aimed at the Jews in Acts [243] is essentially based on this scriptural argument (2:14-36; 3:18-24; 8:28-35; 10:36-43; 13:16-40; 28:23), and the same approach can be found in the controversies of different ages between Jews and Christians, starting with St. Justin's *Dialogue with Trypho*. [244] The situation of modern Judaism is in this regard more complex, in the sense that for some of its members it is no more than an ethnic tradition with no religious character. Those who have lost faith in revelation and the divine character of Scripture are in the same situation as unbelievers of whatever origin. But there remain all the sincere believers of orthodox Judaism, whether

---

[240] This understanding of the baptism of Christians on the basis of the baptism of Christ can be found, for example, in St. Thomas, *Super Evangelium S. Matthaei Lectura* 3,2 (ed. R. Cai, pp. 44-47) and IIIᵃ, q. 39, who himself refers to St. Augustine and St. John Chrysostom. On this relation to the literal sense of the texts, cf. A. Feuillet, "Le baptême de Jésus," *RB* 73 (1964), 348 ff.

[241] Above, pp. 361 ff.

[242] Above, pp. 140-146.

[243] J. Dupont, "L'utilisation apologétique de l'Ancien Testament dans les discours des Actes," *ETL* 29 (1953), 289-327 (= Analecta Lovaniensia, II, 40).

[244] J. Daniélou, *Message évangélique et culture hellénistique aux IIᵉ et IIIᵉ siècles*, pp. 185 ff.; P. Prigent, *Justin et l'Ancien Testament* (Paris: Gabalda, 1964). Concerning this recourse to Scripture in the controversy between Jews and Christians, cf. M. Simon, *Verus Israel: Étude sur les relations entre chrétiens et juifs dans l'empire romain* (Paris: De Boccqal, 1948), pp. 177-187.

conservative or liberal, [245] who are passionately attached to the Scripture they have received from their tradition, and which they interpret, sometimes more rigidly, sometimes more flexibly, according to their own norms.

For some of them, the problem of the critical reading of biblical texts seems more difficult to solve than it is for Catholic theologians of a conservative bent, for their attachment to the Torah, the rule of life given by God to his people, forbids them to question its historical origin or obligatory character. But that is not the essential point. The approach of a Jew to the Christian faith always implies, along with the recognition of Christ as the Messiah promised to Israel, the complete reinterpretation of all of Scripture in the light of the mystery that is revealed in him. In place of a reading "according to the letter," guided by the "tradition of the elders" (Mk 7:5-9), it is necessary to adopt a reading "according to the spirit" (cf. 2 Co 3:6; Rm 2:29), whose principle are the words and deeds of Christ. For "even today, whenever Moses is read, the veil is over their minds. It will not be removed until they turn to the Lord" (2 Co 3:15-16). This passage from the letter to the spirit is in the end, as we have seen, nothing else but the discovery of the fuller sense of the sacred text beneath the outer covering of the literal sense. It is possible that an attentive consideration of the literal sense, undertaken with the profound piety that Jewish faith implies, might reveal an internal dynamism that poses the problem of going beyond that sense, or better, of its eschatological "accomplishment." In this regard the exact role of Christ in the divine plan merits closer examination. But to reach the goal of this process, to discover in faith in Christ the accomplishment of Jewish faith, as St. Paul did on the road to Damascus, the Jew has need of a grace and an interior illumination (cf. Jn 6:44 ff.) which is beyond the Christian apologist's power to provide. He can only be a witness to his own faith, insisting on the fact that he, like the Jew, believes in the Old Testament, but finds it accomplished in Christ. Only God can do the rest. [246]

---

[245] For the diverse tendencies into which modern Judaism has divided, see the historical account by I. Epstein, *Judaism* (a Penguin book, 1959).

[246] The reading of the New Testament similarly poses a problem in which purely critical choices meet the basic religious choice in regard to Jesus, Christian faith and the Church. To pass from a sympathetic approach, which appreciates the biblical echoes in the text at their proper value (e.g., S. Sandmel, *A Jewish Understanding of the New Testament* [New York, 1956]) to a reading in faith which recognizes in it the word of God and the accomplishment of the Scriptures, an interior illumination of grace is needed. But in that case it is no longer a question of the fuller sense of the New Testament; it is the literal sense that is in question.

## II. THE FULLER SENSE AND THEOLOGY [247]

We have seen that biblical criticism could provide a starting point for the systematic study of Christian doctrine, because the study of the literal sense issues in biblical theology. [248] But that is not all there is to theology. Its task is to interpret the word of God for the Christian people by exposing its real content, just as the tradition of the Church preserves it and makes it fruitful. In this sense Scripture is a norm for theology; conversely, its riches must be exploited without expecting that criticism alone will demonstrate them with evidence. Stated thus, the problem of interpretation demands a solution which does justice to the requirements of scientific exegesis, but does not neglect to deepen its conclusions, for the theological interpretation of Scripture consists in setting forth the whole of Christian doctrine on the basis of the writings in which the word of God can be grasped directly. The combination of Scripture and Tradition is necessary for such an operation. [249] From this standpoint, it becomes evident that in many cases the scriptural foundation for doctrine appears only in the fuller sense, as J. Levie [250] and E. Schillebeeckx [251] have noted. In the terminology of St. Thomas, moreover, the *sensus litteralis*, which contains all that is necessary to establish doctrine, corresponds to our fuller sense. [252]

These facts suggest that the notion of scriptural proof, as the Counter-Reform theologians understood it, should be expanded to the dimensions of a more traditional concept. In the controversy between Catholicism and Protestantism, Scripture was consulted principally for texts that would serve as evidence, and from which the doctrine to be proved could incontestably be drawn. The juridical form of such argumentation in itself forbade going beyond the limits of the literal sense without recurring to tradition or the magisterium for indications of its exact meaning. The progress of critical studies, however, tended gradually to reduce scriptural arguments thus constructed. Then there was a move to compensate for this lack by an appeal to tradition, which was then regarded as a "second source" of doctrine. Finally, this evolution of theological method led to the admission that some doctrines might pertain to the faith, and hence to the apostolic deposit,

---

[247] See the bibliography given above, p. 366, note 178.

[248] Above, pp. 366 f.

[249] Tradition is "the ecclesial understanding of Scripture" (Y. Congar, *La foi et la théologie*, p. 25).

[250] J. Levie, *The Bible, Word of God in Words of Men*, pp. 267 ff.

[251] E. Schillebeeckx, "Exegese, Dogmatik und Dogmenentwicklung" in *Exegese und Dogmatik*, pp. 106 ff. Likewise R. Schnackenburg, "Zur dogmatischen Auswertung des Neuen Testaments," *ibid.*, pp. 124 ff.

[252] Above, pp. 313 ff., 317.

without in any manner being found in Scripture: the transmission by tradition, which for that matter is impossible to prove in many cases by an unbroken chain of texts going back to the apostles, [253] would thus suffice to establish the doctrine in question.

But when the relation of Scripture and Tradition are seen in a different light, when it is admitted that Scripture has a real content broader and deeper than that which criticism left to itself can reach, when above all Tradition is consulted for the way it understood Scripture and what point of doctrine it read in it, then the question appears in a new light. Without losing contact with the results of criticism, the interpreter learns in the school of Tradition how to discover the hidden riches of Scripture. He will renounce theological work of any sort independently of it, for every doctrinal, dogmatic or moral exposition must be rooted in it, and, so to speak, emerge from it. Such interpretation, intimately entwined with the whole of theology, obviously implies a recourse to the fuller sense of the text. But establishing the fuller sense cannot be left to the whim of each interpreter; it must follow strict rules. This sort of interpretation aims less to demonstrate propositions with the aid of Scripture than to display all the objects of the knowledge of faith that are present in Scripture, if not explicitly, at least in embryo or in a hidden way. [254] This is the essential task, for which the theologian must become an exegete, and the exegete must rise above the domain of his criticism and become a theologian. [255]

### III. THE FULLER SENSE AND THE APOSTOLATE

The same rule is even more valid for the various aspects of the Church's apostolate. Whether it be in catechetics, preaching, or the liturgy, the goal is to actualize the word of God with Scripture as the starting point, to show, consequently, its existential importance for the men whom God today calls to enter the way of salvation. [256] The guidelines furnished by critical study are

---

[253] See the remarks of K. Rahner, "Virginitas in partu" in *Theological Investigations IV* (Baltimore: Helicon, 1966), pp. 134-162; "Écriture et Tradition: A propos du schéma conciliaire sur la révélation divine" in *L'homme devant Dieu (Mélanges H. de Lubac)*, Vol. 3, pp. 215 ff.

[254] It is "what is implicit in revelation," as Y. Congar writes, *La foi et la théologie*, p. 103, that shows that on this point the modern notion of the fuller sense agrees with the problem of interpretation in Protestant theology, see J. M. Robinson, "Scripture the viewpoint of the fathers and medieval theologians.

[255] For a Protestant estimate of the problem of the fuller sense, compared with the problem of interpretation in Protestant theology, see J. M. Robinson, « Scripture and Theological Method," *CBQ* 27 (1965), 6-27.

[256] This *existential* application of Scripture naturally supposes an *existentialist* interpretation (to use Bultmann's terminology), that is, an interpretation in which the problem of existence serves as introduction to scriptural hermeneutics, and in which Scripture makes possible the hermeneutics of existence. But this point belongs to dogmatic rather than pastoral theology, although it points up the close connection

an indispensable first step in accomplishing that task, for they show how the people of God in other times found in his word a nourishment full of vitality. But it is necessary to go beyond this retrospective point of view and establish a direct connection between the text and the men to whom the gospel is presently announced. In this regard, not all texts are of equal value; that goes without saying. But even when their relative importance has been noted, it is still true that there is no text which does not offer the means of illuminating one or the other aspect of the mystery of Christ, and that is all that matters. Spiritual exegesis, that is, the use of the fuller sense in all its forms, thus constitutes one of the essential functions of the apostolate. To proclaim Jesus Christ on the basis of Scripture in catechetics and preaching, to contemplate Jesus Christ and praise God with the aid of Scripture in the liturgy—these are the activities in which the task of Christian interpretation is accomplished. It is in them that Scripture, as a fixed text, brings to life the living word of God which the Church proclaims for men to hear. [257] While literal exegesis continues to play its role, marking out the way and subjecting the expansiveness of preachers to firm control, it does so only to give way to the action of the Holy Spirit who gives the Church a full understanding of Scripture.

In fact, spiritual exegesis is a prophetic reading of the Bible, in the sense that it is a fruit of the charism of prophecy, which is basically accorded the Church at large, [258] but which is more visibly at work in those members to whom Christ's gift is that they should be "some, prophets; some, evangelists; some, pastors and teachers" in his Church (Ep 4:11). The charism in question does not dispense these persons from exegetical work; on the contrary, it supposes the results of such work for the good of their ministry. But nothing can substitute for the charism. Its action upon the interpreters of Scripture whose works Christian tradition has handed down to us explains why a genuine spiritual vitality can be found in their commen-

---

between them. In this regard, one might profitably consult the interesting comparison between Bultmann's theology and that of K. Rahner in an article by H. Ott, "Existentiale Interpretation und anonyme Christlichkeit" in E. Dinkler (ed.), *Zeit und Geschichte, Dankesgabe an Rudolf Bultmann* (Tübingen: Mohr, 1964), pp. 367-379.

[257] In this we agree with the remark of G. Ebeling, *Word and Faith*, pp. 312 ff., for whom Scripture does not really become the word of God except through preaching, which, by explaining and applying it, makes of it a word-event. On the proclamation of the word in the Church, see the collective volume *Parole de Dieu et liturgie* (Paris: Cerf, 1958), especially the contributions of L. Bouyer, A. M. Roguet, J. Lécuyer, P. A. Lesort. H. Oster, "Aujourd'hui s'accomplit ce passage de l'Écriture..." in *Parole de Dieu et sacerdoce* (Tournai-Paris: Desclée, 1962), pp. 195-213.

[258] That is the meaning of the Pentecost scene, which is explained in Peter's discourse with the aid of the text of Joel (Ac 2:16-21) that explicitly mentions the prophetic Spirit.

taries, even when the methods they employed were faulty, insufficient, or even misleading (as for example, the extended application of the allegorical method). The modern improvement of methods at the level of literal exegesis is an incontestable progress. But that should not prevent us from gathering the positive legacy which interpreters of the past have bequeathed us, and from which the Church can still benefit, nor above all should it prevent us from putting ourselves at the service of the Holy Spirit as they did, and not expect from our science more than it can afford us.

CONCLUSION: EXEGESIS, THEOLOGY AND APOSTOLATE

In recounting the history of Christian interpretation, we underlined the progressive breaking up of the various branches of study which in the ancient Church were a vital part of a reflective reading of Scripture. After the cleft which the 13th century introduced between the popular apostolate and scientific theology [259] the age of the Renaissance began a progressive development of scientific exegesis outside the main current of theology. [260] The results of that situation were not fortunate for any of the subjects involved; the crises equally experienced in modern times by exegesis, theology, and finally the apostolate are perhaps one of its consequences. The present direction of Christian thought is to reestablish their organic unity around Scripture, which will serve as their center point. The good sense of this undertaking merits a moment's reflection.

On the surface, biblical criticism, theology and the apostolate do have well defined fields of competence, to which correspond the methods they employ. How else can they be joined but from without, through a spirit of comprehension and mutual aid, which would nevertheless leave them all to their respective specializations? But the problem changes when it is recognized that all three have the same goal in different forms and at different levels. What is the aim of the Christian exegete? To enable the men of today to enter into contact with Scripture, the word of God in human language. Recognizing that this human language was conditioned by a particular history, he makes use of all the means critical study offers to make this contact possible. But recognizing at the same time the divine origin of that word, he cannot undertake a critical study of Scripture without manifest-

---

[259] Above, pp. 201 f..

[260] Above, pp. 213 ff.    St. Thomas already laid down the principle of a methodological distinction between exegesis and theology (cf. H. de Lubac, *Exégèse médiévale*, Part II, Vol. 2, p. 301).    But it was the development of critical methods in exegesis that brought to completion the process of disintegration which we have in mind here.

ing what signs he considers indicative of God's message, and how he understands that message. Thus the evidence of his belief is inseparable from his specialized work, and the latter necessarily leads to something above the techniques of exegesis. And what is the aim of the theologian? Knowing that his investigation does not deal with some abstract knowledge, but with the revelation of the living God, he seeks to acquire an understanding of the latter in order to share it with the men of his times. He too must establish a connection between the word of God, of which Scripture is the direct witness, and humanity, whose anxieties he shares, whose problems he knows, and whose language he speaks. While he must, even more than the exegete, anchor himself in the living tradition of the Church and at the same time listen to the voice of his age, his task is basically no less than that of interpreter of Scripture who, taking Scripture as his starting point, seeks to discover the fulness of revelation in order to make it accessible to all. This very effort puts him at the heart of the pastoral activity of the Church, whose principal concern is to proclaim the gospel to men and to extend to them an active sharing in the mystery of salvation. Here too, Scripture is the basis of the whole task, so that its ministers can at no time dispense themselves from being its faithful interpreters.

There is, therefore, no break in continuity between biblical criticism, theological explanation and pastoral activity. Despite their specialized duties and the occasional tensions which might appear, they are equally devoted to the whole mission confided the Church. They are also equally involved in the problem of scriptural interpretation, which concerns all three of them. That is why we have devoted so much space to examining that problem, and why we have given as much attention to biblical criticism and literal exegesis as to the question of the fuller sense and spiritual exegesis. This seems to us the way to reestablish the organic unity of criticism, theology and the apostolate, such as existed in the age of the fathers and even in the Middle Ages. [261] Those who attempt to oppose their individual methods

---

[261] We quote here the wish we expressed elsewhere: "The doctrine of the four senses of Scripture, no more in its ancient formulations than in its Thomistic formulation, was not developed with our critical notion of the literal sense in mind. But might we not entertain the hope of seeing it recast about that notion, and on that basis a concept of theological exegesis which would enable us, in different cultural circumstances, to find a common ground with the essential values of ancient Christian exegesis? Has the breakup of disciplines, the separation of exegesis, theology, preaching, spirituality, had such happy results? Let us imagine a time when once again theology, preaching, and spirituality would all develop with Scripture as foundation, by striving to examine the texts to find in them that profound secret which always, in one way or another, speaks to us of the mystery of Jesus Christ. Would that not redound to the benefit of the Church? Perhaps our times will see that unity of Christian thought—whose instrument of old was exegesis—reconstructed" (review of H. de Lubac, *Exégèse médiévale*, Part II, Vol. 2, in *RB* 73 (1964), 416).

actually misunderstand their respective places in the common activity which fulfills the command of Christ to announce the gospel "to all creation" (Mk 16:15). If it is no longer possible for the same men to be pastors, theologians and exegetes at the same time, as was the case in the first centuries of the Christian era, at least those who hold these different offices can properly appreciate the usefulness and understand the methods of all of them, in order to assume their own proper place in the Church and to benefit from the work of others.   The organic unity of the offices directed to the same ministry of the word demands the strictest collaboration between them.

# INDEX OF AUTHORS CITED

# INDEX OF SCRIPTURAL CITATIONS

### (Biblical order — Jerusalem Bible)

NY. 47. — Printed in Belgium by DESCLÉE & CO, ÉDITEURS, S. A., Tournai — 10.972

D—1069—0002—29